Using Computers in Legal Research

A Guide to LEXIS and WESTLAW

Published and distributed by Adams & Ambrose Publishing,
1220 South Park Street, P.O. Box 9684, Madison, Wisconsin 53715.
Telephone (608) 257-5700.

Additional copies of this book, or copies of THE LEGAL RESEARCH MANUAL: A GAME PLAN FOR LEGAL RESEARCH AND ANALYSIS, by the same authors, may be ordered from Adams & Ambrose Publishing.

Acknowledgment of permission to reprint previously published material appears on page iv.

Printed in the United States of America
Printed on acid-free paper
Printing: 20 19 18 17 16 15 14 13 12 11 10 9 8 7 6 5 4 3 2 1

Library of Congress Cataloging-in-Publication Data
Wren, Christopher G., 1950-
Using computers in legal research : a guide to LEXIS and WESTLAW / Christopher G. Wren, Jill Robinson Wren.
p. cm.
Includes bibliographical references and index.
ISBN 0-916951-21-9 (pbk.)
1. Legal research--United States--Data processing. 2. Information storage and retrieval systems--Law--United States. 3. LEXIS (Information retrieval system) 4. WESTLAW (Information retrieval system) I. Wren, Jill Robinson, 1954- . II. Title.
KF242.A1W74 1994
025.06'34--dc20 93-40352
CIP

ISBN 0-916951-21-9 (pbk.)

Using Computers in Legal Research

A Guide to LEXIS and WESTLAW

Christopher G. Wren
J.D., Harvard Law School
Member, Massachusetts and Wisconsin Bars

Jill Robinson Wren
J.D., Boston University School of Law
Member, Wisconsin Bar

Adams & Ambrose Publishing, Madison, Wisconsin

Permissions

The authors gratefully acknowledge the permission granted by the following copyright holders to reprint material in this book:

The State of Alabama and Governor Jim Folsom—for Figures 11.09, 11.10, 11.20, and 11.21. Copyright © 1977-1993 The State of Alabama. All rights reserved.

Bancroft-Whitney Company, a division of Thomson Legal Publishing, Inc.—for Figure 12.17. Copyright © 1982-1991, 1992 Bancroft-Whitney Company. All rights reserved.

Alfred Glossbrenner—for allowing use and adaptation in Chapter 13 of material from HOW TO LOOK IT UP ONLINE. Copyright © 1987 Alfred Glossbrenner. All rights reserved.

Sidney Harris—for Figure 4.02. Copyright © 1987 Sidney Harris and *The Chronicle of Higher Education*. All rights reserved.

Lawyers Cooperative Publishing, a division of Thomson Legal Publishing, Inc.—for Figures 5.15, 5.16, 12.11, and 12.12. Copyright © 1991, 1993 Lawyers Cooperative Publishing. All rights reserved.

Mead Data Central, Inc., provider of the LEXIS®/NEXIS® services—for Figures 5.11, 8.01, 8.02, 9.01, 9.03, 9.05, 9.06, 9.09, 9.12 to 9.14, 10.01, 10.03 to 10.06, 11.01 to 11.08, 11.11 to 11.14, 12.15, 12.16, 12.19, 12.20, 12.22 to 12.28, 14.01, A.01, and A.02. Copyright © 1993 Mead Data Central, Inc. All rights reserved.

Punch Magazine—for Appendix O. Copyright © 1962 *Punch*. All rights reserved.

Shepard's/McGraw-Hill, Inc.—for Figures 12.01 to 12.08, 12.29 to 12.36, and 12.38 to 12.42. Copyright © 1986, 1988, 1993 Shepard's/McGraw-Hill, Inc. All rights reserved.

West Publishing Company—for Figures 5.01 to 5.07, 5.13, 5.14, 5.17, 5.18, 8.03 to 8.07, 9.02, 9.04, 9.07, 9.08, 9.10, 9.11, 9.16, 9.17, 10.07, 10.09 to 10.14, 11.15 to 11.19, 11.22 to 11.27, 12.37, 12.38, 12.44, 12.45, 12.48, 12.50 to 12.53, 12.55, 12.56, 12.58 to 12.60, 14.02, and B.01. Copyright © 1982, 1989, 1992, 1993 West Publishing Company. All rights reserved.

Trademarks

PREFACE

About This Book

To use a computer successfully in legal research, you need to figure out how the computer can help you at each stage of the research process—that is, as you gather your facts and evaluate the legal issues they raise, as you find the law, as you read the law, and as you update the law. If you have done legal research using books, this question will have a familiar ring: it's the same one you ask about books when you use them in your legal research.

Because the computer's value to you depends on its utility in helping you perform a legal research task, learning about using computers in legal research occurs most easily and effectively in the context of the research process. A framework that mirrors the setting in which you actually use computers in your legal research makes the practical value of specific computer features immediately apparent, and their use easier to understand and remember. Consequently, after providing some necessary background information, the explanation in this guide tracks the steps you follow in doing legal research.

What this book offers

Part I. Effective use of a computer in legal research begins before you press the switch that turns the machine on; effective use begins with understanding the components of a computer-assisted legal research system and how they can affect your research efforts. Part I provides this background. Chapters 1, 2, and 3 offer a quick tour of the computer hardware and software, as well as basic principles of searching computer databases. Chapter 4 explains the language you use to create your search instructions. Chapter 5 completes the introduction by explaining the structure of documents in computer databases and how to take advantage of that structure in formulating your search instructions.

Part II. Just as understanding the environment in which you will conduct your computer searching will improve your search skills, an understanding of how to plan a computer search session will enhance the success of your search and minimize the frustration and wasted effort that can overtake you if you lack a game plan. Part II covers the points to keep in mind as you prepare to do a computerized search.

Part III. Building on the foundation created in Parts I and II, Part III shows how to use a computer to find, read, and update the law. The chapter entitled "Using Computers in Finding the Law" explains the techniques for computerizing the law-finding approaches you use when you research with books, as well as some methods for finding the law in ways you cannot use with books. The chapter entitled "Using Computers in Reading the Law" covers the ways in which you can view and preserve the materials you retrieve with the computer. The chapter entitled "Using Computers in Updating the Law" catalogs the numerous methods by which you can use a computer to update legal authorities; some of these methods you can also use in book-based legal research, and others you can use only in computer-assisted legal research. Skimming these chapters will familiarize you with the range of computer activities you can perform.

Because the explanation is organized according to the research task you need to perform, Part III can serve as a user manual for the computer services. So, when you need to implement a particular computerized technique in your own research projects, you can turn to an explanation in Part III. To further simplify locating the explanation you want, each of the chapters on using a computer to find, read, and update the law is divided into two parts—one for LEXIS and one for WESTLAW.

Because legal researchers also need to know how to obtain nonlegal information, Part III concludes with a chapter that explains how to incorporate databases of nonlegal information into your computer-assisted legal research.

Part IV. Part IV contains more tips for effectively using computers in legal research, including pointers about keeping a record of your search session and deciding when to end a search session. Recapping and expanding on points made throughout the book, the final chapter in Part IV canvasses the benefits and drawbacks of using computers in legal research and examines in more detail how to blend books and computers into a comprehensive research strategy.

Part V. Part V closes the book with appendices containing lists and other reference materials to which researchers should have ready access but that would disrupt the explanation of using computers in legal research if the materials were included as part of the main text. Some of the appendices deal in more detail with points addressed briefly elsewhere in the book.

Quick Guides. Throughout the book, Quick Guides summarize key points in chart form. These Quick Guides can also function as refreshers you can quickly scan while you use a computer-assisted legal research service.

A companion volume. Along with standing on its own as a guide to computer-assisted legal research, this book serves as a companion volume to *The Legal Research Manual: A Game Plan for Legal Research and Analysis*, in which we introduce the techniques of researching and analyzing the law. In *The Legal Research Manual*, we present legal research as a process, organizing the explanation according to the steps you follow in actually doing legal research; discussion of law books occurs in connection with the legal research tasks for which you use the books.*

This book continues that approach. Following the pattern of *The Legal Research Manual*, we explain the contents and features of computer-assisted legal research services in the course of explaining the process of using computers in legal research.

To us, this arrangement offers the easiest way to understand when and how to use the myriad of features and documents available in computer-assisted legal research services. Given the vast quantity and variety of materials and search features available through a computer-assisted legal research service, a framework organized according to what you are trying to accomplish in your research project holds an enormous advantage over an organization based on the contents and features of the computer services: most likely, you will know what you want to do (for example, update an authority), but not know the computer resource to use; only rarely are you likely to remember the computer feature but not know what it does.

Correlating book-based and computer-assisted legal research

Throughout, the explanation in this book highlights the parallels between book-based and computer-assisted legal research. In addition, both explicitly in the text and implicitly through the text's organization, the book points up the substantial similarities between LEXIS and WESTLAW. This approach is intended to make it easier to move between books and computers, to move between LEXIS and WESTLAW, and to spot those relatively infrequent points where the two computer services diverge.

In correlating computer-assisted and book-based legal research, this book avoids mingling explanations of the mechanics of using computers with ex-

*For an explanation of the benefits we see flowing from explaining legal research this way, interested readers can refer to *The Teaching of Legal Research*, 80 LAW LIBR. J. 7 (1988), and *Reviving Legal Research*, 82 LAW LIBR. J. 463 (1990).

planations of the mechanics of using law books. Learning to use a computer in legal research means learning to use a software program, which requires developing skills significantly different from those required for using law books. Bouncing between explanations of two systems—law books and computer-assisted legal research services—that require fundamentally different skills for their use interrupts the task of learning how to use either system well.

Of course, in actually doing legal research, you will seek to blend the use of law books and the use of computer-assisted legal research services as you gather your facts, and find, read, and update the law. But the mingling of these research tools can occur in using them, not in learning about their use. For learning purposes, separate explanations of book-based and computer-assisted legal research can bring quickly into focus the skills and information needed to accomplish research tasks with each kind of tool. With that knowledge in place, researchers are in a better position to combine books and computer services successfully in their research strategies.

So, to make it possible to learn efficiently about using books and computer services, we have provided separate explanations: here, an explanation focusing on how to use computer-assisted legal research services, and in *The Legal Research Manual*, an explanation focusing on how to use law books. As a result, you can learn the mechanics of using one research tool without being interrupted by an explanation of the mechanics of using the other research tool.

For those who prefer, however, to alternate between explanations of how to use books and how to use computers, the parallel organization of the two texts coordinates the explanations and allows them to be mingled at the reader's discretion: if you want, you can read about how to carry out a research task with one tool (a computer or a book), then switch to the corresponding section of the other text to read about how to do the same task with the other tool. In addition, as you read an explanation in this text of how to use a computer to accomplish a research task that can be done with either a computer or a book, you will see a brief recap of the book-based procedure, along with a citation to a fuller explanation in *The Legal Research Manual* of how to accomplish the same research task with a book.

A final note

We would have preferred to write a shorter explanation of computer-assisted legal research. But we found that computer-assisted legal research did not lend itself well to a short explanation, which would omit information essential to using computers effectively and efficiently in legal research.

In using computers, as in using books, the legal researcher's critical need is to know *when* to select from the array of available resources the one best suited for doing a particular research task at any given point in a research project. Having made the selection, the researcher then needs to know *how* to use the book or computerized resource.

A researcher who selects a book does not require much additional explanation about how to use it. A lifetime of using books will have created a familiarity with their characteristics and use. For the relatively few characteristics special to law books (such as pocket parts that update main volumes), a researcher does not need much explanation to understand their functions and uses.

By contrast, a researcher who selects a computerized resource needs considerably more information about how to use it. Computer-assisted legal research services offer a wide array of features, and learning how to use one computer feature does not necessarily translate into knowing how to use another computer feature. In addition, activities that occur intuitively when you use a book require knowledge of specific commands when you perform them with a computer. For example, in place of the familiar steps of taking a book off a shelf, opening the book, turning its pages, and returning the book to the shelf and selecting another book, you need to learn the commands to select a computer file, to find a document in the file, to view a particular page, to view a different page, to select a different document to look at, and so on.

Moreover, computer-assisted legal research is an activity in which many obstacles to achieving acceptable search results will not be evident just from using the computer-assisted legal research services. Researchers therefore need to know about potential pitfalls and how to minimize their impact.

The length of this book flows from our desire to provide these sorts of essential details—and to provide them about both LEXIS and WESTLAW. In addition, we have included many pages showing sample screens reproducing what researchers see on the computer monitor when they use the computer services; these screens are intended to allow readers to learn about LEXIS and WESTLAW without having to be hooked up to either service. For the benefit of readers who have LEXIS or WESTLAW access that allows practicing computer-assisted legal research techniques, we have also included illustrative search instructions throughout the book to provide a basis for experimenting with online searching.

As with our earlier book, we hope the information in this guide will help you do your research as effectively and efficiently as possible.

Madison, Wisconsin

C.G.W.
J.R.W.

Acknowledgments

In writing this book, we have felt privileged to receive assistance, generous in both quantity and quality, from many people. We take pleasure in acknowledging their contributions, which made this book possible.

Mead Data Central, provider of the LEXIS/NEXIS services, and West Publishing Company, provider of WESTLAW, made available to us, with no strings attached, an array of resources that allowed us to independently probe the operation of their online services. In addition, in response to the numerous questions we asked as we explored LEXIS and WESTLAW and in connection with reviewing our manuscript for technical accuracy, we received much helpful information from many individuals at Mead Data Central and West Publishing Company. At Mead Data Central, the people whose time and efforts supported this project include James M. Joseph, Manager, Public Communications; Monica Schiffler, Senior Public Communications Specialist; Karen Cejka, Training Media Manager; and Michael Hensley, Senior Legal Specialist-Customer Service. Likewise, at West Publishing Company, many individuals in various departments took time to ensure that we acquired the information we needed. We especially thank members of the following departments at West Publishing: Account Management; Computer Systems & Programming; Customer Support; Editorial; Manuscript; Marketing; and Media Relations.

In connection with our receiving online access to the services of Mead Data Central and West Publishing Company, we extend special thanks to Dean Steven M. Barkan, Professor of Law and former Law Library Director at Marquette University Law School, who facilitated our early contacts with the database vendors.

As with our previous writing projects, we count ourselves extraordinarily fortunate that so many people took time from busy schedules to read the manuscript and offer assessments that reflected great care and insight. For their generosity in reviewing the manuscript for this book, we are indebted to the following people: Dean Steven M. Barkan, of Marquette University Law School; Ellen M. Callinan, Manager of Research Services, Crowell & Moring, Washington, D.C.; Neil A. Campbell, Law Librarian and Associate Professor of Law, University of Manitoba; Jane Colwin, Public Services Librarian, Wisconsin State Law Library; attorney Mathew J. Dew, of Madison, Wisconsin; John Eaton, Reference Librarian, E.K. Williams Law Library, University of

Manitoba; S. Blair Kauffman, Law Library Director and Professor of Law, University of Wisconsin Law School; attorney Noelle E. Lambert, of Charlotte, North Carolina; Mary Mahoney, Deputy Director, Law Library, Marquette University Law School; Thomas McDonnell, Associate Professor of Law, Pace University Law School; Cheryl O'Connor, Circulation/Reference Librarian, University of Wisconsin Law Library; Nancy Paul, Assistant Director, Technical Services, University of Wisconsin Law Library; Duane A. Strojny, Head of Reference, Law Library, Marquette University Law School; and Kenneth J. Vandevelde, Professor of Law, Western State University-San Diego.

For turning our manuscript pages into a book, we express our gratitude to all involved. Evelyn McLean-Cowan designed the book, and Claire Huismann coordinated the transformation of our word-processed pages into typeset ones, a transformation built on a foundation Mary Boss helped create. Tom Linley typeset the text, while Ann Stretton supervised the graphic elements. Judy Waddell brought sharp proofreading skills to the project.

Special thanks are also due Julie Christian, who attended to a wide assortment of administrative responsibilities during our work on this project. Her involvement opened up for us significantly more time to work on the manuscript.

Family, friends, and colleagues also played an important role at every stage of our work by offering encouragement that sustained us as we progressed from the idea of this book to its completion.

Although authors find their names on the cover, a book really results from the collective efforts of many people. To all who helped with this one, our heartfelt thanks.

Summary Table of Contents

PART IV
More Tips for Effectively Using Computers in Legal Research

PART V
Appendices

Detailed Table of Contents

Chapter 4 The Dialects of Database Searching—Cont.

PART II
Preparing for Online Searching

Chapter 8 Modifying Your Search Request—Cont.

Chapter 10 Using Computers in Finding the Law—Cont.

Chapter 11 Using Computers in Reading the Law—Cont.

Chapter 12 Using Computers in Updating the Law—Cont.

Chapter 12 Using Computers in Updating the Law—Cont.

Typeface Conventions in This Book

Throughout this book, we have used the following conventions:

KEYS YOU PRESS — This typeface indicates a key on your keyboard. For example, "Press ENTER."

`What you type` — This typeface indicates words, letters, numbers, or symbols you type to instruct the computer. For example, "Type `m1` and press ENTER." A phrase like "Transmit `shep`" means you would type "shep" and then press the key labelled ENTER or TRANSMIT.

PART I

Background: Understanding the Tools

Part I provides background information essential for effective online searching:

- an introduction to computer hardware, software, and databases (Chapter 2)
- an introduction to basic principles of database searching (Chapter 3)
- an introduction to search terms and logic connectors, and to natural language—the dialects of database searching (Chapter 4)
- an introduction to fields and segments, which allow you to restrict your search to specified parts of documents in a database (Chapter 5)

CHAPTER 1

Introduction

In recent years, computers have lent a high-tech aura to legal research.[1] The computer's massive storage capacities afford researchers access to materials unavailable, in the same quantity or variety, in even the most comprehensive library of printed publications. Moreover, the extraordinary speed with which a computer can manipulate data permits researchers to retrieve these materials with remarkable swiftness. And the computer's ability to compile data according to a wide variety of criteria allows researchers to conduct specialized searches (such as finding all the dissenting opinions written by a specific judge) that would be impossible—or at least tremendously tedious and time-consuming—to perform without a computer.

But these benefits do not come without costs. To use computers effectively, legal researchers need skills and information beyond knowing the sources of the law and understanding the research process (matters covered in more detail in *The Legal Research Manual: A Game Plan for Legal Research and Analysis*).[2] Although the computer services most used in legal research—LEXIS and WESTLAW—are relatively simple to operate on a purely mechanical level, you can easily obtain poor results if you do not understand how each service's computer carries out your instructions. Without this understanding, you will likely end up with a nicely arranged computer-generated report that fails (perhaps without your realizing it) to give you the best results you could obtain. So, to use computers effectively in your legal research, you need to understand such things as the dialect for gaining access to materials stored in the computer, the technique the computer uses to locate information, and some key characteristics of the computer's information-retrieval technique that

[1] For a review of the evolution of the use of computers in legal research, see William G. Harrington, *A Brief History of Computer-Assisted Legal Research*, 77 LAW LIBR. J. 543 (1985).

[2] CHRISTOPHER G. WREN & JILL R. WREN, THE LEGAL RESEARCH MANUAL: A GAME PLAN FOR LEGAL RESEARCH AND ANALYSIS (2d ed. 1986).

will significantly affect your chances of ferreting out the materials you want to locate.

This book explains how to use computers in legal research, an enterprise widely referred to as "computer-assisted legal research" (or "CALR"). The discussion provides an overview of computer systems, summarizes the principal characteristics of LEXIS and WESTLAW, and then explains how to use a CALR service in gathering facts and in finding, reading, and updating the law. The discussion also addresses the relationship between book-based and computer-assisted legal research, indicates the strengths and limitations of computer-assisted legal research, points out the continuing role of printed legal research sources, and notes factors to consider in deciding when and how to fit computers into an overall strategy for legal research.

Because the coverage and features offered by vendors of CALR services continually evolve, this book does not detail *all* the peculiarities of each service. Such a discussion would quickly go out of date. Moreover, researchers who use CALR services have ready access to reference manuals, newsletters, and online aids provided by the vendors to explain their services.

Instead, this book introduces you to LEXIS and WESTLAW by explaining how the principal features of these services work and showing you the part those features can play in fact-gathering and in finding, reading, or updating the law; with that understanding, it's easy to adjust to the steady flow of enhancements the CALR vendors offer and to see where in a research project the new enhancements might prove useful. If you need to know more bibliographic data about the cases, statutes, and other materials stored in the LEXIS or WESTLAW computers, or about a particular feature of these services, the vendors' literature provides a resource for further reading.

As you learn about computer-assisted legal research, remember that it simply amounts to doing research in an electronic law library rather than in one filled with printed materials: in each setting, the underlying research process remains the same. So, whether you use computers or books, you still need to understand the research process—that is, you still need to analyze your research problem, identify legal issues, and then devise appropriate strategies for finding, reading, and updating the relevant law.[3]

The words "legal research" in the phrase "computer-assisted legal research" might suggest that computers can actually *do* research, instead of just retrieving information a researcher requests. As you will discover from this book, however, and through using a computer in your research, a phrase like

[3] This book tracks those steps. A fuller explanation of the steps appears in CHRISTOPHER G. WREN & JILL R. WREN, THE LEGAL RESEARCH MANUAL: A GAME PLAN FOR LEGAL RESEARCH AND ANALYSIS (2d ed. 1986).

"computer-assisted document retrieval" or "computer-assisted legal indexing" would more accurately reflect the computer's function.

In short, even though computers can offer invaluable research assistance, they cannot make you any more skilled at legal research than you are when using printed publications.

CHAPTER 2

Computer Systems: The Nature of the Medium

Although a computer, like a book, functions as a medium for storing information, the nature of the computer establishes a new relationship between researchers and the information they seek. Success at computer-assisted legal research depends in large part on understanding the implications this relationship holds for how you search for and retrieve information stored in a computer. An understanding of this relationship and its implications will, in turn, come more readily if you have a basic knowledge of computer systems.

Hardware and software

Regardless of their individual characteristics, all computer systems permit users to perform the same basic tasks: storing information (commonly referred to as "data") and then, by giving the computer instructions (called "commands"), sifting through and retrieving from that storehouse of data specific items of information. To allow users to accomplish these activities, computer systems rely on two separate but interdependent elements—hardware and software.

At a minimum, the hardware of a computer system consists of:

- a device (ordinarily a typewriter-style keyboard, and sometimes a pointing mechanism called a "mouse") for entering information and commands into the computer
- a device (such as a magnetic disk or tape) for storing information and commands
- a device (*i.e.*, the computing component at the core of the system) for processing information and commands

- devices (such as a television-style screen, *i.e.*, a "monitor," and a printer) for viewing the information the computer retrieves in response to commands

In a computer-assisted legal research service, a keyboard, monitor, and a telecommunications device called a "modem"—collectively known as a "terminal"—are located at the researcher's workplace, as is (usually) a printer. A computer and a storage device containing the material a researcher wants to search are located at the CALR vendor's headquarters and linked to the researcher's terminal by a telecommunications network, *e.g.*, telephone lines.

Computer hardware cannot function without software to tell the computer what operation to perform and how to perform it, based on commands the user supplies. Software for computer-assisted legal research serves principally to search a database for information useful in legal research. A large part of learning how to use computers in legal research consists of mastering the commands for instructing each CALR service's computer.

Figure 2.01 illustrates the components of a CALR service and their relationships to one another.

Databases

Databases lie at the core of computer-assisted legal research. A database consists of information stored in a predefined configuration that facilitates its retrieval, sometimes (as you will see) in arrangements not feasible to achieve through books. The information in a database, like the information in books, can appear in several formats:

- the full text of such materials as cases, statutes, constitutional provisions, administrative regulations, or articles from legal periodicals
- abstracts, such as summaries of bills introduced in Congress
- bibliographic and directory-style entries, such as those found in an index to legal periodicals or in a law dictionary
- statistical, financial, and other numeric data, such as stock market prices

The two leading databases for computer-assisted legal research are LEXIS (a service of Mead Data Central) and WESTLAW (a service of West Publishing Company). Each service's database consists of whatever materials—*e.g.*, cases, statutes, regulations, law review articles and other secondary sources—the vendor has chosen to include.[4] Mead Data and West Publishing continually

[4]Chapters 10 and 12 discuss some of the commonly used materials in the LEXIS and WESTLAW databases.

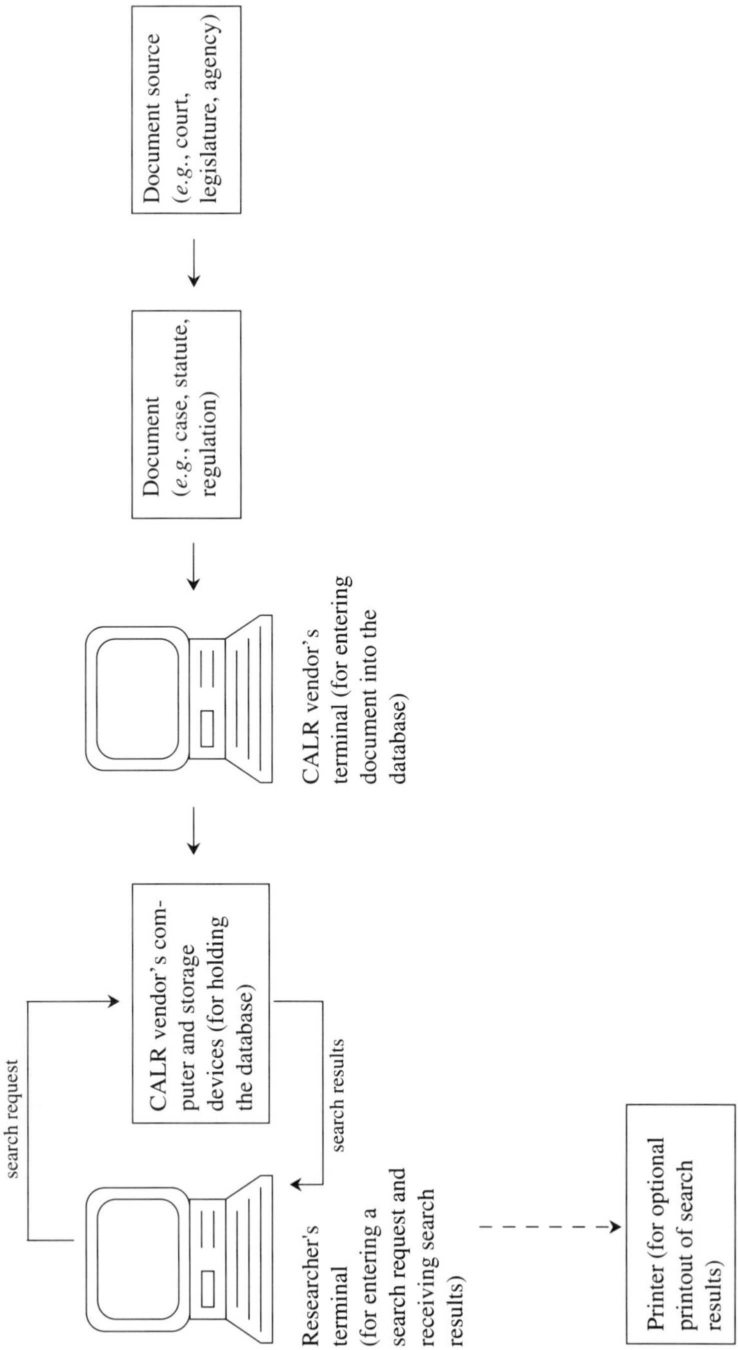

Figure 2.01. Components of a CALR Service

add new materials to their databases and, occasionally, delete material. At regular intervals, the two vendors issue updated printed directories that list the contents of their databases. The vendors also provide directories in the database services themselves; these online directories are updated more frequently than the printed directories, and therefore provide more help in determining the current coverage of LEXIS or WESTLAW. Appendices A and B highlight the printed and online database directories for LEXIS and WESTLAW.

Although a CALR database is an electronic version of a book-filled law library, the contents of your law library's collection and of a CALR database will not coincide. Your library will likely have materials (such as city ordinances or certain treatises) probably not available through a database, and a database will likely have materials (such as cases not published in printed case reporters, cases decided by the International Court of Justice, or attorney general opinions from other states) your library might not contain.

The method of storage in a CALR database differs, of course, from the method of storage in a print medium: the computer stores information as a mass of electronic signals rather than as inked images on pages arranged in bound volumes. Without a mediating mechanism of some sort (a function performed by indexes in printed publications), most researchers would find navigating a database too frustrating to make the voyage worthwhile. Therefore, to facilitate researchers' efforts to find and retrieve database materials, each CALR vendor organizes its electronic signals to create the effect of a collection of information organized along the familiar lines of a traditional law library of printed publications. Mead Data and West Publishing accomplish this by dividing their respective databases into ever-narrowing groupings of related materials.

The organization of the LEXIS and WESTLAW databases

The broadest divisions consist of materials that share a common jurisdictional origin or subject matter. In LEXIS, these broad divisions are called "libraries"; in WESTLAW, they are referred to as "databases."[5] For example, in LEXIS, the "general federal" library (designated GENFED) functions as a jurisdictional division because it includes federal cases, statutes, administrative regulations, and other federal materials, regardless of subject matter; the LEXIS libraries for banking law and insurance law exemplify subject-matter divisions because they contain topically related materials regardless of juris-

[5] In common computer terminology, the term "database" refers generically to a collection of information stored in a computer in a structured arrangement. In WESTLAW, "database" refers to a specific division of the overall database service. Except when specifically referring to subdivisions in WESTLAW, this book uses "database" in its generic sense to signify either CALR vendor's collection of information.

diction. Similarly, WESTLAW contains jurisdictional divisions, such as the ALLFEDS database (which contains cases from all federal courts regardless of subject matter), and subject-matter databases analogous to subject-matter libraries in LEXIS.

In LEXIS, each library is, in turn, further refined into related groupings called "files." For instance, the GENFED library of federal materials contains a file for U.S. Supreme Court cases, a file for U.S. Courts of Appeals cases, a file for the *United States Code*, and a file for each of several other categories of materials in the GENFED library. WESTLAW does not further subdivide its databases at this level because each of its databases already constitutes a grouping analogous to a LEXIS file.

Each LEXIS file and each WESTLAW database is next divided into units called "documents." An individual case, for example, is a document.

As a final division, documents are broken into units called "fields" in WESTLAW and "segments" in LEXIS. Fields and segments contain predetermined types of information, and reflect a recognition that similar kinds of documents share a common structure. For example, all cases have common elements—the case caption, the name of the judge who wrote the opinion, the date of the decision, the text of the opinion, and so forth—and each case in a database therefore contains a separate field or segment corresponding to each of these components. Figure 5.08 (pages 114–18) lists the WESTLAW fields and LEXIS segments for federal cases. Other kinds of documents, such as statutes and administrative regulations, also have recurring elements, which are reflected in fields or segments unique to these materials. *WESTLAW DataBasics*,[6] the *LEXIS Product Guide*,[7] and the online aids in LEXIS and WESTLAW (see Appendices A and B) identify the fields or segments you will encounter in various kinds of documents in LEXIS and WESTLAW.

Figure 2.02 shows the organization of the LEXIS and WESTLAW databases, as well as their organizational parallel in a traditional law library's book-based collection.

CALR databases other than LEXIS and WESTLAW

Although LEXIS and WESTLAW dominate the market for computer-assisted legal research, other CALR services exist.[8] For example:

- Lawyers Cooperative Publishing, Bancroft-Whitney, and the Research Institute of America jointly offer VERALEX 2, through

[6] West Publishing Company, WESTLAW DataBasics (1993).

[7] Mead Data Central, LEXIS Product Guide (1992 & current supp.).

[8] Although containing some now-dated information, a good roundup of key databases likely to be useful to legal researchers appears in S. Blair Kauffman, *Electronic Databases in Legal Research: Beyond LEXIS and WESTLAW*, 13 Rutgers Computer & Tech. L.J. 73 (1987).

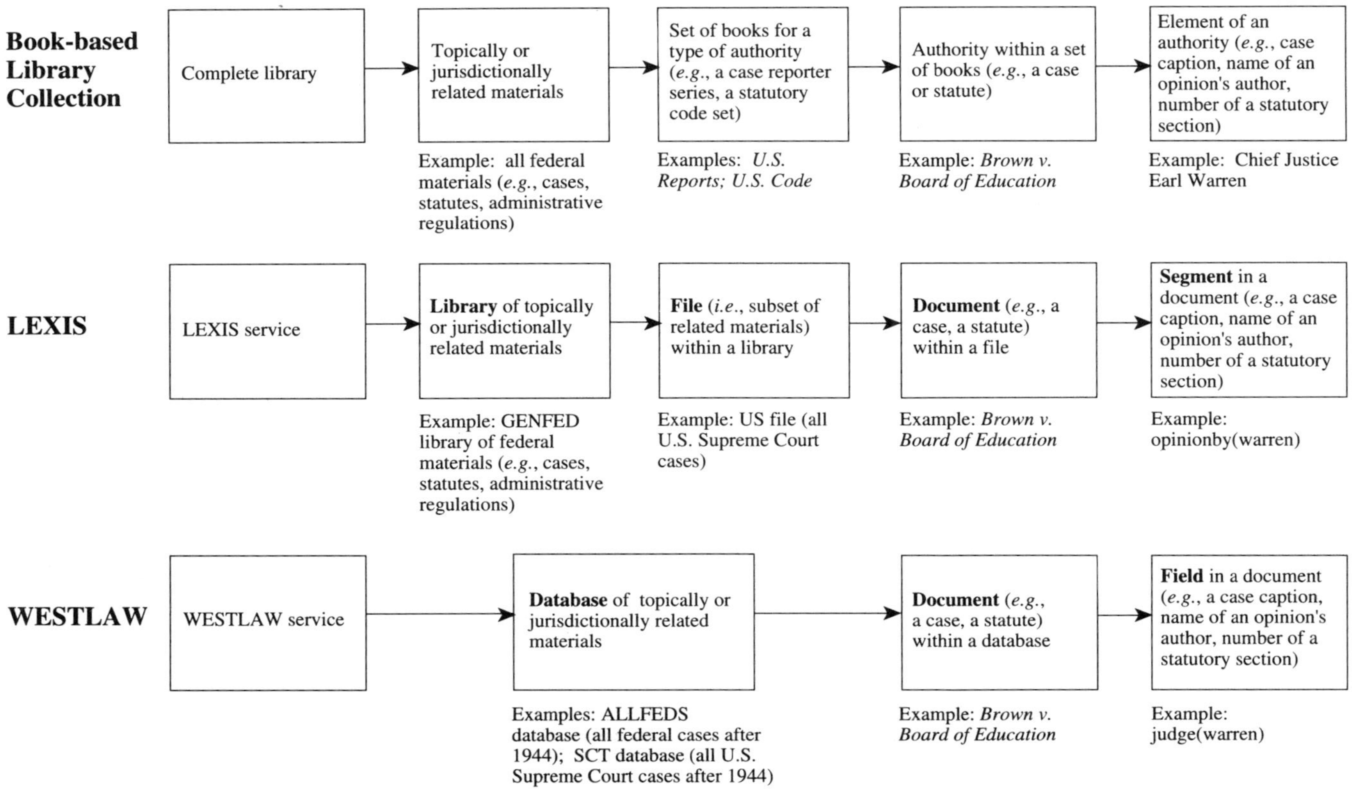

Figure 2.02. The Organization of the LEXIS and WESTLAW Databases

which you can gain access to (among other things) the more recent series of *American Law Reports Annotated*, Auto-Cite (discussed in Chapter 12), LEXIS, or the Research Institute's tax materials (including *Federal Tax Coordinator 2d*).

- Commerce Clearing House (through CCH ACCESS) offers computer access to wide-ranging databases of tax information.
- Commerce Clearing House offers Electronic Legislative Search System (ELSS), a computerized service for tracking federal and state legislative activity. Public Affairs Information offers a similar service.
- Legi-Slate, a service of *The Washington Post*, provides computer access to daily updates of the *Code of Federal Regulations* and the *United States Code*, to online versions of the *Federal Register* and the *Congressional Record*, and to congressional materials such as House and Senate committee reports and the transcripts of significant committee hearings.
- QUICKLAW, a service of QL Systems Limited, provides access to a wide range of databases containing Canadian cases, statutes, regulations, and other legal authorities.
- The federal government provides many of its employees access to its own CALR databases, the contents of which reflect the research interests of the agencies sponsoring the services. The Department of Justice offers a database service called JURIS, the Air Force offers FLITE, and the Internal Revenue Service has RIRA.
- Increasingly, state and local governments are assembling databases for their employees to use in various activities, such as drafting legislation.

Some of these CALR databases are available through LEXIS and WESTLAW. You can learn whether you have access via LEXIS or WESTLAW by checking the vendors' literature or by asking the person who coordinates the subscription to the CALR service you use.

In addition to the databases already mentioned, many law offices create private databases of documents for personal, in-house use. These private databases can consist of a wide array of documents useful in doing legal research. The documents can include legal briefs, memoranda of law, deposition transcripts, documents obtained during litigation—in short, anything for which storage in a database might prove useful in the work of the law office. Some commercial vendors of database services (such as LEXIS and WESTLAW) provide software programs, consultation, and other resources to help offices convert their documents into databases that can be kept on a computer either in house or at a remote location reached through telecommunications links; for example, Mead Data and West Publishing will convert a law office's documents into a database structured like their LEXIS or WESTLAW databases and searchable with LEXIS or WESTLAW commands.

A law office can also use off-the-shelf software programs to create in-house collections of computer-searchable documents. Programs of this sort include ZyINDEX, Folio Views, Isys, Magellan, askSam, and Personal Librarian. With each of these programs, as with database services like LEXIS and WESTLAW, the computer provides powerful new means of storing and retrieving information in ways not always feasible when the information is stored in printed form.

The relationship of CD-ROM to computer-assisted legal research

In doing legal research, in addition to encountering legal materials in books and in database services like LEXIS and WESTLAW, you will encounter legal materials stored in a medium known as "CD-ROM" (which stands for "compact disc-read only memory"). Physically identical to a compact disc used to play music in a stereo system, a CD-ROM disc holds its information on a surface readable by a laser beam.

Using a CD-ROM disc containing legal materials is like using a small legal database service without having to telephone a remote computer. To gain access to information on a CD-ROM disc, you simply insert the disc into a compact-disc drive (sometimes called a "reader" or "player") attached to your computer and then type commands that tell the computer what information you want to retrieve and display on a computer monitor. So, if the same information is available either on a CD-ROM disc or through a database service like LEXIS or WESTLAW, using the CD-ROM disc will avoid the charges you incur when you establish a telecommunications link with, and search in, a database at another location.

Legal publishers are offering an increasing variety of materials in the CD-ROM format, particularly in specialized areas like bankruptcy and taxation. But compared to the storage capacity of database services like LEXIS and WESTLAW, the storage capacity of a CD-ROM disc seems almost trivial, even though it holds the equivalent of between 275,000 and 300,000 pages of text. In addition, despite the growing variety of materials offered through CD-ROM, the range of materials available at this time remains extremely limited compared to the range available through LEXIS, WESTLAW, or a similar database service.

This book does not further address researching with CD-ROM technology. In general, the techniques for retrieving information stored on a CD-ROM disc are similar to the techniques used to retrieve information from LEXIS, WESTLAW, and other CALR database services. Once you understand the principles for retrieving information from LEXIS and WESTLAW, you can adapt those principles to retrieving information from CD-ROM discs.

If you search a CD-ROM disc, check the vendor's manual for an explanation of the specific commands to use with that product. Although searching CD-ROM discs resembles searching CALR databases, you will often find that one CD-ROM product will require you to use a certain command to carry out a research task and another CD-ROM product will require you to use a different command to carry out the same task.

CHAPTER 3

An Orientation to Database Searching

Introduction. Although the databases used in computer-assisted legal research track traditional law libraries of printed materials in terms of coverage and organization, researchers gain access to information in the databases in a way fundamentally different from that used to gain access to information in law books. The difference arises from a key characteristic of CALR databases: unlike most law books, the databases (with rare exceptions) do not provide indexes to guide users to relevant information; instead, users of CALR services construct their own indexes, using instructions explained in the next chapter. Indexing by the user defines the new relationship computer-assisted legal research establishes between researchers and legal information.[9]

Over the years, American law book publishers have provided increasingly fine-tuned and detailed indexes, including case digests (which serve as indexes for case reporters), indexes to statutory and administrative codes, and indexes to legal periodicals, encyclopedias, and other secondary sources. When using American law books, researchers have routinely relied on professional indexers to guide them to the information they want.

By not placing a professional indexer between researchers and the information in the databases, the vendors of CALR services afford researchers the opportunity to circumvent the principal drawbacks sometimes attributed to the indexing systems for printed legal materials: the potential difficulty of accurately anticipating the index headings and legal subject categories to which an indexer has assigned information, and the possibility that a piece of information has been either misindexed or not indexed at all. As independent indexers,

[9] This new relationship reflects a profound change: researchers have relied on prepared indexes since at least 650 B.C., when patrons of the library at Ninevah in ancient Assyria referred to indexes written on clay tablets. *See* RUTH C. CROSS, INDEXING BOOKS 3 (1980).

users of CALR services are free to construct indexes tailored to the precise problems they want to solve. You can index legal material by using any words or phrases contained in the documents you seek. Your research efforts will not be confined either by a limited universe of terms and concepts under which someone else has indexed information, or by your failing to anticipate correctly the index headings and terms to examine.

Thus, computer-assisted legal research offers an alternative to the two choices previously available to researchers seeking access to information. Traditionally, researchers could either rely on prepared indexes or (in theory, at least) read *all* the law for themselves to locate authorities pertaining to their research problems. With CALR, a researcher can instruct the computer to "read" all the material in its collection of information and retrieve just the materials that satisfy the indexing criteria the researcher establishes.

How the computer reads

To instruct the computer successfully, though, requires understanding that the computer does not read the material the way you as a researcher would. At the most fundamental level, what a computer recognizes as a word differs from what you might recognize as a word. For CALR purposes, a computer treats as a word any series of characters (called a "character string" in computer parlance) that conforms to standards established by each CALR vendor in connection with its database.[10] For example, a CALR service would accept a misspelled word or a nonsense word as a valid term by which to index material in a database. Thus, you could instruct the LEXIS or WESTLAW computer to search for references to "defendents" or "borogoves."[11]

In addition to using different standards for recognizing individual words, computers perceive combinations of words differently than researchers do. A researcher reads words contextually, as part of a phrase or sentence or paragraph. By contrast, instead of reading words in the context of surrounding

[10] In LEXIS and WESTLAW, a word can be a single character or multiple characters without intervening spaces. *See* page 27. Under Mead Data's and West's rules for defining a word, some characters are considered spaces in certain contexts. *See* Appendices G and H.

[11] 'Twas brillig, and the slithy toves
Did gyre and gimble in the wabe;
All mimsy were the borogoves,
And the mome raths outgrabe.

LEWIS CARROLL, THROUGH THE LOOKING-GLASS, AND WHAT ALICE FOUND THERE 24 (London, MacMillan & Co. 1872), *reprinted in* CHARLES L. DODGSON, THE COMPLETE WORKS OF LEWIS CARROLL 155 (Vintage Books 1976), MARTIN GARDNER, THE ANNOTATED ALICE: ALICE'S ADVENTURES IN WONDERLAND & THROUGH THE LOOKING GLASS 197 (Meridian 1960), *and* MARTIN GARDNER, MORE ANNOTATED ALICE: ALICE'S ADVENTURES IN WONDERLAND & THROUGH THE LOOKING-GLASS 178 (1990).

words, a computer in a CALR service detects words through a device called a "concordance." This device lists in alphabetical order every word in the database except for a few common ones like "of" and "the." The concordance also records, in connection with each word, every location (called an "address") at which that word appears in the database.

When you instruct the computer to locate documents containing individual words or combinations of words, the computer does not actually inspect the documents for the presence of the specified terms. Rather, the computer searches mechanistically through the concordance, looking for words (*i.e.*, character strings) that match the words in your instructions. Whenever the computer finds a match, it refers to that word's addresses, which direct the computer to the documents in which the word appears.

This matching technique by which the computer searches a database is notable for its literalness. Suppose, for instance, a researcher's instructions (referred to as a "search request" or "query" or "description")[12] tell the computer to look for documents containing the character string "posession." The computer will not look for or retrieve any documents with the word "possession" (unless the documents contain the correctly spelled version in addition to the misspelling used in the search request).

Further, the computer's uncompromising search for identical character strings means a document the computer retrieves as satisfying a search request might not prove pertinent to the research problem. The computer's literalness leaves it oblivious to the meaning, nuance, or ambiguity of the words for which it has been instructed to search. For example, in response to an instruction to search for documents containing the word "court," a computer cannot distinguish among occurrences in which "court" refers to a judicial tribunal, a basketball or other type of athletic arena, a street name, or a romantic enterprise.[13]

In short, when you instruct a computer to "read" a CALR database, the computer simply searches its concordance for references to documents containing character strings that match character strings in your search request. If any matches exist, the computer will report that result but will not indicate whether the documents satisfying your request have any possible relevance to your problem. If the computer does not find a match, it will report that the database contains no documents with the terms specified in your search request; the computer will not guide you in modifying your search for something

[12] A search instruction is called a "search request" in LEXIS. In WESTLAW, a search instruction is called a "query" or (if created with a feature known as "natural language") a "description." For convenience, this book uses "search request" to refer to all search instructions, whether in WESTLAW or LEXIS.

[13] You can minimize the problem of ambiguity through thoughtful construction of search requests (see pages 155–56), but you can never completely avoid the effects of the computer's literalness.

that might prove relevant. In this respect, the computer differs from book indexes and case digests, which (through their cross-references and topical outline organization) explicitly and implicitly suggest additional avenues of research.[14]

Searching effectively

Because researchers want to find information relating to relevant legal concepts and because the computer can only scan for matching character strings, the challenge you confront in making effective use of a computer in legal research is learning how to search for concepts with a tool that does not recognize them. To meet this challenge, you need to construct a search request that expresses concepts in a dialect that allows the computer to perform its task (matching character strings) while still achieving the result you desire (locating conceptually relevant documents and ignoring conceptually irrelevant documents).

The Boolean (or "terms-and-connectors") dialect in LEXIS and WESTLAW. One of the dialects employed for search requests, explained more fully in the next chapter, consists of two components: search terms and logic connectors (also called "Boolean connectors"). The *search terms* are the words you want the computer to locate in the database; these words reflect facts or legal concepts that are pertinent to your research problem and that will therefore presumably appear in the text of relevant cases, statutes, or other legal authorities (referred to as "documents"). To select appropriate search terms, you think from the perspective of a judge, legislator, or other author and try to imagine what words those people would use in a document dealing with a problem like yours.[15]

Logic connectors, the second component of the search request, tell the computer how your search terms should relate to one another during the search—for example, whether the computer should retrieve a document only if it contains all the terms in the search request, or whether the computer should retrieve a document if it contains some combination of the search terms. By carefully selecting and linking search terms and connectors, you translate for

[14] As explained later in this chapter and in more detail in the next chapter, you sometimes have the option in WESTLAW of expressing your search instructions in plain-English statements or questions, using a feature called "natural language." Despite the plain-English nature of natural-language search instructions, the computer still searches mechanistically through a concordance to identify documents satisfying a search instruction, all the while remaining oblivious to the actual meaning of the words for which the search instruction directs the computer to search.

[15] Note that you also engage in a similar kind of anticipatory thinking process in book-based research. In that setting, however, you try to anticipate not the actual text of authorities, but the classifications and headings legal publishers would use to index them in such research sources as case digests, annotated statutes, treatises, and encyclopedias.

the computer the legal concepts with respect to which you want to find cases, statutes, and other authorities.

In effecting this translation, you will obviously want to avoid retrieving either too many irrelevant documents (the reading of which would prove needlessly time-consuming) or too few relevant documents (a circumstance that could deprive you of useful insights or perhaps a controlling authority). You will encounter greater success in striking an appropriate balance if you keep in mind a key principle that applies to Boolean searching in computer-assisted legal research: when you construct a search request designed to retrieve a high number of the relevant documents in a CALR database, your request will generally also retrieve a considerable number of irrelevant documents; on the other hand, when you construct a request designed to retrieve few irrelevant documents, you will also exclude some (perhaps many) relevant documents from your search results.

Example. As an illustration of this principle, consider a simplified series of Boolean search requests based on the following problem:[16]

> A person leases an apartment in Ohio and then discovers the apartment lacks running water. The landlord refuses to make the necessary repairs, and the tenant wants legal advice about possible remedies.

Because the term "lease" will probably appear in any case arising out of a tenant's dissatisfaction with the habitability of a rented apartment, you could begin your search by instructing the computer to locate all Ohio cases containing the term "lease." With this request, the computer will retrieve a high percentage—perhaps even 100 per cent—of the Ohio cases the database includes that resemble the tenant's situation.[17] At the same time, however, the search will also retrieve a substantial—probably unwieldy—number of irrelevant Ohio cases that include the term "lease" in connection with other kinds of rental transactions, such as leases of automobiles.

[16] Although in practice, you would check to see whether statutes or administrative regulations address the problem, our example focuses on cases. The principle applies equally, however, with respect to other kinds of authorities you might search for in LEXIS or WESTLAW.

Also, to illustrate the choices you make in developing effective search instructions, we have divided the hypothetical search into more individual searches than you would likely use for so simple a problem. After analyzing the facts of the hypothetical, you would probably start an actual search based on the same facts by using a single search request constructed after taking into account all the factors discussed in connection with the hypothetical search scenario.

[17] The search might yield less than 100 per cent of relevant Ohio cases. For example, the search request would not retrieve relevant cases containing typographical errors in "lease." For a discussion of typographical errors in documents in CALR databases, see Kelly Warnken, *A Study in LEXIS and WESTLAW Errors*, LEGAL ECON., July/Aug. 1987, at 38, 58. Or, a relevant case might use a synonymous word or phrase in lieu of "lease"—for example, "rental agreement" or "rental contract." In practice, you would consider adding such synonyms to your search request.

Consequently, you will need to make a choice. You could examine all the retrieved cases to find the relevant ones. Or, you could modify your search request in an effort to reduce the total number of cases retrieved, yet increase the likelihood that any given case you retrieve will be relevant. Because a search for the term "lease" would almost certainly retrieve more cases than you could reasonably expect to read, you would undoubtedly elect to modify your search request.

At this point, you could instruct the computer to retrieve all Ohio cases containing both the term "lease" and the term "apartment." The additional term in this modified search request imposes a new, more restrictive condition that will cause the computer to retrieve fewer cases: from the set of cases the computer retrieved when you searched for only the term "lease," the computer will now retrieve just the subset of cases that also include the term "apartment." Using this modified request, a higher percentage of the cases you retrieve is likely to be relevant. Thus, you will have improved the precision of your search. Now, though, your search results might exclude potentially relevant cases the previous search would have retrieved, particularly cases involving relevant analogies (such as leases of condominiums or houses that lack running water).[18] Moreover, even after decreasing the number of retrieved cases and increasing the percentage of relevant cases retrieved, you will probably still retrieve a significant number of irrelevant cases, *i.e.*, cases mentioning leases and apartments but involving issues that are unrelated to the Ohio tenant's problem.

Therefore, you again face the choice of examining all the retrieved cases or further modifying your search. You would undoubtedly decide to modify your search by instructing the computer to look for an additional term—say, "plumbing" or "water." If so, an even higher percentage of the cases you retrieve will likely be relevant, but again you would simultaneously lose some potentially relevant cases. For example, you would probably miss analogous cases involving apartments lacking heat, electricity, or other conditions affecting habitability. And, as with the previous modification, you still might retrieve irrelevant cases. For instance, an actual Boolean search for Ohio cases containing the terms "lease," "apartment," and either "water" or "plumbing" retrieved a case having nothing do to with water or plumbing:[19] the computer located the case because it listed the lawyer for one of the parties as having an office on South Water Street.

More about fine-tuning Boolean search requests. Appendix M explains in more detail the task you encounter in fashioning search terms and logic

[18] For a discussion of using analogies in legal research, see CHRISTOPHER G. WREN & JILL R. WREN, THE LEGAL RESEARCH MANUAL: A GAME PLAN FOR LEGAL RESEARCH AND ANALYSIS 32–33, 80–81 (2d ed. 1986).

[19] *Silver Meadows Properties v. Biney*, No. 1556, slip op. (Ohio Ct. App. Jan. 31, 1986).

connectors into search requests that retrieve a satisfactory number of relevant documents without also retrieving an unwieldy number of irrelevant documents. As you gain experience doing computer-assisted legal research, you will become increasingly adept at constructing search requests that your experience and growing legal knowledge tell you have probably yielded acceptable results. As a backdrop for evaluating the results of your search requests, Appendix N summarizes an influential experiment that systematically assessed the effectiveness of Boolean search requests used to locate documents based on the language they contain.

The "natural language" dialect in WESTLAW. In WESTLAW, you can search with either a Boolean search request or a search request expressed in "natural language" (which WESTLAW also calls "WIN," for "WESTLAW Is Natural"). As with Boolean searching, natural-language searching in WESTLAW requires you to anticipate words that will appear in relevant documents: whether you use a Boolean request or a natural-language request, the computer can only identify and retrieve documents based on words they contain. Consequently, in a natural-language request for researching a given problem, you will normally include many of the same search terms you would include in a Boolean request for researching the same problem. For example, to search for documents relevant to the Ohio landlord-tenant problem presented earlier, a natural-language search request would include words like "lease," "apartment," "plumbing," and "water"—in short, the same words used in the Boolean search request that sought documents relevant to this problem.

Unlike a Boolean search request, however, a natural-language search request does not use logic connectors to tell the computer how the search terms should relate to one another during the search—for example, whether each search term must appear in a document, or whether the search terms should appear in a particular order in a document. Instead, when you use a natural-language search request, you just supply the search terms. As explained in more detail in the next chapter, the WESTLAW computer then applies mathematical formulas based on statistical probabilities to determine whether a document contains search terms in arrangements that indicate the document will likely prove relevant.

By eliminating the need for researchers to select logic connectors to establish relationships among search terms, WESTLAW's natural-language feature simplifies the task of creating search instructions. This change, however, does not alter the fundamental limitation of computer-assisted legal research: the inability of the computer to understand the meaning of the words you include in your search instructions. Thus, natural-language search requests do not guarantee, any more than do Boolean search requests, that search results will include relevant documents or exclude irrelevant ones.

Choosing a search dialect. The ease of using WESTLAW's natural-language feature might suggest that Boolean searching no longer has a significant role in computer-assisted legal research. Currently, however, natural-language searching has some constraints (discussed in more detail in the next chapter). For example, you cannot use natural language to search for every kind of authority or to perform all the research tasks you can perform with Boolean searching. Consequently, natural-language searching and Boolean searching complement rather than replace each other. To conduct fully effective computer-assisted legal research, you need to understand both dialects for searching computer databases.

CHAPTER 4

Search Terms and Logic Connectors, and Natural Language: The Dialects of Database Searching

"Matchmaker, matchmaker, make me a match."
—*Fiddler on the Roof*

As the previous chapter noted, the computer retrieves information by matching words in search requests with words in the documents contained in a CALR database. To make effective use of a computer's information-retrieval capabilities, you need a way to bridge the gap between, on the one hand, the computer's ability to locate documents by performing purely mechanistic matches and, on the other hand, your need to locate documents based on their relevance to a legal research problem. In computer-assisted legal research, words provide this bridge: the computer can locate words, and words express the information and ideas that interest researchers.

Thus, to bridge the gap, you translate relevant concepts into appropriate words and then into instructions the computer can process.

The Boolean (or "terms-and-connectors") dialect. Using Boolean logic,[20] you accomplish this task through two steps:

1. First, you reduce relevant concepts to words that represent the key elements of your research problem. These words constitute the

[20] The Boolean dialect for database searching derives from the form of mathematical logic known as "Boolean algebra" (after the work of British mathematician George Boole).

search terms in your search request and function as a user-created index to the database.

For example, in the Ohio landlord-tenant problem on pages 19–20, "lease," "apartment," "water," and "plumbing" were some possible search terms.

2. Second, because most concepts cannot be fully expressed in a single word, you use logic (or "Boolean") *connectors*, where necessary, to link search terms in appropriate relationships so the terms come to reflect the relevant concepts.

   For instance, in the Ohio example, because "apartment lease" is a relevant concept, you might link the search terms "apartment" and "lease" with a connector that tells the computer to find documents in which these terms occur within, say, ten words of each other. A judge writing an opinion involving an apartment lease will likely use the words "apartment" and "lease" in fairly close proximity—as in the phrases "apartment lease" or "lease of an apartment." Therefore, the ten-word proximity relationship between search terms in this example would probably retrieve most, if not all, cases that mention apartment leases.

Each CALR vendor has developed a special Boolean dialect for communicating search terms to the computer and for establishing relationships among search terms. Though some details differ, the Boolean dialects researchers use to search the LEXIS and WESTLAW databases share fundamental similarities. These similarities arise because the database vendors have had to develop ways for researchers to deal with the same problems stemming from the computer's literalness.

WESTLAW's natural-language dialect. In WESTLAW, to bridge the gap between the computer's mechanistic match-making capability and the researcher's need to locate conceptually relevant documents, you can often use an alternative dialect to translate relevant concepts into instructions the computer can process. This dialect—called "natural language" (or "WIN," for "WESTLAW Is Natural")—allows you to communicate a search instruction as a plain-English statement or question. (Currently, Mead Data does not offer a natural-language dialect for searching LEXIS.)

You fashion a natural-language search request this way:

1. First, as in creating a Boolean search request, you select words that represent the key concepts of your research problem. These words constitute the search terms the computer will use to identify potentially relevant documents in the database.

For example, returning to the Ohio landlord-tenant problem on page 19, possible search terms include "lease," "apartment," "water," and "plumbing."

2. Second, you use these words in a plain-English statement or question that describes the issue you are researching. For instance, in the Ohio example, you might express your natural-language search request like this: "Does a landlord have an obligation to provide running water in a leased apartment?" Or, you can simply list your search terms.

   Unlike a Boolean search request, a natural-language search request does not rely on logic connectors to define the relationships among search terms. Instead, the computer automatically applies formulas based on statistical probabilities to determine which documents to retrieve.

The statistical probability formulas (or, more accurately, "algorithms") used in processing a natural-language search request in WESTLAW have evolved from several decades of research into automated information retrieval and into the nature and structure of human speech.[21] From this research, WESTLAW computer programmers have developed algorithms resting on two assumptions about how to assess the probable relevance of a document to a researcher's issue.[22] These algorithms assume that:

[21] Research into natural-language searching as a method of retrieving information from databases extends back to at least the late 1950s. One of the earliest published reports of this research appears in M.E. Maron & J.L. Kuhns, *On Relevance, Probabilistic Indexing and Information Retrieval*, 7 J. ASS'N COMPUTING MACHINERY 216 (1960). Recent articles discussing natural-language searching include several co-written by Dr. Howard R. Turtle, the architect of WESTLAW's natural-language feature: W. Bruce Croft, Lisa A. Smith & Howard R. Turtle, *A Loosely-Coupled Integration of a Text Retrieval System and an Object-Oriented Database System*, in PROCEEDINGS OF THE FIFTEENTH ANNUAL INTERNATIONAL ACM SIGIR CONFERENCE ON RESEARCH AND DEVELOPMENT IN INFORMATION RETRIEVAL 223 (1992); W. Bruce Croft, Howard R. Turtle & David D. Lewis, *The Use of Phrases and Structured Queries in Information Retrieval*, in PROCEEDINGS OF THE FOURTEENTH ANNUAL INTERNATIONAL ACM/SIGIR CONFERENCE ON RESEARCH AND DEVELOPMENT IN INFORMATION RETRIEVAL 32 (1991); Howard R. Turtle & W. Bruce Croft, *Evaluation of an Inference Network-Based Retrieval Model*, 9 ACM TRANS. ON INFO. SYS. 187 (1991); Howard R. Turtle & W. Bruce Croft, *Inference Networks for Document Retrieval*, in PROCEEDINGS OF THE 13TH ANNUAL INTERNATIONAL CONFERENCE ON RESEARCH AND DEVELOPMENT IN INFORMATION RETRIEVAL 1 (1990). A comparison of Boolean and natural-language searching appears in Howard R. Turtle & W. Bruce Croft, *A Comparison of Text Retrieval Methods*, 35 COMPUTER J. 279 (1992).

[22] The WESTLAW computer might calculate the probable relevance of a document by relying on a set of algorithms tailored to evaluating the type of authority that document represents (*e.g.*, a set of algorithms for evaluating cases, a set of algorithms for evaluating statutes). The principal assumptions underlying the natural-language algorithms remain constant, however.

- The less frequently a search term appears in a WESTLAW database, the more likely that the search term embodies one concept and only one concept—in effect, that the search term will have a constant meaning throughout that database. For example, the term "insemination" appears relatively infrequently in WESTLAW databases; the term also represents a concept that leaves relatively little room for ambiguity.
- The more frequently a search term appears in a given document, the greater the likely relevance of that document to the researcher's issue.

Taken together, these assumptions allow the computer to estimate whether a given document in a database has greater relevance for a researcher's issue than does another document. For instance, suppose Document A contains frequent occurrences of search terms that appear infrequently in the database as a whole. In addition, suppose Document B contains infrequent occurrences of search terms that appear frequently in the database. The computer will identify Document A as probably more relevant than Document B.

Learning both dialects. Although WESTLAW's natural-language feature can simplify the task of communicating search instructions, the feature does not (as explained later in this chapter) supplant Boolean searching. In particular, if your research goal includes obtaining a comprehensive collection of potentially relevant documents, the availability of natural-language searching does not eliminate the need to understand the Boolean dialect of search terms and logic connectors.

The next two sections of this chapter cover the basic dialect rules for formulating Boolean search instructions in LEXIS and WESTLAW. The rules apply regardless of the type of authority (*e.g.*, cases, statutes) for which you are searching. A discussion of the rules that affect natural-language searching in WESTLAW appears after the sections that discuss the Boolean dialect.

The central characteristics of the CALR services, such as the way search terms and logic connectors work, change only rarely. But to be sure you stay abreast of any new developments in the rules governing the use of search terms and logic connectors, you should refer to the CALR vendors' newsletters and announcements and any new editions of the LEXIS and WESTLAW reference manuals; information about new developments also appears online as part of the CALR services themselves. (Appendices A and B highlight these sources of help.) For additional guidance, you can seek assistance from a librarian or a customer service representative of LEXIS or WESTLAW.

Search terms in Boolean searching in LEXIS and WESTLAW

Because the computer will not perceive a match and retrieve a document unless the document contains the words stated in a search request, a CALR dialect needs rules that define what constitute searchable words and how the computer will react to those words in search requests. This section discusses the rules for search terms. A summary of the discussion appears in Figure 4.01 (pages 41–43).

What is a searchable word? The CALR vendors define a word as a single character (*i.e.*, a letter, number, or symbol like "$") or a string of characters unbroken by a space.[23] Thus, a search term can be an abbreviation, number, or symbol, as well as a conventional word. For example, LEXIS and WESTLAW treat the following character strings as search terms:

automobile	McGeorge	2001
habeas	tetrahydrocannabinol	3.75
inc.	C.F.R.	.5
etc.	MBA	18,622

In LEXIS, if a search term exceeds 20 characters, the computer searches for any word that begins with the same 20 characters. In WESTLAW, regardless of a search term's length, the computer will not substitute different endings when a word exceeds a certain length.

Hyphenated words. Asking what constitutes a searchable word (*i.e.*, a search term) leads to considering the effect of a hyphen in a character string.

The LEXIS computer has been programmed to treat a hyphen in a string of letters as a space; because a space indicates to LEXIS the beginning of a new word, LEXIS treats a hyphenated word as if it were two words instead of one. Thus, if you use "post-conviction" as a search term, LEXIS will examine documents for the presence of "post-conviction" or "post conviction" (each of which LEXIS treats as the same two-word phrase), but LEXIS will not search for "postconviction" (which LEXIS perceives as a single term). In short, in LEXIS,

`post-conviction`	searches for	post-conviction post conviction

Of course, the author of a legal document might write "postconviction." Because you cannot be sure which variant the author has used, you should instruct the computer to find documents containing any of the three possible spellings. To do this in LEXIS, you would instruct the computer with a search request containing "postconviction" as an alternative to either "post-conviction" or "post conviction." Your LEXIS search request would take either of the following forms:

```
post-conviction or postconviction
post conviction or postconviction
```

[23] In certain contexts, some characters are considered spaces and therefore represent the start of new words. *See* Appendices G and H.

In WESTLAW, unlike in LEXIS, a hyphen in a string of letters does not function as a space that begins a new word. Rather, the hyphen in WESTLAW indicates to the computer that it should automatically search for all three variants of words that can be written with or without a hyphen—that is, hyphenated, with a space in lieu of a hyphen, or collapsed into a single word without a space or a hyphen. Thus, in WESTLAW

`post-conviction`	searches for	post-conviction post conviction postconviction

The hyphen's effect of automatically standardizing the form of a string of letters in WESTLAW is one aspect of a technique West Publishing calls "normalizing" a search term.[24]

More about symbols in search terms. The preceding discussion covers the basic points about how the LEXIS and WESTLAW computers interpret punctuation marks and other symbols when they occur as part of a search term. In some situations, however, particularly when you search for numbers, you'll need to be aware of variations on the basic rules; for example, in WESTLAW, the hyphen does not "normalize" a string of numbers as it does a string of letters. For a more complete explanation, see Appendices G and H.

Non-searchable words. The CALR vendors have made two kinds of words non-searchable: certain commonly occurring words, and words that serve as computer commands.

Common words. Examples include personal pronouns (he, she, it, they, them), articles (an, the), and forms of the verb "to be" (is, am, are, was, were). LEXIS refers to non-searchable words as *noise words*; WESTLAW calls them *stop words*. Appendices C and D list the current LEXIS noise words and WESTLAW stop words. If the vendors add any noise or stop words to their lists, the additions will appear in the vendors' reference manuals and other literature.

Noise and stop words ordinarily have no legal significance that would make searching for them worthwhile. Moreover, these words occur so frequently in documents that searching for them would substantially slow the computer's response time.

Occasionally, you will want to search for a phrase that includes a noise or stop word. Although the computer will not execute a search request consisting of only a single noise or stop word, you can use these words in a search request if you use them as part of a phrase (as, for example, in a search for

[24] West Publishing Company, WESTLAW Reference Manual 44–45 (5th ed. 1993). A more detailed discussion about normalizing appears later in this chapter. *See* pages 34–36.

the phrase "justice of the peace").[25] The results you obtain in LEXIS will differ from those you obtain in WESTLAW, however.

In LEXIS, the computer will not actually search for the noise words in the phrase. Instead, the LEXIS computer will treat each of the noise words as merely a placeholder for itself or for any other noise word. For instance, if instructed to search for "justice of the peace," the computer would locate documents with the phrase "justice of the peace"; however, because "of" and "the" are noise words that the computer treats as interchangeable with other noise words (such as "is" or "our"), the computer would also locate documents containing a phrase like "justice is our peace."

In WESTLAW, the placement of the stop word in the phrase will determine how the computer treats the stop word. If a stop word other than "the" begins or ends the phrase in the search request (as in "after-acquired property"), the computer will retrieve documents containing that phrase. (The WESTLAW computer will not search for a phrase that begins or ends with "the.") If a stop word occupies any other position in a phrase, the WESTLAW computer will not actually search for the stop word, but will treat the word as merely a placeholder for itself or for *any* other word. For example, in WESTLAW, a search for "justice of the peace" will locate documents containing the same phrases LEXIS would locate, as well as documents containing phrases in which *any* two words separate "justice" and "peace" (such as an opinion in which a judge writes, "The demonstrators chanted, 'We want justice, we want peace.' ").

Command words. The CALR vendors have also made non-searchable a few words, phrases, and characters set aside for use as commands to the computer. For example, "and" and "or" serve as commands, and are non-searchable in LEXIS and WESTLAW.[26] LEXIS refers to these command words as *reserved words.* WESTLAW does not assign a separate label to them, treating them instead as just part of the collection of stop words. Appendices C and D list the command words currently non-searchable in LEXIS and WESTLAW.

A phrase for which you want to search—such as "stop and frisk"—may include a command word. Although the computer will not execute a search request consisting only of command words, you can use a command word in a search request as part of a phrase that also includes searchable words. But you must enclose the command word in quotation marks. By doing so, you override the word's status as a command: rather than respond to the word as an instruction, the computer will treat the word as simply part of a searchable phrase.

[25] The procedure for conducting a search for a phrase, in contrast to a single word, is explained at pages 51–53.

[26] Pages 41–56 discuss the words, phrases, and characters you use as search commands in Boolean (terms-and-connectors) searching in LEXIS and WESTLAW.

Some command words, such as "and," are non-searchable both because they serve as instructions and because they occur commonly. With these command words, placing the word in quotation marks will allow you to use the word as a search term. The computer will treat the command word like an ordinary noise or stop word, and will execute the search request in the manner explained earlier.

For example, in both LEXIS and WESTLAW, if you search for "stop and frisk" by placing quotation marks around the phrase, the computer will not treat "and" as a command word. Instead, the computer will treat "and" as part of the phrase "stop and frisk," and will search for documents containing this phrase. However, the computer will go on and search for documents with other phrases in which the words "stop" and "frisk" are separated by a single noise or stop word (as in "stop or frisk"); in WESTLAW, the computer will additionally search for documents in which "stop" and "frisk" are separated by *any* word (as in "stop, don't frisk").

Search term equivalencies. Through capitalization, abbreviation, pluralization, the use of possessive nouns, and other means, authors of documents can vary the form of words for which you might want the computer to search. So that researchers do not need to instruct the computer with all the possible variations on the spelling of each searchable word, the CALR vendors have embedded in their software programs various unseen search requests—called "equivalencies"—that instruct the computer to treat certain search terms as equivalent to certain other terms. In these situations, you can instruct the computer to search for a given word and the computer will locate documents containing not only that word but additional, software-defined variations of your search term. Thus, if you instruct the LEXIS or WESTLAW computer to search for, say, "drug," you will not miss a document in which the author consistently wrote "drugs."

Some of these embedded search requests are automatically initiated by the computer in every search; others are activated at the user's discretion. The presence of the automatically performed equivalencies in the CALR services can create the impression that the computer responds intelligently—that rather than simply searching for literal matches, it independently initiates a search for desired variations of search terms. Literalness, however, remains the core characteristic of a CALR computer, requiring users to exercise considerable care in formulating Boolean search requests. Except for instances in which the CALR vendors have programmed "fixes" in the form of equivalencies, the computer will only retrieve documents containing words that exactly match the terms used in search requests.

The *automatic equivalencies* in LEXIS and WESTLAW consist of the following:

- *Capitalization.* The LEXIS and WESTLAW computers automatically equate an uppercase letter with its lowercase version, and vice versa. For example, the computers will locate documents containing either "negligence" or "Negligence," regardless of which version you use in your search request.[27]
- *Abbreviations.* Both LEXIS and WESTLAW will automatically search for many (not all) terms that authors might have expressed as abbreviations. For example, if your search term is `chapter` (which is subject to an automatic equivalency search in both LEXIS and WESTLAW), your search request will automatically locate documents containing either "ch" or "chapter." Similarly, the search term `ch` will automatically locate "chapter" in addition to "ch."[28]

  The terms and abbreviations the computers will automatically treat as equivalent cover numbers as well as words: for instance, "tenth" and "10th" are treated as equivalent terms for searching

[27] Occasionally, you might find that in automatically equating uppercase and lowercase letters, the computer retrieves documents because they contain word forms you did not want to retrieve. In LEXIS, you can turn off or modify the automatic equivalency between uppercase and lowercase letters:

- You can instruct the computer to retrieve documents in which your search term does not contain any uppercase letters. For example, `nocaps (des)` will only search for "des," not "DES" or "Des."
- You can instruct the computer to retrieve documents in which your search term does not contain any lowercase letters. For example, `allcaps (des)` will only search for "DES," not "des" or "Des."
- You can instruct the computer to retrieve documents in which your search term contains at least one uppercase letter. For example, `caps (des)` will search for "DES" or "Des," but not "des."

In some databases, especially nonlegal ones (discussed in Chapter 13), information appears in all lowercase or all uppercase letters. For example, in XINHUA (the NEXIS file containing news from the Xinhua News Agency), all text appears lowercase; in LEXIS files containing Secretary of State records from various states, all text appears uppercase. If you inappropriately alter the automatic equivalency of lowercase and uppercase letters when you search in databases like these, you can easily bypass relevant documents.

Currently, West Publishing does not offer WESTLAW researchers the opportunity to control the automatic equivalency for capitalization.

[28] Occasionally, you might find that in automatically equating abbreviated and unabbreviated forms of search terms, the computer retrieves documents with meanings you did not intend. For example, searching for "Arkansas" will also automatically retrieve documents describing a ship as an "ark." In WESTLAW, you can turn off the automatic equivalency for abbreviations by placing the pound symbol (#) before the search term. Thus, `#arkansas` will search for "Arkansas," not "ark"; likewise, `#ark` will search for "ark," not "Arkansas." At this writing, Mead Data does not offer LEXIS researchers a similar feature.

purposes. The following sampling of equivalent terms and abbreviations in LEXIS suggests the range of this type of equivalency:[29]

H.U.D.	= HUD	I.C.C.	= ICC
Thursday	= Thurs	October	= Oct
one	= 1	eighty	= 80
first	= 1st	nineteenth	= 19th
Alabama	= Ala	certiorari	= cert

Appendices E and F reprint from the LEXIS and WESTLAW reference manuals the current lists of selected terms and their automatically equivalent abbreviations; any additions to the vendors' lists will appear in their literature and new editions of their reference manuals. When you search for a word that might be expressed as an abbreviation, check to see whether an automatic equivalency exists. If not, you will need to include the different possible spellings in your search request.

- *Pluralization.* Both LEXIS and WESTLAW will automatically search for the plural forms of most words. In both services, automatic equivalencies exist for the plurals of search terms that form their plurals regularly (that is, by adding "s" or "es" or, in the case of singular terms ending in "y," by changing "y" to "ies").[30] Thus, in LEXIS and WESTLAW,

`drug`	searches for	drug or drugs
`tax`	searches for	tax or taxes
`remedy`	searches for	remedy or remedies

Currently, the pluralization equivalency operates in only one direction in WESTLAW: a singular search term automatically gen-

[29] These examples are drawn from the LEXIS reference manual. MEAD DATA CENTRAL, REFERENCE MANUAL FOR THE LEXIS/NEXIS SERVICES 4 (undated looseleaf ed.).

[30] Occasionally, you might find that in automatically equating plural and singular search terms, the computer retrieves documents with meanings you did not intend. If so, you can alter the automatic search for plurals in LEXIS or WESTLAW.

In LEXIS, you can search for just the singular form of a search term. For example, `singular (damage)` will search for "damage" but not for "damages." Conversely, you can search for just the plural form of a search term. For example, `plural (damage)` will search for "damages" but not for "damage."

In WESTLAW, you can search for just the singular form of a search term: place the pound symbol (#) before the search term. For instance, `#damage` will search for "damage" but not for "damages."

erates a search for its regularly formed plural, but the plural search term does not trigger an automatic search for its singular form. Singular search terms therefore prove more effective than plurals for WESTLAW searching.

In LEXIS, the pluralization equivalency runs in both directions. As the following examples illustrate, a singular search term in LEXIS also retrieves its regularly formed plural, and a regularly formed plural search term also retrieves the singular version:[31]

`corporation`	searches for	corporation or corporations
`branch`	searches for	branch or branches
`city`	searches for	city or cities
`pleads`	searches for	pleads or plead
`scorches`	searches for	scorches or scorch
`stories`	searches for	stories or story

As for irregularly formed plurals (*e.g.*, memorandum/memoranda), LEXIS and WESTLAW automatically equate some—but not all—of these with their singular forms. For example, `memorandum` searches for "memorandum" or "memoranda."

For LEXIS, Appendix E includes automatic equivalencies for some irregular plurals. In connection with irregular plurals listed in the appendix (*e.g.*, "indices," "matrices"), you can search for either the singular or the plural and you will locate both forms. In WESTLAW, some of the automatic equivalencies for irregular plurals (such as memorandum/memoranda) run in both directions, and searching for either the singular or the plural will locate both forms; more often, though, the plural will not trigger a search for the singular.

So far, the CALR vendors have not published complete lists of their automatic equivalencies for irregular plurals. (The *WESTLAW Reference Manual*, for instance, says automatic equivalencies exist for "common" irregular plurals, but does not indicate which irreg-

[31] Note that an exception to the pluralization equivalency exists in LEXIS for singular search terms that end in "us" or "is." LEXIS does not automatically search for the plural form of these terms; for example, `bonus` will not locate "bonuses." To search in LEXIS for the plural of a term ending in "us" or "is," include both the singular and plural forms in your search request: `bonus or bonuses`.

ular plurals are considered common.)[32] Unless you know from experience that an automatic equivalency exists, the safest course when you want to search for an irregular plural in LEXIS or WESTLAW is to include both the singular and plural form in your search request, as in this search instruction:

```
mouse or mice
```

- *Possessive nouns (apostrophe).* Both LEXIS and WESTLAW will automatically search for the possessive form of singular nouns used as search terms. Thus, for example, in LEXIS and WESTLAW,

`tenant`	searches for	tenant or tenant's
`child`	searches for	child or child's

The result is similar for plural nouns. For instance, in LEXIS and WESTLAW,

`victims`	searches for	victims or victims'
`children`	searches for	children or children's

LEXIS and WESTLAW take this automatic equivalency one step further by combining the automatic search for possessives with the automatic search for plurals. Thus, the singular form of a search term also searches automatically for the plural form, the singular possessive form, and the plural possessive form. For example, in LEXIS and WESTLAW,

`tenant`	searches for	tenant tenants tenant's tenants'

In addition to the preceding software-embedded equivalencies for which the LEXIS and WESTLAW computers have been programmed to search automatically, each CALR service provides certain embedded equivalencies that researchers can activate at their discretion. These *discretionary equivalencies*, set out below, afford researchers additional ways to search for variations on search terms.

- *Compound words and acronyms: WESTLAW's "normalized" equivalencies.* With WESTLAW, researchers can choose to acti-

[32] West Publishing Company, WESTLAW Reference Manual 66 (5th ed. 1993).

vate a special type of discretionary equivalency search in connection with two kinds of words: compound words and acronyms. Each of these terms can appear in several configurations. A compound word can appear as, for example, "post conviction," "post-conviction," or "post-conviction"; an acronym can appear as, for instance, "A.I.D.S.," "AIDS," "A I D S," or "A. I. D. S." These variations pose a problem for researchers using a CALR service because, in selecting search terms, researchers cannot know which variation an author of a document has used.

To address this problem, WESTLAW provides researchers the option of using a WESTLAW-designated configuration (referred to as a "normalized" form) that will search for all the variations. Generally, when searching in WESTLAW for an acronym or a compound word, you will find using the normalized form of the term the most effective way to search. The normalized form is least apt to miss your search term in any of its configurations.

For compound words, WESTLAW has selected the hyphenated configuration as the normalized form. As mentioned earlier, if you use the hyphenated configuration in your search request, you activate a search for all three variations of the term. By contrast, if you omit the hyphen, the computer will search for only the form of the term you use in your search request. Thus, in WESTLAW,

`post-conviction`	searches for	post-conviction
		postconviction
		post conviction

The hyphen in LEXIS does not have this effect, but simply signifies the start of a new word. (See page 27 and Appendix G.)

For acronyms, WESTLAW's normalized form uses periods without intervening spaces (for example, "A.I.D.S."). By using this configuration when searching for an acronym in WESTLAW, you activate an equivalency search for all four forms the term may take. Thus, in WESTLAW,

`A.I.D.S.`	searches for	A.I.D.S
		A. I. D. S.
		AIDS
		A I D S

LEXIS does not provide a normalized form for acronyms. In LEXIS, you cannot use a designated form of an acronym to activate a search for a variation of the search term unless LEXIS has included the acronym among the abbreviations selected for an automatic equivalency search. (See pages 31–32.) Even then, the LEXIS computer will search for just one variation. In contrast, WESTLAW's technique for normalizing acronyms works with *any* acronym and searches for all variations.

Using WESTLAW's normalized forms will help you avoid retrieving unwanted results. For instance, searching for A. I. D. S. instead of the normalized A.I.D.S. will retrieve not only A. I. D. S., but other combinations of these letters (such as I. D. S.). The computer will search for the unwanted letter combinations because a space signals the start of a new word and because (as noted in the explanation of the "or" connector on pages 44–45) a space between words in a WESTLAW search request operates as an instruction to the computer to search for documents containing either or both of the words separated by the space.

Using WESTLAW's normalized search terms won't completely eliminate unexpected search results, however. For example, when the WESTLAW computer searches for the normalized acronym A.I.D.S.—and, consequently, for AIDS as one of the equivalencies—the computer will locate not only documents that use "AIDS" to refer to acquired immune deficiency syndrome, but documents that refer, say, to financial "aids" or to a defendant who "aids" and abets the commission of a crime. (Recall that, as discussed on page 31, the computer automatically treats uppercase and lowercase letters as equivalent.)

- *Universal characters (also known as "root expanders").* In both LEXIS and WESTLAW, you can look for variations on search terms by using the asterisk or the exclamation mark as a substitute for one or more characters in a search term.

  The *asterisk* functions as a stand-in for a character anywhere in a search term except for the first character. For example, if you use `kn*w` as a search term, the computer will search for any four-character strings that begin with "kn" and end with "w." Consequently, in LEXIS and WESTLAW,

`kn*w`	searches for	know
		knew

Because an asterisk in the middle of a search term must represent a character, the search term `prof*ession`, for example, will not locate "profession."

You can use more than one asterisk in the middle of a search term, each one substituting for a character. For example,

`bl**d`	searches for	bleed blood blind blend blond

As a practical matter, though, if you want to search only for related terms like "bleed" and "blood" (and avoid "blind," "blend," and "blond"), you will probably search more efficiently if you do not use multiple asterisks in the middle of your search term. Instead, simply instruct the computer to search for each term without using asterisks:

```
bleed or blood
```

In addition to using the asterisk in the middle of a search term, in both LEXIS and WESTLAW you can place one or more asterisks at the end of a search term to expand on the search term's root. Each asterisk substitutes for one character at the end of the root, and the computer will search for any character string that consists of the root plus any number of characters up to the number of asterisks following the root. This feature addresses the situation in which, for example, the author of a document might have expressed a point in any one of the following ways:

> "The plaintiffs *objected* to the introduction of the evidence."
>
> "The plaintiffs raised an *objection* to the evidence."
>
> "In arguing as they did, the plaintiffs were *objecting* to the evidence."

Because you normally will not know the exact language in a document, you will often need to search for the likely variations on the roots of your search terms. To locate variations on the root "object," for example, you could use the asterisk to form various expansions:

`object**`	searches for	object objects objected objector

`object***`	searches for	object objects objected objector objecting objection objective objectors
`object****`	searches for	object objects objected objector objecting objection objective objections objectives

This example illustrates several points. First, when the asterisk appears at the end of a search term, the computer does not require a character to be present in the place the asterisk occupies. Unlike an asterisk in the middle of a search term, an asterisk at the end can substitute for nothing. For instance, `object**` will search for "object," just as `object****` will search for "objected."

Second, the computer will search only for character strings that do not exceed the number of characters in the root plus the number of asterisks attached to the root. For example, with four asterisks after "object," the computer will not search for "objectionable."

Third, using asterisks to expand the roots of search terms can locate irrelevant terms. For example, suppose you want to locate documents dealing with objections to evidence introduced during a trial. Searching for `object****` locates not only documents with relevant terms like "objected" or "objection," but documents with the presumably irrelevant terms "objective" or "objectives."

The other universal character—the *exclamation mark*—also provides a way to expand on the roots of search terms. Unlike the asterisk, though, the exclamation mark is used only at the end of a search term, where it substitutes for an unlimited number of characters after the root of a search term. Thus, in LEXIS and WESTLAW,

`object!` searches for object
objects
objected
objector
objecting
objection
objective
objectors
objections
objectives
objectively
objectivity
objectifiable
objectionable
objectiveness
objectionability

When you use the exclamation mark, you do not need to consider how many characters might appear in all potentially relevant expansions of your search term, as you do when you use asterisks to look for root expansions. The exclamation mark will retrieve any number of characters at the end of your search term. Moreover, the exclamation mark proves convenient if your search term has many different possible endings: you avoid the unwieldiness of relying on a long string of asterisks to ensure that your search does not miss a relevant expansion.[33] With the exclamation mark, however, you run the risk of locating more irrelevant words than you would with four or fewer asterisks.

Finally, as you seek to expand the roots of search terms, remember that it is not always necessary to use either the asterisk or the exclamation mark to achieve your goal. If you only want to locate, say, "executor" or "executrix," just use those words in your search request. You will locate the words you want and avoid a root expander's retrieving irrelevant variations. In other situations, an automatic equivalency will eliminate the need for a root expander. For example, you do not need to use a root expander to search for the possessive form of a search term (tenant/tenant's) or for the

[33] As an earlier edition of the WESTLAW reference manual noted, "[t]here is no limit to the number of asterisks you may use at the end of a term, but for practical use, if more than four asterisks are needed, the root expansion character (!) should probably be used instead." WEST PUBLISHING COMPANY, WESTLAW TEMPORARY REFERENCE MANUAL 7/6 (1985 ed. & 1987 inserts).

regularly formed plural of a singular search term (tax/taxes): automatic equivalencies already perform these tasks. (See pages 32–34.)

Search term frequency in LEXIS. When you search in LEXIS, you can instruct the computer to retrieve documents containing at least a certain number of occurrences of a word. For example, to search for documents containing at least 25 occurrences of "reckless," you would include the following command in your search request:

```
atleast25(reckless)
```

Or, you could search for documents containing at least 25 occurrences of "reckless" and at least 50 occurrences of "wanton":

```
atleast25(reckless) and atleast50(wanton)
```

You can use any number up to 255 in an "atleast" command, although in selecting a number, you face the problematic task of trying to anticipate how many times the author of a relevant document has used your search term.

The use of the "atleast" command rests on an assumption that the more frequently a search term appears in a document, the more likely the document will prove relevant to the issue reflected in the search request. Thus, the "atleast" command shares one of the assumptions underlying natural-language searching in WESTLAW. (See page 26.) But, unlike WESTLAW's natural-language feature, the "atleast" command in LEXIS does not operate in conjunction with the other key assumption (explained on page 26) underlying natural-language searching: that the evaluation of a document's relevance must also take into account how frequently a search term occurs throughout the database in which the search is conducted. This evaluation allows natural-language algorithms to minimize the likelihood of falsely assigning a high probable relevance to a document when the document contains a large number of occurrences of a search term that also appears frequently in documents throughout the entire database. (In that situation, the nondistinctiveness of the search term means it probably does not serve as a good discriminator of relevant documents.)

Because the frequency of a search term's occurrence in a document will not—by itself—necessarily correlate with that document's likely relevance, the usefulness of the "atleast" command is difficult to predict. In addition, using the "atleast" command can easily result in bypassing highly relevant documents that contain fewer occurrences of a search term than required by the command. Consequently, this command might prove less risky when used only after you have retrieved a collection of documents and want to scan them with a FOCUS search (explained in Chapter 11) to find occurrences of particular words.

Summary. Figure 4.01 highlights the rules governing search terms when you search with Boolean logic in LEXIS and WESTLAW.

Logic connectors in Boolean searching in LEXIS and WESTLAW

Search terms constitute only one part of a Boolean search request. The other part consists of logic connectors. Each connector in a search request specifies for the computer a particular relationship that must exist among search terms in a document for the document to satisfy the search request.

The need for logic connectors arises because legal research problems involve concepts that can rarely be expressed in a single word or in a single way. For example, to return to the Ohio landlord-tenant dispute about the lack of running water in a leased apartment (see pages 19–20), the concept of an apartment lease can be expressed, among other ways, as "apartment lease," "apartment rental agreement," "lease of an apartment," and "the plaintiff leased an apartment." Logic connectors are the mechanism by which you link appropriate search terms to express a concept in the same arrangement of words the

What is a searchable word?

You can search for a single character, *i.e.,* a letter, number, or symbol like $. Or you can search for a string of characters unbroken by a space. (Some symbols are treated as spaces in certain situations. See Appendices G and H.) In LEXIS, if a word exceeds 20 characters, the computer searches for any word that begins with the same 20 characters.

Examples: automobile
inc.
2001

What is not a searchable word?

You cannot search for certain commonly occurring words, called "noise" words in LEXIS and "stop" words in WESTLAW. Check the CALR vendors' lists of non-searchable words (see Appendices C and D).

Examples: an, the, it, them

In LEXIS, you cannot search for words that serve as LEXIS commands; in WESTLAW, you cannot search for words that serve as WESTLAW commands. Check the list of LEXIS "reserved" words and WESTLAW "stop" words (see Appendices C and D).

Examples: and, or

(continues)

Figure 4.01. Quick Guide to Search Terms

(continued)

Capital letters

Uppercase and lowercase letters are automatically treated as equivalent.

Example: Negligence = negligence

Abbreviations

Many abbreviations (but not all) are considered the same as their unabbreviated counterparts. Check the CALR vendors' lists of automatic equivalencies (see Appendices E and F).

Examples: ch = chapter
10th = tenth

Acronyms

For some acronyms, LEXIS will automatically search for a predetermined variation. Check the list of automatic equivalencies in LEXIS for acronyms that trigger automatic equivalency searches (see Appendix E).

Example: H.U.D. = HUD

WESTLAW automatically searches for all forms of an acronym if you type it with periods and without spaces.

Example: `H.U.D.` searches for H.U.D.
HUD
H. U. D.
H U D

Compound words

In LEXIS, a hyphen starts a new word; it does not trigger an automatic search for all forms of a compound word.

Example: `post-conviction` searches for post-conviction
post conviction

WESTLAW automatically searches for all forms of a compound word if you type it with a hyphen.

Example: `post-conviction` searches for post-conviction
postconviction
post conviction

Regularly formed plurals

LEXIS and WESTLAW automatically search for the plurals of search terms that form their plurals regularly (that is, by adding "s" or "es" or, in the case of singular search terms ending in "y," by changing "y" to "ies").

Examples: `drug` searches for drug or drugs
`tax` searches for tax or taxes
`remedy` searches for remedy or remedies

(continues)

Figure 4.01. Quick Guide to Search Terms (continued)

(continued)

In LEXIS, the automatic equivalency for regularly formed plurals runs in both directions: a regularly formed plural search term will also search for the singular form. Thus, `drugs` searches for "drugs" or "drug." In WESTLAW, searching for a regularly formed plural will not locate the singular form.

In LEXIS, the automatic pluralization equivalency does not work for the plurals of words that end in "us" or "is." So, searching for `bonus` will not locate "bonuses."

Irregularly formed plurals

LEXIS and WESTLAW automatically search for the irregularly formed plurals of some (but not all) singular search terms. Check the CALR vendors' lists of automatic equivalencies (see Appendices E and F).

Example: `memorandum` searches for memorandum or memoranda

Possessive nouns (apostrophe)

LEXIS and WESTLAW automatically search for the possessive forms of singular and plural nouns.

Examples:	`tenant`	searches for	tenant or tenant's
	`child`	searches for	child or child's
	`victims`	searches for	victims or victims'
	`children`	searches for	children or children's

For singular search terms, LEXIS and WESTLAW combine the automatic search for possessives with the automatic search for plurals.

Example: `tenant` searches for tenant
tenants
tenant's
tenants'

Universal characters, also known as "root expanders" (* and !)

In Boolean search requests, LEXIS and WESTLAW allow you to use an asterisk to substitute for a character anywhere in a search term except for the first character.

Examples:	`kn*w`	searches for	know or knew
	`object***`	searches for	objected, objection, objecting, etc.

Each asterisk in the middle of a search term must substitute for a character; at the end of a search term, an asterisk need not substitute for anything.

LEXIS and WESTLAW allow you to use an exclamation mark to substitute for an unlimited number of characters at the end of a search term in a Boolean search request.

Example: `object!` searches for objected, objection, objectionability, etc.

Figure 4.01. Quick Guide to Search Terms (continued)

author of a document has used to express the concept. This replication creates an instruction that allows the computer to find the document by matching the search terms with the words in the document.

Logic connectors build on three core logic relationships that can exist among search terms. For example:

- A search request can require "plumbing" *or* "water" to appear in a document.
- A search request can require "plumbing" *and* "water" to appear in a document.
- A search request can require "plumbing" but *not* "water" to appear in a document.

The CALR vendors have designated logic connectors to signify each of these relationships, as well as logic connectors signifying several other relationships that flow from the three core ones.[34] This section explains the LEXIS and WESTLAW connectors; a summary of the discussion appears on pages 56–57 and in Figure 4.03 on pages 58–59.

The three core connectors. The following connectors signify the three central logic relationships in LEXIS and WESTLAW:

- `or` (LEXIS)
  `or` or **a space** (WESTLAW)

  Only one of the search terms linked by the connector need appear in a document for it to satisfy the search request. Although the "or" connector requires the presence of only one of the search terms, a document will still satisfy the search request if both terms appear in the document. Thus, either or both of the terms can appear anywhere in the document.

  For example, in response to the following search requests,

LEXIS:	`plumbing or water`
WESTLAW:	`plumbing or water` `plumbing water`

  the computer will locate any document that contains either "plumbing" or "water" (or both) anywhere in the document. The "or" con-

[34] The articulation of the three principal relationships—alternation, conjunction, and negation—traces back to George Boole, who recognized them as existing among all "things" or "propositions." *See* GEORGE BOOLE, AN INVESTIGATION OF THE LAWS OF THOUGHT [*25], [*52] (1854), *reprinted in* II GEORGE BOOLE, COLLECTED LOGICAL WORKS 27, 57 (P. Jourdain ed., 1940); WILLARD V.O. QUINE, MATHEMATICAL LOGIC 14 (1947); WILLARD V.O. QUINE, METHODS OF LOGIC 1–3 (rev. ed. 1959).

Figure 4.02. George Boole in His Office

nector is frequently used. Note that WESTLAW gives you the option of using either the word "or" or a space as the connector.

- **and** or **&** (LEXIS)
  and or **&** (WESTLAW)

  Each search term linked by the connector must appear in a document for it to satisfy the search request; the terms can appear anywhere in the document.

  For example, in response to the following search requests,

LEXIS:	`apartment and lease` `apartment & lease`
WESTLAW:	`apartment and lease` `apartment & lease`

the computer will locate any document in which both search terms—"apartment" and "lease"—appear somewhere in the document.[35] The "and" connector is frequently used. Note that LEXIS and WESTLAW give you the option of using either the word "and" or the "&" symbol as the connector.

- `and not` (LEXIS)
  `but not` or `%` (WESTLAW)

The search term preceding the connector must appear somewhere in the document and the search terms following the connector must not appear anywhere in the document for the document to satisfy the search request.

For example, in response to the following search requests,

LEXIS:	`apartment and not house`
WESTLAW:	`apartment but not house` `apartment % house`

the computer will locate any document containing "apartment" somewhere in it, but in which "house" does not appear anywhere. Note that WESTLAW gives you the option of using either the words "but not" or the "%" symbol as the connector.

You will find relatively little use for the "and not" and "but not" connectors. These exclusionary connectors pose a significant risk of missing relevant documents. First, you cannot always accurately predict the context in which the excluded term might appear; for instance, the computer will pass over a relevant case even if the excluded term appears only as the name of a party, attorney, or street address mentioned in the document.

Similarly, the computer will bypass a relevant document even if the author of the document has used the excluded term in a way that enhances instead of diminishes the document's relevance. Sup-

[35] Although not like a typical connector, which links different search terms, the LEXIS "atleast" command (explained on page 40) operates, in effect, like the "and" connector. For example, `atleast25(reckless)` instructs the computer to locate documents that contain one occurrence of "reckless" *and* a second occurrence of "reckless" *and* a third occurrence of "reckless," and so on, up to at least a 25th occurrence of "reckless."

pose, for example, you are interested in locating cases about civil rather than criminal assault. You could use the search request `assault but not criminal`. This request, however, would fail to locate civil assault cases in which the judge expressly distinguishes criminal assault doctrines from doctrines about civil assault—*e.g.*, by writing that "the burden of proof in a civil assault case, such as this, differs substantially from the burden in a criminal assault case."

Finally, if you exclude a term, you might inadvertently bypass documents in which the excluded term represents an important analogy useful to your research.

As you become familiar with online searching, you will encounter situations in which excluding a search term proves a useful way to eliminate irrelevant documents from your search results. In general, though, you will find it preferable not to exclude search terms, especially before you have had a chance to sample the results retrieved by a search request that does not exclude search terms.

If you opt to use the "and not" or "but not" connector, be sure that any search terms appearing after this connector are words you do not want to appear in retrieved documents. Otherwise, you might inadvertently exclude more search terms than you intend.

Note. As you use LEXIS and WESTLAW, you might notice that the LEXIS computer also accepts the WESTLAW formulation, "but not." "But not" and "and not" do not operate identically in LEXIS, however. If you use "but not" in LEXIS, the search term following the connector can appear in the document so long as that term does not appear in the same segment as the search term preceding the connector.[36] Because of the difference between "and not" and "but not" in LEXIS, you can obtain different search results if you substitute one connector for the other.

In WESTLAW, the computer accepts the LEXIS "and not" connector, which operates just like the WESTLAW "but not" or "%" connector.

Proximity connectors. In addition to the "or," "and," and "and not/but not" logic connectors, which correspond to the three basic logic relationships, the CALR vendors have established several other connectors known variously as "proximity connectors," "distance connectors," "numerical connectors," and "grammatical connectors." (This book calls them "proximity connectors.") Regardless of the designation, all these connectors differ from the core connectors

[36] For a discussion of segments, see Chapter 5.

in one significant respect. The relationships the core connectors establish among search terms do not require the terms to appear in specific positions in the document. For example, the search request `apartment and lease` will locate a document in which both terms appear, regardless of their location in the document: "apartment" could be, say, the first word in the document and "lease" the last (or vice versa), and the document would satisfy the search request.

The proximity connectors, by contrast, require not only the presence or absence of terms in a document, but that the presence or absence of those terms occur within defined distances (or "proximities") within the document. For example, suppose your search request includes a proximity connector to require the term "apartment" to appear in a document within ten words of "lease." If both "apartment" and "lease" appear in the document, but are separated by, say, 15 words, the computer will not locate the document. In this way, proximity connectors can both significantly fine-tune and significantly constrict your search, reducing the number of documents the computer will locate.

LEXIS and WESTLAW have established the following proximity connectors:

- `w/n` or `/n` (LEXIS)
  `w/n` or `/n` (WESTLAW)
  Note: The "n" stands for any number you choose from 1 through 255.

  Both search terms linked by the connector must appear in the document and must appear within "n" words of each other. Either term can precede the other so long as the terms appear within the required distance of each other. (In LEXIS, the terms must also appear in the same segment of the document; WESTLAW does not impose this additional restriction.)[37]

  For example, in response to the following search requests,

LEXIS:	`apartment w/10 lease` `apartment /10 lease`
WESTLAW:	`apartment w/10 lease` `apartment /10 lease`

  the computer will locate any document in which "apartment" and "lease" appear in the document within ten words of each other (and, in LEXIS, within the same segment as well). Thus, in response to the search requests in the examples, the computer will locate doc-

[37] For a discussion of segments, see Chapter 5.

uments that include phrases like "apartment lease" or "lease of an apartment" or "the apartment that plaintiff agreed to lease." Note that LEXIS and WESTLAW give you two options for expressing the connector.

This connector is a frequently used connector, designed to reduce the likelihood the computer will retrieve documents in which your search terms appear so far apart they constitute random occurrences and do not represent the concept for which you are searching.[38] You will find the connector useful when searching for terms that commonly appear near each other, but not necessarily in the same arrangement every time (as in "apartment lease" and "lease of an apartment").

Experience with legal terminology and its usage helps develop proficiency at choosing appropriate numbers to substitute for "n." As an earlier edition of the WESTLAW reference manual noted, "[t]here are no magical numbers for specifying the distance between words. . . . You must simply decide what number seems reasonable, based on how you think the words would occur in a relevant case."[39] The LEXIS reference manual similarly observes that "[t]here is no magic formula for choosing the value of [the 'w/n' connector]."[40] The LEXIS manual offers these guidelines, however, for choosing a value:[41]

- Try a value from 3 to 5 if your search terms are apt to appear as part of a short phrase (*e.g.*, the terms "fair" and "value" in the phrase "fair market value" or "fair rental value") or if the search terms are part of someone's name (*e.g.*, "Lawrence" and "Walsh" in the name "Lawrence A. Walsh").
- Try a value from 10 to 15 if your search terms are apt to appear as part of a longer phrase or within a discussion of roughly sentence length.

[38] The additional requirement LEXIS imposes that the search terms appear within the same segment is designed to minimize further the retrieval of irrelevant documents. If the terms linked by the "w/n" connector appear in a document because they express the concept in which you are interested, the terms will almost necessarily appear within the same segment. If the terms do not appear in the same segment, they likely have no relation to each other and therefore probably do not represent the concept for which you are searching.

[39] West Publishing Company, WESTLAW Temporary Reference Manual 7/8 (1985 ed. & 1987 inserts). *See also* West Publishing Company, WESTLAW Reference Manual 73 (5th ed. 1993).

[40] Mead Data Central, Reference Manual for the LEXIS/NEXIS Services 46 (undated looseleaf ed.); Mead Data Central, LEXIS-NEXIS User's Guide 5–4 (1990 & 1991 Supp.).

[41] Mead Data Central, Reference Manual for the LEXIS/NEXIS Services 46 (undated looseleaf ed.).

- Try a value from 25 to 100 if your search terms are apt to appear in a discussion of approximately paragraph length.

In using the "w/n" (or "/n") connector, you might notice that you obtain different results in LEXIS and WESTLAW with identical search requests. The connector can yield different results in the two services because LEXIS and WESTLAW use different methods of counting the words between your search terms. In LEXIS, "n" refers only to searchable words; noise words do not count. In WESTLAW, "n" refers to all words, including stop words. (See Appendices C and D for lists of noise and stop words, and pages 28–30 for a general discussion of these words.)

For example, consider the following search request: `felon w/10 firearm`. In LEXIS, this request would retrieve a document containing the sentence "A felon is not authorized, unless a pardon has been granted, to possess a firearm." Because the LEXIS computer does not count the noise words "is," "has," "been," and "to," it perceives the search terms as within eight words of each other. The WESTLAW computer, on the other hand, would bypass the sentence because, by counting the words the LEXIS computer ignores, the WESTLAW computer perceives the search terms as being 12 words apart.[42]

- `pre/n` or `+n` (LEXIS)
  `pre/n` or `+n` (WESTLAW)
  Note: The "n" stands for any number you choose from 1 through 255.

  Both search terms linked by the connector must appear in the document, and the term to the left of the connector must precede the term to the right of the connector by not more than "n" words.[43] (In LEXIS, the terms must also appear in the same segment of the document; WESTLAW does not impose this additional restriction.)[44]

  This connector offers a way to search for phrases in which you know certain terms appear, you know the order of the terms, but

[42] MEAD DATA CENTRAL, REFERENCE MANUAL FOR THE LEXIS/NEXIS SERVICES 39, 46 (undated looseleaf ed.); MEAD DATA CENTRAL, LEXIS-NEXIS USER'S GUIDE 5–3 (1990 & 1991 Supp.); WEST PUBLISHING COMPANY, WESTLAW REFERENCE MANUAL 73 (5th ed. 1993).

[43] The discussion (above) of the "w/n" connector explains how the LEXIS and WESTLAW computers count words in order to determine whether search terms are "n" words apart.

[44] For a discussion of segments, see Chapter 5.

you do not know the exact wording of the entire phrase. Thus, the connector can help in searching for citations to cases.[45]

For example, the following search requests will locate documents that refer to the case of *Miranda v. Arizona*, whether the author of the document has written "Miranda v. Arizona" or "Miranda v. State of Arizona":

LEXIS: **miranda pre/6 arizona**
miranda +6 arizona

WESTLAW: **miranda pre/6 arizona**
miranda +6 arizona

Similarly, the following search requests will locate documents that refer to a case citation, whether the author of the document has written "360 U.S. 684 or "360 United States Reports 684":

LEXIS: **360 pre/5 684**
360 +5 684

WESTLAW: **360 pre/5 684**
360 +5 684

Note that LEXIS and WESTLAW give you two options for expressing the connector.

It is also possible, although not always effective, to use the "pre/n" (or "+n") connector to search for citations to statutes or rules. For example, to locate documents referring to 20 U.S.C. § 1080, you could use the search request **20 pre/6 1080**. This request, however, would bypass documents in which the statutory reference appeared in an unconventional format, such as "section 1080 of Title 20 of the United States Code." For locating statutory and administrative citations (in which the order of citation elements is apt to vary), you will generally find the "w/n" connector results in more comprehensive searching than the "pre/n" (or "+n") connector.

- **phrase searching:**
space or **quotation marks** (LEXIS)
quotation marks (WESTLAW)

You can instruct the computer to treat adjacent search terms as a single phrase and to locate documents containing that phrase. To

[45] In many situations, however, the LEXCITE feature in LEXIS (see pages 461–66) and the QuickCite feature in WESTLAW (see pages 596–603) offer more convenient alternatives to using the "pre/n" (or "+n") connector to search for references to case citations.

do this in LEXIS, just leave a space between the search terms in the phrase; if you want, you can also enclose the search terms in quotation marks as a visual reminder that your search instruction includes a phrase. In WESTLAW, leave a space between adjacent terms and enclose them in quotation marks (which are *not* optional for a WESTLAW phrase search).

For example, in response to the following search requests,

LEXIS:	`habeas corpus` `"habeas corpus"`
WESTLAW:	`"habeas corpus"`

the computer will locate any document containing the phrase "habeas corpus."

Although you do not need to use quotation marks to search for a phrase in LEXIS, a useful rule of thumb is to use quotation marks whenever you search for a phrase, whether in LEXIS or WESTLAW. Sometimes, you will want to locate a phrase that includes a word that is non-searchable because it is a noise word, a stop word, or a word that has been reserved for use as a command; as explained on pages 28–30, you can search for such a phrase by placing quotation marks around either the non-searchable word or the entire phrase of which it is part. Thus, a LEXIS search request to locate the phrase "stop and frisk" could be formulated with quotation marks (in either of the following ways) to negate the reserved status of "and":

```
"stop and frisk"
stop "and" frisk
```

Moreover, by routinely using quotation marks in both LEXIS and WESTLAW, you only need to remember one rule for phrase searching.

Note that when you do a phrase search in LEXIS, you can search for a phrase that starts in one sentence and ends in the next. In WESTLAW, the words in the phrase must appear in the same sentence.

Phrase searching, whether in LEXIS or WESTLAW, imposes a high degree of rigidity on search requests. Because the search terms must appear in the document in the identical relationship to one another as in the search request, phrase searching does not offer a useful approach when the concept you want to locate can be expressed in more than one way (*e.g.*, "apartment lease" or "lease of an apartment").

If, however, you are certain that a relevant phrase has an invariable configuration, phrase searching works effectively. Terms of art, such as "habeas corpus," lend themselves to phrase searching. Similarly, if you need to locate documents construing particular language from a statute, regulation, jury instruction, or other source, you might find it helpful to search for a key phrase from the language; you will quickly find documents interpreting the language (assuming, of course, the documents quote the same phrase you include in your search request).[46]

- `w/seg` (LEXIS)

  There is no counterpart in WESTLAW.

  This proximity connector has relatively limited utility.[47] Both search terms it links must appear in the document and must appear in the same segment of the document.[48] So long as the terms satisfy the same-segment requirement, they can appear in any order and be separated by any number of words. The connector does not specify any particular segment in which the search terms must appear. A search request using the "w/seg" connector takes like form:

```
apartment w/seg lease
```

[46] Although phrase searching is intended to retrieve the exact language you use in a search request, you will sometimes retrieve slight variations on the language as well. As explained in the discussion of non-searchable words on pages 28–30, the computer might retrieve variations on a phrase if it contains a noise word, a stop word, or a reserved word.

In addition, because equivalencies (such as the pluralization equivalency) and universal characters (* and !) remain in effect during phrase searching, the computer will retrieve variations on a phrase if you include a universal character in your phrase search or if the computer locates a document in which the phrase is expressed with an equivalency. Thus, the phrase search `"justice of the peace"` would also retrieve "justices of the peace." Similarly, the phrase search `"assum! the risk"` would retrieve "assumed the risk," "assumes the risk," and "assuming the risk." (For a discussion of universal characters, see pages 36–40. For a discussion of other equivalencies, see pages 30–36.)

Even though non-searchable words, universal characters, and equivalencies allow for some variation between the form of words in a phrase search and the form those words take in a document, phrase searching always requires the words to appear in the document in the same sequence found in the search request. Thus, the phrase search `"assum! the risk"` would bypass the phrase "the risk was assumed." By contrast, a search request with a "w/n" connector—such as `assum! w/5 risk`—would retrieve "the risk was assumed" as well as the other phrases retrieved by the phrase search `"assum! the risk"`.

[47] Mead Data Central identifies this connector as one of several connectors that have only "limited application." MEAD DATA CENTRAL, LEARNING LEXIS 8 (1989).

[48] For a discussion of segments, see Chapter 5.

- `not w/n` (LEXIS)
  There is no counterpart in WESTLAW.
  Note: The "n" stands for any number you choose from 1 through 255.

  The document must contain at least one instance in which the search term preceding the connector appears somewhere in the document but does not appear within "n" words of the search term following the connector.[49] The "not w/n" connector has relatively limited utility[50] and (like the "and not" and "but not" connectors) risks excluding relevant documents.[51]

  Nonetheless, the "not w/n" connector sometimes proves helpful in isolating documents in which your search terms appear in relevant contexts. For example, suppose you want to locate cases concerning the drug diethylstilbestrol, commonly referred to as "D.E.S." or "DES." To reduce the likelihood that searching for "DES" will retrieve documents just because they mention, say, Des Moines or Des Plaines, you could use a search request in this form:

  ```
  des not w/2 (moines or plaines)
  ```

  In response to this search request, the computer will locate any document in which "DES" appears somewhere and in which "Moines" or "Plaines" either does not appear anywhere or (if it does appear in the document) in at least one instance does not appear within two words of "DES."

- `not w/seg` (LEXIS)
  There is no counterpart in WESTLAW.

  The document must contain at least one segment in which the search term preceding the connector appears but the search term following the connector does not appear.[52] The "not w/seg" connector has limited utility[53] and (like the "and not" and "but not" connectors) risks excluding relevant documents.[54]

[49] Page 50 explains how the LEXIS computer counts words in order to determine whether search terms are "n" words apart.

[50] *See* note 47.

[51] *See* pages 46–47.

[52] For a discussion of segments, see Chapter 5.

[53] *See* note 47.

[54] *See* pages 46–47.

- `/s` (WESTLAW)
  There is no counterpart in LEXIS, although the LEXIS reference manual suggests using the "w/n" connector with an "n" value from 10 to 15 to achieve similar results.[55]

  Both search terms linked by the "/s" connector must appear in the document, and must appear somewhere in the same sentence. Either term can precede the other in the sentence. A search request using the "/s" connector takes this form:

```
apartment /s lease
```

The "/s" connector is intended to avoid the problem of having to choose an appropriate value for "n" in the "w/n" connector. However, the vagaries of the English language and variations in authors' writing styles pose a challenge to researchers attempting to anticipate whether an author has expressed an idea in, say, one sentence or two. For example, the search request **apartment /s lease** would locate a document in which the author wrote, "Plaintiff signed a one-year lease for an apartment." But the search request would bypass a document expressing the idea in two sentences, such as "Plaintiff rented an apartment. She signed a one-year lease." Moreover, stylistic conventions change over time; applying modern notions of grammar and sentence structure might result in a search request that fails to retrieve older, yet still relevant, documents.

- `+s` (WESTLAW)
  There is no counterpart in LEXIS.

  Both search terms linked by the connector must appear in the document and must appear in the same sentence, with the term to the left of the connector appearing before the term to the right of the connector. A search request using the "+s" connector (which has limited utility) takes this form:

```
apartment +s lease
```

As with the "/s" connector, the "+s" connector can prove problematic for researchers trying to anticipate the order in which an author has arranged words in a sentence. For instance, suppose one document contains the sentence "The apartment was rented pur-

[55] MEAD DATA CENTRAL, REFERENCE MANUAL FOR THE LEXIS/NEXIS SERVICES 46 (undated looseleaf ed.); MEAD DATA CENTRAL, LEXIS-NEXIS USER'S GUIDE 5–4 (1990 & 1991 Supp.).

suant to a one-year lease." Suppose another document says "The plaintiff signed a one-year lease for the apartment." The search request `apartment +s lease` would locate the first document, but skip the second. West Publishing has suggested that researchers rarely use the "+s" connector.[56]

- `/p` (WESTLAW)
  There is no counterpart in LEXIS, although the LEXIS reference manual suggests using the "w/n" connector with an "n" value from 25 to 100 to achieve similar results.[57]

  Both search terms linked by the "/p" connector must appear in the document and must appear somewhere in the same paragraph. Either term can precede the other in the paragraph. A search request using the "/p" connector takes this form:

  ```
  apartment /p lease
  ```

  As with sentence structure, authors vary in how they form paragraphs. In using the "/p" connector, you face a challenge analogous to the one you confront with the "/s" connector.

- `+p` (WESTLAW)
  There is no counterpart in LEXIS.

  Both terms linked by the connector must appear in the document and must appear in the same paragraph, with the term to the left of the connector appearing before the term to the right of the connector. The "+p" connector has limited utility. To use it effectively, you must correctly predict the order in which words will appear in paragraphs in relevant documents, and this task poses difficulties like those you face with "+s."

Summary: Making sense of the connectors. Knowing about the full range of available connectors will give you a feel for the CALR services' capabilities. However, you can formulate most of your Boolean search requests, especially in the beginning, by employing only three of the connectors:

- `or`—either or both of the search terms can appear
- `and`—both search terms must appear

[56] West Publishing Company, WESTLAW Temporary Reference Manual 7/10 (1985 ed. & 1987 inserts). *See also* note 59 and accompanying text.

[57] Mead Data Central, Reference Manual for the LEXIS/NEXIS Services 46 (undated looseleaf ed.); Mead Data Central, LEXIS-NEXIS User's Guide 5–4 (1990 & 1991 Supp.).

- `w/n` (or `/n`)—the search terms must appear within a designated number of words of each other

In addition, you will probably find the phrase connector (*i.e.*, a space or quotation marks in LEXIS, and quotation marks in WESTLAW) helpful if you need to locate a specific phrase.[58] The "pre/n" connector can help if you need to locate a case citation.

You will likely use the remaining connectors (such as "and not" and "but not") less frequently, and you might never use some connectors (such as "w/seg," "not w/seg," and "+p").

In WESTLAW, if time and money are a concern, you might want to avoid using the "/p," "+p," "/s," and "+s" connectors. These connectors operate much more slowly than other connectors, and can significantly increase the time (and therefore the cost) of carrying out a search request.[59]

Figure 4.03 provides a summary of all the connectors for Boolean searching in LEXIS and WESTLAW.

The relative restrictiveness of connectors. Regardless of the connectors you use, you will need to know whether a particular connector (in comparison with other possible connectors) increases or decreases the number of documents a search request will locate. In particular, note that a search request

[58] In fact, the contemporary CALR services trace their roots to a computerized system created to search for all occurrences of the phrase "retarded child" in statutory documents, which the legislature planned to change to read "special child." *See* Jon Bing, *Performance of Legal Text Retrieval Systems: The Curse of Boole*, 79 LAW LIBR. J. 187, 187–88 (1987) (describing a system first demonstrated in 1960).

[59] For some examples of the slower response times, see John Doyle, *Aiming at the Databases*, 3 TRENDS IN LAW LIBR. MGMT. & TECH., Mar. 1990, at 3. For instance, Doyle compared the time the WESTLAW computer took to carry out the following two search requests in the ALLSTATES database:

```
"good faith" /p employ! /s will
"good faith" /90 employ! /20 will
```

The computer needed 8 minutes and 5 seconds to retrieve 1,130 cases with the first search request, but needed only 1 minute and 25 seconds to retrieve 1,161 cases using the second search request. Even at low-end rates of $2 to $3 a minute, the first search would cost roughly $13 to $20 more than the second search.

Instead of using "/s" or "/p" in a WESTLAW search request, you can use the "w/n" connector and experiment with different "n" values. For example, try an "n" value around 15 to 25 to simulate "/s," or an "n" value somewhere between 50 and 125 to simulate "/p." (You might notice these "n" values for approximating sentence and paragraph lengths are larger than the values for similar searching in LEXIS. See pages 49–50. The disparity results because the WESTLAW computer counts every word in a document, while the LEXIS computer counts only searchable words. *Id.*)

Although the informational literature West Publishing provides to WESTLAW users does not mention the slower response times for the "same sentence" and "same paragraph" connectors, a leader of the team that redesigned the WESTLAW system in the early 1980s noted in a 1983 interview that these connectors operate more slowly than other connectors. *See* James A. Sprowl, *The Latest on Westlaw, Lexis and Dialog*, A.B.A. J., Mar. 1984, at 85, 87–88.

Connector		Explanation
LEXIS	WESTLAW	
`or`	`or` space	At least one of the terms linked by the connector must appear in the document.
`and` `&`	`and` `&`	Each term linked by the connector must appear in the document.
`and not`	`but not` `%`	The term preceding the connector must appear in the document, and the terms following the connector must not appear in the document.
`w/n` `/n`	`w/n` `/n`	The terms linked by the connector must appear within "n" words of each other (and, in LEXIS, within the same segment as well).*
`pre/n` `+n`	`pre/n` `+n`	The term preceding the connector must appear in front of, and within "n" words of, the term following the connector. (In LEXIS, the terms must also appear within the same segment.)*
space or quotation marks [phrase searching]	quotation marks [phrase searching]	The phrase must appear in the document. (The search might also retrieve limited variations on the phrase. See page 53 n.46.)
`w/seg`	[no counter-part]	The terms linked by the connector must appear within the same segment.
`not w/n`	[no counter-part]	The term preceding the connector must appear in the document; the term following the connector either must not appear in the document or, if it appears, in at least one instance must not appear within "n" words of the term preceding the connector.*

`not w/seg`	[no counter-part]	The document must contain at least one segment in which the term preceding the connector appears but the term following the connector does not.
[no counter-part]**	`/s`	The terms linked by the connector must appear within the same sentence.
[no counter-part]	`+s`	The term preceding the connector must appear within the same sentence as, and in front of, the term following the connector.
[no counter-part]***	`/p`	The terms linked by the connector must appear within the same paragraph.
[no counter-part]	`+p`	The term preceding the connector must appear within the same paragraph as, and in front of, the term following the connector.

* The "n" stands for any number you choose from 1 through 255. For an explanation of how the LEXIS and WESTLAW computers count words when you use an "n" value in a connector, see page 50.

** Although there is no counterpart in LEXIS, the LEXIS reference manual suggests using the `w/n` connector with an "n" value from 10 to 15 to achieve similar results.

*** Although there is no counterpart in LEXIS, the LEXIS reference manual suggests using the `w/n` connector with an "n" value from 25 to 100 to achieve similar results.

Note. Although not documented in the *WESTLAW Reference Manual* (5th ed. 1993), the `w/n` and `pre/n` connectors work as indicated.

Figure 4.03. Quick Guide to LEXIS and WESTLAW Connectors

using the "or" connector will increase the number of documents located in comparison with a search request using the "and" connector. For example, the search request `apartment or lease` will locate more documents than will the search request `apartment and lease`. Figure 4.04 illustrates this comparison.

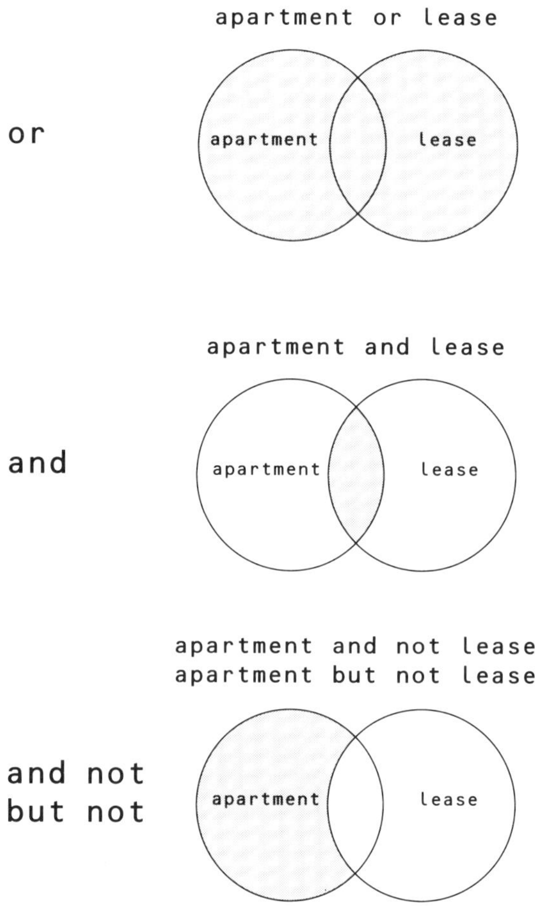

One circle represents the universe of online documents containing the search term `apartment` and the other circle represents the universe of online documents containing the search term `lease`. The shaded areas represent the documents that satisfy Boolean search requests using the three basic logic connectors to link these search terms. A comparison of the shaded areas shows the connectors' relative restrictive impact on the search requests.

Figure 4.04. Venn Diagrams of the Three Core Logic Relationships

By extension, if you know whether a connector is analogous to the "or" connector or to the "and" connector, you can assess its relative broadening or narrowing impact on your search results. Because each connector shares core characteristics with either the "or" or the "and" connector, you can classify all the connectors as establishing either an "or"-type or an "and"-type relationship between search terms. An "or"-type connector establishes an optional condition—that is, a search request based on an "or"-type connector can be satisfied by the presence of either of the search terms linked by the connector. In contrast, an "and"-type connector establishes a mandatory condition with respect to the search terms it links.

Figure 4.05 depicts the classification of connectors into "or"-type and "and"-type categories. As Figure 4.05 shows, except for "or," all the con-

LEXIS		**WESTLAW**	
Or-type	**And-type**	**Or-type**	**And-type**
`or`	`and, &`	`or`, space	`and, &`
	`and not`		`but not, %`
	`w/n, /n`		`w/n, /n`
	`pre/n, +n`		`pre/n, +n`
	space or quotation marks [phrase search]		quotation marks [phrase search]
	`w/seg`		`/s`
	`not w/n`		`+s`
	`not w/seg`		`/p`
			`+p`

The exclusionary connectors (`and not` and `but not`) create "and"-type relationships because they establish a mandatory condition with respect to each search term they link. For instance, `apartment and not house` requires that "apartment" appear in the document *and* that "house" not appear.

Similarly, all the proximity connectors (such as `w/n` or `/p`) are "and"-type connectors because they impose mandatory conditions. For instance, `apartment w/10 lease` requires that "apartment" appear in the document *and* that "lease" appear within ten words of "apartment." Likewise, a phrase search for "habeas corpus" mandates that "habeas" appear in the document *and* that "corpus" appear immediately following "habeas."

The negative proximity connectors (`not w/n` and `not w/seg`) also establish "and"-type relationships. For example, `warrant not w/10 arrest` imposes the following two mandatory conditions: that "warrant" appear in the document *and* that if "arrest" appears, in at least one instance it not appear within ten words of "warrant."

Figure 4.05. Classification of Connectors

nectors are "and"-type connectors. Consequently, compared with a single-word search request, all the connectors except "or" will decrease in varying degrees the number of documents a search request will locate. Even though narrowing a search always creates the potential for bypassing relevant documents, you will often need to use "and"-type connectors to sharpen the focus of your search and avoid locating an unmanageably large number of irrelevant documents. By recognizing, however, that "and"-type connectors might skip some relevant documents as these connectors narrow a search, you will use them more knowledgeably and can evaluate the need to continue your search, perhaps in books.

Finally, in Figure 4.06 you can see in a spectrum format the relative broadening and narrowing effect of the various connectors. As you examine the spectrum, you will be able to construct scenarios in which the relative restrictiveness of some of the connectors could vary from the sequence shown. For example, the same-sentence connector ("/s") would not be more restrictive than the same-paragraph connector ("/p") if a pertinent paragraph consisted of only a single sentence; rather, in that circumstance, the two connectors would prove equally restrictive. Nevertheless, visualizing the connectors on a continuum provides a general sense of their relative impact on search requests.

Using more than one connector in a search request. When (as generally happens) you need to use more than two search terms at a time to express the idea for which you want the computer to search, you will also need to use more than one connector to link the search terms. For example, returning to the hypothetical landlord-tenant dispute about the apartment that lacked running water (pages 19–20), a search request for relevant documents might instruct the computer to search for documents that contain "apartment" and "lease" within ten words of each other and that contain either "plumbing" or "water." This request could be communicated to the computer as:

```
apartment w/10 lease and plumbing or water
```

In a multiple-connector request like this, each connector has the same effect as when you use it in a single-connector search request. However, because the computer cannot process all the connectors simultaneously, a question arises about the order in which the computer will evaluate the connectors. The search request `apartment w/10 lease and plumbing or water` illustrates the problem. For instance, does the search request require that "apartment" appear within ten words of "lease," or does it require that "apartment" appear within ten words of both "lease" and "plumbing"? To avoid this kind of interpretative uncertainty, each CALR vendor has established an order for the computer to follow in executing a multiple-connector search request.

The LEXIS and WESTLAW computers process connectors in the following order:

LEXIS

Least Restrictive ⟷ **Most Restrictive**

or	single search term	not w/n	not w/seg	and not	and &	w/seg	w/n /n	pre/n +n	phrase search (*i.e.*, space or quotation marks)

WESTLAW

Least Restrictive ⟷ **Most Restrictive**

or space	single search term	but not %	and &	/p	/s	w/n /n	+p	+s	pre/n +n	phrase search (*i.e.*, quotation marks)

Note. The less restrictive the logic connector, the more documents it locates. The more restrictive the logic connector, the fewer documents it locates.

Figure 4.06. Relative Restrictiveness of Connectors

LEXIS	WESTLAW
1. phrases	1. phrases
2. terms used with `atleast`[60]	2. `or`
3. `or`	3. `+n`
4. `w/n`, `pre/n`, `not w/n`	4. `/n`
5. `w/seg`	5. `+s`
6. `not w/seg`	6. `/s`
7. `and`	7. `+p`
8. `and not`	8. `/p`
	9. `and`
	10. `but not`

In effect, the computer breaks a multiple-connector request into a series of single-connector requests and carries out each request individually in the order established by the vendors' hierarchies. Given the hierarchies, you can anticipate how the LEXIS or WESTLAW computer would process the sample search request `apartment w/10 lease and plumbing or water`:

- First, because the "or" connector has the highest priority of the connectors in this search request, the computer would begin by evaluating the terms linked by "or." Thus, the computer would first search for documents containing either "plumbing" or "water."
- Next, the computer would evaluate the "w/10" connector, which has the second-highest priority among the connectors in the search request. So, the computer would next search for documents containing "apartment" within ten words of "lease."
- Finally, the computer would evaluate the "and" connector, the lowest-priority connector in the search request. Because the search terms adjacent to "and" ("lease," "plumbing") are already part of other higher-priority connector groupings, "and" does not link "lease" and "plumbing." Rather, it links the results of the computer's evaluations of the adjacent connector *groupings*, in effect treating each grouping as a single search term.

Figure 4.07 illustrates how the LEXIS and WESTLAW computers process the connectors in the example.

Numerous rules amplify the basic hierarchy of connectors by addressing various situations that can arise in multiple-connector search requests.[61] (By

[60] Recall that, although not a true connector, the "atleast" command in LEXIS operates like a connector. *See* page 46 n.35.

[61] The *WESTLAW Reference Manual* contains seven pages of rules elaborating on exceptions and nuances concerning the hierarchy of WESTLAW connectors. West Publishing Company, WESTLAW Reference Manual 319–25 (5th ed. 1993). The LEXIS reference manual contains a similar discussion of the rules governing the hierarchy of LEXIS connectors. Mead Data Central, Reference Manual for the LEXIS/NEXIS Services 56, Appendix F (undated looseleaf ed.); Mead Data Central, LEXIS-NEXIS User's Guide 5–6 (1990 & 1991 Supp.).

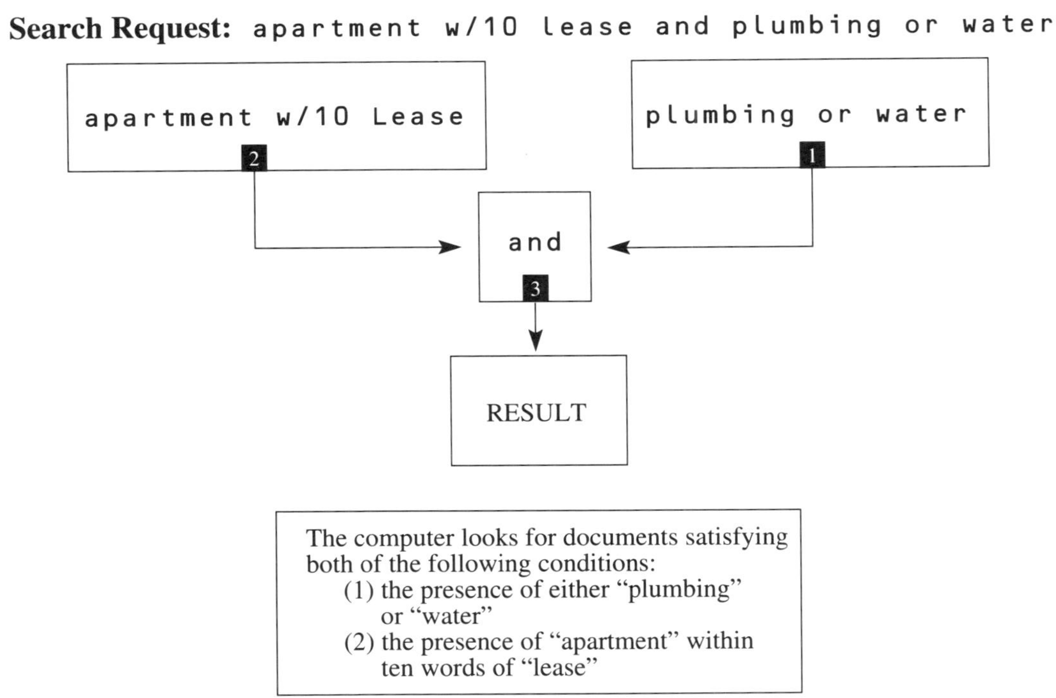

Figure 4.07. How LEXIS and WESTLAW Process a Multiple-Connector Search Request

using parentheses in search requests, as explained in the next paragraph, you can minimize the need to have more than a passing familiarity with the basic hierarchy rules for connectors.) Two situations are especially apt to arise. First, a multiple-connector search request might use a given connector more than once, as in `apartment w/10 lease and plumbing or water or heat or electricity`.[62] Second, a multiple-connector search request might contain more than one connector with a numerical value, as in `risk w/10 warn! w/10 fail!` or `risk w/3 warn! pre/5 fail!`[63] If you want to learn more about the hierarchy of connectors, you will find a detailed explanation in the vendors' reference manuals.[64]

Using parentheses to establish the order for processing connectors. If you are uncertain about the order in which the computer will process a multiple-connector search request, the vendors give you the option of using parentheses to group search terms and connectors so the computer will carry out the request in the order you want:

> [C]onnectors used inside parentheses have priority over—*i.e.*, operate before—connectors used outside. If more than one connector is used inside parentheses, they operate in their standard sequence. Then those outside [the parentheses] operate in their standard sequence.[65]

[62] In this situation, the LEXIS and WESTLAW computers still follow the basic hierarchy; however, when the computers encounter a connector that appears more than once (such as "or" in the example above), the computers process all the like connectors from left to right, *i.e.*, in the order they appear in the search request, before processing whatever connector in the search request has the next highest priority.

An exception to this general rule occurs in WESTLAW with respect to its sentence and paragraph connectors ("+s," "/s," "+p," "/p"). WEST PUBLISHING COMPANY, WESTLAW REFERENCE MANUAL 320 (5th ed. 1993) ("Grammatical connectors are never processed from left to right.").

[63] In this situation in LEXIS, if the numerical values in the connectors are equal, the computer processes the connectors from left to right. If the numerical values differ, the LEXIS computer processes connectors with smaller values before processing connectors with larger values.

In WESTLAW, where the only connectors using numerical values are "+n" and "/n," the computer processes all "+n" connectors before processing any "/n" connectors. When the computer processes "+n" connectors, it follows the rules used in LEXIS for processing connectors having numerical values: if the values are equal, the WESTLAW computer processes them from left to right; if the values differ, the WESTLAW computer processes connectors with smaller values before processing connectors with larger values. Then, if the search request has any "/n" connectors, the WESTLAW computer moves on to processing them, following the same order as for processing "+n" connectors.

Although these LEXIS and WESTLAW rules appear nearly identical, the two services can process the same search request differently. For example, if you apply the rules just discussed to the search request `risk w/3 warn! pre/5 fail!`, you can see that the LEXIS computer will process the "w/3" connector first, while the WESTLAW computer would start by processing the "pre/5" connector.

[64] See note 61.

[65] MEAD DATA CENTRAL, REFERENCE MANUAL FOR THE LEXIS/NEXIS SERVICES 56–57

Thus, for example, if you were unsure of the standard order for processing the search request `apartment w/10 lease and plumbing or water`, you could use parentheses in the following way to achieve the same results as the standard hierarchy (illustrated in Figure 4.07):

```
(apartment w/10 lease) and (plumbing or water)
```

Using parentheses to clarify the normal order for processing connectors is explained in more detail on pages 158–62.

In addition to using parentheses to replicate the standard connector hierarchy, you can use parentheses to vary the hierarchy. Thus, you can use parentheses to relate connectors and search terms to one another in whatever way you want.[66]

In taking advantage of this flexibility, though, keep in mind that even small changes in the placement of the parentheses can yield dramatic differences in search results, as Figure 4.08 illustrates.

Search terms and their arrangements in WESTLAW's natural-language dialect

With natural-language search instructions, as with Boolean search instructions, the computer needs rules for determining what constitute searchable words and how to respond to those words in search instructions. Without these rules, the computer would not have any way to match words in search requests with words in documents and thus would not be able to retrieve potentially relevant documents. Consequently, the computer programmers who created WESTLAW's natural-language search feature had to address the same issues faced in creating a program for searching a database through Boolean logic—whether to equate uppercase and lowercase letters, whether to treat singular and plural forms of a search term as equivalent, what arrangements of words in a document will satisfy a search request, and so on.

The following paragraphs highlight the programming decisions that control the results you obtain through natural-language searching in WESTLAW.

Search terms in natural-language searching. As in Boolean searching, a word in natural-language searching can consist of a single character or a

(undated looseleaf ed.). This rule applies in both LEXIS and WESTLAW. *See also* MEAD DATA CENTRAL, LEXIS-NEXIS USER'S GUIDE 5–7 (1990 & 1991 Supp.); WEST PUBLISHING COMPANY, WESTLAW REFERENCE MANUAL 323–25 (5th ed. 1993).

[66] Only a few situations exist in which you cannot use parentheses to override the standard order for processing connectors. These occur in WESTLAW. *See* WEST PUBLISHING COMPANY, WESTLAW REFERENCE MANUAL 324–25 (5th ed. 1993).

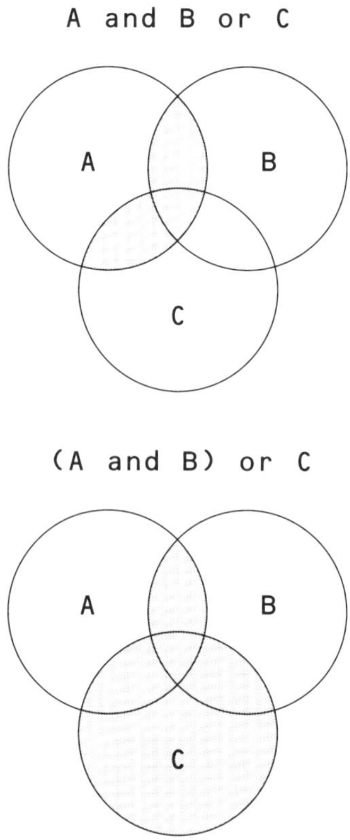

Figure 4.08. "`A and B or C`" is not the same search request as "`(A and B) or C`"

string of characters unbroken by a space.[67] Thus, you can search for "MacPherson" or "C.F.R." or "4.5" or "2001."

As in Boolean searching, the computer will ignore certain words if you use them in a natural-language search request. These non-searchable words, analogous to "stop" words in Boolean searching in WESTLAW, normally do not serve as good indicators of a document's relevance. The list of non-searchable words includes most of the words (such as "about" and "and") treated as stop words in Boolean searching in WESTLAW; the list also includes other words deemed not useful in natural-language searching. At this writing, West Publishing has not released a list of the words for which you cannot search with the natural-language feature. When you transmit a natural-language search request, however, the computer will disregard any non-searchable

[67] Also as in Boolean searching, some characters are considered spaces in certain contexts and therefore represent the start of new words. *See* Appendix H.

words appearing in your search request, and the monitor will redisplay the words for which the computer will search, showing them under the heading "Concepts in your description."

You might want to search for a phrase (such as "stop and frisk") that contains a non-searchable word (like "and"). Although the computer will not carry out a search request consisting only of a non-searchable word, the computer will search for a phrase containing a non-searchable word. In natural-language searching, the computer will treat a non-searchable word in a phrase the same way the word would be treated in a phrase in a Boolean search in WESTLAW. So, the search results might include documents that do not contain the same phrase used in the search request.[68] For example, searching for "stop and frisk" might retrieve documents because they contain the phrase "stop, don't frisk."

When you search with a natural-language request, as when you search with a Boolean request, you do not need to include in your request every possible variation on the spelling of the words you want the computer to locate. Using software-defined equivalencies, the computer will, for example, automatically search for "liability" or "Liability" in response to the search term `liability`, and for "drug" or "drugs" in response to the search term `drug`. Likewise, as in Boolean searching, the computer will "normalize" compound words spelled with hyphens and acronyms spelled with periods: the search term `post-conviction` will also locate "postconviction" and "post conviction"; `H.U.D.` will also locate "H U D," "HUD," and "H. U. D."[69]

Compared to Boolean searching, the natural-language feature automatically searches for more variations on search terms. For example, in both a Boolean search request and a natural-language search request, `drug` will retrieve "drug" or "drugs." But the search term `sold` will retrieve different results depending on whether you use a Boolean or a natural-language request: a natural-language request will also retrieve "sell," a result you would not obtain with a Boolean request. Moreover, because the natural-language feature automatically generates searches for a wider range of variations on search terms than does Boolean searching, a natural-language search for "sold" will also retrieve "Selle's" used as the possessive form of a person named "Selle" (a result you might not want).[70]

Many equivalencies in natural-language searching occur because, unless a search term appears on a special list of exceptions in the computer program, the computer relies on an algorithm to determine whether to truncate (or

[68] *See* pages 28–30 (discussing non-searchable words in Boolean searching).

[69] *See* pages 30–36 (discussing equivalencies in Boolean searching).

[70] For example, using the natural-language search request `sold as is` to search Wisconsin cases will retrieve documents simply because they contain phrases like "Mrs. Selle's attorney."

"stem") a search term to invoke an automatic search for other words sharing the same root. If the computer determines a search term should be truncated, the stemming algorithm also decides what part of the search term should form the basis for the search. For example, with the natural-language feature, the search term `defamation` will retrieve not only "defamation," but variations on the root "defam," such as "defame," "defames," "defamed," "defaming," and "defamatory." In effect, the stemming algorithm replaces the root expanders (* and !) that researchers can choose to use in Boolean searching, where expressing the concept of defamation by using the search term `defam!` will locate the words that the search term `defamation` will locate in natural-language searching.

Relationships among search terms in natural-language searching. In natural-language searching, you do not use logic connectors to establish relationships among search terms, as you do in Boolean searching. Rather, you transmit your search terms in a plain-English question, statement, or list of terms, as in these examples:

```
Does a landlord have an obligation to provide
running water in a leased apartment?

landlord's obligation to provide running water
in a leased apartment

landlord obligation running water leased
apartment
```

The computer then applies a series of algorithms based on statistical probability formulas (see pages 25–26) to analyze the search terms as they appear in the database. Each searchable term or phrase in your search request constitutes a concept. The algorithms focus on retrieving documents that contain the most references to the concepts the computer considers most important.

The computer determines the importance of a concept (*i.e.*, a word or phrase in your search request) in the course of evaluating a document for probable relevance. A concept's importance depends on the frequency with which the concept appears in the document as compared to the frequency with which the concept appears in the database as a whole. So, the computer will treat a concept that occurs frequently in a document but infrequently in the database as more important than a concept that occurs rarely in the document but often in the database.

The computer applies additional algorithms when, as normally happens, a search request includes more than one concept. In that situation, the computer assesses the likely relevance of documents through calculations that consider such factors as the number of concepts in the documents, the relative importance of each concept, and the frequency with which each concept appears in the documents.

The interplay of Boolean logic and natural language

In comparison to the Boolean search feature, WESTLAW's natural-language search feature shields researchers from the need to make as many decisions about expressing and arranging search terms. Because the natural-language feature resolves more issues about search instructions without the researcher's involvement, researchers do not need to specify the forms search terms might take in documents or the arrangements in which the search terms might appear. Researchers need only supply the search terms. Despite the ease of formulating search requests in natural language, however, knowing how to construct a Boolean search request remains an important skill in computer-assisted legal research:

- You might want to search WESTLAW for legal authorities that natural-language searching will not locate. Currently, although you can search most WESTLAW databases with the natural-language feature, some databases still require Boolean searching. For example, at this writing, the WESTLAW databases in which you cannot use the natural-language feature include the USTREATIES database (which contains U.S. treaties and other international agreements) and the INT-EEUROPE database (which contains commercial laws of eastern and central Europe).
- You might want to find facts by searching the nonlegal databases constituting the DIALOG service available through WESTLAW (see Chapter 13). Currently, natural-language searching does not operate in DIALOG.
- You might want to search for material, such as *American Law Reports*, that appears in LEXIS but not in WESTLAW. At this writing, LEXIS does not offer natural-language searching.
- You might want to conduct a WESTLAW search for more documents than natural-language searching allows. Currently, the natural-language feature limits the number of documents you can retrieve with a search request. As explained in Chapter 9 (see page 197), you can tell the WESTLAW computer the number of documents you want a natural-language search to retrieve, but you currently cannot choose a number greater than 100.

Unlike Boolean searching, natural-language searching in WESTLAW is not intended as a means of retrieving comprehensive collections of documents relevant to a research problem. Rather, natural-language searching is intended to conveniently identify the most relevant documents in a larger pool of potentially relevant documents. Thus, a natural-language search is considered successful when it obtains good results, if not complete results.

- Boolean and natural-language search requests on the same issue will normally retrieve many of the same documents. But each collection of documents will also typically include some documents not found in the other collection. Knowing how to search with Boolean logic will give you access to potentially relevant documents you might bypass in natural-language searching.
- You might want to display retrieved documents so the most recent ones appear at the beginning of the collection. When you search with a Boolean search request (but not with a natural-language search request), you can display retrieved documents in reverse chronological order. At this writing, with natural-language searching, results always display according to the statistical relevance of the documents.
- Natural-language searching does not always work as well as Boolean searching when you want to locate documents containing a specific phrase, such as "contempt of court." Unlike the way Boolean searching handles phrases in search requests, the natural-language algorithms break up a phrase into its component words and then treat those individual words as separate search terms. Consequently, a natural-language search for a phrase sometimes retrieves documents that contain only some of the significant words in the phrase instead of the whole phrase.
- You might know the Key Number of a West Digest subtopic that addresses the point you want to research. You can include the Key Number in either a natural-language or Boolean search request. As explained on page 294, however, cases retrieved by a natural-language search request containing a Key Number will not necessarily be digested under that Key Number. To search comprehensively for cases dealing with a particular West subtopic, a Boolean request will operate more effectively.
- You might want to take advantage of the fields in online documents to focus your search on specific pieces of information, such as the names of attorneys who participated in a case. (The next chapter explains how to use fields in online searching.) Even when you use WESTLAW's natural-language feature, you use Boolean logic connectors if you want to search a field for more than one term (say, the last names of two attorneys who represented parties in a case).

- Once you retrieve the results of a search request—whether natural-language or Boolean—you might want to scan the results to find occurrences of particular words that will help you assess the relevance of retrieved documents. In WESTLAW, as explained in Chapter 11, you can scan retrieved documents by using the LOCATE feature. LOCATE uses Boolean, rather than natural-language, search procedures.

In short, despite the advent of natural-language searching in WESTLAW, Boolean searching retains an important role in computer-assisted legal research.[71] For some research tasks, Boolean searching offers the only route to online information. For research tasks you can accomplish with either Boolean or natural-language searching, you can obtain benefits from each search method. Natural-language searching offers convenience in communicating your search instructions. Boolean searching, on the other hand, allows you to exercise greater control over the forms and arrangements of your search terms as they appear in online documents. As you gain experience with online searching, you will develop your own preferences for when to take advantage of the benefits of the Boolean dialect and when to take advantage of the benefits of the natural-language dialect.

Summary of the dialects for searching in LEXIS and WESTLAW

To search for documents in the LEXIS and WESTLAW databases by using *Boolean logic* (also known as the "terms-and-connectors" technique), you use a dialect consisting of:

- *Search terms*, by which you express the key elements of your research problem. Figure 4.01 (pages 41–43) highlights the LEXIS and WESTLAW rules that define searchable words and how the computer will respond to those words in Boolean search requests.
- *Connectors*, by which you link search terms in appropriate relationships. Figure 4.03 (pages 58–59) summarizes the LEXIS and WESTLAW connectors for Boolean searching.

[71] West Publishing's announcements about natural-language searching in WESTLAW remark that this feature does not supplant Boolean searching for locating information in WESTLAW. *See, e.g.*, Richard A. Leiter, *WIN: "It's the Natural Way,"* LEGAL INFO. ALERT, Nov./Dec. 1992, at 1, 1–2 (summarizing observations of WESTLAW representatives that some searches in WESTLAW work better with Boolean logic than with natural language); West Publishing Co., *WESTLAW Takes the Wraps Off a Revolutionary New Breakthrough*, A.B.A. J., Nov. 1992, at 21, 23 (advertisement).

In WESTLAW, you often have the option of using plain English (the *natural-language* feature) as your CALR dialect. Here, you use ordinary questions or statements to tell the computer what terms to search for.

With a knowledge of the two CALR dialects—Boolean logic and natural language—you can formulate search requests. But in doing so, you will also want to consider whether you will enhance the effectiveness and efficiency of your search by instructing the computer to carry out your search request by checking entire documents or by checking just designated parts of documents. The next chapter explains the ability to restrict the operation of your search request to specified LEXIS segments or WESTLAW fields.

CHAPTER 5

Fields and Segments: Restricted Locations for Database Searching

To this point, the discussion of database searching has assumed you will use the computer to search entire documents to see whether they satisfy search requests. In both LEXIS and WESTLAW, unless you instruct the computer otherwise, the computer will automatically search a document from its first character to its last. You can, however, instruct the computer to carry out search requests in only specified portions of documents. The resulting search is analogous to, say, skimming a magazine for articles by a particular author: you would look only at bylines, not entire articles.

As explained on page 10, the CALR vendors have divided documents in their databases into units corresponding to elements that recur in cases and other legal authorities. These units are called "fields" in WESTLAW and "segments" in LEXIS. The term "field," though, is broadly used in computer terminology to refer to divisions within documents in any database; consequently, this chapter uses "field" generically to refer to both WESTLAW fields and LEXIS segments.[72]

Because a given field in all like kinds of documents (*e.g.*, all cases) contains the same type of information, you can use a field-restricted search request in LEXIS or WESTLAW to conduct highly specialized searches that would be nearly impossible—or at least tremendously tedious and time-consuming—to perform without a computer.

A field restriction can also help sharpen the focus of a basic search. Some field restrictions can reduce ambiguity by providing a context in which a search

[72] Similarly, this chapter uses the phrase "field-restricted searching" to refer to searches of either WESTLAW fields or LEXIS segments.

term will likely have the meaning you intend. In addition, when you retrieve an unmanageably large number of documents, a field restriction can cull documents by establishing a screening criterion (such as a date).

The next section explains field-restricted searching in cases in LEXIS and WESTLAW. Pages 109–10 discuss the highly similar techniques for searching fields in statutes and other types of documents in LEXIS and WESTLAW.

In WESTLAW, you can also include field restrictions in your search instructions when you use the natural-language feature for transmitting a search instruction in plain English. Pages 110–11 explain how field-restricted searching operates with WESTLAW's natural-language feature. But for a few minor exceptions noted there, the following explanation of field-restricted searching applies whether you use Boolean or natural-language search requests.

Field-restricted searching in cases

To illustrate searching case-law fields, suppose you wanted to compile a list of all the cases in which a party was represented by attorney William Saxbe. Because one of the fields in each case in the LEXIS and WESTLAW databases contains the name of counsel, you could easily assemble the list by instructing the computer to search for the lawyer's name in the designated field. Your field-restricted search request, formulated to locate the various possible configurations of "William Saxbe" (such as "Saxbe, William" or "William B. Saxbe"), would take this form:

LEXIS:	`counsel(william w/5 saxbe)`
WESTLAW:	`attorney(william w/5 saxbe)` `at(william w/5 saxbe)`

As this example shows, you formulate a field-restricted search request with two components:

- *The name of the field you want the computer to search (or, in WESTLAW, the two-letter abbreviation for the field).*

  Figure 5.08 on pages 114–18 lists the names of the principal fields for cases in the LEXIS and WESTLAW databases. Figures 5.11 (pages 125–27) and 5.13 (pages 131–34) illustrate LEXIS segments and WESTLAW fields in a United States Supreme Court case. Figures 5.12 (pages 128–30) and 5.14 (pages 135–37) show how the contents of the printed versions of the case correlate with the segments and fields in the online versions.

Information about the case-law fields in LEXIS and WESTLAW also appears in the vendors' printed and online informational guides (see Appendices A and B).[73]

- *Your search terms and logic connectors in parentheses after the name (or abbreviation) of the field.* The presence of a field name followed by a parenthetical search request instructs the computer to perform the search in just the designated field.[74]

With field-restricted search requests, you use search terms and logic connectors the same way you use them in unrestricted search requests. A field-restricted search request differs from an unrestricted one only with respect to the area of the document in which the computer conducts its search (*i.e.*, in a specified field rather than throughout the entire document); no difference occurs with respect to how the computer evaluates the search terms and logic connectors within the specified field.

As in unrestricted searching, you can combine as many elements as you want in a restricted search request. For example, you can formulate a field-restricted search request using just one search term, like this:

LEXIS: `opinionby(rehnquist)`

WESTLAW: `judge(rehnquist)`

These search requests would generate a compilation of all cases in which a judge named Rehnquist wrote the opinion for the court.

Or, just as in an unrestricted search request, you can use multiple terms and connectors. For instance, if you wanted to locate cases in which two particular lawyers participated as counsel, your search request would take this form:

LEXIS: `counsel(william w/5 saxbe and lee w/5 bailey)`

WESTLAW: `attorney(william w/5 saxbe and lee w/5 bailey)`

[73] In some documents, some of the segments and fields listed in Figure 5.08 will be empty. For instance, the "dissentby" segment in a case in LEXIS will not contain any information if a judge did not dissent. Similarly, cases in WESTLAW that have not been published in a West case reporter will not have any information in the "topic," "headnote," "digest," or "synopsis" field.

Also, note that the CALR vendors do not divide the documents in their databases into identical units, and usually use different names for fields that contain comparable information. For instance, as you can see from the preceding example, the field containing lawyers' names is called "counsel" in LEXIS and "attorney" in WESTLAW. Nonetheless, fields serve the same purpose in both LEXIS and WESTLAW: they establish fixed locations in which researchers can expect to find specified kinds of information.

[74] In LEXIS, when you restrict your search request by the date field, you have the option of either using or omitting parentheses. See pages 83–84.

Besides linking search terms in a field-restricted search request, you can link field restrictions. For example, if you wanted to locate cases in which a particular judge wrote the court's opinion and in which specific lawyers participated, your search request would have this format:

LEXIS:
```
opinionby(rehnquist) and
counsel(william w/5 saxbe and
lee w/5 bailey)
```

WESTLAW:
```
judge(rehnquist) and
attorney(william w/5 saxbe and
lee w/5 bailey)
```

As a final option, you can combine field-restricted search terms and connectors with unrestricted search terms and connectors. The computer will search the entire document for the unrestricted search terms, and search only in the designated fields for the restricted search terms. As an illustration, say you were searching for a particular kind of case (such as murder cases) in which a certain judge wrote the court's opinion and in which specific lawyers participated. You could instruct the computer to locate murder cases by searching all fields for "murder" or "homicide," and you could refine the search by checking specified fields for the judge's and lawyers' names. Your search request would follow this format:

LEXIS:
```
(murder or homicide) and
opinionby(rehnquist) and
counsel(william w/5 saxbe and
lee w/5 bailey)
```

WESTLAW:
```
(murder or homicide) and
judge(rehnquist) and
attorney(william w/5 saxbe and
lee w/5 bailey)
```

The preceding discussion has illustrated a few of the specialized searches you can conduct with field restrictions. The following list provides a sampling of other field-restricted searches you can perform in case-law databases in LEXIS and WESTLAW. In addition, Figure 5.09 (pages 119–23) summarizes the more common field-restricted searches possible in cases.

- *Searching for a case by the parties' names.* Suppose you know of a case that is relevant to your research, but your only citation information about the case consists of the name of one or more parties. You can locate the case in LEXIS or WESTLAW by instructing the computer to search for the parties' names in the field containing that information—the "name" segment in LEXIS and the "title" field in WESTLAW. By restricting the search to one of these fields, you avoid locating cases that simply refer to your case somewhere in the document.

For example, to locate the case of *Kingsley International Pictures Corporation v. Regents of the State of New York*, you could use the following search requests:

LEXIS: `name(kingsley and regents)`

WESTLAW: `title(kingsley and regents)`

As this example shows, the computer's search technique does not require a complete case name in order to use the name or title field to locate a document. In fact, using the complete case name in your search request is not effective: you will fail to retrieve the case if the name in the database varies in form from the name in your search request. For instance, the search request `name(kingsley international pictures corporation v. regents of the state of new york)` would fail to retrieve the desired case if the name appeared in the name field as "Kingsley International Pictures Corporation v. Regents of New York State." The better approach uses a couple distinctive words from the case name, or perhaps only one word if it is unusual; if the case name does not include any distinctive words, you might need to use more words from the name.

Conducting a field-restricted search of the name or title field is analogous to using a Table of Cases or a Defendant-Plaintiff Table in book-based research to locate a case you know only by party name.[75] With the computer, however, you have added flexibility. To use the printed tables, you need to know the name of a principal plaintiff or defendant; in LEXIS or WESTLAW, you can often find a case when you only know the name of a non-principal party or when you do not know a party's full name.

A field-restricted search using the name or title field also enables you conveniently to compile a list of cases in which a particular person or organization has been a party. For example, the search request `name("kingsley international")` would locate any case in LEXIS in which Kingsley International is listed as a plaintiff or defendant. You could further refine your search to locate, say,

[75] For more information about this "partially known authority" approach to finding the law in book-based legal research, see CHRISTOPHER G. WREN & JILL R. WREN, THE LEGAL RESEARCH MANUAL: A GAME PLAN FOR LEGAL RESEARCH AND ANALYSIS 58, 60 (2d ed. 1986).

just cases in which Kingsley International has litigated a particular kind of issue, such as a constitutional challenge to an obscenity law. Your search request might look like this:

LEXIS:	`name("kingsley international") and obscen!`
WESTLAW:	`title("kingsley international") and obscen!`

Combining a "name" or "title" restriction with unrestricted search terms describing relevant facts or legal issues can also prove helpful in locating a case if the name consists of common words (such as "Jones" or "Smith") or if a party has litigated other kinds of cases in which you are not interested. In each instance, the unrestricted descriptive words will channel the computer's search toward the relevant case.

- *Searching for a case by its citation.* If you know the citation of a case that is relevant to your research, you can locate the case by instructing the computer to search for the citation in the "cite" segment in LEXIS or the "citation" field in WESTLAW. For example, if you wanted to locate *Kingsley International Pictures Corporation v. Regents of the State of New York*, 360 U.S. 684 (1959), you could use the following search requests:

LEXIS:	`cite(360 pre/5 684)`
WESTLAW:	`citation(360 pre/5 684)`

Note that using the "pre/n" connector to search the "cite" or "citation" field generally yields better results than using the standard citation form you would use in writing a brief or other legal document. In addition, note that to retrieve a case using the citation field restriction in WESTLAW, you normally must use a West case reporter citation, not a parallel citation to a non-West source.[76]

At one time, using the "cite" or "citation" field was the only way you could locate a case by its citation in LEXIS or WESTLAW. Now, if you prefer, you can use the LEXSEE command in LEXIS (see pages 238–43) or the FIND command in WESTLAW (see pages 279–84). If you know a case's citation, you will usually retrieve the case more conveniently with one of these commands than with a field-restricted search.

[76] West Publishing Company, WESTLAW Reference Manual 54 (4th ed. 1990).

- *Searching for cases from a particular court.* When you use a computer to search for cases, you often conduct your search in a collection of cases issued by more than one court. For example, LEXIS and WESTLAW each has a grouping that includes cases from all the federal circuit courts of appeals; similarly, LEXIS and WESTLAW each has a grouping consisting of cases from the U.S. Supreme Court, all federal circuit courts of appeals, all federal district courts, and some other federal courts, such as the U.S. Claims Court. When searching such a collection, you will sometimes find it helpful to restrict your search to cases from a specific court (or from specific courts). You can use the "court" field in LEXIS and WESTLAW to accomplish that result.

  For instance, in a collection of cases from all federal circuit courts of appeals, you could search for cases from, say, only the Ninth Circuit or from either the Ninth Circuit or Tenth Circuit. Likewise, in a collection of cases from the courts of several states, you could search for cases from only one of the states. Or, in a collection of cases from several courts within a single state, you could search for cases from only one of the courts in that state.

  In LEXIS, to identify the court or courts whose cases you want to search, use one or two distinctive words from the court name. For example, if you were searching in a collection of cases from all federal courts and wanted to restrict your search to cases from only the United States Courts of Appeals for the Ninth or Tenth Circuits, your restriction could read `court(ninth or tenth)` or, because of the automatic equivalency, `court(9th or 10th)`; you will locate just cases from the desired courts because only one federal court has a name with the word "Ninth" in it, just as only one federal court has a name that includes "Tenth." Similarly, in a collection of cases from all Ohio courts, to search for cases from just the Ohio Supreme Court, your restriction could read `court(supreme)`. Or, for example, to restrict your search to cases from the United States District Courts for the Northern or Southern Districts of California, your restriction could read `court(california and northern or n.d.)` or `court(california and southern or s.d.)`.

  For identifying a court in a court-restricted search request in WESTLAW, the WESTLAW reference manual provides names and abbreviations to use in your court restriction.[77] For example,

[77] WEST PUBLISHING COMPANY, WESTLAW REFERENCE MANUAL 97–108, 307–08, 311–12 (5th ed. 1993).

in a collection of cases from all New York courts, if you wanted to restrict a WESTLAW search to cases from the New York Family Court, your restriction would read `court(n.y.fam.ct.)`.

Normally, researchers combine court restrictions with other search terms or field restrictions. Standing alone, a court restriction would assemble a list of every case issued by the designated court or courts, yielding an indiscriminate compilation unlikely to have any usefulness in solving a legal research problem. Linking a court restriction with a search term that focuses the search on a relevant fact or legal issue results in a search request with the following format:

LEXIS:	`court(9th or 10th) and obscen! and "first amendment"`
WESTLAW:	`court(ninth or tenth) and obscen! and "first amendment"`

You could also refine this court-restricted search request by adding a field restriction limiting the search to, say, cases decided by a particular judge on the court or cases decided after a particular date.

Note that if a LEXIS file or a WESTLAW database contains cases from just the courts in which you are interested, you do not need to use a court restriction to limit your search to those courts. Conducting your search in the appropriate file or database will have the same effect as using a court restriction. For example, if you wanted to search for cases issued only by courts in Pennsylvania, you could proceed in two ways. You could use a court-restricted search request in the LEXIS file or WESTLAW database that includes all state court cases. Or, you could take the more efficient approach of simply selecting the LEXIS file or WESTLAW database containing only cases from Pennsylvania courts.

- *Searching for cases based on the date of decision.* In both LEXIS and WESTLAW, you can restrict your search to cases decided on, before, after, or between particular dates. Date-restricted searching can prove useful, for example, if you want to limit your search to cases decided after a date on which a court changed a legal rule or if your research involves examining the historical development of a legal principle during a specified period. Because a date alone does not generate an effective search, you use a date restriction in combination with one or more other search terms or field restrictions.

You conduct a date-restricted search in essentially the same way in both LEXIS and WESTLAW. In LEXIS, however, you do not have to enclose the date-restricted search terms in parentheses. Thus, to search for obscenity cases decided after 1985 by the United States Court of Appeals for the Ninth Circuit, your search request could take the following form:

LEXIS:

```
court(9th) and obscen! and
"first amendment" and
date(aft 1985)

court(9th) and obscen! and
"first amendment" and date
aft 1985
```

WESTLAW:

```
court(ninth) and obscen!
and "first amendment" and
date(aft 1985)
```

The date in a date-restricted search request can consist of a year, of a month and year, or of a month, day, and year. In both LEXIS and WESTLAW, you can express the date in alternative ways, which the vendors' reference manuals explain in detail.[78] For instance, all of the following expressions work equally well in a date restriction in LEXIS and WESTLAW:

april 30, 1988
apr 30, 1988
4–30–88
4/30/88

Similarly, you can express the scope of a date restriction in a variety of ways.[79] To search for cases decided on a specific date, you could use the following formats:

[78] MEAD DATA CENTRAL, REFERENCE MANUAL FOR THE LEXIS/NEXIS SERVICES 97–99 (undated looseleaf ed.); MEAD DATA CENTRAL, LEXIS-NEXIS USER'S GUIDE 7–1 to 7–3 (1990 & 1991 Supp.); WEST PUBLISHING COMPANY, WESTLAW REFERENCE MANUAL 109–12 (5th ed. 1993).

[79] MEAD DATA CENTRAL, REFERENCE MANUAL FOR THE LEXIS/NEXIS SERVICES 97–99 (undated looseleaf ed.); MEAD DATA CENTRAL, LEXIS-NEXIS USER'S GUIDE 7–1 to 7–3 (1990 & 1991 Supp.); WEST PUBLISHING COMPANY, WESTLAW REFERENCE MANUAL 109–12 (5th ed. 1993).

LEXIS:
```
date(is 4/30/88)
date is 4/30/88
date = 4/1/88
```

WESTLAW:
```
date(is 4/30/88)
date(= 4/30/88)
date(4/30/88)
```

To search for cases decided before a specific date, you could use the following formats:

LEXIS:
```
date(bef 1980)
date bef 1980
date < 1980
```

WESTLAW:
```
date(before 1980)
date(bef 1980)
date(< 1980)
```

To search for cases decided after a specific date, you could use the following formats:

LEXIS:
```
date(aft 4/30/88)
date aft 4/30/88
date > 4/30/88
```

WESTLAW:
```
date(after 4/30/88)
date(aft 4/30/88)
date(> 4/30/88)
```

Finally, to search for cases decided between specific dates, you could use the following formats:

LEXIS:
```
date(aft 1954) and date(bef
1/1/88)
date > 1954 and date <
1/1/88
```

WESTLAW:
```
date(after 1954 and before
1/1/88)
date(aft 1954 and bef
1/1/88)
date(> 1954 and < 1/1/88)
```

Note that if your date indicates a year but not the century (as in "4/30/88"), the computer will assume your date occurs in the twentieth century. If you want your date restriction to refer to an earlier century, you must specify it, as in `4/30/1888`.

WESTLAW's "Full Text Plus" fields in cases. For court opinions published in West's case reporters, WESTLAW includes several fields containing *editor*-prepared information that supplements the court-authored text. Cases in LEXIS do not contain analogous editorial features.

In compiling court opinions for publication in the volumes comprising its National Reporter System, West adds to the opinions several editorial features familiar to book-based researchers—*e.g.*, digest topics and key numbers, headnotes, and synopses of opinions. As a consequence of its ownership by West Publishing Company, WESTLAW incorporates these features in its database versions of the published opinions; when WESTLAW promotes its database as "full text plus," the "plus" refers to the editorial enhancements derived from West's case reporters.[80]

Each type of editorial enhancement appears in a separate field in WESTLAW. The editorial fields are:

- topic field (which includes Key Numbers)
- headnote field
- digest field
- synopsis field

You can conduct field-restricted searches using these fields just as you use any other field.

The following discussion describes the fields containing editorial additions in WESTLAW. A summary of the WESTLAW "Plus" fields, along with some practical guidelines for when to use which field restriction, appears on pages 107–09.

- **Topic field (including Key Numbers).** This WESTLAW field includes the name of a West digest topic (*e.g.*, "Weapons," "Arbitration," "Consumer Protection"), the identification number West assigns to the topic for use in searching WESTLAW, a Key Number subtopic within the topic, and the phrase West uses to describe the subject matter covered by that Key Number;[81] the topics, Key Num-

[80] The "full text plus" features are not present in *all* cases in the WESTLAW database. For a small percentage of cases published in West case reporters (*e.g.*, Tax Court Memoranda), West's editors do not prepare synopses; the WESTLAW versions of these cases do not include synopses, either. In addition, the WESTLAW database contains some cases that West does not publish in its reporters; these cases do not include any of the "full text plus" features. Finally, "full text plus" features are also absent from cases in WESTLAW that West will publish in its reporters, but that have not yet gone through the editorial process that produces the information in "full text plus" fields; when West publishes the cases, the online versions are revised to include the editorial enhancements.

[81] Early cases do not contain identification numbers for the topics under which the cases are digested. For example, at this writing, topic numbers do not appear in federal cases decided before the mid-1920s.

bers, and phrases describing the subject matter of Key Numbers in WESTLAW track those in the printed West digests. In addition, to show the position the Key Number assigned to a specific headnote occupies in the outline of the digest topic, the topic field lists all topic and Key Number classifications to which the Key Number is subordinate. An excerpt from a typical digest outline appears in Figure 5.03 on page 102.

As the law evolves, West occasionally reclassifies material in its topic and Key Number system by, for example, adding new topics or adding new subdivisions to existing Key Numbers. If the current topic or Key Number classification for a case represents a reclassification from an earlier topic or Key Number, the topic field will include a cross-reference to the earlier classification, as in this example:

> 92k83(4) k. Freedom of movement; right to travel.
> Formerly 92k83(1)

Figure 5.01 shows a West digest topic ("Weapons"), Key Number ("4"), and descriptive phrase ("Manufacture, sale, gift, loan, possession, or use") as they appear in a West digest. Figure 5.13 (pages 131–34), which depicts several screens of a case in WESTLAW, illustrates the topic field (as well as other WESTLAW fields).

Using a topic field restriction will retrieve cases that contain a headnote classified under the West digest topic you selected. A listing of West digest topics and the numbers assigned to the topics in WESTLAW appears in Appendix A of the *WESTLAW Reference Manual*[82] and can be viewed online in WESTLAW in the TOPIC database and through the Topic and Key Number Service (explained on pages 100–07). You can also find the listing in the West digests themselves and at pages 165–67 of *The Legal Research Manual* (2d ed.).

If you conducted a WESTLAW search using only a topic number as your search request, the computer would retrieve all cases digested under that topic—in effect, recreating online the coverage you would find for that topic in the printed West digest for the jurisdiction in which you performed your WESTLAW search. For example, the search request

```
topic(406)
```

[82] West Publishing Company, WESTLAW Reference Manual 301–05 (5th ed. 1993).

80 F P D 2d—7

WEAPONS ⚿4

two years, or both, does not deny equal protection or due process, or violate any constitutional provision. 18 U.S.C.A.App. § 1202(a)(1); U.S.C.A.Const. Amends. 5, 14.—U. S. v. Kozerski, 518 F.Supp. 1082.

D.C.N.J. 1979. Statute prohibiting unlawful receipt of firearms shipped or transported in interstate commerce by person under indictment for offense punishable by imprisonment exceeding one year did not deny equal protection as applied to person under indictment for nonviolent offenses. 18 U.S.C.A. § 922(h)(1).—U. S. v. Weingartner, 485 F.Supp. 1167, appeal dismissed 642 F.2d 445.

Statute prohibiting receipt of firearms shipped or transported in interstate commerce by person under indictment for offense punishable by imprisonment exceeding one year did not create unconstitutional irrebuttable presumption that any person under indictment for specified offenses had propensity for violence. 18 U.S.C.A. § 922(h)(1).—Id.

D.C.N.Y. 1982. Provisions of New York Penal Law raising criminal possession of a weapon in the third degree from a misdemeanor to a felony on the basis of a prior conviction and calling for second felony offender treatment because of the same prior felony conviction do not violate due process or double jeopardy. N.Y. McKinney's Penal Law §§ 70.15, 265.01, 265.02(1, 4).—Cassesse v. People of State of New York, 530 F.Supp. 694.

D.C.N.Y. 1981. State statute providing that pistol license may be revoked and cancelled at any time in city of New York by licensing officer is not unconstitutionally vague. N.Y.Penal Law § 400.00, subd. 11.—Brescia v. McGuire, 509 F.Supp. 243.

D.C.Pa. 1977. Ordinary standard of administrative review does not apply to decisions of Bureau of Alcohol, Tobacco and Firearms revoking license to sell firearms and ammunition; since statute provides for introduction of evidence beyond that contained in administrative record, district court's review is "de novo." 18 U.S.C.A. § 923(f)(3).—Shyda v. Director, Bureau of Alcohol, Tobacco and Firearms, U. S. Dept. of Treasury, 448 F.Supp. 409.

On de novo review of decision of Bureau of Alcohol, Tobacco and Firearms revoking dealer's license to sell firearms and ammunition, court would treat Bureau's motion for summary judgment as any other motion for summary judgment by examining matter afresh, using entire record to determine whether there was material issue of fact necessitating further proceedings. 18 U.S.C.A. §§ 921 et seq., 923(f)(3); Fed.Rules Civ.Proc. rule 56, 28 U.S.C.A.—Id.

In order to prove "willful" violation of recordkeeping requirements of Gun Control Act sufficient to support revocation of license to sell firearms and ammunition, Bureau of Alcohol, Tobacco and Firearms must prove that licensee knew of his legal obligation and purposefully disregarded or was plainly indifferent to recordkeeping requirements; there is no requirement of bad purpose as might be imposed with respect to determination of willfulness in criminal prosecution. 18 U.S.C.A. § 923(g).—Id.

Where licensee admitted on stand under oath that he was aware of specific legal obligations under Gun Control Act to record dispositions of firearms within seven days and to maintain dispositional records for ammunition, and where there was no substantial controversy as to proof that extremely serious breaches of recordkeeping practices occurred in that licensee sold or delivered more than 1,600 firearms without recording their disposition and in that ammunition-disposition records were not maintained in a bound book or in chronological order, licensee was guilty of "willful" violation of such recordkeeping requirements. 18 U.S.C.A. § 923(g).—Id.

⚿4. Manufacture, sale, gift, loan, possession, or use.

U.S.Pa. 1980. Statute authorizing imposition of enhanced penalties on a defendant who uses or carries a firearm while committing a federal felony may not be applied to a defendant who uses a firearm in the course of a felony that is proscribed by a statute which itself authorizes enhancement if a dangerous weapon is used; sentence received by such a defendant may be enhanced only under enhancement provision in statute defining felony he has committed. 18 U.S.C.A. § 924(c).—Busic v. U. S., 100 S.Ct. 1747, 446 U.S. 398, 64 L.Ed.2d 381, on remand 639 F.2d 940, certiorari denied 101 S.Ct. 3055, 452 U.S. 918, 69 L.Ed.2d 422.

Where, through combination of aiding and abetting statute and statute making it unlawful to assault a federal officer, defendant was found guilty as a principal of using a firearm to assault undercover agents, codefendant's gun became defendant's gun as a matter of law for purposes of assault statute, which provided for enhanced punishment when the assaulter "uses" a deadly weapon, and thus statute authorizing imposition of enhanced penalties on a defendant who "uses" or "carries" a firearm while committing a federal felony could not be applied against defendant on theory that defendant was merely "carrying," as opposed to "using," his gun. 18 U.S.C.A. §§ 2, 111, 924(c), (c)(1, 2).—Id.

U.S.Va. 1980. Federal firearms statute prohibits felon from possessing a firearm despite the fact that the predicate felony may be subject to collateral attack on constitutional grounds. 18 U.S.C.A. App. § 1202(a)(1).—Lewis v. U. S., 100 S.Ct. 915, 445 U.S. 55, 63 L.Ed.2d 198.

C.A.Ala. 1981. Government must prove both willingness to deal and more than occasional sale in order to prove status of accused as one engaged in business of dealing in firearms. 18 U.S.C.A. § 922(a)(1), 924(a).—U. S. v. Berry, 644 F.2d 1034.

C.A.Ala. 1981. Under statute prohibiting a convicted felon from receiving, possessing, or transporting any firearm that has moved in interstate commerce, separate prosecution units can arise either from showing of separate receipts or separate possessions; separate receipts can be established by showing that the weapons were acquired at different times or places, and separate possessions can be established by showing either that the weapons were stored in different places or that the weapons were acquired at different times or places. 18 U.S.C.A.App. § 1202(a)(1).—U. S. v. McCrary, 643 F.2d 323.

C.A.Ala. 1979. In proceedings to accept guilty plea to charge of receiving firearms transported in interstate commerce, Government was not required to demonstrate that defendant was aware of interstate character of weapon. 18 U.S.C.A. § 922(h); Fed.Rules Crim.Proc. rule 11, 18 U.S.C.A.—Lambert v. U. S., 600 F.2d 476.

C.A.Ala. 1979. Defendant had constructive possession of weapons if he had intent and power to exercise dominion and control over weapons. 18 U.S.C.A. App. § 1202(a).—U. S. v. Smith, 591 F.2d 1105.

C.A.Ala. 1977. U. S. v. Woods, 560 F.2d 660, certiorari denied 98 S.Ct. 1452, 435 U.S. 906, 55 L.Ed.2d 497.

C.A.Ariz. 1981. As used in statute which prohibits the receipt by a convicted felon of a firearm that has been shipped in interstate commerce, the term "receipt" includes any knowing acceptance or taking of possession of a weapon. 18 U.S.C.A. § 922(h).—U. S. v. Lipps, 659 F.2d 960.

Source: West Publishing Company © 1982

Figure 5.01. Sample Page from a West Digest, Which Contains the Same Information Found in the Topic, Headnote, and Digest Fields in Cases in WESTLAW

would retrieve all cases digested under the topic "Weapons" (to which West has assigned the topic number 406). The online digest coverage would be more current, however, than the coverage of the printed digest on hand at the time you performed your WESTLAW search: the WESTLAW versions of West digest summaries become available sooner than the versions in the West digest volumes.

In formulating a search request using the topic field, you can use the name of the topic instead of the topic number.[83] Your search request would look like this:

```
topic(weapons)
```

Using the topic name yields the same result as using the topic number, *i.e.*, a collection of all cases digested under the topic. But the topic name might also retrieve cases digested under other topics. This occurs when the topic name you have selected is part of the name of another topic or is part of a phrase describing a Key Number subtopic under another topic. For example, with the search request `topic(jury)`, you would retrieve not only cases digested under the West digest topic "Jury," but cases digested under the West digest topic "Grand Jury" and under the subtopic "questions for jury" in the West digest topic "Bankruptcy," among others. Thus, searching for a topic name will generally yield more cases (some relevant and some irrelevant) than searching for a topic number.

You will rarely, if ever, want to recreate online an entire West digest topic, much less an entire topic plus an unpredictable number of cases culled from other topics. Ordinarily, whether you use a topic number or a topic name in a search request based on the topic field, you refine your search by linking the topic number or name with one or more additional search terms.

These additional terms could reflect significant facts or issues in your research problem. For example, if you were researching the range of damages awarded in spinal injury cases, you could use a topic field restriction this way:

```
topic(damages) and (spine or spinal)
topic(115) and (spine or spinal)
```

[83] If you want your topic field search to retrieve early cases that do not contain identification numbers for West digest topics, you must use the topic name rather than its identification number in your search request. For additional advice about searching for West digest topics and Key Numbers in early cases, see WEST PUBLISHING COMPANY, WESTLAW REFERENCE MANUAL 193 (5th ed. 1993).

These searches would retrieve cases classified under the digest topic "Damages" and containing the words "spine" or "spinal" anywhere in the document.

Alternatively, you could combine a topic field restriction with another topic field restriction. For example

```
topic(negligence) and topic(broker)
```

would locate cases having to do with negligence and brokers. Or, you could combine a topic field restriction with a non-topic field restriction to screen cases by, say, date, court, authoring judge, or participating lawyer:

```
topic(damages) and (spine or spinal)
and date(after 1989)
```

Thus, topic field restrictions allow you to fine-tune your examination of a West digest. In book-based research, the functional equivalent of a topic field search would require you to collect all the cases digested under a particular topic in a West digest and then to read all the cases to find the ones that mention a specific fact word (such as "spine" or "spinal") or that satisfy specific criteria (such as authorship by a particular judge).

In addition to offering speed and convenience, a topic field search in WESTLAW can increase the likelihood that when looking for a search term having more than one meaning, the computer will locate only documents in which the term has been used in the sense you desire. Linking the ambiguous search term with a digest topic establishes a context in which the term is apt to occur and thus tends to reduce the range of possible meanings the term will have.

In doing topic field searches, you can also *exclude* a topic or topics as a way of focusing your search. For example, suppose you were researching a liability or damage question in a tort action involving a personal injury. The standards for liability and damages for personal injuries covered by workers' compensation statutes differ from tort standards that would otherwise apply. So you might want to look only for torts cases and exclude from your search any cases originating as workers' compensation claims. Because workers' compensation is a West digest topic (to which West has assigned topic number 413), you could use a search request along the following lines to accomplish this exclusion:[84]

[84] If you decide to exclude cases digested under a certain topic, using the number of the topic instead of the topic name will minimize the risk of inadvertently excluding more documents than you actually want to eliminate. This is the flip side of the fact (discussed earlier) that using a topic name for finding cases digested under that topic might also turn up cases digested under other topics: you will discover that using a topic name to exclude cases digested under the topic might also exclude relevant cases digested under other topics.

```
injur! w/15 arm or leg but not
topic(413)
```

Suppose, however, that West digested a tort case under the topic "Workers' Compensation" because the judge analyzed a workers' compensation principle in the course of contrasting it with a governing tort doctrine. This search request would bypass that case. Thus, an exclusionary topic field search carries the same risk of bypassing relevant cases that you face with the exclusionary connectors "and not" and "but not," discussed on pages 46–47.

Finally, note that whether you include or exclude topics in a topic field search, this kind of search requires the same familiarity with the body of American law and the scope of the various digest topics that you need in order to use the "known topic" approach successfully in book-based research:[85] as with topic searches in printed digests, online topic searches are generally less effective than other approaches unless you are certain you know what area of law your research problem involves.

Key Number searching. If you have identified a particular subtopic under a West topic as addressing a point you want to research, you can use the Key Number component of the topic field (illustrated in Figure 5.13 on page 132) to retrieve only cases digested under the Key Number corresponding to that subtopic. For example, suppose you have identified Key Number 4 under the topic "Weapons" as a relevant or potentially relevant Key Number. You could retrieve all the cases digested under this Key Number by using the following search request:

```
406k4
```

As this search request shows, a West Key Number as expressed for WESTLAW purposes consists of three elements:

- the number corresponding to a West digest topic (here, "406," which corresponds to the West topic "Weapons")
- the letter "k," which substitutes for the Key Number symbol West uses in its printed digests
- the Key Number corresponding to a subtopic under the West topic (here, "4," which corresponds to the Weapons subtopic "Manufacture, sale, gift, loan, possession, or use")

[85] *See* CHRISTOPHER G. WREN & JILL R. WREN, THE LEGAL RESEARCH MANUAL: A GAME PLAN FOR LEGAL RESEARCH AND ANALYSIS 60–62, 63 (2d ed. 1986).

Note that there are no spaces between the elements of the Key Number and that, unlike the typical field-restricted search term, the Key Number is not enclosed in parentheses or prefaced with the field name.

You will usually want to refine a Key Number search by linking a Key Number with a word expressing a relevant fact or issue or with another field restriction. With this refinement, instead of retrieving all the cases digested under the Key Number, you will retrieve only those cases that are digested under the Key Number and that satisfy the additional criteria in your search request. For example, the search request

```
406k4 and molotov w/5 cocktail or
explosive or incend!
```

would retrieve only cases digested under Weapons Key Number 4 that mention Molotov cocktails, explosives, or other incendiary devices. Similarly, the search request

```
406k4 and explosive and judge(breyer)
and date(after 12/31/79)
```

would retrieve only cases digested under Weapons Key Number 4 that mention explosives, that were decided after December 31, 1979, and in which a judge named Breyer wrote the opinion for the court.

As you formulate Key Number search requests, keep in mind that the sweep of your search will depend on the position your Key Number occupies in the hierarchy of the West digest topic outline, such as the outline excerpted in Figure 5.03 on page 102. A Key Number search will retrieve not only cases digested under the Key Number you use in your search request, but cases digested under any Key Numbers that appear as subdivisions under that Key Number. For instance, in Figure 5.05 on page 104, the indentations of Key Numbers 1.1, 2, and 3 indicate their status as subdivisions of Key Number 1. Thus, the Key Number search request

```
92k1
```

would retrieve cases digested under Constitutional Law Key Numbers 1, 1.1, 2, and 3, as well as any other subdivisions existing at the time of the search. By contrast, if you search for a Key Number that does not have any subdivisions, you will retrieve only cases digested under that Key Number. Thus, at this writing, the Key Number search request

```
92k3
```

retrieves only cases digested under Constitutional Law Key Number 3.

Although a Key Number search will retrieve cases digested under subdivision Key Numbers, relevant cases might be digested under other nearby Key Numbers that the search will not retrieve. For example, returning to Figure 5.05 on page 104, searching for Constitutional Law Key Number 7 will not find cases digested under Key Number 8 (unless those cases have been digested under both Key Number 7 and Key Number 8). Some overlap exists among Key Number classifications, however, especially among those in close numerical proximity. As in doing a Key Number search in West digest volumes, browsing through entries under adjoining Key Numbers often proves informative. In a computerized Key Number search, to achieve the effect of browsing through neighboring Key Number entries in a digest volume, include in your search request *all* the potentially relevant Key Numbers you would have scanned in the digest. As a practical matter, you will often obtain these Key Numbers by examining a topic in a West digest volume before formulating your WESTLAW search request; consequently, engaging in book-based Key Number searching frequently serves as a precursor to doing a Key Number search in WESTLAW. If you want to identify appropriate Key Numbers while using WESTLAW, you can do so through WESTLAW's Topic and Key Number Service (explained on pages 100–07).

Finally, using a reclassified Key Number in your search request can leave gaps in the results of your online search. When West reassigns cases from an existing Key Number, cases formerly grouped together might be dispersed among several new Key Numbers. In that situation, searching for cases digested under one of the new Key Numbers will bypass cases assigned to other new Key Numbers. To ensure that you retrieve potentially relevant cases assigned to new Key Numbers other than the Key Number in your search request, search for the old Key Number. The old Key Number will appear as a cross-reference in the topic field of any case digested under a new classification derived from that Key Number. Consequently, your search will retrieve all cases formerly classified under that Key Number, regardless of their new Key Number classifications.

- **Headnote field.** This WESTLAW field contains the same material as headnotes in a case printed in a West case reporter: one-paragraph summaries (prepared by West editors) of specific points of law decided in the case, along with citations to any statutes or rules the court construed when deciding the points of law summarized in the headnotes. The text of a WESTLAW headnote and of the corresponding headnote in a West case reporter are identical, as you can see by comparing the WESTLAW screens in Figure 5.13 (pages 131–34) and the corresponding case reporter pages in Figure 5.14 (pages 135–37).

You construct a search request restricted to the headnote field just as you construct other field-restricted search requests. Type the name of the field, followed parenthetically by the terms you want the computer to search the field for:

```
headnote(firearm and felon and
possess!)
```

For a case to satisfy this search request, the search terms must appear somewhere in the headnotes to the case; if the search terms appear in the actual text of the case, but not in the headnotes, the computer will not retrieve the case.

You can also use a headnote field restriction with an unrestricted term or with another field restriction. For example, the following search request will locate cases that interpret 18 U.S.C. App. § 1202, that have been digested under the West topic "Weapons," and that mention firearms:

```
headnote(18 pre/10 1202) and
topic(406) and firearm
```

Note that the headnote field of a given case consists of *all* the headnotes accompanying that case. Thus, the search request `headnote(firearm and felon and possess!)` would be satisfied if all the search terms either appeared in a single headnote or were dispersed among several headnotes (*e.g.*, if "firearm" appeared in one headnote, "felon" appeared in another headnote, and "possession" appeared in yet a third headnote). Because each WESTLAW headnote is considered a separate paragraph in the headnote field, you should use the "same paragraph" connector ("/p") if you want all your search terms to appear in a single headnote:

```
headnote(firearm /p felon /p
possess!)
```

Looking for your search terms in a single headnote can help if you find that an unrestricted search request retrieves more irrelevant cases than you can effectively screen. West's editors seek to compress within an individual headnote the significant elements of a given point of law. As a result of this compression, word combinations in headnotes sometimes reflect legal concepts even when the same words in the text of cases do not. Therefore, using a "same paragraph" connector to locate your search terms in a single headnote can reduce the number of irrelevant cases the computer retrieves, while minimizing the loss of relevant cases.[86]

For instance, the search terms "firearm," "felon," and "possession" in a single headnote are apt to relate to an issue of the lawfulness of a felon's possessing a firearm. In the text of a case, by contrast, these search terms might relate to this issue—or, they might just describe unrelated background facts. For example, imagine a case concerning whether alleged misconduct by a prosecutor warrants a new trial for a criminal defendant. As context for the misconduct issue, the judge might summarize the underlying case, writing that "defendant, a twice-convicted *felon*, was arrested and found in *possession* of numerous items stolen during a burglary of the home of complainant, a collector of antique *firearms*." An unrestricted search for "felon," "firearm," and "possession" would retrieve this case, although it sheds no light on the issue of whether a felon can lawfully possess a firearm. By contrast, requiring the search terms to appear in a single headnote would likely exclude the case; its headnotes are apt to summarize facts and issues directly related only to the issue of misconduct by prosecutors.

A headnote field restriction can also help when you want to locate cases in which a court has construed a particular statute or rule. For example, suppose you are searching for cases that have interpreted 29 U.S.C. § 253. An unrestricted search request designed to retrieve such cases might take the following form:

```
29 pre/10 253
```

This search request would retrieve cases mentioning 29 U.S.C. § 253. In addition, though, the search request would retrieve cases that have not cited your statute but have cited, say, 29 Yale L.J. 253 or a case reported at 29 Cal. Rptr. 253. Restricting the search

[86] For related observations suggesting why restricting a search to the headnote field can have this effect, see Craig E. Runde & William H. Lindberg, The Curse of Thamus: *A Response*, 78 LAW LIBR. J. 345, 346–47 (1986).

to the headnote field, however, makes it more likely the numerical terms will refer to the statute: numerical references in a headnote field normally relate to citations (as opposed to, say, measurements or times); moreover, the only citations in a headnote field are to statutes and rules, and West's editors put these in conventional citation form. Thus, the field-restricted search request

```
headnote(29 pre/10 253)
```

is more likely to retrieve just cases that construe your statute.

In summary, the headnote field can aid your research efforts when you search for cases interpreting statutes and rules or when you want to reduce the number of irrelevant cases retrieved by an unrestricted search request.

You will generally find, however, that including a headnote field restriction in a search request does not offer significant benefits in other situations. Indeed, West does not expect researchers routinely to use headnote field restrictions. West designed the headnote field to function primarily as an additional location in which the computer will automatically look for search terms.[87] (Recall that unless you instruct the computer to search for a term in only a specified field, the computer will search for the term everywhere in the document.)

The principal value of the headnote field, according to West, derives from "vocabulary enrichment" found in the headnotes.[88] The "enriched vocabulary" consists of words that West's editors include to describe significant facts or issues discussed in the case. For example, a judge in a medical malpractice case might use only the word "ophthalmologist" to refer to the defendant and only the word "Bufferin" to describe an allegedly misprescribed drug. West's editors, however, might use the more general words "physician" and "aspirin" in the headnotes. When West headnotes include words that do not appear in the case itself, the headnotes enhance the likelihood of the terms in a search request matching the words in the document, thus increasing the chance the search request will retrieve the document.[89]

[87] As shown on page 132 in Figure 5.13, the headnote field is an element of the digest field, which West says "is most helpful simply as an extra component for searching." WEST PUBLISHING COMPANY, WESTLAW TEMPORARY REFERENCE MANUAL 9/23 (1985 ed. & 1987 inserts).

[88] *See, e.g.*, Craig E. Runde & William H. Lindberg, The Curse of Thamus: *A Response*, 78 LAW LIBR. J. 345, 346 (1986).

[89] Not every West headnote adds words beyond those used in the case. Many West headnotes simply repeat significant words from the case. Daniel P. Dabney, *The Curse of Thamus: An*

- **Digest field**. This WESTLAW field corresponds to the digest paragraphs found in West digest volumes. The top screen on page 132 in Figure 5.13 shows a typical WESTLAW digest paragraph. Figure 5.01 on page 87 reproduces a sample page from a West digest volume; in the middle of the right-hand column of the sample page, you'll find the printed version of the WESTLAW digest paragraph in Figure 5.13. You can see by comparing the two figures that a WESTLAW digest paragraph contains the same information as the corresponding digest volume paragraph.

  The digest field in WESTLAW functions as an umbrella field that encompasses several other fields. As Figure 5.13 shows, the digest field contains the following fields:

  - topic field
  - court field
  - headnote field

  In addition, the digest field includes the case's short title (identifying the principal plaintiff and the principal defendant, not any additional parties who might be listed in the title field) and the year of decision (although not the month and day, which appear in the date field).

  You can do in the digest field any search you can do in the fields comprising the digest field. A search request restricted to the digest field could take this form:

```
digest(firearm /p felon /p possess!)
```

Analysis of Full-Text Legal Document Retrieval, 78 LAW LIBR. J. 5, 32 (1986); Craig E. Runde & William H. Lindberg, The Curse of Thamus: *A Response*, 78 LAW LIBR. J. 345, 346 (1986); *cf.* Arnold O. Ginnow, *The West Computer-Assisted Legal Retrieval System*, LAW & COMPUTER TECH., July/Aug. 1975, at 82, 82 ("The headnotes contain the language used in the opinion to the fullest possible extent.").

The proportion of headnotes that add new words instead of tracking judicial language remains unknown. West instructs its headnote editors to use designated alternative words in headnotes if a judge does not use the designated words in the text of the case. Craig E. Runde & William H. Lindberg, *supra*, at 346. The frequency with which West editors find it necessary to provide alternatives to the judicially selected words has not been established, however. Thus, the actual extent of the benefit flowing from vocabulary enrichment in WESTLAW is still a subject of dispute. *Compare* Craig E. Runde & William H. Lindberg, *supra*, at 345–46 *with* Daniel P. Dabney, *supra*, at 32 *and* Daniel P. Dabney, *A Reply to West Publishing Company and Mead Data Central on* The Curse of Thamus, 78 LAW LIBR. J. 349, 350 (1986). *See also* James A. Sprowl, *WESTLAW vs. LEXIS: Computer-Assisted Legal Research Comes of Age*, 68 ILL. B.J. 156, 159 (1979) ("comparative tests of the WESTLAW headnote system and the LEXIS full-text system have shown little difference in the ability of the two systems to capture the most pertinent cases").

This search request would retrieve each case in which the search terms appear in a single paragraph in the digest field; the terms need not appear in the actual text of the case. You can also link a digest field restriction with an unrestricted search term or with another field restriction.

The digest field for a given case contains a separate paragraph for each headnote in the case; because most cases have more than one headnote, the digest field for a case usually consists of more than one paragraph. As with searching in the headnote field, using the "same paragraph" connector ("/p") ensures your search terms will appear in a single paragraph, where their presence together is more apt to signify the meaning you intend.[90] By contrast, the search request `digest(firearm and felon and possess!)` would be satisfied if every search term appeared in one paragraph of the digest field or if the search terms appeared dispersed throughout several paragraphs in the field.

Because the information in the digest field also appears in other WESTLAW fields, searching the digest field offers minimal advantages beyond those associated with separately searching the fields that constitute this field. In fact, using a digest field restriction can undermine your research efforts by introducing uncertainty: sometimes, search terms whose significance you can anticipate fairly successfully when they appear in one of the fields that make up the digest field become less predictable when you search for the terms in the digest field.

For example, if you search for "firearm" in the context of the headnote field, you can be fairly certain the term, if present, will signify an important fact in the case. But if you search for "firearm" in the context of the digest field, you cannot predict whether the term, if present, will represent a significant fact in the case (as summarized in a headnote) or whether it will simply occur as, say, part of the case title (*e.g.*, "*Internal Revenue Service v. Acme Firearms & Hunting Supplies, Inc.*"). A search of the digest field might also locate the term in the topic field as part of the topic name or as part of a phrase describing a Key Number subtopic.

As this example implies, a search restricted to the digest field will usually retrieve more cases—some relevant and some irrelevant—than will a search restricted to one of the fields that constitute the digest field. Because the digest field contains more information, the computer has more opportunities to match search terms with

[90] See pages 93–94.

terms in the field; thus, the computer will generally retrieve more cases, a portion of which will likely prove relevant. On the other hand, because terms in the digest field can take on a broader range of meanings, some of which might not pertain to the research problem, searching in the digest field can increase the number of irrelevant cases retrieved.

In considering whether to use a digest field restriction, keep in mind that West designed the digest field (like the headnote field) to function mainly as an additional location the computer can check for search terms.[91] Even if you do not use a digest field restriction in your search request, the computer will automatically look in the digest field for your unrestricted search terms.

- **Synopsis field**. This WESTLAW field contains a brief overview of the case. Written by West editors, the information in the synopsis field summarizes the key facts and issues of the case, the progression of the case through the appellate courts, the court's resolution of each issue, and the court's decision (*e.g.*, affirmed, reversed).

  In addition, the synopsis field includes the name of the judge who wrote the opinion summarized by the synopsis; if an appellate court issued the opinion, the synopsis also identifies any appellate judges who concurred or dissented, and usually identifies the trial court judge and the appellate judges who wrote the majority opinions in any intermediate appeals.[92]

  Some courts, such as the United States Supreme Court and a few state courts, prepare their own summaries in the form of a "syllabus." In those instances, the court-prepared syllabus appears in the synopsis field along with the West-prepared summary.

  Pages 131 and 133 in Figure 5.13 show a typical WESTLAW synopsis field. Pages 135 and 136 in Figure 5.14 show the corresponding material from a West case reporter. As you can see by comparing the figures, the information in the WESTLAW synopsis field replicates the information in the synopsis portion (and, when available, syllabus portion) of a case published in a West reporter.

  A search request restricted to the synopsis field takes this form:

```
synopsis(firearm and felon and
possess!)
```

[91] *See* page 95.

[92] In LEXIS, United States Supreme Court cases and cases from some state courts contain a segment called "syllabus," which includes information similar to that found in the synopsis field in WESTLAW. Unlike the editorially prepared material in the WESTLAW synopsis field, however, the contents of a LEXIS syllabus segment are written by the court that decided the accompanying case. For more information about the coverage of the LEXIS syllabus segment, see Figure 5.08.

For a case to satisfy this search request, the search terms must appear somewhere in the synopsis field; if the search terms appear in the actual text of the case, but not in the synopsis, the computer will not retrieve the case. As with other field-restricted searches, you can link a synopsis field restriction with an unrestricted search term or with another field restriction.

A synopsis field restriction can serve two purposes. First, you can use it to find cases in which specific judges have written concurring or dissenting opinions or in which the decisions of specific lower court judges have been affirmed or reversed on appeal.[93] At this time, cases in WESTLAW do not contain fields that isolate this kind of information, so you need to extract it from the synopsis field with search requests like these examples:[94]

```
synopsis(stevens /s concur!)
synopsis(brennan /s dissent!)
synopsis(doyle and affirmed)
synopsis(jackson and reversed)
```

You can also link these synopsis field restrictions with unrestricted search terms or with other field restrictions.

The synopsis field restriction serves a second function: reducing the number of cases retrieved if you find that an unrestricted search request yields more cases than you can effectively review. As with headnotes, West's editors strive to compress within a synopsis the significant factual and legal points in the accompanying case. Because of this distillation, word combinations in a synopsis sometimes reflect legal concepts even when the same words in the text of the accompanying case do not. (This result arises for essentially the same reasons as those discussed on page 94 in connection with the headnote field restriction.) Consequently, using a synopsis field

[93] You can also use the synopsis field to locate cases in which specific judges have written the majority opinions, but you will generally find using the "judge" field (as explained on page 77) more effective for this purpose: because the "judge" field contains only the name of the judge who wrote the opinion, no possibility exists for ambiguity in the meaning of the search term.

[94] You can perform similar searches in LEXIS. There, separate segments exist for locating names of judges who have written various types of opinions. In LEXIS, the name of the judge who writes the opinion for the court appears in the "opinionby" segment of a case, the name of a judge who writes a concurring opinion appears in the "concurby" segment, and the name of a judge who writes a dissenting opinion appears in the "dissentby" segment. In addition, LEXIS includes a segment designated "writtenby," through which you can locate all opinions—majority, concurring, and dissenting—written by a particular judge. Figure 5.09 on pages 119–23 illustrates search requests in these LEXIS segments.

restriction with your search terms can reduce the number of irrelevant cases the computer retrieves.

Looking in only the synopsis field for search terms reflecting key aspects of your research problem might also pass over too many *relevant* cases, however. Synopses often express significant facts and legal issues in broad, categorical terms. For example, a synopsis might characterize a case by referring to it as "an antitrust prosecution" instead of as "a prosecution for fixing prices." Unless the search terms you use in a synopsis field restriction represent sufficiently broad legal concepts (such as antitrust), the terms might not appear in the synopses of some relevant cases; your search request might therefore bypass relevant law. Because of this drawback, WESTLAW has advised caution when using the synopsis field to restrict a search for legal concepts.[95]

When not used as a field restriction, the synopsis field serves simply as an additional location the WESTLAW computer can check for search terms, thus increasing the likelihood a search request will retrieve relevant cases. The WESTLAW computer automatically looks in the synopsis field (as well as in all other fields) for unrestricted search terms. Because the synopsis field, like the headnote and digest fields, might include terms that do not appear in the text of the accompanying case, the additional terms (referred to as "enriched vocabulary") provide further opportunities for the computer to match search terms with terms in the document.[96]

Using the Topic and Key Number Service in WESTLAW to identify West topics or Key Number subtopics for topic-field searching in cases. In addition to the TOPIC database (which provides an online list of all West digest topics), WESTLAW offers the Topic and Key Number Service, which complements the TOPIC database by providing online access to West's Key Number outline of the law, including all of West's digest topics *and subtopics.* You can use the Topic and Key Number Service to verify online whether you have selected an appropriate West topic for a search that includes a topic field restriction; you can also verify whether you have selected an appropriate Key Number for a Key Number search, and you can view neighboring Key Numbers to determine whether other subtopics pertain to the issue you are researching.

[95] "[A synopsis field restriction] should be used only when dealing with such major concepts as search and seizure, antitrust, discrimination, insurance, and so on." WEST PUBLISHING COMPANY, WESTLAW TEMPORARY REFERENCE MANUAL 9/17 (1985 ed. & 1987 inserts).

[96] When a synopsis does not add terms beyond those appearing in the text of the case, however, the synopsis field will not confer the benefit of vocabulary enrichment. *Cf.* note 89 (discussing enriched vocabulary in West headnotes).

Gaining access to the Topic and Key Number Service in WESTLAW. You can gain access to the Topic and Key Number Service at any time while using WESTLAW. To do so, type **key** and press the ENTER key. The monitor will display a screen like the one shown in Figure 5.02, which is the first screen of the list of West digest topics.

Displaying a West digest topic outline. Through the Topic and Key Number Service, you can see the online version of the outline you would see for a digest topic in a printed West digest. (Figure 5.03 on page 102 shows part of a typical outline from a West digest.) After invoking the Topic and Key Number Service by transmitting **key**, you can follow either of two routes to select and display the outline you want:

- Suppose you are viewing the list of West digest topics (illustrated in Figure 5.02). You can press the TAB key to position the cursor (the short bar of light that indicates your typing position on the monitor) under the JUMP marker (the ">" symbol or triangle) next to the topic for which you want to see an outline. Then press the ENTER key. For example, at the screen in Figure 5.02, you would press the TAB key to position the cursor on the ">" symbol next to "Accession" and press ENTER if you wanted to see the outline for that topic.

```
                      Copyright (c) 1993 West Publishing Company
                               Key Number Service
>                                   Topic List
-------------------------------------------------------------------------------
>    1  ABANDONED AND LOST PROPERTY
>    2  ABATEMENT AND REVIVAL
>    4  ABORTION AND BIRTH CONTROL
>    5  ABSENTEES
>    6  ABSTRACTS OF TITLE
>    7  ACCESSION
>    8  ACCORD AND SATISFACTION
>    9  ACCOUNT
>   10  ACCOUNT, ACTION ON
>   11  ACCOUNT STATED
>   11A ACCOUNTANTS
>   12  ACKNOWLEDGMENT
>   13  ACTION
>   14  ACTION ON THE CASE

If you wish to:
   View an item in more detail, select its jump marker
   View the next or previous page, type P or P- and press ENTER
   View the list of Key Number commands, type CMDS and press ENTER
   Go back to the previously accessed service, type GB and press ENTER
```

Source: West Publishing Company © 1993

Figure 5.02. First Screen of the List of West Digest Topics in WESTLAW's Topic and Key Number Service

3 F P D 4th—4

ARBITRATION

SUBJECTS INCLUDED

Submission of controversies by the parties thereto to persons chosen by themselves, for determination

Agreements to arbitrate disputes, and enforcement thereof

Rights, powers, duties and proceedings of arbitrators, umpires, etc.

Requisites, validity, operation and effect of such submission and the award thereon

Pleading arbitration and award as defense

Enforcing, modifying, or setting aside award

SUBJECTS EXCLUDED AND COVERED BY OTHER TOPICS

Architects, engineers, or others, determination of performance of contracts by, see CONTRACTS

Labor disputes, arbitration of, see LABOR RELATIONS

Particular classes of contracts, stipulations for arbitration in, see INSURANCE, LABOR RELATIONS, LANDLORD AND TENANT, PARTNERSHIP, and other specific topics

Public bodies, arbitration of claims against, see STATES, MUNICIPAL CORPORATIONS, and other specific topics

Reference of issues in pending actions under provision of statutes or rules or orders of courts, see REFERENCE

For detailed references to other topics, see Descriptive-Word Index

---

Analysis

I. NATURE AND FORM OF PROCEEDING, 🔑1–5.

II. AGREEMENT AND SUBMISSION, 🔑6–25.

(A) AGREEMENTS TO ARBITRATE, 🔑6–10.15.

(B) SUBMISSION, 🔑11–21.

(C) PERFORMANCE, BREACH, ENFORCEMENT, AND CONTEST, 🔑22–25.

III. ARBITRATORS AND PROCEEDINGS, 🔑26–47.

IV. AWARD, 🔑48–89.

I. NATURE AND FORM OF PROCEEDING.

🔑1. Nature and right to arbitration in general.

1.1. Contractual or consensual basis.

1.2. Arbitration favored; public policy.

2. Constitutional and statutory provisions; rules of court.

2.1. Common law or statutory arbitration.

2.2. What law governs.

Source: West Publishing Company © 1989

Figure 5.03. Sample First Page of a Topic (Arbitration) in a West Digest, Showing West Key Numbers You Can Use to Search the Topic Field in WESTLAW

If the topic you want does not appear on the part of the list you are viewing, you can move forward through the list by pressing the ENTER key, by pressing the PAGE DOWN key, or by typing `p` and pressing the ENTER key; to move backward through the list, press the PAGE UP key or type `p-` and press the ENTER key. Then, when you see your topic displayed on the screen, you can use the JUMP feature to select that topic.

- If you know the name or number of the digest topic, you can type the name or number and press the ENTER key. For instance, to see the outline for "Weapons" (which is topic number 406), you could type **`weapons`** and press ENTER, or you could type **`406`** and press ENTER.[97]

After you select a digest topic, the monitor will display the first screen of the outline for that topic. Figure 5.04 shows a typical screen displayed at this point.

Digest topics in the Topic and Key Number Service can display in two formats: in a summary outline or in a detailed outline. Initially, a topic outline displays in the summary format illustrated in Figure 5.04. The summary format is known as the "Outline" mode (identified by the phrase "Mode: Outline" in the upper right corner of the screen). To switch to the detailed outline format (known as the "All" mode), type **`all`** and press the ENTER key. Figure 5.05 shows the first screen of the topic "Constitutional Law" in the "All" mode. To return to "Outline" mode, type **`outline`** and press the ENTER key. You can switch between "Outline" mode and "All" mode as often as you want.

When you are viewing a topic outline in the Topic and Key Number Service, you might see JUMP markers (the ">" symbols or triangles) in the left margin of the outline. Each marker indicates that you can see more detail for the portion of the outline adjacent to the marker. To see the additional details for an outline entry marked with a JUMP symbol, press the TAB key to position the cursor under the JUMP marker next to the entry you want to select, then press the ENTER key. For instance, in Figure 5.04, the JUMP marker next to the outline entry "Vested Rights" indicates the existence of additional subtopic entries (namely, the subtopic entries for Key Numbers 92 through 112). If you used the JUMP feature to display the additional entries under "Vested Rights," you would see the screen in Figure 5.06.

While viewing a topic outline in the Topic and Key Number Service, you can display a specific Key Number within that topic by transmitting `k` and the Key Number you want to view. So, for example, if you were viewing the

[97] Currently, if you transmit a West topic name that does not exist, the monitor will display the topic list beginning with the topic name that would follow alphabetically the nonexistent topic name you transmitted.

```
                         Copyright (c) 1993 West Publishing Company
                              Key Number Service
> Topic List                                                       Mode: Outline
-------------------------------------------------------------------------------
>                             92  CONSTITUTIONAL LAW
                                     Analysis

>        I. ESTABLISHMENT AND AMENDMENT OF CONSTITUTIONS, k1-k10.32
>       II. CONSTRUCTION, OPERATION, AND ENFORCEMENT OF CONSTITUTIONAL
                PROVISIONS, k11-k49
>      III. DISTRIBUTION OF GOVERNMENTAL POWERS AND FUNCTIONS, k50-k80(4)
>       IV. POLICE POWER IN GENERAL, k81-k81
>        V. PERSONAL, CIVIL AND POLITICAL RIGHTS, k82-k91
>       VI. VESTED RIGHTS, k92-k112
>      VII. OBLIGATION OF CONTRACTS, k113-k185
>     VIII. RETROSPECTIVE AND EX POST FACTO LAWS, k186-k203
>       IX. PRIVILEGES OR IMMUNITIES, k204-k207
>        X. CLASS LEGISLATION, k208-k208

If you wish to:
   View an item in more detail, select its jump marker
   View the next or previous page, type P or P- and press ENTER
   Run a search using a topic and key number, type DB followed by a database
     identifier and the number and press ENTER (e.g., DB ALLFEDS 410k196.1)
```

Source: West Publishing Company © 1993

Figure 5.04. First Screen of WESTLAW's Topic and Key Number Service Outline for West's "Constitutional Law" Digest Topic (in "Outline" Mode)

```
                         Copyright (c) 1993 West Publishing Company
                              Key Number Service
> Topic List                                                       Mode: All
>  92  CONSTITUTIONAL LAW
-------------------------------------------------------------------------------
      I. ESTABLISHMENT AND AMENDMENT OF CONSTITUTIONS, k1-k10.32
        k1     Nature, authority, and adoption
        k1.1   --In general
        k2     --Constitutional conventions
        k3     --Submission to popular vote
        k4     Amendment and revision of state Constitutions
        k5     --In general
        k6     --Constitutional provisions as to resubmission and revision
        k7     --Legislative powers and proceedings
        k8     --Conventions to revise Constitution
        k9     --Submission to popular vote
             (0.5) In general
             (1)   Method of submission and form of ballots

If you wish to:
   View an item in more detail, select its jump marker
   View the next or previous page, type P or P- and press ENTER
   Run a search using a topic and key number, type DB followed by a database
     identifier and the number and press ENTER (e.g., DB ALLFEDS 410k196.1)
```

Source: West Publishing Company © 1993

Figure 5.05. First Screen of WESTLAW's Topic and Key Number Service Outline for West's "Constitutional Law" Digest Topic (in "All" Mode)

```
                   Copyright (c) 1993 West Publishing Company
                              Key Number Service
> Topic List                                              Mode: Outline
>  92  CONSTITUTIONAL LAW
>     VI. VESTED RIGHTS, k92-k112
--------------------------------------------------------------------------------
        k92   Constitutional guaranties in general
>       k93   Estates and interests in property in general
        k94   Rules of descent
        k95   Dower and curtesy
        k96   Community property
        k97   Betterment laws
        k98   Redemption laws
        k99   Exemption and homestead laws
        k100  Exemptions from taxation
        k101  Franchises and privileges
>       k102  Public offices
        k103  Disposition of public moneys

If you wish to:
   View an item in more detail, select its jump marker
   View the next or previous page, type P or P- and press ENTER
   Run a search using a topic and key number, type DB followed by a database
     identifier and the number and press ENTER (e.g., DB ALLFEDS 410k196.1)
```

Source: West Publishing Company © 1993

Figure 5.06. Sample Screen in WESTLAW's Topic and Key Number Service, Showing Key Number Entries in a West Digest Topic Outline

```
                   Copyright (c) 1993 West Publishing Company
                              Key Number Service
 Topic List                                               Mode: All
>  92  CONSTITUTIONAL LAW
>     VII. OBLIGATION OF CONTRACTS, k113-k185
>       (A) POWERS OF STATES IN GENERAL, k113-k119
>         k114  The law impairing the obligation
--------------------------------------------------------------------------------
          k116  --Judicial decisions
          k117  Exercise of police power
          k118  Exercise of power of eminent domain
          k119  Exercise of power of taxation
        (B) CONTRACTS OF STATES AND MUNICIPALITIES, k120-k144
          k120  Nature of contracts protected in general
          k121  Contracts of state or municipality with individuals in
                  general
            (0.5) In general
            (1)   State

If you wish to:
   View an item in more detail, select its jump marker
   View the next or previous page, type P or P- and press ENTER
   Run a search using a topic and key number, type DB followed by a database
     identifier and the number and press ENTER (e.g., DB ALLFEDS 410k196.1)
```

Source: West Publishing Company © 1993

Figure 5.07. Sample Screen in WESTLAW's Topic and Key Number Service, Showing Key Number Entries in a West Digest Topic Outline

screen shown in Figure 5.04, you could type `k116` and press ENTER to display the screen shown in Figure 5.07.

Switching to the outline for a different West digest topic. While you are in the Topic and Key Number Service, you can switch from the topic outline you are viewing to the outline for another topic. To do that, type the name or number of the new topic, then press the ENTER key. So, if you were viewing the outline for Constitutional Law and wanted to switch to the outline for Weapons (topic 406), you could transmit either `weapons` or `406` to make the switch.

If you know the Key Number you want to view in the outline for the new topic, you can go directly to that portion of the topic outline. To do so, type the number of the topic to which you want to switch, the letter "k", and the Key Number you want to view within the new topic; then press the ENTER key. For instance, you could transmit `92k117` to switch to the outline for the "Constitutional Law" topic and view the portion of the outline beginning with Key Number 117.

Shortcuts for gaining access to an outline in WESTLAW's Topic and Key Number Service. WESTLAW offers several shortcuts for going directly to an outline in the Topic and Key Number Service without first displaying the list of digest topics (Figure 5.02). If you have not already invoked the Topic and Key Number Service, you can use any of these shortcuts:

- When you know the name or number of the digest topic for which you want to view an outline, you can type `key` followed by the topic name or number, and then press the ENTER key. The monitor will display the first screen of the outline for that topic. For example, transmitting `key 92` or `key constitutional law` would display the screen shown in Figure 5.04.
- When you know the number of the digest topic *and* the Key Number you want to view in that topic, you can transmit `key` followed by the topic number and Key Number. The monitor will display the topic outline beginning with that Key Number. For instance, transmitting `key 92k116` would display the screen shown in Figure 5.07.
- When you are viewing the contents of a digest field in a case in WESTLAW (as on page 132 in Figure 5.13), you might see a digest topic for which you want to view an outline, or you might see a Key Number you want to view in the context of neighboring Key Number subtopics. If so, you can gain access to the Topic and Key Number Service by using the JUMP marker (the ">" symbol or triangle) next to the topic or Key Number in which you are interested. Simply press the TAB key to position the cursor under the

JUMP marker next to that topic or Key Number, then press the ENTER key. The monitor will display the portion of the topic outline corresponding to your selection.

Checking the scope of coverage of a West topic outline. In printed West digests, the scope analysis at the beginning of a topic outline (such as the one shown in Figure 5.03 on page 102) alerts you to subjects covered by the topic, as well as to subjects excluded. When you use the Topic and Key Number Service in WESTLAW, you can view an online version of the scope analysis for a topic outline. To see the scope analysis for an outline you are viewing, type `scope` (or `sc`) and press the ENTER key. To see the scope analysis for an outline you are not viewing, type `scope` (or `sc`) followed by the topic name or number, then press ENTER; for example, you could transmit `scope weapons` or `sc 406`.

Sometimes, specific Key Numbers in printed West digests are accompanied by short scope analyses indicating subjects included in or excluded from those Key Number subtopics. The Topic and Key Number Service contains these analyses, with their locations marked on the screen by "(NOTE)." You can display the text of Key Number scope analyses by typing `notes` and pressing the ENTER key. If you then want to turn off this display, you can type `xnotes` and press ENTER.

Leaving WESTLAW's Topic and Key Number Service. When you want to leave the Topic and Key Number Service, type `gb` (for "go back") and press the ENTER key. The monitor will redisplay the screen you were viewing when you transmitted a "key" command to gain access to the Topic and Key Number Service.

Summary of WESTLAW's "Full Text Plus." The fields in WESTLAW that editorially enhance the text of cases have varying implications for searching in WESTLAW. In summary, these editorially prepared fields—the topic, headnote, digest, and synopsis fields—hold the following significance for researchers.

Using the *topic* field parallels searching through a topic in a West digest volume. In WESTLAW, though, you can link a topic field restriction with terms representing important facts or legal concepts in your research problem or with other field restrictions (*e.g.*, date of decision, name of judge, name of attorney, or even another topic); thus, you can tailor your search in ways that would be inconvenient or even impossible with printed digests. In short, you can pinpoint, according to a variety of screening criteria, particular cases abstracted under a given digest topic.

You can also refine a topic field search by looking for cases digested under specific subtopic Key Numbers. Because of overlap in the coverage of many Key Numbers, however, you need to exercise caution when choosing Key

Numbers; to ensure a comprehensive search, you might need to include in your search request several Key Numbers (which you can find by browsing in a West digest volume or by checking the Topic and Key Number Service in WESTLAW).

To conduct either a topic or Key Number search effectively, you need to know in advance the West digest topics under which to categorize your research problem—often a problematic task for researchers confronting unfamiliar areas of law. Moreover, selecting an appropriate topic requires familiarity with the scope of the topic's coverage. Consequently, unless you know the range of a topic's coverage, it's a good idea to check the scope analysis at the beginning of a topic in a West digest volume or to use the "scope" command in WESTLAW's Topic and Key Number Service before beginning a topic search online. (An example of a scope analysis appears in the top half of Figure 5.03 on page 102.)

The *headnote*, *digest*, and *synopsis* fields in WESTLAW offer additional opportunities to match search terms with terms in the document and, therefore, to retrieve additional relevant cases. The extent of the benefit of this "enriched vocabulary" remains unknown, however, given the uncertainty about how often the West editors who write headnotes and synopses include words that do not appear in the text of the accompanying case. In any event, because the WESTLAW computer automatically searches the headnote, digest, and synopsis fields for all unrestricted terms, you do not need to include a headnote, digest, or synopsis field restriction as part of your search request to obtain the benefit of any enriched vocabulary.

You might want to use a *headnote* field restriction in two situations, however. First, because headnotes cite relevant statutes and rules, a headnote restriction can help you find cases in which a court has construed a particular statute or rule. Second, because headnotes distill legal concepts, a headnote restriction can sometimes reduce the number of irrelevant cases retrieved by an unrestricted search request (while minimizing the loss of relevant cases).

The *digest* field encompasses the topic, headnote, and court fields. You can search the digest field for any information contained in the component fields, but (because of the various categories of information included) searching with a digest field restriction can introduce unanticipated ambiguities you would not encounter by separately searching each of the underlying fields.

Including a *synopsis* field restriction in your search request can serve two purposes. First, you can use this restriction to locate cases in which particular judges have participated in specified ways (*e.g.*, by concurring, by dissenting). By searching the database according to such criteria, the computer will quickly locate cases you could pinpoint through book-based research only with considerably more time and effort.[98] Second, you can use a synopsis field restric-

[98] Recall that you can also screen cases according to judge-related criteria in LEXIS. *See* note 94.

tion to reduce the number of irrelevant cases retrieved if an unrestricted search request yields more cases than you can practically evaluate. Because of the broad, categorical language in which West's editors frequently write synopses, however, this use of a synopsis field restriction might also bypass too many relevant cases; a headnote field restriction can prove more effective for paring an unmanageably large collection of cases retrieved by an unrestricted search request.

Field-restricted searching in other kinds of authorities in LEXIS and WESTLAW

As with cases, you can perform field-restricted searches in other materials in LEXIS and WESTLAW, such as statutes, administrative regulations, and articles in law reviews and newspapers. The CALR vendors also divide these documents into segments or fields that reflect recurring elements. For example, LEXIS and WESTLAW divide their annotated versions of the *United States Code* into the segments and fields shown in Figure 5.10 on page 124; illustrations of these segments and fields appear in Figures 5.15 on page 138 and 5.17 on pages 140–41. Figures 5.16 on page 139 and 5.18 on page 142 show how the contents of the printed statutes correlate with the segments and fields in the online statutes.

For complete lists of LEXIS segments in various kinds of documents, check the *LEXIS Product Guide*.[99] Online, you can also press the SEGMTS key on the LEXIS keyboard after you have gained access to a LEXIS file to see a list of segments for that file; in addition, some files in the GUIDE library (and the GUIDE file found in some libraries) contain sample documents showing the available segments.[100]

For WESTLAW, complete lists of the fields for various kinds of documents appear in *WESTLAW DataBasics*.[101] A list of WESTLAW fields also appears in the online descriptions of WESTLAW databases (type `scope` and press ENTER to see it). Or, after you have gained access to a WESTLAW database, you can display a list of fields for that database by typing `f` (for "fields") and pressing ENTER.

Conducting a search in nonjudicial authorities. To perform a field-restricted search in documents other than cases, you start by familiarizing yourself with the names and contents of the LEXIS segments or WESTLAW fields in the kind of documents you want to search. Then you formulate your search request by using the same technique explained on pages 76–77 for field-

[99] MEAD DATA CENTRAL, LEXIS PRODUCT GUIDE (1992 & current supp.).
[100] For an explanation of GUIDE, see Appendix A.
[101] WEST PUBLISHING COMPANY, WESTLAW DATABASICS (1993).

restricted searches in cases: enclose your search terms and connectors in parentheses after the segment or field name (or, in WESTLAW, after the abbreviation for the field name).

For example, the "history" segment in a *United States Code* provision in LEXIS contains the public law number under which the provision was enacted; in WESTLAW, the information appears in the "credit" field in *United States Code* provisions. Thus, in LEXIS, if you wanted to find all *United States Code* provisions enacted under Public Law 99–514, you could transmit

```
history(99-514)
```

in the USCS or USCODE file in the GENFED library or the USCODE file in the CODES library. In WESTLAW, you could transmit

```
credit(99-514)
```

in the USC database. As with field-restricted searching in cases, you could combine the field restriction with unrestricted search terms or with another field restriction.

The vendors' literature provides additional examples of searching LEXIS segments or WESTLAW fields in documents other than cases. To get a feel for the range of field-restricted searches you can perform in statutes, administrative regulations, newsletters, and other nonjudicial materials, check the *LEXIS Product Guide*;[102] pages 93 to 101 of the LEXIS reference manual;[103] pages 143 to 150 and pages 154 to 157 of the *WESTLAW Reference Manual 5th*; and *WESTLAW DataBasics.*

Using field restrictions in natural-language searching in WESTLAW

If you use the natural-language feature (explained on pages 24–26 and 67–71) for searching in WESTLAW with plain-English instructions, you can include field restrictions in your search. A field restriction in a natural-language search instruction follows the same format as in a Boolean terms-and-connectors search instruction: the identification of the field you want the computer to search, followed by the terms (and, if appropriate, connectors) enclosed in parentheses.

To include a field restriction in a natural-language search instruction, type `res` (for "restriction") and press ENTER. You can transmit this command either while viewing a retrieved document or when the monitor displays the screen

[102] MEAD DATA CENTRAL, LEXIS PRODUCT GUIDE (1992 & current supp.).

[103] MEAD DATA CENTRAL, REFERENCE MANUAL FOR THE LEXIS/NEXIS SERVICES (undated looseleaf ed.).

for transmitting natural-language searches, illustrated in Figure 9.11 on page 202. (If any search instructions already appear in the area of the screen for typing instructions, first erase those words from the screen by pressing the HOME key and then the F9 key, or by using the DELETE key or the BACKSPACE key.) After you transmit `res`, the monitor will display a screen showing the fields available as restrictions in natural-language searching. On-screen prompts guide you in a fill-in-the-blank fashion through the steps for including the field restrictions you want. Later, if you want to modify or delete a field restriction, transmit `res` again, press the TAB key to move to the restriction, and then modify or delete it.

At this time, the natural-language feature does not allow field-restricted searching in some kinds of authorities (such as international treaties in the USTREATIES database). In addition, field-restricted searching with natural language currently operates less flexibly than field-restricted searching outside the natural-language feature; for example, you cannot base field restrictions on all the fields available in cases, and you cannot use a search instruction consisting just of field restrictions.

Because WESTLAW's natural-language searching capability is relatively new and departs significantly from the longer-established Boolean searching methods, researchers who use this feature should watch WESTLAW newsletters, press releases, online announcements, and other promotional materials for information about new developments.[104]

Closing thoughts on field-restricted searching

As the discussion of field-restricted searching has suggested, this kind of searching allows you to take advantage of the computer's formidable ability to search rapidly through masses of information. In minutes or even seconds, a field-restricted search can yield a compilation of documents you could spend hours or days assembling by non-computerized methods—*e.g.*, decisions of a specific judge in cases in which a particular lawyer represented one of the parties. Moreover, when you restrict your search for a term to a field containing a specific, narrowly defined type of information (such as a date or name), you can predict with considerable accuracy the connotation of that search term. For example, although you cannot anticipate whether "burger" as an unrestricted search term will locate references to, say, a food, a lawyer, or a restaurant chain, you know that searching for the term "burger" in LEXIS's "opi-

[104] Appendix B identifies various sources of information about WESTLAW.

nionby" segment or WESTLAW's "judge" field will locate only references to judges named "Burger."[105]

Field-restricted searching is not suitable for every research problem, though. Whenever you use field restrictions, you risk bypassing relevant documents because the computer searches in only selected portions of the document: you will miss relevant documents when your search terms appear in the documents but not in the fields to which you have restricted your search. For instance, because cases in WESTLAW that have not been published in a West case reporter will not have information in the "topic," "headnote," "digest," or "synopsis" field, using one of these editorially created fields as a restriction would skip all unpublished cases in WESTLAW, regardless of their relevance. Similarly, in some state statutes in WESTLAW, several fields are combined into one field with its own name;[106] because this combination renders the absorbed fields functionally nonexistent, using the name of an absorbed field instead of the combined field as a search restriction could bypass relevant statutes.

Before using a field-restricted search request, consider whether it will advance your research effort. Field-restricted searches generally work most effectively when your research involves locating documents based on information for which narrowly defined segments or fields exist (*e.g.*, using the "opinionby" segment in LEXIS to compile a list of opinions written by a particular judge, or using the WESTLAW "date" field to limit your search for housing discrimination cases to only those decided on or after a particular date).

If your research does not depend on locating documents based on such specific information, you will often search more effectively by not including field restrictions in your search requests. Because the computer responds to an unrestricted search request by searching through all segments or fields, using an unrestricted search request maximizes the number of locations in the document the computer can inspect for search terms, thus reducing the chances of passing over relevant documents. If your unrestricted search retrieves more documents than you can review, you can always revise your search request at that point by adding a field restriction to focus your results. Even then, however, better methods might exist for modifying your search. For example, you

[105] The problem of accurately predicting the meaning of search terms still exists, however, when you restrict your search to a field (such as the "digest" or "synopsis" field in WESTLAW, or the "opinion" field in LEXIS or WESTLAW) that is not limited to information as discrete as dates or names. Fields that include a range of information in a prose format (*e.g.*, summaries of significant facts and legal issues) present the opportunity for a single search term to be used in more than one sense.

[106] *See* West Publishing Company, WESTLAW Reference Manual 143 n.* (5th ed. 1993).

could change your search terms or connectors (or both) or conduct your search in a different WESTLAW database or LEXIS library or file. Chapter 8 discusses ways to modify search requests.

If you decide to use a field restriction, be sure to base it on up-to-date information about the name and contents of the LEXIS segment or WESTLAW field you plan to search. Because segments and fields serve as fixed locations in which researchers can confidently expect to locate defined pieces of information, the CALR vendors keep these features relatively constant. Occasionally, however, the vendors rename or rearrange a segment or field. Researchers need to check the vendors' informational literature and online explanations periodically for possible changes that could affect the effectiveness of a field-restricted search.

In short, although field-restricted searching can function as a powerful instrument for navigating LEXIS or WESTLAW, the utility of this kind of search depends on the researcher's making appropriate choices about when and how to use the available field restrictions.

LEXIS		WESTLAW		
Segment Name	**Contents**	**Field Name**	**Abbre-viation**	**Contents**
cite	• citation of the case (*e.g.*, 360 U.S. 684)	citation	ci	• citation of the case (*e.g.*, 360 U.S. 684)
name	• names of all the parties in the case	title	ti	• names of all the parties in the case
court	• name of the court that issued the case	court	co	• name of the court that issued the case
number	• docket number of the case (*e.g.*, 78-1595)	opinion	op	among other items of information, • docket number of the case (*e.g.*, 78-1595)
date	• date of the court's decision	date	da	• date of the court's decision
disposition	• court's decision (*e.g.*, affirmed, reversed)	synopsis	sy	among other items of information, • court's decision (*e.g.*, affirmed, reversed)
history	• summary of facts • prior and subsequent appellate history • name of lower court • name of lower-court judge	synopsis	sy	among other items of information, • West-prepared overview of the case, including: • significant facts and issues • appellate history • name of lower-court judge
notice	• additional information about the case (*e.g.*, appeal pending, decision not final until expiration of period for petitioning for rehearing)	[no comparable field]		
opinionby	• last name of the judge who wrote the majority opinion in the case	judge	ju	• last name of the judge who wrote the majority opinion in the case

concurby	• last names of judges who wrote concurring opinions in the case	synopsis	sy	among other items of information, • names of judges who wrote concurring opinions in the case
dissentby	• last names of judges who wrote dissenting opinions in the case	synopsis	sy	among other items of information, • names of judges who wrote dissenting opinions in the case
writtenby	• combination of opinionby, concurby, and dissentby segments—allows searching for all types of opinions written by a specific judge	[no comparable field]		[all opinions written by a specific judge can be located by searching the judge and synopsis fields together]
judges	• last names of all participating judges (including those who joined but did not write an opinion)	opinion	op	among other items of information, • names of all participating judges (including those who joined but did not write an opinion)
counsel	• names of attorneys (and law firms, if known) who participated in the case	attorney	at	• names of attorneys (and law firms, if known) who participated in the case
opinion	• text of the majority or plurality opinion in the case • name of the judge writing the opinion • names of other judges participating in the case	opinion	op	among other items of information, • text of the majority or plurality opinion in the case • name of the judge writing the opinion • names of other judges participating in the case
concur	• text of all concurring opinions in the case • names of judges who wrote or joined in them	opinion	op	among other items of information, • text of all concurring opinions in the case • names of judges who wrote or joined in them

(continues)

Figure 5.08. Quick Guide to LEXIS Segments and WESTLAW Fields for Cases

(continued)

LEXIS		WESTLAW		
Segment Name	**Contents**	**Field Name**	**Abbre-viation**	**Contents**
dissent	• text of all dissenting opinions in the case • text of all opinions dissenting in part and concurring in part in the case • names of judges who wrote or joined in them	opinion	op	among other items of information, • text of all dissenting opinions in the case • text of all opinions dissenting in part and concurring in part in the case • names of judges who wrote or joined in them
opinions	• combination of opinion, concur, and dissent segments—allows searching the text of all opinions in the case (majority, plurality, concurrences, dissents, dissents in part, and concurrences in part) • names of all participating judges	opinion	op	among other items of information, • text of all opinions in the case (majority, plurality, concurrences, dissents, dissents in part, and concurrences in part) • names of all participating judges
headnotes	• summaries the court prepares of individual points of law in the case	synopsis	sy	among other items of information, • summaries the court prepares of individual points of law in the case
[no comparable segment]		headnote	he	• summaries that West prepares of individual points of law in the case • citations to statutes or rules construed in the case

[no comparable segment]		topic	to	• name of a West digest topic (*e.g.*, Weapons) under which the case is digested • identification number that West assigns to the topic (*e.g.*, 406) • the Key Number that West assigns to the sub-topic within the topic (*e.g.*, 17) • the phrase West uses to describe the sub-topic (*e.g.*, Criminal prosecutions)
[no comparable segment]		digest	di	• combination of topic, court, and headnote fields • short title of the case (*i.e.*, principal plaintiff and principal defendant) • year of the decision

[no comparable segment]		synopsis	sy	among other items of information,
				• West-prepared overview of the case, consisting of:
				  • significant facts and issues
				  • appellate history
				  • court's resolution of each issue
				  • court's decision (*e.g.*, affirmed, reversed)
				  • name of judge who wrote the court's opinion
				  • names of any judges who concurred or dissented
				  • names of appellate judges who wrote majority opinions in any intermediate appeals
				  • name of lower-court judge

(continues)

Figure 5.08. Quick Guide to LEXIS Segments and WESTLAW Fields for Cases (continued)

(continued)

LEXIS		WESTLAW		
Segment Name	**Contents**	**Field Name**	**Abbre-viation**	**Contents**
syllabus*	• court-prepared overview (when the court prepares one) of the case, including such items as: • significant facts and issues • appellate history • court's resolution of each issue • court's decision (*e.g.*, affirmed, reversed) • name of judge who wrote the court's opinion • names of any judges who concurred or dissented • names of attorneys who participated in the case	synopsis	sy	among other items of information, • court-prepared overview (when the court prepares one) of the case, including such items as: • significant facts and issues • appellate history • court's resolution of each issue • court's decision (*e.g.*, affirmed, reversed) • name of judge who wrote the court's opinion • names of any judges who concurred or dissented • names of attorneys who participated in the case
[no comparable segment]		image**	im	a non-searchable field that contains a drawing, chart, or other image you can view by printing the image on certain laser printers or on a fax machine

* This segment is found in United States Supreme Court cases and in cases decided by some state courts.
** This field is available in certain cases only.

Figure 5.08. Quick Guide to LEXIS Segments and WESTLAW Fields for Cases (continued)

Task You Want to Perform	Restriction You Can Use				
	LEXIS		WESTLAW		
	Segment Name	Example	Field Name	Abbreviation	Example
Finding a case by the name of a party or parties in the case	name	name(kingsley and regents)	title	ti	ti(kingsley & regents)
Finding all cases in which a particular person or organization (*e.g.*, Kingsley International Pictures Corporation) has been a party	name	name("kingsley international")	title	ti	ti("kingsley international")
Finding a case by its citation (*e.g.*, 360 U.S. 684)	cite*	cite(360 pre/6 684)	citation*	ci	ci(360 +6 684)
Finding cases issued by a particular court (*e.g.*, U.S. Court of Appeals for the Ninth Circuit)	court**	court(9th)	court**	co	co(ninth)
Finding a case by its docket number (*e.g.*, 78-1595)	number	number(78-1595)	opinion*	op	op(78-1595)

(continues)

* For retrieving a case by its citation in LEXIS, the LEXSEE command (see pages 238–43) operates more conveniently and efficiently than a cite-field restriction; for retrieving a case by its citation in WESTLAW, the FIND command (see pages 279–84) offers similar advantages over a citation-field restriction. For retrieving a case by its docket number in WESTLAW, the FIND command offers an alternative to an opinion-field restriction.

** Instead of using a court restriction, you can select an appropriate LEXIS case file or WESTLAW case database. *See* page 82.

Figure 5.09. Scenarios for Field-Restricted Searching in Cases

(continued)

Task You Want to Perform	Restriction You Can Use				
	LEXIS		WESTLAW		
	Segment Name	Example	Field Name	Abbreviation	Example

Finding cases decided on, before, or after a specified date, or between two specified dates	date	`date is 4/30/89`
		`date bef 1980`
		`date aft 4/30/89`
		`date aft 1954 and date bef 1/1/89`
			date	da	`da(is 4/30/89)`
					`da(before 1980)`
					`da(after 4/30/89)`
					`da(after 1954 and before 1/1/89)`

Finding all cases in which a particular judge participated (even if the judge did not write an opinion)	judges	`judges(abrahamson)`	opinion	op	`op(abrahamson)`
Finding all cases in which a particular judge wrote a majority, plurality, concurring, or dissenting opinion	writtenby	`writtenby(hastie)`	combination of judge and synopsis***	ju sy	`ju(hastie) or sy(hastie /s concur! or dissent!)`
Finding all cases in which a particular judge wrote the majority or plurality opinion	opinionby	`opinionby(rehnquist)`	judge	ju	`ju(rehnquist)`
Finding all cases in which a particular judge wrote a concurring opinion	concurby	`concurby(stevens)`	synopsis***	sy	`sy(stevens /s concur!)`

Finding all cases in which a particular judge wrote or joined in a concurring opinion	concur	`concur(powell)`	synopsis	sy	`sy(powell /s concur!)`
Finding all cases in which a particular judge wrote a dissenting opinion	dissentby	`dissentby(brennan)`	synopsis***	sy	`sy(brennan /s dissent!)`
Finding all cases in which a particular judge wrote or joined in a dissenting opinion or an opinion dissenting in part	dissent	`dissent(posner)`	synopsis	sy	`sy(posner /s dissent!)`
Finding all cases in which a particular attorney or law firm participated	counsel	`counsel(lee w/5 bailey)`	attorney	at	`at(lee w/5 bailey)`
Finding all cases in which your search terms appear in the majority or plurality opinion	opinion	`opinion(firearm and felon and possess!)`	opinion†Δ	op	`op(firearm & felon & possess!)`

(continues)

*** In connection with concurring and dissenting opinions, the synopsis field in WESTLAW contains not only the names of the judges who wrote these opinions, but the names of judges who joined in them. Consequently, restricting your search to the synopsis field in WESTLAW will retrieve cases in which the judge *either* wrote a concurring or dissenting opinion *or* joined in one.

† Because WESTLAW groups different kinds of opinions in the opinion field, restricting your search to the opinion field in WESTLAW might retrieve cases in which your search terms appear in opinions other than the kind you want.

Δ Because the opinion field restriction forces the computer to bypass WESTLAW's editorial fields, using this restriction diminishes the benefit you might otherwise obtain from enriched vocabulary found in the headnote, digest, and synopsis fields. *See* pages 95, 98, and 100.

Figure 5.09. Scenarios for Field-Restricted Searching in Cases (continued)

(continued)

Task You Want to Perform	Restriction You Can Use				
	LEXIS		WESTLAW		
	Segment Name	Example	Field Name	Abbreviation	Example
Finding all cases in which your search terms appear in a concurring opinion	concur	`concur(firearm and felon and possess!)`	opinion†Δ	op	`op(firearm & felon & possess!)`
Finding all cases in which your search terms appear in a dissenting opinion or in an opinion dissenting in part	dissent	`dissent(firearm and felon and possess!)`	opinion†Δ	op	`op(firearm & felon & possess!)`
Finding all cases in which your search terms appear in the text of a majority, plurality, concurring, or dissenting opinion (*e.g.*, excluding cases in which some of your search terms appear in an opinion and some appear in a non-opinion field or segment, such as the title field or name segment)	opinions	`opinions(firearm and felon and possess!)`	opinionΔ	op	`op(firearm & felon & possess!)`

Finding cases digested under a particular West digest topic or Key Number	[no comparable segment]		topic	to	`to(weapons)`
					`to(406)`
					`406k17`

Finding all cases in which your search terms appear in West's headnote summaries of significant points of law decided in a case	[no comparable segment]		headnote *or* digest	he di	`he(firearm /p felon /p possess!)` `di(firearm /p felon /p possess!)`
Finding all cases construing a particular statute or rule (*e.g.*, 29 U.S.C. § 201)	[no comparable segment]		headnote	he	`he(29 pre/10 201)`

† Because WESTLAW groups different kinds of opinions in the opinion field, restricting your search to the opinion field in WESTLAW might retrieve cases in which your search terms appear in opinions other than the kind you want.

Δ Because the opinion field restriction forces the computer to bypass WESTLAW's editorial fields, using this restriction diminishes the benefit you might otherwise obtain from enriched vocabulary found in the headnote, digest, and synopsis fields. *See* pages 95, 98, and 100.

Figure 5.09. Scenarios for Field-Restricted Searching in Cases (continued)

LEXIS	WESTLAW		
Segment Name	**Field Name and Abbreviation**		**Contents**
cite	citation	ci	citation of a statutory section
heading	prelim	pr	*United States Code* title and other headings preceding the section number and section heading
section	caption	ca	section number and section heading
text	text	te	text of the statutory section
history	credit	cr	references to session laws that created, amended, or otherwise affected the statutory section
	historical notes	hn	historical and other notes about the statutory section, including information about legislative changes
notes	references	re	research references (*e.g.*, cross-references to other statutes, citations to law review articles) relating to the statutory section
casenotes	annotations	an	summaries of cases deciding issues under the statutory section
status	[comparable information available through the Related Materials Directory and the UPDATE feature]		references to legislation that has affected the statutory section
unanno	[achieve same result by searching in a database of unannotated statutes]		combination of all segments except notes and casenotes—allows searching an unannotated version of a statute

Figure 5.10. Quick Guide to LEXIS Segments and WESTLAW Fields in Annotated Versions of the *United States Code*

```
                    LEVEL 1 - 11 OF 12 CASES

                    LEWIS v. UNITED STATES          — name

                        No. 78-1595                 — number

             SUPREME COURT OF THE UNITED STATES     — court

   445 U.S. 55; 100 S. Ct. 915; 1980 U.S. LEXIS 85; 63 L. Ed.   — cite
                          2d 198

                  January 7, 1980, Argued
                  February 27, 1980, Decided        — date

PRIOR HISTORY:   [***1]                                          — history

   CERTIORARI TO THE UNITED STATES COURT OF APPEALS FOR THE FOURTH CIRCUIT.

DISPOSITION:  <=1>  591 F.2d 978, affirmed.         — disposition

SYLLABUS:  Held: Even though petitioner's extant prior state-court felony   — syllabus
conviction may be subject to collateral attack under  <=2>  Gideon v.       — headnotes
Wainwright, 372 U.S. 335, it could properly be used as a predicate for his
```

```
                445 U.S. 55, *; 100 S. Ct. 915, **;
             1980 U.S. LEXIS 85, ***1; 63 L. Ed. 2d 198
subsequent conviction for possession of a firearm in violation of @ 1202 (a)(1)
of Title VII of the Omnibus Crime Control and Safe Streets Act of 1968.  Pp.    — syllabus
60-68.

   (a) The plain meaning of @ 1202 (a)(1)'s sweeping language proscribing the   — head-
possession of firearms by any person who "has been convicted by a court of the    notes
United States or of a State . . . of a felony," is that the fact of a felony
conviction imposes firearm disability until the conviction is vacated or the
felon is relieved of his disability by some affirmative action.  Other
provisions of the statute demonstrate and reinforce its broad sweep, and there
is nothing in @ 1202 (a)(1)'s legislative history to suggest that Congress was
willing to allow a defendant to question the validity of his prior conviction as
a defense to a charge under @ 1202 (a)(1).  Moreover, the fact that there
[***2]   are remedies available to a convicted felon -- removal of the firearm
disability by a qualifying pardon or the Secretary of the Treasury's consent, as
specified in the Act, or a challenge to the prior conviction in an appropriate
court proceeding -- suggests that Congress intended that the defendant clear his
status before obtaining a firearm, thereby fulfilling Congress' purpose to keep
firearms away from persons classified as potentially irresponsible and
dangerous.  Pp. 60-65.
```

(continues)

Source: Mead Data Central, Inc. © 1993

Figure 5.11. Sample Screens from the LEXIS Version of a U.S. Supreme Court Case, Showing the Contents of LEXIS Segments

(continued)

syllabus — head-notes

```
                         445 U.S. 55, *; 100 S. Ct. 915, **;
                       1980 U.S. LEXIS 85, ***2; 63 L. Ed. 2d 198
   (b) The firearm regulatory scheme at issue here is consonant with the concept
of equal protection embodied in the Due Process Clause of the Fifth Amendment,
since Congress could rationally conclude that any felony conviction, even an
allegedly invalid one, is a sufficient basis on which to prohibit the possession
of a firearm.  And use of an uncounseled felony conviction as the basis for
imposing a civil firearms disability, enforceable by criminal sanction, is not
inconsistent with <=3> Burgett v. Texas, 389 U.S. 109; <=4> United States v.
Tucker, 404 U.S. 443; and <=5> Loper v. Beto, 405 U.S. 473. Pp. 65-67.
```

counsel

```
COUNSEL: Andrew W. Wood argued the cause   [***3]   for petitioner.  With him on
the briefs was Neal P. Rutledge.

   Andrew J. Levander argued the cause pro hac vice for the United States.  With
him on the brief were Solicitor General McCree, Assistant Attorney General
Heymann, Deputy Solicitor General Frey, Jerome M. Feit, and Joel M. Gershowitz.
```

judges

```
JUDGES: BLACKMUN, J., delivered the opinion of the Court, in which BURGER, C.
J., and STEWART, WHITE, REHNQUIST, and STEVENS, JJ., joined.  BRENNAN, J., filed
a dissenting opinion, in which MARSHALL and POWELL, JJ., joined, post, p. 68.

OPINIONBY: BLACKMUN
```

opinionby

opinion

```
                         445 U.S. 55, *; 100 S. Ct. 915, **;
                       1980 U.S. LEXIS 85, ***3; 63 L. Ed. 2d 198
OPINION:   [*56]      [**916]   MR. JUSTICE BLACKMUN delivered the opinion of
the Court.

   This case presents the question whether a defendant's extant prior
conviction, flawed because he was without counsel, as required by <=6> Gideon
v. Wainwright, 372 U.S. 335 (1963), may constitute the predicate for a
subsequent conviction under @ 1202 (a)(1), as amended, of Title VII of the
Omnibus Crime Control and Safe Streets Act of 1968, <=7> 18 U. S. C. App. @
1202 (a)(1). n1

- - - - - - - - - - - - - - - - - -Footnotes- - - - - - - - - - - - - - - - - -

   n1 Section 1202 (a) reads in full:

"Any person who --

   "(1) has been convicted by a court of the United States or of a State or any
political subdivision thereof of a felony, or

   "(2) has been discharged from the Armed Forces under dishonorable conditions,
or
```

(continues)

Source: Mead Data Central, Inc. © 1993

Figure 5.11. Sample Screens from the LEXIS Version of a U.S. Supreme Court Case, Showing the Contents of LEXIS Segments (continued)

(continued)

445 U.S. 55, *68; 100 S. Ct. 915, **922;
1980 U.S. LEXIS 85, ***21; 63 L. Ed. 2d 198

Prior Convictions and the Gun Control Act of 1968, [*68] 76 Colum. L. Rev. 326, 338-339 (1976). Cf. <=90> Walker v. City of Birmingham, 388 U.S. 307 (1967).

The judgment of the Court of Appeals is affirmed.

It is so ordered.

opinion

DISSENTBY: BRENNAN **dissentby**

DISSENT: MR. JUSTICE BRENNAN, with whom MR. JUSTICE MARSHALL and MR. JUSTICE POWELL join, dissenting.

In disagreement with every other Court of Appeals that has addressed the issue, n1 the Court of Appeals for the Fourth Circuit, held, by a divided vote, that an uncounseled and hence unconstitutional felony conviction may form the predicate for conviction under @ 1202 (a)(1) of the Omnibus Crime Control and Safe Streets Act of 1968. Today the Court affirms that judgment, but by an analysis that cannot be squared with either the literal language of the statute or controlling decisions of this Court. I respectfully [***22] dissent.

- - - - - - - - - - - - - - - - - -Footnotes- - - - - - - - - - - - - - - - -

dissent

Source: Mead Data Central, Inc. © 1993

Figure 5.11. Sample Screens from the LEXIS Version of a U.S. Supreme Court Case, Showing the Contents of LEXIS Segments (continued)

LEWIS *v.* UNITED STATES 55

Syllabus

name — LEWIS *v.* UNITED STATES

history — CERTIORARI TO THE UNITED STATES COURT OF APPEALS FOR THE FOURTH CIRCUIT

number — No. 78–1595. Argued January 7, 1980—Decided February 27, 1980 — date

syllabus / headnotes —

Held: Even though petitioner's extant prior state-court felony conviction may be subject to collateral attack under *Gideon* v. *Wainwright,* 372 U. S. 335, it could properly be used as a predicate for his subsequent conviction for possession of a firearm in violation of § 1202 (a)(1) of Title VII of the Omnibus Crime Control and Safe Streets Act of 1968. Pp. 60–68.

(a) The plain meaning of § 1202 (a)(1)'s sweeping language proscribing the possession of firearms by any person who "has been convicted by a court of the United States or of a State . . . of a felony," is that the fact of a felony conviction imposes firearm disability until the conviction is vacated or the felon is relieved of his disability by some affirmative action. Other provisions of the statute demonstrate and reinforce its broad sweep, and there is nothing in § 1202 (a)(1)'s legislative history to suggest that Congress was willing to allow a defendant to question the validity of his prior conviction as a defense to a charge under § 1202 (a)(1). Moreover, the fact that there are remedies available to a convicted felon—removal of the firearm disability by a qualifying pardon or the Secretary of the Treasury's consent, as specified in the Act, or a challenge to the prior conviction in an appropriate court proceeding—suggests that Congress intended that the defendant clear his status *before* obtaining a firearm, thereby fulfilling Congress' purpose to keep firearms away from persons classified as potentially irresponsible and dangerous. Pp. 60–65.

(b) The firearm regulatory scheme at issue here is consonant with the concept of equal protection embodied in the Due Process Clause of the Fifth Amendment, since Congress could rationally conclude that any felony conviction, even an allegedly invalid one, is a sufficient basis on which to prohibit the possession of a firearm. And use of an uncounseled felony conviction as the basis for imposing a civil firearms disability, enforceable by criminal sanction, is not inconsistent with *Burgett* v. *Texas,* 389 U. S. 109; *United States* v. *Tucker,* 404 U. S. 443; and *Loper* v. *Beto,* 405 U. S. 473. Pp. 65–67.

disposition — 591 F. 2d 978, affirmed.

(continues)

Figure 5.12. Sample Pages from the Print Version of a U.S. Supreme Court Case Corresponding to the LEXIS Version and Correlating the Contents with LEXIS Segments

(continued)

56 OCTOBER TERM, 1979

Opinion of the Court 445 U. S.

judges — BLACKMUN, J., delivered the opinion of the Court, in which BURGER, C. J., and STEWART, WHITE, REHNQUIST, and STEVENS, JJ., joined. BRENNAN, J., filed a dissenting opinion, in which MARSHALL and POWELL, JJ., joined, *post*, p. 68.

counsel — *Andrew W. Wood* argued the cause for petitioner. With him on the briefs was *Neal P. Rutledge*.

Andrew J. Levander argued the cause *pro hac vice* for the United States. With him on the brief were *Solicitor General McCree, Assistant Attorney General Heymann, Deputy Solicitor General Frey, Jerome M. Feit,* and *Joel M. Gershowitz.*

opinionby

opinion — MR. JUSTICE BLACKMUN delivered the opinion of the Court.

This case presents the question whether a defendant's extant prior conviction, flawed because he was without counsel, as required by *Gideon* v. *Wainwright,* 372 U. S. 335 (1963), may constitute the predicate for a subsequent conviction under § 1202 (a)(1), as amended, of Title VII of the Omnibus Crime Control and Safe Streets Act of 1968, 18 U. S. C. App. § 1202 (a)(1).[1]

I

In 1961, petitioner George Calvin Lewis, Jr., upon his plea of guilty, was convicted in a Florida state court of a felony

[1] Section 1202 (a) reads in full:

"Any person who—

"(1) has been convicted by a court of the United States or of a State or any political subdivision thereof of a felony, or

"(2) has been discharged from the Armed Forces under dishonorable conditions, or

"(3) has been adjudged by a court of the United States or of a State or any political subdivision thereof of being mentally incompetent, or

"(4) having been a citizen of the United States has renounced his citizenship, or

"(5) being an alien is illegally or unlawfully in the United States,

"and who receives, possesses, or transports in commerce or affecting commerce, after the date of enactment of this Act, any firearm shall be fined not more than $10,000 or imprisoned for not more than two years, or both."

(continues)

Figure 5.12. Sample Pages from the Print Version of a U.S. Supreme Court Case Corresponding to the LEXIS Version and Correlating the Contents with LEXIS Segments (continued)

(continued)

68 OCTOBER TERM, 1979

BRENNAN, J., dissenting 445 U. S.

opinion

76 Colum. L. Rev. 326, 338–339 (1976). Cf. *Walker* v. *City of Birmingham,* 388 U. S. 307 (1967).

The judgment of the Court of Appeals is affirmed.

It is so ordered.

dissentby

MR. JUSTICE BRENNAN, with whom MR. JUSTICE MARSHALL and MR. JUSTICE POWELL join, dissenting.

In disagreement with every other Court of Appeals that has addressed the issue,[1] the Court of Appeals for the Fourth Circuit, held, by a divided vote, that an uncounseled and hence unconstitutional felony conviction may form the predicate for conviction under § 1202 (a)(1) of the Omnibus Crime Control and Safe Streets Act of 1968. Today the Court affirms that judgment, but by an analysis that cannot be squared with either the literal language of the statute or controlling decisions of this Court. I respectfully dissent.

dissent

I

Two longstanding principles of statutory construction independently mandate reversal of petitioner's conviction. The first is the precept that "when choice has to be made between two readings of what conduct Congress has made a crime, it is appropriate, before we choose the harsher alternative, to require that Congress should have spoken in language that is clear and definite." *United States* v. *Universal C. I. T. Credit Corp.,* 344 U. S. 218, 221–222 (1952). The Court has repeatedly reaffirmed this "rule of lenity." See, *e. g., Simpson* v. *United States,* 435 U. S. 6, 14 (1978); *United States* v. *Bass,* 404 U. S. 336, 347–349 (1971); *Rewis* v. *United States,* 401 U. S. 808, 812 (1971); *Ladner* v. *United States,* 358 U. S. 169,

[1] See, *e. g., Dameron* v. *United States,* 488 F. 2d 724 (CA5 1974); *United States* v. *Lufman,* 457 F. 2d 165 (CA7 1972); *United States* v. *DuShane,* 435 F. 2d 187 (CA2 1970); *United States* v. *Thoresen,* 428 F. 2d 654 (CA9 1970). See generally Comment, 92 Harv. L. Rev. 1790 (1979).

Figure 5.12. Sample Pages from the Print Version of a U.S. Supreme Court Case Corresponding to the LEXIS Version and Correlating the Contents with LEXIS Segments (continued)

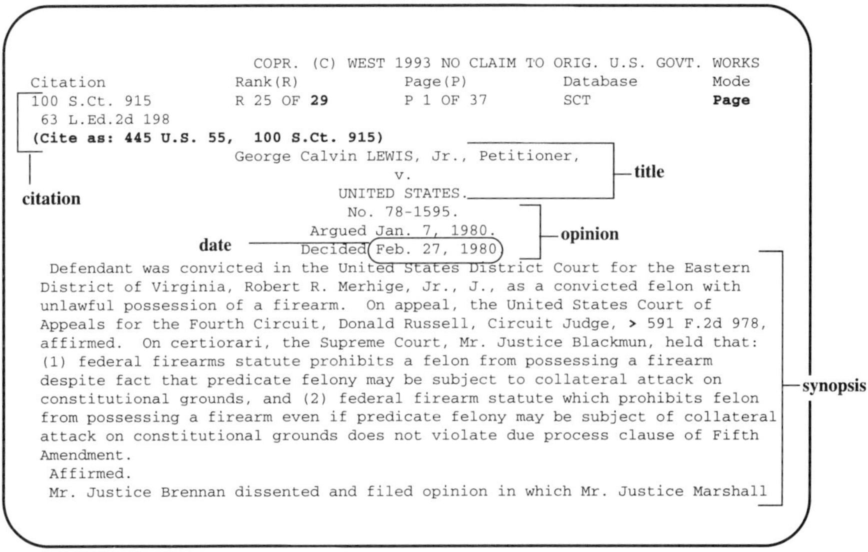

```
                              COPR. (C) WEST 1993 NO CLAIM TO ORIG. U.S. GOVT. WORKS
Citation                      Rank(R)            Page(P)           Database        Mode
100 S.Ct. 915                 R 25 OF 29         P 1 OF 37         SCT             Page
 63 L.Ed.2d 198
(Cite as: 445 U.S. 55,  100 S.Ct. 915)
                              George Calvin LEWIS, Jr., Petitioner,
                                               v.
                                       UNITED STATES.
                                        No. 78-1595.
                                    Argued Jan. 7, 1980.
                                   Decided Feb. 27, 1980.
 Defendant was convicted in the United States District Court for the Eastern
District of Virginia, Robert R. Merhige, Jr., J., as a convicted felon with
unlawful possession of a firearm.  On appeal, the United States Court of
Appeals for the Fourth Circuit, Donald Russell, Circuit Judge, > 591 F.2d 978,
affirmed.  On certiorari, the Supreme Court, Mr. Justice Blackmun, held that:
(1) federal firearms statute prohibits a felon from possessing a firearm
despite fact that predicate felony may be subject to collateral attack on
constitutional grounds, and (2) federal firearm statute which prohibits felon
from possessing a firearm even if predicate felony may be subject of collateral
attack on constitutional grounds does not violate due process clause of Fifth
Amendment.
 Affirmed.
 Mr. Justice Brennan dissented and filed opinion in which Mr. Justice Marshall
```


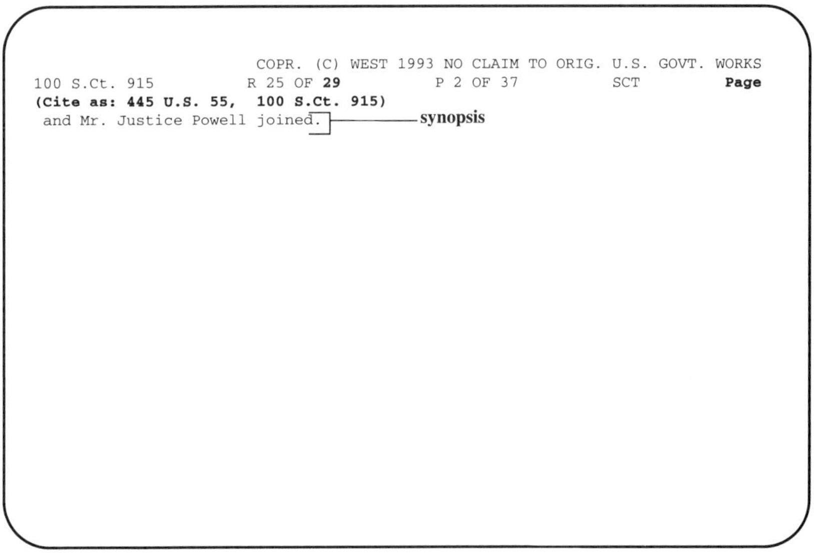

```
                              COPR. (C) WEST 1993 NO CLAIM TO ORIG. U.S. GOVT. WORKS
100 S.Ct. 915                 R 25 OF 29         P 2 OF 37         SCT             Page
(Cite as: 445 U.S. 55,  100 S.Ct. 915)
 and Mr. Justice Powell joined.
```


(continues)

Source: West Publishing Company © 1993

Figure 5.13. Sample Screens from the WESTLAW Version of a U.S. Supreme Court Case, Showing the Contents of WESTLAW Fields

(continued)

```
                         COPR. (C) WEST 1993 NO CLAIM TO ORIG. U.S. GOVT. WORKS
100 S.Ct. 915            R 25 OF 29            P 3 OF 37          SCT          Page
(Cite as: 445 U.S. 55,  100 S.Ct. 915)
 Lewis v. U. S.
 > [1]
 > 406    WEAPONS

 > 406k4  k. Manufacture, sale, gift, loan, possession, or use.
 U.S.Va.,1980.
 Federal firearms statute prohibits felon from possessing a firearm despite the
 fact that the predicate felony may be subject to collateral attack on
 constitutional grounds.  18 U.S.C.A. App. § 1202(a)(1).
```

title — **topic** — **court** — **digest** — **head-note**

```
                         COPR. (C) WEST 1993 NO CLAIM TO ORIG. U.S. GOVT. WORKS
100 S.Ct. 915            R 25 OF 29            P 4 OF 37          SCT          Page
(Cite as: 445 U.S. 55,  100 S.Ct. 915)
 Lewis v. U. S.
 > [2]
 > 110    CRIMINAL LAW
 > 110XX    Trial
 > 110XX(B)   Course and Conduct of Trial in General
 > 110k641      Counsel for Accused

 > 110k641.1  k. In general.
 U.S.Va.,1980.
 Under Sixth Amendment, an uncounseled felony conviction cannot be used for
 certain purposes;  however, that uncounseled conviction is not invalid for all
 purposes.  U.S.C.A.Const. Amend. 6.
```

listing of the West digest topic and Key Number classifications to which Criminal Law Key Number 641.1 is subordinate

topic

(continues)

Source: West Publishing Company © 1993

Figure 5.13. Sample Screens from the WESTLAW Version of a U.S. Supreme Court Case, Showing the Contents of WESTLAW Fields (continued)

(continued)

```
                         COPR. (C) WEST 1993 NO CLAIM TO ORIG. U.S. GOVT. WORKS
100 S.Ct. 915           R 25 OF 29           P 8 OF 37          SCT          Page
(Cite as: 445 U.S. 55,  100 S.Ct. 915, **915)
                              **915 Syllabus [FN*]

    FN* The syllabus constitutes no part of the opinion of the Court but has
   been prepared by the Reporter of Decisions for the convenience of the
   reader.  See > United States v. Detroit Lumber Co., 200 U.S. 321, 337, 26
   S.Ct. 282, 287, 50 L.Ed. 499.

 *55 Held:  Even though petitioner's extant prior state-court felony
conviction may be subject to collateral attack under > Gideon v. Wainwright,
372 U.S. 335, 83 S.Ct. 792, 9 L.Ed.2d 799, it could properly be used as a
predicate for his subsequent conviction for possession of a firearm in
violation of § 1202(a)(1) of Title VII of the Omnibus Crime Control and Safe
Streets Act of 1968.  Pp. 918-922.
 (a) The plain meaning of § 1202(a)(1)'s sweeping language proscribing the
possession of firearms by any person who "has been convicted by a court of the
United States or of a State  . . .  of a felony," is that the fact of a felony
conviction imposes firearm disability until the conviction is vacated or the
felon is relieved of his disability by some affirmative action.  Other
provisions of the statute demonstrate and reinforce its broad sweep, and there
is nothing in § 1202(a)(1)'s legislative history to suggest that Congress was
willing to allow a defendant to question the validity of his prior conviction
```

synopsis

```
                         COPR. (C) WEST 1993 NO CLAIM TO ORIG. U.S. GOVT. WORKS
100 S.Ct. 915           R 25 OF 29           P 9 OF 37          SCT          Page
(Cite as: 445 U.S. 55, *55,  100 S.Ct. 915, **915)
as a defense to a charge under § 1202(a)(1).  Moreover, the fact that there are
remedies available to a convicted felon--removal of the firearm disability by
**916 a qualifying pardon or the Secretary of the Treasury's consent, as
specified in the Act, or a challenge to the prior conviction in an appropriate
court proceeding--suggests that Congress intended that the defendant clear his
statusbefore obtaining a firearm, thereby fulfilling Congress' purpose to keep
firearms away from persons classified as potentially irresponsible and
dangerous.  Pp. 918-921.
 (b) The firearm regulatory scheme at issue here is consonant with the concept
of equal protection embodied in the Due Process Clause of the Fifth Amendment,
since Congress could rationally conclude that any felony conviction, even an
allegedly invalid one, is a sufficient basis on which to prohibit the
possession of a firearm.  And use of an uncounseled felony conviction as the
basis for imposing a civil firearms disability, enforceable by criminal
sanction, is not inconsistent with > Burgett v. Texas, 389 U.S. 109, 88 S.Ct.
258, 19 L.Ed.2d 319;  > United States v. Tucker, 404 U.S. 443, 92 S.Ct. 589,
30 L.Ed.2d 592;  and > Loper v. Beto, 405 U.S. 473, 92 S.Ct. 1014, 31 L.Ed.2d
374.  Pp. 921-922.
 4 Cir., > 591 F.2d 978, affirmed.
 *56 Andrew W. Wood, Richmond, Va., for petitioner.
 Andrew J. Levander, Washington, D. C., pro hac vice, for respondent, by
```

synopsis

attorney[†]

(continues)

[†] The information in this field is also part of the opinion field.

Source: West Publishing Company © 1993

Figure 5.13. Sample Screens from the WESTLAW Version of a U.S. Supreme Court Case, Showing the Contents of WESTLAW Fields (continued)

(continued)

```
                         COPR. (C) WEST 1993 NO CLAIM TO ORIG. U.S. GOVT. WORKS
100 S.Ct. 915           R 25 OF 29           P 10 OF 37          SCT          Page
(Cite as: 445 U.S. 55, *56,  100 S.Ct. 915, **916)
 special leave of Court.
```

attorney†

judge

opinion

```
   Mr. Justice BLACKMUN delivered the opinion of the Court.
  This case presents the question whether a defendant's extant prior conviction,
 flawed because he was without counsel, as required by > Gideon v. Wainwright,
 372 U.S. 335, 83 S.Ct. 792, 9 L.Ed.2d 799 (1963), may constitute the predicate
 for a subsequent conviction under § 1202(a)(1), as amended, of Title VII of the
 Omnibus Crime Control and Safe Streets Act of 1968, 18 U.S.C. App. §
 § 1202(a)(1). [FN1]

      FN1. Section 1202(a) reads in full:
     "Any person who--
     "(1) has been convicted by a court of the United States or of a State or
     any political subdivision thereof of a felony, or
     "(2) has been discharged from the Armed Forces under dishonorable
     conditions, or
     "(3) has been adjudged by a court of the United States or of a State or any
     political subdivision thereof of being mentally incompetent, or
     "(4) having been a citizen of the United States has renounced his
     citizenship, or
     "(5) being an alien is illegally or unlawfully in the United States,
```

```
                         COPR. (C) WEST 1993 NO CLAIM TO ORIG. U.S. GOVT. WORKS
100 S.Ct. 915           R 25 OF 29           P 29 OF 37          SCT          Page
(Cite as: 445 U.S. 55, *67,  100 S.Ct. 915, **922)
 not open the predicate conviction to a new form of collateral attack.  See
 Note, Prior Convictions and the Gun Control Act of 1968, *68 76
 Colum.L.Rev. 326, 338-339 (1976).  Cf. > Walker v. City of Birmingham, 388
 U.S. 307, 87 S.Ct. 1824, 18 L.Ed.2d 1210 (1967).
  The judgment of the Court of Appeals is affirmed.
  It is so ordered.

  Mr. Justice BRENNAN, with whom Mr. Justice MARSHALL and Mr. Justice POWELL
 join, dissenting.
  In disagreement with every other Court of Appeals that has addressed the
 issue, [FN1] the Court of Appeals for the Fourth Circuit, held, by a divided
 vote, that an uncounseled and hence unconstitutional felony conviction may form
 the predicate for conviction under § 1202(a)(1) of the Omnibus Crime Control
 and Safe Streets Act of 1968.  Today the Court affirms that judgment, but by an
 analysis that cannot be squared with either the literal language of the statute
 or controlling decisions of this Court.  I respectfully dissent.

      FN1. See, > e. g., Dameron v. United States, 488 F.2d 724 (CA5 1974);
     > United States v. Lufman, 457 F.2d 165 (CA7 1972);  > United States v.
     DuShane, 435 F.2d 187 (CA2 1970);  > United States v. Thoresen, 428 F.2d
     654 (CA9 1970).  See generally Comment, 92 Harv.L.Rev. 1790 (1979).
```

opinion

† The information in this field is also part of the opinion field.

Source: West Publishing Company © 1993

Figure 5.13. Sample Screens from the WESTLAW Version of a U.S. Supreme Court Case, Showing the Contents of WESTLAW Fields (continued)

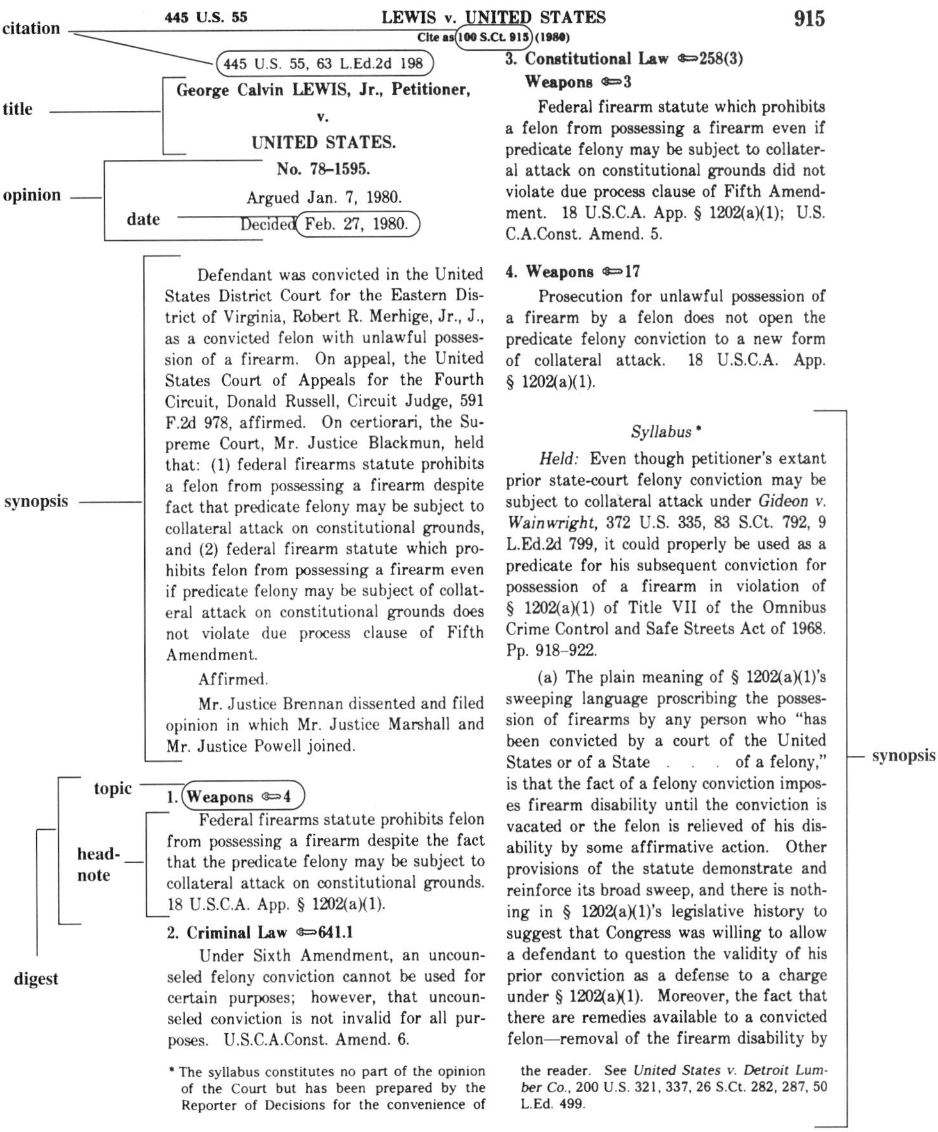

445 U.S. 55 **LEWIS v. UNITED STATES** **915**

Cite as 100 S.Ct. 915 (1980)

445 U.S. 55, 63 L.Ed.2d 198

George Calvin LEWIS, Jr., Petitioner,

v.

UNITED STATES.

No. 78–1595.

Argued Jan. 7, 1980.

Decided Feb. 27, 1980.

Defendant was convicted in the United States District Court for the Eastern District of Virginia, Robert R. Merhige, Jr., J., as a convicted felon with unlawful possession of a firearm. On appeal, the United States Court of Appeals for the Fourth Circuit, Donald Russell, Circuit Judge, 591 F.2d 978, affirmed. On certiorari, the Supreme Court, Mr. Justice Blackmun, held that: (1) federal firearms statute prohibits a felon from possessing a firearm despite fact that predicate felony may be subject to collateral attack on constitutional grounds, and (2) federal firearm statute which prohibits felon from possessing a firearm even if predicate felony may be subject of collateral attack on constitutional grounds does not violate due process clause of Fifth Amendment.

Affirmed.

Mr. Justice Brennan dissented and filed opinion in which Mr. Justice Marshall and Mr. Justice Powell joined.

1. **Weapons ⚿4**

Federal firearms statute prohibits felon from possessing a firearm despite the fact that the predicate felony may be subject to collateral attack on constitutional grounds. 18 U.S.C.A. App. § 1202(a)(1).

2. **Criminal Law ⚿641.1**

Under Sixth Amendment, an uncounseled felony conviction cannot be used for certain purposes; however, that uncounseled conviction is not invalid for all purposes. U.S.C.A.Const. Amend. 6.

3. **Constitutional Law ⚿258(3)**

Weapons ⚿3

Federal firearm statute which prohibits a felon from possessing a firearm even if predicate felony may be subject to collateral attack on constitutional grounds did not violate due process clause of Fifth Amendment. 18 U.S.C.A. App. § 1202(a)(1); U.S.C.A.Const. Amend. 5.

4. **Weapons ⚿17**

Prosecution for unlawful possession of a firearm by a felon does not open the predicate felony conviction to a new form of collateral attack. 18 U.S.C.A. App. § 1202(a)(1).

Syllabus *

Held: Even though petitioner's extant prior state-court felony conviction may be subject to collateral attack under *Gideon v. Wainwright*, 372 U.S. 335, 83 S.Ct. 792, 9 L.Ed.2d 799, it could properly be used as a predicate for his subsequent conviction for possession of a firearm in violation of § 1202(a)(1) of Title VII of the Omnibus Crime Control and Safe Streets Act of 1968. Pp. 918–922.

(a) The plain meaning of § 1202(a)(1)'s sweeping language proscribing the possession of firearms by any person who "has been convicted by a court of the United States or of a State . . . of a felony," is that the fact of a felony conviction imposes firearm disability until the conviction is vacated or the felon is relieved of his disability by some affirmative action. Other provisions of the statute demonstrate and reinforce its broad sweep, and there is nothing in § 1202(a)(1)'s legislative history to suggest that Congress was willing to allow a defendant to question the validity of his prior conviction as a defense to a charge under § 1202(a)(1). Moreover, the fact that there are remedies available to a convicted felon—removal of the firearm disability by

* The syllabus constitutes no part of the opinion of the Court but has been prepared by the Reporter of Decisions for the convenience of the reader. See *United States v. Detroit Lumber Co.*, 200 U.S. 321, 337, 26 S.Ct. 282, 287, 50 L.Ed. 499.

(continues)

Source: West Publishing Company © 1982

Figure 5.14. Sample Pages from the Print Version of a U.S. Supreme Court Case Corresponding to the WESTLAW Version and Correlating the Contents with WESTLAW Fields

(continued)

916 **100 SUPREME COURT REPORTER** **445 U.S. 55**

synopsis —

a qualifying pardon or the Secretary of the Treasury's consent, as specified in the Act, or a challenge to the prior conviction in an appropriate court proceeding—suggests that Congress intended that the defendant clear his status *before* obtaining a firearm, thereby fulfilling Congress' purpose to keep firearms away from persons classified as potentially irresponsible and dangerous. Pp. 918–921.

(b) The firearm regulatory scheme at issue here is consonant with the concept of equal protection embodied in the Due Process Clause of the Fifth Amendment, since Congress could rationally conclude that any felony conviction, even an allegedly invalid one, is a sufficient basis on which to prohibit the possession of a firearm. And use of an uncounseled felony conviction as the basis for imposing a civil firearms disability, enforceable by criminal sanction, is not inconsistent with *Burgett v. Texas*, 389 U.S. 109, 88 S.Ct. 258, 19 L.Ed.2d 319; *United States v. Tucker*, 404 U.S. 443, 92 S.Ct. 589, 30 L.Ed.2d 592; and *Loper v. Beto*, 405 U.S. 473, 92 S.Ct. 1014, 31 L.Ed.2d 374. Pp. 921–922.

4 Cir., 591 F.2d 978, affirmed.

---

attorney† —

Andrew W. Wood, Richmond, Va., for petitioner.

Andrew J. Levander, Washington, D. C., pro hac vice, for respondent, by special leave of Court.

judge —

⊥Mr. Justice BLACKMUN delivered the opinion of the Court. ⊥56

opinion —

This case presents the question whether a defendant's extant prior conviction, flawed because he was without counsel, as required by *Gideon v. Wainwright*, 372 U.S. 335, 83 S.Ct. 792, 9 L.Ed.2d 799 (1963), may constitute the predicate for a subsequent conviction under § 1202(a)(1), as amended, of Title VII of the Omnibus Crime Control and Safe Streets Act of 1968, 18 U.S.C. App. § 1202(a)(1).[1]

I

In 1961, petitioner George Calvin Lewis, Jr., upon his plea of guilty, was convicted in a Florida state court of a felony⊥for breaking and entering with intent to commit a misdemeanor. See Fla.Stat. § 810.05 (1961). He served a term of imprisonment. That conviction has never been overturned, nor has petitioner ever received a qualifying pardon or permission from the Secretary of the Treasury to possess a firearm. See 18 U.S.C. App. § 1203(2) and 18 U.S.C. § 925(c). ⊥57

In January 1977, Lewis, on probable cause, was arrested in Virginia, and later was charged by indictment with having knowingly received and possessed at that time a specified firearm, in violation of 18 U.S.C. App. § 1202(a)(1).[2] He waived a jury and was given a bench trial. It was stipulated that the weapon in question had been shipped in interstate commerce. The

1. Section 1202(a) reads in full:

"Any person who—

"(1) has been convicted by a court of the United States or of a State or any political subdivision thereof of a felony, or

"(2) has been discharged from the Armed Forces under dishonorable conditions, or

"(3) has been adjudged by a court of the United States or of a State or any political subdivision thereof of being mentally incompetent, or

"(4) having been a citizen of the United States has renounced his citizenship, or

"(5) being an alien is illegally or unlawfully in the United States,

"and who receives, possesses, or transports in commerce or affecting commerce, after the date of enactment of this Act, any firearm shall be fined not more than $10,000 or imprisoned for not more than two years, or both."

2. The indictment also charged petitioner with a violation of 18 U.S.C. § 922(h)(1). That statute reads in pertinent part:

"It shall be unlawful for any person—

"(1) who is under indictment for, or who has been convicted in any court of, a crime punishable by imprisonment for a term exceeding one year;

. . . . .

"to receive any firearm . . . which has been shipped or transported in interstate . . . commerce."

Petitioner was acquitted on the § 922(h)(1) charge and it is not before us here.

†The information in this field is also part of the opinion field.

(continues)

Figure 5.14. Sample Pages from the Print Version of a U.S. Supreme Court Case Corresponding to the WESTLAW Version and Correlating the Contents with WESTLAW Fields (continued)

(continued)

sanction, is not inconsistent with *Burgett, Tucker,* and *Loper.* In each of those cases, this Court found that the subsequent conviction or sentence violated the Sixth Amendment because it depended upon the reliability of a past uncounseled conviction. The federal gun laws, however, focus not on reliability, but on the mere fact of conviction, or even indictment, in order to keep firearms away from potentially dangerous persons. Congress' judgment that a convicted felon, even one whose conviction was allegedly uncounseled, is among the class of persons who should be disabled from dealing in or possessing firearms because of potential dangerousness is rational.[9] Enforcement of that essentially civil disability through a criminal sanction does not "support guilt or enhance punishment," see *Burgett,* 389 U.S., at 115, 88 S.Ct., at 262, on the basis of a conviction that is unreliable when one considers Congress' broad purpose. Moreover, unlike the situation in *Burgett,* the sanction imposed by § 1202(a)(1) attaches immediately upon the defendant's first conviction.

[4] Again, it is important to note that a convicted felon may challenge the validity of a prior conviction, or otherwise remove his disability, before obtaining a firearm. We simply hold today that the firearms prosecution does not open the predicate conviction to a new form of collateral attack. See Note, Prior Convictions and the Gun
⌊68 Control Act of 1968, ⌊76 Colum.L.Rev. 326, 338–339 (1976). Cf. *Walker v. City of Birmingham,* 388 U.S. 307, 87 S.Ct. 1824, 18 L.Ed.2d 1210 (1967).

The judgment of the Court of Appeals is affirmed.

It is so ordered.

Mr. Justice BRENNAN, with whom Mr. Justice MARSHALL and Mr. Justice POWELL join, dissenting.

In disagreement with every other Court of Appeals that has addressed the issue,[1] the Court of Appeals for the Fourth Circuit, held, by a divided vote, that an uncounseled and hence unconstitutional felony conviction may form the predicate for conviction under § 1202(a)(1) of the Omnibus Crime Control and Safe Streets Act of 1968. Today the Court affirms that judgment, but by an analysis that cannot be squared with either the literal language of the statute or controlling decisions of this Court. I respectfully dissent.

I

Two longstanding principles of statutory construction independently mandate reversal of petitioner's conviction. The first is the precept that "when choice has to be made between two readings of what conduct Congress has made a crime, it is appropriate, before we choose the harsher alternative, to require that Congress should have spoken in language that is clear and definite." *United States v. Universal C. I. T. Credit Corp.,* 344 U.S. 218, 221–222, 73 S.Ct. 227, 229, 97 L.Ed. 260 (1952). The Court has repeatedly reaffirmed this "rule of lenity." See, *e. g., Simpson v. United States,* 435 U.S. 6, 14, 98 S.Ct. 909, 914, 55 L.Ed.2d 70 (1978); *United States v. Bass,* 404 U.S. 336, 347–349, 92 S.Ct. 515, 522, 30 L.Ed.2d 488 (1971); *Rewis v. United States,* 401 U.S. 808, 812, 91 S.Ct. 1056, 1059, 28 L.Ed.2d 493 (1971); *Ladner v. United States,* 358 U.S. 169, ⌊177, 79 S.Ct. 209, 213, 3 L.Ed.2d 199 ⌊69
(1958); *Bell v. United States,* 349 U.S. 81, 75 S.Ct. 620, 99 L.Ed. 905 (1955). Indeed, the principle that "ambiguity concerning the ambit of criminal statutes should be

9. The dissent's assertion that Congress' judgment in this regard cannot rationally be supported, *post,* at 924–925, is one we do not share. Moreover, such an assertion seems plainly inconsistent with the deference that a reviewing court should give to a legislative determination that, in essence, predicts a potential for future criminal behavior.

1. See, *e. g., Dameron v. United States,* 488 F.2d 724 (CA5 1974); *United States v. Lufman,* 457 F.2d 165 (CA7 1972); *United States v. DuShane,* 435 F.2d 187 (CA2 1970); *United States v. Thoresen,* 428 F.2d 654 (CA9 1970). See generally Comment, 92 Harv.L.Rev. 1790 (1979).

opinion

Figure 5.14. Sample Pages from the Print Version of a U.S. Supreme Court Case Corresponding to the WESTLAW Version and Correlating the Contents with WESTLAW Fields (continued)

```
To be able to browse preceding or succeeding code sections, transmit B.  The
first page of the document you are currently viewing will be displayed in FULL.
--------------------------------------------------------------------------------

                              LEVEL 1 - 1 OF 1 SECTION

                              UNITED STATES CODE SERVICE
                    Copyright (c) 1993, Lawyers Cooperative Publishing

     *** THIS SECTION IS CURRENT THROUGH P.L. 103-23, APPROVED 4/16/93 ***   status

                              TITLE 16.  CONSERVATION
     CHAPTER 1.  NATIONAL PARKS, MILITARY PARKS, MONUMENTS, AND SEASHORES   heading
                              YELLOWSTONE NATIONAL PARK

                  cite        16 USCS @ 36a (1993)

@ 36a. Disposition of surplus elk   section

     The Secretary of the Interior is authorized in his discretion, and under
text regulations to be prescribed by him, to sell or otherwise dispose of the surplus
     elk from the Yellowstone National Park herd, and all moneys received from the
     sale of any such surplus elk shall be deposited in the Treasury of the United
     States as miscellaneous receipts.
```

```
                              16 USCS @ 36a (1993)

HISTORY: (March 4, 1929, ch 707, 45 Stat. 1644.)   history

NOTES:

CODE OF FEDERAL REGULATIONS
   Disposal of certain wild animals, 36 CFR Part 10.

CROSS REFERENCES                                                    casenotes
notes  National Elk Refuge and Wyoming Elk Reserve, 16 USCS @@ 673--673c.

                         INTERPRETIVE NOTES AND DECISIONS
   Suit for injunction brought against superintendent of Yellowstone National
Park and his agents and employees restraining them from continuing
elk-slaughtering program in park, was in fact suit against United States in
which it was indispensable party, and federal district court lacked jurisdiction
of matter since United States had not consented to be sued in that type of
action.  Frost v Garrison (1962, DC Wyo) 201 F Supp 389.
```

Source: Mead Data Central, Inc.; © 1993 Lawyers Cooperative Publishing

Figure 5.15. LEXIS Version of a Federal Statute (16 U.S.C. § 36a) from *United States Code Service*, Showing the Contents of LEXIS Segments

section — **§ 36a. Disposition of surplus elk**

text — The Secretary of the Interior is authorized in his discretion, and under regulations to be prescribed by him, to sell or otherwise dispose of the surplus elk from the Yellowstone National Park herd, and all moneys received from the sale of any such surplus elk shall be deposited in the Treasury of the United States as miscellaneous receipts.

history — (March 4, 1929, ch 707, 45 Stat. 1644.)

notes —

CODE OF FEDERAL REGULATIONS

Disposal of certain wild animals, 36 CFR Part 10.

CROSS REFERENCES

National Elk Refuge and Wyoming Elk Reserve, 16 USCS §§ 673–673c.

case-notes —

INTERPRETIVE NOTES AND DECISIONS

Suit for injunction brought against superintendent of Yellowstone National Park and his agents and employees restraining them from continuing elk-slaughtering program in park, was in fact suit against United States in which it was indispensable party, and federal district court lacked jurisdiction of matter since United States had not consented to be sued in that type of action. Frost v Garrison (1962, DC Wyo) 201 F Supp 389.

Source: Lawyers Cooperative Publishing © 1991

Figure 5.16. Printed *United State Code Service* Version of a Federal Statute (16 U.S.C. § 36a) Corresponding to the LEXIS *United State Code Service* Version and Correlating the Contents with LEXIS Segments

```
Citation                 Rank(R)            Page(P)          Database        Mode
16 USCA § 36a             R 3 OF 30          P 1 OF 2         USCA            Page
 16 U.S.C.A. § 36a

                            UNITED STATES CODE ANNOTATED
                               TITLE 16.  CONSERVATION
       CHAPTER 1--NATIONAL PARKS, MILITARY PARKS, MONUMENTS, AND SEASHORES
                     SUBCHAPTER V--YELLOWSTONE NATIONAL PARK
              COPR. (c) WEST 1993  No Claim to Orig. Govt. Works
                 Current through P.L. 103-30, approved 5/7/93

§ 36a. Disposition of surplus elk

 The Secretary of the Interior is authorized in his discretion, and under
regulations to be prescribed by him, to sell or otherwise dispose of the
surplus elk from the Yellowstone National Park herd, and all moneys received
from the sale of any such surplus elk shall be deposited in the Treasury of the
United States as miscellaneous receipts.

                        1992 Main Volume Credit(s)

(Mar. 4, 1929, c. 707, 45 Stat. 1644.)
```

citation, **prelim**, **caption**, **text**, **credit**

```
16 USCA  36a             R 3 OF 30            P 2 OF 3          USCA            Page
 REFERENCES

                                  REFERENCES

                               CROSS REFERENCES

 Conservation of elk in Wyoming, National Elk Refuge in Wyoming, and Wyoming Elk
    Reserve, see 16 USCA §§ 673 to 673c.

                              LIBRARY REFERENCES

 Administrative Law

 Disposal of certain wild animals, see 36 C.F.R. § 10.1 et seq.

 American Digest System

 Game on public lands or waters, see Game k2 1/2.

 Encyclopedias

 Protection and regulation of game;  constitutional and statutory provisions,
```

refer-ences

(continues)

Source: West Publishing Company © 1993

Figure 5.17. WESTLAW Version of a Federal Statute (16 U.S.C. § 36a) from *United States Code Annotated*, Showing the Contents of WESTLAW Fields

(continued)

```
16 USCA § 36a          R 3 OF 30          P 3 OF 3          USCA          Page
 REFERENCES

    see C.J.S. Game § 8.  ---------------- references

 16 U.S.C.A. § 36a
 16 USCA § 36a          ---- citation
END OF DOCUMENT
```

Source: West Publishing Company © 1993

Figure 5.17. WESTLAW Version of a Federal Statute (16 U.S.C. § 36a) from *United States Code Annotated*, Showing the Contents of WESTLAW Fields (continued)

caption — **§ 36a. Disposition of surplus elk**

text — The Secretary of the Interior is authorized in his discretion, and under regulations to be prescribed by him, to sell or otherwise dispose of the surplus elk from the Yellowstone National Park herd, and all moneys received from the sale of any such surplus elk shall be deposited in the Treasury of the United States as miscellaneous receipts.

credit — (Mar. 4, 1929, c. 707, 45 Stat. 1644.)

references —

CROSS REFERENCES

Conservation of elk in Wyoming, National Elk Refuge in Wyoming, and Wyoming Elk Reserve, see 16 USCA §§ 673 to 673c.

LIBRARY REFERENCES

Administrative Law

Disposal of certain wild animals, see 36 C.F.R. § 10.1 et seq.

American Digest System

Game on public lands or waters, see Game ⇔2½.

Encyclopedias

Protection and regulation of game; constitutional and statutory provisions, see C.J.S. Game § 8.

WESTLAW ELECTRONIC RESEARCH

Game cases: 187k[add key number].
See, also, WESTLAW guide following the Explanation pages of this volume.

Source: West Publishing Company © 1992

Figure 5.18. Printed *United State Code Annotated* Version of a Federal Statute (16 U.S.C. § 36a) Corresponding to the WESTLAW *United State Code Annotated* Version and Correlating the Contents with WESTLAW Fields

PART II.

Preparing for Online Searching

Part II covers the following subjects:

- the importance of developing your facts and legal issues before you go online (Chapter 6)
- guidelines for selecting and arranging search terms when you formulate search requests (Chapter 7)
- guidelines for modifying search requests (Chapter 8)
- a checklist summarizing the steps in a computer-assisted legal research session (Chapter 9)

CHAPTER 6

Developing Your Facts and Legal Issues

The preceding chapters cover the basic features of computer-based information storage, the organization of CALR databases, and the dialect (search terms and connectors, or WESTLAW's natural language) used to gain access to information in the databases. Before going online to find, read, or update the law, however, researchers need to develop the facts and legal issues of their research problems. Developing your facts and legal issues, whether in preparation for book-based or computer-based legal research, consists of four tasks:[107]

(1) gathering the facts (a task that can include searching a database of nonlegal information, as explained in Chapter 13);

(2) analyzing the facts;

(3) identifying the legal issues raised by the facts; and

(4) when feasible, arranging the legal issues in a logical order for research.

New facts and issues will often become apparent once the research is underway, but conducting a preliminary fact analysis and issue identification is essential to provide direction for starting the legal research itself.

You will find that conducting the initial fact-related tasks normally takes on even greater importance when you anticipate doing research in a CALR database than when you expect to do your research in books. Through your

[107] Chapter 3 of *The Legal Research Manual* explains the purpose of each of these tasks and offers suggestions for carrying them out. CHRISTOPHER G. WREN & JILL R. WREN, THE LEGAL RESEARCH MANUAL: A GAME PLAN FOR LEGAL RESEARCH AND ANALYSIS 29–38 (2d ed. 1986).

preliminary assessment of the facts and issues, you develop a collection of descriptive words (also referred to as "fact words") that describe the important aspects of your research problem. When you research in books, these descriptive words serve as the terms you look up in indexes (such as the descriptive word index to a case digest, to a set of annotated statutes, or to a legal encyclopedia), which in turn lead you to the legal authorities themselves. When you conduct your research in a CALR database, whether you search with a Boolean or natural-language search request, your descriptive words serve as the search terms by which you index the database.

As you use descriptive words in CALR databases, as opposed to using them in book indexes, you will discover a significant difference in how the words assist you in gaining access to legal authorities. Book indexes, through their cross-references, implicitly and explicitly suggest additional avenues of research, including additional descriptive words. Because of the cross-referencing, you can still make progress in book-based research even if your initial selection of descriptive words proves a bit fuzzy: the cross-references will often guide you to more appropriate descriptive words and even new ideas, and, ultimately, to authorities pertinent to your research problem.

By contrast, the computer locates authorities in a database solely on the basis of the words you use in your search request. And, in reporting the results of its search, the computer does not suggest other, possibly more fruitful tacks for your research.[108]

[108] An online thesaurus, similar to those found in many word processing programs, can provide on-the-spot assistance to a legal researcher looking for useful search terms. WESTLAW offers an online thesaurus through which researchers can add synonyms to search requests. LEXIS does not currently provide an online thesaurus, but will undoubtedly offer such a thesaurus in the future.

Even when available, however, a thesaurus does not offer all the benefits of an index. Although a thesaurus can supply useful synonyms, it will not necessarily supply terms that represent concepts analogous to concepts relevant to your research problem. Nor will a thesaurus necessarily supply conceptual links between terms that might otherwise appear unrelated. A good index often features both kinds of guidance.

At some point, research and development in the areas of artificial intelligence and expert systems might enable the CALR vendors to refine their services to provide responses that more effectively aid researchers in formulating and modifying search requests. Although WESTLAW's natural-language feature is a byproduct of research into artificial intelligence and expert systems, the feature does not reach the level of either artificial intelligence or an expert system.

At this writing, general-purpose expert systems for legal research appear to be at least several years away. Artificial intelligence is even farther down the road, and some experts doubt that an artificial intelligence approaching human intelligence is possible at all. *See, e.g.*, HUBERT L. DREYFUS, WHAT COMPUTERS *STILL* CAN'T DO: A CRITIQUE OF ARTIFICIAL REASON (1992); ROGER PENROSE, THE EMPEROR'S NEW MIND: CONCERNING COMPUTERS, MINDS, AND THE LAWS OF PHYSICS (1989); Roger Penrose, *Precis of* The Emperor's New Mind: Concerning computers, minds, and the laws of physics, 13 BEHAV'L & BRAIN SCI. 643, 643–55 (1990); Roger Penrose, *The Nonalgorithmic Mind*, 13 BEHAV'L & BRAIN SCI. 692, 692–705 (1990) (response to critiques

In short, the indexes used in book-based research afford you a margin of error not available in computer-based research. In searching a CALR database, you are responsible for selecting the index terms, and the success of your online legal research will depend in large part on how thoroughly you gather and analyze your facts and appraise your legal issues. The better you develop your facts and issues before going online, the greater the likelihood you will select effective search terms and create search requests that will yield satisfactory results.[109]

---

of *The Emperor's New Mind*); Barbara Wallraff, *The Literate Computer*, ATLANTIC MONTHLY, Jan. 1988, at 64, 70–71. *But see* DANIEL C. DENNETT, CONSCIOUSNESS EXPLAINED (1991); Open Peer Commentary, 13 BEHAV'L & BRAIN SCI. 655, 655–92 (1990) (critiques of *The Emperor's New Mind*). For an example of an effort to apply principles of artificial intelligence to legal analysis (specifically, the analysis of offer-and-acceptance questions in contract law), see ANNE VON DER L. GARDNER, AN ARTIFICIAL INTELLIGENCE APPROACH TO LEGAL REASONING (1987). *See also* KEVIN D. ASHLEY, MODELING LEGAL ARGUMENT: REASONING WITH CASES AND HYPOTHETICALS (1990) (similar effort in trade-secrets law). *See* generally ADVANCED TOPICS OF LAW AND INFORMATION TECHNOLOGY (G.P.V. Vandenberghe ed., 1989); COMPUTING POWER AND LEGAL REASONING (Charles Walter ed., 1985); THE FOUNDATIONS OF ARTIFICIAL INTELLIGENCE: A SOURCEBOOK (Derek Partridge & Yorick Wilks eds., 1990).

[109] Careful preparation will also help reduce the expense of using a CALR service: the vendors charge for the time you spend online, and effective search requests achieved through advance preparation will minimize the amount of online time the computer uses executing search requests, as well as the amount of online time you need to spend modifying poorly constructed search requests.

CHAPTER 7

Formulating Your Search Request: Selecting and Arranging Search Terms

"The difference between the right word and the almost right word is the difference between lightning and the lightning bug."
—*Mark Twain*[110]

Introduction. Once you have assessed the facts and issues in your research problem, you are ready to communicate to the computer the descriptive words generated by your assessment. To do that in a format and arrangement that will reflect the concepts you want to research (*i.e.*, the relevant legal and factual aspects in your research problem), you take the following steps, which build on the dialect rules explained in Chapter 4 for search terms and connectors:

1. For each concept, select the term or terms you believe the authors of the documents you want to locate would have used to express the concept.

2. If you are planning a Boolean terms-and-connectors search, consider whether to instruct the computer to search for other forms of these search terms. For example, do you want to include a universal character or root expander in a search term? (When you

[110] THE WIT AND WISDOM OF MARK TWAIN 252 (Alex Ayres ed., 1987).

perform a natural-language search in WESTLAW, the computer automatically looks for most of the variants of your search terms.)

3. Consider whether any search terms pose semantic problems. For instance, will a term with more than one meaning (such as "court") present an ambiguity?

4. Establish the relationships among your search terms. If you are preparing a Boolean search, use logic connectors to link search terms. If you are preparing to search with WESTLAW's natural-language feature, simply use your search terms in a plain-English question, statement, or list; in response, the computer will automatically apply algorithms to determine what relationships among search terms in documents will satisfy the search request.

This chapter offers guidelines to assist in the art of selecting and arranging search terms to meet the unique requirements of each legal research problem. The guidelines provide help in molding search requests that represent relevant concepts so they can be found by a computer, which neither recognizes concepts nor appreciates the subtleties of a system of law and language in which legal concepts can be expressed in different ways, often using words with multiple meanings. The guidelines also assist in creating search requests that retrieve as many as possible of the relevant documents in the database and minimize as much as possible the number of irrelevant documents you retrieve.

Step 1. Select search terms

Define your concepts. Your definitions of the relevant concepts in your research problem will establish the range of search terms you select to reflect concepts. Ideally, as in book-based research, you want to locate authorities in which the facts and legal issues match those in your research problem. As a practical matter, however, you will frequently rely on authorities that apply only by analogy, whether because there are no authorities on point or because you want to supplement on-point authorities. Therefore, you normally need to define the concepts in your research problem specifically enough to yield authorities with facts and issues highly similar to yours, yet generally enough to allow you to capture authorities containing relevant analogies.[111]

For example, returning to the hypothetical Ohio landlord-tenant problem on pages 19–20, you could define the problem as involving an apartment and a lack of running water. These narrowly defined concepts would yield search

[111] For a discussion of reasoning by analogy, see CHRISTOPHER G. WREN & JILL R. WREN, THE LEGAL RESEARCH MANUAL: A GAME PLAN FOR LEGAL RESEARCH AND ANALYSIS 33, 81 (2d ed. 1986).

terms specific to the problem, *e.g.*, "apartment," "water," "plumbing." On the other hand, you could define the concepts more generally as a place of habitation and as a condition affecting habitability. Each of these concepts is broad enough to stimulate the selection of search terms that not only reflect the particular facts and legal issues in the problem, but analogies as well. Thus, the concept of a place of habitation could be reflected not only by the problem-specific term "apartment," but by analogous terms such as "condominium" or "rooming house." Similarly, the condition affecting habitability could be represented not only by "water" or "plumbing," but by terms such as "light," "heat," or "electricity" to retrieve analogous authorities.

Properly defined concepts constitute the starting point for selecting appropriate search terms:

> Prior to the formulation of a search request, there is some legal problem or issue in the mind of the [researcher]. . . . [This] problem can be described as an intersection of ideas [*i.e.*, concepts]. In a case concerning the possible liability of the owner of a dog that has inflicted an injury on an old person, the problem may be seen as the idea of a dog, the idea of liability, and the idea of personal injury. Obviously, the [evaluation] of a problem may result in different formulations of these ideas by different [researchers], according to their understanding of the problem. But we now have a rather interesting basic thesis: to be relevant, a document has to contain all three ideas. If we think a document can be relevant without containing all three ideas, our initial [evaluation] of the problem is not appropriate and should be changed.[112]

Generate additional search terms. After you have identified an initial set of search terms based on your assessment of the facts and legal issues in your problem, you can expand your universe of search terms by thinking of synonyms. For instance, with respect to the concept of a landlord-tenant relationship, synonymous terms for "landlord" and "tenant" would include "lessor," "lessee," and "leaseholder."[113]

[112] Jon Bing, *Performance of Legal Text Retrieval Systems: The Curse of Boole*, 79 LAW LIBR. J. 187, 197 (1987). Bing's article offers a detailed discussion of "conceptor-based retrieval strategy" in the context of Boolean searching and explains how focusing on concepts as the foundation for a search request enhances a researcher's odds of retrieving a high percentage of the relevant documents in a database and simultaneously minimizes the likelihood of retrieving irrelevant documents.

A similar assumption about the relationship between concepts and a document's relevance underlies the computer's operation when you search with WESTLAW's natural-language feature: if a document contains each of your search terms, the computer treats that document as probably more relevant to your research issue than a document that contains fewer of your search terms.

[113] In WESTLAW, if you search with the natural-language feature, you can include synonyms in a search request in either of two ways. You can simply include synonyms in your plain-English instruction. Or, you can enclose one or more synonyms in parentheses after the search term for which the words serve as synonyms. Using parentheses to identify synonyms in a natural-language search request affects the computer's statistical estimation of a document's relevance. See page 177 n.129.

Thinking of antonyms can also generate search terms: sometimes, you can get at a concept indirectly by describing what it isn't. Thus, the absence of "heat" or the presence of "cold" describes the same condition affecting habitability.

Keep in mind that the way people use language changes over time. For example, documents written many years ago would likely refer to "Indians," while more recent writing might refer instead to "Native Americans."

In selecting terms to include in your search request, you can get ideas from sources other than your own evaluation of your research problem. For instance, a law dictionary or a thesaurus of legal or nonlegal words can help you think of relevant search terms.[114] In addition, some treatises, hornbooks, and other printed research tools include suggested search requests you might want to use or adapt.

As you select terms by which to index a database, don't overlook indexes to primary and secondary authorities as sources of search terms. The index terms you find there will often be drawn from the text of the underlying cases, statutes, and other authorities you want the computer to search, and will therefore contain many of the terms you want the computer to locate. Also, because many index entries consist of pithy characterizations of facts and legal issues, indexes can suggest other ways of thinking about your research problem and thus lead you to additional search terms.

For example, suppose your problem concerned a blind person refused a ticket to ride a train because the person required the assistance of a Seeing Eye dog. You would certainly identify "train," "ride," "blind," "passenger," "ticket," and "refusal" as some potential search terms. By checking the index to, say, *Corpus Juris Secundum*, you would find entries such as these:

Blind persons
    . . . .
    Carriers,
        Duty of transporting, Carr § 538
        Moving trains, partial blindness as requiring
            carrier to prevent leaving, Carr § 725
        Wrongful ejection, defense, Carr § 832
        Highways, injuries from defects or
            obstructions, High § 269

[114] As noted earlier, WESTLAW offers an online thesaurus. LEXIS does not yet offer an online thesaurus, but will surely add one.

For an example of a print publication designed to assist online researchers in selecting useful search terms, see ANNE L. MCDONALD, LYNDA THOMPSON & MARY E. ZIEBARTH, COMMUNICATING WITH LEGAL DATABASES: TERMS AND ABBREVIATIONS FOR THE LEGAL RESEARCHER (1987).

Reviewing these entries would present you with possible search terms you might have overlooked, such as "carrier." In addition, the brief characterizations in the phrases "duty of transporting" and "wrongful ejection" suggest legal theories for which additional search terms (such as "eject!" or "transport!") would be appropriate. Moreover, the reference to "highways" might prompt you to consider search terms for analogous situations, such as denial of passage on a bus or in a taxi, or (by further analogy) on a ship or airplane. And, thinking of "taxi" might remind you of "fare" as a synonymous search term for "ticket."

Thus, you can often enhance your indexing of a database by referring to professionally prepared indexes of the corresponding print materials. Similarly, scanning the summaries under an appropriate topic in a case digest can yield helpful search terms.

The documents themselves that you retrieve from LEXIS or WESTLAW will also suggest additional terms to use in subsequent search requests, but the charges for being connected to LEXIS or WESTLAW place a premium on careful initial selection of search terms before beginning your online search.

Think about the nature of relevant documents. As you select search terms, consider whether they are appropriate to the kind of authorities (*e.g.*, cases, statutes) you plan to search. The authors of different kinds of authorities often have different purposes and audiences, and sometimes use different language to express the same thought. For instance, when crafting a criminal statute, legislators often use precise, uniform language to define a standard of future conduct for all persons within the jurisdiction covered by the statute. By contrast, when writing an opinion involving the same subject as the statute, a judge would focus primarily on the conduct in which the defendant in the immediate litigation had already engaged; rather than create a standard, the judge need only interpret the one established by the legislature.[115] The judge therefore has more flexibility in describing the statutorily defined conduct and can use less precise language than the statute might contain. Thus, when a legislature prohibits "transfers" of a drug statutorily identified only in terms of its active chemical ingredient, "tetrahydrocannabinol," a judge writing about a defendant who engaged in this prohibited conduct might describe the activity instead as "buying or selling marijuana."

In short, when you search the text of documents directly (as you do in LEXIS or WESTLAW) rather than indirectly (as you do when you use an index in book-based research), you need to anticipate the language likely to

[115]The line between legislative and judicial activities is not always this neatly drawn. *See* CHRISTOPHER G. WREN & JILL R. WREN, THE LEGAL RESEARCH MANUAL: A GAME PLAN FOR LEGAL RESEARCH AND ANALYSIS 83 (2d ed. 1986). But a distinction nonetheless exists, and it constitutes a factor in online searching.

appear in the documents. As you engage in this anticipatory thinking, a sensitivity to the characteristics of the types of documents you plan to search will help you select appropriate search terms.

Step 2. Consider various forms of search terms

After you have identified the terms you want to use in your search request, think of ways in which the computer might fail to perceive your terms in relevant documents. Because of the computer's literalness, you need to anticipate various forms in which a search term might appear: for example, a judge might have written "postconviction" rather than "post-conviction." In constructing your search request, consider whether to instruct the computer to look for additional configurations of any of your search terms.

As already discussed (pages 30–34 and 69–70), the LEXIS and WESTLAW computers automatically treat certain variations of search terms as equivalent to the search terms themselves; even if you do not instruct the computers to do so, they will search for these alternative configurations. The automatic equivalencies cover capitalization, specified abbreviations, certain plurals, and possessive forms of nouns. So, for instance, if you use the term `lease` in a search request, the computer will automatically search for "leases" as well; however, if your search term forms its plural irregularly (as with "knife" and "knives"), you might need to include the plural form as part of your search request.

The LEXIS and WESTLAW computers also recognize some equivalencies that researchers can invoke at their discretion, as explained earlier (pages 34–40 and 69.) In WESTLAW, you can create equivalencies for compound words (*e.g.*, "post-conviction") or acronyms (*e.g.*, "A.I.D.S.") by choosing the term's "normalized" form as your search term. For example, if you use the normalized search term `post-conviction` in your WESTLAW search request, the computer will also search for "postconviction" and "post conviction." In addition, when you formulate a Boolean search request in either LEXIS or WESTLAW, you can create equivalencies for any search term by substituting a universal character or root expander (*, !) for letters in the term. Thus, if you use `kn*w` in a Boolean search request, the computer will search for either "know" or "knew."

Familiarizing yourself with the automatic and discretionary equivalencies that operate in a particular CALR service will help you formulate effective search requests. For example, if you are performing a Boolean search for a word you think might appear in relevant documents in an abbreviated form, check whether the word and its abbreviation are automatic equivalencies. If not, or if you have any doubt, include both forms in your search request.

Also consider, however, ways in which equivalent forms of a search term might retrieve *irrelevant* documents. For instance, suppose you want to perform a Boolean search for cases dealing with "detrimental reliance," which can be expressed in several ways (as in "a person may not cause another person to detrimentally rely"). The search term `rel!` would locate all forms of "reliance," but would also locate unrelated terms such as "relevant," "release," "reliable," and "relief." If you want assistance in anticipating what words the computer will look for when you use a particular root in a Boolean search request, checking a dictionary, preferably an unabridged one, can guide you in deciding where, or even whether, to truncate a search term.

As explained on pages 69–70, when you search with WESTLAW's natural-language feature, the computer often looks automatically for more forms of a search term than the computer would look for if you used the same term in a Boolean search request. Consequently, in contrast to Boolean searching, natural-language searching usually does not require you to specify variations on search terms. For example, the search term `defamation` in a natural-language search request will automatically retrieve variations like "defame," "defamed," and "defamatory"; to achieve this result, you do not need to use (indeed, cannot use) a search term formulation like `defam!` Keep in mind, however, that you must still use the normalized form of an acronym or compound word in a natural-language search request if you want the computer to search for each variation on the term.

Step 3. Consider semantic problems

Because words serve as the bridge between the concepts in which you are interested and the character strings the computer can locate, formulating an effective search request requires you to consider language problems that can interfere with words performing the bridging function. These semantic problems fall into four categories:[116]

- ambiguous words
- synonyms
- nondistinctive words
- finding words to express implicit concepts

This section looks at each of these categories of semantic problems in turn. In practice, as you will discover when you prepare search requests, the categories often overlap.

[116] For a more in-depth discussion of these problems, see Jon Bing, *Performance of Legal Text Retrieval Systems: The Curse of Boole*, 79 LAW LIBR. J. 187 (1987).

Ambiguous words. Ambiguity arises when a single word can have more than one meaning, such as "court," which can refer to a judicial tribunal, an athletic arena, a street name, or an amorous activity. When your search request includes a term that can reflect multiple concepts, you need to create a context for the term to improve the likelihood that each document the computer locates will use the term the way you intend.

Combining an ambiguous term with other search terms can often establish the necessary context. For example, suppose your research problem involved an issue of contempt of court. Individually, "court" and "contempt" are ambiguous words—"court" for reasons already mentioned, and "contempt" because it can mean either a willful disobedience of a public authority or a sense of scorn. But linking "court" with "contempt" would probably eliminate most documents in which "court" means something other than a judicial tribunal or in which "contempt" means a scornful emotion. Thus, a Boolean search request could include `court w/5 contempt!`, and a natural-language search request in WESTLAW could include `contempt of court`. The documents retrieved would most likely deal with contempt of court, although a document could still satisfy the search request if it contained the sentence "Defendant's language and conduct, as he advanced menacingly toward the official on the basketball court, were contemptible."

In a Boolean search request, using the phrase `"contempt of court"` would further reduce ambiguity and retrieve fewer irrelevant documents than would the Boolean search request `court w/5 contempt!` But by establishing too exact a context for the search terms, the phrase search also increases the likelihood of bypassing relevant documents. For example, the phrase search would not retrieve a case in which the judge expressed the concept only by writing "defendant exhibited contempt for the court" or "defendant acted contemptuously toward the court."

If you include the phrase `contempt of court` in a natural-language search request when you search in WESTLAW, the computer might retrieve documents that contain not only the phrase, but documents that contain any of the significant words in the phrase. So, `contempt of court` might retrieve documents that contain the word "court" but not the word "contempt" or any of its variant forms. In short, the computer does not treat a phrase in a natural-language search request as literally as a phrase in a Boolean search request.

As these examples suggest, combining an ambiguous term with other search terms can reduce, but not necessarily eliminate, problems caused by a word's ambiguity. Success with this technique depends on the particular search term involved and on the experience and creativity of the researcher.

You can also provide a context for ambiguous search terms by restricting your search for them to particular fields, although not every research problem lends itself to this technique. (See Chapter 5.) For instance, if you intend the search term `white` to refer to a judge who has written a court opinion, rather than to an object's color, searching for "white" in just the "judge" field in WESTLAW or the "opinionby" segment in LEXIS will establish your intended meaning. Similarly, in WESTLAW, linking search terms with a topic field restriction[117] or restricting a search to the headnote field when looking for citations to statutes or rules can diminish ambiguity.[118] Different fields will reduce ambiguity with different degrees of effectiveness.[119] Proficiency at using field restrictions to reduce ambiguity depends on understanding the nature of the contents of the available fields so you can select a field restriction that will provide an appropriate context.

Synonyms. To express a single concept, such as the idea of a tenant, writers can use a variety of words, such as "lessee," "tenant," or "leaseholder." If you do not include among your search terms the words the authors of relevant documents used to express the concept in which you are interested, your search request will not retrieve the documents.

On the other hand, including every conceivable synonym an author might have used will simply slow down your search, increasing its cost without appreciably enhancing its effectiveness. For example, suppose you want to find cases involving a stable's liability for injuries a customer suffered when thrown from a horse. "Mare" and "stallion" are possible synonyms for the search term "horse." But because a judge will almost certainly not use either of those words without also using "horse," adding these synonyms to your search request is not apt to improve your results.

Consequently, you need to review your search terms to ensure you have included appropriate synonyms. With experience in online searching and increased familiarity with the language authors tend to use to write about the subject you are researching, you will develop a better feel for which synonyms to include in your search requests.

Nondistinctive words. These can present difficulties as search terms by causing the computer to retrieve an unusually high number of irrelevant documents. When the words you can use to express the concepts in your research problem also reflect many other issues unrelated to your problem, a substantial number of irrelevant documents will satisfy your search request.

For instance, suppose your research problem concerns a civil complaint that alleges one of two possible causes of action based on a single set of facts. On the ground that the complaint failed to state a cause of action, the court has dismissed it with prejudice (*i.e.*, without permission to replead). You want to determine whether the plaintiff may file a new complaint alleging the pre-

[117] For a refresher on the topic field, see pages 85–92.

[118] *See* pages 94–95.

[119] *See* pages 111–12.

viously unpleaded cause of action, or whether the plaintiff was obligated to plead both causes initially and has therefore waived the right to sue now on the second one. The obvious search terms you could use to research this problem—such as "complaint," "cause of action," "dismiss," "prejudice," "res judicata," "waiver"—pervade statutory and case law. In a search of LEXIS or WESTLAW, these terms will therefore retrieve an enormous number of documents completely unrelated to your research problem.

To minimize the complications created by using nondistinctive words as search terms, you can try to extract from your research problem additional search terms that will distinguish your problem from other, unrelated problems the nondistinctive words describe. You might discover, though, that you cannot conjure up search terms that overcome the predicament—that your problem does not lend itself to online searching as well as it does to book-based research, where success does not depend on matching descriptive words with the language in relevant documents.

Implicit concepts. A similar predicament can arise in connection with the final category of semantic problems: selecting search terms when you want the computer to locate implicit concepts. These concepts acquire their substance when someone reads "between the lines" or perceives a meaning in a subtle interplay among words rather than in the words themselves.

As you review your selection of terms to use in search requests, keep in mind the predicament posed by implied meaning. Although this semantic problem occurs fairly infrequently,[120] when it does occur, you might find that even with carefully chosen terms, you simply cannot formulate a search request that will effectively target documents containing implicit concepts relevant to your research problem.[121] In short, your research problem might be less suited to online searching than to research in books, where authorities are indexed by the ideas they represent instead of simply by the words they contain.

Step 4. Establish relationships among search terms

Natural-language searching in WESTLAW. If you search with WESTLAW's natural-language feature, the computer uses algorithms (see pages 25–26) to establish the relationships among your search terms after you transmit them in a plain-English question, statement, or list, such as these:

```
Does a landlord have an obligation to provide
running water in a leased apartment?
```

[120] As Bing notes, "implicity is a minor cause of recall failure." Jon Bing, *Performance of Legal Text Retrieval Systems: The Curse of Boole*, 79 LAW LIBR. J. 187, 198 (1987).

[121] "[S]ituations where the meaning is 'between the lines' or otherwise implied by the text . . . [present] an absolute limit to [retrieving documents based on the language they contain]." *Id.* at 193.

```
Does a tenant have the right to running water
in an apartment?

leased apartment obligation landlord running
water
```

With one exception, the way you arrange your search terms in natural-language search requests does not affect the way the computer searches for those words in documents. The exception occurs when your search request includes adjacent search terms (such as "probable cause") that the computer has been programmed to treat as a single phrase. If you do not want the computer to treat search terms as a phrase, you need to arrange those terms in your search request so they do not appear adjacent to one another.

Compared to the way you formulate natural-language search requests, the way you arrange your search terms in Boolean search requests has, as explained in the rest of this section, a far greater impact on your search results.

Boolean searching in LEXIS and WESTLAW. If you use Boolean logic to search in LEXIS or WESTLAW, once you have chosen and evaluated your search terms, you complete your search request by using logic connectors as follows to establish the relationships among the search terms:

1. Group together the search terms that relate to the same concept (*e.g.*, "tenant," "lessee"). Place an "or" connector between these search terms, and enclose the grouping of terms in parentheses.
2. Repeat this procedure for each grouping of search terms that relate to a single concept.
3. Then, between your groupings of search terms, insert "and" or an "and"-type connector (*i.e.*, any connector except "or").[122]

For instance, returning to the hypothetical landlord-tenant problem on pages 19–20, recall that central to the problem were the concept of an apartment, the concept of a lease between a landlord and tenant, and the concept of a lack of running water as a condition affecting habitability. Depending on the synonyms, antonyms, and analogous terms you choose to reflect each of these concepts, a Boolean search request for this problem would link the terms like this search request does:

```
(apartment or dwelling or roominghouse or
"rooming house") and (lease! or contract or
agree! or rent! or tenant or lessee or
landlord or lessor) and (water or plumbing or
heat or light or electric!)
```

[122] For a discussion of "and"-type connectors, see pages 57 and 60–62.

In practice, you might not include this many terms in a search request dealing with such simple facts. Nevertheless, the sample search request illustrates the principle for linking search terms with Boolean logic: you use "or" to link terms corresponding to a single concept, and you use "and" (or an "and"-type connector) to link groupings of terms.

Using multiple parentheses in a Boolean search request. Note that instead of being contained in a single word, the thought you want to express in a search term might require a phrase, such as "rental contract" or "rooming house." When the words in a multiple-word search term are linked by a Boolean proximity connector, as in `rental w/10 contract`, confusion can arise over how the connector interacts with the rest of the search request. To make sure your meaning is clear, you can place additional parentheses around the multiple-word search term to identify it as a single element within a Boolean search request, as is done here with `rent! w/10 contract`:

```
(apartment or "rooming house") and (lease! or
(rent! w/10 contract) or tenant or landlord)
and (water or plumbing)
```

You could also place additional parentheses around a phrase enclosed in quotation marks, such as "rooming house." But with a phrase search, confusion is not apt to arise over the relationship of the phrase to the rest of the search request: the quotation marks already denote the phrase as a single element.

The effect of "or" and "and." In Boolean searching, a search request constructed by linking alternative search terms with "or" and then linking your groupings of alternative terms with "and" or an "and"-type connector enhances the likelihood of retrieving as many relevant documents, and as few irrelevant documents, as possible.[123] Moreover, so long as you link your search terms appropriately, you will achieve this result whether or not you enclose your search-term groupings in parentheses. But the parentheses help ensure clarity in the arrangements of your search terms.

By using the "or" connector to link the search terms corresponding to a given concept, you give the computer a choice of alternative expressions that might indicate a relevant document. The presence of even one of the terms in a document indicates the possibility the document deals with a concept you have identified as relevant. Thus, assuming you have selected suitable search terms, the "or" connector creates the largest possible universe of documents that might have some conceivable relevance to your research problem.

[123] A search request formulated with this technique yields a "conceptor-based" search. Jon Bing, *Performance of Legal Text Retrieval Systems: The Curse of Boole*, 79 LAW LIBR. J. 187, 198 (1987). Bing's article explains in detail why a Boolean search of a database usually proceeds most effectively with a search request "specifying a . . . string of disjunctive search terms within each [set of] parenthes[e]s and combining these with conjunctions." *Id.*

This universe, however, will inevitably include irrelevant documents as well. By next linking your groupings of alternative search terms with "and" or an "and"-type connector, you narrow the computer's search in a way that excludes as many irrelevant documents as possible. Inserting "and" or an "and"-type connector between groupings instructs the computer to retrieve only documents that contain at least one term from each grouping of search terms—that is, documents in which each relevant concept presumably appears. By requiring retrieved documents to contain at least one expression of each relevant concept, you significantly enhance the likelihood that any given document you retrieve will actually be relevant.

In short, your search request first creates a universe of every conceivably relevant document, and then extracts from that universe the set of documents most likely to prove relevant to your research problem.

Caveat. As you construct Boolean search requests, keep in mind the key to ensuring that logic connectors have the effect you intend. This key consists of distinguishing search terms that simply represent alternative ways of expressing a given concept (and that therefore belong in the same grouping) from search terms that actually represent a different concept (and that therefore belong in some other grouping). Unless you align your search terms appropriately, your search request can easily bypass relevant documents.

For example, in the landlord-tenant hypothetical, you might have viewed "lease" and its synonyms (such as "rental contract") as expressions of one concept, with "tenant," "landlord," and their synonyms (such as "lessee," "lessor") as expressions of an unrelated concept. This arrangement (reflecting four concepts instead of the three discussed on page 158) would have resulted in a search request along these lines:

```
(apartment or dwelling or roominghouse or
"rooming house") and (lease! or contract or
agree! or rent!) and (tenant or lessee or
leaseholder or landlord or lessor) and (water
or plumbing or heat or light or electric!)
```

However, the existence of a lease (or its synonyms) implies the existence of a landlord and tenant (and their synonyms): the lease states the landlord-tenant relationship; where the lease exists, so must a landlord and tenant. All of these search terms therefore relate to the same concept—the concept of a lease—and belong together as alternative expressions of this concept. If you split these related search terms into groupings reflecting distinct concepts and require a document to contain at least one term from each grouping, your search request would bypass relevant documents. For instance, you would fail to retrieve a relevant case in which a judge used the terms "lease," "apartment," and "water" but only referred to the parties as "plaintiff" and "defendant," not as, say, "landlord" or "tenant."[124]

As this example suggests, even seemingly slight changes in how you group your search terms—that is, in how you translate your research problem for the computer—can substantially alter the meaning of your search instructions and misdirect the computer in its search for relevant documents. Further, every Boolean search request consisting of more than a single search term contains at least one grouping of search terms whose alignments you need to understand. If you opt not to use parentheses to define the groupings in your search requests, the connectors you use to link your search terms will automatically establish groupings; unless overridden by parentheses in a search request, each CALR vendor's hierarchy rules for processing connectors dictate the groupings that exist in the search request. (See pages 62, 64–66.) Figure 4.07 on page 65 depicts an example of how these rules establish groupings if parentheses do not define them.

In formulating Boolean search requests, you can rely either on your mastery of the connector hierarchy rules or on parentheses to align your search terms. Especially in the beginning, using parentheses offers several advantages. First, by requiring you to consciously organize your search terms by concept, using parentheses helps you retain maximum control over the relationship among search terms—and, therefore, over the computer's execution of your search request. As a result, you enhance the likelihood your search request will locate the documents you want. If you do not deliberately group your search terms by concept, you surrender control of your Boolean search request to the CALR vendors' hierarchy rules. Unless you thoroughly understand these rules, the default groupings they create can result in ineffective or inaccurate translations of your research problems.

Second, using parentheses to differentiate search terms relating to different concepts visually reinforces the relationship among search terms, making the search request easier to read. With parentheses, you can clearly see which concepts your search request reflects and, therefore, more easily detect ways in which the computer might generate unintended results.

Finally, unlike the hierarchy rules (which differ in subtle but sometimes important ways between LEXIS and WESTLAW), using parentheses to establish relationships among search terms works the same way in each CALR service. You do not need to modify your technique for grouping search terms when you move from one CALR service to another.

Whether you use parentheses or not, however, the key to formulating successful Boolean search requests remains the same: link alternative search

[124] For another illustration of how linking search terms inappropriately can fail to retrieve relevant documents, see Jon Bing, *Performance of Legal Text Retrieval Systems: The Curse of Boole*, 79 LAW LIBR. J. 187, 200 n.39 (1987).

terms relating to a single concept with "or," and combine these search-term groupings with "and" or an "and"-type connector. By paying careful attention to the concepts your search terms relate to, you address the challenge in using a computer in legal research: finding concepts with a machine that does not recognize them. While conceptual thinking drives legal research, mechanistically matching character strings drives the retrieval of documents through a CALR service. Search requests that correctly reflect the concepts in your research problems bridge this gulf to the greatest degree possible.

Summary of formulating search requests

Step 1. Select search terms you think the authors of relevant documents have used to express the concepts in which you are interested.

- Consider synonyms and analogous terms (*e.g.*, "apartment," "roominghouse," "dwelling"), or even antonyms if you think you can get at an idea indirectly by words reflecting what it is not (*e.g.*, "cold" instead of "heat"). Remember that language usage might change over time.
- Consider whether your terms are appropriate to the kind of authority you plan to search. For example, a legislature might use the term "tetrahydrocannabinol"; a judge is more apt to use the less technical term "marijuana."
- If you need ideas for search terms, check a legal thesaurus or law dictionary, skim indexes or case summaries in printed digests, or do background reading in a printed secondary source (such as a legal encyclopedia, a treatise or hornbook, *Restatements of the Law*, law reviews, or *American Law Reports Annotated*). Some treatises, hornbooks, and other printed research tools offer suggestions for selecting search terms.

Step 2. Consider whether to search for variant forms of your search terms.

- Familiarize yourself with the LEXIS and WESTLAW equivalency rules for abbreviations, acronyms, compound words, plurals, and possessive nouns. See pages 30–36 and 69–70. If a variation on one of your search terms is not automatically equivalent to the term itself, consider whether to include the variation as an alternative search term. When you search with WESTLAW's natural-language feature, the computer automatically looks for most of the variants of your search terms, although you should still take care to use normalized forms of search terms.

- For a Boolean search in LEXIS or WESTLAW, consider whether to use universal characters or root expanders (* and !) to stand in for characters in search terms. See pages 36–40. Universal characters and root expanders do not operate in natural-language search requests in WESTLAW; instead, the computer automatically looks for variants that universal characters and root expanders would generate in Boolean searching.

Step 3. Consider whether any of your search terms pose semantic problems.

- *Ambiguous words*—When a search term has more than one meaning, create a context for the term to improve the likelihood that retrieved documents will use it the way you intend. Combining the ambiguous term with one or more other search terms can often establish your meaning (*e.g.*, searching for "contempt" in close proximity to "court" will tend to focus on documents in which "court" means judicial tribunal instead of, say, a street). Sometimes, you can restrict your search to a field where the ambiguous term is more apt to be used in the desired sense (*e.g.*, search for Judge White's last name in the "judge" field in WESTLAW or the "opinionby" segment in LEXIS).
- *Synonyms*—If the author of a relevant document might have used a synonym instead of your search term, include the synonym as an alternative term in your search request.
- *Nondistinctive words (such as "complaint," "cause of action," "dismiss")*—If possible, extract from your research problem additional search terms that will distinguish your problem from other, unrelated problems the nondistinctive words describe. Otherwise, perform your search in books instead of a database.
- *Implicit concepts*—If you want to locate concepts that acquire their substance when someone reads between the lines or perceives a meaning in a subtle interplay among words rather than in the words themselves, selecting effective search terms can prove difficult or impossible. You will proceed more efficiently and effectively by researching in books instead of online.

Step 4. Establish the relationships among your search terms. In Boolean searching in LEXIS or WESTLAW, use this technique:

- First, group together search terms that relate to the same concept (*e.g.*, "tenant," "lessee"). Place an "or" between these search terms. Although not necessary, enclosing the grouping in parentheses helps ensure accuracy and visual clarity.

- Repeat this procedure for each grouping of search terms that stands for a single concept.
- Then, between your groupings of search terms, insert "and" or an "and"-type connector.

Example:

```
(apartment or dwelling or roominghouse or
"rooming house") and (lease! or contract or
agree! or rent! or tenant or lessee or
landlord or lessor) and (water or plumbing or
heat or light or electric!)
```

In natural-language searching in WESTLAW, establish relationships among your search terms by using them in a plain-English question, statement, or list:

```
Does a landlord have an obligation to provide
running water in a leased apartment?
```

```
landlord obligation running water leased
apartment
```

In response, the computer will automatically apply algorithms (see pages 25–26) to determine what relationships among search terms in documents will satisfy the search request.

CHAPTER 8

Modifying Your Search Request

Introduction. After the computer processes your search request, the monitor will display the number of documents the computer retrieved in response to the request. You might conclude that the computer located more documents than you can reasonably hope to read, or that it located fewer documents than you had expected to find. Or, the number of documents might be manageable but, after skimming several of them, you might find their contents less useful than you had anticipated. In these situations, you will want to modify your search request.

You might want to do this even if you got satisfactory results from your original request: experimenting with different formulations might achieve even better results, or confirm that you have already obtained the most promising results possible. By going this extra measure, you simply do in your computerized search what you do when researching in books. There, when you look for descriptive words in an index, you don't necessarily consider your index search complete as soon as you find your first word listed, even if it has several index entries under it. You also look for some other descriptive words, which might lead you to still other relevant sources.

This chapter explains how to modify a search request in LEXIS or WESTLAW. Making changes to a search request the computer has already executed constitutes part of the online phase of computer-assisted legal research (a phase outlined in the next chapter). But modifying a search request is also an extension of the analytical preparation (covered in the previous chapter) that goes into formulating a search request before you begin using LEXIS or WESTLAW.

In developing modifications of a search request, you need to pay as much attention to selecting and arranging your search terms as you did when you created your original search request. In particular, when you modify a Boolean (*i.e.*, terms-and-connectors) search request, you need to consider the effect that introducing new search terms will have on the organization of your original request. Grouping terms inappropriately in a modified Boolean search request (see pages 178–80) will bypass relevant documents or retrieve irrelevant documents as readily as grouping terms inappropriately when you initially formulate a Boolean search request (see pages 160–61).

A summary of the procedures for modifying search requests appears in Figure 8.08 on pages 186–87.

Options for modifying a search request

Options for modifying Boolean search requests in LEXIS and WESTLAW. Several options exist for modifying Boolean search requests in LEXIS and WESTLAW:

- You can change the connectors.
- You can add, delete, or edit search terms.
- You can add, delete, or change a field restriction.
- You can implement any combination of these modifications.

Whether one of these adjustments is likely to increase or decrease the number of documents retrieved depends on the kind of modification you make:

- Substituting a more restrictive connector for a less restrictive one (for example, using "w/10" instead of "and") will decrease the number of documents retrieved. See Figure 4.06 on page 63.
- Substituting a less restrictive connector for a more restrictive one (for example, using "and" instead of "w/10") will increase the number of documents retrieved. See Figure 4.06 on page 63.
- Adding a search term whose presence in the document will be required (*i.e.*, a term linked with "and" or an "and"-type connector) will decrease the number of documents retrieved. Pages 61–62 discuss "and"-type connectors.
- Adding a search term whose presence in the document will be optional (*i.e.*, a term linked with "or") will increase the number of documents retrieved.
- Deleting a search term whose presence in the document was optional (*i.e.*, a term linked with "or") will decrease the number of documents retrieved.
- Deleting a search term whose presence in the document was required (*i.e.*, a term linked with "and" or an "and"-type connector) will increase the number of documents retrieved.

- Replacing a general search term with a more specific one (for example, replacing "horse" with "Clydesdale") will most likely decrease the number of documents retrieved.
- Replacing a specific search term with a more general one (for example, replacing "homicide" with "felony") will most likely increase the number of documents retrieved.
- Editing a search term by adding a root expander or universal character will increase the number of documents retrieved.
- Editing a search term by removing a root expander or universal character will decrease the number of documents retrieved.
- Adding a field restriction (for example, modifying your search to retrieve only cases decided by a certain judge) will normally decrease the number of documents retrieved.
- Deleting a field restriction will normally increase the number of documents retrieved.
- The effect of substituting one field restriction for another will vary depending on the fields involved.

Options for modifying natural-language search requests in WESTLAW. As in Boolean searching, you have several options for modifying natural-language search requests in WESTLAW:

- You can add or delete search terms.
- You can add, delete, or change a field restriction.
- You can implement any combination of these modifications.

Modifying a natural-language search request generally has no effect on the number of documents you retrieve. Instead, modifications affect which documents the computer includes in the retrieved collection and the order in which those documents display. After modifying a natural-language search request, you usually will still retrieve whatever number of documents (up to 100) you previously instructed the computer to retrieve in response to a natural-language search request (as explained on page 197).

The mechanics of modifying a search request

The mechanics of modifying in LEXIS. In LEXIS, the procedure for modifying a search request depends on where in the search request you want to introduce the change.

Modifying at the end of a LEXIS search request. If you want to add new search terms and connectors to the end of a search request:

1. Type `m` (for "modify").

2. Press TRANSMIT. Your search request will appear on the monitor, and you can then type your modification (which must begin with a connector). The first screen in Figure 8.01 illustrates the monitor's appearance at this stage.

3. After you type your change, press TRANSMIT again. The monitor will display the change (but not the unchanged part of the search request); the second screen in Figure 8.01 illustrates what you will see. Although the change appears detached from the rest of the search request, the computer in fact combines the original search request with the modification and treats the combination as a single search request.

Thus, when you modify a LEXIS search request by adding a change to the end, the modification does not supersede the original search request. Rather, this kind of modification creates a new "level" of search. LEXIS designates the original search request as "level 1"; LEXIS then labels the first modification as "level 2," the next modification as "level 3," and so forth. You can create up to 255 levels in LEXIS, although you will rarely need to go beyond four or five to achieve satisfactory results.

For example, your original search request (level 1) might be

```
tenant or landlord or lease! and apartment
```

Your first modification (level 2) might be

```
and water or plumbing
```

Your second modification (level 3) might be

```
and habitable or uninhabitable or habitability
```

Each level incorporates each previous level, resulting in one ever-lengthening search request. So, in the preceding example, the three search levels would locate the same documents you would have found if you had originally formulated the search request like this:

```
tenant or landlord or lease! and apartment and
water or plumbing and habitable or
uninhabitable or habitability
```

At each level of your LEXIS search, the computer informs you of the number of documents located at that level and allows you to view the docu-

Type your modification here.

```
Your search request is:
 TENANT OR LANDLORD OR LEASE! AND APARTMENT

Number of CASES found with your search request through:
   LEVEL   1...     1190

Please transmit the modification to your search request (Level 2).
REMEMBER to start your modification with a CONNECTOR.

For further explanation, press the H key (for HELP) and then the TRANSMIT key.
```

```
AND WATER OR PLUMBING

LEXIS is working on the displayed request.
If it is not what you intended to transmit, please press the STOP key.
```

Source: Mead Data Central, Inc. © 1993

Figure 8.01. Sample Screens in LEXIS: Modifying at the End of a Search Request

ments located at that level.[125] This information lets you evaluate the effect each modification has on your search so you can make any appropriate adjustments.

Modifying at the beginning or in the middle of a LEXIS search request ("back modifying").[126] To edit a LEXIS search request other than by adding search terms and connectors to the end of the most recent level of your search:

1. Decide which search level you want to modify. For example, after searching through three levels, you might want to go back and modify level 1 of your search request, perhaps to change a connector, to add or delete a term, or to edit a term by adding or deleting a universal character.

2. Once you have decided which level you want to modify, instruct the LEXIS computer to recall the terms and connectors you used at that level: type the number of the search level and the letter `m` (or type `m` followed by the number), then press the TRANSMIT key. To edit level 1, you would type `1m` (or `m1`) and press TRANSMIT.

3. After you transmit your instruction, the monitor will display near the top of the screen the terms and connectors from the search level you specified, as well as those from all subsequent levels. In addition, farther down the screen, you will see all levels of your search. The screen will look like the one in Figure 8.02.

   If you discover that you selected the wrong level at which to make your modification, you can select the correct level by once again transmitting the number of a search level and the letter `m` (or `m` followed by the number).

4. You can now make your modification at the top of the screen by moving the cursor (the short bar of light that indicates your typing position on the monitor) to the place in the search request you want to edit and then making the desired change.

For example, suppose you have reviewed the documents the LEXIS computer retrieved after processing the three-level search request on page 168. Based on your review, you decide to modify level 1 to insert `or (rental w/5 (contract or agree!))` before `and apartment`. You would transmit

[125] To view the documents the LEXIS computer found at a level of search *other* than the level you just performed, you type the number of the level and then press the key labelled DIF LEVEL or, on older keyboards, DISP DIF LEVEL (for "display different level"). Pages 319 to 347 explain more about how to view documents in LEXIS.

[126] Mead Data Central uses the phrase "back modify" to refer to editing an earlier search level. MEAD DATA CENTRAL, REFERENCE MANUAL FOR THE LEXIS/NEXIS SERVICES 85 (undated looseleaf ed.); MEAD DATA CENTRAL, LEXIS-NEXIS USER'S GUIDE 12–4 (1990 & 1991 Supp.); *id.* at Glossary-1.

the instruction `1m`, after which the monitor would display levels 1, 2, and 3, with each level beginning on a new line:

```
tenant or landlord or lease! and apartment
and water or plumbing
and habitable or uninhabitable or habitability
```

Figure 8.02 shows how the monitor will look. To make your modification, you would move the cursor before **and apartment** and insert your change. The monitor would then show:

```
tenant or landlord or lease! or (rental w/5
(contract or agree!)) and apartment
and water or plumbing
and habitable or uninhabitable or habitability
```

To complete your modification, you would move the cursor past the last term you wanted to retain in your modified search request and press TRANSMIT.

The contents of the resulting search request will depend on the cursor's location when you pressed TRANSMIT. In LEXIS, whenever you transmit a search request (whether your original one or a modified version), the computer ignores all search terms and connectors displayed to the right of or below the

```
TENANT OR LANDLORD OR LEASE! AND APARTMENT
AND WATER OR PLUMBING
AND HABITABLE OR UNINHABITABLE OR HABITABILITY

Your search request is:
TENANT OR LANDLORD OR LEASE! AND APARTMENT
AND WATER OR PLUMBING
AND HABITABLE OR UNINHABITABLE OR HABITABILITY

Number of CASES found with your search request through:
LEVEL 1... 1190 LEVEL 2... 172 LEVEL 3... 28

Please type your search request then press the TRANSMIT key.
What you transmit will be Search Level 1.

For further explanation, press the H key (for HELP) and then the TRANSMIT key.
```

Type the desired changes to the search request.

Source: Mead Data Central, Inc. © 1993

Figure 8.02. Sample Screen in LEXIS: "Back Modifying" at the Beginning or in the Middle of a Search Request

cursor's position on the monitor. For example, in the preceding illustration, if you placed the cursor after, say, `habitable` and then pressed TRANSMIT, the computer would drop `or uninhabitable or habitability` from the search request. Consequently, before you press TRANSMIT, make sure you have positioned the cursor at the end of the search terms and connectors you want to include in your search request.

Transmitting a modification of a multiple-level search request not only eliminates the search terms and connectors that appear after the cursor. The change also reorganizes the levels, so you end up with a different number of levels than you had when you started.

For instance, consider again the original three-level search request on page 168. Suppose you went back to level 2 to modify it by adding `or heat or light or electric!` The modified search request would consist of two levels rather than three. Level 1 in the modified search request would remain the same as the original level 1 search:

```
tenant or landlord or lease! and apartment
```

The cursor's location would determine what constitutes level 2 after your modification. If you transmitted the change with the cursor at the end of the line you edited, your new level 2 search would be:

```
and water or plumbing or heat or light or
electric!
```

If, instead, you transmitted your modification with the cursor positioned after `habitability`, the new level 2 search would be:

```
and water or plumbing or heat or light or
electric! and habitable or uninhabitable or
habitability
```

In short, when you return to an earlier level of a LEXIS search request and transmit a modification, the computer constructs a new, reorganized search request that begins with level 1 and continues through subsequent levels (up to the position of the cursor). You end up with as many search levels as the number you used in the instruction to recall the search level for modification. Thus, `1m` yields a one-level search request, `2m` a two-level request, `3m` a three-level request, and so on.

The mechanics of modifying in WESTLAW. In WESTLAW, you take the following steps whenever you want to modify your search requests, whether you formulate them with terms and connectors or in natural language:

1. Type `q` (for "query," the WESTLAW designation for a search request).

2. Press ENTER. Your search request will appear on the monitor, which will look like the screen in Figure 8.03 (if you formulated a Boolean search request) or like the screen in Figure 8.04 (if you formulated a natural-language search request). You can then make whatever modifications you want, anywhere in the search request.

3. When you finish editing, transmit the new, modified search request to the computer by pressing ENTER again. At that point, the modified search request will supersede any earlier search requests you used.

   In WESTLAW, the cursor's location makes no difference when you transmit a search request or modification. (This contrasts with the situation in LEXIS; see pages 171–72.) Regardless of the cursor's location, the WESTLAW computer treats as the intended search request any words that appear in the typing area of the screen when you press ENTER. If any words appear that you do *not* want to include in your search request, use the DELETE key or the BACKSPACE key to erase those words from the monitor before pressing ENTER to transmit your modification.

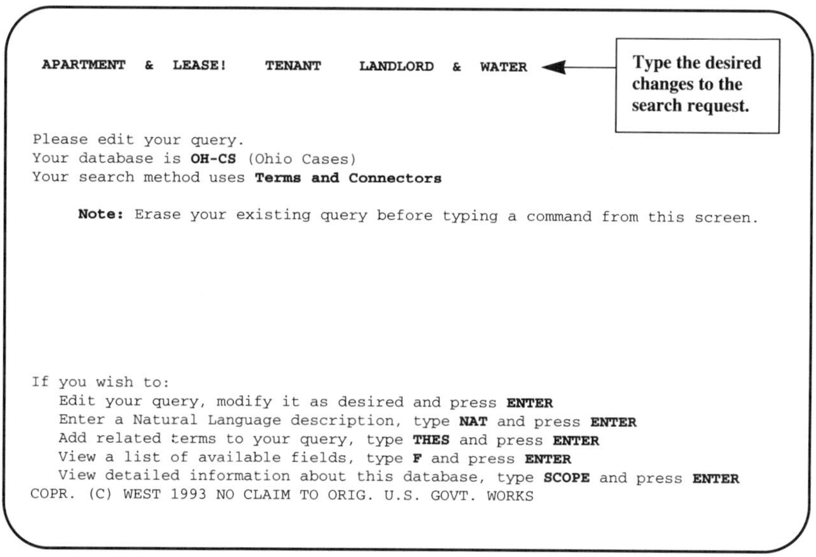

APARTMENT & LEASE! TENANT LANDLORD & WATER

Type the desired changes to the search request.

Please edit your query.
Your database is **OH-CS** (Ohio Cases)
Your search method uses **Terms and Connectors**

Note: Erase your existing query before typing a command from this screen.

If you wish to:
Edit your query, modify it as desired and press **ENTER**
Enter a Natural Language description, type **NAT** and press **ENTER**
Add related terms to your query, type **THES** and press **ENTER**
View a list of available fields, type **F** and press **ENTER**
View detailed information about this database, type **SCOPE** and press **ENTER**
COPR. (C) WEST 1993 NO CLAIM TO ORIG. U.S. GOVT. WORKS

Source: West Publishing Company © 1993

Figure 8.03. Sample Query Modification Screen for Boolean Searching in WESTLAW

```
DOES A LANDLORD HAVE AN OBLIGATION TO PROVIDE RUNNING WATER TO A TENANT IN A
LEASED APARTMENT?

Please edit your description.
Your database is OH-CS (Ohio Cases)
Your search method uses Natural Language.                  Maximum Result:  100

     NOTE: Erase your existing description before typing a command from this
     screen.




If you wish to:
   Edit your description, modify it as desired and press ENTER
   Add related concepts to your description, type THES and press ENTER
   Add restrictions to your description, type RES and press ENTER
   Enter a Terms and Connectors query, type TC and press ENTER
   View detailed information about this database, type SCOPE and press ENTER
COPR. (C) WEST 1993 NO CLAIM TO ORIG. U.S. GOVT. WORKS
```

Type the desired changes to the search request.

Source: West Publishing Company © 1993

Figure 8.04. Sample Query Modification Screen for Natural-Language Searching in WESTLAW

You can repeat this sequence for making modifications until you achieve results you consider satisfactory.[127]

[127] Because a modification of a WESTLAW search request supersedes any previous search request, modifications do not result in creating different "levels" of a search request, as occurs in LEXIS. (See pages 168–70.) If you want to evaluate the effect each modification has on your search so you can make appropriate adjustments, you can achieve the effect of searching by levels in WESTLAW if you divide a Boolean search request into components and communicate them to the computer in separate steps. For instance, to replicate in WESTLAW the three LEXIS search levels shown in the earlier illustration, you would begin by entering the following search request (equivalent to the level 1 LEXIS search in the example on page 168):

```
tenant or landlord or lease! and apartment
```

In response to this search request, the WESTLAW computer would indicate the number of documents it located and allow you to view them. After reviewing the results, you could type `q` and press ENTER (to recall the search request for editing), then modify the search request by adding `and water or plumbing` at the end and pressing ENTER. Your search request (now equivalent to the level 2 search in the LEXIS illustration) would be:

```
tenant or landlord or lease! and apartment and water or plumbing
```

After examining the results of this search, you could modify the search request again by recalling it to the monitor and adding `and habitable or uninhabitable or habitability`. Your new search request (equivalent to the level 3 search in the LEXIS example) would then be:

```
tenant or landlord or lease! and apartment and water or
plumbing and habitable or uninhabitable or habitability
```

Using WESTLAW's thesaurus in modifying search requests. WESTLAW provides an online thesaurus you can use to select synonyms for search terms in your search request. To use the WESTLAW thesaurus, first transmit a search request.[128] Then follow this procedure:

1. While viewing a document your search request retrieved, type `thes` and press ENTER to invoke the thesaurus.

   Alternatively, transmit `q` (for "query") to return to the screen for typing search instructions (Figure 8.03 or 8.04). At that screen, press the F9 key or use the DELETE key to remove your search request from the area of the screen for typing instructions. Then transmit `thes` to invoke the thesaurus.

2. The monitor will display a screen listing those of your search terms for which the thesaurus offers synonyms. Figure 8.05 depicts a typical screen displayed at this point. To select the search term for which you want to view synonyms, type the number for that search term and then press ENTER.

3. When the monitor displays a synonym list, such as the one in Figure 8.06, type the numbers for the synonyms you want to add to your search request; then press ENTER.

4. The monitor will redisplay your search request, with each synonym you selected shown after the search term to which the synonym corresponds. This screen will resemble Figure 8.07, which shows "lessor" as a synonym for "landlord." When you use the thesaurus to add synonyms to a natural-language search request, the synonyms will appear in parentheses after the corresponding search terms (as shown in Figure 8.07).

   At this screen, you can repeat the process to select additional synonyms. Or, you can press ENTER to return to the screen for typing search instructions, where you can view and transmit your modified search.

Of course, you do not need to go through the online thesaurus to add synonyms to a search request. You can modify your request by simply typing new search terms.

If you add synonymous terms to a natural-language search request without using the thesaurus, you can type the new terms without parentheses, or you

[128] If you gain access to WESTLAW through the version of the WESTMATE software designed for use with Microsoft Windows, you do not need to transmit a search request before you can invoke the thesaurus. Similarly, a forthcoming non-Windows version of the WESTMATE software—version 4.8 for MS-DOS—will allow you to invoke the thesaurus without having to first transmit a search request.

```
                         WESTLAW Thesaurus

Your description is:
DOES A LANDLORD HAVE AN OBLIGATION TO PROVIDE RUNNING WATER TO A TENANT IN A
LEASED APARTMENT?

The concepts in your description that have related concepts are:

 1  LANDLORD
 2  OBLIGATION
 3  PROVIDE
 4  RUNNING
 5  WATER
 6  TENANT
 7  APARTMENT

If you wish to:
   View related concepts for a concept listed above, type the concept number
      and press ENTER
   Return to the description screen, press ENTER
```

Source: West Publishing Company © 1993

Figure 8.05. Sample List of Search Terms for Which WESTLAW's Thesaurus Offers Synonyms

```
                         WESTLAW Thesaurus

Related concepts for LANDLORD are:

 1  LANDHOLDER
 2  LANDLADY
 3  LANDOWNER
 4  LESSOR
 5  OWNER
 6  PROPRIETOR
     -----
 7  SLUMLORD
 8  TENEMENT

If you wish to:
   Add related concepts to your description, type one or more concept numbers
      (e.g. 2,3) and press ENTER
   Return to the Thesaurus concept list, press ENTER
```

Source: West Publishing Company © 1993

Figure 8.06. Sample List of Synonyms Suggested by WESTLAW's Thesaurus

```
                         WESTLAW Thesaurus

Your description is:
DOES A LANDLORD (LESSOR) HAVE AN OBLIGATION TO PROVIDE RUNNING WATER TO A
TENANT IN A  LEASED APARTMENT?

The concepts in your description that have related concepts are:

 1  LANDLORD
 2  OBLIGATION
 3  PROVIDE
 4  RUNNING
 5  WATER
 6  TENANT
 7  APARTMENT



If you wish to:
   View related concepts for a concept listed above, type the concept number
      and press ENTER
   Return to the description screen, press ENTER
```

Source: West Publishing Company © 1993

Figure 8.07. Sample Natural-Language Search Request with a Synonym Added Through WESTLAW's Thesaurus

can enclose the new terms in parentheses (which creates synonyms the computer will treat as though you had added them through the thesaurus). So, if you had originally transmitted `who is a public figure for the purposes of defamation`, you could type a modification like one of these:

```
who is a public figure for the purposes of
defamation or libel
```

```
who is a public figure for the purposes of
defamation (libel)
```

Although these two modifications might look like they would retrieve identical results, the natural-language feature handles these search requests differently, and they could retrieve slightly different collections of documents or collections in which the documents appear in different orders. The differences can occur because of the way the natural-language algorithms calculate the statistical relevance of documents.[129]

[129] In the natural-language feature, each word in a WESTLAW database receives a numerical value based on the frequency with which the word occurs in that database. The computer uses this value in its algorithms (see pages 25–26) to determine which documents to retrieve. When you add a synonym to a natural-language search request by using WESTLAW's thesaurus or by

Summary. Although some differences exist in the mechanics of modifying search requests in LEXIS and WESTLAW, the result of any modification in either service is ultimately the same: whether you tack on changes to the end of a search request or insert them at the beginning or in the middle, or whether your modified search request appears on the monitor as one undivided entity (as in WESTLAW) or divided into levels (as can occur in LEXIS), the modification always results in a revised set of instructions for searching the database. The computer will respond by retrieving a new collection of documents, telling you the number of documents retrieved, and offering you the opportunity to view the documents and, if you want, to commence another round of modifications.

Aligning terms when you modify search requests

Boolean alignments in LEXIS and WESTLAW. As you modify a Boolean search request in LEXIS or WESTLAW, be sure not to inadvertently undo appropriate alignments you established among the terms in your original search request. Just as with your original Boolean request (see pages 67 and 160–61), if the terms in your modified Boolean request are not correctly linked, you are less apt to retrieve relevant documents and more apt to retrieve irrelevant documents: linking a new search term to the wrong part of a previous Boolean search request enters the researcher into a "Boolean lottery, where it is quite incidental whether [the researcher] actually wins a relevant document as a prize."[130]

An example drawn from the LEXIS reference manual illustrates the point, which applies equally to Boolean searching in WESTLAW (although the WESTLAW monitor would not display your modifications in levels).[131] Sup-

---

typing the synonym in parentheses yourself, the synonym takes on the value of the search term that appears in front of it in the search request (*i.e.*, the search term for which the new word serves as a synonym). If a search term and one of its synonyms have different values, your search results can differ depending on whether the synonym appears in parentheses in your search request.

For instance, in the defamation example, suppose the word "defamation" had a value of .1 and the word "libel" had a value of .2. In the first modification, where the synonym does not appear in parentheses, the computer would assign "defamation" a value of .1 and "libel" a value of .2 when calculating the statistical relevance of a document. But in the second modification, where the synonym appears in parentheses, the computer would assign "defamation" and "libel" equal values (.1) when calculating a document's statistical relevance. You could even obtain a third outcome if you used "defamation" as a synonym of "libel," as in `who is a public figure for the purposes of libel (defamation)`: the computer would give "libel" its normal value of .2 and reassign "defamation" a value of .2.

[130] Jon Bing, *Performance of Legal Text Retrieval Systems: The Curse of Boole*, 79 LAW LIBR. J. 187, 200 (1987) (footnote omitted).

[131] *See* MEAD DATA CENTRAL, REFERENCE MANUAL FOR THE LEXIS/NEXIS SERVICES 86–87 (undated looseleaf ed.). For another example, see Jon Bing, *Performance of Legal Text Retrieval Systems: The Curse of Boole*, 79 LAW LIBR. J. 187, 199–200 (1987).

pose you searched in the ALLREG file in the GENFED library in LEXIS with the following search request:

```
ceramic w/5 "gallium arsenide"
```

In reviewing the documents retrieved, you discover that some authors used the chemical abbreviation "GaAs" for gallium arsenide. To expand your search to retrieve documents in which an author used the chemical abbreviation instead of the full chemical name, you could modify your request by adding

```
or gaas
```

at the end. After transmitting this modification, your search request would be:

```
ceramic w/5 "gallium arsenide" or gaas
```

Under the connector hierarchy rules discussed on pages 62 and 64–66, this modified search request achieves the result you want: treating the chemical abbreviation "GaAs" as an alternative way of expressing "gallium arsenide," and retrieving documents in which the author used one or both of these expressions within five words of "ceramic." Adding parentheses, as explained on pages 66–67, to visualize the search-term groupings the Boolean connectors establish in the modified request highlights that the terms are correctly aligned:

```
ceramic w/5 ("gallium arsenide" or gaas)
```

Suppose, however, that your original request had been:

```
"gallium arsenide" w/5 ceramic
```

If you modified that search request by adding `or gaas` at the end, your new search request would be:

```
"gallium arsenide" w/5 ceramic or gaas
```

Adding parentheses to visualize the search-term groupings the Boolean connectors establish in this search request highlights that now the terms are incorrectly aligned:

```
"gallium arsenide" w/5 (ceramic or gaas)
```

Thus, the modification did not achieve your objective: "GaAs" is now treated as an alternative way of expressing "ceramic," and "ceramic" does not need to appear in retrieved documents.

In short, failing to focus on the alignment of your search terms when you modify a Boolean search request can result in a search that significantly diverges from what you intend.

Your research goal and the structure of your search request will influence how you effect a modification to achieve your intended result. For example, in the illustration, if you had started with the search request `"gallium arsenide" w/5 ceramic` and then decided to add "GaAs" as an alternative expression of "gallium arsenide," you could accomplish this change by adding the new term immediately before or after "gallium arsenide," instead of tacking it on at the end. This modification would align the search terms to produce the desired effect, as highlighted by the parentheses used in either version of the resulting modified search request:

```
("gallium arsenide" or gaas) w/5 ceramic
(gaas or "gallium arsenide") w/5 ceramic
```

Search term alignments in natural-language searching in WESTLAW. When you search with WESTLAW's natural-language feature, you do not need to keep your search terms arranged in appropriate conceptual groupings, either when you formulate your requests or when you later modify them. In either instance, instead of relying on relationships the researcher establishes by using Boolean connectors, the computer applies statistical algorithms to determine automatically what arrangements among words in documents will satisfy the request.

Modifying to narrow a search

Narrowing a Boolean search in LEXIS or WESTLAW. In modifying Boolean search requests, consider whether a modification will broaden or narrow your research. Sometimes it makes sense to broaden a search to increase the number of documents the computer will retrieve. For example, in the research scenario in the previous section, skimming the documents retrieved by the search request `ceramic w/5 "gallium arsenide"` revealed that "GaAs" was an alternative search term that should be added to expand the scope of the search.

In general, though, the most effective search strategy starts with a request designed to sweep in as many potentially relevant documents as possible, with each modification designed to locate successively fewer documents. By searching this way, you can see whether a particular arrangement of terms and connectors has narrowed the search either less than you wanted or more than you wanted. You also minimize the likelihood of bypassing relevant documents, as could occur if your initial request focused your search too narrowly.

For instance, suppose you need to research whether a motion picture studio can claim an investment tax credit for chemicals used in producing movies.[132] A Boolean request for researching this problem in LEXIS or WESTLAW might read as follows:

[132] This hypothetical is drawn from MEAD DATA CENTRAL, LEARNING LEXIS: A HANDBOOK FOR MODERN LEGAL RESEARCH 18–19 (Jan. 1989).

```
(investment w/5 credit) and (production w/5
cost) and (movie or film or "motion picture")
and (chemical or solution)
```

You could transmit the entire search request at one time in an appropriate LEXIS file or WESTLAW database. But transmitting the search request in stages designed to move from broad to narrow results could prove more informative. Using a broad-to-narrow searching technique, you might begin with

```
(investment w/5 credit)
```

as your original search request. If that search retrieved more documents than you wanted, you could modify your search request by adding

```
and (production w/5 cost)
```

After seeing the results of that modification, you could decide whether to restrict your search to the movie industry by adding

```
and (movie or film or "motion picture")
```

Finally, based on the results of that search, you could decide whether to further narrow your search by adding

```
and (chemical or solution)
```

Narrowing a natural-language search in WESTLAW. Because WESTLAW's natural-language feature currently cuts off search results at 100 documents, the Boolean strategy of first performing a broad search designed to sweep in as many potentially relevant documents as possible and then modifying the search to reduce the number of documents retrieved has little practical application in natural-language searching. In all but rare instances, any natural-language search you transmit will retrieve whatever number of documents (up to 100) you previously instructed the computer to retrieve.

The most promising tactic for natural-language searching usually involves transmitting a search request you believe best reflects the precise issue you want to research. If you need to modify the search request to focus even more narrowly on your research issue, the modification will typically involve adding more search terms appropriate to your issue, a modification that can cause the collection of retrieved documents to prove increasingly relevant to your research needs.

Other ways to revise search results

Adding, deleting, or changing the terms, connectors, or field restrictions in a search request can alter the collection of documents retrieved. You can also alter the collection in other ways.

Change the LEXIS file or WESTLAW database. You can revise your search results by switching to a different LEXIS file or WESTLAW database, where you can repeat your current search request or try a modified version. For example, you might want to search for cases on the same issue but from a different jurisdiction. Or, if a Boolean search in a file or database of statutes from multiple jurisdictions retrieves more documents than you can evaluate, you can reduce the number of documents retrieved if you repeat your search in a file or database containing statutes from only one jurisdiction.

LEXIS. In LEXIS, to search in a different file in the library you are in:

1. Press the key labelled CHG FILE (for "change file").
2. Type the abbreviated name of the new file, as shown on the monitor.
3. Press TRANSMIT.

If you want to search in a different file in another library:

1. Press the key labelled CHG LIB (for "change library").
2. Type the abbreviated name of the new library, as shown on the monitor.
3. Press TRANSMIT.
4. Type the abbreviated name of the new file, as shown on the monitor.
5. Press TRANSMIT.

Whether you switch to a different file in the same library or in another library, your current search request will appear on the monitor, along with on-screen instructions offering you the opportunity to transmit that request in the new file or to edit the request before you transmit it in the new file.

WESTLAW. In WESTLAW, whether you search with a Boolean request or a natural-language request, you can repeat your current search request in a different database by following this sequence:

1. Type the command **sdb** followed by the abbreviated name (called an "identifier") of the new database. Appendix B lists sources from which you can obtain database indentifiers.
2. Press ENTER, which will cause the computer to switch to the new database and run your search there.

To run an edited version of a Boolean or natural-language search request in a different database:

1. Type the command **qdb** followed by the identifier of the new database.

2. Press ENTER. Your current search request will appear on the monitor, at which point you can edit the request and press ENTER to run the modified search in the new database.

Start a new search. You can revise your search results by discarding all versions of your search request and starting over with a new search request. For instance, if you aren't satisfied with the results of previous searches and you anticipate making a lot of changes to your search instructions, you might proceed more quickly by simply typing a new search request instead of making further modifications.

LEXIS. In LEXIS, to start a new search in the same file:

1. Press the NEW SEARCH key.

2. Type your new search request.

3. Press TRANSMIT.

To start a new search in a different LEXIS file:

1. First follow the procedure described on page 182 for changing files.

2. Then press the NEW SEARCH key.

3. Type your new search request.

4. Press TRANSMIT.

WESTLAW. In WESTLAW, to start a new search (whether Boolean or natural-language) in the same database:

1. Type the command **s**.

2. Press ENTER.

3. Type your new search request.

4. Press ENTER.

To start a new Boolean or natural-language search in a different WESTLAW database:

1. Type the command **db** followed by the identifier of the new database.

2. Press ENTER.

3. Type your new search request.

4. Press ENTER.

In WESTLAW, switch between Boolean and natural-language searching. When you research the same issue with Boolean and natural-language searches, you will normally retrieve many of the same documents, but each collection of documents will also likely include some documents not found in the other collection. Consequently, you might want to switch between Boolean and natural-language searching as a way of revising your search results in WESTLAW.

The WESTLAW software chooses a search method (currently, Boolean searching) that will automatically apply unless you change it by making a different selection through the Options Directory, as explained on pages 197–98. In addition, during an online session, you can switch from Boolean searching to natural-language searching, or vice versa. You make this switch when the monitor displays the screen for transmitting search requests (Figures 9.10 and 9.11 on pages 201 and 202) or for transmitting changes to search requests (Figures 8.03 and 8.04 on pages 173 and 174):

1. If any words appear in the area of the screen for typing search instructions, remove those words by pressing the F9 key after positioning the cursor at the upper left of the screen, or by using the DELETE key or BACKSPACE key.

2. Type `nat` to switch to natural-language searching, or type `tc` to switch to Boolean (terms-and-connectors) searching.

3. Press ENTER.

When you use this technique to switch search methods, your selection remains in effect for the rest of your online session, or until you select a different search method.

Switch CALR services. You can revise your search results by switching CALR services (*e.g.*, from LEXIS to WESTLAW, or vice versa) and repeating your current search request or trying a modified version. The next chapter explains how to enter and exit the LEXIS and WESTLAW services.

Even when you use the same search request in comparable files or databases in LEXIS and WESTLAW, you can retrieve different collections of documents. At any given time, the coverage of comparable LEXIS files and WESTLAW databases can differ: Mead Data Central and West Publishing Company do not add documents to their services in the same order or at the same speed and, in any event, do not always add the same documents. In addition, a document in one of the CALR services might include a typographical or other data-entry mistake that (as explained on page 665 n.412) could leave the document invisible to the search request; the other CALR service might contain the document without the data-entry error.

Summary of modifying searches

As this chapter shows, several techniques exist for modifying searches in LEXIS and WESTLAW. Figure 8.08 summarizes these procedures.

If you want to:	Follow this procedure	
	LEXIS	**WESTLAW**
Modify your search request for use in the current LEXIS file or WESTLAW database	To add a modification to the end of the request, type `m` (for "modify") and press TRANSMIT. To insert a change elsewhere in the request, type the number of the search level and the letter `m` (or type `m` followed by the number). Then press TRANSMIT.	Type `q` (for "query") and press ENTER.
Use the same search request in a different LEXIS file or WESTLAW database	To switch to a different file in the same library, press CHG FILE (for "change file"), type the name of the new file, and press TRANSMIT. To switch to a different file in another library, press CHG LIB (for "change library"), type the name of the new library, press TRANSMIT, type the name of the new file, and press TRANSMIT.	Type `sdb` followed by the identifier of the new database, and press ENTER.
Modify your search request for use in a different LEXIS file or WESTLAW database	First, switch files as described immediately above. Then edit the request.	Type `qdb` followed by the identifier of the new database, and press ENTER.

Start over with a new search request in the current LEXIS file or WESTLAW database	Press the NEW SEARCH key.	Type `s` and press ENTER.
Start over with a new search request in a different LEXIS file or WESTLAW database	First, switch files (see above). Then press the NEW SEARCH key.	Type `db` followed by the identifier of the new database, and press ENTER.
Switch between Boolean (terms-and-connector) searching and natural-language searching in WESTLAW	[not applicable]	Type `opt` and press ENTER to invoke the Options Directory; then select a new search method. *or* At the screen for transmitting search requests or modifications to search requests, type `nat` or `tc` and press ENTER.
Switch CALR services	Log off LEXIS by pressing the SIGN OFF key. Then log on to WESTLAW (see pages 191–94).	Log off WESTLAW by typing `off` and pressing ENTER. Then log on to LEXIS (see pages 191–94).

Figure 8.08. Quick Guide to Modifying Searches in LEXIS and WESTLAW

CHAPTER 9

Overview of a Computer-Assisted Legal Research Session: A Checklist

Introduction. So far, the discussion has set the stage for going online to find, read, and update the law. This chapter and the following ones explain how to actually perform computer-assisted research activities in each of these phases of research.

Your online searching will progress more effectively and efficiently if—before going online—you know the complete sequence for conducting a computer-assisted research session. With this background, you will minimize confusion and wasted time during your CALR searches and avoid unnecessary online charges.

Each CALR session will proceed a little differently, depending on what you seek to accomplish. For example, for one research problem, you might use books to find the relevant law, and only use LEXIS or WESTLAW to update your authorities. This chapter's overview of a CALR session presumes you want to do a descriptive-word search to find authorities, then skim the authorities you locate, and finally update the ones that appear relevant. Even if you choose to follow a different tack, reading the checklist that begins on page 191 will familiarize you with the basic steps you will encounter in using computers in legal research. A summary of the checklist appears on page 206.

A few words about keyboards, Windows, and mice

Keyboards. In LEXIS and WESTLAW, you can use either a personal computer or a dedicated computer terminal specifically designed for using

LEXIS or WESTLAW (such as the UBIQ terminal for LEXIS or the WALT II terminal for WESTLAW). If you use a dedicated terminal, you will find that the keyboard has, in addition to the letter and number keys found on a standard typewriter keyboard, many keys specially designated for CALR functions. When you press one of these dedicated keys, the computer carries out a particular function, such as displaying the next document in a collection of documents retrieved by a search request.

If you use a personal computer for computer-assisted legal research, Mead Data Central and West Publishing Company provide special software that allows your computer to communicate with the CALR computer. This software also controls the keys on your keyboard so some of them will perform the same CALR functions as the special keys on the dedicated CALR keyboards. If you use a personal computer not supplied by Mead Data or West Publishing, however, the keys on your keyboard will not be labelled as keys that perform CALR functions; for this situation, Mead Data and West Publishing provide templates (paper or plastic overlays) you can place on your keyboard to identify the keys that perform specific CALR functions.

The figures at the end of the chapter show the principal keyboards and templates in use with LEXIS and WESTLAW. Of those figures, the following ones illustrate the keyboard configurations for LEXIS:

- Figure 9.12 shows the keyboard for the LEXIS 2000 terminal, an IBM-compatible personal computer available from Mead Data Central for use with LEXIS.
- Figure 9.13 shows a LEXIS keyboard template for use on IBM-compatible personal computers other than the LEXIS 2000 terminal.
- Figure 9.14 shows the LEXIS keyboard for the UBIQ, an early dedicated LEXIS terminal still in use but which Mead Data will eventually phase out.

The following figures illustrate the keyboard configurations for WESTLAW:

- Figure 9.15 shows the keyboard for the WALT PC terminal, an IBM-compatible personal computer available from West Publishing Company for use with WESTLAW.
- Figure 9.16 shows a WESTLAW keyboard template for use on IBM-compatible personal computers other than the WALT PC terminal.
- Figure 9.17 shows the keyboard for WALT II, the current dedicated terminal used with WESTLAW.

In both LEXIS and WESTLAW, nearly every CALR function can be carried out either by pressing a function key or by typing a combination of letters and numbers that will send an equivalent instruction to the CALR computer. This book generally refers to typed commands, rather than function keys, in illustrating how to carry out CALR functions. The typed commands for each CALR service operate the same way on any of the keyboards you might use with that service. By contrast, the use of function keys can vary from one keyboard to another. For example, on one keyboard, you might press a function key by itself to carry out a CALR activity, but you might need to press a function key in combination with, say, the SHIFT key to carry out the same activity when you use a different keyboard. Also, if you use a recently manufactured dedicated CALR keyboard, it might include CALR function keys not found on an older model of the same keyboard. Consequently, using typed commands to explain how to perform CALR operations provides more consistency than using function keys for the explanation.

For certain functions in LEXIS, the typed command consists of a period followed by a two-letter combination, known collectively as a "dot command." Once researchers gain familiarity with using LEXIS, they often prefer using dot commands (explained in Appendix I). But novice or infrequent LEXIS users often find dot commands difficult to remember. When a researcher can perform a LEXIS function with either a dot command or a function key, this book generally refers to the function key.

If you want to correlate a function key with a typed command, or vice versa, Mead Data and West Publishing provide reference cards and pamphlets that show this information. In this book, you will find a complete list of function keys and corresponding typed commands in Appendix K for LEXIS and in Appendix L for WESTLAW. In addition, Figures I.01 and I.02 on pages 726 and 727 list the LEXIS function keys and the corresponding dot commands.

A shortcut for typing commands in LEXIS and WESTLAW. Once you become familiar with the organization of LEXIS and WESTLAW and with the commands for searching them, you might want to combine separate commands into a single typed instruction (a technique sometimes called "stacking" commands). Appendices I and J explain how this technique works in each CALR service.

Windows and mice. LEXIS and WESTLAW also offer versions of their personal-computer software that you can use with Microsoft Windows, a software program developed by Microsoft Corporation. If you use the Windows version of the LEXIS or WESTLAW software, you can use a pointing device (called a "mouse") instead of a keyboard to perform most CALR functions. These Windows versions create a screen display (known generically as a "graphical user interface," or "GUI") distinguished by the presence of boxes labeled with LEXIS or WESTLAW functions. By maneuvering the mouse on a flat surface near the computer, you move an arrow on the screen so the arrow points to the box for the operation you want the computer to carry out. By pressing a button on the mouse (sometimes called "clicking" the mouse), you instruct the computer to perform the function to which the arrow was pointing.

The mouse does not replace the keyboard for all purposes, however. For instance, you would still need the keyboard to type the words for which you want the computer to search. Moreover, even when you have a mouse attached to your computer, you can still use the keyboard instead of the mouse to carry out LEXIS or WESTLAW functions.

The LEXIS and WESTLAW screens shown in this book are typical of those you will see when you use non-Windows versions of LEXIS and WESTLAW. The Windows versions of LEXIS and WESTLAW modify these screens by adding boxes and borders to the displays. Otherwise, the information you will see on the screens is the same.

A computer-assisted legal research sequence

Step 1. Formulate and write out your search request. (See Chapter 7.) Doing this before you go online is key to saving time and money. A worksheet, such as that in Figures 9.18 and 9.19 on pages 214–17, can assist with this step.

Step 2. Log on. To establish communication with a CALR service, find the on/off button on the terminal you are using, and turn the machine on. If you are working on a dedicated terminal (that is, a terminal used only for searching in one of the CALR services), the terminal will automatically establish a telecommunications link with the CALR service's computer when you switch on the terminal. If you are working on non-dedicated equipment (such as your personal computer), the reference manuals for your computer hardware and the CALR vendors' communications software will provide specific instructions for establishing a connection with the LEXIS or WESTLAW computer.

Transmit your identification number. Once you are electronically linked with the LEXIS computer, the monitor will display instructions (called "prompts") asking you to type your LEXIS identification number and press the TRANSMIT key. Figure 9.01 shows the monitor's appearance. Similarly, once you are electronically linked with the WESTLAW computer, the monitor will display prompts asking you to type your WESTLAW password and press the ENTER key. Figure 9.02 shows how the monitor looks.

As you log on, the monitor will display brief announcements about recent changes in the CALR service, such as the addition of new files or features. Typical announcements appear in Figures 9.03 and 9.04. Reading this information when you log on will help you keep current with changes that occur in the CALR services.

Type your LEXIS identification number here.

```
WELCOME TO LEXIS AND NEXIS.
LEXIS and NEXIS will be available until  2:00 A.M. Eastern Time.

Please type your personal identification number (7 characters) and press the
TRANSMIT key.
```

Source: Mead Data Central, Inc. © 1993

Figure 9.01. LEXIS Log-On Screen

Type your WESTLAW password here.

```
A COMPUTER-ASSISTED LEGAL RESEARCH SERVICE OF WEST PUBLISHING COMPANY

COPYRIGHT (C) 1993 BY WEST PUBLISHING COMPANY.  COPYRIGHT IS NOT CLAIMED AS
TO ANY PART OF THE ORIGINAL WORK  PREPARED BY A U. S. GOVERNMENT OFFICER OR
EMPLOYEE  AS PART  OF THAT PERSON'S OFFICIAL DUTIES.   ALL RIGHTS RESERVED.
NO  PART  OF A  WESTLAW TRANSMISSION MAY BE COPIED, DOWNLOADED, STORED IN A
RETRIEVAL  SYSTEM, FURTHER  TRANSMITTED  OR  OTHERWISE  REPRODUCED, STORED,
DISSEMINATED, TRANSFERRED  OR  USED, IN ANY FORM  OR  BY ANY MEANS, WITHOUT
WEST'S PRIOR WRITTEN AGREEMENT.  EACH REPRODUCTION OF ANY PART OF A WESTLAW
TRANSMISSION MUST  CONTAIN NOTICE  OF  WEST'S COPYRIGHT AS  FOLLOWS: "COPR.
(C) WEST 1993 NO CLAIM TO ORIG. U.S. GOVT. WORKS".  WESTLAW AND WESTNET ARE
REGISTERED SERVICE MARKS OF WEST PUBLISHING CO. REG. U.S. PAT. AND TM. OFF.

           AVAILABLE 24 HOURS MONDAY THROUGH SATURDAY
                  AND SUNDAY FROM 8 AM, CST
PLEASE TYPE YOUR PASSWORD AND PRESS ENTER:  (PASSWORD MAY NOT BE DISPLAYED)
```

Source: West Publishing Company © 1993

Figure 9.02. WESTLAW Log-On Screen

Type an identification for your research session here.

1...5...10...15...20...25...30..

announcements of recent changes to the LEXIS service

NOW - New Jersey Agency decisions for 45 agencies in the **NJAGEN** file in the **NJ** and **STATES** libraries! Search free of charge, **ENTER: PRACT; NJAGEN.**
New **TAX** file now available in the **EASY SEARCH(TM)** library! Track Governor Pete Wilson's (R-CA) campaign finance receipts, ENTER: **cmpgn;cafin;name(wilson w/2p)**
Call **1-800-34NEXIS** for a free list of new files in NEXIS, request doc #107.

To identify the research to follow, please type and transmit up to 32 characters identifying the client or matter.

For further explanation, press the H key (for HELP) and then the TRANSMIT key.

Figure 9.03. Research Identification Screen in LEXIS

Type an identification for your research session here.

WELCOME TO WESTLAW

Check **Daily Labor Report (BNA-DLR)** for the Full-Text of Interim Final Regulations Implementing the Family and Medical Leave Act of 1993; Analysis:6/4/93; Full-Text:6/7/93. Both Text and Analysis in 6/8/93 edition of **Daily Report for Executives (BNA-DER).**

Complete Shepard's citations for **New York Supplement** and **Northeastern Reporter** (First and Second Series) now available on WESTLAW!

West's Legal Directory now features a nationwide directory of **judicial clerkships.** To access this database type **DB WLD-CLERK.**

announcements of recent changes to the WESTLAW service

In **DJH: Assault** launched on **Somali** warlord's compound; **Reports** of **Pepsi tampering** claims faked; **National service** plan; **Ginsburg; Syria**

DATABASE ANNOUNCEMENTS (For more information, enter **NEW** from the Directory.)

WLD-CLERK	WLD-Judicial Clerkships	**VA-BILLS**	VA Bill Tracking-Summaries & Full Text Combined
CERCLA-LH	Comprehensive Envtl Response, Compensation & Liability Act of 1980	**BANKR78-LH**	Bankr. Act of 1978-Leg. Hist.
		BANKR84-LH	Bankr. Act of 1984-Leg. Hist.
VA-BILLTXT	VA Bill Tracking-Full Text	**BANKR86-LH**	Bankr. Act of 1986-Leg. Hist.

Identify this research session. Type your **CLIENT** billing information and press **ENTER**

Figure 9.04. Research Identification Screen in WESTLAW

Identify your research session. At this point, as you can see in Figures 9.03 and 9.04, the monitor will show a prompt inviting you to identify your research session by typing in and transmitting an identification of your choosing (*e.g.*, a client's name or file number, or your research topic). Identifying each research session allows you to keep track of the time and online charges you spend on various research problems; the information will appear on your LEXIS or WESTLAW bill.

If you encounter difficulty logging on to LEXIS or WESTLAW, you can obtain assistance from a librarian, from the person who coordinates your CALR service subscription, or from a customer service representative of LEXIS or WESTLAW (whose telephone numbers appear in Appendices A and B).

With a small number of exceptions, once you are logged on, you start incurring charges that will continue to mount until you log off.[133]

Step 3. Gain access to the LEXIS file or WESTLAW database in which you want to begin your search.

LEXIS. In LEXIS, after you finish logging on, the monitor displays a list of libraries; Figure 9.05 depicts the appearance of the monitor at this point. The list, known as the "library menu," actually contains more information than the monitor can display on one "page" (*i.e.*, on one computer screen); you can view additional pages of the menu by pressing the key labelled NEXT PAGE or PgDn (for "page down").

You do not search directly in a LEXIS library, but in a file within the library. To gain access to a LEXIS file:

1. At the library menu, type the name of the library that contains the file you want to search. (Spell the library name the way it appears on the monitor in the library menu; some names will be abbreviated.)
2. Press TRANSMIT. The monitor will then display the menu of LEXIS files in the library you selected. If you selected the STATES library, for instance, the monitor would display a file list like the one shown in Figure 9.06.
3. Type the file name (spelling it the way it appears in the file menu).
4. Press TRANSMIT. You will now have gained access to the file, and the monitor will display an instruction to begin your search by transmitting a search request.

[133] Some or all online charges are suspended when you use certain LEXIS files or WESTLAW databases designed to provide online help in using the CALR service (*e.g.*, files in the GUIDE library in LEXIS, or the IDEN database in WESTLAW). The vendors' literature provides up-to-date information about billing practices.

```
                        LIBRARIES -- PAGE 1 of 2
Please TRANSMIT the NAME (only one) of the library you want to search.
 - For more information about a library, TRANSMIT its page (PG) number.
 - To see a list of additional libraries, press the NEXT PAGE key.
 NAME   PG NAME   PG NAME   PG NAME   PG NAME   PG NAME   PG NAME   PG NAME   PG

 -------General Legal-------- --Public Records--- --Helps-- Financial --News--
 MEGA    1 ALR     6 LAWREV  6 ASSETS  6 LEXDOC  9 EASY    1 COMPNY 17 NEXIS  14
 GENFED  1 BNA     6 MARHUB  6 DOCKET  6 LIENS   6 GUIDE  13 NAARS  12 LEGNEW 15
 STATES  1 ABA     6 LEXREF  6 INCORP  6 VERDCT  9 PRACT  13 QUOTE  17 CMPGN  15
 CODES   1 CAREER  6 HOTTOP  1                                         WORLD  18
 CITES   6 BEGIN   6
 LEGIS   1 CUSTOM  9

 ----------------------------Area of Law-------------------------------------
 ADMRTY  2 ENERGY  2 FEDSEC  3 INSRLW  3 MEDLNE 16 PRLIAB  4 STTAX   4 UCC     5
 BANKNG  2 ENVIRN  2 FEDSEN  3 INTLAW  3 MEDMAL  3 PUBCON  4 TAXANA  6 UTILTY  5
 BKRTCY  2 ESTATE  2 FEDTAX  3 ITRADE  3 MILTRY  4 PUBHW   4 TAXRIA  6
 COPYRT  2 ETHICS  2 GENMED 16 LABOR   3 MSTORT  5 REALTY  4 TRADE   5
 CORP    2 FAMILY  2 HEALTH  3 LEXPAT  3 PATENT  4 STENV   4 TRANS   5
 EMPLOY  2 FEDCOM  3 IMMIG   3 M&A     4 PENBEN  4 STSEC   4 TRDMRK  5

 Enter .NP for Individual States, International Law and more News information
```

Source: Mead Data Central, Inc. © 1993

Figure 9.05. First Screen of the LEXIS Library Menu

```
Please TRANSMIT, separated by commas, the NAMES of the files you want to search.
You may select as many files as you want, including files that do not appear
below, but you must transmit them all at one time.  To see a description of a
file, TRANSMIT its page (PG) number.
            FILES - PAGE 1 of 8 (NEXT PAGE for additional files)

NAME   PG DESCRIP                   NAME   PG NAME   PG NAME   PG NAME   PG

------ COURT GROUP FILES -------  ------------ STATE CASE LAW ----------
MEGA   65 Federal & State Courts  ALA     1 ILL    15 MONT   30 RI     43
OMNI   65 State Courts & ALR      ALAS    2 IND    16 NEB    31 SC     44
COURTS 65 State Courts            ARIZ    3 IOWA   17 NEV    32 SD     44
HIGHCT 65 State Cts of Last Resort ARK    4 KAN    18 NH     33 TENN   45
-------- GROUP FILES -----------  CAL     5 KY     20 NJ     34 TEX    46
ALLCDE 65 All State Codes         COLO    7 LA     21 NM     35 UTAH   47
ALLAG  64 Attorney General Ops.   CONN    8 ME     22 NY     35 VT     48
STTRCK 55 State Bill Tracking     DEL     9 MD     23 NC     37 VA     49
ALLPUC 64 Public Utility Decisions DC    10 MASS   24 ND     37 VI     50
ALLTAX 64 Taxing Authority Decs.  FLA    11 MICH   25 OHIO   38 WASH   51
ALLSOS 64 Corp & Ltd. Partnership GA     12 MINN   27 OKLA   39 WVA    52
-------- ANNOTATIONS -----------  HAW    13 MISS   28 ORE    40 WISC   53
ALR    75 ALR & L.Ed. Annos       IDA    14 MO     29 PA     41 WYO    54
```

Source: Mead Data Central, Inc. © 1993

Figure 9.06. First Screen of the LEXIS File Menu for the STATES Library

In some LEXIS libraries, you can gain access to more than one file at the same time: while in the file menu, type the name of each file you want to search, joining them with a comma, and then press TRANSMIT. This technique is called "custom file selection." For example, if you want to conduct a search simultaneously in the files for Alabama and Georgia cases, you would first select the STATES library at the library menu and then transmit **ala,ga** when the file menu prompted you to type the name of the file or files you want to search. The online file menus and the printed *LEXIS/NEXIS Library Contents and Alphabetical List* indicate the libraries in which you can combine files for searching.

WESTLAW. Gaining access to a WESTLAW database involves a procedure similar to that for gaining access to a LEXIS file. After you log on, the monitor displays the first page of the directory of materials in WESTLAW. As Figure 9.07 shows, this page lists, according to several broad categories, the areas of interest for which WESTLAW provides databases. To view the next page of the directory, press ENTER; to skip to another page, type **p** followed by a page number, and press ENTER.

To gain access to a WESTLAW database:

1. At the WESTLAW Directory, type the identifier (*i.e.*, the abbreviation) for the database you want to search. For example, type

```
_______________________ WELCOME to the WESTLAW DIRECTORY ____________P1_________

   GENERAL MATERIALS          SPECIALIZED MATERIAL    TEXTS, PERIODICALS AND NEWS
 Federal              P3     BNA                 P494   Law Reviews, Texts,     P441
  Case Law            P3     Other Publishers    P527    Journals & CLEs
  Statutes & Regs     P5     Careers             P532   Newspapers & Mags       P254
  Administrative      P9     Dialog Databases    P203
 State                P12    Gateways (e.g.,     P509           CITATORS
 Combined Federal     P11     Dow Jones)                Insta-Cite, Shepard's P490
  & State                    Highlights          P559    Citations, Shepard's
                             Public Records      P548    PreView, & QuickCite
   TOPICAL MATERIAL          Restatements &      P489
 Bankruptcy           P270    Uniform Laws                      SERVICES
 Environmental        P309                              Dictionaries            P501
 Labor & Employment   P371         DIRECTORIES          EZ ACCESS               P562
 Securities           P408   West's Legal        P505   Key Number Service      P561
 Taxation             P422    Directory                 Other Services          P561
 ....More Topics      P2     Other Directories   P502   Customer Service        P563

If you wish to:
   Select the searchable WESTLAW database list, type IDEN and press ENTER
   Select a known database, type its identifier and press ENTER
   Obtain further information, type HELP and press ENTER
```

Source: West Publishing Company © 1993

Figure 9.07. First Screen of the WESTLAW Directory

`az-cs` if you want to search the database containing Arizona cases. If you do not know the database identifier, you can get the information from several of the sources listed in Appendix B.

2. Press ENTER. You will now have gained access to the database, and the monitor will display an instruction to begin your search by transmitting a search request.

As you gain access to a WESTLAW database, note that WESTLAW allows you to select certain options for using the service and for displaying information on the monitor. Once you have logged on and the monitor has displayed the WESTLAW Directory (Figure 9.07), you have your first opportunity to choose, among other things, the following from the Options Directory:

- which search method (Boolean, *i.e.*, terms-and-connectors searching, or natural-language searching) you want to use for descriptive-word searches
- the maximum number of documents (up to 100) you want the computer to retrieve in response to a natural-language search request
- the order in which you want to view documents retrieved by search requests (see pages 353–55 for more about document display order in WESTLAW)
- whether you want to display or print "star-page" numbers (see pages 356–58 for more about star paging in WESTLAW)
- whether you want the monitor to display instructions (called "prompts") about using WESTLAW—Opting to have explanatory messages appear on the monitor will slightly alter the appearance of the screens; the WESTLAW screens reproduced in this book do not show the explanatory messages that will appear if you choose to display them.
- whether you want to implement the EZ ACCESS feature for communicating your WESTLAW search instructions (see pages 303–11 and 603–09 for explanations of EZ ACCESS)—If you implement EZ ACCESS, the "Welcome to EZ ACCESS" screen (see Figure 10.10 on page 304) will display instead of the WESTLAW Directory screen (Figure 9.07) the next time you log on to WESTLAW.

WESTLAW will automatically select default options unless you instruct the computer to use different ones. To change the default options, or just to see what the current options are:

1. Type `options` (or `opt`).

2. Press ENTER.

The monitor will then display the Options Directory, the first two screens of which are illustrated in Figure 9.08. On-screen prompts will describe the available choices and explain how to make your selection. The options you choose will remain in effect throughout your search session unless you transmit `options` (or `opt`) again and make different choices. You can change options at any point in your research. The options in effect when you end a search session by leaving WESTLAW will be in effect when you return to WESTLAW and start another search session.

Sources of information about LEXIS files and WESTLAW databases. To gain access to and make effective use of an appropriate LEXIS file or WESTLAW database, you need to know:

- which files and databases exist
- the names, abbreviations, or codes that identify them
- the coverage of the files or databases, *i.e.*, the kinds of documents they contain, the earliest and latest documents included, and the contents of fields in the documents (in case you want to conduct a field-restricted search)

Several sources, highlighted in Appendices A and B, provide these details.

Knowing the coverage of a LEXIS file or WESTLAW database—both in terms of the types of materials included and the time span covered—is vital to assessing the thoroughness of an online search. Be wary of judging coverage only by the name of a file or database: the name can create the impression that documents are present that in fact are not. For instance, a LEXIS file or WESTLAW database might not cover the same period as the printed equivalent (if one exists). As an example, the WESTLAW database for South Carolina cases at this writing includes South Carolina Supreme Court cases from 1945 to the present, even though the printed case reporter (*South Carolina Reports*) contains South Carolina Supreme Court cases dating back to 1868, with predecessor reporters extending coverage back to 1783.

In short, conducting an online search without verifying the current coverage of a file or database can cause you to erroneously conclude the computer has searched through documents it has not. Unless you know the coverage of the files or databases you search, you can't know whether you need to search other files or databases—or books—to complete your research.

Choose the smallest appropriate LEXIS file or WESTLAW database. In deciding which LEXIS file or WESTLAW database to search, choose the smallest one that will meet your research needs. Confining your search to the smallest appropriate file or database will retrieve fewer irrelevant documents,

```
                          OPTIONS DIRECTORY                    Page 1 of 3

Select one of the following features to customize your research session:

General Features                                      Current Setting
 1  Designate a topical "Welcome to WESTLAW" screen...Standard
 2  Display explanatory messages.....................Noprompts
 3  Display or print Star Paging.....................Display and print
 4  Select time zone for displaying time of day.......Central

Search Features                                       Current Setting
 5  Select a search method...........................Terms and Connectors
 6  Select Terms and Connectors result rank order.....Terms
 7  Allow you to interrupt Terms and Connectors
            searches.................................Yes
 8  Set the number of documents retrieved for
            Natural Language search..................100

If you wish to:
   Change a feature, type its number and press ENTER
   View a different page, type P followed by a number and press ENTER
   Obtain further information, type HELP and press ENTER
   Continue your research, press ENTER
```

```
                          OPTIONS DIRECTORY                    Page 2 of 3

Select one of the following features to customize your research session:

Search Features  (cont.)                              Current Setting
 9  Receive assistance from EZ ACCESS................No
10  Select a search method for EZ ACCESS.............Natural Language
11  Specify the action taken with your search result..Ask at sign off
12  Display Citations List when search completes......No

Offline Printing and Downloading Features             Current Setting
13  Choose a fax machine.............................Ask at sign off
14  Assign your print request destination............Ask at sign off
15  Gather and print chargeable time information......No
16  Assign your downloading format...................Standard
17  Assign your fax machine printing format..........Composed


If you wish to:
   Change a feature, type its number and press ENTER
   View a different page, type P followed by a number and press ENTER
   Obtain further information, type HELP and press ENTER
   Continue your research, press ENTER
```

Source: West Publishing Company © 1993

Figure 9.08. Options Directory in WESTLAW

speed the computer's processing of your search request, and minimize the vendors' online charges you incur.

For example, if you want to search in LEXIS for cases decided only by the Washington Court of Appeals, select the file for Washington Court of Appeals cases (APP) in the Washington library (WASH) rather than the file for all Washington cases (WASH) in the States library (STATES). Similarly, to search WESTLAW for articles published only in the *Georgetown Law Journal*, search in the *Georgetown Law Journal* database (GEOLJ) rather than in the texts and periodicals database (TP-ALL). Or, to search WESTLAW materials involving a specialized area, such as federal taxation, look for (and, if available, select) the database that covers just the specialized materials. For all federal tax materials, this would be the FTX-ALL database; otherwise, you will have to run your search in each database (*e.g.*, the databases for various federal courts, the *U.S. Code*, the *Code of Federal Regulations*) from which federal tax materials have been extracted to create FTX-ALL.

Step 4. Type and transmit your first search request. After you gain access to a LEXIS file or a WESTLAW database, the monitor will display a message indicating that you can type your search request. Figure 9.09 shows the appearance of the LEXIS monitor at this point. Figures 9.10 and 9.11 show

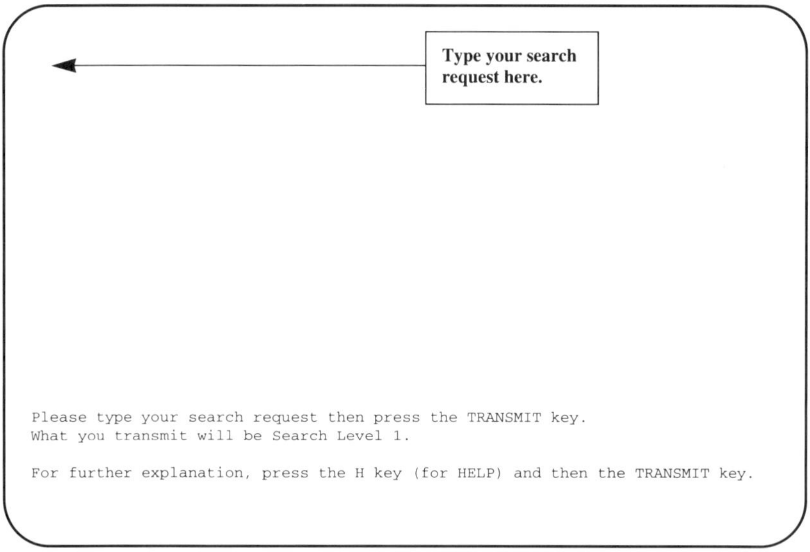

Source: Mead Data Central, Inc. © 1993

Figure 9.09. Search Request Entry Screen in LEXIS

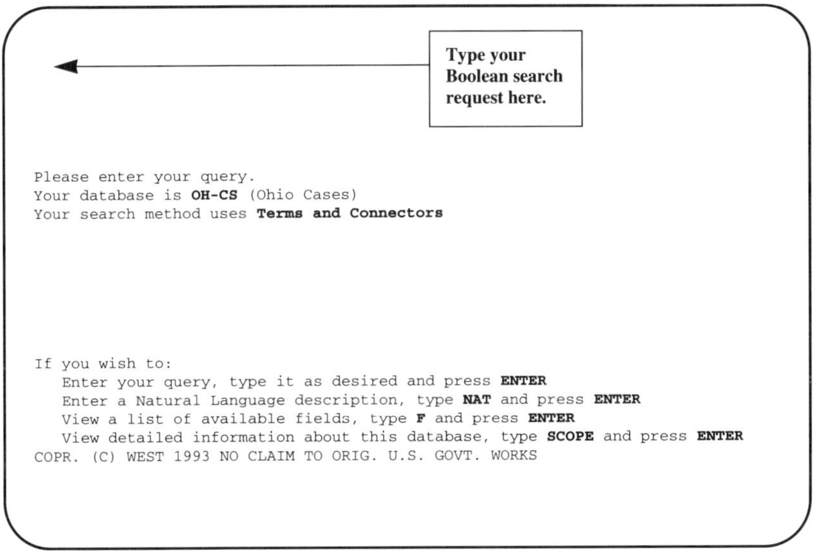

Source: West Publishing Company © 1993

Figure 9.10. Query Entry Screen for Boolean Searching in WESTLAW

the WESTLAW monitor's appearance, which will depend on whether you have selected Boolean logic (terms and connectors) or natural language as your search method.

The cursor will appear in the upper left corner of the LEXIS or WESTLAW monitor, a position referred to as the "home" position. That's where you begin typing your search request. When you type, you need not concern yourself with capitalization: the computer will automatically treat lower- and uppercase versions of a letter as equivalent. Do not, however, substitute letters (l, O) for numbers (1, 0), or vice versa: the computer will not treat these as interchangeable.

When you finish typing your search request, checking it carefully will help ensure that you have expressed your search instructions as you intended and that you have not made typographical errors. The LEXIS or WESTLAW computer will search for misspelled words as readily as for correctly spelled ones—but misspellings can result in bypassing potentially relevant documents and in incurring charges for the wasted search effort.

If you need to make a correction in your search request, use the cursor keys to move the cursor to the place at which you want to make the change. The cursor keys, also sometimes referred to as the "arrow" or "editing" keys, are located on the right side of the keyboard; each cursor key is marked with

Type your natural-language search request (also called a "description") here.

```
Please describe your issue.
Your database is OH-CS (Ohio Cases)
Your search method uses Natural Language.                Maximum Result:  100





If you wish to:
   Run a search, type your description as desired and press ENTER
   Add restrictions to your description, type RES and press ENTER
   Enter a Terms and Connectors query, type TC and press ENTER
   View detailed information about this database, type SCOPE and press ENTER
COPR. (C) WEST 1993 NO CLAIM TO ORIG. U.S. GOVT. WORKS
```

Source: West Publishing Company © 1993

Figure 9.11. Query Entry Screen for Natural-Language Searching in WESTLAW

a double arrowhead (») or an arrow to indicate the direction in which the key moves the cursor.

Once you have positioned the cursor where you want it, you can type corrections or other changes in your search request. In most respects, the LEXIS and WESTLAW keyboards respond the same way. If you want to delete text (whether a character or a space), you press the DEL CHAR or DELETE key once for each character or space you want to delete. If you want to replace existing text with new text, simply type the new text, which will automatically replace (or "overwrite") the old.

To insert new text without replacing the old text when you use a LEXIS 2000 keyboard, press the INSERT key, type your insertion, and then press the INSERT key again when you finish inserting the new text; on a LEXIS UBIQ keyboard, press the INS CHAR key once for each character or a space you want to insert, and then type the new text. On the WESTLAW keyboard, press the INSERT MODE key, type your insertion, and then press the INSERT MODE key again when you finish inserting the new text.

If you want to make a lot of changes or corrections, you might proceed more efficiently by erasing everything you have typed and starting over. To clear the screen in LEXIS, press the NEW SEARCH key on the LEXIS 2000 keyboard or press the CLEAR key on the UBIQ keyboard. To clear the screen in WESTLAW, press the CLEAR key on the WALT II keyboard; if you are using a WALT PC keyboard, place the cursor in the upper left corner of the monitor and press the F9 key.

Transmitting your search request. When you are ready to transmit your search request for processing, press the TRANSMIT key on a LEXIS keyboard or the ENTER key on the WESTLAW keyboard. In LEXIS, before pressing TRANSMIT, remember to place the cursor past the end of all the terms and connectors you want to include in your search request; in WESTLAW, it does not matter where the cursor is when you press ENTER.

After you transmit your search request, the monitor will redisplay the request, along with a message advising that the computer is carrying out the search. In WESTLAW, when the monitor redisplays a Boolean search request, some of the connectors might appear in a format different from what you typed. (Recall that some WESTLAW connectors can be expressed more than one way. See pages 44–51.) For example, if you typed `or` as a connector, you will now see it as a space between search terms in the redisplayed search request; similarly, `and` will redisplay as `&`.

While conducting a search, the LEXIS and WESTLAW computers only respond to certain commands:

- In LEXIS, you can cancel a search by pressing the STOP key (although this command will not work if you delay too long after the search has begun).
- In WESTLAW, you can cancel a search by typing `x` and pressing ENTER, or you can exit the WESTLAW service by typing `off` and pressing ENTER. If you transmitted a search request using terms and connectors rather than natural language, you can interrupt the search and see the results the computer has retrieved to that point: type `i` and press ENTER.

Step 5. View your search results. Once the computer has assembled the documents that satisfy a search request, the monitor will display (among other things) a message indicating the number of documents retrieved:

- In LEXIS, the number appears in a message specifically stating how many documents were retrieved. See Figure 11.01 on page 319.
- In WESTLAW, the number appears at the top of the monitor as the second number under the heading "Rank." See Figure 11.15 on page 348.

Knowing the number of documents retrieved can help you make a preliminary determination whether your search has swept too broadly or too narrowly. But before deciding whether or how to modify your search request, skim several retrieved documents to see whether you have located the kinds of documents you want; the context in which your search terms appear in a document can suggest ways to modify your search request.

In both LEXIS and WESTLAW, you can choose various formats for displaying your search results on the monitor. You can opt to view as little as simply the citations of the documents, or selected parts of the documents (such as places your search terms appear), or as much as the full text of documents. Chapter 11, "Using Computers in Reading the Law," explains the procedures for viewing search results.

Step 6. If necessary, modify your search. After you evaluate your search results, make any necessary modifications to your search. A modification can consist of such changes as adding, deleting, or substituting search terms, connectors, or field restrictions. Or you can start over with a new request, or switch to a different LEXIS file or WESTLAW database and transmit the same request or a modified version. See Chapter 8.

Step 7. Update your search results. Just as with your research in books, you need to make sure that any relevant authorities the computer locates are still valid law. LEXIS and WESTLAW both provide several updating capabilities, including these:

- Both services offer online versions of *Shepard's Citations* for updating certain kinds of authorities.
- Both services (through "Auto-Cite" in LEXIS and "Insta-Cite" in WESTLAW) also allow you to retrieve a list of prior and subsequent proceedings that occurred as the case you are updating progressed through the courts. Frequently, this list will also include citations to cases that have commented critically on the case you are updating.
- Both services allow you to update any kind of authority—whether primary (*e.g.*, case, statute) or secondary (*e.g.*, treatise, law review article)—by instructing the computer to search the text of documents in the database for references to the authority in whose current status you are interested.

Chapter 12, "Using Computers in Updating the Law," explains these three principal procedures (as well as some others) for online updating of your search results.

Step 8. Continue to modify your search request, and to view and update the results. As with book-based research, computer-assisted searching repeatedly cycles through finding, reading, and updating the law. After transmitting an initial search request, you review the documents retrieved and decide whether to transmit a modified search request or to check the current validity of any relevant documents found by the initial request. You continue to modify your search request as necessary and to view and update the results until you decide to terminate your online search session.

Step 9. Keep a record of your work. At each point in your online searching, it helps to keep track of significant aspects of your work, including the search requests you transmit, the files or databases you search, and the results you obtain. You can keep this record by:

- taking notes (see Chapter 14 for tips on using the computer as a note-taking aid)
- producing a computer printout or requesting one from the CALR vendors (see pages 340–46 and 371–79)
- downloading information to your computer if you are using a personal computer with a storage device like a floppy or hard disk (see pages 346–47 and 379–82)

Step 10. Log off. When you have finished searching online, you log off the CALR service. Logging off terminates the communications link between your terminal and the CALR vendor's computer, and stops the vendor's online charges from running. Whenever you want to log off:

- Press the key labelled SIGN OFF to log off LEXIS.
- Type `off` and press ENTER to log off WESTLAW.

In both services, the monitor will then display instructions guiding you through the rest of the procedure for logging off.

Saving your results. One of the instructions you see when you log off LEXIS or WESTLAW offers you the option of saving, for a designated period, the results of your most recent search request. If you choose to retain your results, and if you log back onto the service before the designated period expires, you can either resume your search where you left off or start a new search. The option of resuming a search session with the results of a previous search does not apply to certain kinds of online activities.

Elapsed time. As part of logging off, the monitor displays the amount of time spent online during the search session. LEXIS and WESTLAW calculate their charges differently and base them on varying factors, such as the amount of time spent online, the number of searches performed, and the number of files or databases searched. Nonetheless, the CALR vendors' charges for online searches roughly correlate with the amount of time spent online, so the information about elapsed online time will help you gauge the charges incurred during a search session.

Especially in the beginning, you might be surprised how quickly online time—and charges—accrue. Consequently, you should periodically review the rates for searching whatever CALR services you use. Generally, you can safely assume that your search session will cost no less than $2.00 to $3.00 per minute, and most likely will cost more.

Summary

The following list summarizes the steps you can take during a basic search session on LEXIS or WESTLAW:

1. Formulate and write out your search request. Familiarize yourself with the available LEXIS files and WESTLAW databases, and decide which ones you want to search.
2. Log on to the CALR service.
3. Gain access to the LEXIS file or WESTLAW database in which you want to begin your search.
4. Type and transmit your first search request.
5. View your search results.
6. If necessary, modify your search.
7. Update your search results.
8. Continue to modify your search request and to view and update the results as you feel necessary.
9. Keep a record of the search requests you transmit, the files or databases you search, and the results you obtain. Take notes, and consider whether to generate a computer printout or download information to your computer.
10. Log off.

Not every online session will involve each of these steps; you might not use a computer in each phase (finding the law, reading the law, and updating the law) of your research project. Also, as later chapters will explain, some of the things you can do in LEXIS and WESTLAW do not require you to first gain access to a file or database.

Now, to go online . . .

Having prepared for online searching, the next step is to actually use LEXIS or WESTLAW in finding, reading, or updating the law. Part III explains how to do that.

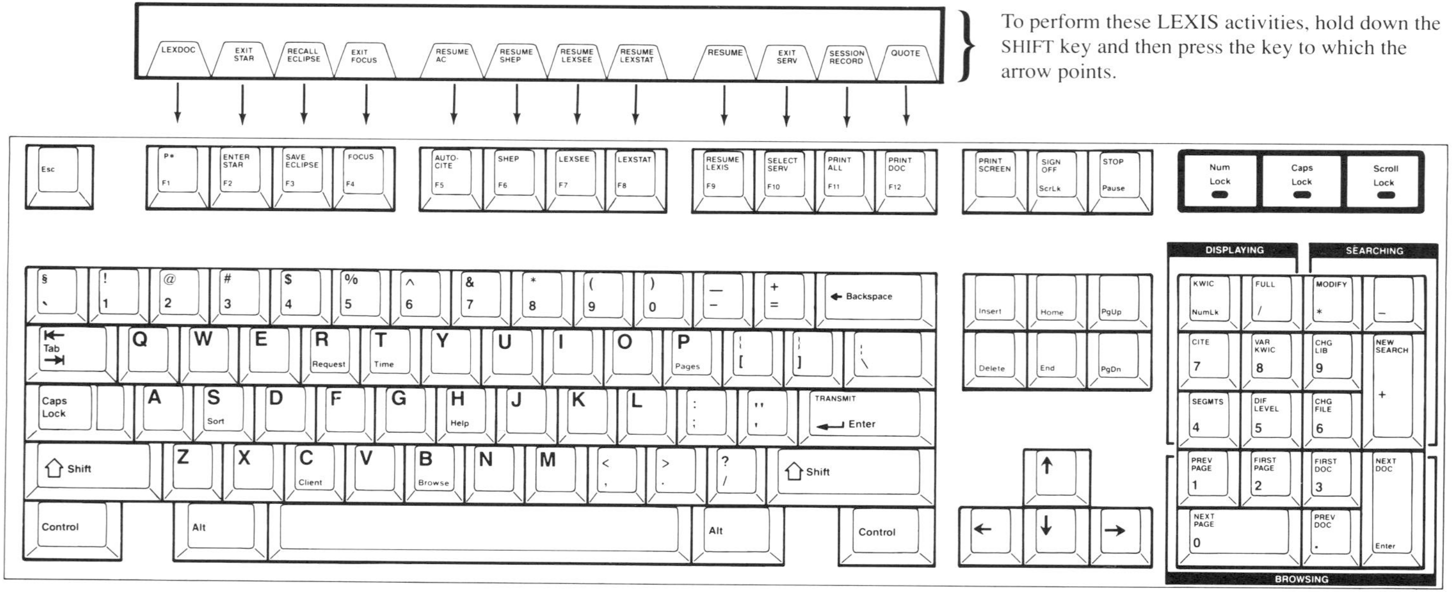

Source: Mead Data Central, Inc.

Figure 9.12. Keyboard for the LEXIS 2000 Terminal, an IBM-Compatible Personal Computer Available from Mead Data Central for Use with LEXIS

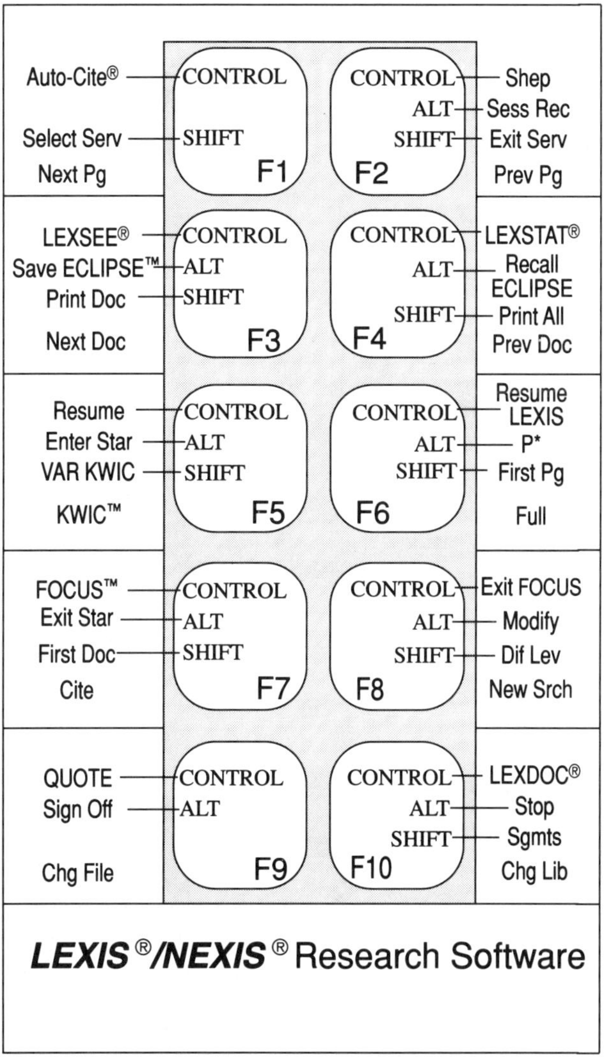

To carry out some activities, you press a function key by itself. For example, you press F1 by itself to move to the next page in a document. To carry out other activities, you hold down the SHIFT, ALT, or CONTROL key and then press a function key. For example, you press CONTROL and F1 to invoke Auto-Cite.

This template accompanies version 2.7 of the LEXIS/NEXIS Technology Series Research Software for MS-DOS.

Source: Adapted from template created by Mead Data Central, Inc.

Figure 9.13. LEXIS Function Key Template for Keyboards on IBM-Compatible Personal Computers

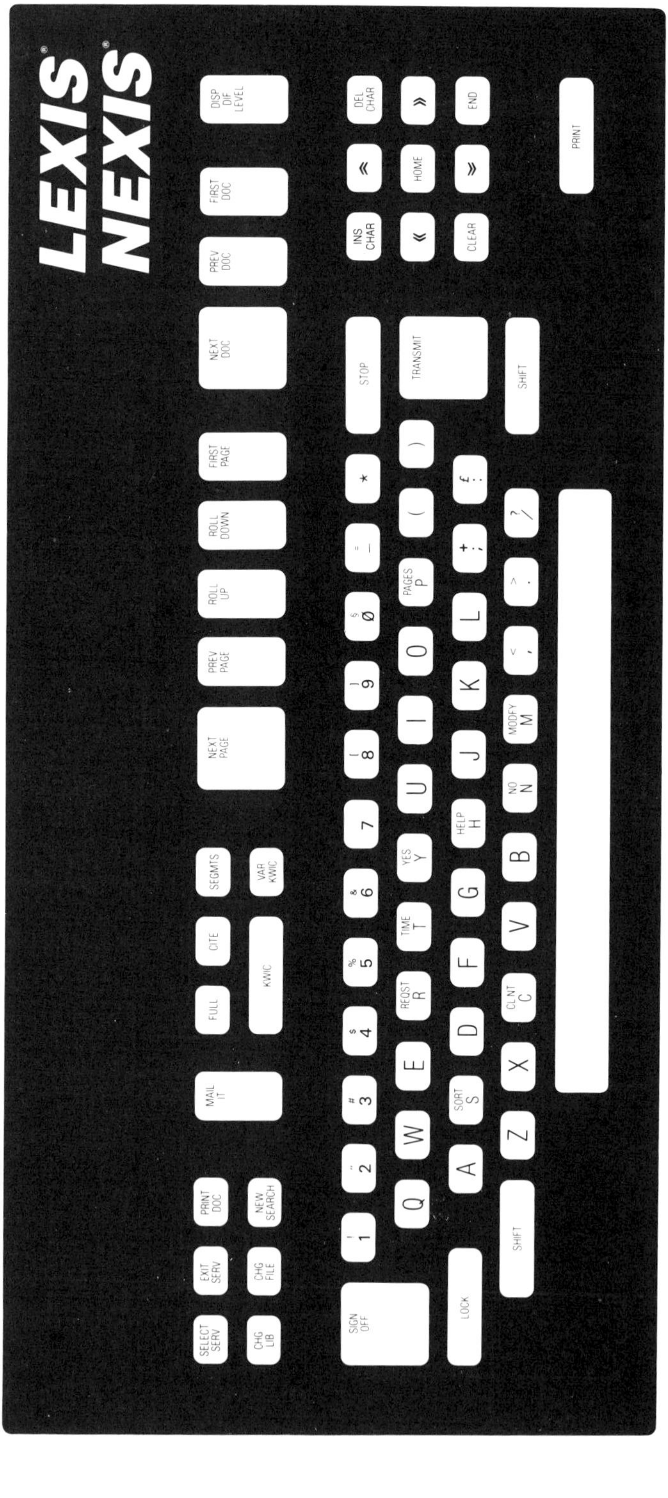

Source: Mead Data Central, Inc.

Figure 9.14. Keyboard for the LEXIS UBIQ, Mead Data Central's Early Dedicated Terminal

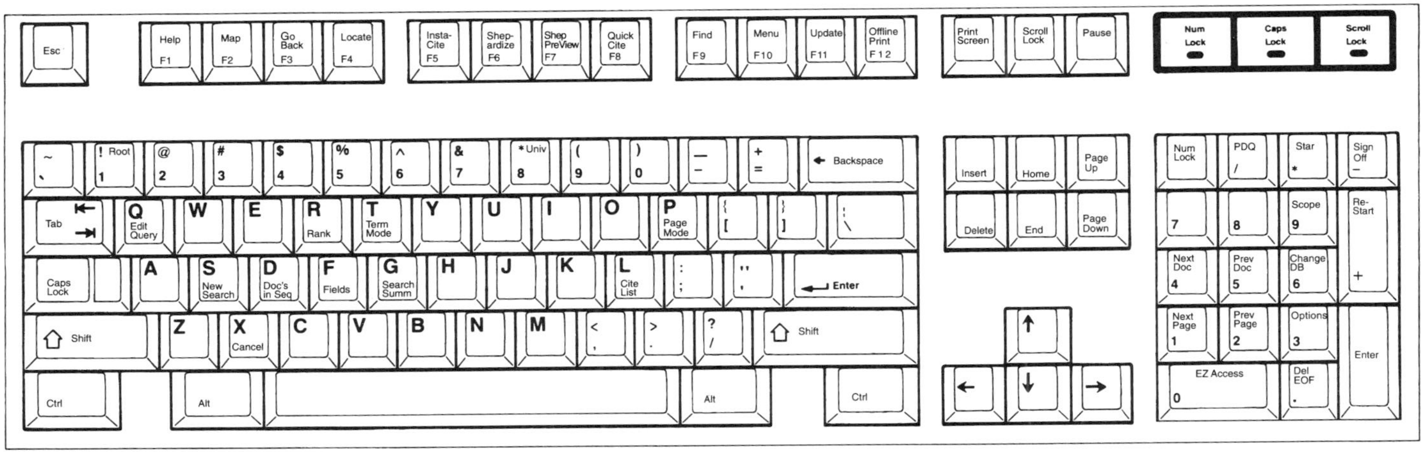

Figure 9.15. Keyboard for the WALT PC Terminal, an IBM-Compatible Personal Computer Available from West Publishing Company for Use with WESTLAW

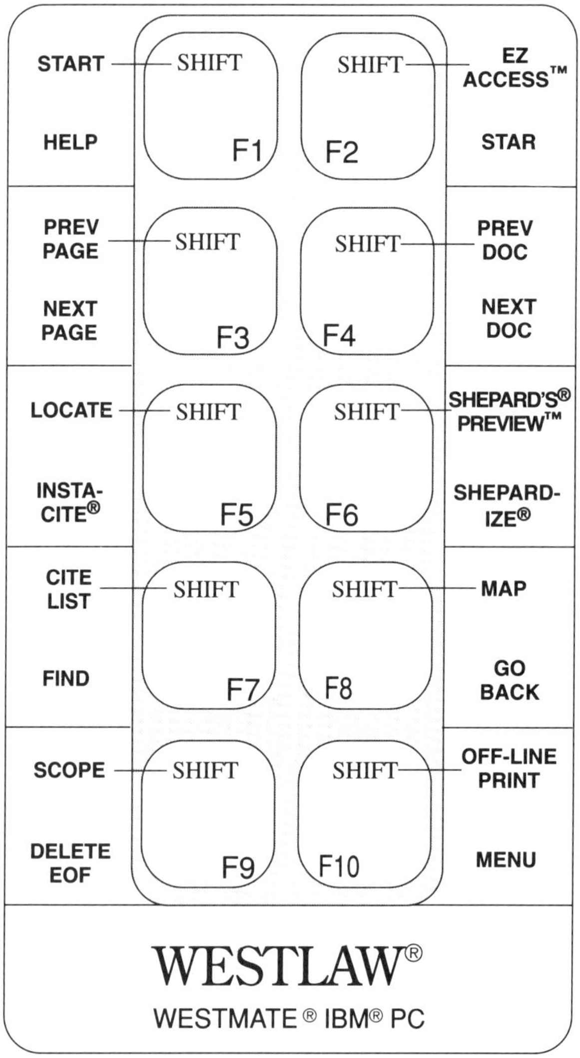

To carry out some activities, you press a function key by itself. For example, you press F3 by itself to move to the next page in a document. To carry out other activities, you hold down the SHIFT key and then press a function key. For example, you press SHIFT and F3 to move to the previous page in a document.

This template accompanies version 4.5 of the WESTMATE Communications Software for the IBM PS/2, IBM PC and Compatibles.

Source: Adapted from template created by West Publishing Company

Figure 9.16. WESTLAW Function Key Template for Keyboards on IBM-Compatible Personal Computers

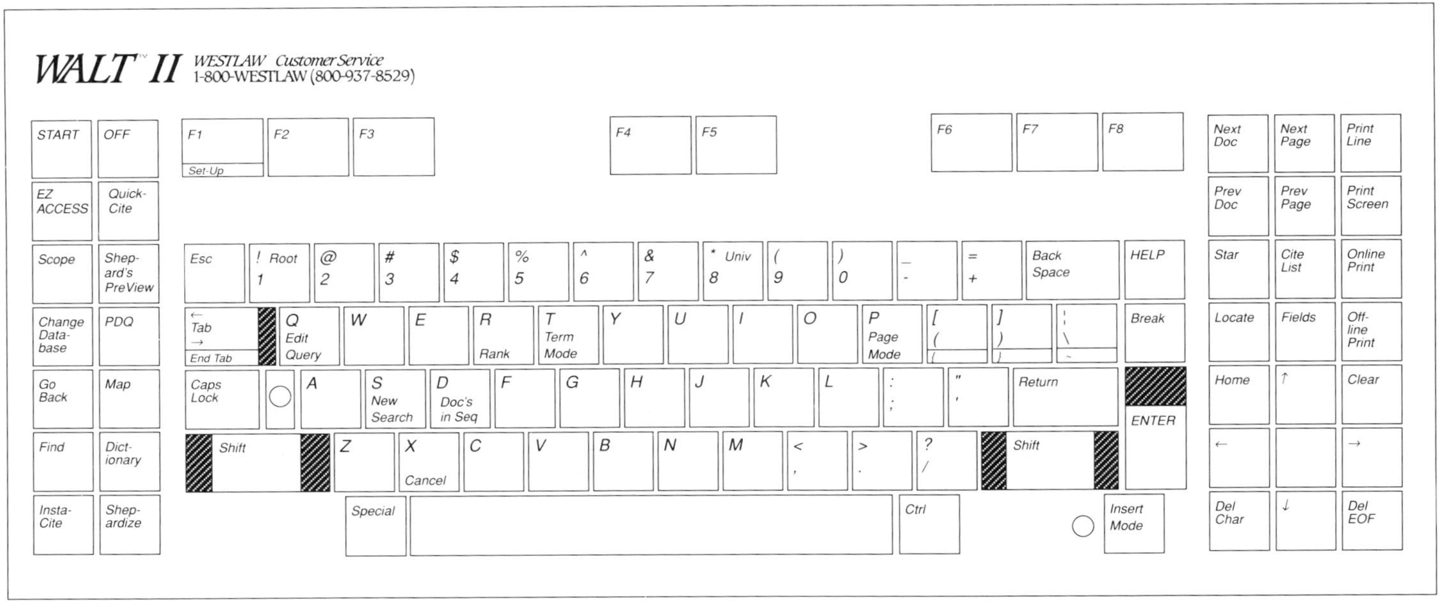

Source: West Publishing Company

Figure 9.17. Keyboard for WALT II, the Dedicated Terminal Used with WESTLAW

Boolean Search Request Planning Worksheet

LEXIS
Customer Service: 1-800-543-6862
Telecommunications for the deaf: 1-800-732-5306

WESTLAW
Customer service: 1-800-937-8529
Telecommunications for the deaf: 1-800-333-4656
Reference attorneys: 1-800-REF-ATTY (1-800-733-2889)
1-800-688-6363

Date ____________

Client I.D. ____________

Research session I.D. ____________

Your name ____________

Procedure:

1. At the top of the chart below, write out your issue and describe the concepts it involves. (See pages 149–53.)
2. Decide what type of document (*e.g.*, case, statute) you want to search, and in what jurisdiction. Then identify appropriate LEXIS libraries and files, or appropriate WESTLAW databases: ____________

   ____
3. In the chart below, write out potential search terms reflecting the concepts in your problem. Keep in mind variant forms (hyphens, irregular plurals, root expanders, universal characters, etc.); noise, stop, and reserved words; ambiguity and other language problems; and characteristics of documents to be searched. (See pages 152–57.)
4. Consider whether to include any field restrictions. (See Chapter 5.)
5. Link desired search terms with connectors. Use the "or" connector to link terms corresponding to a single concept. Use "and" or an "and"-type connector to link conceptual groupings. (See pages 158–62.) Write out the resulting search request:

   ____

   ____

   ____

   ____

   ____
6. Decide whether to transmit your entire search request in one step, or whether to transmit the request in stages—that is, in "levels" in LEXIS, or in component parts in WESTLAW. (See pages 167–72, 174 n.127, and 180–81.)
7. Log on, and begin your search.

Issue: ____________________

Concept (describe)		**Concept** (describe)		**Concept** (describe)	
Search terms (including synonyms and analogous terms)	**Variant forms** (root expanders, abbreviations, etc.)	**Search terms** (including synonyms and analogous terms)	**Variant forms** (root expanders, abbreviations, etc.)	**Search terms** (including synonyms and analogous terms)	**Variant forms** (root expanders, abbreviations, etc.)

Figure 9.18. Boolean Search Request Planning Worksheet (See also Figure 9.19.)

Boolean Search Request Planning Worksheet

LEXIS
Customer Service: 1-800-543-6862
Telecommunications for the deaf: 1-800-732-5306

WESTLAW
Customer service: 1-800-937-8529
Telecommunications for the deaf: 1-800-333-4656
Reference attorneys: 1-800-REF-ATTY (1-800-733-2889)
1-800-688-6363

Date ____________________

Client I.D. ____________________

Research session I.D. ____________________

Your name ____________________

Procedure:

1. At the top of the chart below, write out your issue and describe the concepts it involves. (See pages 149–53.)

2. Decide what type of document (*e.g.*, case, statute) you want to search, and in what jurisdiction. Then identify appropriate LEXIS libraries and files, or appropriate WESTLAW databases: OHIO library, CASES file (LEXIS); OH-CS (WESTLAW)

3. In the chart below, write out potential search terms reflecting the concepts in your problem. Keep in mind variant forms (hyphens, irregular plurals, root expanders, universal characters, etc.); noise, stop, and reserved words; ambiguity and other language problems; and characteristics of documents to be searched. (See pages 152–57.)

4. Consider whether to include any field restrictions. (See Chapter 5.)

5. Link desired search terms with connectors. Use the "or" connector to link terms corresponding to a single concept. Use "and" or an "and"-type connector to link conceptual groupings. (See pages 158–62.) Write out the resulting search request:
(apartment or "rooming house")
w/10 lease! and
(water or plumbing)

6. Decide whether to transmit your entire search request in one step, or whether to transmit the request in stages—that is, in "levels" in LEXIS, or in component parts in WESTLAW. (See pages 167–72, 174 n.127, and 180–81.)

7. Log on, and begin your search.

Issue: Does a landlord have a legal obligation to provide running water to a tenant who leases an apartment?

Concept (describe)		**Concept** (describe)		**Concept** (describe)	
place of habitation		lease between a tenant and a landlord		condition affecting habitability	
Search terms (including synonyms and analogous terms)	**Variant forms** (root expanders, abbreviations, etc.)	**Search terms** (including synonyms and analogous terms)	**Variant forms** (root expanders, abbreviations, etc.)	**Search terms** (including synonyms and analogous terms)	**Variant forms** (root expanders, abbreviations, etc.)
apartment		lease	lease!	plumbing	
dwelling		contract		water	
roominghouse	"rooming house"	rental	rent!	heat	
		agreement	agree!	light	
		tenant		electricity	electric!
		lessee			
		landlord			
		lessor			

Figure 9.19. Completed Boolean Search Request Planning Worksheet (See also Figure 9.18.)

PART III

Conducting Online Searches

Part III explains the ways you can use LEXIS, WESTLAW, or nonlegal databases in legal research:

- using computers in finding the law (Chapter 10)
- using computers in reading the law (Chapter 11)
- using computers in updating the law (Chapter 12)
- incorporating nonlegal databases into computer-assisted legal research (Chapter 13)

CHAPTER 10

Using Computers in Finding the Law

Introduction. Whether you use books or computers, the approaches for finding relevant authorities remain the same.[134] The principal approaches are:

- descriptive word or fact word approach
- known authority approach
- known topic approach

Each law-finding approach, whether you use it in book-based research or online searching, offers certain advantages. The approach that will work best will depend on the particular matter being researched, as well as on how much or how little you know about the subject you are researching.

Of course, even though you use the same approaches to find law online as you do to find law in books, when you work online, you need to adapt your law-finding approaches to accommodate the characteristics of computers and of database searching. First, the mechanics of gaining access to sources in a database obviously differ from the mechanics of gaining access to sources in books.

Second, you won't have access online to all the sources you might find in a book-filled law library. For instance, at this time, LEXIS and WESTLAW do not include all state cases, have relatively few state administrative regulations, and do not have either of the leading legal encyclopedias (*Corpus Juris Secundum* and *American Jurisprudence 2d*) or many of the treatises and other

[134] See Chapter 4 of CHRISTOPHER G. WREN & JILL R. WREN, THE LEGAL RESEARCH MANUAL: A GAME PLAN FOR LEGAL RESEARCH AND ANALYSIS (2d ed. 1986). In addition, whether you search in books or in a database, your research goal remains the same: to find mandatory primary authorities or, if none exist or if you want to supplement your research, to find persuasive primary authorities or secondary authorities. *Id.* at 41.

secondary authorities used in book-based research. Consequently, you need to review frequently the scope of coverage of the CALR services you use and to supplement your online search with book-based research, especially if the database lacks some of the sources in which you are interested.

This chapter explains the three principal law-finding approaches (along with a few other available ones) as they apply online. The first part of the chapter shows how to use these approaches in LEXIS; the second part of the chapter shows their use in WESTLAW. Throughout, the discussion notes when online searching offers research capabilities not readily available without a computer.

Summary. A summary of using LEXIS and WESTLAW in finding the law appears at the end of the chapter (pages 312–16).

Finding the Law through LEXIS

Descriptive word or fact word approach in LEXIS

Unless you already know the citation of a case, statute, or other authority that bears on your research problem, you will generally find the descriptive or fact word approach the most fruitful way to start finding relevant primary authorities.[135] If you have followed the procedures for developing your facts and issues and for formulating search requests (see Chapter 7), this approach should follow naturally.

The idea here is to take the words (called "descriptive words" or "fact words") you selected to describe key aspects of your research problem, and use them as the search terms in your search request. For example, returning to the hypothetical landlord-tenant problem on pages 19–20, involving a lack of running water in an apartment, your analysis of the problem might lead you to select and arrange terms in a search request like this:

```
(tenant or landlord or lease!) and (apartment
or roominghouse or "rooming house") and (water
or plumbing)
```

This online law-finding technique corresponds to the book-based legal research approach in which you look up descriptive or fact words in an index.[136]

After constructing your search request, you transmit it in an appropriate LEXIS file. In response to the search request, the computer will retrieve documents containing your descriptive or fact words in the relationship prescribed

[135] If you already know of a relevant authority, the "known authority" approach (see pages 237–51) offers a good starting point.

[136] *See* CHRISTOPHER G. WREN & JILL R. WREN, THE LEGAL RESEARCH MANUAL: A GAME PLAN FOR LEGAL RESEARCH AND ANALYSIS 46–51 (2d ed. 1986).

by your request. The kind of documents you retrieve will depend on where you transmit your search request:

- *Cases.* In a file of cases, a document will consist of the court's opinion, along with any concurring or dissenting opinions.
- *Statutes.* In a file of *unannotated* statutes, a document will consist of a statutory section, its subsections, and (sometimes) cross-references to other research sources (*e.g.*, related statutes, session laws, or administrative regulations; notes about the statute's history). The document might also include references to selected secondary sources, such as law review articles, *American Jurisprudence 2d*, or annotation articles in *American Law Reports Annotated.*

  In a file of *annotated* statutes, a document will also include annotations accompanying each statutory section retrieved (*i.e.*, brief summaries of cases and attorney general opinions that have interpreted and applied the statute). The document might also include references to selected secondary sources, such as texts and law review articles.

  Note that the statutes for a jurisdiction usually include that jurisdiction's constitution and court rules (such as rules of evidence or civil procedure). Consequently, in certain statutory files, a document can also consist of a constitutional provision or a court rule.
- *Administrative regulations.* In a file consisting of an administrative code (*i.e.*, administrative regulations arranged by subject matter), a document will consist of an administrative regulation and its subsections. In addition, a document will likely contain cross-references to the corresponding administrative register (*i.e.*, the chronological arrangement of regulations) and to statutes authorizing the regulation.

  In a file consisting of an administrative register, a document will consist of an administrative regulation and its subsections, a proposed regulation, a notice of an administrative agency meeting or hearing, or an announcement of other agency activity. A document might also include related information, such as cross-references to sections of the administrative code the document affects, or the name of a person to contact at the agency that issued the document.

As you conduct descriptive or fact word searches for authorities in LEXIS, the tips provided from here to page 237 can help you search more effectively and efficiently.

Tips for descriptive or fact word searching in LEXIS: refining searches in annotated statutes. When you search for statutes by using the descriptive or fact word approach in a file of annotated statutes, you might retrieve irrelevant statutes because your search terms appear in accompanying annotations. If you encounter this problem, add a field restriction confining your search to the segment containing just the statutory text.

Tips for descriptive or fact word searching in LEXIS: where to find constitutions. To conduct a descriptive or fact word search for constitutional provisions, you can follow either of two routes:

- You can search in a file consisting of just constitutional provisions.
- You can search in files that combine statutory-type documents (*e.g.*, statutes, session laws, constitutional provisions). In this kind of file, you extract the constitutional provisions by adding a field restriction to your search request.

In LEXIS, the United States Constitution appears in the USCNST file in the GENFED library. Similarly, each state's library includes a file (named CONST) consisting of that state's constitution. These files provide direct access to constitutional provisions when you perform descriptive or fact word searches.

Constitutional provisions also appear in LEXIS files combining various statutory-type documents. For example, the United States Constitution also appears in the USCODE file in the GENFED and CODES libraries, and Tennessee constitutional provisions also appear in the TNCODE file in the STATES, CODES, and TENN libraries.

When you perform a descriptive or fact word search for constitutional provisions in a LEXIS file containing a variety of statutory-type documents, you isolate the constitutional provisions by using a field-restricted search based on the "cite" segment, which contains citation information about each document. In a combined statutory file, a constitutional provision's citation appears with the abbreviation "Const" in the "cite" segment. Consequently, when you search a combined statutory file, the field restriction in the following example will confine your search to constitutional provisions (here, provisions mainly concerning freedom of speech):

```
speech and cite(const)
```

Tips for descriptive or fact word searching in LEXIS: where to find court rules. At the federal level and for some states, to locate court rules (*e.g.*, rules of evidence, rules of civil and criminal procedure) through a descriptive or fact word search, you have the option of searching in LEXIS files consisting exclusively of court rules. To perform a descriptive or fact word search for the court rules of some states, though, you must search in LEXIS files consisting of statutory codes (which contain the rules).

LEXIS makes federal court rules available as part of the federal statutory code, *i.e.*, in the online versions of *United States Code*:

- The USCODE file in the GENFED and CODES libraries contains federal court rules.
- The USCS file in the GENFED library contains the Federal Rules of Evidence.

Federal court rules also appear in LEXIS files separate from the statutory code files:

- The RULES file in the GENFED library combines all the files for federal court rules.
- Other files in the GENFED library isolate specific sets of federal court rules. For example, the FRCP file contains civil procedure rules, the FRE file contains evidence rules, and the SUPRUL file contains the rules for the United States Supreme Court.

At the state level, you can find the court rules for some states in a LEXIS file consisting of just the state's court rules. For other states, you can find the court rules only as part of the state's statutory code.

When you search for court rules in a statutory code file, you isolate the rules by using a field restriction based on citation information. For example, to locate rules of evidence governing hearsay, you can try searching in a LEXIS state statutory code file with a request like this:

```
hearsay and heading(evidence)
```

However, states use different names for comparable court rules (*e.g.*, "Rules of Civil Procedure," "Code of Procedure"), so you will need to experiment to find the right combination of search terms and field restrictions to segregate particular kinds of court rules in a given state.

Tips for descriptive or fact word searching in LEXIS: where to find administrative regulations. To locate federal administrative regulations through a descriptive or fact word search in LEXIS, you search in a file consisting of material from the *Code of Federal Regulations* or from the *Federal Register*, or in a file consisting of material from both publications. You will find federal administrative regulations in several places in LEXIS:

- The CFR file in either the GENFED library or the CODES library contains the current edition of the *Code of Federal Regulations*.
- The FEDREG file in either the GENFED library or the CODES library contains the *Federal Register*.

- For the *Code of Federal Regulations*, the GENFED library also includes separate files (*e.g.*, CFR87, CFR86, CFR85) containing previous years' versions of the code.
- The ALLCFR file in the GENFED library permits simultaneous searching through all previous years' versions of the *Code of Federal Regulations*, except for the version immediately preceding the current year's version.
- The ALLREG file in either the GENFED library or the CODES library allows you to search in one pass through the *Federal Register* and the *Code of Federal Regulations*.
- Files in many of the LEXIS libraries covering specialized topics contain federal administrative regulations. For example, the CFR file in the federal communications library (FEDCOM) consists of federal regulations governing telecommunications. Similarly, the CFR file in the environmental law library (ENVIRN) contains federal regulations related to environmental matters.

At the state level, LEXIS currently provides few administrative codes or registers. Mead Data will undoubtedly add more state administrative regulations to LEXIS, and checking Mead Data's descriptions of LEXIS materials will alert you to new additions. To determine whether a state's administrative regulations are online in LEXIS, check the file menu for a particular state library, for the CODES library, or for the STATES library. Also check the coverage of specialized libraries and files in LEXIS: libraries and files in areas such as state taxation or state securities regulation sometimes include state administrative materials.

Until more state administrative codes and registers appear in LEXIS, you will generally need to take an indirect route when using descriptive or fact words in LEXIS to find state administrative regulations relevant to your problem. If the state administrative regulations you want are not in LEXIS, online statutes might provide leads in the form of cross-references to state administrative regulations interpreting or implementing the statutes. For example, the "notes" segment or "references" segment in annotated statutes in LEXIS sometimes includes citations to related state administrative regulations.

Even if searching a file of state statutes does not turn up references to specific regulations, your search might uncover relevant statutes that authorize administrative agencies to formulate, issue, and enforce regulations implementing statutory objectives. If so, you can log off LEXIS and check the printed version of the appropriate administrative code or register.

Finally, you might find research leads by searching in a file containing an online version of a relevant looseleaf publication addressing a specialized area of law where regulations play an important role. Check, for example, LEXIS files containing publications of the Bureau of National Affairs (BNA) or Commerce Clearing House (CCH).

Tips for descriptive or fact word searching in LEXIS: simultaneously searching all online jurisdictions. In addition to allowing you to conduct descriptive or fact word searches in the authorities of a single jurisdiction, LEXIS offers you the ability to search simultaneously the authorities of multiple jurisdictions. For example, in one pass, you could search all the online cases from every state for any decisions dealing with the admissibility of videotaped depositions of child witnesses in criminal trials. (This kind of search presents an online variation of looking for state cases in *Decennial Digests* and *General Digests* in book-based legal research, although when performed online, the technique avoids the need to check multiple, non-cumulative volumes.)[137] Or you could, say, simultaneously search all the online state statutes for provisions concerning drunk driving.

LEXIS provides numerous multi-jurisdictional files that afford this capability for comparative law research. The following paragraphs highlight some of the files most commonly used for multi-jurisdictional searching. As you familiarize yourself with the contents of LEXIS, you will discover other multi-jurisdictional files.

- *Cases.* The OMNI and COURTS files in the STATES library include cases from all states, the OMNI and COURTS files in the GENFED library include cases from all federal courts, and the MEGA file in the GENFED and STATES libraries combines all online federal and state cases in a single file. In the GENFED library, LEXIS also provides the USAPP file for cases from all United States Courts of Appeals and the DIST file for cases from all United States District Courts.
- *Statutes.* For simultaneously searching all online state statutes, LEXIS provides the ALLCDE file, available in the CODES library and in the STATES library.
- *Constitutions.* Although LEXIS currently does not offer a multiple-jurisdiction file consisting only of constitutions, you can search simultaneously for comparable provisions in all state constitutions that are online. To do so, select the ALLCDE file in either the CODES or STATES library; then focus the search on constitutional provisions by using the `cite(const)` restriction, as explained on page 224.
- *Court rules.* Although LEXIS currently does not offer a multiple-jurisdiction file consisting only of state court rules, you can search

[137] *See* CHRISTOPHER G. WREN & JILL R. WREN, THE LEGAL RESEARCH MANUAL: A GAME PLAN FOR LEGAL RESEARCH AND ANALYSIS 15 (2d ed. 1986).

simultaneously for comparable court rules from all states with statutes online. To do so, select the ALLCDE file in either the CODES or STATES library; then isolate court rules by adding an appropriate field restriction to your search request, as explained on page 225.

- *Administrative regulations.* At this time, LEXIS offers few state administrative regulations, and the option of simultaneously searching regulations from all states is not available. Mead Data will undoubtedly add more state administrative regulations to LEXIS, however. When that happens, you will likely be able to conduct multi-jurisdictional searches for these materials, probably in much the same way you now can for state statutes.

Tips for descriptive or fact word searching in LEXIS: simultaneously searching in a customized selection of jurisdictions. You are not limited to the extremes of searching either in a single jurisdiction or in every jurisdiction LEXIS includes in a multi-jurisdictional file. You can also customize your selection of jurisdictions in which to search. The following paragraphs summarize the techniques for customizing multi-jurisdictional searches in LEXIS, and highlight some of the files most commonly used for this kind of searching.

- *Cases.* You can customize your selection of jurisdictions in one of two ways. First (as explained on page 196), at the file menu for a LEXIS library, you have the option of designating more than one state case-law file in which to conduct your search. For instance, if you wanted to search simultaneously for cases from Texas, Montana, and Washington, you could designate the case-law file from each of these states when you transmit your file selection at the file menu for the STATES library. Likewise, at the file menu for the GENFED library, you could designate case-law files for specific federal appellate circuits (*e.g.*, the Courts of Appeals for the Second Circuit, the Fifth Circuit, and the Ninth Circuit).

  Second, you can use the "court" segment (which identifies the jurisdiction in which the case was decided) as a restriction when you search in a multi-jurisdictional file. For instance, in the OMNI file (which contains cases from all states) in the STATES library, you can use the "court" segment to designate the states in which you want to search. So, for example, suppose you wanted to find cases from Texas, Montana, and Washington (rather than from every state) dealing with whether videotaped testimony in a criminal trial deprives a defendant of the right to confront adverse witnesses. You could use the following search request in the OMNI file:

```
court(texas or montana or washington)
and (videotap! w/20 confront!)
```

Similarly, in the file for all federal courts of appeals cases (USAPP) in the GENFED library, you can use a court restriction to specify which federal appellate circuits you want to search. Your search request would take this form:

```
court(5th or 6th or 9th) and
(videotap! w/20 confront!)
```

- *Statutes*. You can use either of two ways to customize your selection of state statutes in which to search. First (as explained on page 196), at the file menu for the CODES or STATES library, you have the option of designating more than one state statutory code file in which to conduct your search. For instance, if you wanted to search simultaneously the statutes of Connecticut, Delaware, and Maryland, you could designate the statutory code file from each of these states when you transmit your file selection at the file menu for the CODES or STATES library.

  Second, you can use a "cite" restriction when you search in the LEXIS file containing all online state statutes (ALLCDE) in the CODES or STATES library. Because the "cite" segment for a statutory provision contains the name of the state (either in full or abbreviated form), a "cite" restriction can isolate statutory provisions from each state you want. For example, say you wanted to search simultaneously for statutes from Connecticut, Delaware, and Florida concerning the use of blood or breath alcohol levels to prove an automobile driver's intoxication. You could use the following search request in the ALLCDE file to confine your search to the statutes from just the desired states:

  ```
  cite(connecticut or delaware or florida)
  and ((blood or breath) w/5 alcohol)
  ```

  For some states, you can use either the full name or an abbreviation for the state in the "cite" restriction; for other states, you must use a specific abbreviation.[138]

[138] In the "cite" segment, the LEXIS computer usually allows you to identify a state by using either its full name or an abbreviation. In other instances, however, the computer currently will not treat an abbreviation and the state's full name as interchangeable; instead, you must use an abbreviation, which might differ from the standard one that operates as an equivalency elsewhere in LEXIS. (See Appendix E for the standard LEXIS equivalencies.) For example, "my" is the standard LEXIS equivalency for Maryland, but you have to use "md" or "md." in a "cite" restric-

- *Constitutions.* If you want to find constitutional provisions from just selected states, you can use one of two techniques. First, you can select either the CODES or STATES library, and (as explained on page 196) select the statutory code files for each jurisdiction you want to search. For instance, if you wanted to search simultaneously the constitutional provisions of Minnesota, Iowa, and Nebraska, you could designate the statutory code files from each of these states when you transmit your file selection at the file menu for the CODES or STATES library. Then, because the "cite" segment for a constitutional provision includes the abbreviation "Const," you could use the restriction `cite(const)` in your search request to isolate constitutional provisions found in the statutory codes of the states you selected. For example, the following search request would locate constitutional provisions on free speech:

```
speech and cite(const)
```

As a second technique, you can search in the ALLCDE file (which contains all online state statutes) in the CODES or STATES library, again using the "cite" segment as a restriction. Because the "cite" segment for a constitutional provision contains the name of the state (either in full or abbreviated form) in addition to the abbreviation "Const," a "cite" restriction can isolate constitutional provisions found in the statutory codes of each state you want.

---

tion. Other quirks exist as well: for instance, the computer at this time will accept "s.d." but not "sd" as an abbreviation for South Dakota in the "cite" segment, although "ny" and "n.y." function equally well as abbreviations for New York.

To minimize retrieval errors when you use a state identification in the statutory "cite" segment, be sure you know the appropriate identifications for the states you want to search. The online GUIDE file for a state's statutory code normally indicates the state abbreviation that appears in the "cite" segment in that state's statutes. (For an explanation of GUIDE, see Appendix A.) Because the identification systems sometimes change, ask a LEXIS customer service representative if you encounter unexpected search results. At this writing, in a statutory "cite" restriction, you can use the full name of the state for every state except the following, for which you should use only these abbreviations:

Arizona	a.r.s.	Massachusetts	mass *or* mass.	Oklahoma	okl *or* okl.
Colorado	c.r.s.	Michigan	mcl	Oregon	ors
District of Columbia	d.c.	Mississippi	miss *or* miss.	Puerto Rico	l.p.r.a.
Georgia	o.c.g.a.	New Hampshire	rsa	Rhode Island	r.i.
Hawaii	hrs	New Jersey	n.j.	South Carolina	s.c.
Illinois	ilcs	New Mexico	n.m.	South Dakota	s.d.
Kansas	k.s.a.	New York	ny *or* n.y.	Vermont	v.s.a.
Kentucky	krs	North Carolina	n.c.	Virgin Islands	v.i.c.
Maine	m.r.s.	North Dakota	n.d.	Washington	rcw
Maryland	md *or* md.	Ohio	orc	West Virginia	w.va.

Also, note that "va" or "virginia" will retrieve references to either Virginia or West Virginia. Use `cite(virginia but not w.)` to retrieve only Virginia provisions from a multi-jurisdictional file.

Thus, the following search request in the ALLCDE file would locate state constitutional provisions dealing with free speech in California and New York:

```
speech and cite(const and (california
or ny))
```

For some states, you can use either the full name or an abbreviation for the state in the "cite" restriction; for other states, you must use a specific abbreviation.[139]

- *Court rules.* To search simultaneously for court rules from specific states, you can use either of two techniques. First (as explained on page 196), at the file menu for the CODES or STATES library, you can designate more than one file in which to conduct your search. For instance, if you wanted to search simultaneously the court rules of Georgia, Iowa, and Nebraska, you could designate the statutory code files from each of these states when you transmit your file selection at the file menu for the CODES or STATES library. Then, you could add a field restriction that will isolate the court rules from the rest of the statutory code (see page 225).

  As a second technique, you can search in the file containing all online state statutory codes (ALLCDE) in the CODES or STATES library. Because the "cite" segment in a statutory code provision contains the name of the state (either in full or abbreviated form), you can use a "cite" restriction to isolate the statutory code for each state you want. For example, you could use the restriction `cite(georgia or iowa or nebraska)` to confine your search in ALLCDE to just those states. For some states, you can use either the full name or an abbreviation for the state; for other states, you must use a specific abbreviation.[140] Along with the field restriction to segregate the statutory codes of the states you want to search, you also use a field restriction to isolate the court rules from the rest of the statutory code provisions, as explained on page 225. Your resulting search request would take a form like this: `cite(georgia or iowa or nebraska) and heading (evidence) and hearsay`.

- *Administrative regulations.* At this time, LEXIS offers few state administrative regulations, so searching a customized selection of state administrative regulations is a limited option. Mead Data will undoubtedly add more state administrative regulations to LEXIS,

[139] *See* note 138.
[140] *See* note 138.

however. When that happens, you should be able to customize your multi-jurisdictional searches by adapting the techniques for simultaneously searching selected state statutory codes.

Tips for descriptive or fact word searching in LEXIS: online indexes for statutory and administrative codes. The CALR vendors generally tout computer-assisted legal research as a way of escaping the potential drawbacks of printed indexes.[141] Nonetheless, for the *United State Code* and for some state statutory codes, LEXIS provides online versions of the print indexes; in addition, LEXIS currently provides an online index for the *Code of Federal Regulations* and for Ohio's administrative code. To determine which codes have associated online indexes, you can check the LEXIS file descriptions.

An online index serves the same principal purpose as its printed counterpart: to direct you to relevant code provisions you can then look up in either an online or printed version of the code itself. Browsing an online index can also suggest additional search terms you can use in searching a code.[142] Of course, if you have access to the index in printed form, you will often proceed just as well—and avoid online charges—by using it instead of the online index.

If you want to search in an online statutory or administrative code index, you select search terms by thinking like an indexer. Instead of anticipating the language used in the actual text of a relevant statute or regulation (as you normally do in computer-assisted legal research), you anticipate the terms legal publishers have used to index authorities. In short, when you search an online index, you simply select terms as you would when you look up something in the index of a book.

Using the United States Code index in LEXIS. To search the index in LEXIS for the *United States Code*, gain access to the USINDX file, which contains the General Index to Lawyers Cooperative Publishing's *United States Code Service*. This file appears in the CODES and GENFED libraries.

Once you enter the USINDX file, you will see a menu (shown in Figure 10.01) offering you several choices:

- the option of viewing an alphabetical list of the main index entries beginning with "a," an alphabetical list of the main index entries beginning with "b," an alphabetical list of the main index entries beginning with "c," and so on—choices 2 through 27 in Figure 10.01
- the option of viewing all the alphabetical lists, a choice that retrieves all the alphabetical lists as 26 separate documents—the first choice in Figure 10.01

[141] *See* pages 15–16.
[142] *See* pages 151–52.

```
                    LEVEL 1 - 1 OF 1 DOCUMENT

              UNITED STATES CODE SERVICE -- GENERAL INDEX
            Copyright (c) 1993 Lawyers Cooperative Publishing
   *** THE INDEX IS CURRENT THROUGH P.L. 102-439, APPROVED 10/23/92 ***

To select a desired item, enter "=" and the number: e.g. =1

<=1>    Review all lists of Major Terms.
<=2>    Review list of Major Terms for the letter "A".
<=3>    Review list of Major Terms for the letter "B".
<=4>    Review list of Major Terms for the letter "C".
<=5>    Review list of Major Terms for the letter "D".
<=6>    Review list of Major Terms for the letter "E".
<=7>    Review list of Major Terms for the letter "F".
<=8>    Review list of Major Terms for the letter "G".
<=9>    Review list of Major Terms for the letter "H".
<=10>   Review list of Major Terms for the letter "I".
<=11>   Review list of Major Terms for the letter "J".
<=12>   Review list of Major Terms for the letter "K".
<=13>   Review list of Major Terms for the letter "L".
<=14>   Review list of Major Terms for the letter "M".
<=15>   Review list of Major Terms for the letter "N".
<=16>   Review list of Major Terms for the letter "O".
```

```
<=17>   Review list of Major Terms for the letter "P".
<=18>   Review list of Major Terms for the letter "Q".
<=19>   Review list of Major Terms for the letter "R".
<=20>   Review list of Major Terms for the letter "S".
<=21>   Review list of Major Terms for the letter "T".
<=22>   Review list of Major Terms for the letter "U".
<=23>   Review list of Major Terms for the letter "V".
<=24>   Review list of Major Terms for the letter "W".
<=25>   Review list of Major Terms for the letter "X".
<=26>   Review list of Major Terms for the letter "Y".
<=27>   Review list of Major Terms for the letter "Z".
<=28>   Perform a word search in the index without the help of <LINK>.
<=29>   HELP - How to use this index.
```

Source: Mead Data Central, Inc.; © 1993 Lawyers Cooperative Publishing

Figure 10.01. First Two Screens in the USINDX File in LEXIS

- the option of performing a Boolean search for words appearing in the index—choice 28 in Figure 10.01

If you choose to view one or all of the alphabetical lists of main index entries, you can scan the entries in any of several ways:

- You can press the NEXT PAGE key or use one of the other standard LEXIS techniques for moving within a document or between documents. (See pages 332–36.)
- You can move to a specified portion of a displayed list by transmitting `p*` followed by the first three letters of the descriptive or fact word you think might begin a main index entry. For example, while viewing the list of main index entries beginning with "c," you would transmit `p*civ` to move to the portion of the list containing main index entries beginning with the words "civil rights."
- In the alphabetical list or lists you chose to view, you can locate potentially relevant main index entries by using the FOCUS feature (explained in more detail on pages 336–40): type `focus` followed by your descriptive or fact words, linked by logic connectors (if appropriate); then press TRANSMIT. For example, you could transmit `focus "civil rights"` to locate any main index entries that include the phrase "civil rights."

Once you arrive at the main index entry in which you are interested, you can display its subordinate entries, including citations to (among other things) *United States Code Service* provisions. To do so, use the LINK marker associated with the main entry: type an equal sign followed by the number preceding the entry, then press TRANSMIT.[143] For example, suppose you were viewing the following list of main index entries:

. . . .
<=**613**> CIVIL RIGHTS AND DISCRIMINATION
<=**614**> CIVIL RIGHTS ATTORNEY'S FEES AWARDS ACT OF 1976
<=**615**> CIVIL RIGHTS AUTHORIZATION ACT OF 1992, COMMISSION ON
<=**616**> CIVIL RIGHTS COMMISSION
<=**617**> CIVIL RIGHTS OF INSTITUTIONALIZED PERSONS ACT
. . . .

If you transmitted `=613`, the monitor would display the main index entry "Civil Rights and Discrimination" and its subordinate entries:

[143] For more about the LINK feature, see pages 244–45.

MAJOR-TERM: CIVIL RIGHTS AND DISCRIMINATION

Generally, <=**5**> 42 USCS 1981 et seq.

Abortion, <=**6**> 20 USCS 1688; <=**7**> 42 USCS 300a-7, <=**8**> 42 USCS 1975c

Actions

- generally, <=**9**> 28 USCS 1343, <=**10**> 28 USCS 1344, <=**11**> 28 USCS 1443, <=**12**> 28 USCS 1447
- civil actions, infra
- exhaustion of remedies, infra
- parties to actions, infra
- personal suits for relief against discrimination, infra

Adjusted test scores, employment practice, prohibition against discriminatory use, <=**13**> 42 USCS 2000e-2

. . . .

At this point, you could retrieve a cited statute by using the LINK marker preceding the statute's citation in the index. For instance, in the preceding illustration, you could transmit `=5` to retrieve 42 U.S.C.S. § 1981.

Instead of searching the index by moving through lists of main index entries, you can perform a Boolean search for your descriptive or fact words in the index. To do so, press the key labelled NEW SEARCH, then transmit a search request based on the terms you want to locate. Or, if you are viewing the menu in Figure 10.01, you can implement a Boolean search by selecting the 28th choice on the menu.

If you transmit an unrestricted search request, you will locate every occurrence of your search terms in the index, along with corresponding citations. For example, an unrestricted search for "adoption" might locate the word in connection with adoption of children, of the Constitution, of export standards, and so on.

If you prefer, you can use a restricted search request to find index entries (including citations) collected under a main index entry. Two segments exist for restricting searches in USINDX:

- The "major-term" segment contains the main index entries used in USINDX.
- The "minor-term" segment contains the index entries appearing under the main index entries.

Thus, for example, the search request `major-term(adoption)` would locate any main index entries that contain the word "adoption."

Using state statutory code indexes in LEXIS. To search a state statutory code index in LEXIS, select the library for the state in which you want to search; in that library, transmit the name of the index file, which will be called

INDEX. Once in the INDEX file, you will first see the "Index Guide," an alphabetical listing of the main index entries, such as this:

ADOPTION
ADULT ENTERTAINMENT ESTABLISHMENTS
ADULTERATION
ADULTERATION OR MISBRANDING
ADULTERY
ADULT PROTECTIVE SERVICES
ADULTS
ADVANCED PLANNING FUND
    See ECONOMIC DEVELOPMENT
ADVANCEMENTS

This listing, which for most entries does not provide references to code provisions, functions as an index to the index.[144] On-screen instructions explain how to browse the Index Guide.

To find citations to code provisions, you must leave the Index Guide and use the "General Index" portion of the INDEX file. To do so, press the key labelled NEW SEARCH, then transmit a search request based on the terms you want to locate.

If you transmit an unrestricted search request, you will locate every occurrence of your search terms in the General Index, along with corresponding citations. For example, an unrestricted search for "adoption" might locate the word in connection with adoptions of children, ordinances, corporate bylaws, and so on.

If you prefer, you can use a restricted search request to find index entries (including citations) collected under a main index entry. Two segments exist for restricting searches in INDEX files:

- The "main-term" segment contains the main index entries listed in the Index Guide. In the INDEX files for Ohio and Kentucky, the segment named "main-heading" corresponds to the "main-term" segment found in other states' INDEX files.
- The "text" segment contains the index entries appearing under the main index entries.

Thus, for example, in the index for Florida statutes, the search request `main-term(adoption)` would locate the portion of the General Index at which the main index entry for "adoption" begins:

[144] The Index Guides in the INDEX files for Ohio and Kentucky currently look a bit different from the Index Guides for other states. Nonetheless, the Index Guides for these two states operate similarly to other Index Guides.

main-term → ADOPTION
text → . . (See also FOSTER CARE)
text → . Adopted children
text → . . Aliens, 382.017
text → . . Annulment, 382.015
text → . . Birth certificates, See BIRTH CERTIFICATES
. . . .

In addition, the search request would locate any other main index entries containing the word "adoption" (*e.g.*, "Adoption, Advisory Council on").

Using administrative code indexes in LEXIS. For administrative regulations, the two online indexes currently available in LEXIS—the INDEX file in the GENFED library (for the *Code of Federal Regulations*) and the OHADMX file in the OHIO library (for Ohio's administrative code)—operate in essentially the same way as the state statutory code indexes in LEXIS. Mead Data will likely add more administrative code indexes to LEXIS. When that happens, you should have little difficulty using the administrative indexes if you understand how to use the online statutory indexes.

Known authority approach in LEXIS

If you know the citation of a legal authority that might apply to your problem, you won't necessarily log on to a CALR service to find or read that authority: you will often just pull the appropriate book off the library shelf and begin reading. This technique, called the "known authority" approach, is the most direct method for finding an authority, and leads quickly and easily to related authorities (for example, by checking annotations accompanying a known statute, or by checking authorities you find cited in a known case).[145]

In some instances, however, you won't be able to turn directly to a printed source containing your known authority, or you might find it more convenient not to use an available printed version of the authority. Perhaps your library's collection does not include the publication you want, or maybe the authority was issued too recently to be published in a printed version yet. Alternatively, while reading something online, you might come across a reference to another authority and want to quickly review that authority without the extra steps of logging off the CALR service, retrieving a book, and later logging back on to continue your research.

In situations like these, using a CALR service can prove the only way, or the most practical way, to take advantage of the "known authority" approach. LEXIS provides several means for using citation elements (*e.g.*, the name and

[145] *See* CHRISTOPHER G. WREN & JILL R. WREN, THE LEGAL RESEARCH MANUAL: A GAME PLAN FOR LEGAL RESEARCH AND ANALYSIS 51–60 (2d ed. 1986).

volume of a case reporter and the page number on which an authority begins) to go directly to a known authority.[146]

Finding known cases and other non-code authorities through LEXSEE in LEXIS. You can use the LEXSEE feature to retrieve cases, law review articles, annotations in *American Law Reports* and *Lawyers' Edition 2d*, documents in the *Federal Register*, decisions of several administrative agencies, and any other authority to which Mead Data Central has assigned a "LEXIS Cite." (Figure 10.02 explains LEXIS Cites.) Mead Data will undoubtedly continue to increase the authorities for which the LEXSEE feature is available.[147]

LEXSEE performs one function: retrieving and displaying a specific authority in response to your transmitting the authority's citation in an appropriate format. Unlike other methods of retrieving documents in LEXIS, LEXSEE does not require you to specify a library or file in which to search.

You can invoke LEXSEE at any point after identifying the research session when you log on to LEXIS (as explained on pages 191–94). For instance, when the library menu first appears on the monitor after you log on, instead of selecting a library and file in which to transmit a search request, you can use LEXSEE to retrieve your known authority. Or, suppose you have already transmitted a search request and are skimming one of the cases you retrieved; if you then encounter a citation to another case you want to check while the reference is fresh in your mind, you can use LEXSEE to go directly from the case you are viewing to the case you want to check.

When you finish using LEXSEE, you return to wherever you had been in your research when you gave the LEXSEE command; for example, if you had been reading a case and moved via LEXSEE to a second case, you would return to the first case. In effect, LEXSEE temporarily stores your current research result in the background while you pursue a new research lead.

LEXSEE works simply:

1. Type `lexsee` (or `lxe`) followed by the citation of the authority you want to retrieve.

[146] As with the "known authority" approach in book-based legal research, you need to know and recognize the elements of a citation to find legal authorities through a known-authority search in a CALR service. Although the abbreviations, punctuation, and spacing in citations for CALR purposes sometimes differ from their book-based counterparts, the elements of a citation (*e.g.*, volume number, page number, section number) remain the same. For a refresher on citations, see Chapter 2 in CHRISTOPHER G. WREN & JILL R. WREN, THE LEGAL RESEARCH MANUAL: A GAME PLAN FOR LEGAL RESEARCH AND ANALYSIS (2d ed. 1986).

[147] To retrieve known provisions from statutory or administrative codes, you use the LEXSTAT feature, which works similarly to LEXSEE. (Pages 243–44 explain LEXSTAT.) If Mead Data combines LEXSEE and LEXSTAT into a single feature capable of retrieving both non-code and code authorities, the combined feature will probably operate like LEXSEE and LEXSTAT do now.

Mead Data Central developed LEXIS Cites because many authorities, particularly cases and administrative law decisions, appear in LEXIS before they are published in printed versions and acquire traditional, book-based citations. For instance, Mead Data adds each United States Supreme Court case to LEXIS within a few hours after the Court announces the decision; by contrast, the printed reporters for U.S. Supreme Court cases (*United States Reports*, *Supreme Court Reporter*, and *Lawyers' Edition 2d*) do not become available for weeks or even months. To promptly provide researchers a standardized, unique identification for a document, Mead Data in 1988 began assigning LEXIS Cites to cases and selected administrative materials upon their addition to the LEXIS service.

On screen, a LEXIS Cite appears as part of a document's heading. If the authority is later published in a standard printed source, Mead Data supplements the document's heading with the traditional citation as a parallel citation to the LEXIS Cite. The LEXIS Cite, however, will remain the only citation available for some authorities in LEXIS, such as cases not slated for publication in a printed case reporter.

A LEXIS Cite contains the following elements:

- the name or title of the authority
- the year the authority was issued
- the jurisdiction or forum from which the authority issued
- the name of the Mead Data Central service ("LEXIS")
- the identification number Mead Data assigns to the authority

For example, as you can see in Figure 11.02 on page 321, the LEXIS Cite for *United States v. Mendoza-Lopez* is:

United States v. Mendoza-Lopez, 1987 U.S. LEXIS 2262

When you use a LEXIS Cite in your own writing, you should add the following elements to the citation:†

- Add the court's docket number for the authority (*e.g.*, C.A. No. 88-2322).
- If the identification of the jurisdiction or forum could refer to more than one tribunal (as with "U.S. Dist.," which could refer to any of the federal district courts), identify the specific tribunal. This citation convention parallels the one used in citing to a printed case reporter when the court's identification is not clear from the name of the reporter.††
- Add the full date on which the court issued the authority.

Thus, you would write the LEXIS Cite for *Michigan Citizens for an Independent Press v. Thornburgh*, a

† *See* THE BLUEBOOK: A UNIFORM SYSTEM OF CITATION Rule 10.8.1(b) (15th ed. 1991).

†† *Id.* at Rule 10.4.

(continues)

Figure 10.02. LEXIS Cites

(continued)

case decided in 1988 by the U.S. District Court for the District of Columbia, this way:

> *Michigan Citizens for an Independent Press v. Thornburgh*, C.A. No. 88-2322, 1988 U.S. Dist. LEXIS 16576 (D.D.C. Aug. 17, 1988)

Within a document in LEXIS, Mead Data also assigns LEXIS page numbers (referred to as "star-page" numbers), which on the monitor appear embedded in the document's text as asterisked numbers enclosed in brackets—such as [*2]. (You can see these page numbers, for example, in Figure 11.02 on page 321.) If you want to use a LEXIS Cite to refer someone to a specific portion of a document in LEXIS, you can include the document's internal LEXIS page number in your LEXIS Cite, as in this example, which directs the reader to LEXIS page 2 of *Michigan Citizens*:

> *Michigan Citizens for an Independent Press v. Thornburgh*, C.A. No. 88-2322, 1988 U.S. Dist. LEXIS 16576, at *2 (D.D.C. Aug. 17, 1988)

West Publishing Company uses a similar citation system for documents in WESTLAW. See Figure 10.08 on pages 281–82.

Figure 10.02. LEXIS Cites (continued)

2. Press TRANSMIT.

Alternatively (and less directly), you can gain access to LEXSEE by pressing the key labelled SELECT SERV. The monitor will display a list of services available in LEXIS, as shown in Figure 10.03.[148] To invoke LEXSEE, type `lexsee` and press TRANSMIT. A screen will then appear on which you can complete your LEXSEE instruction by typing the citation of the authority you want to retrieve and then pressing TRANSMIT.

LEXSEE allows some flexibility in citation format. You can generally use the citation to any official or unofficial reporter (for a case reprinted in more

[148] Mead Data uses the term "service" as a catch-all label for various features and collections of information available online. In its broadest sense, "service" refers to LEXIS and other collections of information available through Mead Data, such as NEXIS (a collection of non-legal information) and MEDIS (a collection of medically related information). Within LEXIS, "service" refers to certain features, such as LEXSEE, LEXSTAT, DEBUT, online tutorials, an online version of *Shepard's Citations*, and Auto-Cite. For more information about services, see MEAD DATA CENTRAL, REFERENCE MANUAL FOR THE LEXIS/NEXIS SERVICES 30, C-1 (undated looseleaf ed.).

```
Please transmit the NAME (only one) of the service that you want to use. If you
transmit the NAME of a service that is indicated as inappropriate (I) or
unavailable (U), further information will be provided.

NAME   CITATION SERVICES               NAME   FREE SERVICES
AC     AUTO-CITE Citation Service      CAI    Computer Assisted
       to verify a citation.                  Instructions.
SHEP   SHEPARD's Citation Service      TUTOR  LEXIS/NEXIS TUTORIALS
       to list citing references              to assist searching.
       to a case citation.             DEBUT  What is new in LEXIS
LEXSEE LEXSEE Citation Service                and NEXIS.
       to see the full text of a
       case, as identified by its             ECLIPSE SERVICES
       citation.                       SAV    Save a search for
LXSTAT LXSTAT Citation Service                automatic updates.
       to see the full text            REC    RECALL a previously
       of a code section, as                  saved ECLIPSE search.
       identified by its citation

If you have changed your mind and do not want to select a service, press the
EXIT SERV key.
```

Source: Mead Data Central, Inc. © 1993

Figure 10.03. Menu of Services Available in LEXIS

than one reporter),[149] the citations to leading looseleaf services that reported the case, or the LEXIS Cite (where available). For example, any of the following LEXSEE instructions will retrieve *Zacchini v. Scripps-Howard Broadcasting Company*, 433 U.S. 562, 97 S. Ct. 2849, 53 L. Ed. 2d 965 (1977), also reported in *United States Patents Quarterly* (205 U.S.P.Q. 741):

```
lexsee 433 us 562
lxe 97 sct 2849
lxe 53 led2d 965
lexsee 1977 us lexis 145
lexsee 205 uspq 741
```

LEXSEE will also accept some variations in the spacing and punctuation of the abbreviation of the source in which the document appears, although you cannot omit a hyphen if it appears as part of the citation. Thus, if you wanted to use LEXSEE to retrieve the article beginning on page 2099 of volume 87 of the *Michigan Law Review*, the instructions that would work include these:

[149] Mead Data recommends using the official citation, however. MEAD DATA CENTRAL, REFERENCE MANUAL FOR THE LEXIS/NEXIS SERVICES 131 n.3 (undated looseleaf ed.). For a refresher on official and unofficial reporters, see CHRISTOPHER G. WREN & JILL R. WREN, THE LEGAL RESEARCH MANUAL: A GAME PLAN FOR LEGAL RESEARCH AND ANALYSIS 10–11 (2d ed. 1986).

```
lexsee 87 mich.l.rev. 2099
lexsee 87 mich. l.rev. 2099
lexsee 87 mich. l. rev. 2099
lexsee 87 michlrev 2099
lexsee 87 mich l rev 2099
```

For some types of authorities (notably, cases and law review articles), LEXSEE will retrieve the document you want even if your LEXSEE instruction uses a page number within the document rather than the first page of the document. For instance, suppose you wanted to find the *Zacchini* case via LEXSEE, but you transmitted `lexsee 433 us 564` instead of `lexsee 433 us 562`. Because the LEXIS computer is programmed to retrieve whatever case includes the page number transmitted in a LEXSEE instruction, you would still retrieve *Zacchini*.

Help with LEXSEE. What if you do not know an acceptable abbreviation for the source of the authority you want to retrieve through LEXSEE (such as "Mar. Law." for *Tulane Maritime Law Journal*)? You can view an online list of abbreviations to use in LEXSEE commands. As soon as you gain access to LEXSEE, type `h` (for "help") and press TRANSMIT. The monitor will display a list of options, along with instructions to follow. Currently, the instructions direct you to transmit `h` again to bring you to another help screen, and then to transmit `l` (for "list") to display more options, including the choice of viewing a list of LEXSEE citation formats. On-screen instructions explain how to navigate the list and how to exit when you are done.

You can also review the online list of LEXSEE citation formats while viewing a document you retrieved through LEXSEE. Transmit `h` (for "help"), then transmit `m` (for "master list of LEXSEE tutorial topics") and follow the on-screen instructions.

Leaving LEXSEE. Once you have invoked the LEXSEE feature, you can do as many LEXSEE searches in a row as you want. When you have found all the authorities you want to locate through LEXSEE, you end your LEXSEE session either by pressing the EXIT SERV key or by typing `resume` (or `res`) and pressing TRANSMIT.

Pressing EXIT SERV will take you out of LEXSEE (and out of any other service you might also have used) and return you to wherever you had been in your research when you invoked a service.[150]

Depending on the sequence of your research activities, transmitting `resume` (or `res`) will cause the computer either (1) to return you to your most recent research activity or (2) to present you with the "Resume Options" screen, where you can select from a list of your previous research activities

[150] In addition to LEXSEE, a service could be, for instance, Shepard's or Auto-Cite. *See* note 148.

the one to which you want to return. For example, suppose you had begun your online session by using a Boolean search to retrieve a law review article and then used LEXSEE to retrieve a case you saw mentioned in the article. Transmitting `resume` (or `res`) while viewing the case would take you back to the law review article. On the other hand, if you had used a Boolean search to retrieve the law review article and then used two or more services before invoking LEXSEE, transmitting `resume` (or `res`) while viewing your LEXSEE result would produce the Resume Options screen.

Finding known statutes and administrative code sections through LEXSTAT in LEXIS. If you know the citation of a relevant statutory or administrative code section available in LEXIS, you can use the LEXSTAT feature to retrieve and display the section's text.[151] LEXSTAT works much like LEXSEE. As with LEXSEE, you can invoke LEXSTAT at any point after identifying your research session when you log on to LEXIS. To begin a LEXSTAT search:

1. Type `lexstat` (or `lxstat`, `lextat`, `lxtat`, or `lxt`) followed by the citation of the code section you want to retrieve.

2. Press TRANSMIT.

Alternatively, you can invoke LEXSTAT by pressing the key labelled SELECT SERV and following the on-screen prompts when the menu of services (shown in Figure 10.03 on page 241) appears.

LEXSTAT accommodates some variation in citation format, although you cannot omit a hyphen that is part of a citation. For example, any of the following LEXSTAT instructions will retrieve section 2254 in title 28 of the *United States Code*:

```
lexstat 28 uscs sec 2254
lxt 28 uscs @ 2254
lexstat 28 u. s. c. s. 2254
lxstat 28 u.s.c.s. 2254
lexstat 28 u s c s 2254
lexstat 28 uscs 2254
```

Help with LEXSTAT. If you do not know the citation format that will retrieve the statutory or administrative code section you want to find through LEXSTAT, you can review an online list of acceptable formats. At any time during a LEXSTAT session, you can type `h` (for "help"), press TRANSMIT, and

[151] To retrieve known non-code authorities (such as cases), you use the LEXSEE feature explained on pages 238 and 240–43. If Mead Data Central combines LEXSTAT and LEXSEE into a single feature capable of retrieving both code and non-code authorities, the combined feature will probably operate like LEXSTAT and LEXSEE do now.

follow the on-screen instructions, which will explain how to view and exit the list of citation formats.

Leaving LEXSTAT. When you have finished finding all the code sections you want to retrieve through LEXSTAT, you end your LEXSTAT session either by pressing the EXIT SERV key or by typing `resume` (or `res`) and pressing TRANSMIT.

Pressing EXIT SERV will take you out of LEXSTAT (and out of any other service you might also have used) and return you to wherever you had been in your research when you invoked a service.[152]

Depending on the sequence of your research activities, transmitting `resume` (or `res`) will cause the computer either (1) to return you to your most recent research activity or (2) to present you with the "Resume Options" screen, where you can select from a list of your previous research activities the one to which you want to return. For example, suppose you had begun your online session by using a Boolean search to retrieve a case and then used LEXSTAT to retrieve a statutory section you saw mentioned in the case. Transmitting `resume` (or `res`) while viewing the statute would take you back to the case. On the other hand, if you had used a Boolean search to retrieve the case and then used two or more services before invoking LEXSTAT, transmitting `resume` (or `res`) while viewing your LEXSTAT result would produce the Resume Options screen.

LINK: Automating the use of LEXSEE and LEXSTAT in LEXIS. LEXIS offers a feature called LINK that can speed up using LEXSEE and LEXSTAT. While viewing an authority in LEXIS, you might see a reference to another authority you want to retrieve. You can use LINK to retrieve the text of that authority if the reference to it has a LINK marker nearby. A LINK marker looks like this:

<=4>

The marker numbers increase sequentially throughout a document. An example of a LINK marker appears in front of the first citation to *Lewis v. United States* in Figure 11.03 on page 321.[153]

LEXIS offers two ways to use LINK to retrieve an authority through LEXSEE or LEXSTAT:

1. Type an equal sign followed by the number in the LINK marker you want to use. For example, type `=3`.

[152] In addition to LEXSTAT, a service could be, for instance, Shepard's or Auto-Cite. *See* note 148.

[153] LEXIS automatically displays LINK markers but offers the option of not displaying them. To suppress LINK markers, type `.linkoff` and press TRANSMIT; to redisplay the LINK markers, type `.linkon` and press TRANSMIT.

2. Press TRANSMIT.

Alternatively:[154]

1. Press the TAB key to position the cursor under the LINK marker preceding the citation of the authority you want to retrieve.

2. Press TRANSMIT.

The computer will automatically formulate a LEXSEE or LEXSTAT instruction based on the citation for the reference for which you transmitted a marker number or on which you positioned the cursor. The computer will then retrieve and display the authority.

If the citation you selected includes a cite to a page other than the first page of the authority (as in "26 S. Ct. 282, 287"), the display will begin with the internal page. If the LINK marker precedes a string citation of statutes (as in "21 U.S.C. @@ 842(c)(2)(b), 843(c), 844(a)"), the LINK feature will read in only the first citation—in this instance, creating the LEXSTAT instruction "21 U.S.C. 842." Also, if you use LINK to retrieve the text of a statute, the computer will retrieve the statute's text as it appears in the *current* online version of the statutory code. The current version might differ, though, from the version of the statute to which the original authority referred.

Currently, the convenience offered by LINK exists when you are viewing federal or state cases, law review articles, and *A.L.R.* annotations. In these documents, the LINK markers allow you to retrieve federal and state cases, statutes in the *United States Code Service*, documents in the *Federal Register*, law review articles, attorney general opinions, and selected tax-related documents. For situations in which LINK is not available, you can retrieve most known authorities by transmitting a LEXSEE or LEXSTAT instruction.

Leaving LINK. Once you retrieve an authority using LINK, you can do anything you could have done if you had retrieved the document using a LEXSEE or LEXSTAT instruction without the assistance of LINK. If you want to resume viewing the results of an earlier descriptive-word search, you can leave the LINK-invoked service (LEXSEE or LEXSTAT) by pressing the EXIT SERV key or by typing `resume lexis` (or `res lexis`) and pressing ENTER.

Finding known authorities in LEXIS by using citation information in a field-restricted search request. The LEXSEE and LEXSTAT features in LEXIS do not work for all authorities. When you cannot use LEXSEE or LEXSTAT to retrieve an authority for which you know the citation, you can retrieve the authority by using a search request that includes the citation in-

[154] This alternative does not work with versions earlier than version 2.7 of the LEXIS/NEXIS Technology Series Research Software for MS-DOS.

formation in a field restriction based on the LEXIS segment containing the authority's citation. You can use this kind of field restriction to find any known authority available in LEXIS, regardless of whether the LEXSEE or LEXSTAT feature (or their automated counterpart, LINK) would also retrieve the authority you want.

In LEXIS, citation information for most authorities appears in the "cite" segment. So, for instance, if you wanted to use the cite segment to retrieve *Varnell v. Young*, 839 F.2d 1245 (7th Cir. 1988), you would select an appropriate file of federal courts of appeals cases (such as USAPP) and use one of the following search requests, which are based on the *Federal Reporter* citation and the LEXIS Cite (1988 U.S. App. LEXIS 2197):

```
cite(839 pre/3 1245)

cite(1988 pre/5 2197)
```

Page 80 explains more about using the cite segment in a search request.

Using the cite segment to retrieve a known authority is not as efficient as using LEXSEE or LEXSTAT. First, with a field-restricted search request, you must initially gain access to a LEXIS file that includes the authority you want to retrieve; by contrast, you can invoke LEXSEE or LEXSTAT from anywhere in LEXIS, and you do not need to select an appropriate file in which to search. Second, if you use a page number within a case rather than the page on which the case begins, searching the cite segment will not retrieve the case, whereas LEXSEE would. Third, a field-restricted search request (unlike LEXSEE or LEXSTAT) will not hold your current research results in the background while you check another authority, or allow you to return directly to your earlier research results when you finish pursuing the new research lead.

Consequently, if LEXSEE or LEXSTAT is available to retrieve the known authority you want, you will probably find using one of these features more advantageous than conducting a field-restricted search of the cite segment.

Finding partially known authorities in LEXIS. What if you know of a particular case, statute, or other authority that holds potential relevance for your research problem, but you don't know the citation information (*e.g.*, reporter volume and page number, or statutory code section) that would allow you to retrieve the authority by using LEXSEE or LEXSTAT, or by searching the cite segment? For example, someone might suggest you look at the "Steelworkers Trilogy" of cases or the federal "Equal Credit Opportunity Act," but not be able to tell you the exact citation. Or, you might only remember that during a particular period, a certain judge wrote an opinion addressing an issue relevant to your research.

When you search online, you can use elements of a citation to track down a partially known authority. The technique parallels using incomplete citation information in book-based legal research to find a partially known authority by checking a table of case names or a table of popular names for cases or statutes.[155] Online, however, you can often locate a partially known authority by working with even fewer clues than you would need to find the authority in a printed source.

Partially known cases. To find partially known cases in LEXIS, you can take one of several courses, depending on what information you know. For each technique, you will first need to gain access to an appropriate LEXIS file. If you know the jurisdiction in which the case you are tracking down was decided, you would select a file containing cases from that jurisdiction. If you know your case was decided by a state court, but do not know which state, the OMNI file in the STATES library would be an appropriate choice. If you know your case was decided by a federal court, but do not know which court, you could select the COURTS file in the GENFED library. If you do not know whether your case was decided by a state or federal court, you could select the MEGA file in the GENFED or STATES library.

Once you have gained access to an appropriate file, you can use one of the following techniques:

- *Search for the name of a party to the case.* If you know the name of at least one party in a case, you can locate the case by searching for that name in the "name" segment.[156] For example, if you know the name of the plaintiff in *Kingsley International Pictures Corporation v. Regents of the State of New York*, you could retrieve the case by transmitting

```
name("kingsley international pictures")
```

  In most instances, if a case has multiple plaintiffs or defendants, the names of all the parties will appear in this segment. Consequently, you can often find a case even if you don't know the name of the principal plaintiff or principal defendant. In this respect, a CALR search offers a capability not available in book-based research: with books, to use a party's name to find a case, you must know the name of a principal plaintiff or defendant in order to use the party tables in a case digest.

- *Search for the case's popular name.* If the case you want to locate is known by a popular name (such as the "Steelworkers Trilogy"), you can conduct an unrestricted search for the popular name in an

[155] *See* Christopher G. Wren & Jill R. Wren, The Legal Research Manual: A Game Plan for Legal Research and Analysis 58, 60 (2d ed. 1986).

[156] For a refresher on conducting a field-restricted search in the "name" segment, see pages 78–80.

appropriate file. The computer might locate a reference to the popular name in, say, a case or law review article. If so, the reference will probably appear with the case's official name and citation, which you can then use to retrieve the case through the "known authority" approach explained on pages 238, 240–43, and 245–46.

When the popular name and the official name and citation appear together online, this technique achieves the same result as using a popular name to locate a case in book-based research by checking *Shepard's Acts and Cases By Popular Names* or a Popular Names Table in a digest.

- *Search for other bits of information identifying the case.* You might be able to locate a partially known case if you have other items of information—such as the docket number of the case, the name of a judge who wrote an opinion in the case, the names of the attorneys who participated, or the period during which the case was decided. For instance, suppose you knew that Laurence Tribe had served as counsel to one of the parties in a possibly relevant federal court of appeals case involving a constitutional challenge to a requirement that lawyers join a bar association. Even without knowing which court issued the decision, the name of any judge or party involved, or when the case was decided, you could locate the case in LEXIS with the clues you have available. You could search the USAPP file in the GENFED library with the following search request to find the case:

```
counsel((laurence or lawrence) w/3
tribe) and "bar association"
```

  As this example implies, you can incorporate whatever information you have into various field restrictions to locate a partially known case. Moreover, you can often find a partially known case online when you only have clues that would prove too sparse to locate the case through book-based research. Chapter 5 provides more information about using field restrictions in search requests.

Partially known statutes. Suppose you do not know the citation of a potentially relevant statute, but know its popular name (such as the "Equal Credit Opportunity Act"). For *federal statutes*, LEXIS provides an online version of the "Table of Acts by Popular Names" from *United States Code Service*, published by Lawyers Cooperative Publishing; this table appears in the USNAME file in the GENFED and CODES libraries. Through the popular-names file in LEXIS, you can obtain citation and other information for finding a statute you know only by its popular name.

The USNAME file consists of twenty-six documents, one for each letter of the alphabet; the document for letter "e," for example, contains all the popular names beginning with "e." When you select the USNAME file, the monitor will automatically display the first screen for the document for letter "a," as shown in the first screen in Figure 10.04. At this point, you can locate a popular name in either of two ways, depending on what you know about the popular name of the statute you seek:

- If you know the exact popular name of the statute, begin by selecting the document for the letter with which the popular name begins. For instance, at the first screen shown in Figure 10.04, you would start by typing **19** and pressing TRANSMIT if you wanted to locate a reference to the "Science and Engineering Equal Opportunities Act."

  The monitor will display the first screen of the document for the letter you selected. You can then locate the popular name by transmitting **p*** followed by the first three letters of the popular name. For example, to locate the portion of the table referring to the "Science and Engineering Equal Opportunities Act," you would transmit

  ```
  p*sci
  ```

  At that point, to locate the popular name you seek when several statutes have popular names beginning with the same three letters, you might need to scan the list of popular names by pressing the NEXT PAGE key or using one of the other standard LEXIS techniques for moving within a document. (See pages 332–33.)

- If you do not know the exact popular name of the statute but know some of the words in the popular name, you can use the FOCUS feature (explained in more detail on pages 336–40) to locate the popular name: type **focus** followed by words in the popular name, linked by logic connectors (if appropriate); then press TRANSMIT. The computer will retrieve any of the file's 26 documents (A through Z) that contain references satisfying your FOCUS request.

  For example, if you knew that the popular name referred to opportunities in science or engineering, you could transmit

  ```
  focus science or engineer! w/5
  opportun!
  ```

  To see a popular name after the computer retrieves a document or documents containing popular names that satisfy your request,

```
                    LEVEL 1 - 1 OF 26 DOCUMENTS

                    UNITED STATES CODE SERVICE
            Copyright (c) 1992 Lawyers Cooperative Publishing

                TABLE OF ACTS BY POPULAR NAMES -- LETTER A
   *** THIS TABLE INCLUDES ALL NAMES ENACTED THROUGH P.L. 103-22, 4/12/93 ***

This document contains all popular names that begin with the letter A.

To find a POPULAR NAME enter p* and the first three letters of the first word.
   Example:   To jump to:   "Army Housing Act" ........... enter:   p*arm
              To jump to:   "Aviation Service Act" ....... enter:   p*avi

Use the FOCUS feature to find a POPULAR NAME when the exact name is not known.
   Example:   focus employ! w/5 retirement

To review popular names beginning with a different letter enter the number of
the letter as it appears in the alphabet.  (Must have 26 documents)
  A = 1    D = 4    G = 7    J = 10   M = 13   P = 16   S = 19   V = 22   Y = 25
  B = 2    E = 5    H = 8    K = 11   N = 14   Q = 17   T = 20   W = 23   Z = 26
  C = 3    F = 6    I = 9    L = 12   O = 15   R = 18   U = 21   X = 24
```

```
                    USCS Pop. Name A 1992, *

               TABLE OF POPULAR NAMES -- LETTER A
[*A]       Popular Names beginning with "A".
[*AA]      Popular Names beginning with "AA".
[*AAA]     Enter p* and up to three letters to jump elsewhere.
           To view a P.L. after 100-242 use LEXSEE  -- e.g.  lexsee 102 pl 166
           To view a USCS section use LXSTAT        -- e.g.  lxstat 42 uscs 5101

AAA FARM RELIEF AND INFLATION ACT
   May 12, 1933, ch 25, 48 Stat. 31, 7 USCS @@ 601--604, 607--620; 12 USCS @@
347, 636, 723, 771, 781, 810, 992, 993, 1016--1019; 31 USCS @@ 462, 821--823.

[*AB]      Popular Names beginning with "AB".
[*ABA]     Enter p* and up to three letters to jump elsewhere.
           To view a P.L. after 100-242 use LEXSEE  -- e.g.  lexsee 102 pl 166
           To view a USCS section use LXSTAT        -- e.g.  lxstat 42 uscs 5101

ABACA PRODUCTION ACT
   Aug. 10, 1950, ch 673, 64 Stat. 435, 50 USCS @@ 541--546.

ABANDONED BARGE ACT OF 1992
   Nov. 4, 1992, P.L. 102-587, 46 USCS @ 4701 note.
```

Source: Mead Data Central, Inc.; © 1992 Lawyers Cooperative Publishing

Figure 10.04. First Two Screens for the Letter "A" in the USNAME File in LEXIS, Containing the *United States Code Service* "Table of Acts by Popular Names"

press the key labelled KWIC to use the "key word in context" display format (explained on pages 319–20).

Once you find a popular name in the online popular-names table, you can use the citation information accompanying the popular name to retrieve the text of the statute in LEXIS. To retrieve the statutory text as published in *United States Code Service*, transmit a LEXSTAT instruction with U.S.C.S. citation information—for example, `lxstat 42 uscs 1861`. To retrieve the statutory text as published in *Statutes at Large*, transmit a LEXSEE instruction with the public-law citation information—for instance, `lxe 100 pl 570`.

For *state statutes*, LEXIS at this time does not offer a popular-names table. However, searching in various LEXIS files for the popular name of a state statute might locate either the statute itself or a reference to its official citation, which you can then use to retrieve the statute through the "known authority" approach explained on pages 243–44 and 245–46. To avoid bypassing unconventional references (such as a reference to the "Equal Credit Opportunity Law" instead of the "Equal Credit Opportunity Act"), omit words like "act," "law," or "statute" from the popular name in your search request.

The information you retrieve will depend on where you search. For example:

- Searching in a LEXIS file of statutes from the jurisdiction that enacted the statute you want will retrieve the statute itself if its popular name appears in the statute. (Legislators often include a statutory section designating a "short title" for the statute; the short title often becomes the statute's popular name.)
- Searching in an annotated statutory code in LEXIS might yield references to the popular name in the statutory annotations, which could also contain the statute's official citation or a citation to, say, a law review article or *A.L.R.* annotation that would provide the statute's citation.
- Searching for the statute's popular name in a LEXIS file of federal or state cases might retrieve cases that refer to the statute by its popular name, along with the statute's official citation.

When the popular name and the citation appear together online, you achieve the same result you would in book-based legal research by checking a statute's popular name in *Shepard's Acts and Cases By Popular Names*, in tables of Acts By Popular Names or Short Titles in individual Shepard's citators, or in Popular Names tables in annotated statutes.[157]

[157] *See* CHRISTOPHER G. WREN & JILL R. WREN, THE LEGAL RESEARCH MANUAL: A GAME PLAN FOR LEGAL RESEARCH AND ANALYSIS 60 (2d ed. 1986).

Known topic approach in LEXIS

In book-based legal research, if you feel confident you know what area of law your problem involves (*e.g.*, sales, wills, taxation, civil rights), you can find relevant cases by skipping the index to a case digest, going directly to the appropriate case digest topic, and perusing the table of contents until you find a subtopic that relates to your research problem.[158] Similarly, you can find relevant statutory or administrative law by skipping a code's index and going directly to an appropriate topical grouping of statutes or regulations within the code.[159]

You can also use a "known topic" approach online, although the same caveat applies there as in book-based legal research: the approach is most useful to experienced researchers working in a familiar area of law. Researchers who lack familiarity with the array of legal topics are generally better off using one of the other law-finding approaches explained in this chapter.[160]

Cases: the known topic approach in LEXIS. Occasionally, search terms you select for a descriptive-word search for cases in LEXIS will simulate a known topic search. Some words—such as "replevin" or "eminent domain" (which are examples of topics in West case digests)—are so closely aligned with a particular legal topic that they will almost certainly appear in cases dealing with that topic, but not in cases unrelated to the topic. When you use such words as search terms in a LEXIS search of a case file, you will retrieve many, perhaps most, of the cases you would find digested under the corresponding topics in a case digest.

In addition, when a LEXIS topical file (see page 254) covers the area of law you want to research, searching in that file can simulate researching in a case digest topic.

Statutes and administrative regulations: the known topic approach in LEXIS. For book-based research in statutes and administrative regulations, if you know that some topical grouping within a statutory or administrative code applies to your research problem, you can go straight to that part of the code. To implement this "known topic" approach to find statutes or regulations in LEXIS, you would use a field restriction to confine your search to the group of statutes or regulations in which you are interested. The LEXIS segment used in this type of search will contain the name of, or citation information for, the topical grouping.

[158] For more information about the known topic approach in book-based research, see *id.* at 60–63.

[159] *Id.*

[160] See *id.* at 60, 62 (discussing the drawbacks of the "known topic" approach in book-based legal research). These drawbacks apply equally to computer-assisted legal research.

For example, suppose you want to research whether a copyright holder is required to register the copyright before commencing a civil action alleging copyright infringement. Suppose you also knew that in the *United States Code*, Title 17 (entitled "Copyright") contained the federal statutes governing copyright, and that in the *Code of Federal Regulations*, Title 37 (entitled "Patents, Trademarks, and Copyrights") contained federal regulations dealing with copyright. You could find the code sections addressing your issue by using a field restriction instructing the computer to look for your search terms in only 17 U.S.C. or 37 C.F.R.[161] In LEXIS, your search request for statutes in the USCS or USCODE file in the GENFED library, or in the USCODE file in the CODES library, could take any of these forms:

```
heading(copyright) and (infringe! w/25 regist!)

heading("title 17") and (infringe! w/25 regist!)

cite("17 uscs") and (infringe! w/25 regist!)
```

Your LEXIS search request for regulations in the CFR file in the GENFED library could take any of these forms:

```
title(copyright) and (infringe! w/25 regist!)

title("title 37") and (infringe! w/25 regist!)

cite("37 cfr") and (infringe! w/25 regist!)
```

State statutory and administrative codes also organize statutes and regulations by grouping them together topically according to common subject matter, although the methods of numbering and naming topical groupings vary from state to state. If you know the name of, or citation information for, a relevant grouping within a state statutory or administrative code, you can conduct a known topic search in that code by using field restrictions similar to those used for known topic searches in the federal codes. Of course, you will need to modify the field restrictions to take into account differences between the federal and state codes, such as different ways of numbering and naming topical groupings.

For federal and state statutory codes, LEXIS offers an online version of the tables of contents, which you can use to identify groupings of statutes that deal with the topic you are researching. To check the online table of contents for the *United States Code*, gain access to either the GENFED or CODES

[161] For a complete list of names and numbers of titles in the *United States Code*, see CHRISTOPHER G. WREN & JILL R. WREN, THE LEGAL RESEARCH MANUAL: A GAME PLAN FOR LEGAL RESEARCH AND ANALYSIS 175 (2d ed. 1986). For a complete list of names and numbers of titles in the *Code of Federal Regulations*, see *id.* at 176.

library and transmit the file name (USTOC) for the table of contents. To check the online table of contents for a state statutory code, gain access to the CODES library and transmit the file name for the table of contents you want to view; the file name will consist of the state's two-letter postal abbreviation followed by "TOC" (*e.g.*, VATOC for the table of contents for Virginia statutes). Once you are in a table of contents file, you'll first see a list of broad topical categories. At this screen, you can transmit a Boolean search for words describing your topic, or you can select from the topical list the category likely to encompass statutes relevant to your research issue. If you choose a category from the list, on-screen prompts will lead you through menus of increasingly narrow topical categories until you arrive at a grouping of statutes dealing with a particular topic. At that point, you can retrieve a statute by using its LINK marker to implement a LEXSTAT search (as explained on pages 244–45).

Topical files: the known topic approach in LEXIS. In carrying out a known topic search online, you might also find topical files in LEXIS worthwhile sources. LEXIS pulls together various related materials into topical collections in such specialized areas as insurance, taxation, energy, environmental law, and labor. For instance, the BANKNG library in LEXIS offers access to a collection of files containing cases, statutes, administrative regulations, looseleaf services, law review articles, and other materials relating to banking and financial services. For a complete listing of the topical collections available in LEXIS, check Mead Data's printed and online guides to LEXIS; Appendix A highlights these sources of information.

A specialized approach in LEXIS: Words and Phrases

Sometimes, your research issue will involve or turn on a legal definition of a term. For instance, suppose local officials propose locating a half-way house in a residential neighborhood where zoning regulations prohibit locating a jail. You would want to know whether a half-way house constituted a jail, and would therefore want to find definitions of "jail" or "half-way house" (or, by analogy, "prison" or "penitentiary").

In book-based legal research, if you need to find a judicial definition of a term, you can go straight to *Words and Phrases*, West Publishing Company's multi-volume "dictionary" that contains common-law definitions, along with citations to the cases in which the words and phrases were construed. In addition to the *Words and Phrases* series of volumes, case digests usually contain either a topic entry or a separate volume entitled "Words and Phrases" that lists significant terms interpreted by courts in the jurisdiction covered by the particular digest.[162]

[162] *See* CHRISTOPHER G. WREN & JILL R. WREN, THE LEGAL RESEARCH MANUAL: A GAME PLAN FOR LEGAL RESEARCH AND ANALYSIS 63–65 (2d ed. 1986).

But what if you don't have access to *Words and Phrases* (or to a digest counterpart)? Or what if the term you want is not defined in *Words and Phrases* (or in a digest counterpart)? Or suppose you simply want to supplement a book-based "words and phrases" search (perhaps to find more recent definitions). You can try one of the following techniques to implement the "words and phrases" approach in LEXIS.

Finding judicial definitions in LEXIS. You can search in LEXIS for judicial definitions of your term:

- Try linking your term in a search request with words that can indicate the presence of a definition. When judges define a term, their opinions usually include, near the word or phrase being defined, words such as "means," "meaning," "define," "defined," "definition," "construe," "construing," "interpret," or "interpretation." Consequently, you can sometimes find judicial definitions by searching a case-law file in LEXIS with a search request along these lines:

  ```
  ((half-way or halfway) pre/2 house)
  w/10 (mean* or meaning or defin*** or
  definition or constru*** or interpret!)
  ```

  Because judges sometimes cite *Words and Phrases* when defining a term, you might also want to include `"words and phrases"` in your search request to enhance the likelihood of retrieving definitional cases, as in this example:

  ```
  ((half-way or halfway) pre/2 house)
  w/10 (mean* or meaning or defin*** or
  definition or constru*** or interpret!
  or "words and phrases")
  ```

- If you want to find judicial definitions of a word or phrase you think occurs relatively infrequently in cases, you can simply search for the word or phrase in LEXIS without including additional search terms (like "mean" or "define") that suggest a definitional context. Although you will undoubtedly retrieve some cases that mention your word or phrase without defining it, you are less likely to bypass cases that contain relevant definitions but do not include words like "mean" or "define" near your word or phrase. Moreover, if your word or phrase actually occurs infrequently, the number of cases retrieved will likely be small enough that you can screen all of them to find the ones containing definitions.

  Searching for a word or phrase without adding a search term like "means" can prove especially helpful if you need to find judicial interpretations of key phrases from statutes, administrative regulations, or jury instructions.

Finding statutory and administrative definitions in LEXIS. You can also use a "words and phrases" approach in LEXIS to search for definitions that legislatures or administrative agencies assign to words or phrases in statutes or administrative regulations:

- Try linking your term with words that can indicate the presence of a definition. Statutes and administrative regulations often contain sections defining salient terms for the purpose of interpreting and applying the statutes or regulations. Terms defined in statutes or regulations typically appear near words like "means," "meaning," "define," or "definition," as in these examples:

> **450.01 Definitions.** In this chapter:
>
> . . . .
>
> **(8)** "Distribute" means to deliver, other than by administering or dispensing.
>
> . . . .
>
> **(10)** "Drug" means:
>
> (a) Any substance recognized as a drug in the official U.S. pharmacopoeia and national formulary or official homeopathic pharmacopoeia of the United States or any supplement to either of them;
>
> . . . .
>
> **939.22 Words and phrases defined.** In chs. 939 to 948 and 951, the following words and phrases have the designated meanings unless the context of a specific section manifestly requires a different construction or the word or phrase is defined in s. 948.01 for purposes of ch. 948:
>
> . . . .
>
> **(11)** "Drug" has the meaning specified in s. 450.01(10).
>
> . . . .
>
> **939.24 Criminal recklessness. (1)** In this section, "criminal recklessness" means that the actor creates an unreasonable and substantial risk of death or great bodily harm to another human being and the actor is aware of that risk.
>
> . . . .

Consequently, you might be able to find relevant statutory or administrative definitions by searching in a LEXIS file of statutes or administrative regulations with a request linking the term you want defined (for example, "drug") and words designed to locate definitions:

```
drug w/10 (mean or meaning or define*
or definition)
```

If a search request in this form retrieves more code sections than you can reasonably expect to review, you can try using field restrictions to narrow your search—in particular, restrictions limiting the search to sections in which the term you want defined appears in the text of the section and in which a word like "definition" appears in the segment containing the title of the section. For example, your restricted search request in a statutory file in LEXIS could take this form:

```
text(drug) and section(mean or
meaning or define* or definition)
```

- If you want to find legislative or administrative definitions of a word or phrase you think occurs relatively infrequently in a code (such as, say, "criminal recklessness"), you can simply search for the word or phrase in a statutory or administrative code file in LEXIS without including additional search terms (like "mean" or "define") that suggest a definitional context. Although you will undoubtedly retrieve some code sections that mention your word or phrase without defining it, you are less likely to bypass sections that contain relevant definitions but do not include words like "mean" or "define" near your word or phrase. Moreover, if your word or phrase actually occurs infrequently, the number of sections retrieved will likely be small enough that you can screen all of them to find the ones containing definitions.

Suggestion: the words and phrases approach online. As a practical matter, a "words and phrases" search (whether in cases, statutes, or regulations) will often prove less efficient in a CALR service than in books. For judicial definitions, if you have access to *Words and Phrases* or a digest counterpart, you might find it more productive to search there than online. First, with *Words and Phrases*, you do not need to screen out cases that do not contain definitions; editors have already performed that screening, allowing you to simply turn to the entry for your word or phrase as easily as you would turn to a definition in a dictionary. Second, in a book-based search, you will find definitional cases even if they do not spotlight a definition with words such as "mean" or "define"; editors generally include cases if the discussions of words or phrases function as definitions, whether or not they are called that. Finally, *Words and Phrases* and its digest counterparts subdivide entries to permit researchers to find definitions quickly in specific contexts—for instance, entries under "jail" might include "city jail," "county jail," and "state jail."

Likewise, you might find legislative and administrative definitions more readily in a print version of a code than in a CALR service: a good index to a printed code will normally direct you faster to relevant definitions of words and phrases. (If you have a choice of printed codes for a given jurisdiction, you will often find better indexes in a commercially published, annotated code than in a code published by a government agency.)

A Generalized Approach in LEXIS: law reviews, *American Law Reports*, looseleaf services, *Restatements of the Law*, and other secondary legal sources

The research approaches discussed so far are mainly designed to lead you directly to primary sources of law (cases, statutes, administrative regulations, constitutional provisions), not to secondary sources (writings or commentaries about the law found in primary sources). If you want to gain perspective on the primary law involved in your research problem, however, you might find it helpful to obtain some generalized background information from secondary sources.

LEXIS offers online versions of several of the secondary sources you can use in book-based legal research to locate commentaries on the law.[163] The secondary sources in LEXIS include:

- law reviews
- legal magazines and newsletters
- looseleaf services (such as those published by the Bureau of National Affairs and by Commerce Clearing House)
- case annotations from both *American Law Reports* and *U.S. Supreme Court Reports, Lawyers' Edition*
- *Restatements of the Law*
- briefs filed in the United States Supreme Court

Currently, LEXIS does not provide access to either of the leading legal encyclopedias (*Corpus Juris Secundum* and *American Jurisprudence 2d*). At the state level, LEXIS offers access to various legal encyclopedias that deal with legal doctrines of particular states.

As with other materials available in LEXIS, the coverage of secondary sources continually evolves. Mead Data's printed and online guides to LEXIS

[163] Pages 65 to 74 of CHRISTOPHER G. WREN & JILL R. WREN, THE LEGAL RESEARCH MANUAL: A GAME PLAN FOR LEGAL RESEARCH AND ANALYSIS (2d ed. 1986), cover the "generalized approach" as it applies in book-based legal research and highlight some of the secondary sources most commonly used in this law-finding approach.

(highlighted in Appendix A) provide timely information about the secondary sources offered. When checking the availability of secondary materials in LEXIS, pay particular attention to possible omissions in a publication's coverage: the licensing arrangements between Mead Data and the publishers of secondary sources sometimes require the exclusion of specified items from the online versions of certain publications. Also, when checking Mead Data's descriptions of secondary materials in LEXIS, note the segments available in these materials; the wide range of secondary sources has spawned a variety of searchable segments.

Despite the array of secondary sources in LEXIS, if you are searching these materials to gather background information in an area of law unfamiliar to you (rather than to improve your understanding of an area of law already familiar to you), you will often proceed more efficiently and effectively by starting in books, assuming you have access to them. Sometimes, you will have information (such as the name of the author of a law review article) that will enable you to locate a helpful secondary source online even if you have little knowledge of the area you are researching. Just as likely, however, a lack of familiarity with the key concepts and terms relevant to a particular research problem will hinder you in developing successful search requests; you can waste considerable time and online charges trying to gain an introduction to a new area of law through database searching. In book-based research, by contrast, you can rely on scope notes, cross-references in indexes, and other editorially prepared features to orient you to the subject matter and suggest avenues of inquiry.

If you decide to search for secondary sources in LEXIS, you apply the search techniques already discussed for finding primary authorities. For example, you can perform an unrestricted search in secondary sources for the descriptive or fact words you have identified as relevant to your problem. Or, you can include a field restriction to limit a search to, say, law review articles written by a specific author.

The following paragraphs spotlight some of the secondary sources you can search in LEXIS.

Law reviews and other legal periodicals. LEXIS offers online access to the text of articles, book reviews, and other items appearing in law reviews and other legal periodicals (such as bar association publications). You will find legal periodicals in several places, including these:

- The LAWREV library contains files for numerous law reviews.
- Topical and other specialized libraries (*e.g.*, the HEALTH and ABA libraries) often contain files with legal periodicals relevant to the library's focus.
- NEXIS, the companion service to LEXIS, offers access to some legal periodicals, such as the *National Law Journal*.

You can locate articles in law reviews and other legal periodicals in LEXIS several ways:

- You can search for fact or descriptive words in the text of these publications in a file that contains legal periodicals.
- You will encounter references to legal periodical articles in many of the cases you retrieve through LEXIS, as well as in the annotations at the end of many statutory code sections in LEXIS. You can use these citations to find the articles in files containing legal periodicals.
- You can use the online versions of indexes to legal periodicals to search more systematically in LEXIS for references to articles, book reviews, and other items appearing in law reviews and other legal periodicals. Like their print versions, the online periodical indexes consist of citations (not the text of the indexed materials) and allow you to locate citations according to various criteria, including subject, title, author, or the citation of a case or statute that has been the principal subject of an article.

  You will find *Index to Legal Periodicals* in the ILP file in either the LAWREV or LEXREF library, and you will find *Legal Resource Index* in the LGLIND file in either the LAWREV or LEXREF library.

  Although each index entry is brief, it consists of several segments. In LEXIS, this characteristic means that, as a rule of thumb, you should search with the "and" connector instead of a "w/n" connector. Each term you link with a "w/n" connector in LEXIS must appear in the same segment; given the brevity of the segments in the periodical indexes, terms linked with a "w/n" connector can easily occur within the prescribed number of words of each other, yet appear in different segments, thus causing your search request to miss potentially relevant index entries. The "and" connector presents less risk of bypassing relevant citations because this connector does not impose a same-segment requirement.

To ensure a comprehensive LEXIS search for articles in law reviews and other legal periodicals, search the periodical indexes *and* the text of the periodicals themselves. The indexes might refer you to articles in periodicals not available in LEXIS. On the other hand, searching the text of periodicals might locate articles that have not been indexed in a way that identifies them as relevant to your research.

Case annotations in *American Law Reports* and *U.S. Supreme Court Reports, Lawyers' Edition*. In *A.L.R.* and *Lawyers' Edition, Second Series*, Lawyers Cooperative Publishing provides articles (*i.e.*, "annotations") that analyze legal issues from selected cases published in *A.L.R.* and *Lawyers' Edition 2d*. You can gain access to these annotations in LEXIS in a couple of ways:

- You can search in the ALR file in either the ALR library or the BEGIN library (which contains various secondary sources). The ALR file contains all the *A.L.R.* and *Lawyers' Edition 2d* annotations available in LEXIS.
- When you search in some combined case-law files, the computer will also retrieve any annotations that satisfy your search request. This situation occurs, for instance, when you search in the OMNI file in either the STATES library or the GENFED library. You will see the annotations identified as a separate group of documents when the monitor displays your search results. An example of this kind of display appears in Figure 11.01 on page 319.

  For a list of the LEXIS files in which you can opt to see *A.L.R.* and *Lawyers' Edition 2d* annotations as part of your search results, check the entries for *American Law Reports* or *Lawyers' Edition* in the alphabetical listing in the *LEXIS/NEXIS Library Contents and Alphabetical List.*

Looseleaf services. LEXIS offers access to numerous looseleaf services. You can find them in topical collections of LEXIS files (see page 254) and in collections of LEXIS files grouped according to publisher, such as Bureau of National Affairs (BNA) and Commerce Clearing House (CCH).

Restatements of the Law. LEXIS offers access to *Restatements of the Law*, the treatise-like publications produced by committees of distinguished judges, law professors, and practicing lawyers, all working under the auspices of the American Law Institute. At this writing, *Restatements* appear in the RESTAT file in the BEGIN library (which contains various secondary sources).

U.S. Supreme Court briefs. In the BRIEFS file in the GENFED library in LEXIS, you can gain access to briefs filed in U.S. Supreme Court cases.

Finding the law in LEXIS through updating

As you update the law to make sure the legal authorities you've located in your "finding the law" phase still constitute valid statements of the law, you will also be finding more new authorities. Therefore, just as in book-based legal research, updating the law also functions as a technique for finding the law. Chapter 12 explains how to update the law online.

Finding the law in LEXIS by using Easy Search

When you use LEXIS to find authorities, you have the option of using the Easy Search feature to simplify the task.[164] Intended for novice or infrequent users of LEXIS, Easy Search provides a fill-in-the-blank method of implementing some of the law-finding techniques already explained in this chapter. (As explained in Chapter 12, you can also use Easy Search to update authorities.)

Easy Search presents menus of research activities and asks you to specify the task the computer should perform. For the research activities available through Easy Search, you do not need to know an array of commands to use LEXIS. Once you finish typing responses to the "plain English" prompts Easy Search displays, the computer translates your choices into LEXIS commands, carries out a search, and displays the results.

Easy Search is a relatively new feature, and the arrangement of the Easy Search menus has evolved since Mead Data added the feature to LEXIS. The basic menu-driven operation of Easy Search has remained unchanged, however.

Using Easy Search to find authorities in LEXIS. To use Easy Search, begin by selecting the Easy Search library (EASY) just as you would any other LEXIS library. When the monitor displays a screen listing the files in the EASY library, type the name of the file you want to select, then press TRANSMIT. Currently, the LEGAL file in the EASY library allows you to perform law-finding activities in LEXIS files of cases, statutes, annotations in *American Law Reports*, and other materials useful in researching United States law. This discussion assumes that you will be using the LEGAL file.

After you select the LEGAL file, the monitor will display a menu from which you can select a category of documents to search. For law-finding activities, select the category designated "General Cases, Codes, Cite Verification." You will then see a screen similar to the one shown in Figure 10.05. You can then use Easy Search to find the law in several ways, including these:

- You can find a known case or *A.L.R.* annotation by transmitting a citation or other information you know about the authority. Select the menu choice "Specific case or ALR annotation."
- You can find a known statute by transmitting its citation. Select the menu choice "Find a statute or view a statutory table of contents."

[164] Long-time LEXIS users might notice similarities between the Easy Search feature and Legal Research Assistant, a component of the Easy Search software program Mead Data offers as part of its LEXIS/NEXIS Technology Series Research Software for MS-DOS. The Easy Search feature, which functions while you are logged on to LEXIS, derives from the Legal Research Assistant software that Mead Data developed so researchers could prepare search instructions offline, before logging on to LEXIS.

```
                    LEVEL 1 - 1 OF 1 ITEM

                    EASY SEARCH - LEGAL
          General Cases, Codes, Cite Verification

<=1>  Specific case or ALR annotation
<=2>  Verify a case using the Shepard's (R) or Auto-Cite (R) service
<=3>  References to a case using the LEXCITE (R) feature
<=4>  Find a statute or view a statutory table of contents

<=5>  Main Menu  <=6>  Sign Off
```

Source: Mead Data Central, Inc. © 1993

Figure 10.05. Menu for Selecting Law-Finding Activities in the LEGAL File in the EASY Library in LEXIS

- You can conduct a descriptive-word search for cases. Select the menu choice "Specific case or ALR annotation."
- You can find authorities through updating. Select the menu choice "Verify a case using the Shepard's (R) or Auto-Cite (R) service," or select the menu choice "References to a case using the LEXCITE (R) feature."

To convey your menu choice at the screen shown in Figure 10.05:

1. Use the TAB key to move the cursor to the LINK marker next to the activity you want to select. Alternatively, type the number of the LINK marker corresponding to the activity you want to select. For example, to select "Specific case or ALR annotation," move the cursor to the LINK marker labelled "<=1>," or type =1.

2. Press TRANSMIT.

The next screen you see will depend on the selection you made at the screen shown in Figure 10.05. For instance, if you selected "Specific case or ALR annotation," you would see a screen like the one shown in Figure 10.06. As you proceed through the sequence of screens displayed by the Easy Search

```
                    LEVEL 1 - 1 OF 1 ITEM

                    EASY SEARCH - LEGAL
           General Cases, Codes, Cite Verification
              Specific case or ALR annotation

<=1>  The official or unofficial case citation is known
<=2>  The docket number is known
<=3>  The case name, judge, lawyer, law firm or decision date is known
<=4>  Find cases about any topic
<=5>  Find an ALR annotation

<=6>  Previous Step  <=7>  Main Menu  <=8>  Sign Off
```

Source: Mead Data Central, Inc. © 1993

Figure 10.06. Menu for Selecting a Method for Retrieving Cases or ALR Annotations through Easy Search in LEXIS

feature, you construct your search instructions by selecting choices from additional menus or by typing responses to on-screen "plain English" prompts.

To illustrate using Easy Search, suppose you want to retrieve *Lewis v. United States* and you know its citations—445 U.S. 55, 100 S. Ct. 915, 63 L. Ed. 2d 198. At the menu in Figure 10.05, you would move the cursor to the LINK marker labelled "< = 1>" (or type `=1`) and press TRANSMIT. At that point, you would see a screen like the one shown in Figure 10.06. There, you would select "The official or unofficial case citation is known": either move the cursor to the corresponding LINK marker or type `=1`, then press TRANSMIT. The monitor would then display a screen where you would type one of the citations for *Lewis* and press TRANSMIT. On-screen prompts would then guide you through the rest of the Easy Search procedure, at the end of which the computer would implement a LEXSEE search to retrieve *Lewis.*

After you retrieve a document through Easy Search, you can return to the Easy Search menus by typing `.log` and pressing TRANSMIT.

The role of Easy Search in finding the law. For new or infrequent users, the menus and on-screen prompts in Easy Search can simplify using LEXIS: once you have typed your responses to the on-screen prompts, the computer constructs a search request (including segment restrictions where appropriate) and selects an appropriate library and file or service (such as Shepard's) for the search. Thus, Easy Search reduces the number of LEXIS commands, logic connectors, segment names, and library, file, and service names you have to know to use LEXIS.

At this time, however, Easy Search has some drawbacks:

- For experienced LEXIS users, using the Easy Search menus will often prove slower than carrying out the research task without the help of Easy Search.
- When you conduct a descriptive-word search through Easy Search, the computer automatically makes important decisions about your search request, such as selecting logic connectors or using universal characters to truncate search terms. Some of these choices, however, might not prove as well-suited for your research goal as the choices you would make in formulating a search request on your own. For example, at this writing, Easy Search automatically selects "and" to link search terms in situations in which you might prefer to use a connector like "w/10."
- Because of its simplicity and automation, Easy Search invites researchers who do not know how a CALR service operates to use LEXIS for fairly sophisticated law-finding searches. But as earlier chapters have noted, effective use of a CALR service calls for knowledge of such points as how logic connectors work, what factors can affect the selection of search terms (*e.g.*, a word's ambiguity or lack of distinctiveness), and how the computer's literalness affects its response to search instructions. Easy Search is designed, however, for users least likely to have this knowledge. Thus, Easy Search could encourage LEXIS use by those most likely to find searching online a waste of time and money, whether through Easy Search or otherwise.

Finding the Law through WESTLAW

Descriptive word or fact word approach in WESTLAW

Unless you already know the citation of a case, statute, or other authority that bears on your research problem, you will generally find the descriptive or fact word approach the most fruitful way to start finding relevant primary authorities.[165] If you have followed the procedures for developing your facts and issues and for formulating search requests (see Chapter 7), this approach should follow naturally.

[165] If you already know of a relevant authority, the "known authority" approach (see pages 278–92) offers a good starting point.

The idea here is to take the words (called "descriptive words" or "fact words") you selected to describe key aspects of your research problem, and use them as the search terms in your search request. For example, returning to the hypothetical landlord-tenant problem on pages 19–20, involving a lack of running water in an apartment, your analysis of the problem might lead you to select and arrange terms in a Boolean search request like this:

```
(tenant or landlord or lease!) and (apartment
or roominghouse or "rooming house") and (water
or plumbing)
```

In most WESTLAW databases, you have the option of expressing your descriptive-word search request in plain English, using WESTLAW's natural-language feature. For example, you could transmit this search request:

```
Does a landlord have an obligation to provide
running water in a leased apartment?
```

This online law-finding technique, whether implemented with a Boolean (terms-and-connectors) search request or with a natural-language search request, corresponds to the book-based legal research approach in which you look up descriptive or fact words in an index.[166]

After constructing your search request, you transmit it in an appropriate WESTLAW database. In response to a Boolean search request, the computer will retrieve documents containing your descriptive or fact words in the relationship you prescribed in your request; in response to a natural-language search request, the computer will prescribe the relationship by applying statistical probability algorithms (see pages 25–26) and then retrieve documents satisfying that relationship.

The kind of documents you retrieve will depend on where you transmit your search request:

- *Cases*. In a database of cases, a document will consist of the court's opinion, along with any concurring or dissenting opinions. The document will also often include editorial enhancements, such as headnotes or a synopsis. (Pages 85–109 describe these WESTLAW enhancements.)
- *Statutes*. In a database of *unannotated* statutes, a document will consist of a statutory section, its subsections, and (sometimes) cross-references to other research sources (*e.g.*, related statutes, session laws, or administrative regulations; notes about the statute's history).

[166] *See* CHRISTOPHER G. WREN & JILL R. WREN, THE LEGAL RESEARCH MANUAL: A GAME PLAN FOR LEGAL RESEARCH AND ANALYSIS 46–51 (2d ed. 1986).

In a database of *annotated* statutes, a document will also include annotations accompanying each statutory section retrieved (*i.e.*, brief summaries of cases and attorney general opinions that have interpreted and applied the statute). The document might also include references to selected secondary sources, such as texts, *Corpus Juris Secundum*, and law review articles.

Note that the statutes for a jurisdiction usually include that jurisdiction's constitution and court rules (such as rules of evidence or civil procedure). Consequently, a document in a statutory database can also consist of a constitutional provision or a court rule.

- *Administrative regulations.* In a database consisting of an administrative code (*i.e.*, administrative regulations arranged by subject matter), a document will consist of an administrative regulation and its subsections. In addition, a document will likely contain cross-references to the corresponding administrative register (*i.e.*, the chronological arrangement of regulations) and to statutes authorizing the regulation.

  In a database consisting of an administrative register, a document will consist of an administrative regulation and its subsections, a proposed regulation, a notice of an administrative agency meeting or hearing, or an announcement of other agency activity. A document might also include related information, such as cross-references to sections of the administrative code the document affects, or the name of a person to contact at the agency that issued the document.

As you conduct descriptive or fact word searches for authorities in WESTLAW, the tips provided from here through page 278 can help you search more effectively and efficiently.

Tips for descriptive or fact word searching in WESTLAW: statutes. When you search for statutes by using the descriptive or fact word approach, keep in mind a couple of points.

Refining searches in annotated statutes. When you search in a database of annotated statutes, you might retrieve irrelevant statutes because your search terms appear in accompanying annotations. If you encounter this problem, add a field restriction confining your Boolean search to the field containing just the statutory text, or perform your search in a database of unannotated statutes, where your search terms will most likely appear only in statutory text. (Currently, you cannot use a "text" field restriction when you search statutes with a natural-language request.)

Expanding searches through the Related Materials Directory in WESTLAW. For its statutory databases, WESTLAW provides a feature called the

"Related Materials Directory," which allows you to gain access to related materials in other WESTLAW databases. These related materials consist of such things as session laws amending or repealing the statute you are viewing, notes about the statute's history, references to related administrative regulations or law review commentaries, and annotations of relevant cases.[167]

While viewing a statute, you can invoke the Related Materials Directory by typing **rm** and pressing ENTER. The monitor will then display a directory of related materials grouped in several categories, with each category constituting a service. Figure 10.07 shows the Related Materials Directory for WESTLAW's database of unannotated California statutes (CA-ST). The selections you will see in a Related Materials Directory will vary in different databases.

You gain access to a Related Materials service by typing its command (shown in the Related Materials Directory) and pressing ENTER. The monitor will then display the first page of the related materials in the service you selected. When you finish viewing the materials, you return to the Related Materials Directory by typing **gb** (for "go back") and pressing ENTER. Back

[167] For more details about the Related Materials Directory, see WEST PUBLISHING COMPANY, WESTLAW REFERENCE MANUAL 157–60 (5th ed. 1993).

```
                         RELATED MATERIALS              Only Page

   CITATION: CA BUS & PROF § 101

   Command:            Service:
   UPDATE              Update Materials (Legislative service documents and court
                       orders)
   GM                  General Materials (Major headings with general
                       information applicable to this document)
   REFS                References (Miscellaneous references to secondary sources)
   ANNOS               Annotations (Notes of Decisions)

        Note:  The services listed relate to the current document. You are
               viewing Related Materials for the CA-ST database.


  If you wish to:
     Select a Related Materials service for your citation, type its command and
       press ENTER
     Go back to the previously accessed service, type GB and press ENTER
     View the list of previously accessed services, type MAP and press ENTER
     Obtain further information on Related Materials, type HELP and press ENTER
```

Source: West Publishing Company © 1993

Figure 10.07. Related Materials Directory in the CA-ST Database in WESTLAW

at the directory, you can select another service, or you can again type `gb` and press ENTER to return to the statute you were viewing before you invoked Related Materials.

If you know the command for gaining access to a category of related materials you want to examine, you can bypass the Related Materials Directory and go straight to those related materials by typing the command while viewing a statute and then pressing ENTER. For example, as you can see in Figure 10.07, `refs` is the command that allows you to see references related to statutes in the CA-ST database; if you type `refs` and press ENTER while viewing a statute in CA-ST, the monitor will display citations to law review or legal encyclopedia articles and other secondary sources that relate to your statute. To return to the statute you were viewing before you invoked Related Materials, type `gb` and press ENTER.

Tips for descriptive or fact word searching in WESTLAW: where to find constitutions. In WESTLAW, constitutional provisions currently appear only in databases containing statutory codes. For instance, federal constitutional provisions appear in the databases containing the *United States Code* (USC and USCA). Likewise, Florida constitutional provisions appear in the databases containing unannotated and annotated Florida statutes (FL-ST and FL-ST-ANN, respectively).

You can extract constitutional provisions from a statutory database by using a Boolean search request that includes a field restriction based on the "citation" field, which contains citation information about each document. In a statutory database, a constitutional provision's citation appears with the abbreviation "Const" in the "citation" field. Consequently, when you search a statutory database, the field restriction in the following examples will confine your search to constitutional provisions (here, provisions mainly concerning freedom of speech):

```
speech and citation(const)

speech and ci(const)
```

Currently, you cannot use a "citation" field restriction when you search statutes with a natural-language request.

Tips for descriptive or fact word searching in WESTLAW: where to find court rules. To locate federal court rules (*e.g.*, rules of evidence, rules of civil and criminal procedure) through a descriptive or fact word search in WESTLAW, you can search in databases consisting exclusively of court rules or in databases consisting of the federal statutory code:

- Federal court rules appear in the US-RULES database, which consists exclusively of federal court rules.

At this writing, the frequently used federal court rules (*e.g.*, for evidence or civil procedure) do not appear in separate databases in WESTLAW. To isolate these rules within the US-RULES database, use a citation field restriction in a Boolean search request. For instance, the restriction `citation(fre)` would focus a search on the Federal Rules of Evidence. *WESTLAW DataBasics* provides a list of recommended field restrictions for retrieving specific kinds of rules from the US-RULES database;[168] to see more current tips on which field restrictions to use for this purpose, type `scope` and press ENTER while you are in the US-RULES database.

- Federal court rules also appear in the USC database, which contains the unannotated version of the *United States Code*, and in the USCA database, which contains the annotated version.

  When you search for federal court rules in the USC or USCA database, you isolate the rules by using a field restriction based on citation information. For example, to locate federal rules of evidence governing hearsay, you can use a Boolean search request like `hearsay and prelim(evidence)`.

- Separate databases contain federal court rules in some specialized areas, such as securities law and bankruptcy.[169]

At the state level, you can find the court rules for some states in a WESTLAW database consisting of just a state's court rules. To perform a descriptive or fact word search for the court rules of other states, though, you must search in WESTLAW databases consisting of statutory codes (which contain the rules). To search for state court rules in a statutory code database, isolate the rules by using a field restriction based on citation information. Thus, to locate rules of evidence governing hearsay in a given state, you can try a Boolean search request like `hearsay and prelim(evidence)` in that state's statutory code database in WESTLAW. However, states use different names for comparable court rules (*e.g.*, "Rules of Civil Procedure," "Code of Procedure"), so you will need to experiment to find the right combination of search terms and field restrictions to segregate particular kinds of court rules in a given state.

Tips for descriptive or fact word searching in WESTLAW: where to find administrative regulations. To locate federal administrative regulations through a descriptive or fact word search in WESTLAW, you search in a database consisting of provisions from the *Code of Federal Regulations* or of

[168] WEST PUBLISHING COMPANY, WESTLAW DATABASICS 285–86 (1993).

[169] For a list of these databases, see WEST PUBLISHING COMPANY, WESTLAW DATABASICS 285 (1993).

material from the *Federal Register.* You will find federal administrative regulations in several places in WESTLAW:

- The CFR database contains the current edition of the *Code of Federal Regulations.*
- The FR database contains the *Federal Register.*
- Previous years' versions of the *Code of Federal Regulations* appear in separate databases (*e.g.*, CFR87, CFR86, CFR85).
- Many WESTLAW databases covering specialized topics contain federal administrative regulations. For example, the FSEC-CFR database consists of federal securities regulations found in the *Code of Federal Regulations.* Likewise, the FTRAN-FR database contains transportation-related provisions found in the *Federal Register.*

At the state level, WESTLAW currently provides few administrative codes or registers. West Publishing will undoubtedly add more state administrative regulations to WESTLAW, and checking West's descriptions of WESTLAW materials will alert you to new additions. To determine whether a state's administrative regulations are online in WESTLAW, check the portion of the WESTLAW Directory dealing with state-level databases. Also check the coverage of specialized databases in WESTLAW: databases in areas such as state taxation or state securities regulation sometimes include state administrative materials.

Until more state administrative codes and registers appear in WESTLAW, you will generally need to take an indirect route when using descriptive or fact words in WESTLAW to find state administrative regulations relevant to your problem. If the state administrative regulations you want are not in WESTLAW, online statutes might provide leads in the form of cross-references to state administrative regulations interpreting or implementing the statutes. For example, the "references" field in annotated statutes in WESTLAW cites various related authorities, sometimes including state administrative regulations. Similarly, you might find references to relevant administrative regulations by invoking WESTLAW's Related Materials feature (see pages 267–69) while viewing a statute online.

Even if searching a database of state statutes does not turn up references to specific regulations, your search might uncover relevant statutes that authorize administrative agencies to formulate, issue, and enforce regulations implementing statutory objectives. If so, you can log off WESTLAW and check the printed version of the appropriate administrative code or register.

Finally, you might find research leads by searching in a database containing an online version of a relevant looseleaf publication addressing a specialized area of law where regulations play an important role. Check, for example, WESTLAW databases containing publications of the Bureau of National Affairs (BNA) or Commerce Clearing House (CCH).

Tips for descriptive or fact word searching in WESTLAW: simultaneously searching all online jurisdictions. In addition to allowing you to conduct descriptive or fact word searches in the authorities of a single jurisdiction, WESTLAW offers you the ability to search simultaneously the authorities of multiple jurisdictions. For example, in one pass, you could search all the online cases from every state for any decisions dealing with the admissibility of videotaped depositions of child witnesses in criminal trials. (This kind of search presents an online variation of looking for state cases in *Decennial Digests* and *General Digests* in book-based legal research, although when performed online, the technique avoids the need to check multiple, noncumulative volumes.)[170] Or you could, say, simultaneously search all the online state statutes for provisions concerning drunk driving.

WESTLAW provides numerous multi-jurisdictional databases that afford this capability for comparative law research. The following paragraphs highlight some of the databases most commonly used for multi-jurisdictional searching. As you familiarize yourself with the contents of WESTLAW, you will discover other multi-jurisdictional databases.

- *Cases.* In WESTLAW, the ALLSTATES database includes cases decided from 1945 to the present from all states, while ALLSTATES-OLD includes cases decided before 1945 from all states. The ALLFEDS database includes cases decided by all federal courts from 1945 to the present, while ALLFEDS-OLD includes cases decided by all federal courts from 1789 through 1944. WESTLAW also provides the CTA database for cases decided by all United States Courts of Appeals from 1945 to the present, the CTA-OLD database for cases decided by all United States Courts of Appeals from 1891 through 1944, the DCT database for cases decided by all United States District Courts from 1945 to the present, and the DCT-OLD database for cases decided by all United States District Courts from 1789 through 1944.
- *Statutes.* For simultaneously searching all online state statutes, WESTLAW provides two databases: STAT-ALL covers unannotated state statutes, and ST-ANN-ALL covers the annotated versions.
- *Constitutions.* Although WESTLAW currently does not offer a multiple-jurisdiction database consisting only of constitutions, you

[170] *See* Christopher G. Wren & Jill R. Wren, The Legal Research Manual: A Game Plan for Legal Research and Analysis 15 (2d ed. 1986).

can search simultaneously for comparable provisions in all state constitutions that are online. To do so, select the STAT-ALL or ST-ANN-ALL database; then focus the search on constitutional provisions by using the `citation(const)` restriction in a Boolean search request, as explained on page 269.

- *Court rules.* Although WESTLAW currently does not offer a multiple-jurisdiction database consisting only of state court rules, you can search simultaneously for comparable court rules from all states with statutes online. To do so, select the STAT-ALL or ST-ANN-ALL database; then isolate court rules by adding an appropriate field restriction to a Boolean search request, as explained on page 270.
- *Administrative regulations.* At this time, WESTLAW offers few state administrative regulations, and the option of simultaneously searching regulations from all states is not available. West Publishing will undoubtedly add more state administrative regulations to WESTLAW, however. When that happens, you will likely be able to conduct multi-jurisdictional searches for these materials, probably in much the same way you now can for state statutes.

Tips for descriptive or fact word searching in WESTLAW: simultaneously searching in a customized selection of jurisdictions. You are not limited to the extremes of searching either (on the one hand) in a single jurisdiction or (on the other hand) in all state jurisdictions or all federal jurisdictions. You can also customize your selection of jurisdictions in which to search. The following paragraphs summarize the techniques for customizing multi-jurisdictional searches in WESTLAW, and highlight some of the databases most commonly used for this kind of searching.

- *Cases.* You can customize your selection of jurisdictions by choosing a multiple-jurisdiction database of cases and including in a Boolean search request a field restriction that identifies each jurisdiction in which you want to search. For instance, suppose you wanted to search simultaneously for cases from California, New York, and Florida dealing with whether videotaped testimony in a criminal trial deprives a defendant of the right to confront adverse witnesses. You could select the ALLSTATES database (which contains cases from all states) and include in your search request a field restriction using the "court" field, which identifies the jurisdiction in which the case was decided:

```
court(ca ny fl) and (videotap! w/20
confront!)
```

With this technique, use a space (not the word "or") as the "or" connector between state abbreviations. Because WESTLAW equates a state's two-letter postal abbreviation in the "court" field with the name of the state, the computer in this context will treat the word "or" as a reference to the state of Oregon rather than as a logic connector, and will therefore search for cases from Oregon courts. Only use the word "or" in searching the court field if you want to refer to the state of Oregon.

Through its regional reporter databases, WESTLAW provides another avenue for simultaneously searching cases from selected states. These databases group cases according to the jurisdictions found in West Publishing Company's printed regional reporters, which contain cases from courts in specific geographical regions of the country. Thus, the SO database contains cases from the same states covered by West's *Southern Reporter*—Alabama, Florida, Louisiana, and Mississippi.[171]

At the federal level, if you wanted to limit your WESTLAW search to selected federal appellate circuits, you could select a database of cases from all federal courts of appeals (CTA or CTA-OLD) and include in a Boolean search request a field restriction using the "court" field. For instance, if you wanted to retrieve cases from the Fifth, Sixth, and Ninth Circuits dealing with the relationship between the right of confrontation and the use of videotaped testimony in criminal trials, you could use the following search request in the CTA database:

```
court(5th 6th 9th) and (videotap!
w/20 confront!)
```

WESTLAW also offers databases that allow you to search simultaneously for both state and federal cases from selected jurisdictions. For each state, WESTLAW offers a multiple-jurisdiction database identified by that state's two-letter postal abbreviation followed by "-CS-ALL" (*e.g.*, TX-CS-ALL). The database contains cases decided by the state courts of that state, by the federal district courts and bankruptcy courts located in that state, by the federal circuit court of appeals for the circuit in which that state is located, by the Judicial Panel on Multidistrict Litigation, and by the United

[171] Each of WESTLAW's regional reporter databases includes not only the cases published in the corresponding West regional reporter, but slip opinions and cases that West has not published in the reporter. WEST PUBLISHING COMPANY, WESTLAW REFERENCE MANUAL 102 (5th ed. 1993).

States Supreme Court. For each federal circuit court of appeals, WESTLAW offers a multiple-jurisdiction database identified by that circuit's number followed by "-ALL" (*e.g.*, CTA7-ALL), or, for the D.C. Circuit, CTADC-ALL. The database contains cases decided by the state courts of all the states located in that circuit, by the federal district courts and bankruptcy courts located in that circuit, by that federal circuit court of appeals, by the Judicial Panel on Multidistrict Litigation, and by the United States Supreme Court.

- *Statutes*. In WESTLAW, you customize your selection of state statutes by choosing the STAT-ALL database (for all online unannotated state statutes) or the ST-ANN-ALL database (for all online annotated state statutes); then you include in a Boolean search request a field restriction using the "state" field, which contains the state's two-letter postal abbreviation. For example, suppose you wanted to search simultaneously for statutes from Connecticut, Delaware, and Florida concerning the use of blood or breath alcohol levels to prove an automobile driver's intoxication. You could use the following search request in the STAT-ALL or ST-ANN-ALL database to confine your search to the statutes from just the desired states:

  ```
  state(ct de fl) and ((blood or breath)
  w/5 alcohol)
  ```

  Use a space (not the word "or") as the "or" connector between state abbreviations. Because the computer treats the word "or" in the state field as a reference to Oregon rather than as a logic connector, you should only use the word "or" in searching the state field if you want to refer to Oregon.

- *Constitutions*. In WESTLAW, if you want to search simultaneously for constitutional provisions from selected states, you use field restrictions in a Boolean search of the STAT-ALL database (which contains all online unannotated state statutory codes) or the ST-ANN-ALL database (which contains all online annotated state statutory codes). Because the "citation" field for a constitutional provision contains the abbreviation "Const" and because the "state" field contains the state's two-letter postal abbreviation, you can use these restrictions together to isolate constitutional provisions found in the statutory code of each state you want. For example, the following search request in STAT-ALL or ST-ANN-ALL would locate state constitutional provisions dealing with free speech in California and New York:

```
speech and citation(const) and
state(ca ny)
```

Use a space (not the word "or") as the "or" connector between state abbreviations. The computer treats the word "or" in the state field as a reference to Oregon rather than as a logic connector, so you should only use the word "or" in searching the state field if you want to refer to Oregon.

- *Court rules.* In WESTLAW, to search simultaneously for court rules from selected states, you search in the STAT-ALL database (for all online unannotated state statutory codes) or the ST-ANN-ALL database (for all online annotated state statutory codes). To customize your selection of states, include in a Boolean search request a field restriction using the "state" field, which contains the state's two-letter postal abbreviation. Thus, if you wanted to search simultaneously for court rules from Florida, Georgia, and Louisiana, you would use the restriction `state(fl ga la)`. (Use a space, not the word "or," as the "or" connector between state abbreviations; in the state field, the computer will treat "or" as a reference to Oregon. Only use the word "or" in searching the state field if you want to refer to Oregon.) Along with the field restriction to segregate the statutory codes of the states you want to search, you also use a field restriction to isolate the court rules from the rest of the statutory code provisions, as explained on page 270. Your resulting search request would take a form like this: `state(fl ga la) and prelim(evidence) and hearsay`.
- *Administrative regulations.* At this time, WESTLAW offers few state administrative regulations and does not provide the option of searching a customized selection of state administrative regulations. West Publishing will undoubtedly add more state administrative regulations to WESTLAW, however. When that happens, WESTLAW might offer an option for searching a customized selection of state administrative regulations; if so, you should be able to customize your multi-jurisdictional searches for regulations by adapting the techniques for simultaneously searching selected state statutory codes.

Tips for descriptive or fact word searching in WESTLAW: online indexes for statutory codes. The CALR vendors generally tout computer-assisted legal research as a way of escaping the potential drawbacks of printed indexes.[172] Nonetheless, for the *United States Code Annotated* and for almost

[172] *See* pages 15–16.

every state statutory code, WESTLAW provides an online version of the print index. To verify whether a state statutory code has an associated online index, check the WESTLAW database descriptions (available through the sources highlighted in Appendix B).

An online index serves the same principal purpose as its printed counterpart: to direct you to relevant code provisions you can then look up in either an online or printed version of the code itself. Browsing an online index can also suggest additional search terms you can use in searching a code.[173] Of course, if you have access to the index in printed form, you will often proceed just as well—and avoid online charges—by using it instead of the online index.

If you want to search in an online statutory code index, you select search terms by thinking like an indexer. Instead of anticipating the language used in the actual text of a relevant statute (as you normally do in computer-assisted legal research), you anticipate the terms legal publishers have used to index statutes. In short, when you search an online index, you simply select terms as you would when you look up something in the index of a book.

Using statutory code indexes in WESTLAW. To search in a statutory code index in WESTLAW, gain access to the database containing the statutory index you want to search: USCA-IDX identifies the online index for the *United States Code Annotated*; for a state statutory index database, the standard WESTLAW identifier consists of a state's two-letter postal abbreviation followed by "-ST-IDX" (such as FL-ST-IDX for the index to Florida statutes). After you have gained access to an index database, the monitor will display a screen for entering a search request. If you want to view on-screen instructions before beginning a search in the index, you can type `scope` and press ENTER.

An index database in WESTLAW includes two components: an alphabetical listing of the main entries in the index, and the actual index (which includes the citations to statutory code provisions). In addition, WESTLAW index databases contain two fields you can use to fine-tune your search for index entries:

- The "title" field contains the main index entries. In the USCA-IDX database, you can use either the "title" or "citation" field.
- The "index" field contains the index entries appearing under the main entries.

At the screen for entering a search request, you can instruct the WESTLAW computer either to display the list of main index entries or to conduct a search of the index itself. To display the listing, type the search request `citation(heading)` and press the ENTER key. On-screen instructions will explain how to browse the list, which will include entries such as these:

[173] *See* pages 151–52.

ADOPTION
ADRIFT
ADULT
ADULT CARE FACILITIES
ADULT CONGREGATE LIVING FACILITIES
ADULT CORRECTIONS, DIVISION OF
ADULT DAY CARE CENTERS
ADULT EDUCATION
ADULT FOSTER HOME CARE ACT
ADULT FOSTER HOMES

When you finish reviewing the list, you can search the index: to do so, transmit `q` to redisplay your search request for modification, then type and transmit the request you want to use to find terms in the index.

If you want to locate every occurrence of a search term (such as "adoption") and corresponding citations to statutory code provisions, do not use a field restriction in your search request; just transmit the terms you want the computer to search for. If you want to find index entries (and citations) grouped under a main index entry, use a restriction in your search request. For instance, in the index for Florida statutes, the search request `title(adoption)` would locate the point in the index at which the main index entry for "adoption" begins:

```
title→      ADOPTION
  index→      Generally, FL ST 63.012 et seq.
  index→    Access to information, voluntary registry
  index→      of adoption information, FL ST 382.027
  index→    Acknowledgments,
  index→      Intermediaries, FL ST 63.085
            . . . .
```

In addition, the search request would locate any other main index entries containing the word "adoption" (*e.g.*, "State-Wide Adoption Exchange").

Note that you can bypass the alphabetical list of main index entries and start searching immediately in the index for your search terms. When you first gain access to an index database and the initial screen appears for entering a search request, instead of transmitting the search request `citation(heading)`, simply transmit the request you intend to use to locate your search terms in the index.

Known authority approach in WESTLAW

If you know the citation of a legal authority that might apply to your problem, you won't necessarily log on to a CALR service to find or read that authority: you will often just pull the appropriate book off the library shelf and begin reading. This technique, called the "known authority" approach, is the most direct method for finding an authority, and leads quickly and easily to related authorities (for example, by checking annotations accompanying a known statute, or by checking the authorities you find cited in a known case).[174]

In some instances, however, you won't be able to turn directly to a printed source containing your known authority, or you might find it more convenient not to use an available printed version of the authority. Perhaps your library's collection does not include the publication you want, or maybe the authority was issued too recently to be published in a printed version yet. Alternatively, while reading something online, you might come across a reference to another authority and want to quickly review that authority without the extra steps of logging off the CALR service, retrieving a book, and later logging back on to continue your research.

In situations like these, using a CALR service can prove the only way, or the most practical way, to take advantage of the "known authority" approach. WESTLAW provides several means for using citation elements (*e.g.*, the name and volume of a case reporter and the page number on which an authority begins) to go directly to a known authority.[175]

Finding known authorities through FIND in WESTLAW. You can use the FIND feature to retrieve various types of authorities, which currently include cases, statutes, slip laws,[176] constitutional provisions, administrative regulations, decisions of some administrative agencies, and several looseleaf services (particularly those published by the Bureau of National Affairs). West Publishing continues to increase the number of authorities with which you can use FIND.

FIND performs one function: retrieving and displaying a specific authority in response to your transmitting the authority's citation in an appropriate format. Unlike other methods of retrieving documents in WESTLAW, FIND does not require you to specify a database in which to search.

You can invoke the FIND feature at any point after identifying the research session when you log on to WESTLAW (as explained on pages 191–

[174] *See* CHRISTOPHER G. WREN & JILL R. WREN, THE LEGAL RESEARCH MANUAL: A GAME PLAN FOR LEGAL RESEARCH AND ANALYSIS 51–60 (2d ed. 1986).

[175] As with the "known authority" approach in book-based legal research, you need to know and recognize the elements of a citation to find legal authorities through a known-authority search in a CALR service. Although the abbreviations, punctuation, and spacing in citations for CALR purposes sometimes differ from their book-based counterparts, the elements of a citation (*e.g.*, volume number, page number, section number) remain the same. For a refresher on citations, see Chapter 2 in CHRISTOPHER G. WREN & JILL R. WREN, THE LEGAL RESEARCH MANUAL: A GAME PLAN FOR LEGAL RESEARCH AND ANALYSIS (2d ed. 1986).

[176] At this writing, FIND retrieves slip laws only when they appear in a current legislative service database (such as US-PL for federal slip laws); FIND will not retrieve slip laws when they appear only in historical legislative service databases (such as US-PL90). For more about legislative service databases, see pages 611–16.

94). For example, when the WESTLAW Directory first appears on the monitor after you log on, instead of selecting a database in which to transmit a search request, you can use FIND to retrieve your known authority. Or, suppose you have already transmitted a search request and are skimming one of the cases you retrieved; if you then encounter a citation to another case you want to check while the reference is fresh in your mind, you can use FIND to go directly from the case you are viewing to the case you want to check.

When you finish using FIND, you return to wherever you had been in your research when you transmitted the FIND command; for example, if you had been reading a case and moved via FIND to a second case, you would return to the first case. In effect, FIND temporarily stores your current research result in the background while you pursue a new research lead.

To retrieve a known authority through FIND, you use a single technique, regardless of the type of authority:

1. Type `find` (or `fi`) followed by the citation of the authority.
2. Press ENTER.

You have considerable flexibility in the spacing and punctuation you can use in a FIND instruction, although you must include any hyphens that appear as part of a citation.

To retrieve a known case through FIND, you can use the citation to any official or unofficial reporter (for a case reprinted in more than one reporter),[177] the citations to leading looseleaf services that reported the case, a docket number, or (where available) the WESTLAW Cite. (Figure 10.08 explains WESTLAW Cites.) Suppose you wanted to retrieve *Doe v. United States*, 487 U.S. 201, 108 S. Ct. 2341, 101 L. Ed. 2d 184 (1988), also reported in *United States Law Week* (56 U.S.L.W. 4708), *American Federal Tax Reports, Second Series* (62 A.F.T.R.2d ¶ 88–5744), and *United States Tax Cases* (88–2 U.S. Tax Cas. ¶ 9545), and having docket number 86–1753. You could use any of the following FIND instructions:

```
find 487 us 201
find 487 u.s. 201
fi 487 u s 201
find 108 sct 2341
fi108sct2341
find 101 led2d 184
find 1988 wl 61708
```

[177] For a refresher on official and unofficial reporters, see CHRISTOPHER G. WREN & JILL R. WREN, THE LEGAL RESEARCH MANUAL: A GAME PLAN FOR LEGAL RESEARCH AND ANALYSIS 10–11 (2d ed. 1986).

In 1988, West Publishing Company began assigning WESTLAW Cites to selected authorities upon their addition to the WESTLAW service. A WESTLAW Cite serves the same purpose in WESTLAW as a LEXIS Cite serves in LEXIS: to provide a standardized, unique identification for an authority before it acquires a traditional, book-based citation. See Figure 10.02 on pages 239–40.

A WESTLAW Cite contains the following elements:

- the name or title of the authority
- the year the authority was issued
- the abbreviation "WL" (for "WESTLAW")
- the WESTLAW identification number for the authority
- the jurisdiction or forum from which the authority issued

Thus, the WESTLAW Cite for *Michigan Citizens for an Independent Press v. Thornburgh*, a case decided in 1988 by the U.S. District Court for the District of Columbia, would read:

> *Michigan Citizens for an Independent Press v. Thornburgh*, 1988 WL 90388 (D.D.C.)

When you use a WESTLAW Cite in your own writing, you should add the following elements to the citation:[†]

- the court's docket number for the authority (*e.g.*, C.A. No. 88-2322)
- the full date on which the court issued the authority

So, you would write the WESTLAW Cite for *Michigan Citizens* this way:

> *Michigan Citizens for an Independent Press v. Thornburgh*, C.A. No. 88-2322, 1988 WL 90388 (D.D.C. Aug. 17, 1988)

Within an authority in WESTLAW, West also assigns WESTLAW page numbers (referred to as "star-page" numbers), which you can instruct the computer to display on the monitor as highlighted, asterisked numbers—*e.g.*, *5—embedded in the authority's text. (You can see examples of star-page numbers in Figure 11.19 on page 356.) If you want to use a WESTLAW Cite in your own writing to refer someone to a specific portion of an authority in WESTLAW, you can include the authority's internal WESTLAW page number, as in this example, which directs the reader to WESTLAW page 2 of *Michigan Citizens*:

> *Michigan Citizens for an Independent Press v. Thornburgh*, C.A. No. 88-2322, 1988 WL 90388, at *2 (D.D.C. Aug. 17, 1988)

The WESTLAW Cite for an authority does not always appear on the monitor. For a case that West has not published in one of its reporters, the WESTLAW Cite will automati-

[†] *See* THE BLUEBOOK: A UNIFORM SYSTEM OF CITATION Rule 10.8.1(b) (15th ed. 1991).

(continues)

Figure 10.08. WESTLAW Cites

(continued)

cally display in the upper left corner of the monitor. If West eventually publishes the case in a reporter, whether the WESTLAW Cite will automatically appear on the monitor depends on how you retrieve the case: the WESTLAW Cite will automatically display only if you retrieve the case with a FIND instruction using the WESTLAW Cite. Even if the monitor does not automatically display the WESTLAW Cite, it remains a permanent citation for the authority, and can still be used to search in WESTLAW.

If you want to display the WESTLAW Cite information—*i.e.*, the WESTLAW Cite and the WESTLAW page numbers throughout an authority—in situations in which these items do not automatically show on the monitor, you can instruct the computer to display this information: while the authority appears on the monitor, type `star wl` and press ENTER.

Figure 10.08. WESTLAW Cites (continued)

```
fi 56 uslw 4708
fi 62 aftr2d 88-5744
fi 88-2 ustc 9545
fi dn 86-1753 (us)
```

Your FIND instruction can use a page number within the case instead of the page on which the case begins. If you use an internal page number, the computer will retrieve the case and begin the display with the internal page rather than with the first page of the case. So, the FIND instruction

```
find 487 us 205
```

would retrieve *Doe* and initially display text appearing on page 205 of the *United States Reports* version of the case.

You also have some flexibility in the form of your instruction when you use FIND to retrieve a known statute or administrative regulation available in WESTLAW. Thus, for example, any of the following FIND instructions would retrieve section 1-1-1 of Alabama's statutory code:

```
find alabama statutes s 1-1-1
fi alabama statutes s 1-1-1
find al st s 1-1-1
fi al st s 1-1-1
fi alsts1-1-1
find al st 1-1-1
```

Help with FIND. If you do not know an acceptable abbreviation for the source of the authority you want to retrieve through FIND (such as "ATD" for *Antitrust & Trade Regulation Daily*), you can refer to Appendix K of the *WESTLAW Reference Manual.*[178] WESTLAW also provides online a more current list of the publications—and their abbreviations—that you can use with the FIND feature. You can view the online list at any time (for example, while you are at the WESTLAW Directory or while you are viewing a document): type **find pubs** (or **fi pubs**) and press ENTER. On-screen instructions explain how to obtain information from the list and how to exit when you are done.

Returning to earlier FOUND documents. After you begin a FIND session, you can perform as many successive FIND searches as you want. The WESTLAW computer will keep track of each of the authorities you retrieve through FIND (they are called "FOUND documents"), and you can return to an authority you retrieved earlier in your FIND session. You return to a previous authority in either of two ways. One way, you:

1. Type **gb** (for "go back").
2. Press ENTER.

For example, suppose you had retrieved five authorities in a single FIND session. Transmitting **gb** while the fifth authority is displayed on the monitor would redisplay the fourth authority you retrieved through FIND; transmitting **gb** again would redisplay the third authority. Continuing to transmit **gb** would eventually return you to the first document you retrieved during your FIND session.

Alternatively, if you want to avoid transmitting multiple **gb** commands, you can:

1. Type **map** while viewing an authority located through FIND.
2. Press ENTER.

The monitor will display a list of your previous research results, including each of the authorities you retrieved through FIND. On-screen instructions explain how to return to authorities retrieved earlier in your FIND session.

Leaving FIND. When you have retrieved all the authorities you want to locate through FIND, you can return to wherever you were in your research before you began your FIND session. For instance, if you had been checking the annotations accompanying a statute in WESTLAW and had encountered a reference to a case you then retrieved through FIND, returning to your previous research would take you back to the statutory annotations.

[178] WEST PUBLISHING COMPANY, WESTLAW REFERENCE MANUAL 389–424 (5th ed. 1993).

You have two ways to leave the FIND feature and resume your previous research. You can keep transmitting **gb** commands until you have returned to the first authority retrieved through FIND; at that point, transmitting **gb** one more time will take you out of the FIND feature and back to your previous research. Or, you can exit FIND by transmitting **map**; when the monitor displays a list of your previous research results, select the point in your research you were at when you invoked the FIND feature.[179]

JUMP: Automating the use of FIND in WESTLAW. WESTLAW offers a feature called JUMP that can speed up using FIND. While viewing an authority in WESTLAW, you might see a reference to another authority you want to retrieve. You can use JUMP to retrieve the text of that authority if the reference to it has a "greater than" symbol (">") or a triangle ("➤") nearby (as occurs in the reference to 8 U.S.C. § 1326 in Figure 11.17 on page 350). To use JUMP to retrieve an authority through FIND:

1. Press the TAB key to position the cursor under the ">" symbol or triangle next to the citation of the authority you want to retrieve.

2. Press ENTER.

The computer will automatically formulate a FIND instruction based on the citation for the reference on which you positioned the cursor. The computer will then retrieve and display the authority. If the citation you selected includes a cite to a page other than the first page of the authority (as in "26 S.Ct. 282, 287"), the display will begin with the internal page.

If you use JUMP to retrieve the text of a statute cited in the authority you are viewing, the computer will retrieve the statute's text as it appears in the *current* online version of the statutory code. The current version might differ, though, from the version of the statute to which the original authority referred.

Currently, the convenience offered by JUMP exists only when you are viewing a case, and then only to retrieve cases and federal statutes, although West Publishing will undoubtedly extend the availability of JUMP. For situations in which JUMP is not available, you can retrieve most known authorities by transmitting a FIND instruction.

Leaving JUMP. Once you retrieve an authority using JUMP, you can do anything you could have done if you had retrieved the document using a FIND instruction without the assistance of JUMP. If you want to return to the authority you were most recently viewing, you can type **gb** (for "go back") and press ENTER.

[179] The *WESTLAW Reference Manual* provides more details about the MAP feature. WEST PUBLISHING COMPANY, WESTLAW REFERENCE MANUAL 30–31 (5th ed. 1993). For example, transmitting **map1** will end your FIND session by returning you straight to the WESTLAW Directory (without an intervening display of the MAP list of research results).

Finding known authorities in WESTLAW by using citation information in a field-restricted search request. The FIND feature in WESTLAW does not work for all authorities. When you cannot use FIND to retrieve an authority for which you know the citation, you can retrieve the authority by using a search request that includes the citation information in a field restriction based on the WESTLAW field containing the authority's citation. You can use this kind of field restriction to find any known authority available in WESTLAW, regardless of whether the FIND feature (or its automated counterpart, JUMP) would also retrieve the authority you want.

In WESTLAW, citation information for most authorities appears in the "citation" field. So, for instance, if you wanted to use the citation field in WESTLAW to retrieve *Varnell v. Young*, 839 F.2d 1245 (7th Cir. 1988), you would select an appropriate database of federal courts of appeals cases (such as CTA or CTA7) and use one of the following search requests, which are based on the *Federal Reporter* citation and the WESTLAW Cite (1988 WL 13280):[180]

```
citation(839 pre/3 1245)

citation(1988 pre/3 13280)
```

Page 80 explains more about using the citation field in a search request.

Using the citation field to retrieve a known authority is not as efficient as using FIND. First, with a field-restricted search request, you must initially gain access to a WESTLAW database that includes the authority you want to retrieve; by contrast, you can invoke FIND from anywhere in WESTLAW, and you do not need to select an appropriate database in which to search. Second, if you use a page number within a case rather than the page on which the case begins, searching the citation field will not retrieve the case, whereas FIND would. Third, a field-restricted search request (unlike FIND) will not hold your current research results in the background while you check another authority, or allow you to return directly to your earlier research results when you finish pursuing the new research lead.

Consequently, if FIND is available to retrieve the known authority you want, you will probably consider using this feature more advantageous than conducting a field-restricted search of the citation field.

Using the Related Materials Directory in WESTLAW for a known statute or administrative regulation. If you have retrieved a federal or state statute or a provision in the *Code of Federal Regulations*, you can proceed from your known authority to other, related information by using WESTLAW's Related Materials Directory. While viewing the statute or regulation,

[180] Figure 10.08 on pages 281–82 explains WESTLAW Cites.

type `rm` and press ENTER. The monitor will display the Related Materials Directory (as illustrated in Figure 10.07 on page 268); the directory will describe the related materials available through this feature and identify the commands for gaining access to the materials. The materials available to you through the Related Materials Directory will vary depending on the database you are in when you transmit the "rm" command. For example, transmitting `rm` while viewing a statute in a database of unannotated statutes will allow you to expand your research to annotations of cases applying or interpreting your statute.

For an explanation of how to use the Related Materials Directory with a known statute, see pages 267–69; in addition, pages 611–13 explain UPDATE, one of the selections available through the Related Materials Directory. For an explanation of how to use the Related Materials Directory with a known regulation, see pages 620 and 622, which explain how to use UPDATE with a regulation.

Finding partially known authorities in WESTLAW. What if you know of a particular case, statute, or other authority that holds potential relevance for your research problem, but you don't know the citation information (*e.g.*, reporter volume and page number, or statutory code section) that would allow you to retrieve the authority by using FIND or by searching the citation field? For example, someone might suggest you look at the "Steelworkers Trilogy" of cases or the federal "Equal Credit Opportunity Act," but not be able to tell you the exact citation. Or, you might only remember that during a particular period, a certain judge wrote an opinion addressing an issue relevant to your research.

When you search online, you can use elements of a citation to track down a partially known authority. The technique parallels using incomplete citation information in book-based legal research to find a partially known authority by checking a table of case names or a table of popular names for cases or statutes.[181] Online, however, you can often locate a partially known authority by working with even fewer clues than you would need to find the authority in a printed source.

Partially known cases. To find partially known cases in WESTLAW, you can take one of several courses, depending on what information you know. For each technique, you will first need to gain access to an appropriate WESTLAW database. If you know the jurisdiction in which the case you are tracking down was decided, you would select a database containing cases from that jurisdiction. If you know your case was decided by a state court, but do not know which state, the ALLSTATES or ALLSTATES-OLD database would

[181] *See* CHRISTOPHER G. WREN & JILL R. WREN, THE LEGAL RESEARCH MANUAL: A GAME PLAN FOR LEGAL RESEARCH AND ANALYSIS 58, 60 (2d ed. 1986).

be an appropriate choice. If you know your case was decided by a federal court, but do not know which court, you could select the ALLFEDS or ALLFEDS-OLD database.

Once you have gained access to an appropriate database, you can use one of the following techniques:

- *Search for the name of a party to the case.* If you know the name of at least one party in a case, you can locate the case by searching for that name in the "title" field.[182] For example, if you know the name of the plaintiff in *Kingsley International Pictures Corporation v. Regents of the State of New York*, you could retrieve the case by transmitting

```
title("kingsley international pictures")
```

  In most instances, if a case has multiple plaintiffs or defendants, the names of all the parties will appear in this field. Consequently, you can often find a case even if you don't know the name of the principal plaintiff or principal defendant. In this respect, a CALR search offers a capability not available in book-based research: with books, to use a party's name to find a case, you must know the name of a principal plaintiff or defendant in order to use the party tables in a case digest.
- *Search for the case's popular name.* If the case you want to locate is known by a popular name (such as the "Steelworkers Trilogy"), you can conduct an unrestricted search for the popular name in an appropriate database. The computer might locate a reference to the popular name in, say, a case or law review article. If so, the reference will probably appear with the case's official name and citation, which you can then use to retrieve the case through the "known authority" approach explained on pages 278–84 and 285.

  When the popular name and the official name and citation appear together online, this technique achieves the same result as using a popular name to locate a case in book-based research by checking *Shepard's Acts and Cases By Popular Names* or a Popular Names Table in a case digest.
- *Search for other bits of information identifying the case.* You might be able to locate a partially known case if you have other items of information—such as the name of a judge who wrote an opinion in the case, the names of the attorneys who participated, or the

[182] For a refresher on conducting a field-restricted search in the "title" field, see pages 78–80.

period during which the case was decided. For instance, suppose you knew that Laurence Tribe had served as counsel to one of the parties in a possibly relevant federal court of appeals case involving a constitutional challenge to a requirement that lawyers join a bar association. Even without knowing which court issued the decision, the name of any judge or party involved, or when the case was decided, you could locate the case in WESTLAW with the clues you have available. You could search the CTA database with the following search request to find the case:

```
attorney((laurence or lawrence) w/3
tribe) and "bar association"
```

As this example implies, you can incorporate whatever information you have into various field restrictions to locate a partially known case. Moreover, you can often find a partially known case online when you only have clues that would prove too sparse to locate the case through book-based research. Chapter 5 provides more information about using field restrictions in search requests.

Partially known statutes. Suppose you do not know the citation of a potentially relevant statute, but know its popular name (such as the "Equal Credit Opportunity Act"). For *federal statutes,* WESTLAW provides an online version of the "Popular Name Table for Acts of Congress" from West Publishing's *United States Code Annotated*; this table appears in the USCA-POP database. Through the popular-names table in WESTLAW, you can obtain citation and other information for finding a statute you know only by its popular name.

In the USCA-POP database, each popular name and its corresponding citation information constitutes a document. USCA-POP also contains a document that lists alphabetically all the popular names in the USCA-POP database but without providing any citation information.

To locate a popular name in the USCA-POP database, begin by selecting the database. The monitor will then display the standard WESTLAW screen for typing either a Boolean search request (see Figure 9.10 on page 201) or a natural-language search request (see Figure 9.11 on page 202). At this point, you can locate a popular name in several ways:

- If you know the exact popular name of the statute, you can locate references to the statute by searching the "citation" field for a phrase from the popular name.[183] For instance, if you wanted to locate a reference to the "Science and Engineering Equal Oppor-

[183] For a refresher on field-restricted searching, see Chapter 5.

tunities Act," you could transmit either of these Boolean search requests:

```
ci("engineering equal opportunities")

citation("engineering equal opportunities")
```

With a request like these, the computer will retrieve documents for popular names containing the phrase you transmitted. (Currently, you cannot use a "citation" field restriction in a natural-language request.)

Alternatively, you could transmit the phrase without restriction in a Boolean or natural-language search request:

```
"engineering equal opportunities"
```

With this request, the computer will also retrieve the document containing the alphabetical list of all popular names in the USCA-POP database; the second screen in Figure 10.09 illustrates a portion of the list. By viewing the list, you might notice some popular names that do not include your phrase, but that include close variations on the phrase that identify possibly relevant statutes.

- If you do not know the exact popular name of the statute but know some of the words in the popular name, you can locate references to the statute by searching the citation field for words from the popular name. For instance, if you knew that the popular name referred to opportunities in science or engineering, you could transmit one of these Boolean search requests:

```
ci(science or engineer! w/5 opportun!)

citation(science or engineer! w/5
opportun!)
```

With a request like these, the computer will retrieve documents for popular names that satisfy the search request you transmitted.

Alternatively, you could transmit a Boolean search request without restricting your search to the citation field:

```
science or engineer! w/5 opportun!
```

With this request, the computer will also retrieve the document containing the alphabetical list of all popular names in the USCA-POP database. By viewing entries near the popular names that satisfy your search request, you might notice other popular names suggesting additional, possibly relevant statutes.

```
Citation                        Rank(R)        Page(P)          Database      Mode
USCA POPULAR NAME TABLE         R 1 OF 1       P 1 OF 395       USCA-POP      Term
 USCA POPULAR NAME HEADINGS

                     UNITED STATES CODE ANNOTATED
                POPULAR NAME TABLE FOR ACTS OF CONGRESS
                         Through Pub. L. 103-5
             COPR. (c) 1993  No Claim to Orig. Govt. Works

 To view subjects beginning with
      A . . . . . enter p2            N . . . . . enter p254
      B . . . . . enter p29           O . . . . . enter p280
      C . . . . . enter p38           P . . . . . enter p287
      D . . . . . enter p69           Q . . . . . enter p308
      E . . . . . enter p124          R . . . . . enter p308
      F . . . . . enter p142          S . . . . . enter p326
      G . . . . . enter p177          T . . . . . enter p354
      H . . . . . enter p185          U . . . . . enter p370
      I . . . . . enter p197          V . . . . . enter p375
      J . . . . . enter p215          W . . . . . enter p383
      K . . . . . enter p222          X . . . . . enter p
      L . . . . . enter p223          Y . . . . . enter p394
      M . . . . . enter p234          Z . . . . . enter p395
```

```
USCA POPULAR NAME TABLE         R 1 OF 1       P 2 OF 395       USCA-POP      Page
 USCA POPULAR NAME HEADINGS

 - A -

 AAA Farm Relief and Inflation Act
 AAIA
 AAPA
 Abaca Production Act of 1950
 Abandoned Barge Act of 1992
 Abandoned Infants Assistance Act of 1988
 Abandoned Infants Assistance Act Amendments of 1991
 Abandoned Military Reservations Acts
 Abandoned Mine Reclamation Act of 1990
 Abandoned Property Collection Act
 Abandoned Shipwreck Act of 1987
 Able Seamen Act
 Abolition of Slavery Acts (District of Columbia)
 Abolition of Slavery Act (Territories)
 Abraham Lincoln Birthplace National Historic Site Acts
 Academic Research Facilities Modernization Act of 1988
 Acadia National Park Acts
 Accident Reports Acts (Railroads)
```

Source: West Publishing Company © 1993

Figure 10.09. First Two Screens of the Alphabetical List of Popular Names in the USCA-POP Database in WESTLAW, Containing the *United States Code Annotated* "Popular Name Table for Acts of Congress"

- If you want to retrieve just the alphabetical list of popular names, transmit either of these Boolean search requests:

  `ci(headings)`

  `citation(headings)`

  The monitor will display the first page of the alphabetical list, as shown in the first screen in Figure 10.09. At this point, WESTLAW offers the following two ways of locating a popular name on the list.

  You can type the page number (shown on the first screen of the list) corresponding to the first letter of the popular name you want to locate. For example, at the first screen in Figure 10.09, you would transmit `p326` to go to the portion of the alphabetical list with popular names beginning with "s." Once at that portion of the list, to find the popular name you seek, you might have to page through the popular names by pressing the ENTER key or using one of the other standard WESTLAW techniques for moving within a document. (See pages 360–63.)

  Alternatively, you can use the LOCATE feature (explained in more detail on pages 367–71): type `locate` (or `loc`) followed by words in the popular name, linked by logic connectors (if appropriate); then press ENTER. The computer will search through the alphabetical list for word combinations that satisfy your LOCATE request. For instance, to locate references on the list to "Science and Engineering Equal Opportunities Act," transmit

  `loc science or engineer! w/5 opportun!`

Once you find a popular name in USCA-POP, you can use the citation information accompanying the popular name to retrieve the text of the statute in WESTLAW. To retrieve the statutory text as published in *United States Code Annotated*, transmit a FIND instruction with the U.S.C.A. citation information—for example, `fi 42 usca 1861`.

For *state statutes*, WESTLAW at this time does not offer a popular-names table. However, searching in various WESTLAW databases for the popular name of a state statute might locate either the statute itself or a reference to its official citation, which you can then use to retrieve the statute through the "known authority" approach explained on pages 278–84 and 285. To avoid bypassing unconventional references (such as a reference to the "Equal Credit Opportunity Law" instead of the "Equal Credit Opportunity Act"), omit words like "act," "law," or "statute" from the popular name in your search request.

The information you retrieve will depend on where you search. For example:

- Searching in a WESTLAW database of statutes from the jurisdiction that enacted the statute you want will retrieve the statute itself if its popular name appears in the statute. (Legislators often include a statutory section designating a "short title" for the statute; the short title often becomes the statute's popular name.)
- Searching in an annotated statutory code in WESTLAW might yield references to the popular name in the statutory annotations, which could also contain the statute's official citation or a citation to, say, a law review article that would provide the statute's citation.
- Searching for the statute's popular name in a WESTLAW database of federal or state cases might retrieve cases that refer to the statute by its popular name, along with the statute's official citation.

When the popular name and the citation appear together online, you achieve the same result you would in book-based legal research by checking a statute's popular name in *Shepard's Acts and Cases By Popular Names*, in tables of Acts By Popular Names or Short Titles in individual Shepard's citators, or in Popular Names tables in annotated statutes.[184]

Known topic approach in WESTLAW

In book-based legal research, if you feel confident you know what area of law your problem involves (*e.g.*, sales, wills, taxation, civil rights), you can find relevant cases by skipping the index to a case digest, going directly to the appropriate case digest topic, and perusing the table of contents until you find a subtopic that relates to your research problem.[185] Similarly, you can find relevant statutory or administrative law by skipping a code's index and going directly to an appropriate topical grouping of statutes or regulations within the code.[186]

You can also use a "known topic" approach online, although the same caveat applies there as in book-based legal research: the approach is most useful to experienced researchers working in a familiar area of law. Researchers who lack familiarity with the array of legal topics are generally better off using one of the other law-finding approaches explained in this chapter.[187]

[184] *See* CHRISTOPHER G. WREN & JILL R. WREN, THE LEGAL RESEARCH MANUAL: A GAME PLAN FOR LEGAL RESEARCH AND ANALYSIS 60 (2d ed. 1986).

[185] For more information about the known-topic approach in book-based research, see *id.* at 60–63.

[186] *Id.*

[187] See *id.* at 60, 62 (discussing the drawbacks of the "known topic" approach in book-based legal research). These drawbacks apply equally to computer-assisted legal research.

Cases: the known topic approach in WESTLAW. In WESTLAW, to use the "known topic" approach to find cases online, select an appropriate case-law database and then:

- in a Boolean search request, include a "topic" field restriction or a Key Number subtopic; or
- in a natural-language search request, include a Key Number subtopic.[188]

Pages 85–92 and 100–07 explain how to use the topic field and where to find lists of the available digest topics.

As discussed on pages 86 and 88, if your Boolean search request consists only of a topic field restriction, you will indiscriminately retrieve all the cases digested under the topic you designated, thus recreating online the entire coverage you would find for that topic in the West digest for the jurisdiction in which you performed your WESTLAW search. Normally, therefore, you will want to narrow your search by linking the topic field restriction with one or more other search terms that will screen cases by the facts involved, by the date of decision, by the court, by the name of the authoring judge or a participating attorney, or by some other criterion. So, for instance, if you were researching the range of damages awarded throughout the country in spinal injury cases, you could select the ALLSTATES database and focus your search by linking the topic "damages" with a search term describing a relevant fact. Depending on whether you used the topic name or number (see pages 86 and 88), your search request might look like one of these:

```
topic(damages) & (spine or spinal) &
date(aft 12/31/1987)

topic(115) & (spine or spinal) &
date(aft 12/31/1987)
```

If you have identified a particular subtopic under a West digest topic as addressing a point you want to research, you can use the Key Number component of the topic field in WESTLAW to focus a Boolean or natural-language search on cases digested under the Key Number corresponding to that subtopic. (Pages 90–92 explain online searching using Key Numbers.) As with a field restriction based on a pertinent topic, you will often refine a Key Number search for a subtopic by linking a Key Number with words expressing relevant facts or with one or more additional field restrictions. For example, the search request

[188] At this writing, you cannot use a "topic" field restriction in natural-language searching.

```
406k4 & ((molotov w/5 cocktail) or explosive
or incend!)
```

would retrieve only cases that mention Molotov cocktails, explosives, or other incendiary devices and that are digested under Key Number 4 in topic 406 ("Weapons").

If you use natural language to search for a Key Number, your request could take this form:

```
406k4 molotov cocktail explosive incendiary
```

Under the algorithms that currently direct the computer's natural-language searching, not every case the computer retrieves in response to a natural-language search request that contains a Key Number will necessarily be digested under that Key Number, however; other search terms might carry so much more statistical weight than the Key Number that the search results could include documents retrieved solely on the strength of search terms other than the Key Number. In addition, given the current 100-document limit on the number of documents the computer will retrieve when you search with a natural-language request, a natural-language search for cases digested under a certain Key Number might prove incomplete. Consequently, if you want to search either precisely or comprehensively for cases digested under a particular Key Number, Boolean searching offers a better route than natural-language searching.

Statutes and administrative regulations: the known topic approach in WESTLAW. For book-based research in statutes and administrative regulations, if you know that some topical grouping within a statutory or administrative code applies to your research problem, you can go straight to that part of the code. To implement this "known topic" approach to find statutes or regulations in WESTLAW, you can use a field restriction to confine a Boolean search to the group of statutes or regulations in which you are interested. The WESTLAW field used in this type of search will contain the name of, or citation information for, the topical grouping. (Currently, you cannot use this kind of field restriction in a natural-language search for statutes or regulations.)

For example, suppose you want to research whether a copyright holder is required to register the copyright before commencing a civil action alleging copyright infringement. Suppose you also knew that in the *United States Code*, Title 17 (entitled "Copyright") contained the federal statutes governing copyright, and that in the *Code of Federal Regulations*, Title 37 (entitled "Patents, Trademarks, and Copyrights") contained federal regulations dealing with copyright. You could find the code sections addressing your issue by using a field restriction instructing the computer to look for your search terms in only

17 U.S.C. or 37 C.F.R.[189] In WESTLAW, your search request for statutes in the USC or USCA database could take any of these forms:

```
prelim(copyright) and (infringe! w/25 regist!)

prelim("title 17") and (infringe! w/25 regist!)

citation("17 usca") and (infringe! w/25 regist!)
```

Your WESTLAW search request for regulations in the CFR database could take any of these forms:

```
prelim(copyright) and (infringe! w/25 regist!)

prelim("title 37") and (infringe! w/25 regist!)

citation("37 cfr") and (infringe! w/25 regist!)
```

State statutory and administrative codes also organize statutes and regulations by grouping them together topically according to common subject matter, although the methods of numbering and naming topical groupings vary from state to state. If you know the name of, or citation information for, a relevant grouping within a state statutory or administrative code, you can conduct a known-topic search in that code by using field restrictions similar to those used for known topic searches in the federal codes. Of course, you will need to modify the field restrictions to take into account differences between the federal and state codes, such as different ways of numbering and naming topical groupings.

Topical databases: the known topic approach in WESTLAW. In carrying out a known-topic search online, you might also find topical databases in WESTLAW worthwhile sources. WESTLAW pulls together various related materials into topical collections in such specialized areas as insurance, taxation, energy, environmental law, and labor. For instance, in topically related databases grouped under the heading "Financial Services" in the WESTLAW Directory, WESTLAW offers access to a collection of banking- and finance-related cases, statutes, administrative regulations, looseleaf services, law review articles, and other materials. For a complete listing of the topical collections available in WESTLAW, check West Publishing's printed and online guides to WESTLAW; Appendix B highlights these sources of information about WESTLAW.

[189] For a complete list of names and numbers of titles in the *United States Code*, see CHRISTOPHER G. WREN & JILL R. WREN, THE LEGAL RESEARCH MANUAL: A GAME PLAN FOR LEGAL RESEARCH AND ANALYSIS 175 (2d ed. 1986). For a complete list of names and numbers of titles in the *Code of Federal Regulations*, see *id.* at 176.

A specialized approach in WESTLAW: Words and Phrases

Sometimes, your research issue will involve or turn on a legal definition of a term. For instance, suppose local officials propose locating a half-way house in a residential neighborhood where zoning regulations prohibit locating a jail. You would want to know whether a half-way house constituted a jail, and would therefore want to find definitions of "jail" or "half-way house" (or, by analogy, "prison" or "penitentiary").

In book-based legal research, if you need to find a judicial definition of a term, you can go straight to *Words and Phrases*, West Publishing Company's multi-volume "dictionary" that contains common-law definitions, along with citations to the cases in which the words and phrases were construed. In addition to the *Words and Phrases* series of volumes, case digests usually contain either a topic entry or a separate volume entitled "Words and Phrases" that lists significant terms interpreted by courts in the jurisdiction covered by the particular digest.[190]

But what if you don't have access to *Words and Phrases* (or to a digest counterpart)? Or what if the term you want is not defined in *Words and Phrases* (or in a digest counterpart)? Or suppose you simply want to supplement a book-based "words and phrases" search (perhaps to find more recent definitions). You can try one of the following techniques to implement the "words and phrases" approach in WESTLAW.

Finding judicial definitions in WESTLAW. You can search in WESTLAW for judicial definitions of your term:

- Try linking your term in a search request with words that can indicate the presence of a definition. When judges define a term, their opinions usually include, near the word or phrase being defined, words such as "means," "meaning," "define," "defined," "definition," "construe," "construing," "interpret," or "interpretation." Consequently, you can sometimes find judicial definitions by searching a case-law database in WESTLAW with a Boolean search request along these lines:

```
(half-way pre/2 house) w/10 (mean* or
meaning or defin*** or definition or
constru*** or interpret!)
```

  Or, if you search with natural language, you could try a request like this:

[190] *See* CHRISTOPHER G. WREN & JILL R. WREN, THE LEGAL RESEARCH MANUAL: A GAME PLAN FOR LEGAL RESEARCH AND ANALYSIS 63–65 (2d ed. 1986).

```
What is the definition of a half-way
house?
```

Because judges sometimes cite *Words and Phrases* when defining a term, you might also want to include `"words and phrases"` in your search request to enhance the likelihood of retrieving definitional cases, as in this example:

```
(half-way pre/2 house) w/10 (mean* or
meaning or defin*** or definition or
constru*** or interpret! or "words
and phrases")
```

If search requests like these retrieve more cases than you can reasonably expect to review, you can try restricting your search to the headnote field, which might contain a citation to *Words and Phrases* (although this restricted search request will bypass cases that do not contain a headnote field):

```
headnote((half-way pre/2 house) and
(mean* or meaning or defin*** or
definition or constru*** or "words
and phrases"))
```

- If you want to find judicial definitions of a word or phrase you think occurs relatively infrequently in cases, you can simply search for the word or phrase in WESTLAW without including additional search terms (like "mean" or "define") that suggest a definitional context. Although you will undoubtedly retrieve some cases that mention your word or phrase without defining it, you are less likely to bypass cases that contain relevant definitions but do not include words like "mean" or "define" near your word or phrase. Moreover, if your word or phrase actually occurs infrequently, the number of cases retrieved will likely be small enough that you can screen all of them to find the ones containing definitions.

  Searching for a word or phrase without adding a search term like "means" can prove especially helpful if you need to find judicial interpretations of key phrases from statutes, administrative regulations, or jury instructions.

Finding statutory and administrative definitions in WESTLAW. You can also use a "words and phrases" approach in WESTLAW to search for definitions that legislatures or administrative agencies assign to words or phrases in statutes or administrative regulations:

- Try linking your term with words that can indicate the presence of a definition. Statutes and administrative regulations often contain sections defining salient terms for the purpose of interpreting and applying the statutes or regulations. Terms defined in statutes or regulations typically appear near words like "means," "meaning," "define," or "definition," as in these examples:

> **450.01 Definitions.** In this chapter:
>
> . . . .
>
> **(8)** "Distribute" means to deliver, other than by administering or dispensing.
>
> . . . .
>
> **(10)** "Drug" means:
>
> (a) Any substance recognized as a drug in the official U.S. pharmacopoeia and national formulary or official homeopathic pharmacopoeia of the United States or any supplement to either of them;
>
> . . . .
>
> **939.22 Words and phrases defined.** In chs. 939 to 948 and 951, the following words and phrases have the designated meanings unless the context of a specific section manifestly requires a different construction or the word or phrase is defined in s. 948.01 for purposes of ch. 948:
>
> . . . .
>
> **(11)** "Drug" has the meaning specified in s. 450.01(10).
>
> . . . .
>
> **939.24 Criminal recklessness. (1)** In this section, "criminal recklessness" means that the actor creates an unreasonable and substantial risk of death or great bodily harm to another human being and the actor is aware of that risk.
>
> . . . .

Consequently, you might be able to find relevant statutory or administrative definitions by searching in a WESTLAW database of statutes or administrative regulations with a request linking the term you want defined (such as "drug") and words designed to locate definitions, as in this example:

```
drug w/10 (mean or meaning or define*
or definition)
```

If a search request in this form retrieves more code sections than you can reasonably expect to review, you can try using field restrictions to focus your search—in particular, restrictions limiting the search to sections in which the term you want defined appears in the text of the section and in which a word like "definition" appears in the field containing the title of the section. For example, your restricted search request in a WESTLAW statutory database could take this form:

```
text(drug) and caption(mean or
meaning or define* or definition)
```

- If you want to find legislative or administrative definitions of a word or phrase you think occurs relatively infrequently in a code (such as, say, "criminal recklessness"), you can simply search for the word or phrase in a statutory or administrative code database in WESTLAW without including additional search terms (like "mean" or "define") that suggest a definitional context. Although you will undoubtedly retrieve some code sections that mention your word or phrase without defining it, you are less likely to bypass sections that contain relevant definitions but do not include words like "mean" or "define" near your word or phrase. Moreover, if your word or phrase actually occurs infrequently, the number of sections retrieved will likely be small enough that you can screen all of them to find the ones containing definitions.

Suggestion: the words and phrases approach online. As a practical matter, a "words and phrases" search (whether in cases, statutes, or regulations) will often prove less efficient in a CALR service than in books. For judicial definitions, if you have access to *Words and Phrases* or a digest counterpart, you might find it more productive to search there than online. First, with *Words and Phrases*, you do not need to screen out cases that do not contain definitions; editors have already performed that screening, allowing you to simply turn to the entry for your word or phrase as easily as you would turn to a definition in a dictionary. Second, in a book-based search, you will find definitional cases even if they do not spotlight a definition with words such as "mean" or "define"; editors generally include cases if the discussions of words or phrases function as definitions, whether or not they are called that. Finally, *Words and Phrases* and its digest counterparts subdivide entries to permit researchers to find definitions quickly in specific contexts—for instance, entries under "jail" might include "city jail," "county jail," and "state jail."

Likewise, you might find legislative and administrative definitions more readily in a print version of a code than in a CALR service: a good index to a printed code will normally direct you faster to relevant definitions of words and phrases. (If you have a choice of printed codes for a given jurisdiction, you will often find better indexes in a commercially published, annotated code than in a code published by a government agency.)

A Generalized Approach in WESTLAW: law reviews, *Restatements of the Law*, looseleaf services, and other secondary legal sources

The research approaches discussed so far are mainly designed to lead you directly to primary sources of law (cases, statutes, administrative regulations, constitutional provisions), not to secondary sources (writings or commentaries about the law found in primary sources). If you want to gain perspective on the primary law involved in your research problem, however, you might find it helpful to obtain some generalized background information from secondary sources.

WESTLAW offers online versions of several of the secondary sources you can use in book-based legal research to locate commentaries on the law.[191] The secondary sources in WESTLAW include:

- law reviews
- legal magazines and newsletters
- looseleaf services (such as those published by the Bureau of National Affairs and by Commerce Clearing House)
- *Restatements of the Law*
- treatises (notably, works published by the Clark Boardman Company)

Currently, WESTLAW does not provide access to either of the leading legal encyclopedias (*Corpus Juris Secundum* and *American Jurisprudence 2d*).

As with other materials available in WESTLAW, the coverage of secondary sources continually evolves. West Publishing's printed and online guides to WESTLAW (highlighted in Appendix B) provide timely information about the secondary sources offered. When checking the availability of secondary materials in WESTLAW, pay particular attention to possible omissions in a publication's coverage: the licensing arrangements between West Publishing and the publishers of secondary sources sometimes require the exclusion of specified items from the online versions of certain publications. Also, when checking West Publishing's descriptions of secondary materials in WESTLAW, note the fields available in these materials; the wide range of secondary sources has spawned a variety of searchable fields.

Despite the array of secondary sources in WESTLAW, if you are searching these materials to gather background information in an area of law unfa-

[191] Pages 65 to 74 of CHRISTOPHER G. WREN & JILL R. WREN, THE LEGAL RESEARCH MANUAL: A GAME PLAN FOR LEGAL RESEARCH AND ANALYSIS (2d ed. 1986), explain the "generalized approach" as it applies in book-based legal research and highlight some of the secondary sources most commonly used in this law-finding approach.

miliar to you (rather than to improve your understanding of an area of law already familiar to you), you will often proceed more efficiently and effectively by starting in books, assuming you have access to them. Sometimes, you will have information (such as the name of the author of a law review article) that will enable you to locate a helpful secondary source online even if you have little knowledge of the area you are researching. Just as likely, however, a lack of familiarity with the key concepts and terms relevant to a particular research problem will hinder you in developing successful search requests (whether formulated with Boolean logic or natural language); you can waste considerable time and online charges trying to gain an introduction to a new area of law through database searching. In book-based research, by contrast, you can rely on scope notes, cross-references in indexes, and other editorially prepared features to orient you to the subject matter and suggest avenues of inquiry.

If you decide to search for secondary sources in WESTLAW, you apply the search techniques already discussed for finding primary authorities. For example, you can perform an unrestricted search in secondary sources for the descriptive or fact words you have identified as relevant to your problem. Or, you can include a field restriction to limit a search to, for example, law review articles written by a specific author.

The following paragraphs spotlight some of the secondary sources you can search in WESTLAW.

Law reviews and other legal periodicals. WESTLAW offers online access to the text of articles, book reviews, and other items appearing in law reviews and other legal periodicals (such as bar association publications). You will find legal periodicals in several places, including these:

- Individual databases contain specific law reviews. For instance, the VALR database contains the *Virginia Law Review*.
- The TEXTS AND PERIODICALS database (TP-ALL) encompasses numerous periodicals.
- Topical and other specialized databases contain periodicals (and texts) on specific topics. For example, the HTH-TP database contains texts and periodicals relating to health services, and the AMBAR-TP database contains selected periodicals published by the American Bar Association.
- "Gateway" database services (such as DIALOG) to which you can gain access through WESTLAW (see Chapter 13) include legal periodicals.

You can locate articles in law reviews and other legal periodicals in WESTLAW several ways:

- You can search for fact or descriptive words in the text of these publications in a database that contains legal periodicals.

- You will encounter references to legal periodical articles in many of the cases you retrieve through WESTLAW, as well as in the annotations at the end of many statutory code sections in WESTLAW. You can use these citations to find the articles in databases containing legal periodicals.
- You can use the online versions of indexes to legal periodicals to search more systematically in WESTLAW for references to articles, book reviews, and other items appearing in law reviews and other legal periodicals. Like their print versions, the online periodical indexes consist of citations (not the text of the indexed materials) and allow you to locate citations according to various criteria, including subject, title, author, or the citation of a case or statute that has been the principal subject of an article.

  You will find *Index to Legal Periodicals* in the ILP database, *Legal Resource Index* in the LRI database, and *Current Index to Legal Periodicals* in the CILP database.

To ensure a comprehensive WESTLAW search for articles in law reviews and other legal periodicals, search the periodical indexes *and* the text of the periodicals themselves. The indexes might refer you to articles in periodicals not available in WESTLAW. On the other hand, searching the text of periodicals might locate articles that have not been indexed in a way that identifies them as relevant to your research.

Looseleaf services and treatises. WESTLAW offers access to numerous looseleaf services. WESTLAW also offers online versions of some treatises that, in their printed form, appear as looseleaf publications. You can find looseleaf services in topical collections of databases (see page 295) and in collections of databases grouped according to publisher, such as Bureau of National Affairs (BNA) and Commerce Clearing House (CCH). Currently, the treatises in WESTLAW consist principally of publications from the Clark Boardman Company and can be found in a grouping of databases of Clark Boardman materials, as well as in topical databases, in the texts database (TEXTS), and in the TEXTS AND PERIODICALS database (TP-ALL).

Restatements of the Law. WESTLAW offers access to *Restatements of the Law*, the treatise-like publications produced by committees of distinguished judges, law professors, and practicing lawyers, all working under the auspices of the American Law Institute. *Restatements* are available in a combined database (REST), which contains all the online *Restatements*, and in individual databases for each online *Restatement* (*e.g.*, REST-TORT for the *Restatement of the Law of Torts*, or REST-CONTR for the *Restatement of the Law of Contracts*).

Finding the law in WESTLAW through updating

As you update the law to make sure the legal authorities you've located in your "finding the law" phase still constitute valid statements of the law, you will also be finding more new authorities. Therefore, just as in book-based legal research, updating the law also functions as a technique for finding the law. Chapter 12 explains how to update the law online.

Finding the law in WESTLAW by using EZ ACCESS

In WESTLAW, you have the option of using EZ ACCESS to find authorities. (As explained in Chapter 12, you can also use EZ ACCESS to update authorities.) Intended for novice or infrequent users of WESTLAW, EZ ACCESS provides a fill-in-the-blank method of implementing many of the law-finding techniques already explained in this chapter. EZ ACCESS presents menus of research tasks and asks researchers to specify the tasks the computer should perform. With EZ ACCESS, you do not need to know an array of commands to use WESTLAW; once you type a response to the "plain English" prompts EZ ACCESS displays, the computer translates your choices into WESTLAW commands, carries out a search, and displays the results. Thus, EZ ACCESS allows you to use WESTLAW by remembering just one command: `ez`.

As explained at the end of this section, however, experienced online researchers can find that EZ ACCESS diminishes the effectiveness and efficiency of their WESTLAW research. In addition, when you transmit Boolean search requests through EZ ACCESS, you sometimes give up flexibility in creating search requests that fully accomplish what you want to do.

Gaining access to EZ ACCESS. After you log on to WESTLAW, you can invoke EZ ACCESS at any point during your research:

1. Type `ez`.
2. Press ENTER.

The monitor will display a screen like the one shown in Figure 10.10. Depending on the choice you select from this menu, you can retrieve documents using one of the three principal law-finding approaches discussed in this chapter:

- descriptive word or fact word approach (the "significant words" choice on the menu)
- known authority approach (the "title or citation" choice on the menu)

```
                    COPR. (C) 1993 West Publishing Co. All Rights Reserved

                         *** WELCOME TO EZ ACCESS ***

EZ ACCESS is West Publishing Company's easy-to-use menu driven research system.
You can quickly retrieve information by making a selection from a list of
options.  When you are unsure of the next step, type EZ to see available
choices.

       What would you like to do?

                  Retrieve cases, statutes or other documents using:

                      1.  A Title or Citation
                      2.  A West Topic and Key number
                      3.  Significant words

                  Retrieve references to your document citation using:

                      4.  Insta-Cite, Shepard's, Shepard's PreView or QuickCite

                  Leave EZ ACCESS, type 5 and press ENTER

        Type a number and press ENTER
```

Source: West Publishing Company © 1993

Figure 10.10. Opening Screen for EZ ACCESS in WESTLAW

- known topic approach (the "West Topic and Key Number" choice on the menu)

If you prefer, you can use the Options Directory (discussed at pages 197–99) to invoke EZ ACCESS automatically as part of the WESTLAW sign-on procedure. If you implement that option, the first screen you will see after you log on to WESTLAW is the "Welcome to EZ ACCESS" screen (Figure 10.10) instead of the WESTLAW Directory screen (Figure 9.07 on page 196).

Getting help in using EZ ACCESS. While using EZ ACCESS, you might find yourself unsure of what to do next. By transmitting `ez` again, you can display a menu of EZ ACCESS choices that will help you decide what your next step should be. For additional information about using EZ ACCESS, you can also consult WESTLAW's publication entitled *Guide to EZ ACCESS* (1990).

Using the descriptive or fact word approach to find authorities through EZ ACCESS. If you want to retrieve documents based on words that describe important facts or issues in your research problem, choose "significant words" as your menu selection at the screen shown in Figure 10.10. The computer will then offer you a menu of documents and jurisdictions you can search. You can select the "specific database" choice and then specify the database by its WESTLAW identifier (if you know it), or you can select one of the other choices and let the computer guide you to a database through a series of on-screen instructions.

After you choose your database, the monitor will display a screen allowing you to type significant words or phrases. The screen will look like Figure 10.11 if the Options Directory (see pages 197–99) indicates Boolean terms-and-connectors searching as your EZ ACCESS search method. The screen will look like Figure 10.12 if the Options Directory indicates natural-language searching as your EZ ACCESS search method; if natural-language searching is not available in the database you have chosen, however, the computer will display the screen for typing your descriptive-word search instructions using Boolean terms and connectors.

Once you have typed your words and phrases, press ENTER. The computer will convert those words and phrases into a WESTLAW search request.

In creating a natural-language search request through EZ ACCESS, the computer will eliminate any terms the natural-language feature treats as non-searchable. The computer will also enclose in quotation marks any series of words the feature treats as a phrase.

In creating a Boolean search request through EZ ACCESS, the computer will convert regularly formed plural terms to their singular forms and substitute universal characters in some search terms. If you transmit a phrase without

WORD SEARCH: Word or Phrase

The jurisdiction: **Fed. Case Law** is the **ALLFEDS** database

What are the key words or phrases from your area of interest?

You may choose from one to four words or phrases.
Do not use synonyms. Type one word or phrase per line.

Press **TAB** to move to a choice

Word or **phrase**

Choice 1: **freedom of the press**

Choice 2: **license**

Choice 3: **sexual immorality**

Choice 4: **movie**

Type your **choices** and press **ENTER**
For more choices, type **EZ** and press **ENTER**

Source: West Publishing Company © 1993

Figure 10.11. WESTLAW EZ ACCESS Screen for Typing Descriptive or Fact Words for a Boolean Search

```
Natural Language WORD SEARCH:  Issue

The jurisdiction:  Fed. Case Law is the ALLFEDS database

What is your issue?  ( Does denying a movie an exhibition license because of
sexual immorality violate freedom of the press?

Type a brief description of your issue between the parentheses and press ENTER

              For additional options, type EZ and press ENTER
```

Source: West Publishing Company © 1993

Figure 10.12. WESTLAW EZ ACCESS Screen for Typing Descriptive or Fact Words for a Natural-Language Search

enclosing it in quotation marks, the computer will discard any non-searchable words and insert a "w/n" connector between searchable words in the phrase. Finally, the computer will link your individual search terms and phrases with a "/p" connector.[192] So, at the screen in Figure 10.11, if you transmitted `freedom of the press` as your first entry, `license` as your second entry, `sexual immorality` as your third entry, and `movie` as your fourth entry, the computer would convert your choices into this search request:

```
FREEDOM /5 PRESS /P LICENSE /P SEXUAL /5
IMMORALITY /P MOVIE
```

If you wanted the computer to search for `freedom of the press` as a literal phrase,[193] you would enclose the phrase in quotation marks, which would cause the computer to formulate the search request this way:

```
"FREEDOM OF THE PRESS" /P LICENSE /P SEXUAL /5
IMMORALITY /P MOVIE
```

After you develop your initial search request using the "significant words" technique in EZ ACCESS, the monitor will guide you with messages explain-

[192] See notes 197 and 198 and accompanying text.

[193] For a discussion of phrase searching, see pages 51–53.

ing how you can modify your EZ ACCESS search request. For example, you can add synonyms to existing search terms or add new, different search terms.

Using the known or partially known authority approach to find authorities through EZ ACCESS. Suppose you know the citation (such as 42 U.S.C. § 1981) or, for cases, the name of a party. You can retrieve a document based on that information by choosing "title or citation" as your menu selection at the screen shown in Figure 10.10. The computer will then ask you what kind of document (*e.g.*, a state or federal case, a state or federal statute) you want to retrieve. Depending on the type of authority you indicate, the computer will present a series of screens for typing identifying information about the authority; Figure 10.13 shows the first screen you will see if you want to retrieve a case. If the information about the authority does not establish the database in which to search, the computer will also guide you in selecting an appropriate database.

For example, suppose you have learned that *Kingsley International Pictures Corp. v. Regents of the University of the State of New York* might apply to your research problem. If you know a citation for *Kingsley* (*e.g.*, 360 U.S. 684), you can type that citation on the "citation" line in Figure 10.13; when you press ENTER, the computer will use the citation to retrieve *Kingsley* by carrying out a FIND search.[194] Alternatively, you can type a party name (or

[194] See pages 279–84 for an explanation of the FIND feature.

```
FIND Case Law:  Citation or Party Names

        What do you know about the case you want to find?

                           Press TAB to move to a choice

                CITATION:  360 us 684
                           ______________________________

                                     OR

             PARTY NAMES:  __________________________________________________
                                     First party

                           __________________________________________________
                                Second party (optional)

        Type a citation or party name and press ENTER

                 For more choices, type EZ and press ENTER
```

Source: West Publishing Company © 1993

Figure 10.13. WESTLAW EZ ACCESS Screen for Typing Citation Information about a Known Authority

two parties' names) on the "party names" lines in Figure 10.13; after you press ENTER, the computer will formulate a field-restricted search request using the names you typed, will guide you through the selection of an appropriate database, and will search that database for the party-name information in the "title" field.[195] For instance, if you transmit `kingsley international` at the screen in Figure 10.13, the computer will convert that name into the field-restricted search request

```
TITLE(KINGSLEY W/5 INTERNATIONAL)
```

and then run it in the database you select. If you want EZ ACCESS to search for the exact phrase `kingsley international`, you can enclose the words in quotation marks. The computer will formulate this field-restricted phrase search:

```
TITLE("KINGSLEY INTERNATIONAL")
```

Using the known topic approach to find cases through EZ ACCESS. If you have already learned that a topic and subtopic in a West digest cover a point you want to research, you can choose "West Topic and Key Number" as your menu selection at the screen shown in Figure 10.10.[196] You will then see a screen like that in Figure 10.14, where you can type the name or number of a West topic on one line and, on the other line, the Key Number or a descriptive term corresponding to a subtopic. After you press ENTER to transmit the topic and subtopic information, the computer will convert your choices into a WESTLAW search request, guide you through the selection of an appropriate database, and search that database for cases digested under the West topic and subtopic you chose.

The search request the computer formulates will depend on how you identify the topic and subtopic. If you type a topic name, the computer will convert that name to its corresponding topic number. So, if you type `weapons` as your topic, the computer will convert that to "406," the corresponding number for the topic. If you identify a subtopic by its Key Number, the computer will combine the topic and subtopic numbers into a precise Key Number search. For instance, if you transmit `406` to identify "Weapons" as the topic and `4` as the Key Number identifying a subtopic, the computer will formulate the following search request:

```
406K4
```

This search request will retrieve all cases digested under Key Number 4 of the topic "Weapons." On the other hand, if you identify a subtopic by using words

[195] See pages 78–80 for an explanation of field-restricted searching in the "title" field.

[196] See pages 86 and 100 for information about locating lists of West digest topics and subtopics.

```
TOPIC & KEY

        What general topic and specific point of law (key)
        would you like to search?

                          Press TAB to move to a choice

                TOPIC: 406
                       ______________________________
                              (name or number)

                                   AND

                  KEY: 4
                       ______________________________
                        (descriptive word or number)

        Type your topic and key and press ENTER



            For more choices, type EZ and press ENTER
```

Source: West Publishing Company © 1993

Figure 10.14. WESTLAW EZ ACCESS Screen for Typing Information about a Known Topic

from the Key Number's descriptive line in the West digest, the computer will link those words with the topic number in a descriptive-word search. For instance, the descriptive line "Manufacture, sale, gift, loan, possession, or use" identifies Key Number 4 under the topic "Weapons." If you transmit `weapons` or `406` as your topic and, say, `manufacture` as your Key Number subtopic, the computer will formulate the following search request:

```
TOPIC(406) /P MANUFACTUR!
```

This search request will retrieve not only cases digested under Key Number 4 under the topic "Weapons," but any other case in which a word with the root "manufactur" appears in a headnote digested under the topic "Weapons"—a result almost certain to encompass more cases than the search request `406k4`.

Once you run a search using the "West Topic and Key Number" technique in EZ ACCESS, you can transmit `ez` to have the monitor display messages explaining how you can modify your EZ ACCESS search request. For example, if you want to retrieve only certain kinds of cases digested under the West topic and Key Number you selected, you can add search terms based on significant facts or issues in your research problem. You can also limit your search to cases decided before, during, or after a certain year.

Using the words and phrases approach to find authorities through EZ ACCESS. If your research problem turns on a definition and you want to find authorities by using the "words and phrases" approach explained on pages 296–99, choose "significant words" as your menu selection at the screen shown in Figure 10.10. For your search terms, include the word or phrase you want defined, along with terms—such as `mean`, `meaning`, or `definition`—that can indicate the presence of a definition. Remember, though, that when you implement the "words and phrases" approach online, regardless of whether you use EZ ACCESS, your search results are apt to contain many irrelevant documents. As a practical matter, you will often search for definitions more effectively by using the printed *Words and Phrases* publication or its corresponding volume or topic in a case digest. (See page 299.)

Using the generalized approach to find secondary authorities through EZ ACCESS. If you want to obtain generalized background information from secondary sources (such as law reviews or other legal periodicals), choose "significant words" as your menu selection at the screen shown in Figure 10.10. The computer will then offer you a menu of documents and jurisdictions you can search. You can select "other" (which will allow you to choose an appropriate database from a list of secondary authorities) or "specific database" (which will allow you to designate a database by its identifier).

Once you have selected a database, you can retrieve secondary authorities by performing an unrestricted search for descriptive or fact words that reflect significant aspects of your research problem. Or, if you are looking for a particular secondary authority, you can find it by including a restriction limiting a Boolean search to fields containing information about the title, citation, or author of the authority; for example, you could locate law review articles written by Derrick Bell by typing `au(derrick)` as one search term at the screen shown in Figure 10.11 and `au(bell)` as another.

Using EZ ACCESS to find the law through updating. You can also update an authority through EZ ACCESS, and when you update, you will find new authorities. Pages 603–09 discuss using EZ ACCESS for updating your research.

Running subsequent searches through EZ ACCESS. When you transmit a search request through EZ ACCESS, the computer leaves the EZ ACCESS feature and carries out the search as an ordinary WESTLAW search. Once the monitor displays the results of the search you initiated through EZ ACCESS, you can do anything you could ordinarily do in WESTLAW (*e.g.*, view or print the results, use FIND to retrieve another document, Shepardize an authority). If you want to initiate another search through EZ ACCESS, type `ez` again and press ENTER.

Leaving EZ ACCESS. As just noted, you leave EZ ACCESS whenever you transmit an EZ ACCESS search request. You might, however, gain access to EZ ACCESS and then decide not to transmit an EZ ACCESS search request after all. In that situation, you can leave EZ ACCESS by selecting that choice from an EZ ACCESS menu. If you are not viewing a menu that offers that choice, transmitting `ez` again will move you to a menu that does.

The role of EZ ACCESS in finding the law. For new or infrequent users, EZ ACCESS can simplify using WESTLAW. Its menu-oriented method of selecting a database and formulating a search request guides researchers through each step of the procedure. EZ ACCESS has some drawbacks, however:

- For experienced WESTLAW users, wending through the EZ ACCESS menus will almost always prove slower than selecting a database and formulating a search request without the help of EZ ACCESS.
- EZ ACCESS automatically makes important decisions about Boolean search requests, such as selecting logic connectors or using universal characters to truncate search terms. Some of these choices, however, might not prove as well-suited for your research goal as the choices you would make in formulating a Boolean search request on your own.[197] Moreover, the computer might select a connector (such as "/p") that could slow your search and increase its cost without improving the quality of your search results.[198]
- Currently, you must run a Boolean search request in the form EZ ACCESS creates it before you can edit the request. Transmitting a request just so you can reach a point where the computer will allow you to modify your search is inefficient and costly.
- Because of its simplicity and automation, EZ ACCESS invites researchers who do not know how a CALR service operates to use WESTLAW for fairly sophisticated law-finding searches. But as earlier chapters have noted, effective use of a CALR service calls for knowledge of such points as how logic connectors work, what factors can affect the selection of search terms (*e.g.*, a word's ambiguity or lack of distinctiveness), and how the computer's literalness affects its response to search instructions. EZ ACCESS is designed, however, for users least likely to have this knowledge. Thus, EZ ACCESS could encourage WESTLAW use by those most likely to find searching online a waste of time and money, whether through EZ ACCESS or otherwise.

[197] For example, during the writing of this book, the "/p" connectors EZ ACCESS selected for the illustrative EZ ACCESS search requests on page 306 caused the computer not to retrieve any documents from the ALLFEDS database. However, the same search terms linked with "and" instead of "/p" (a search request you can formulate if you do not use EZ ACCESS) will retrieve relevant documents from ALLFEDS.

[198] See page 57 n.59 for a discussion of how the "/s," "+s," "/p," and "+p" connectors can slow the computer's search and increase online costs.

Summary: developing a strategy for finding the law in LEXIS and WESTLAW

This chapter has covered the major law-finding approaches as a researcher would implement them in LEXIS and WESTLAW. In finding the law online, as in book-based law finding, not every approach will come into play in every research problem. Whether you perform legal research using computers or books or both, your selection of a law-finding approach from among the following approaches will depend on what you know and what you seek to accomplish.[199]

Known authority approach. (See pages 237–51 for LEXIS, and 278–92 for WESTLAW.) If you start your research knowing the citation of a constitutional provision, case, statute, or administrative regulation that might apply to your research problem, you will probably find it most helpful to start your primary-source research by reading the known constitutional provision, case, statute, or regulation. By doing so, you will also likely find leads to other relevant authorities.

To examine the known authority, you will not necessarily log on to LEXIS or WESTLAW. Sometimes, however, checking the authority in a printed source might not be convenient or possible. In those instances, LEXIS and WESTLAW provide several means of using citation information to turn directly to a known authority.

In LEXIS, you can use the LEXSEE feature to retrieve known cases and other non-code authorities, and the LEXSTAT feature to retrieve known statutes and administrative regulations. Similarly, in WESTLAW, the FIND feature provides an easy way to retrieve various kinds of known authorities. Unlike other methods of retrieving documents in LEXIS or WESTLAW, you do not need to first gain access to a file or database; you can transmit a LEXSEE, LEXSTAT, or FIND instruction at any point in your online research.

For known authorities with which these convenient retrieval features do not operate, you can gain access to an appropriate LEXIS file or WESTLAW database and use a search request that includes citation information in a field restriction based on the LEXIS segment or WESTLAW field containing an authority's citation. Usually, this means using the "cite" segment in LEXIS, and the "citation" field in WESTLAW.

If you know of a potentially relevant authority but lack complete citation information for it, you still might be able to retrieve the authority in LEXIS or WESTLAW by searching for its popular name—*e.g.*, the "Equal Credit Opportunity Act" or the "Steelworkers Trilogy" of cases. When looking for a popular name online, you can search a variety of LEXIS files or WESTLAW

[199] *See* CHRISTOPHER G. WREN & JILL R. WREN, THE LEGAL RESEARCH MANUAL: A GAME PLAN FOR LEGAL RESEARCH AND ANALYSIS 76–78 (2d ed. 1986).

databases likely to contain the authority you want or a mention of its popular name (along with the official name or citation); for federal statutes, you can check the tables of popular names in LEXIS and WESTLAW. Or, you might locate a partially known authority by using a search request that incorporates into appropriate field restrictions whatever identifying information you have—*e.g.*, the name of a party, a judge, or an attorney; the court; the date of the authority's issuance. By using available clues about an authority, you can sometimes find a partially known authority in LEXIS or WESTLAW even though you would need more information to find the authority in printed sources through a table of popular names or party names.

To ensure thoroughness in your research, you can supplement your "known authority" or "partially known authority" approach with a "descriptive or fact word" search.

Descriptive word or fact word approach. (See pages 222–37 for LEXIS, and pages 265–78 for WESTLAW.) You will generally use this as the first approach in your primary-source research unless you start out knowing the citation of a relevant primary authority. Take the descriptive or fact words you selected to describe key aspects of your research problem, and use them as the terms in your CALR search request. Then gain access to a LEXIS file or WESTLAW database containing the kind of primary authorities you want to find, and transmit your search request.

The coverage of numerous LEXIS files and WESTLAW databases focuses on cases, statutes, or administrative regulations, so locating collections of these authorities in which to search online is straightforward. To find federal or state constitutional provisions in LEXIS, you can search files consisting only of these authorities; currently, in WESTLAW, you need to search in databases containing federal or state statutory codes and isolate the constitutional provisions by using a field restriction based on citation information. For some court rules, both LEXIS and WESTLAW provide files and databases consisting exclusively of court rules; to locate other court rules, you need to search in LEXIS files or WESTLAW databases that combine a variety of statutory-type authorities and isolate the court rules by using a field restriction based on citation information.

With descriptive or fact word searching for some authorities (*e.g.*, cases, statutes), you have the option of searching not only in one jurisdiction, but simultaneously in all state-level jurisdictions with online coverage of the kind of authorities you want to find. To do this, select a multi-jurisdictional LEXIS file or WESTLAW database. For example, to simultaneously search cases from all states, use the OMNI or COURTS file in the STATES library in LEXIS or the ALLSTATES or ALLSTATES-OLD database in WESTLAW; to simultaneously search all online state statutes, use the ALLCDE file in the CODES or STATES library in LEXIS or the STAT-ALL or ST-ANN-ALL database in WESTLAW.

For cases, this kind of online multi-jurisdictional searching can prove more convenient than checking multiple, non-cumulative volumes of *Decennial Digests* and *General Digests*, as you do in book-based legal research to search across jurisdictions.[200] For finding other kinds of authorities in a single pass, the multi-jurisdictional LEXIS files and WESTLAW databases offer a capability not available in book-based legal research.

In addition to searching for descriptive or fact words in a single jurisdiction or in every jurisdiction the CALR vendors include in a multi-jurisdictional file or database, you can customize your selection of jurisdictions in which to search. This technique involves searching in a multi-jurisdictional LEXIS file or WESTLAW database and using a field restriction based on the LEXIS segment or WESTLAW field that identifies the jurisdiction that issued the authority. In many libraries in LEXIS, you also have the alternative of designating at the file menu which files you want to search simultaneously.

Finally, although the CALR vendors tout computer-assisted legal research as a way of escaping the potential drawbacks of printed indexes, LEXIS and WESTLAW offer access to some statutory and administrative code indexes you can search for your descriptive or fact words. These online indexes offer an alternative to searching for your descriptive or fact words in the text of an online statute or administrative regulation.

Known topic approach. (See pages 252–54 for LEXIS, and pages 292–95 for WESTLAW.) If you feel quite confident you know what area of law your research problem involves, this approach provides another way of proceeding.

To use the "known topic" approach to find cases in WESTLAW, select an appropriate case-law database and then include a "topic" field restriction in your search request. To avoid indiscriminately recreating the entire coverage you would find for the topic in the West digest for the jurisdiction in which you performed your search, link the "topic" field restriction with one or more other search terms that will screen cases by the facts involved, by the date of decision, by the court, by the name of the authoring judge or a participating attorney, or by some other criterion. (Directing the computer in this way to "skim" cases digested under a given West digest topic often avoids retrieving more information than you can feasibly read online, and holds the potential for culling cases faster or more selectively than you could in a printed digest.) You can also use a West Key Number to restrict your search to one or more subtopics under a topic. In LEXIS, cases do not include a segment comparable to the WESTLAW "topic" field; sometimes, though, your search terms (*e.g.*, "replevin" or "eminent domain") will be so closely associated with a particular

[200] *See* CHRISTOPHER G. WREN & JILL R. WREN, THE LEGAL RESEARCH MANUAL: A GAME PLAN FOR LEGAL RESEARCH AND ANALYSIS 15 (2d ed. 1986).

legal topic that searching for them will retrieve many of the same cases you would find by using the "topic" field as a restriction in WESTLAW.

If you know which topical grouping of provisions in a statutory or administrative code applies to your research problem but do not know the exact statutes or regulations that apply, you can use the "known topic" approach in LEXIS or WESTLAW to turn directly to the portion of the code you want. Select an appropriate LEXIS file or WESTLAW database, then use a field restriction to confine your search to the topical grouping of statutes or regulations in which you are interested. The LEXIS segment or WESTLAW field used in this kind of search will contain the name of, or citation information for, the topical grouping (*e.g.*, "copyright," "title 17," "17 uscs," "17 usca").

In using the "known topic" approach online, you might also find topical files in LEXIS and topical databases in WESTLAW worthwhile sources. These pull together various materials (such as cases, statutes, regulations, looseleaf services, and law review articles) into topical collections in certain specialized areas of law, such as taxation or labor law.

Words and phrases approach. (See pages 254–58 for LEXIS, and pages 296–99 for WESTLAW.) If your research problem involves or turns on a legal definition of a word or phrase, you can try this approach in LEXIS or WESTLAW to focus your search on cases, statutes, or other authorities that define the term in which you are interested.

Link your term with words that can indicate the presence of a definition—*e.g.*, "means," "meaning," "define," "defined," "definition." In court opinions, other words that can signal a definition include "construe," "construing," "interpret," "interpretation," and "words and phrases" (if a judge has cited West Publishing Company's *Words and Phrases* in defining a term). Transmit your search request in a LEXIS file or WESTLAW database that contains the kinds of authorities in which you want to find definitions (*e.g.*, a case-law collection if you want judicial definitions, or a statutory collection if you want legislative definitions).

If you retrieve an unmanageable number of authorities, you can try further focusing your search by adding a field restriction. In searching for judicial definitions in WESTLAW, you can restrict your search to the headnote field. In searching for statutory or administrative definitions in LEXIS or WESTLAW, you can use field restrictions to limit your search to code sections in which the term you want defined appears in the text of the section and in which a word like "definition" appears in the field or segment containing the title of the section.

To use the "words and phrases" approach to locate definitions of terms that occur infrequently in legal authorities, you can simply search for your word or phrase without using additional search terms (like "mean" or "define") that suggest a definitional context.

Even if you are looking for a definition of a unique word or phrase, however, you will often discover that the "words and phrases" approach works just as well or better in books. For judicial definitions, if you have access to the *Words and Phrases* volumes or to case digests with a "Words and Phrases" topic entry or volume, you can find definitions readily: you won't have to screen out authorities that mention your term without defining it; you will find authorities that contain definitions even if they do not include words like "mean" or "define"; and the editorial organization will often help you turn directly to definitions that occur in specific contexts. Similarly, in looking for legislative or administrative definitions, printed indexes in statutory or administrative codes, especially commercially prepared ones, will often cite you directly to relevant definitions.

A generalized approach. (See pages 258–61 for LEXIS, and 300–02 for WESTLAW.) If you want to locate commentaries on the primary law involved in your research problem, you can turn to a variety of secondary sources. In LEXIS and WESTLAW, the secondary sources you can search include law reviews, other legal periodicals, looseleaf services, and *Restatements of the Law*. In addition, in LEXIS, you can research in *American Law Reports*. But the CALR services currently do not offer some of the basic secondary sources you can use in book-based research; for example, at this writing, you will not find the major legal encyclopedias or many of the leading treatises in either LEXIS or WESTLAW.

In any event, if you want to use secondary sources to acquaint yourself with an unfamiliar area of law, rather than to gain perspective on an area of law with which you are already familiar, you will often proceed more effectively and efficiently in printed materials. Developing effective CALR search requests without incurring excessive online charges can be tricky when you do not know the key terms and concepts you should be searching for. To avoid wasting time and money with this approach online, you can browse in books and use their editorial features (such as scope notes and cross-references in indexes) to orient yourself to a new subject matter before you log on to LEXIS or WESTLAW.

Finding the law through updating. As you update the law to make sure the legal authorities you've located in your "finding the law" phase still constitute valid statements of the law, you will also be finding more new authorities. Consequently, as in book-based legal research, updating the law online is also a law-finding technique. Chapter 12 explains how you can update through LEXIS and WESTLAW.

Easy Search in LEXIS, and EZ ACCESS in WESTLAW. (See pages 262–65 for LEXIS, and pages 303–11 for WESTLAW.) In LEXIS, you can use Easy Search to implement some of these law-finding approaches, just as you can use EZ ACCESS in WESTLAW to implement law-finding approaches. Experienced LEXIS and WESTLAW users, however, will probably find Easy Search and EZ ACCESS too constraining for most research projects.

CHAPTER 11

Using Computers in Reading the Law

Introduction. The analytical aspect of reading legal authorities you retrieve through LEXIS or WESTLAW does not differ from the analytical aspect of reading legal authorities you retrieve through book-based research. Whether you find the law by using books or by using a CALR service, you read what you have found and decide what significance to attach to it.[201]

In computer-assisted legal research, though, reading the law takes on a new mechanistic aspect in addition to the old analytical one. This chapter explains the mechanics of reading in LEXIS and WESTLAW.

Once the LEXIS or WESTLAW computer has retrieved documents in response to a search request, you have several options for viewing the results:

- You can note the results, log off (and stop incurring online charges), and read the authorities in books or other offline publications.
- You can display the results on the monitor and read them while you remain logged on to the CALR service.
- You can print out the results on a printer linked to the CALR computer so you can read them later, after you log off. If you don't have a printer, you can have Mead Data Central or West Publishing Company print your search results and mail them to you.
- You can save ("download") the results to a storage device in a personal computer so that after you log off, you can read the authorities, either on the computer monitor or after printing them out.

[201] Chapter 5 of CHRISTOPHER G. WREN & JILL R. WREN, THE LEGAL RESEARCH MANUAL: A GAME PLAN FOR LEGAL RESEARCH AND ANALYSIS (2d ed. 1986) explains the basic principles of reading the law in the sense of analyzing legal authorities.

If you have access to books or other offline publications that contain the authorities retrieved by your search request, you should log off LEXIS or WESTLAW when you need to carefully read and analyze your results. The online charges that would result from engaging in extensive analytical reading while connected to a CALR service would quickly exhaust the resources of all but the deepest pocket. In addition, analytically reading online can be inefficient: according to industrial psychologists, people read material on a computer screen about 20 to 30 per cent more slowly than they read the same material on paper.[202]

Because of the cost and inefficiency of reading authorities online, using a computer in reading the law tends not to consist of analyzing authorities in depth to make a final judgment about their usefulness. Rather, online reading usually amounts to quickly viewing documents to make an initial assessment of their likely significance.

When you scan your search results while connected to LEXIS or WESTLAW, you use commands to accomplish online the actions you take when reading books (*e.g.*, turning a page, skipping across several pages, switching to a different document, marking a page to read later). The commands allow you to:

- view a document on the monitor
- move around within a document
- move between documents
- print one or more documents to read later
- download one or more documents to read later

You can accomplish each of these actions in both LEXIS and WESTLAW, although the commands differ between the two services. The rest of this chapter explains first the options and corresponding commands for LEXIS, and then those for WESTLAW.

Summary. A summary of reading the law in LEXIS appears in Figure 11.28 on pages 383–89, and a summary of reading the law in WESTLAW appears in Figure 11.29 on pages 390–98.

[202] Edward Tenner, *The Paradoxical Proliferation of Paper*, HARV. MAG., Mar.-Apr. 1988, at 23, 24, *excerpted as* Edward Tenner, *The Revenge of Paper*, N.Y. Times, Mar. 5, 1988, at 27. Improvements in screen display might narrow the gap between reading material on a monitor and in a book, but a gap will likely persist for quite a while. *Id. See also* John Tierney, *In Multimedia Storm, Text Thrives*, N.Y. Times, Jul. 5, 1993, at 21, 21 ("[E]xperts in mass communications are . . . discovering that, for many purposes, nothing is as technologically advanced as ink on paper.").

Reading the Law in LEXIS

Viewing documents in LEXIS

Once the computer has assembled the collection of documents that satisfies a search request, the monitor will display a message indicating the number of documents retrieved, as shown in Figure 11.01. In files in which a search can retrieve *A.L.R.* annotations, the computer arranges search results into two groups. As you can see in Figure 11.01, Group 1 consists of the cases retrieved and Group 2 consists of the *A.L.R.* annotations retrieved. Unless you instruct it otherwise, the LEXIS computer will automatically treat Group 1 as the collection you want to work with. You can select Group 2 as the preferred collection by typing `group2` and pressing TRANSMIT. You can switch back to Group 1 by typing `group1` and pressing TRANSMIT. You can switch from one group to another whenever you choose.

Display formats in LEXIS. To view the results of your search, you indicate (while viewing the screen illustrated in Figure 11.01) how you want your results displayed on the monitor. You can select from among several formats:

- *Key word in context (KWIC).* In the KWIC format, the monitor displays your search terms highlighted in the text and surrounded

```
There are a total of 20 documents that satisfy your search request
through Level 1, grouped as follows:
GROUP: (1)    17 CASES
       (2)     3 ALR ANNOTATIONS

TO DISPLAY DOCUMENTS IN THE FIRST GROUP, press any format key (e.g. FULL).
TO GO DIRECTLY TO A PARTICULAR GROUP at any time, transmit the word
GROUP and then the group number (e.g., GROUP2).

USE OF THE REQST KEY WITH GROUPED RESULTS:
- To recall this summary while browsing, transmit the REQST (R) key.
- To review your search request from a GROUP summary screen, transmit
  the REQST key.
For further explanation, press the H key (for HELP) and then the TRANSMIT key.
```

Source: Mead Data Central, Inc. © 1993

Figure 11.01. Report of Search Results in LEXIS

on each side by 25 searchable words (*i.e.*, not counting noise words or reserved words). Figures 11.02 and 11.03 illustrate the first and second screens in a typical KWIC display of a case.[203]

The KWIC display format allows you to determine quickly whether you are retrieving documents that use your search terms in the sense you intended and whether the search terms you selected are retrieving relevant documents. By using KWIC, you can skim through a document (especially a long one) for possible relevance in less time than it would take to scan the full text of the document page by page online. Thus, using KWIC can alert you to the need to modify your search request before you spend a lot of time reading the full text of irrelevant documents. Because KWIC speeds up the assessment of relevance, researchers use this display format frequently.

If you decide you want to start viewing your search results by looking at documents in the KWIC format, press the key labelled KWIC. (Alternatively, at the screen shown in Figure 11.01, you can press TRANSMIT.) The monitor will display the first document in the collection your search request retrieved. As shown in Figures 11.02 and 11.03, you will see identifying information about the document (*e.g.*, case caption, citation, date of decision) followed by whichever of your search terms occurs first in the document, along with the 25 searchable words on each side of the term.

- *Variable key word in context (VAR KWIC).* With VAR KWIC, you can display documents in a KWIC format, but with more or fewer than the 25 searchable words KWIC displays on each side of your search terms. In all other respects, VAR KWIC operates like KWIC.

  VAR KWIC offers two options for selecting the number of adjoining words displayed. If you simply press the VAR KWIC key, the monitor will show each occurrence of a search term with 50 searchable words on each side. Alternatively, if you want to see your search terms surrounded by a different number of adjoining words (from 1 to 999), type that number and then press the VAR KWIC key. Figure 11.04 shows the portion of the text illustrated in Figure 11.03, but with 35 searchable words displayed on each side of the search term instead of 25.

[203] Note that the KWIC format will not include as part of the 25 searchable words any words from adjoining segments. So, for example, if a search term were the last word in the opinion segment of a case, the KWIC display would show that term with the 25 searchable words preceding it and none following it.

```
                 LEVEL 1 - GROUP 1 - 1 OF 17 CASES

               UNITED STATES v. MENDOZA-LOPEZ ET AL.

                            No. 85-2067

                 SUPREME COURT OF THE UNITED STATES

      481 U.S. 828; 107 S. Ct. 2148; 1987 U.S. LEXIS 2262; 95 L.
                    Ed. 2d 772; 55 U.S.L.W. 4688


                      March 3, 1987, Argued
                       May 26, 1987, Decided

DISPOSITION: <=1> 781 F.2d 111, affirmed.

SYLLABUS:

   ... [***3]   judgment by respondents, the Immigration Judge completely
deprived them of their right to judicial review  [***4]   of the deportation
proceeding.  This deprivation precludes the use of the deportation orders to
prove @ 1326 violations.  Pp. 839-840.
```

Source: Mead Data Central, Inc. © 1993

Figure 11.02. Key Word in Context (KWIC) Display in LEXIS

```
              481 U.S. 828, *; 107 S. Ct. 2148, **;
           1987 U.S. LEXIS 2262, ***4; 95 L. Ed. 2d 772
   (c) <=4>  Lewis v. United States, 445 U.S. 55, is distinguishable from
the instant case since it assumed the opportunity to challenge the underlying
decision in a judicial forum, precisely that which was denied respondents here.
Pp. 840-842.

OPINION:

   ... [*840] [**2156] [***21]   considered or intelligent, respondents were
deprived of judicial review of their deportation proceeding.  The Government may
not, therefore, rely on those orders as reliable proof of an element of a
criminal offense.

   C

   The United States asserts that our decision in <=64> Lewis v. United
States, 445 U.S. 55 (1980), answered any constitutional objections to the
scheme employed in @ 1326.  In Lewis , the Court held that a state-court
conviction, even though it was uncounseled and therefore obtained in violation
of the Sixth and Fourteenth Amendment rights of the defendant under <=65>
Gideon v. Wainwright, 372 U.S. 335 (1963), could be ...
```

Source: Mead Data Central, Inc. © 1993

Figure 11.03. Second Screen in a Key Word in Context (KWIC) Display in LEXIS

```
                481 U.S. 828, *; 107 S. Ct. 2148, **;
             1987 U.S. LEXIS 2262, ***4; 95 L. Ed. 2d 772
   (c) <=4> Lewis v. United States, 445 U.S. 55, is distinguishable from
the instant case since it assumed the opportunity to challenge the underlying
decision in a judicial forum, precisely that which was denied respondents here.
Pp. 840-842.

OPINION:

   ... [*840] [**2156] [***21]   properly of their eligibility  to apply for
suspension of deportation.  Because the waivers of their rights to appeal were
not considered or intelligent, respondents were deprived of judicial review of
their deportation proceeding.  The Government may not, therefore, rely on those
orders as reliable proof of an element of a criminal offense.

   C

   The United States asserts that our decision in <=64> Lewis v. United
States, 445 U.S. 55 (1980), answered any constitutional objections to the
scheme employed in @ 1326.  In Lewis , the Court held that a state-court
conviction, even though it was uncounseled and therefore obtained in violation
of the Sixth and Fourteenth Amendment rights of the defendant under <=65>
Gideon v. Wainwright, 372 U.S. 335 (1963), could be used as a predicate for a
subsequent conviction under @ 1202(a)(1) of Title VII of the Omnibus Crime
```

Source: Mead Data Central, Inc. © 1993

Figure 11.04. Variable Key Word in Context (VAR KWIC) Display in LEXIS

You can change the number of adjoining words in a VAR KWIC display at any time either by typing the new number and pressing the VAR KWIC key, or by just pressing the VAR KWIC key alone if you want to change to a VAR KWIC value of 50.

- *Full text (FULL).* You also have the option of viewing the complete text of a document online. This option is particularly useful if you do not have offline access to a document.

  If you decide you want to start viewing your search results by looking at documents in the FULL format, press the key labelled FULL. The monitor will display the first document in the collection your search request retrieved. You will see identifying information about the document (*e.g.*, case caption, citation, date of decision) followed by the full text of the document. When you come across your search terms in the text, you will see them highlighted on the monitor.

  Figure 11.05 illustrates a typical first screen of a case in full-text display.

- *Full text in selected segments (SEGMTS).* You might want to view the full text of just selected segments of a document. For instance, you might want to see only the dissenting opinions in the cases retrieved by your search request.

```
                         LEVEL 1 - 1 OF 17 CASES

                 UNITED STATES v. MENDOZA-LOPEZ ET AL.

                             No. 85-2067

                    SUPREME COURT OF THE UNITED STATES

     481 U.S. 828; 107 S. Ct. 2148; 1987 U.S. LEXIS 2262; 95 L.
                    Ed. 2d 772; 55 U.S.L.W. 4688


                         March 3, 1987, Argued
                          May 26, 1987, Decided

PRIOR HISTORY:    [***1]

   CERTIORARI TO THE UNITED STATES COURT OF APPEALS FOR THE EIGHTH CIRCUIT.

DISPOSITION: <=1> 781 F.2d 111, affirmed.

SYLLABUS:  Title <=2> 8 U. S. C. @ 1326 provides that any alien who has been
deported and thereafter enters the United States is guilty of a felony.
Respondents, Mexican nationals, were arrested and deported after a group
```

Source: Mead Data Central, Inc. © 1993

Figure 11.05. Full-Text (FULL) Display in LEXIS

To limit the display to selected segments, press the key labelled SEGMTS. The monitor will then show a list of the segments available for display. Figure 11.06 illustrates a typical segments list for cases. Type the name of each segment you want to view (placing a comma between segment names), and press TRANSMIT. The monitor will then display your document, showing only a heading with identifying information about the document (*e.g.*, case caption, citation, date of decision) followed by the text contained in the segment or segments you selected. Figure 11.07 shows the first screen of a case for which just the dissent segment was selected for viewing.

If you change your mind about the segment or segments you want to view, press the SEGMTS key again, type the name of each segment you now want to view (placing a comma between segment names), and press TRANSMIT.

If any of your search terms appear in the selected segments, the monitor will display these terms highlighted in the text; if your search terms are not present, you will simply see whatever text appears in the segments you chose to view.

In other words, your search terms do not have to appear in a particular segment for you to view the contents of that segment through the SEGMTS display format. Thus, the SEGMTS display

```
Please transmit, separated by commas, the segment(s) you want displayed.

NAME                NUMBER              COURT               CITE
DATE                NOTICE              HISTORY             DISPOSITION
HEADNOTES           SYLLABUS            COUNSEL             JUDGES
OPINIONBY           OPINION             CONCURBY            CONCUR
DISSENTBY           DISSENT             OPINIONS            WRITTENBY
PUBLICATION         CONTENTS            TABLE-OF-CASES      TITLE
TCSL-REFS           JUR-TABLE           INDEX               BYLINE
REFERENCES          TEXT

For further explanation, press the H key (for HELP) and then the TRANSMIT key.
```

Source: Mead Data Central, Inc. © 1993

Figure 11.06. Sample List of Segments You Can Display in LEXIS

```
                          LEVEL 1 - 1 OF 17 CASES

                   UNITED STATES v. MENDOZA-LOPEZ ET AL.

                                No. 85-2067

                      SUPREME COURT OF THE UNITED STATES

        481 U.S. 828; 107 S. Ct. 2148; 1987 U.S. LEXIS 2262; 95 L.
                      Ed. 2d 772; 55 U.S.L.W. 4688


                         March 3, 1987, Argued
                          May 26, 1987, Decided

DISPOSITION:  <=1>  781 F.2d 111, affirmed.

DISSENT: CHIEF JUSTICE REHNQUIST, with whom JUSTICE WHITE and JUSTICE O'CONNOR
join,   [***25]   dissenting.

   I agree with the Court's ruling that the language of  <=72>  8 U. S. C. @
1326, its history, and other provisions of the Immigration and Nationality Act
suggest that Congress did not intend to allow challenges to the validity of a
deportation order in a @ 1326 proceeding.  I also agree with the view that
```

Source: Mead Data Central, Inc. © 1993

Figure 11.07. Display of a Selected Segment ("Dissent" Segment) in LEXIS

format differs from a search request restricted to a particular segment (see Chapter 5). A segment *search* restriction requires the restricted search terms to appear in the designated segment in order to retrieve the document; the segment *display* restriction, however, simply displays the text of selected segments, regardless of whether those segments contain any search terms.

Note, though, that in a given document, a segment you select for viewing might be empty (that is, not contain any text). For instance, in a case in which none of the judges dissented, the dissent segment would be empty; if you had selected only this segment for viewing through SEGMTS, just the heading for the case would show on the monitor, with the rest of the screen blank.

In addition, a segment you select for viewing might not exist in a given document, in which case, of course, you will not be able to view the segment's contents. In some files, you will be given the option of displaying a segment that does not exist in all documents in the file. In that situation, selecting a segment for viewing can also result in displaying only the heading for some documents, with the rest of the screen blank.

- *Citation list (CITE or REFS).* Instead of viewing documents retrieved by your search request, you can opt to see just a list of their citations. The information contained in a citation will vary depending on the type of document (*e.g.*, case, law review article, *American Law Reports* annotation), but the information will always allow you to locate the cited document. Figure 11.08 shows the first screen of a typical list of citations for a collection of cases.

  The CITE option lets you quickly assess the character of the collection of documents retrieved. For instance, with a collection of cases, a citation list will let you see at a glance the following: whether the highest court in a given jurisdiction issued any of the cases; which jurisdictions are represented in the collection (if you conducted a multi-jurisdictional search); or what time span the documents cover. Information such as this can help you decide, before you spend time reviewing documents, whether to modify your search request. You can also use the information from a citation list to retrieve offline versions (if they exist) of the documents cited online.

  To view a citation list, press the key labelled CITE. (On some LEXIS terminals, the key will be labelled REFS instead of CITE.) The monitor will display the citation list, which will resemble Figure 11.08. The list might extend across several screens.

```
                    LEVEL 1 - GROUP 1 - 17 CASES

1. UNITED STATES v. MENDOZA-LOPEZ ET AL., No. 85-2067, SUPREME COURT OF THE
UNITED STATES, 481 U.S. 828; 107 S. Ct. 2148; 1987 U.S. LEXIS 2262; 95 L. Ed. 2d
772; 55 U.S.L.W. 4688,   Argued March 3, 1987,   May 26, 1987

2. BALDASAR v. ILLINOIS, No. 77-6219, SUPREME COURT OF THE UNITED STATES, 446
U.S. 222; 100 S. Ct. 1585; 1980 U.S. LEXIS 124; 64 L. Ed. 2d 169,   Argued
November 26, 1979,   April 22, 1980; Petition for Rehearing Denied June 16,
1980.

3. James Alfonso GREENE, Petitioner-Appellant, v. UNITED STATES of America,
Respondent-Appellee, No. 88-8475, UNITED STATES COURT OF APPEALS FOR THE
ELEVENTH CIRCUIT, 880 F.2d 1299; 888 F.2d 1398; 1989 U.S. App. LEXIS 12362,
August 21, 1989; Rehearing En Banc Denied September 28, 1989; Reported at 1989
U.S. App. LEXIS 19917

4. United States of America, Plaintiff-Appellee, v. Hughes Anderson Bagley,
Defendant-Appellant, No. 87-3922, UNITED STATES COURT OF APPEALS FOR THE NINTH
CIRCUIT, 837 F.2d 371; 1988 U.S. App. LEXIS 207, Argued December 8, 1987;
Submitted December 11, 1987, January 13, 1988, Filed

5. JOSEPH FREDERICK ROBARDS, Petitioner-Appellant, v. JOHN REES, SUPERINTENDANT,
KENTUCKY STATE REFORMATORY and DAVID L. ARMSTRONG, ATTORNEY, GENERAL,
```

Source: Mead Data Central, Inc. © 1993

Figure 11.08. Sample Citation List in LEXIS

In files in which a search can retrieve *A.L.R.* annotations, you will obtain two lists of citations because the computer arranges your search results into two groups. As explained on page 319, Group 1 will consist of cases retrieved, and Group 2 will consist of *A.L.R.* annotations retrieved. Each group will have a separate citation list.

Pressing the CITE key will produce a citation list for whichever group of documents you have directed the LEXIS computer to treat as the preferred collection. (See page 319.) So, pressing the CITE key will normally produce a citation list of the cases retrieved by your search request (*i.e.*, Group 1, the default group). But if you have made Group 2 the preferred collection, pressing the CITE key will produce a citation list of the *A.L.R.* annotations retrieved.

After viewing a collection of documents in the citation list format, you can use the list to select a document for viewing. Here, you have two options. First, you can type the document's identification number (found in front of the document's citation on the list) and press TRANSMIT; the monitor will display the document in KWIC format. For example, if you wanted to view *Greene v. United States* (document 3 in Figure 11.08), you would transmit **3**. Second, if the citation for the document you want to view appears at the top of the monitor (such as *United States v. Mendoza-*

Lopez in Figure 11.08), you can simply press one of the format keys (such as KWIC or FULL) to see the document in the format you requested.

Changing display formats in LEXIS. Once you select a display format for viewing the results of a search request, all documents retrieved by that search request will display in the format you chose until you select a new format. At any time, you can switch the display format by pressing the key for the desired format, at which point you will see the document you were viewing redisplayed in the new format. For example, if you are viewing a document in the KWIC display format, you could press the key labelled FULL to see the document's complete text.

Where in the document you will find yourself after changing display formats will depend on the change you have made, as these examples show.

- For some changes, the new display will pick up at roughly the point in the text the previous format was displaying when you switched. (This occurs when you switch from KWIC, VAR KWIC, or SEGMTS to FULL; from KWIC to VAR KWIC, and vice versa; and from one VAR KWIC value to a different VAR KWIC value.) You might need to page up or down in the document to return to the precise part of the text you were viewing when you changed display formats.
- When you switch to CITE from another display format, the citation of the document you were most recently viewing will appear at the top of the monitor. When you switch from CITE by pressing the key for a different display format, the monitor will display in the selected format the first screen of whatever document had its citation at the top of the monitor when you changed display formats.

Display formats for documents retrieved through LEXSEE and LEXSTAT. Currently, when you retrieve a document through LEXSEE (a feature explained on pages 238–43), you can view that document only in the FULL display format. When you retrieve a document through LEXSTAT (a feature explained on pages 243–44), the monitor will first display that document in the FULL display format; you can then select either the SEGMTS or CITE display format.

Display order for documents retrieved in LEXIS. Regardless of the display format you select (*e.g.*, KWIC, FULL, CITE), the documents your search requests retrieve will display in a predictable order. Knowing this order can help you browse through the retrieved documents more efficiently.

- *Cases.* When you run a search request in a file containing cases from only one court (say, the ORE file, containing cases from the Oregon Supreme Court only, in the ORE library), the cases will display in reverse chronological order—that is, with the most recently decided case displayed first.

  When you run a search request in a file that contains cases from more than one court in a single jurisdiction (such as the CASES file in the NY library, where you can search all online cases from the New York Court of Appeals, the New York Supreme Court (Appellate Division), and various lower courts, such as the New York Criminal Court), the cases will display in the following sequence: first, cases from the highest court will display in reverse chronological order; then cases from the next-highest court will display in reverse chronological order; then cases from the next-highest court will display in reverse chronological order; and so on. An example of this display order appears in Figure 11.08.

  When you run a search request in a file containing cases from more than one court in more than one jurisdiction (as can happen, for example, in the OMNI or COURTS file in the STATES library, where you can search all online cases from all states), the retrieved cases will be arranged according to the alphabetical order of the jurisdictions. Within each jurisdiction, the cases will be arranged by court and then, within each arrangement by court, in reverse chronological order. For example, if a search in the OMNI file retrieved cases from Florida's and Georgia's appellate courts, the cases would display in this order: cases from Florida's highest appellate court, in reverse chronological order; cases from Florida's intermediate appellate court, in reverse chronological order; cases from Georgia's highest appellate court, in reverse chronological order; and cases from Georgia's intermediate appellate court, in reverse chronological order.

  If you customize your selection of case-law files (as explained on page 196), the order in which you specified the files will affect the order in which retrieved documents will display. For instance, if you instructed the computer to search simultaneously in the case files for Alabama, California, Indiana, Maine, Nebraska, and New Mexico, the order in which you transmitted the file names will determine the order in which the retrieved documents will display. If you customized your file selection by transmitting

  ```
  ind,ala,neb,cal,nm,me
  ```

  the cases will display in this order: cases from Indiana's highest appellate court, in reverse chronological order; cases from Indiana's intermediate appellate court, in reverse chronological order; cases from Alabama's highest appellate court, in reverse chronological order; cases from Alabama's intermediate appellate court, in reverse chronological order; and so on.

- *Statutes.* Unlike cases, statutes retrieved by search requests do not display in reverse chronological order. Rather, the display order for statutory sections in a given jurisdiction tracks the order in which those sections appear in that jurisdiction's printed statutory code. For example, 18 U.S.C. § 2331 would display before 18 U.S.C. § 2385, and both these sections would precede 42 U.S.C. § 1985.

  Your search request might retrieve statutes from more than one jurisdiction (as can happen in the ALLCDE file in the STATES library, where you can search all online state statutes). In that situation, the retrieved statutes will be grouped alphabetically by jurisdiction. For instance, Alabama statutes will display before Kentucky statutes. Within each jurisdiction, statutory sections will display as explained in the preceding paragraph.
- *Administrative regulations.* The display order for administrative regulations follows the pattern for displaying statutes.
- *Law review materials.* When your search request retrieves articles and other materials from just one law review, the documents will display in reverse chronological order, with documents from the most recent volume appearing first.

  When your request retrieves materials from more than one law review (as can happen in the ALLREV file in the LAWREV library), the documents will be arranged according to the alphabetical order of the law reviews' names; within a given law review, documents will display in reverse chronological order by volume number.
- *A.L.R. and Lawyers' Edition annotations.* When your search request retrieves case annotations from *A.L.R.* and *Lawyers' Edition 2d*, the annotations will display in the following order: annotations from *A.L.R. Federal*; annotations from *Lawyers' Edition 2d*; annotations from *A.L.R.5th*; annotations from *A.L.R.4th*; annotations from *A.L.R.3d*; and annotations from *A.L.R.2d*. Within each of these series, documents will display in reverse chronological order, with annotations from the most recent volume appearing first.

In general, other kinds of documents retrieved by your LEXIS search requests will display in reverse chronological order. If you are uncertain about the organization of a collection of retrieved documents, press the CITE key. You can then review the citation list to see what pattern exists.

Star paging in LEXIS. "Star pagination" numbers display on the monitor if they are available for the document you are viewing. A star-page number serves as a reference point in the text, allowing you quickly to find in a document a specified location to which someone has referred you, or, likewise, allowing you to refer someone else to a specified location.

Star-page numbers appear embedded in the document's text as asterisked numbers enclosed in brackets. For example, Figure 11.03 on page 321 shows star-page numbers [*840], [**2156], [***21]. Documents for which LEXIS provides star paging include all cases decided after 1987, many earlier cases, some law review articles, and *A.L.R.* annotations.

For a document other than a case (*e.g.*, a law review article), only one set of star-page numbers will appear on the monitor. These numbers correspond to the page numbers of the print version of the document.

A case, however, might have more than one set of star-page numbers, with each set of numbers preceded by a different number of asterisks. For example, a U.S. Supreme Court case might have three star-page sets: one set corresponding to the page numbers of the case as it appears printed in the official *United States Reports*; one corresponding to the page numbers of the case as it appears printed in West Publishing Company's unofficial *Supreme Court Reporter*; and one corresponding to the LEXIS version of the case, using LEXIS page numbers assigned by Mead Data Central.[204] These three sets of star pages would appear in the following form:

`[*840]` for *U.S. Reports* pagination
`[**2156]` for *Supreme Court Reporter* pagination
`[***21]` for LEXIS pagination

The number of asterisks identifying a pagination set will vary depending on how many star-page sets exist in a given case. For instance, using the preceding illustration, if the *U.S. Reports* pagination were unavailable in LEXIS, but the other two pagination sets were present, the sets of page numbers would appear in this form:

`[*2156]` for *Supreme Court Reporter* pagination
`[**21]` for LEXIS pagination

If you want to find out which star-page sets exist for a case you are viewing,

1. Type p (for "pages").
2. Press TRANSMIT.

The monitor will display a message telling you the number of LEXIS screens the case occupies (useful information if, for example, you are considering

[204] LEXIS pages were discussed in Figure 10.02 on pages 239–40.

printing the case); if any star-page sets exist for the case, the message will also indicate the number of pages in each set. Thus, if you transmitted `p` while viewing a U.S. Supreme Court case, you might see a message like this:

```
The 2ND CASE for Search Level 1 contains:
   - 49 LEXIS screens in FULL format.
   - 25 U.S. pages.
   - 41 LEXIS pages.
   - 17 L.Ed.2D pages.
```

In this example, you would know that the case has star paging tied to *U.S. Reports*, LEXIS pagination, and *United States Supreme Court Reports, Lawyers' Edition*. Because the message does not provide the number of pages for the version of the case printed in *Supreme Court Reporter*, you would also know the case does not have star paging tied to that publication. If the message had only indicated the number of LEXIS screens, you would have known the case had *no* star paging at all (whether tied to a printed reporter or to LEXIS pagination).

If you are viewing a case that has multiple star-paging sets and only want to see one set of page numbers, you can remove the other page numbers from the monitor. To do so:

1. Type `star` followed by the identification for the set of star-page numbers you want displayed.

2. Press TRANSMIT.

For example, you would transmit `star us` to display page numbers from just *U.S. Reports*. Similarly, transmitting `star lexis` would cause only LEXIS page numbers to display. You can switch from one star-page display to another whenever you want. Most reasonable abbreviations for a publication will work with the "star" command; if you encounter difficulty, try using the abbreviation you would use for that publication when you invoke Shepard's or Auto-Cite.[205] To return to the standard display of star-page numbers (*i.e.*, displaying all available star-page numbers on the monitor):

1. Type `xstar` (for "exit star").

2. Press TRANSMIT.

[205] See pages 400–22 for a discussion of the Shepard's service in LEXIS; see pages 422 and 426–37 for a discussion of the Auto-Cite service in LEXIS. Publication abbreviations that work with Shepard's and Auto-Cite appear in Appendices G and H of MEAD DATA CENTRAL, REFERENCE MANUAL FOR THE LEXIS/NEXIS SERVICES (undated looseleaf ed.).

Moving within a document in LEXIS

Once the monitor has displayed a document or a citation list, you have several options for moving around within the document or list:[206]

- *Move forward one screen.* Press the key labelled NEXT PAGE or the key labelled PgDn (for "page down"). Alternatively, you can press the TRANSMIT key.

  The display format you have chosen determines what constitutes a "page" when you press the NEXT PAGE, PgDn, or TRANSMIT key. For example, in the FULL display format, a page consists of as much of the document's text as can fit on the screen, and pressing NEXT PAGE, PgDn, or TRANSMIT is analogous to turning a page in a book. In the KWIC format, on the other hand, a page consists of one or more occurrences of a search term surrounded on each side by 25 searchable words (as shown in Figure 11.03 on page 321). Pressing NEXT PAGE, PgDn, or TRANSMIT while in KWIC will move you to the next screen that contains one of your search terms, and is analogous to skipping through a book to find only those pages containing certain words.
- *Move back one screen.* Press the key labelled PREV PAGE (for "previous page") or the key labelled PgUp (for "page up").

  As with the NEXT PAGE (or PgDn) key, the display format you have chosen determines what constitutes a "page" when you press the PREV PAGE (or PgUp) key. (See above.)
- *Move forward more than one screen.* Type the number of screens you want to advance in the document; then press the NEXT PAGE (or PgDn) key. For example, if you were viewing the third screen of a document and wanted to skip ahead 5 screens, you would type 5 and press NEXT PAGE (or PgDn); the monitor would then display the eighth screen of the document.

  If you are viewing a citation list rather than a document, this technique will not work: you cannot use the NEXT PAGE (or PgDn) key to skip ahead multiple screens in the CITE display format.
- *Move back more than one screen.* Type the number of screens you want to move back in the document; then press the PREV PAGE (or PgUp) key. For example, if you were viewing the eighth screen of a document and wanted to skip back 5 screens, you would type 5

[206] If you want to find out how long a document is, type p and press TRANSMIT. As explained on pages 330–31, the monitor will display a message telling you the number of LEXIS screens the document occupies in the current display format. On-screen instructions explain how to return to the document you were viewing.

and press PREV PAGE (or PgUp); the monitor would then display the third screen of the document.

If you are viewing a citation list rather than a document, this technique will not work: you cannot use the PREV PAGE (or PgUp) key to skip back multiple screens in the CITE display format.

- *Return to the first screen.* Press the key labelled FIRST PAGE to return to the beginning of a document or citation list.
- *Move to a specific "star" page.* If you have selected the FULL display format and are viewing a document that contains star paging (explained on pages 330–31), you can move directly to a specific star page. Type `p` followed by the star-page number, including its asterisks; then press TRANSMIT. For instance, referring to the star-paging examples on page 330, if you wanted to see page 840 of the *U.S. Reports* version of the case, you would transmit `p*840`, or if you wanted to view LEXIS page 21 of the case, you would transmit `p***21`.

  This technique works a bit differently when you are viewing an *A.L.R.* annotation. Instead of indicating a specific page number, you indicate a specific section number within the annotation; for example, you would transmit `p*3c` to move to section 3[c]. In addition, you can move to the table of cases for a given *A.L.R.* annotation by transmitting `p*cases`; you can move to the annotation's index (if there is one) by transmitting `p*index`.
- *Move forward or back one line.* Press the key labelled ROLL UP to move ahead one line. Press the key labelled ROLL DOWN to move back one line. These keys are found only on the UBIQ keyboard.

In most instances, a command for moving within a document will result in your continuing to view the same document. Sometimes, however, a command will bump you to another document. For example, if your search results include more than one document and you are viewing the last screen of a document when you press the NEXT PAGE (or PgDn) key, the monitor will display the first screen of the next document in your collection. Likewise, if you are viewing the first screen of a document when you press the PREV PAGE (or PgUp) key, the monitor will display the last screen of the preceding document. Ordinarily, however, to move between documents, you use the commands explained in the next section.

Moving between documents in LEXIS

When your search request retrieves more than one document, you have several options for moving from one document to another.[207] You can:

- *Move forward one document.* Press the key labelled NEXT DOC (for "next document"). (On some LEXIS terminals, the key will be labelled NEXT CASE instead of NEXT DOC.)
- *Move back one document.* Press the key labelled PREV DOC (for "previous document"). (On some LEXIS terminals, the key will be labelled PREV CASE instead of PREV DOC.)
- *Move forward more than one document.* Type the number of documents you want to advance in the collection retrieved by your search request; then press the NEXT DOC key. For example, if you were viewing the third document and wanted to skip ahead 5 documents, you would type 5 and press NEXT DOC; the monitor would then display the eighth document.

  If you use this technique while viewing a citation list (rather than a document), the number you transmit will cause the CITE display to skip ahead that number of citations past the last citation appearing on the monitor when you transmitted the number. Thus, if the sixth citation appeared at the bottom of the monitor and you wanted to skip ahead 20 citations, typing 20 and pressing NEXT DOC would cause the citation list to redisplay with the 26th citation at the top of the monitor.
- *Move back more than one document.* Type the number of documents you want to move back in the collection retrieved by your search request; then press the PREV DOC key. For example, if you were viewing the eighth document and wanted to skip back 5 documents, you would type 5 and press PREV DOC; the monitor would then display the third document.

  If you use this technique while viewing a citation list (rather than a document), the number you transmit will cause the CITE display to skip back that number of citations past the first citation appearing on the monitor when you transmitted the number. Thus, if the 26th citation appeared at the top of the monitor and you wanted to skip back 20 citations, typing 20 and pressing PREV DOC

[207] These navigating options are possible because, as discussed on pages 327–29, documents retrieved by a search request are displayed in a fixed order, and each document is assigned an identification number (which appears on the citation list you can display through the CITE format, as explained at pages 325–27).

would cause the citation list to redisplay with the sixth citation at the bottom of the monitor.

- *Return to the first document.* Press the key labelled FIRST DOC to return to the first document in the collection retrieved by your search request or (if you are viewing a citation list) to return to the first screen of the list. (On some LEXIS terminals, the key will be labelled FIRST CASE instead of FIRST DOC.)
- *Move to a specific document.* If you know the identification number of a document in the collection retrieved by your search request (having gotten the number from a citation list, like the one in Figure 11.08 on page 326), you can go directly from the document you are viewing to the new document. Type the new document's identification number and press TRANSMIT. For example, returning to the collection of cases listed in Figure 11.08, if you were viewing *United States v. Mendoza-Lopez* and wanted to move to *Greene v. United States*, you could do so by typing 3 and pressing TRANSMIT.

  You can also move from a citation list to a specific document by transmitting that document's number, as explained on pages 326–27. Conversely, you can move from a document to a citation list by pressing the CITE key; the monitor will display a citation list, with the citation of the document you were viewing shown as the first citation on the monitor.
- *Move to other statutory or administrative code sections, whether or not retrieved ("Browse").* When viewing a federal or state statute or administrative regulation, you can move to other sections of the code—even those *not* included in your search results. This capability, which Mead Data Central calls "browsing," is analogous to skipping to other sections of a printed code after you have located the section in which you were originally interested. Thus, "browsing" allows you to read statutory and administrative code sections in the context of surrounding, presumably related, provisions.

  By permitting you to move between a retrieved document and an unretrieved document, Browse differs from other navigational techniques (which only permit you to move between documents actually retrieved by a search request).

  You invoke the browsing feature while viewing a statutory or administrative code section, whether retrieved by a search request or through LEXSTAT. To implement the feature, type b and press TRANSMIT. The monitor will redisplay the section you were viewing, but this time in the browse mode. At that point, you can move anywhere in the statutory or administrative code by using the navigating techniques already discussed.

For example, suppose the first two statutory provisions your search request retrieved were sections 12-21-43 and 12-21-72 of the Code of Alabama. If you were viewing section 12-21-43 and pressed the NEXT DOC key, you would normally move to section 12-21-72. But if you had invoked the browsing feature while viewing section 12-21-43, pressing NEXT DOC would move you to section 12-21-44 (the next section in the Code of Alabama), even though your search request had not retrieved that section.

When you use the browsing feature, documents will automatically appear in the FULL display format. You can switch to the SEGMTS or CITE display formats; however, you cannot select either KWIC or VAR KWIC to display documents in the browse mode (because not all the documents available for viewing through the browse feature will have your search terms).

While you are in the browse mode, the legend =B= will appear in the upper right corner of the monitor on the second and subsequent screens of each document you view. To leave the browse mode, transmit **b** again; the legend =B= will disappear from the monitor.

Figure 11.09 shows the first and second screens of a statutory section as it appears before invoking the browsing feature. Figure 11.10 shows the first and second screens of the same section after invoking the browsing feature.

Moving between search levels in LEXIS. So far, the techniques presented for moving between documents in LEXIS assume you are moving between documents on the same search level. (Recall that when you modify a search request in LEXIS, you create a different search level. See page 168.) If you have searched on more than one level and want to return to the documents retrieved at a level other than the one you are viewing:

1. Type the number of the search level you want to view.
2. Press the key labelled DIF LEVEL or, on older keyboards, DISP DIF LEVEL (for "display different level").

The monitor will display a screen indicating the number of documents retrieved at the search level you selected. At that point, you can use any of the techniques for moving between documents.

The FOCUS feature in LEXIS: viewing a subset of documents

When you are viewing a collection of documents retrieved by a search request in LEXIS (or the citation list for those documents), you can use the

```
To be able to browse preceding or succeeding code sections, transmit B.  The
first page of the document you are currently viewing will be displayed in FULL.
-------------------------------------------------------------------------------

                          LEVEL 1 - 1 OF 1 SECTION

                              CODE OF ALABAMA
                Copyright (c) 1977-1993 by The State of Alabama
                            All rights reserved.

      *** THIS SECTION IS CURRENT THROUGH THE 1992 SPECIAL SUPPLEMENT ***
          *** (1992 REGULAR, ORGANIZATIONAL AND SPECIAL SESSIONS) ***

                            TITLE 12.  COURTS
                     CHAPTER 21.  EVIDENCE AND WITNESSES
                        ARTICLE 1.  GENERAL PROVISIONS
                            DIVISION 1.  EVIDENCE
                 SUBDIVISION 2.  COMPETENCY AND ADMISSIBILITY

                        Code of Ala. @ 12-21-43 (1992)

@12-21-43. Writings or records made in regular course of business --Originals
```

message before invoking "Browse"

```
                        Code of Ala. @ 12-21-43 (1992)

   Any writing or record, whether in the form of an entry in a book or
otherwise, made as a memorandum or record of any act, transaction, occurrence or
event, shall be admissible in evidence in proof of said act, transaction or
event if it was made in the regular course of any business and it was the
regular course of the business to make such memorandum or record at the time of
such act, transaction, occurrence or event, or within a reasonable time
thereafter. All other circumstances of the making of such writing or record,
including lack of personal knowledge by the entrant or maker, may be shown to
affect its weight, but they shall not affect its admissibility. The term,
"business" shall include a business, profession, occupation and calling of every
kind.

HISTORY: Code 1940, T. 7, @ 415.

 NOTES:
CODE COMMISSIONER'S NOTE. --This section is superseded by A.R.C.P., Rule 44, as
to civil proceedings, but has been retained for possible applicability in
criminal or probate proceedings.
I. General Consideration.
II. Specific Writings or Records.

I. GENERAL CONSIDERATION.
```

Source: Mead Data Central, Inc.; © 1977–1993 State of Alabama

Figure 11.09. Display of a Statute Before Invoking "Browse" in LEXIS

message after invoking "Browse"

```
This is the first page of the document you were viewing in the FULL format.
To see a preceding or succeeding code section, press the PREV DOC (.PD) or
NEXT DOC (.ND) key.  To return to your LEXIS search results, transmit B.
-------------------------------------------------------------------------------

                              CODE OF ALABAMA
                  Copyright (c) 1977-1993 by The State of Alabama
                             All rights reserved.

       *** THIS SECTION IS CURRENT THROUGH THE 1992 SPECIAL SUPPLEMENT ***
           *** (1992 REGULAR, ORGANIZATIONAL AND SPECIAL SESSIONS) ***

                             TITLE 12.  COURTS
                       CHAPTER 21.  EVIDENCE AND WITNESSES
                          ARTICLE 1.  GENERAL PROVISIONS
                              DIVISION 1.  EVIDENCE
                     SUBDIVISION 2.  COMPETENCY AND ADMISSIBILITY

                          Code of Ala. @ 12-21-43 (1992)

@ 12-21-43. Writings or records made in regular course of business --Originals

   Any writing or record, whether in the form of an entry in a book or
otherwise, made as a memorandum or record of any act, transaction, occurrence
```

indicates "Browse" mode

```
                          Code of Ala. @ 12-21-43 (1992)                  =B=

or event, shall be admissible in evidence in proof of said act, transaction or
event if it was made in the regular course of any business and it was the
regular course of the business to make such memorandum or record at the time of
such act, transaction, occurrence or event, or within a reasonable time
thereafter. All other circumstances of the making of such writing or record,
including lack of personal knowledge by the entrant or maker, may be shown to
affect its weight, but they shall not affect its admissibility. The term,
"business" shall include a business, profession, occupation and calling of every
kind.

HISTORY: Code 1940, T. 7, @ 415.

 NOTES:
CODE COMMISSIONER'S NOTE. --This section is superseded by A.R.C.P., Rule 44, as
to civil proceedings, but has been retained for possible applicability in
criminal or probate proceedings.
I. General Consideration.
II. Specific Writings or Records.

I. GENERAL CONSIDERATION.

CROSS REFERENCES. --As to rules of supreme court relative to admissibility of
```

Source: Mead Data Central, Inc.; © 1977–1993 State of Alabama

Figure 11.10. Display of a Statute After Invoking "Browse" in LEXIS

FOCUS feature to confine your viewing to a selected subset of documents within the collection.[208] For example, suppose you had carried out a search for personal injury cases and retrieved cases reflecting various kinds of personal injuries. If you wanted to view just the cases mentioning spinal injuries, but still wanted to keep the original collection of cases intact for subsequent viewing, you could use the FOCUS command to isolate the subset of cases mentioning spinal injuries.

In effect, FOCUS allows you to perform a subsidiary search within a collection of retrieved documents so that you can quickly scan for occurrences of a particular word or words. These words can differ from the search terms you used to retrieve the original collection of documents.

FOCUS also works with a document retrieved by a LEXSEE or LEXSTAT command. Because LEXSEE and LEXSTAT retrieve a document through its citation rather than its text (see pages 238 and 240–245), you cannot know immediately whether a document retrieved through LEXSEE or LEXSTAT contains words that would suggest the document's relevance. By performing a FOCUS search in the document, you can determine quickly whether it contains such words and thereby speed up your assessment of the document's relevance.

Using FOCUS. You formulate a FOCUS request the same way you formulate an ordinary Boolean search request. Thus, you can use logic connectors, universal characters, field restrictions, and so on (as explained in Chapter 7).

You can transmit a FOCUS search request in one of two ways:

- You can type `focus` at the top of the monitor, followed by a space and the word or words you want the computer to scan for; then press TRANSMIT. So, returning to the earlier research scenario, you could transmit

```
focus spine or spinal
```

- You can just type `focus` and press TRANSMIT. The monitor will redisplay your original search request. You can then modify that request and transmit it as a FOCUS request, or you can type and transmit an entirely different request as your FOCUS request. Either way, the original request remains intact; any modifications operate only while you use the FOCUS feature.

If you want to use FOCUS to confine your viewing to a subset of documents that cite a certain authority, you can often use a LINK marker (explained on page 244) as an alternative to typing the desired citation in your

[208] Currently, you cannot use FOCUS when your search request retrieves 1,000 or more documents.

FOCUS request. While viewing an authority in your retrieved collection, you might see a citation whose other occurrences you want to locate in the retrieved collection. If the citation is preceded by a LINK marker, such as <=4>, you can use the LINK feature to simplify the typing of your FOCUS request:

1. At the top of the monitor, type `focus` followed by an equal sign and the number in the LINK marker appearing in front of the citation you want to use in your FOCUS search. For example, type `focus =4`.
2. Press TRANSMIT.

The computer will automatically formulate a FOCUS request based on the citation associated with the LINK marker you selected.[209]

Viewing documents through FOCUS. After you transmit a FOCUS request, the monitor will display a message (similar to the one in Figure 11.01 on page 319) identifying the number of documents in the original collection that satisfy your FOCUS request. Once you choose a display format (*e.g.*, KWIC, FULL), the monitor will display in that format the first document in your FOCUS collection. You can move within a document and between documents by using the techniques already explained for moving in a collection of documents retrieved by an ordinary search request.

When documents satisfying a FOCUS request are displayed, the words used in the FOCUS request—not the terms used in the original search request—will appear highlighted in the text. In addition, the word "FOCUS" will appear on the top line of the monitor as a reminder that you are viewing a document in the subsidiary collection of documents that satisfy the FOCUS request.

Leaving FOCUS. To leave the FOCUS feature and resume your previous research activity:

1. Type `exit`.
2. Press TRANSMIT.

At that point, the word "FOCUS" will disappear from the top of the monitor.

Printing search results in LEXIS

During an online search session, you might decide you want to print some or all of your search results (*e.g.*, one or more documents, or a list of citations),

[209] In doing so, the computer employs the LEXCITE feature explained on pages 461–66.

especially if the information is not readily available to you in a book or other offline source.

Although you have several options in terms of *what* to print in LEXIS, the computer hardware you are using and the LEXIS subscription agreement between you (or your employer) and Mead Data Central will determine *where* the results will print and *when* they will print (*i.e.*, before or after you end a search session by logging off). Printing can occur either centrally (at a Mead Data office, which mails the print-out to the subscriber) or locally (at your office). Local printing takes place either on an attached printer, which receives printing instructions through the terminal at which you are working, or on a stand-alone printer, which receives instructions through a separate telecommunications link with Mead Data. This discussion assumes you are printing locally.

For additional guidance about printing search results, consult the LEXIS reference manual,[210] the *LEXIS/NEXIS Technology Series Research Software User's Guide*,[211] the person who coordinates your LEXIS subscription, or a LEXIS customer service representative.

Keep in mind that the charges you incur as you print can mount rapidly. In general, you should avoid printing documents (especially lengthy ones) you can readily obtain offline. Printing a list of citations for documents retrieved by a search request, however, can be cost-effective: after ending your LEXIS search session, you can use the list to retrieve authorities from other sources, such as printed case reporters.

In printing search results in LEXIS, you can:

- *Print displayed screens.* If you are looking at a document or citation list and want to print just what appears on the screen you are viewing, press the key labelled PRINT SCREEN or, on older keyboards, PRINT. Printing will begin immediately if you are using an attached printer; printing will occur after you log off LEXIS if you are using a stand-alone printer. If you want to print more than one screen, you can repeat the procedure for each screen.

  If you are using a computer with a disk for storing information, you can use a LEXIS feature called "session recording" to print each screen automatically as it displays. You invoke session recording by holding down the ALT key and pressing the F2 function key. The computer will then prompt you to assign a name to the

[210] MEAD DATA CENTRAL, REFERENCE MANUAL FOR THE LEXIS/NEXIS SERVICES 133–41 (undated looseleaf ed.); MEAD DATA CENTRAL, LEXIS-NEXIS USER'S GUIDE 14–1 to 14–13 (1990 & 1991 Supp.).

[211] See Chapter 3 in MEAD DATA CENTRAL, LEXIS/NEXIS TECHNOLOGY SERIES RESEARCH SOFTWARE USER'S GUIDE (1993) (version 2.7 for MS-DOS).

recording session; at that point, type either LPT1 or LPT2 to designate the printer port through which your printer is connected to your computer, then press TRANSMIT. From then on, until you end the recording session, each screen will print as soon as the monitor displays it. To turn off session recording, hold down the ALT key and press the F2 function key again.

- *Print the displayed document.* If you want to print the document you are viewing, press the key labelled PRINT DOC. The monitor will display a message like the one shown in Figure 11.11, asking where you want the printing to occur. After you transmit your selection, you will see a message like the one in Figure 11.12, advising you that LEXIS will print your document in the FULL format unless you select a different format (*i.e.*, KWIC, VAR KWIC, CITE, or SEGMTS). To select a format other than FULL, press the key for that format. Once you have selected the format you want, type y to confirm that you want to print the document; then press TRANSMIT. If you want to print another displayed document, you can repeat the procedure for that document.

  If you are viewing a citation list when you press the PRINT DOC key, the computer will select for printing the document whose citation appeared at the top of the monitor when you pressed the key. Messages like those in Figures 11.11 and 11.12 will appear, and you then follow the procedure explained in the previous paragraph.

  When you use the PRINT DOC procedure, printing will begin after you log off LEXIS. During a single search session, if you have used the procedure to instruct the computer on more than one occasion to print a displayed document, all the documents you have chosen will print together after you log off.

- *Print selected documents at a given search level.* As discussed on page 168, you create a new search level each time you modify a search request in LEXIS. If you want to print selected documents retrieved at your current search level, press the key labelled PRINT ALL or, on older keyboards, MAIL IT. Then press the key for the format in which you want the documents printed (*i.e.*, KWIC, VAR KWIC, CITE, FULL, or SEGMTS); pressing CITE, for example, will produce a list of citations for the documents. The monitor will display a message asking where you want the printing to occur. After you transmit your choice, another message will appear, offering you the opportunity to print selected documents; Figure 11.13 shows the monitor's appearance. At this screen, transmit sel. The monitor will then display a screen like the one shown in Figure

```
          Choosing a Document Delivery Option

      Enter the number of a delivery option:

          1.   Printed on the printer attached to this terminal or
               computer, after you sign off.
                                OR
               Copied to a disk, after you sign off (if this option
               is available to you).

          2.   Printed on the stand-alone printer assigned to
               your personal identification number.

      Press TRANSMIT to accept selection.
-------------------------------------------------------------------------------
To cancel your document delivery request, press N and then the TRANSMIT key.
For further explanation, press the H key (for HELP) and then the TRANSMIT key.
```

Source: Mead Data Central, Inc. © 1993

Figure 11.11. Printing a Displayed Document in LEXIS

```
          Confirming Your Document Delivery Order

            Document:   1ST
        Print Format:   FULL
Number of Printed Pages:   9
        NOTE:  You may change the print format by pressing the
               desired format key.


        TRANSMIT:     Y   To confirm your order.

                      N   To cancel your order.



 -->  Your destination is the attached printer or disk.
-------------------------------------------------------------------------------
For further explanation, press the H key (for HELP) and then the TRANSMIT key.
```

Source: Mead Data Central, Inc. © 1993

Figure 11.12. Screen for Confirming a Request to Print a Displayed Document in LEXIS

```
            Confirming Your Document Delivery Order

Number of CASES:     37
Print format:     KWIC

         TRANSMIT:   Y     To confirm your order.

                   MANY    To confirm this order and request that more than one
                           CASE may be printed on a page.

                     N     To cancel your order.

                   SEL     To print selected documents.

 -->  Your destination is the attached printer or disk.
----------------------------------------------------------------------------
For further explanation, press the H key (for HELP) and then the TRANSMIT key.
```

Source: Mead Data Central, Inc. © 1993

Figure 11.13. Screen for Confirming a Request to Print All or Selected Documents in LEXIS

```
            Selecting Documents for Delivery

 Number of CASES:  37
 Print Format:  KWIC

 To select documents for delivery, Transmit:

     -   A single document number (example: 3)

     -   Multiple document numbers separated by commas (example: 1,3,5)

     -   A range of document numbers separated by a hyphen (example: 1-5)

     -   A combination of the above, separated by commas (example: 1,3-5,7)

----------------------------------------------------------------------------
For further explanation, press the H key (for HELP) and then the TRANSMIT key.
```

Source: Mead Data Central, Inc. © 1993

Figure 11.14. Screen for Specifying Which Documents to Print in LEXIS

11.14. Follow the on-screen instructions for specifying the documents you want to print.

For example, to print the first, third, and fifth documents in your collection of retrieved documents, you would type 1,3,5 and press TRANSMIT. If you wanted to print documents 1 through 5, you would transmit 1-5. The order in which you specify the documents will be the order in which they will print.

After you specify the documents to print, the monitor will display a message asking you to confirm or cancel your printing order. Transmit y to confirm, or n to cancel.

If your search results are grouped by cases and *A.L.R.* annotations (as shown in Figure 11.01 on page 319), the PRINT ALL or MAIL IT procedure will cause documents in Group 1 (cases) to print. To select a different group of documents for printing, type group followed by the group number, and press TRANSMIT. Then, to print selected documents from the new group, press PRINT ALL or MAIL IT, and proceed as explained in the previous paragraphs.

If you have searched on more than one level, you can use PRINT ALL or MAIL IT to print selected documents from a search level other than the current one. First, switch to the other level by typing the number for that level, then pressing the key labelled DIF LEVEL or DISP DIF LEVEL (for "display different level"). The monitor will display a screen indicating the number of documents retrieved at the search level you selected. At that point, you can press PRINT ALL or MAIL IT, and proceed as explained above.

When you print with PRINT ALL or MAIL IT, printing will begin within a minute or so if you are using a stand-alone printer; printing will occur after you log off LEXIS if you are using an attached printer.

- *Print all documents at a given search level.* If you want to print all the documents retrieved at your current search level, press the key labelled PRINT ALL or, on older keyboards, MAIL IT. Then press the key for the format in which you want the documents printed (*i.e.*, KWIC, VAR KWIC, CITE, FULL, or SEGMTS); pressing CITE, for example, will produce a list of citations for the documents. The monitor will display a message asking where you want the printing to occur. After you transmit your choice, another message will appear, like that in Figure 11.13, offering you the opportunity to confirm or cancel your printing order; transmit y to confirm, or n to cancel.

If your search results are grouped by cases and *A.L.R.* annotations (as shown in Figure 11.01 on page 319), the PRINT ALL or

MAIL IT procedure will cause documents in Group 1 (cases) to print. To select a different group of documents for printing, type `group` followed by the group number, and press TRANSMIT. Then, to print all documents from the new group, press PRINT ALL or MAIL IT, and proceed as explained in the previous paragraph.

If you have searched on more than one level, you can use PRINT ALL or MAIL IT to print all documents from a search level other than the current one. First, switch to the other level by typing the number for that level, then pressing the key labelled DIF LEVEL or DISP DIF LEVEL (for "display different level"). The monitor will display a screen indicating the number of documents retrieved at the search level you selected. At that point, you can press PRINT ALL or MAIL IT, and proceed as explained above.

When you print with PRINT ALL or MAIL IT, printing will begin within a minute or so if you are using a stand-alone printer; printing will occur after you log off LEXIS if you are using an attached printer.

Downloading search results in LEXIS

If you search in LEXIS with a computer that has a disk for storing information, you can save ("download") to your computer's disk some or all of the results of your search. Downloading is analogous to printing, except that instead of storing the results on paper, you store them on your computer's disk, incurring a downloading charge as you do so. After downloading, you can log off LEXIS (so you stop incurring charges) and then read your results, either on your computer monitor or on a print-out you generate from the downloaded file.

In downloading search results in LEXIS, you can:

- *Download displayed screens.* To download the screen you are viewing, as well as individual subsequent screens as you display them, use the LEXIS "session recording" feature. To invoke session recording, hold down the ALT key and press the F2 function key. Each screen will download as soon as the monitor displays it. To turn off session recording, hold down the ALT key and press the F2 function key again. For more details about session recording, see the LEXIS reference manual[212] and the *LEXIS/NEXIS Technology Series Research Software User's Guide.*[213]

[212] MEAD DATA CENTRAL, REFERENCE MANUAL FOR THE LEXIS/NEXIS SERVICES 143–49 (undated looseleaf ed.).

[213] MEAD DATA CENTRAL, LEXIS/NEXIS TECHNOLOGY SERIES RESEARCH SOFTWARE USER'S GUIDE 3–1, 3–3 (1993) (version 2.7 for MS-DOS).

- *Download the displayed document.* To download the document you are viewing, use the same procedure you would use to print that document (as discussed in the previous section), except that when you log off LEXIS, select the option for downloading your research results. Downloading will occur after you log off.
- *Download selected documents at a given search level.* Use the same procedure you would use to print selected documents (as discussed in the previous section), except that when you log off LEXIS, select the option for downloading your research results. Downloading will occur after you log off.
- *Download all documents at a given search level.* Use the same procedure you would use to print all documents (as discussed in the previous section), except that when you log off LEXIS, select the option for downloading your research results. Downloading will occur after you log off.

For additional guidance about downloading in LEXIS, you can consult the LEXIS reference manual,[214] the *LEXIS/NEXIS Technology Series Research Software User's Guide*,[215] the person who coordinates your LEXIS subscription, a LEXIS customer service representative, or the user manuals for your computer's hardware and software.

Reading the Law in WESTLAW

Viewing documents in WESTLAW

Status line. Once the computer has assembled the collection of documents that satisfies a search request in WESTLAW, the monitor will display the first screen of the first document in the collection. At the top of the monitor, you will see a "status line," which provides information about the displayed document and the collection of which it is a part. Figure 11.15 shows a screen typical of what you see after completing a WESTLAW search.

The status line, which appears at the top of each screen of a document, displays the following information:[216]

- *Citation*—the citation of the document.

[214] MEAD DATA CENTRAL, REFERENCE MANUAL FOR THE LEXIS/NEXIS SERVICES 143–49 (undated looseleaf ed.).

[215] MEAD DATA CENTRAL, LEXIS/NEXIS TECHNOLOGY SERIES RESEARCH SOFTWARE USER'S GUIDE 3-1 to 3-6 (1993) (version 2.7 for MS-DOS).

[216] If you want to learn more about the status line, consult WEST PUBLISHING COMPANY, WESTLAW REFERENCE MANUAL 118–19 (5th ed. 1993).

status line

```
                         COPR. (C) WEST 1993 NO CLAIM TO ORIG. U.S. GOVT. WORKS
Citation               Rank(R)           Page(P)          Database        Mode
107 S.Ct. 2148         R 1 OF 17         P 1 OF 48        ALLFEDS         Term
95 L.Ed.2d 772, 55 USLW 4688
(Cite as: 481 U.S. 828,  107 S.Ct. 2148)
                             UNITED STATES, Petitioner
                                         v.
                  Jose MENDOZA-LOPEZ and Angel Landeros-Quinones.
                                    No. 85-2067.
                                Argued March 3, 1987.
                                Decided May 26, 1987.
 Government appealed from order of the United States District Court for the
District of Nebraska which dismissed indictments charging aliens with reentry
after deportation.  The Court of Appeals for the Eighth Circuit, > 781 F.2d
111, affirmed and certiorari was granted.  The Supreme Court, Justice Marshall,
held that:  (1) statute did not require that deportation have been lawful;  (2)
Congress did not intend to permit challenge to validity of prior deportation in
a prosecution for reentry after deportation;  but (3) statute permitting
imposition of criminal penalty for reentry after any deportation regardless of
how violative of the rights of the alien the deportation proceeding may have
been did not comport with due process.
 Affirmed.
 Chief Justice Rehnquist dissented and filed an opinion in which Justice White
and Justice O'Connor joined.
```

Source: West Publishing Company © 1993

Figure 11.15. Illustrative First Screen of Search Results in WESTLAW

- *Rank*—the displayed document's position (or "rank") within the collection retrieved by the search request, and the number of documents in the collection. For example, the document displayed in Figure 11.15 is the first document in a collection of 17 documents ("R 1 of 17").

  If you did not retrieve a displayed document through a search request using terms and connectors or natural language, the rank column in the status line will reflect the feature you used to retrieve the document. For example, instead of a rank number, you will see the phrase "Found Document" in the status line of a document retrieved through FIND.
- *Page*—the number of WESTLAW screens in the displayed document, and the number of the screen you are viewing. For example, Figure 11.15 shows the first screen of a 48-screen document ("P 1 of 48").
- *Database*—the identifier of the database in which you conducted the search that retrieved the displayed document. If you retrieved the document through a method other than a terms-and-connectors or natural-language search request (for instance, through the FIND feature), the database column in the status line will indicate the database that contains the displayed document.

- *Mode*—the technique being used to move from screen to screen in the retrieved documents. The four techniques are TERM mode, PAGE mode, LOCATE mode ("T LOCATE" for "TERM LOCATE," or "P LOCATE" for "PAGE LOCATE"), and BEST mode. The TERM, PAGE, and BEST modes are explained at pages 358–59; the LOCATE mode is explained at pages 367–71.

Display formats in WESTLAW. To view documents retrieved in WESTLAW, you can choose among three display formats:

- *Full text.* In this format, the monitor displays the full text of the document you are viewing. Unless you indicate a different preference through the Options Directory (see pages 197–99), the WESTLAW computer initially displays search results in full-text format; once the first document appears on the monitor, you can select a different format if you wish.

  In full-text format, you see the status line at the top of the monitor; on the first screen of a document, you also see additional identifying information about the displayed document (*e.g.*, case caption, date of decision). When you page through the document (as explained on pages 360–63), you will see your search terms highlighted on the monitor.

  Figure 11.15 depicts the first screen of a typical full-text display of a case.

- *Full text in selected fields.* You might want to view the full text of just selected fields of a document. For instance, you might want to see only the headnotes in the cases retrieved by your search request.

  To limit the display to selected fields, type `f` and press ENTER. You will see a list of the fields available for display. Figure 11.16 illustrates a typical list of fields for cases. Type the name of each field you want to view (placing a comma between field names), and press ENTER. The monitor will then display your document, showing the status line and the text contained in only the field or fields you selected. Figure 11.17 shows the first screen of a case for which just the opinion field was selected for viewing.

  If you change your mind about the field or fields you want to view, type `f` and press ENTER again. The monitor will redisplay a screen like that in Figure 11.16. Type the name of each field you now want to view (placing a comma between field names), then press ENTER.

  When selecting the field display format, if you know the name of each field you want to view, you can bypass the screen listing the fields available for viewing. To use this shortcut, type `f` fol-

```
                         COPR. (C) WEST 1993 NO CLAIM TO ORIG. U.S. GOVT. WORKS
                                  FIELDS

     TI  TITLE          CO  COURT         TO  TOPIC        DI  DIGEST
     CI  CITATION       JU  JUDGE         HE  HEADNOTE     IM  IMAGE
     SY  SYNOPSIS       AT  ATTORNEY      OP  OPINION

If you wish to:
   Display a single field, type its abbreviation and press ENTER
   Display multiple fields, type their abbreviations separated by commas
     and press ENTER
   Cancel the display of requested fields, type XF and press ENTER
   Continue, press ENTER
```

Source: West Publishing Company © 1993

Figure 11.16. Sample List of Fields You Can Display in WESTLAW

```
                         COPR. (C) WEST 1993 NO CLAIM TO ORIG. U.S. GOVT. WORKS
Citation               Rank(R)            Page(P)          Database        Mode
107 S.Ct. 2148         R 1 OF 17          P 1 OF 35        ALLFEDS         Term
 95 L.Ed.2d 772, 55 USLW 4688
(Cite as: 481 U.S. 828,  107 S.Ct. 2148)
                                     No. 85-2067.
                                 Argued March 3, 1987.
                                 Decided May 26, 1987.
  **2150 Christopher J. Wright, for petitioner.
  Kathy Goudy, Lincoln, Neb., for respondents.
  In this case, we must determine whether an alien who is prosecuted under > 8
 U.S.C. § 1326 for illegal entry following deportation may assert in that
 criminal proceeding the invalidity of the underlying deportation order.
                                    **2151 I
  Respondents, Jose Mendoza-Lopez and Angel Landeros-Quinones, were arrested at
 separate locations in Lincoln, Nebraska, on October 23, 1984, by agents of the
 Immigration and Naturalization Service.  On October 30, 1984, they were
 transported to Denver, Colorado, where a group deportation hearing was held for
 respondents along with 11 other persons, all of whom were, like respondents,
 Mexican nationals. [FN1]  After the hearing, respondents were ordered deported
 and were bused to El Paso, Texas.  They were deported from El Paso on November
 1, 1984.  Each received, at the time of his deportation, a copy of Form I-294,
 which advised, in both Spanish and English, that a return to the United States
 without permission following deportation would constitute a felony.
```

Source: West Publishing Company © 1993

Figure 11.17. Display of a Selected Field ("Opinion" Field) in WESTLAW

lowed by a space and the name of each field you want to view (placing a comma between field names). Then press ENTER.

With a field display, your search terms do not have to appear in a particular field for you to view the contents of that field through the field display format. Thus, the field display format differs from a search request restricted to a particular field (see Chapter 5). A field *search* restriction requires the restricted search terms to appear in the designated field in order to retrieve the document; the field *display* restriction, however, simply shows the text of selected fields, regardless of whether those fields contain any search terms.

Note, though, that in a given document, a field you select for viewing might be empty (that is, not contain any text). For instance, in an unpublished case available in WESTLAW, the headnote field would be empty.[217] If you had selected just this field for viewing, only the status line for the case would show on the monitor; no text from the case would appear.

To cancel the field display format and return the document you are viewing to the full-text display format, type `xf` (for "exit field display"); then press ENTER.

- *Citation list.* Instead of viewing documents retrieved by your search request, you can opt to see just a list of their citations. The information contained in a citation will vary depending on the type of document (*e.g.*, case, law review article, statute), but the information will always allow you to locate the cited document. Figure 11.18 shows a typical list of citations for a collection of cases.

  To view a citation list, type the letter `l` and press ENTER. The monitor will display the citation list, beginning with the citation of the first document in your collection. The list might extend across several screens.

  Two variations on the `l` command—`lr`, and `lr` followed by a document number—are discussed at page 365. Unlike the `l` command, these variations allow you to begin displaying the citation list with a specified citation.

  You can use a citation list to select a document for viewing. Type the document's identification number (referred to as its "rank number"), which appears in front of the document's citation on the list. Then press ENTER. For example, if you wanted to view *Robards v. Rees* (document 5 in Figure 11.18), you would type `5` and press ENTER.

[217] *See* page 85 n.80.

```
                       COPR. (C) WEST 1993 NO CLAIM TO ORIG. U.S. GOVT. WORKS
CITATIONS LIST (Page 1)             Search Result Documents: 17
Database: ALLFEDS

  1.  U.S. v. Mendoza-Lopez, 481 U.S. 828, 107 S.Ct. 2148, 95 L.Ed.2d 772,
      55 USLW 4688 (U.S.Neb., May 26, 1987) (NO. 85-2067)

  2.  Baldasar v. Illinois, 446 U.S. 222, 100 S.Ct. 1585, 64 L.Ed.2d 169
      (U.S.Ill., Apr 22, 1980) (NO. 77-6219)

  3.  Greene v. U.S., 880 F.2d 1299 (11th Cir.(Ga.), Aug 21, 1989) (NO. 88-8475)

  4.  U.S. v. Bagley, 837 F.2d 371 (9th Cir.(Wash.), Jan 13, 1988) (NO. 87-3922)

  5.  Robards v. Rees, 789 F.2d 379 (6th Cir.(Ky.), Apr 25, 1986) (NO. 85-5529)

  6.  U.S. v. Mendoza-Lopez, 781 F.2d 111 (8th Cir.(Neb.), Dec 31, 1985)
      (NO. 85-1436, 85-1437)

  7.  U.S. v. Garcia, 771 F.2d 1369 (9th Cir.(Cal.), Sep 23, 1985) (NO. 84-1275)

  8.  Santillanes v. U.S. Parole Com'n, 754 F.2d 887
      (10th Cir.(N.M.), Feb 11, 1985) (NO. 83-1838)
```

Source: West Publishing Company © 1993

Figure 11.18. Sample Citation List in WESTLAW

If you prefer, you can instruct the computer to initially display as a citation list (rather than in full text) the results of each search you perform during your current and subsequent online search sessions. To indicate this preference, transmit `options` (or `opt`) to invoke the Options Directory and then follow the on-screen instructions.

Changing display formats in WESTLAW. Search results in WESTLAW initially display in whichever format—full text or citation list—the Options Directory indicates. Currently, unless you change the setting in the Options Directory, the computer will initially display the first retrieved document in the full-text format, and will continue to display documents in the full-text format until you select the fields display format. Once you choose the fields display format, documents will display in that format until you switch back to full-text display. At any time, you can switch between these display formats by transmitting the appropriate command for the desired format, at which point you will see the document you were viewing redisplayed in the new format. So, if you have been viewing documents in full-text display, you can transmit the `f` command to switch to fields display. Conversely, if you have been viewing selected fields in documents, you can transmit `xf` to cancel field display and return to full-text display.

If you transmit the l command to see a citation list for your retrieved documents and then select a document for viewing, the document will appear in whichever display format (full-text or fields) you were using before viewing the citation list. For example, if you were viewing documents in full-text display when you transmitted the letter l to see a list of their citations, the next document you select for viewing would display in the full-text format.

Display order for retrieved documents in WESTLAW. The order in which documents display differs depending on whether you search with a Boolean (terms-and-connectors) request or a natural-language request. Knowing the display order (referred to as "ranking" in WESTLAW) can help you browse more efficiently through your search results.

Display order in Boolean searching. With Boolean searching, regardless of the display format you select (*i.e.*, full text, full text in selected fields, or citation list), WESTLAW offers four ways of ordering retrieved documents for display. In any given database, up to three of the following four choices for display order will be available:

- AGE—Documents display in reverse chronological order (that is, with the most recently issued document displayed first).
- TERMS—The document with the greatest number of different search terms displays first (the idea being that the greater the number of different search terms in a document, the greater that document's probable relevance to the researcher). Then the document with the next greatest number of different search terms displays, and so on.[218]
- COURT—The computer divides the display of cases into two categories: all state cases and all federal cases. State cases display in reverse chronological order. Federal cases are further divided according to court level (district court, court of appeals, and so on), with cases at each level displaying in reverse chronological order.
- PUBLICATION—Documents display in the order in which they were published. For example, 18 U.S.C. § 2331 would display before 18 U.S.C. § 2385, and both of these sections would precede 42 U.S.C. § 1985.

The display order you can select depends on the type of authority contained in the database you are searching:

[218] The ranking formula the computer uses to display documents in TERMS order closely tracks the algorithm the computer uses in natural-language searching to display documents in the order of their statistical relevance. So, if you perform a Boolean search and a comparable natural-language search in the same database, you will usually see much overlap in your search results if you display your Boolean search results in TERMS order.

- *Cases.* AGE and TERMS are display-order options available for documents retrieved from any case-law database; in some case-law databases, COURT is also a display-order option. In most case-law databases, cases will automatically display in reverse chronological order (AGE), unless you specifically change the display order. In other case-law databases, cases will automatically display in COURT order, unless you switch to AGE or TERMS order.
- *Statutes.* PUBLICATION and TERMS are the display-order options for documents retrieved from databases of statutes. Statutory sections will automatically display in the order in which those sections appear in a jurisdiction's printed statutory code (PUBLICATION), unless you specifically change the display order to TERMS.

  With the PUBLICATION display order, when your search request retrieves statutes from more than one jurisdiction (as can happen, for example, in the STAT-ALL database), the statutes will first be grouped alphabetically by jurisdiction. For instance, Alabama statutes will appear before Kentucky statutes. Within each jurisdiction, statutory sections will display in PUBLICATION order.
- *Administrative regulations.* PUBLICATION and TERMS are the display-order options for documents retrieved from databases of administrative regulations. The display order follows the pattern for displaying statutes.
- *Law review materials.* AGE and TERMS are the display-order options for documents retrieved from databases of law review materials. These materials will automatically display in reverse chronological order (AGE), unless you specifically change the display order to TERMS.
- *Other materials.* With a few exceptions,[219] other kinds of documents retrieved by Boolean search requests will display in reverse chronological order (AGE), with TERMS as the alternative display-order option.

If you are uncertain about the display-order options available in the database you are searching, type `options` (or `opt`) and press ENTER. When the Options Directory appears on the monitor, follow the on-screen instructions for changing the rank order of your search results. The next screen you see will display a message stating the current display order and indicating the display-order options available for the database. At that point, if you want to

[219] *See* WEST PUBLISHING COMPANY, WESTLAW REFERENCE MANUAL 12 (5th ed. 1993) (listing databases for which PUBLICATION is the standard option for display order).

change the display order of your documents, you can do so, following the on-screen instructions. (The change will take effect with the next search you run and will remain in effect until you change the display order again.) If you do not want to change the display order, you can resume your research simply by pressing ENTER.

Display order in natural-language searching. When you search WESTLAW with a natural-language request, the computer always displays retrieved documents in order of their statistical relevance. The computer determines the statistical relevance of a document by applying formulas that take into account such factors as the frequency with which your search terms appear in the database and in each document the computer has identified for retrieval. This method of ranking corresponds to the ranking method the computer uses when you choose the TERMS display order in Boolean searching.

Document display limitation in WESTLAW. The number of documents you can view with a WESTLAW search request differs depending on whether you search with a Boolean (terms-and-connectors) request or with a natural-language request.

Document display limitation in Boolean searching. If your Boolean search request in WESTLAW retrieves more than 10,000 documents, the computer will not allow you to view more than the first 10,000 documents in the collection. Generally, if you retrieve that many documents, you will want to modify your search request to reduce the number to a more manageable quantity.[220] But if you want to see more than the 10,000 documents WESTLAW allows (because, say, you're engaged in statistical research), you can circumvent the display limitation by carrying out a series of more limited searches that, taken together, will retrieve all the documents in your original collection.

For instance, suppose you had run a search request that retrieved more than 10,000 documents from the CTA database (which contains cases from each of the federal circuit courts of appeals). You could carry out sequential searches in the databases for each of the courts of appeals (*i.e.*, in CTA1, then in CTA2, and so on). Or, you could use a date restriction. For example, in the ALLSTATES database (which contains cases decided from 1945 to the present from all 50 states and the District of Columbia), you could carry out a series of searches with a date restriction like `date(aft 1969 and bef 1980)` to retrieve just a decade's worth at a time of the cases that constituted the original collection.

Document display limitation in natural-language searching. The WESTLAW computer limits the number of documents you can view in response to a natural-language search request. Currently, WESTLAW automatically sets

[220] Chapter 8 explains how to modify search requests.

the limitation at 20 documents, but you can use the Options Directory (see pages 197–99) to change that limitation to any other number from 1 to 100.

The 100-document ceiling highlights an important characteristic of natural-language searching: West Publishing does not intend this search method to operate as a vehicle for comprehensive searching, but as a way to identify the most relevant documents in a larger pool of potentially relevant documents. If you need to ensure comprehensiveness in your online search results, Boolean terms-and-connectors searching will normally achieve your goal more effectively.

Star paging in WESTLAW. "Star pagination" numbers display on the monitor if they are available for the document you are viewing. A star-page number serves as a reference point in the text, allowing you quickly to find in a document a specified location to which someone has referred you, or, likewise, allowing you to refer someone else to a specified location. Star-page numbers appear embedded in the text as highlighted asterisked numbers. For example, Figure 11.19 shows star-page numbers *834 and **2153.

For the online versions of cases published in West Publishing's case reporters, WESTLAW provides star-page numbers corresponding to page numbers in those case reporters. In addition, WESTLAW supplies star-page numbers for many official state reporters not published by West Publishing. For cases to which WESTLAW Cites have been assigned, WESTLAW also makes

```
                         COPR. (C) WEST 1993 NO CLAIM TO ORIG. U.S. GOVT. WORKS
107 S.Ct. 2148          R 1 OF 17         P 20 OF 48         ALLFEDS        Page
(Cite as: 481 U.S. 828, *833,  107 S.Ct. 2148, **2152)
     barred in prosecutions under § 1326);  see also > United States v. Rosal-
     Aguilar, 652 F.2d 721, 723 (CA7 1981) (trial de novo on the factual basis
     of the underlying deportation is not a constitutional prerequisite to
     conviction under § 1326, but "the Government must prove the underlying
     deportation to have been based on a valid legal predicate and obtained
     according to law");  > Petrella v. United States, 464 U.S. 921, 922, 104
     S.Ct. 289, 78 L.Ed.2d 265 (1983) (WHITE, J., dissenting from denial of
     certiorari) (internal quotation omitted).

                                    II
  In > United States v. Spector, 343 U.S. 169, 72 S.Ct. 591, 96 L.Ed. 863
 (1952), we left open whether the validity of an underlying order of deportation
 may be challenged in a criminal prosecution in which that prior deportation is
 an element of the crime. [FN7]  Today, we *834 squarely confront
 **2153 this question in the context of § 1326, which imposes a criminal
 penalty on any alien who has been deported and subsequently enters, attempts to
 enter, or is found in, the United States.  The issue before us is whether a
 federal court must always accept as conclusive the fact of the deportation
 order, even if the deportation proceeding was not conducted in conformity with
 due process. [FN8]
```

Source: West Publishing Company © 1993

Figure 11.19. Examples of Star-Page Numbers in WESTLAW

available star-page numbers tied to those citations.[221] Finally, for U.S. Supreme Court cases, WESTLAW provides up to three sets of star-page numbers: one set corresponding to the page numbers of the case as it appears printed in the official *U.S. Reports*; one corresponding to the page numbers of the case as it appears printed in West's unofficial *Supreme Court Reporter*; and one corresponding to the WESTLAW version of the case, using WESTLAW page numbers.

Which star-page numbers will display for a case depends on the case's publication status:

- If a case has not yet been published in a West case reporter, but has been assigned a WESTLAW Cite, you will just see star-page numbers tied to the WESTLAW Cite.
- If a case has been published in a West case reporter (in either an advance sheet or a permanent, hardbound volume), one set of star-page numbers, corresponding to the page numbers in that reporter, will display. In U.S. Supreme Court cases, two sets of star-page numbers might display—one set corresponding to page numbers in West's *Supreme Court Reporter*, and the other set corresponding to page numbers in the official *U.S. Reports* (when the official pagination becomes available).

When more than one set of star-page numbers displays in a case, each set will be distinguished by a different number of asterisks. For instance, in a case with star paging tied to both *U.S. Reports* and *Supreme Court Reporter*, the sets of star pages would appear in the following form:

`*834` for *U.S. Reports* pagination
`**2153` for *Supreme Court Reporter* pagination

If only one set of star-page numbers displays in a case, that set will be identified by a single asterisk. For instance, using the preceding illustration, if only the *Supreme Court Reporter* pagination displayed, the star-page numbers would appear in this form:

`*2153` for *Supreme Court Reporter* pagination

If you are viewing a case that has multiple star-page sets and only want to see one set of page numbers, you can remove the other page numbers from the monitor. To do so:

1. Type `star` (or `st`) followed by the identification for the star paging you want displayed.

[221] WESTLAW Cites were discussed in Figure 10.08 at pages 281–82.

2. Press ENTER.

For instance,

`st us`	will display only *U.S. Reports* star pages
`st sct`	will display only *Supreme Court Reporter* star pages
`st wl`	will display only WESTLAW star pages
`st f2d`	will display only *Federal Reporter 2d* star pages
`st fsupp`	will display only *Federal Supplement* star pages

You can switch from one star-page display to another whenever you want. If you are unsure about how to identify a publication, use the abbreviation that would work with the FIND feature (explained on pages 279–84). To return to the star-page display as it existed before you customized it:

1. Type `star` (or `st`).
2. Press ENTER.

If you want to remove *all* star-page numbers from the monitor:

1. Type `xstar` or `xst` (for "exit star paging").
2. Press ENTER.

The monitor will redisplay your case without showing star-page numbers.[222] If you change your mind and want to see star-page numbers again, type `star` (or `st`) and press ENTER.

Viewing images in cases in WESTLAW. In West's printed reporters, cases might contain drawings, charts, or other images. In WESTLAW, the online version of some of these cases will include those illustrations in the "image" field. Currently, the image will not display on the screen, but the computer will display a message indicating the presence of an image. To see an image, you must print it on a specified kind of laser printer or on a fax machine. Pages 371 to 379 explain how to print documents in WESTLAW.

Moving within a document in WESTLAW

TERM, PAGE, or BEST mode. Movement within a document in WESTLAW depends initially on whether you are viewing the document in TERM

[222] You can also use the Options Directory (explained on pages 197–99) to suppress the display of star-page numbers during your search session.

mode (indicated by "Term" in the status line), in PAGE mode (indicated by "Page" in the status line), or in BEST mode (indicated by "Best" in the status line).[223] In TERM mode, you move only to screens that contain your search terms. In PAGE mode, you move through each screen in a document, regardless of whether the screen contains a search term. In BEST mode, available just for documents retrieved with a natural-language search, you move only to screens in the statistically "best" portion of a document.[224]

Moving through a document in TERM mode allows you to determine quickly whether you are retrieving documents that use your search terms in the sense you intended and whether the search terms you selected are retrieving relevant documents. By using TERM mode, you can scan a document (especially a long one) for possible relevance in less time than it would take to scan the full text of the document page by page online. Thus, using TERM mode can alert you to the need to modify your search request before you spend a lot of time reading the full text of irrelevant documents.

When you retrieve a document by using a Boolean or natural-language search request, the document will first display in TERM mode. While viewing a document, you can switch to PAGE mode at any time:

1. Type `p`.
2. Press ENTER.

Likewise, you can switch back to TERM mode at any time:

1. Type `t`.
2. Press ENTER.

While viewing a document you retrieved with a natural-language search request, you also have the option of switching to BEST mode at any time:

1. Type `best` or `b`.
2. Press ENTER.

If you retrieve a document through FIND (a feature explained on pages 279–84), the document will display in PAGE mode.

[223] For an illustration of a status line, see Figure 11.15 on page 348.

[224] For a document retrieved through a natural-language search, West uses a mathematical formula to define "portions" of the document. Because math defines a portion, portions will not necessarily correspond to a document's syntactical or other divisions, such as paragraphs, pages, or screens. Rather, the size of a portion depends on the number of words between occurrences of your search terms in the document. These mathematical calculations can result in a document having numerous portions of varying sizes. After the computer identifies the portions in a document, other statistical probability algorithms determine which one of these portions (*i.e.*, the "best" portion) qualifies as the one most likely to contain information relevant to a search request.

Choices for moving within a document in WESTLAW. Once the monitor has displayed a document or a citation list, you have several choices for moving around within the document or list. You can:

- *Move forward one screen.* Press ENTER. In TERM mode, the screen you see next will depend on whether you retrieved the document with a Boolean or natural-language request. If you searched with a Boolean request, the monitor will display the next screen that contains your search terms. If you searched with a natural-language request, pressing ENTER in TERM mode will display the next screen in the document's portions (up to five portions) that the computer determines are statistically most likely to contain information relevant to your search request.[225]

  In PAGE mode, when you press ENTER (or the PAGE DOWN or PgDn key), the monitor will display the next screen in the document, regardless of whether the screen contains a search term. PAGE mode works the same whether you obtain your search results through Boolean or natural-language searching.

  In BEST mode, when you press ENTER, the monitor will display the next screen in the single "best" portion of a document retrieved with a natural-language search request.
- *Move back one screen.* In TERM mode, type `t-` and press ENTER. The screen you see next will depend on whether you retrieved the document with a Boolean or natural-language request. If you searched with a Boolean request, the monitor will display the previous screen that contained your search terms. If you searched with a natural-language request, transmitting `t-` in TERM mode will display the previous screen in the document's portions (up to five portions) that the computer determines are statistically most likely to contain information relevant to your search request. (You can also transmit `t-` while you are in PAGE or BEST mode; the instruction will have the same effect, but it will first switch the display from PAGE or BEST mode to TERM mode.)

  In PAGE mode, type `p-` and press ENTER (or just press the PAGE UP or PgUp key) to display the previous screen in the document, regardless of whether the screen contains a search term. (You can

[225] After the computer determines the number of portions in a document (as explained in note 224), another formula calculates which five of these portions are statistically most likely to contain information relevant to a search request. Pressing ENTER in TERM mode allows you to move to occurrences of your search terms in these five portions. At this writing, if a document contains more than five portions, TERM mode will not allow you to see every occurrence of your search terms.

also transmit p− or press the PAGE UP or PgUp key while you are in TERM or BEST mode; the instruction will have the same effect, but it will first switch the display from TERM or BEST mode to PAGE mode.)

In BEST mode, type b− and press ENTER. The monitor will display the previous screen in the portion of the document that the computer determines is statistically most likely to contain information relevant to your search request. (You can also transmit b− while you are in TERM or PAGE mode; the instruction will have the same effect, but it will first switch the display from TERM or PAGE mode to BEST mode.)

- *Move forward more than one screen.* Type p+ followed by the number of screens you want to advance in the document; then press ENTER. Alternatively, type the number of screens you want to advance and then press the PAGE DOWN or PgDn key. For example, if you were viewing the third screen of a document and wanted to skip ahead 5 screens, you could type p+5 and press ENTER; the monitor would then display the eighth screen of the document. (If you are in TERM or BEST mode when you transmit this instruction, the instruction will also switch the display from TERM or BEST mode to PAGE mode.)

  At this time, WESTLAW does not offer a comparable instruction for advancing a specific number of screens in TERM or BEST mode—that is, an instruction like t+5 or b+2 will not work.

- *Move back more than one screen.* Type p− followed by the number of screens you want to move back in the document; then press ENTER. Alternatively, type the number of screens you want to move back and then press the PAGE UP or PgUp key. For example, if you were viewing the eighth screen of a document and wanted to skip back 5 screens, you could type p−5 and press ENTER; the monitor would then display the third screen of the document. (If you are in TERM or BEST mode when you transmit this instruction, the instruction will also switch the display from TERM or BEST mode to PAGE mode.)

  At this time, WESTLAW does not offer a comparable instruction for moving back a specific number of screens in TERM or BEST mode—that is, an instruction like t−5 or b−2 will not work.

- *Move forward half a screen.* Type h+ and press ENTER. The monitor will display the lower half of the screen you were viewing, followed by the upper half of the next screen in the document. For example, if you were viewing the third screen of a document when you transmitted h+, the monitor would display the bottom half of the third screen and the top half of the fourth screen. When you move forward half a screen, a plus sign will appear in the page column of the status line (*e.g.*, "P 3+ of 12"). (If you transmit h+ while you are in TERM or BEST mode, the instruction will also switch the display from TERM or BEST mode to PAGE mode.)

Half-screen paging does not work on a citation list.

- *Move back half a screen.* Type h− and press ENTER. The monitor will display the upper half of the screen you were viewing, preceded by the lower half of the previous screen in the document. For example, if you transmitted h− while viewing the sixth screen of a document, the monitor would display the bottom half of the fifth screen and the top half of the sixth screen. When you move back half a screen, a plus sign will appear in the page column of the status line (*e.g.*, "P 5+ of 17"). (If you transmit h− while you are in TERM or BEST mode, the instruction will also switch the display from TERM or BEST mode to PAGE mode.)

  Half-screen paging does not work on a citation list.
- *Move to a specific screen.* Type p followed by the number of the screen you want to view, then press ENTER. For example, to move to the tenth screen, type p10 and press ENTER. (If you are in TERM or BEST mode when you transmit this instruction, the instruction will also switch the display from TERM or BEST mode to PAGE mode.)

  When viewing a citation list, you can also use another method of moving to a specific screen in the list. This technique lets you move to a screen where a specified document's citation appears as the first one on the monitor. Type the letters lr (for "list rank") followed by the document's identification number (or "rank number"); then press ENTER. For instance, suppose you were viewing the screen with the first five citations on the list and you transmitted lr35 (for "list rank number 35"). You would move to a screen where the citation for the 35th document would be the first one displayed.
- *Move to a specific "star" page.* If you are viewing in full-text display format a document that contains star paging (explained on pages 356–58), you can move directly to a specific star page. Type star (or st) followed by the number of the star page you want to see; then press ENTER. For instance, if the case you were viewing covered pages 450 to 460 in a printed case reporter whose star-page numbers appear online, you could transmit st 458 to see page 458.

If a document has more than one set of star-page numbers, you can add the identification for the star-paging set that includes the page you want to view. For example, you could transmit `st us 458` if you wanted to see page 458 of the *U.S. Reports* version of a case.

If you are in TERM or BEST mode when you transmit an instruction to move to a specific star page, the instruction will also switch the display from TERM or BEST mode to PAGE mode.

- *Move from a case headnote to the text of the opinion, or from the opinion to a headnote.* Researchers familiar with West case reporters will know that in a case printed there, headnote numbers serve as an internal indexing system for locating the discussion of points of law within the case. For example, on page 137, the bracketed number "4" on the last page of the figure indicates where in the case the discussion of the issue summarized in the fourth headnote of that case occurs. These headnote numbers also appear online in cases in WESTLAW.

  If you are viewing a case headnote in WESTLAW, you can use the JUMP feature to move directly to the part of the opinion dealing with the issue summarized in that headnote. Conversely, you can use JUMP to move to a headnote if you are viewing the part of an opinion dealing with the issue summarized in that headnote. A JUMP marker (a ">" or "➤" symbol) next to a headnote number indicates the availability of the JUMP feature for moving to and from that headnote.

  So, suppose you were viewing the first headnote in WESTLAW's version of *Lewis v. United States* (shown on page 132 in Figure 5.13). If you wanted to see the opinion's discussion of the point of law summarized in that headnote, you could move to the discussion by pressing the TAB key to position the cursor under the JUMP marker next to "[1]" and then pressing ENTER. Likewise, if you were viewing *Lewis*'s discussion of the issue summarized in the case's first headnote, you could move to that headnote by pressing the TAB key to position the cursor under the JUMP marker next to "[1]" in the text of the opinion and then pressing ENTER.

In most instances, a command for moving within a document will result in your continuing to view the same document. Sometimes, however, a command will bump you to another document. For example, if your search results include more than one document and you are viewing the last screen of a document when you instruct the computer to move forward one screen, the monitor will display the first screen of the next document in your collection.

Ordinarily, however, to move between documents, you use the commands explained in the next section.

Moving between documents in WESTLAW

When your search request retrieves more than one document, you have several ways of moving from one document to another.[226] You can:

- *Move forward one document.* Type **r** (for next "ranked" document) and press ENTER.

  If you use this technique while viewing a citation list, the monitor will display the document following the one you were viewing when you transmitted your instruction to display the citation list. For example, suppose you had been viewing document 15 in your collection and then displayed the citation list. If you transmitted **r** while viewing the list, the monitor would display document 16.
- *Move back one document.* Type **r–** (for previous "ranked" document) and press ENTER.

  If you use this technique while viewing a citation list, the monitor will display the document preceding the one you were viewing when you transmitted your instruction to display the citation list. For example, suppose you had been viewing document 16 in your collection and then displayed the citation list. If you transmitted **r–** while viewing the list, the monitor would display document 15.
- *Move forward more than one document.* Type **r+** followed by the number of documents you want to advance in the collection retrieved by your search request; then press ENTER. For example, if you were viewing the third document and wanted to skip ahead 5 documents, you would type **r+5** and press ENTER; the monitor would then display the eighth document.

  If you use this technique while viewing a citation list, the number you transmit with **r+** will skip the display ahead that many documents past the document you were viewing when you transmitted your instruction to display the citation list. For example, suppose you had been viewing document 15 in your collection and then displayed the citation list. If you transmitted **r+10** while viewing the list, the monitor would display document 25.

[226] These navigating techniques are possible because, as discussed on pages 353–55, documents retrieved by a search request are displayed in a fixed order, and each document is assigned an identification number (called a "rank number" in WESTLAW) that appears when you display a citation list, as explained at pages 351–52.

- *Move back more than one document.* Type `r-` followed by the number of documents you want to move back in the collection retrieved by your search request; then press ENTER. For example, if you were viewing the eighth document and wanted to skip back 5 documents, you would type `r-5` and press ENTER; the monitor would then display the third document.

  If you use this technique while viewing a citation list, the number you transmit with `r-` will skip the display back that many documents past the document you were viewing when you transmitted your instruction to display the citation list. For example, suppose you had been viewing document 25 in your collection and then displayed the citation list. If you transmitted `r-10` while viewing the list, the monitor would display document 15.
- *Move to a specific document.* You might know the identification number (*i.e.*, "rank number") of a document in the collection retrieved by your search request (having gotten the number from a citation list, like the one in Figure 11.18 on page 352). If so, you can go directly from the document you are viewing to the new document: type `r` (for "rank") followed by the new document's identification number (or type the number alone); then press ENTER.

  For example, returning to the collection of cases listed in Figure 11.18, if you were viewing *United States v. Mendoza-Lopez* and wanted to move to *Greene v. United States*, you could type `r3` (or just `3`) and press ENTER. The monitor would display *Greene*.

  You can also use this technique while viewing a citation list. Conversely, you can move from a document you are viewing to a citation list; the command you use depends on the part of the citation list to which you want to move. If you want to move from a document to the top of a citation list, type the letter `l` (for "list") and press ENTER. If you want to move from a document to the portion of the citation list beginning with that document's citation, type the letters `lr` (for "list rank") and press ENTER; for example, transmitting `lr` while viewing the 20th document would move you to the part of the citation list beginning with the citation for the 20th document. If you want to move from a document to the portion of the citation list beginning with another document's citation, type the letters `lr` followed by that document's identification number, and then press ENTER; for instance, transmitting `lr35` while viewing the 20th document would move you to the part of the citation list beginning with the citation for the 35th document.
- *Move to other statutory or administrative code sections, whether or not retrieved (DOCUMENTS IN SEQUENCE).* When viewing

a statute or administrative regulation, you can move to other sections of the code—even those *not* included in your search results. This capability, provided through the DOCUMENTS IN SEQUENCE feature, is analogous to skipping to other sections of a printed code after you have located the section in which you were originally interested. Thus, the feature allows you to read statutory and administrative code sections in the context of surrounding, presumably related, provisions.

By permitting you to move between a retrieved document and an unretrieved document, DOCUMENTS IN SEQUENCE differs from other navigational techniques (which only permit you to move between documents actually retrieved by a search request).

You invoke DOCUMENTS IN SEQUENCE while viewing a statutory or administrative code section, whether retrieved by a search request or through FIND. To implement the feature, type **d** and press ENTER. The monitor will then display the code section that immediately follows the section you were viewing when you transmitted **d**. Each time you want to move forward to the next section of the code, transmit **d** again.

For example, suppose the first two statutory provisions your search request retrieved were sections 12-21-40 and 12-21-72 of the Code of Alabama. Ordinarily, if you were viewing section 12-21-40 and instructed the computer to display the next document, you would move to section 12-21-72. But if you had invoked DOCUMENTS IN SEQUENCE by transmitting **d** while viewing section 12-21-40, you would move to section 12-21-41 (the next section in the Code of Alabama), even though your search request had not retrieved that section. If you transmitted **d** again, you would move to the next code section (12-21-42), even if your search request had not retrieved that section, either.

While in DOCUMENTS IN SEQUENCE, you can move anywhere in the code by transmitting variations on the **d** command. Transmitting **d–** will move you back one section in the code (*e.g.*, from section 12-21-40 to section 12-21-39). Transmitting **d+** followed by a number will move you forward that number of sections in the code (*e.g.*, **d+5** would move you from section 12-21-40 to section 12-21-45). Transmitting **d–** followed by a number will move you back that number of sections in the code (*e.g.*, **d–5** would move you from section 12-21-45 to section 12-21-40).

While viewing a code section in DOCUMENTS IN SEQUENCE, you can move from screen to screen by using the techniques already explained for moving around within a document.

Movement will automatically occur in PAGE mode; you cannot select TERM mode because not all the sections available for viewing will have your search terms.

As long as you remain in DOCUMENTS IN SEQUENCE, the phrase "DOCUMENTS IN SEQUENCE" (or an abbreviation of it) will appear in the rank column of the status line. You can see the rank message, for example, in Figure 11.21, which shows the statute that displayed after invoking DOCUMENTS IN SEQUENCE while viewing the statute in Figure 11.20.

To leave the DOCUMENTS IN SEQUENCE feature and return to the code section you were viewing when you invoked the feature, type `xd` (for "exit DOCUMENTS IN SEQUENCE") and press ENTER. Alternatively, to resume your viewing at a specific ranked document (say, the fifth code section in your search results), type `r` followed by the section's rank number (*e.g.*, `r5`); then press ENTER.

The LOCATE feature in WESTLAW: viewing a subset of documents

When you are viewing a collection of documents retrieved by a search request in WESTLAW (or the citation list for those documents), you can use the LOCATE feature to confine your viewing to a selected subset of documents within the collection. For example, suppose you had carried out a search for personal injury cases and retrieved cases reflecting various kinds of personal injuries. If you wanted to view just the cases mentioning spinal injuries, but still wanted to keep the original collection of cases intact for subsequent viewing, you could use the LOCATE command to isolate the subset of cases mentioning spinal injuries.

In effect, LOCATE allows you to perform a subsidiary search within a collection of retrieved documents so that you can quickly scan for occurrences of a particular word or words. These words can differ from the search terms you used to retrieve the original collection of documents.

LOCATE also works with a document retrieved by a FIND command. Because FIND (explained on pages 279–84) retrieves a document through its citation rather than its text, you cannot know immediately whether a "found" document contains words that would suggest the document's relevance. By performing a LOCATE search in the document, you can determine quickly whether it contains such words and thereby speed up your assessment of the document's relevance.

Using LOCATE. You formulate and modify a LOCATE request the same way you formulate and modify an ordinary Boolean search request. Thus, you

```
Citation                  Rank(R)          Page(P)        Database         Mode
AL ST § 12-21-40          R 1 OF 2         P 1 OF 2       AL-ST            Term
 Code 1975 § 12-21-40

                              CODE OF ALABAMA 1975
                                TITLE 12. COURTS.
                       CHAPTER 21. EVIDENCE AND WITNESSES.
                         ARTICLE 1. GENERAL PROVISIONS.
                              Division 1. Evidence.
                  Subdivision 2. Competency and Admissibility.
       Copyright (c) 1977-1993 by State of Alabama.  All rights reserved.
                  Current through Act 92-720, approved 10-9-92

 § 12-21-40. Handwriting -- Comparison of disputed writing with genuine.

   Comparison of a disputed writing with any writing admitted to be genuine or
 proven to the reasonable satisfaction of the court to be genuine shall be
 permitted to be made by witnesses who are qualified as experts or who are
 familiar with the handwriting of the person whose handwriting is in question,
 and such writings and the evidence of witnesses respecting the same may be
 submitted to the court or jury trying the case as evidence of the genuineness
 or otherwise of the writings in dispute.
```

Source: West Publishing Company; © 1977–1993 State of Alabama

Figure 11.20. Display of a Statute Before Invoking DOCUMENTS IN SEQUENCE in WESTLAW

```
Citation                 DOCUMENTS         Page(P)        Database        Mode
AL ST § 12-21-41        IN SEQUENCE        P 1 OF 2       AL-ST           Page
 Code 1975 § 12-21-41

                              CODE OF ALABAMA 1975
                                TITLE 12. COURTS.
                       CHAPTER 21. EVIDENCE AND WITNESSES.
                         ARTICLE 1. GENERAL PROVISIONS.
                              Division 1. Evidence.
                  Subdivision 2. Competency and Admissibility.
       Copyright (c) 1977-1993 by State of Alabama.  All rights reserved.
                  Current through Act 92-720, approved 10-9-92

 § 12-21-41. Evidence of title to lands.

   Copies of the field notes of the original government surveys of lands or
 other evidences of title to lands furnished by the secretary of state or by the
 United States, or any department thereof, to the probate judge, when certified
 by such judge, are admissible in evidence.

   (Code 1876, § 3050; Code 1886, § 2786; Code 1896, § 1817; Code 1907, § 3984;
 Code 1923, § 7682; Code 1940, T. 7, § 395.)
```

rank message

Source: West Publishing Company; © 1977–1993 State of Alabama

Figure 11.21. Display of a Statute After Invoking DOCUMENTS IN SEQUENCE in WESTLAW

can use logic connectors, universal characters, field restrictions, and so on (as explained in Chapter 7).

You can transmit a LOCATE search request in one of several ways:

- You can type `locate` (or `loc`) at the top of the monitor, followed by a space and the word or words you want the computer to scan for; then press ENTER. So, returning to the earlier research scenario, you could transmit

  ```
  loc spine or spinal
  ```

  If your LOCATE request exceeds a certain length—currently, 23 characters—this technique will not work, and you will have to use one of the techniques explained below.
- You can just type `locate` (or `loc`) and press ENTER. The monitor will then display a screen with a message asking you to type and transmit your LOCATE request. This technique accommodates lengthy LOCATE requests.
- You can recall your original search request and edit it for use as a LOCATE request. Type `locate q` or `loc q` (for "LOCATE query"), and press ENTER. The monitor will redisplay your original search request, which you can then modify and transmit as a LOCATE request. If you recall a natural-language search request for use as a LOCATE request, you will have to recast the request into a form appropriate for Boolean (terms-and-connectors) searching.

  Editing an original search request for use as a LOCATE request leaves the original request intact. The modifications operate only while you use the LOCATE feature.

After you have performed a LOCATE search, you might want to edit your LOCATE request. To do so:

1. Type `locate` (or `loc`).
2. Press ENTER. The monitor will display your LOCATE request for editing.
3. When you finish making the modifications you want, press ENTER to carry out the new LOCATE search.

Viewing documents through LOCATE. After you transmit a LOCATE request, the monitor will redisplay the document you were viewing (if it satisfies the LOCATE request), or will display the first screen of the next-ranked document that satisfies the LOCATE request. By using techniques explained on pages 360–67 for moving in a collection of documents retrieved by an ordinary search request, you can move within a document and between documents retrieved by your LOCATE request: press ENTER to advance from screen to screen, transmit `t-` or `p-` to move backwards through screens, transmit `r` to advance through documents, or transmit `r-` to move to previous documents. If you want to see a list of documents that satisfy your LOCATE request, type `lloc` and press ENTER.[227]

Although a LOCATE search identifies all documents in the original collection that satisfy the LOCATE request, the display of these documents begins only from the point at which you transmit your LOCATE request. For instance, in a collection of 50 documents retrieved by your original search request, a LOCATE request transmitted while you were viewing the 20th document would begin displaying the results of the LOCATE search with the 20th document. This response can leave the impression (which might be incorrect) that none of the first 19 documents satisfies the LOCATE request. To be sure you don't inadvertently overlook any documents that satisfy a LOCATE request, start by displaying the first document in the collection retrieved by your original search request (type the number `1` and press ENTER); then transmit your LOCATE request.

When documents satisfying a LOCATE request are displayed, the words used in the LOCATE request—not the terms used in the original search request—will appear highlighted in the text. In addition, "T LOCATE" or "P LOCATE" will appear in the mode column of the status line.

"T LOCATE" and "P LOCATE" serve as reminders that when you move from screen to screen, whether in TERM or PAGE mode, you are moving within the subsidiary collection of documents that satisfy the LOCATE request, *not* throughout the entire collection satisfying your original search request.[228] For example, in TERM mode (identified by "T LOCATE"), pressing ENTER will move you to the next screen containing text that satisfies your LOCATE request, not to the next screen containing text that satisfies your original search request. In PAGE mode (identified by "P LOCATE"), pressing ENTER moves you screen by screen through only the documents satisfying your LOCATE request, not through all the documents satisfying the original search request.[229]

[227] Alternatively, you can transmit `l`, the standard WESTLAW command for viewing a citation list. The monitor will display a list of all the documents retrieved by the original search request; arrows in the left margin will point to documents in the subset satisfying the LOCATE request.

[228] When a document satisfying a LOCATE request first appears on the monitor, the document will automatically display in TERM mode. While viewing a document, you can switch to PAGE mode at any time by typing `p` and pressing ENTER; you can switch back to TERM mode at any time by typing `t` and pressing ENTER.

[229] The LOCATE feature does not operate in conjunction with BEST mode. Thus, if you transmit a LOCATE request while viewing a document in BEST mode, the computer will automatically switch to TERM mode for moving from screen to screen in your LOCATE results.

Leaving LOCATE. To leave the LOCATE feature and resume your previous research activity:

1. Type `xloc` or `xl` (for "exit LOCATE").

2. Press ENTER.

At that point, you will leave LOCATE and the word "LOCATE" will disappear from the mode column of the status line.

Printing search results in WESTLAW

During an online search session, you might decide you want to print some or all of your search results (*e.g.*, one or more documents, or a list of citations), especially if the information is not readily available to you in a book or other offline source.

Although you have several choices in terms of *what* to print in WESTLAW, the computer hardware you are using and the subscription agreement between you (or your employer) and WESTLAW will determine *where* the results will print. Printing can occur either centrally (at West Publishing Company, which mails the print-out to the subscriber) or locally (at your office). Local printing takes place either on an attached printer, which receives printing instructions through the terminal at which you are working, or on a stand-alone printer, which receives instructions through a separate telecommunications link with WESTLAW. You can also have your WESTLAW results printed through a fax machine at any telephone number you designate. This discussion assumes you are printing locally.

For additional guidance about printing search results, consult the WESTLAW publication entitled *Guide to Printing and Downloading*, the WESTMATE software manuals,[230] the person who coordinates your WESTLAW subscription, or a WESTLAW customer service representative.

Keep in mind that the charges you incur as you print can mount rapidly. In general, you should avoid printing documents (especially lengthy ones) you can readily obtain offline. Printing a list of citations for documents retrieved by a search request, however, can be cost-effective: after ending your WESTLAW search session, you can use the list to retrieve authorities from other sources, such as printed case reporters.

In printing search results in WESTLAW, you can:

[230] West Publishing Company, WESTMATE: WESTLAW Communications Software for the IBM PS/2, IBM PC and Compatibles 6–1 to 7–4 (1990) (version 4.5); West Publishing Company, WESTMATE User Guide for the IBM PS/2, IBM PC and Compatibles 14–17 (1990) (version 4.5).

- *Print a single line.* If you are using a WALT II terminal and want to print just a single line of a document or citation list you are viewing, move the cursor to the line you want to print and press the PRINT LINE key. Printing will begin immediately. You can repeat this procedure for each line you want to print.
- *Print displayed screens.* If you are looking at a document or citation list and want to print just what appears on the screen you are viewing, press the key labelled PRINT SCREEN (or, on some keyboards, the key labelled PRT SC); depending on the keyboard you use, you might need to hold down the SHIFT key while you press PRINT SCREEN (or PRT SC). Printing will begin immediately. You can repeat the procedure to print any screen you display.

  WESTLAW also allows you to print each screen automatically as you display it. Press the key labelled CONTROL (or CTRL) and, while holding down that key, press the key labelled PRINT SCREEN (or PRT SC); on some keyboards, you press only the key labelled ONLINE PRINT. The phrase "Log: Printer" will appear at the bottom of the monitor. Now, each time you display a new screen, it will automatically print without your giving the computer any additional printing instructions. This automatic screen printing will continue until you turn the function off. To do so, press the same keys you used to turn the function on: press CONTROL (or CTRL) and, while holding down that key, press PRINT SCREEN (or PRT SC); on some keyboards, you press only ONLINE PRINT. The phrase "Log: Printer" will disappear from the bottom of the monitor.
- *Print the displayed document.* If you want to print the document or citation list you are viewing, type `pr` (for "print offline") and press ENTER.[231] The monitor will display the WESTLAW Offline Printing and Downloading Menu, which offers choices for (among other things) printing the current document or citation list. The menu choices will vary slightly, depending on the database you are searching, on the point at which you invoke the printing function, and on whether you used a terms-and-connectors or natural-language search request. Figure 11.22 shows what a typical menu of printing choices looks like when invoked while viewing a document retrieved with a terms-and connectors search; Figure 11.23 shows what a typical menu of printing choices looks like when invoked while viewing a citation list.

[231] You can also print a displayed "scope" description using the "print offline" command because the WESTLAW computer treats a "scope" description as a document.

```
Select one of the following commands to store information for later offline
printing or downloading:

Current document                           Selected documents
  T   All Term mode pages                    T#  All Term mode pages
  D   All pages                              D#  All pages
  P   Last displayed page                    F#  First page including West
  P#  Selected pages                             synopsis (if available)
                                             L#  List of citations
All documents
  AT  All Term mode pages
  AD  All pages
  F   First page including West synopsis (if available)
  L   List of all citations

      Note:  # represents a range or selection of pages or documents.
               EXAMPLE:  P1-4 = Pages 1 through 4; P1,4 = Pages 1 and 4


If you wish to:
   Store information, type a command and press ENTER
   Cancel this request and resume your research, press ENTER
```

Source: West Publishing Company © 1993

Figure 11.22. Typical WESTLAW Printing and Downloading Menu Invoked From a Document

```
Select one of the following commands to store information for later offline
printing or downloading:

Current citation list                      Selected documents
  P   Last displayed page                    T#  All Term mode pages
  L#  List of selected citations             D#  All pages
  L   List of all citations                  F#  First page including West
                                                 synopsis (if available)
All documents
  AT  All Term mode pages
  AD  All pages
  F   First page including West synopsis (if available)

      Note:  # represents a range or selection of documents.
               EXAMPLE:  D1-4 = Documents 1 through 4; D1,4 = Documents 1 and 4


If you wish to:
   Store information, type a command and press ENTER
   Cancel this request and resume your research, press ENTER
```

Source: West Publishing Company © 1993

Figure 11.23. Typical WESTLAW Printing and Downloading Menu Invoked From a Citation List

To implement a printing choice for your current document or citation list, type the appropriate command from the menu and then press ENTER. For example, returning to Figure 11.22, transmitting `t` would result in printing screens in your document that have one or more of your search terms.[232] Or, for instance, transmitting `p` followed by one or more numbers would result in printing the screens corresponding to those numbers; transmitting `p3-6` would yield a printout of screens 3 through 6, while transmitting `p3,6-8` would yield a printout of screen 3 and screens 6 through 8.

In West's printed reporters, cases might contain drawings, charts, or other images. In WESTLAW, the online version of some of these cases will include those illustrations in the "image" field. Currently, the image will not display on the screen, but the computer will display a message indicating the presence of an image. To see an image in the case you are viewing, you must print the image on a specified kind of laser printer or on a fax machine. To print the images in the case you are viewing, you can print the whole document, print just the pages containing the images, or restrict the display of the case to the image field and then print just that field.

After you make your printing choices, the monitor will display a summary of your printing selection and allow you to designate a destination for printing that selection (*e.g.*, to a printer attached to your computer). Figure 11.24 illustrates the appearance of the monitor. If you want to designate a destination at this point, follow the on-screen instructions. If you do not designate a destination at this point, you can do so later in your search session through the Offline Print Directory (see pages 377–79) or when you log off WESTLAW.

Once you have finished making your printing choices, you can either resume your research or immediately log off WESTLAW. The WESTLAW computer will store your printing instructions until you finish your search session and log off.

You might prefer not to go through the step of designating a destination for each document you want to print during a single search session. In that case, you can use the Options Directory at any time to instruct the computer to designate a printing destination

[232] With a document retrieved through Boolean searching, all screens containing your search terms will print. With a document retrieved through natural-language searching, screens from the five "best portions" of the document will print. For a refresher on "portions" in documents retrieved through natural-language searching, see note 225 on page 360.

```
Your request to store information has been completed and approximately 85 lines
have been stored.

   Summary of Your Request
   Client Identifier:   Abdul/Eljohn Rentals
   Database:            OH-CS
   Lines:               85
   Command:             T
   Destination:         ???

   Note:  All requests, excluding "Print it Now on STP", will be sent to the
          specified destination after you sign off.



If you wish to:
   Continue your research, press ENTER
   Assign a destination, type the command and press ENTER
     FAX  Fax Machine             DLD  Download to Disk       SAV  Save
     ATP  Attached Printer        DIS  Discard
   Sign off WESTLAW, type OFF and press ENTER
```

Source: West Publishing Company © 1993

Figure 11.24. WESTLAW Screen for Designating a Destination for Offline Printing

to use unless you override it by indicating a destination when the monitor displays a screen like that in Figure 11.24. To go to the Options Directory, type `options` (or `opt`) and press ENTER.

- *Print selected documents.* To print selected documents from your search results, or to print a citation list for selected documents, type `pr` (for "print offline") and press ENTER. The monitor will display the WESTLAW Offline Printing and Downloading Menu, which lists printing choices like those in Figure 11.22 or 11.23. The menu choices will vary slightly, depending on the database you are searching, on the point at which you invoke the printing function, and on whether you used a terms-and-connectors or natural-language search request.

  To implement a choice for printing selected documents, or a list of their citations, type the appropriate command from the menu and then press ENTER. For example, returning to Figure 11.22, transmitting `t` followed by the identification (*i.e.*, rank) numbers of your selected documents would result in printing screens that have one or more of your search terms in the selected documents.[233] Thus,

[233] See note 232.

transmitting `t6,20,23` would yield a printout of TERM-mode screens from documents ranked 6, 20, and 23. Likewise, transmitting `L2-5,9` would yield a list containing the citations of documents ranked 2, 3, 4, 5 and 9.

Currently, to print drawings, charts, or other images contained in the "image" field of selected cases, you must print the images on a specified kind of laser printer or on a fax machine. To print the images in selected cases, you can print the cases in their entirety, or you can restrict the display of the cases to the image field and then print just that field.

After you make your printing choices, you follow the procedure (already discussed under printing a displayed document) for designating a destination for your printing. You can then either resume your research or immediately log off WESTLAW.

- *Print all documents.* To print all documents from your search results, or a citation list for all the documents, type `pr` (for "print offline") and press ENTER. The monitor will display the WESTLAW Offline Printing and Downloading Menu, which lists printing choices like those in Figure 11.22 or 11.23. The menu choices will vary slightly, depending on the database you are searching, on the point at which you invoke the printing function, and on whether you used a terms-and-connectors or natural-language search request.

  To implement a choice for printing all documents, or their citations, type the appropriate command from the menu and then press ENTER. For example, returning to Figure 11.22, transmitting `at` would result in printing screens that have one or more of your search terms in all retrieved documents.[234] Likewise, transmitting `L` would yield a list containing the citations of all retrieved documents.

  Currently, to print drawings, charts, or other images contained in the "image" field of the cases you retrieved, you must print the images on a specified kind of laser printer or on a fax machine. To print the images, you can print the cases in their entirety, or you can restrict the display of the cases to the image field and then print just that field.

  After you make your printing choices, you follow the procedure (already discussed under printing a displayed document) for designating a destination for your printing. You can then either resume your research or immediately log off WESTLAW.

[234] See note 232.

The WESTLAW Offline Print Directory ("OPD"). When you use the "pr" command to instruct the computer to print search results after you log off WESTLAW, the WESTLAW computer stores your printing instructions in the Offline Print Directory. You can use the OPD during your search session to:

- review a summary of your printing instructions
- designate a destination for printing your search results (*e.g.*, to a printer attached to your computer) if you did not designate a destination when you originally set up your printing instructions with the "pr" command
- change the destination for printing your search results (*e.g.*, switch from an attached printer to a stand-alone printer)
- discard a printing instruction

To display the Offline Print Directory:

1. Type **opd**.
2. Press ENTER.

The monitor will display a screen like that in Figure 11.25. As the illustration shows, the OPD lists the following information about each of your printing (and downloading) requests:

```
                         OFFLINE PRINT DIRECTORY                    Only Page

Request  Created   Service/Database  Lines  Command  Destination
   1     06/19/93  ALLFEDS             195  T        Save until 07/19/93
   2     06/10/93  OH-CS                85  T          ???
   3     06/01/93  SCT                  95  L        Download to Disk

If you wish to:
   View a summary or change the destination of a single request, type its
     number and press ENTER
   Change multiple request destinations, type a range or selection of
     request numbers (e.g., 1-4 or 1,4) and press ENTER
   View a complete list of destination commands, type CMDS and press ENTER
   Continue, press ENTER
```

Source: West Publishing Company © 1993

Figure 11.25. Offline Print Directory in WESTLAW

- a WESTLAW-assigned OPD number for the request
- the date the request was created
- the service or database containing the material you want to print
- the approximate number of lines that will print
- the choice you transmitted at the WESTLAW Offline Printing and Downloading Menu (shown in Figures 11.22 and 11.23), such as T to print retrieved screens containing one or more of your search terms
- the destination you designated for your printing at the screen shown in Figure 11.24, or "???" if you did not designate a destination at that point

To display a summary of an OPD request so you can review the request, assign or change a destination, or discard the request:

1. Type the OPD request number (listed in the first column in Figure 11.25).
2. Press ENTER.

The monitor will then display a screen like that in Figure 11.26. Follow the on-screen instructions for carrying out whichever task you want to accomplish.

```
               OFFLINE PRINT DIRECTORY - SUMMARY OF REQUEST         Only Page

Request Number:  2                          Approximate Number of Lines:  85
Created:  06/10/93  02:01 pm  (Central)     Command:  T
Client Identifier:  Abdul/Eljohn Rentals
Database:  OH-CS
Citation:  Slip Copy
Query:  APARTMENT W/10 LEASE  &  PLUMBING    WATER

Star Paging Request:  All Available Publications

Destination:    ???



If you wish to:
   Change the destination, type the command and press ENTER
     FAX  Fax Machine            DLD  Download to Disk       SAV  Save
     ATP  Attached Printer       DIS  Discard
   View a complete list of destination commands, type CMDS and press ENTER
   Return to your Offline Print Directory, type OPD and press ENTER
   Continue, press ENTER
```

Source: West Publishing Company © 1993

Figure 11.26. Summary of an Offline Print Directory Request in WESTLAW

For example, returning to Figure 11.25, if you wanted to designate an attached printer as the destination for OPD request 2 (which does not yet have a destination), you would type `2` and press ENTER. When the summary of OPD request 2 appears (Figure 11.26), you would type `atp` and press ENTER. The monitor would then redisplay Figure 11.26, but would show "Attached Printer" instead of "???" as the destination. On-screen instructions explain how to continue your online research session.

Downloading search results in WESTLAW

If you search in WESTLAW with a computer that has a disk for storing information, you can save ("download") to your computer's disk some or all of the results of your search. Downloading is analogous to printing in WESTLAW, except that instead of storing the results on paper, you store them on your computer's disk, incurring a downloading charge as you do so. With downloading, you can log off WESTLAW (so you stop incurring charges) and then read your results, either on your computer monitor or on a print-out you generate from the downloaded file.

For additional guidance about downloading in WESTLAW, you can consult WESTLAW's *Guide to Printing and Downloading*, the WESTMATE software manual,[235] the person who coordinates your WESTLAW subscription, a WESTLAW customer service representative, or the user manuals for your computer's hardware and software.

In downloading search results in WESTLAW, you can:

- *Download displayed screens.* To download only the screen you are viewing, press the F10 function key. When the monitor displays the WESTMATE menu (illustrated at the top of Figure 11.27), select the "File/Accessing" heading by either typing `f` or pressing ENTER; when the sub-menu appears (as illustrated at the bottom of Figure 11.27), select the "Store Screen to Disk" option. Downloading will occur immediately.

  If you want to download the screen you are viewing *and* subsequent screens as you display them, press F10 to display the WESTMATE menu, select the "File/Accessing" heading, and then select the "Log Screens to Disk" option. Each screen will download as soon as the monitor displays it. To stop this automatic downloading of displayed screens, press F10 to display the WESTMATE menu, and then select the "File/Accessing" heading again; this

[235] WEST PUBLISHING COMPANY, WESTMATE USER GUIDE FOR THE IBM PS/2, IBM PC AND COMPATIBLES 14–15 (1990) (version 4.5).

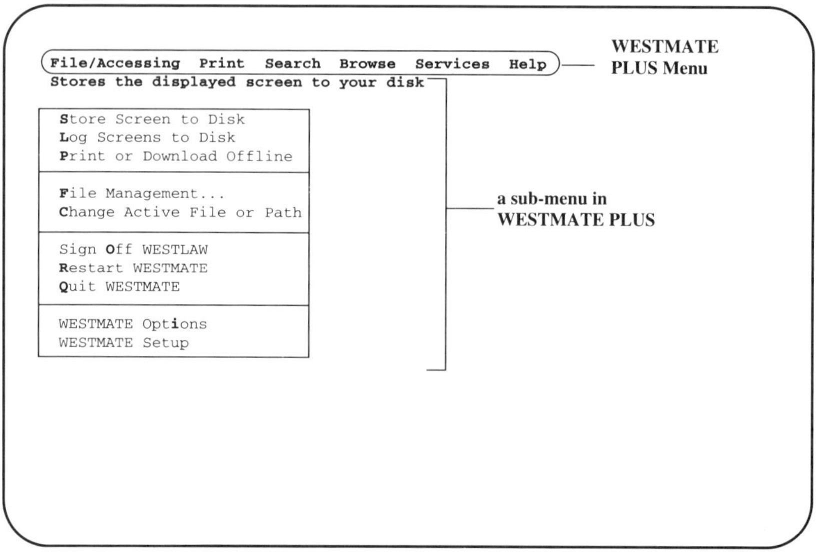

Source: West Publishing Company © 1993

Figure 11.27. "File/Accessing" Sub-Menu in the WESTMATE Plus Menu

time, you will have an opportunity to select a "Stop Disk Logging" option.

For more details about downloading individual displayed screens, see WESTLAW's *Guide to Printing and Downloading* and the WESTMATE software manual.[236]

- *Download the displayed document.* To download the document you are viewing, use the same procedure you would use to print that document (as explained in the previous section), except that when you designate a destination for storing the document, select the option for downloading to a disk. Downloading will occur after you log off.
- *Download selected documents.* Use the same procedure you would use to print selected documents (as explained in the previous section), except that when you designate a destination for storing the documents, select the option for downloading to a disk. Downloading will occur after you log off.
- *Download all documents.* Use the same procedure you would use to print all documents (as explained in the previous section), except

[236] West Publishing Company, WESTMATE User Guide for the IBM PS/2, IBM PC and Compatibles 13–15 (1990) (version 4.5).

that when you designate a destination for storing the documents, select the option for downloading to a disk. Downloading will occur after you log off.

Using the WESTLAW Offline Print Directory ("OPD") in downloading. When you use the "pr" command to instruct the computer to download search results after you log off WESTLAW, the WESTLAW computer stores your downloading instructions in the Offline Print Directory. You can use the OPD during your search session to:

- review a summary of your downloading instructions
- designate downloading as the destination for your search results if you did not designate a destination when you originally set up your instructions with the "pr" command
- change the destination for your search results (*e.g.*, switch from an attached printer to downloading)
- discard a downloading instruction

To display the Offline Print Directory:

1. Type opd.
2. Press ENTER.

The monitor will display a screen like that in Figure 11.25 on page 377. As the illustration shows, the OPD lists the following information about each of your downloading (and printing) requests:

- a WESTLAW-assigned OPD number for the request
- the date the request was created
- the service or database containing the material you want to download
- the approximate number of lines that will download
- the choice you transmitted at the WESTLAW Offline Printing and Downloading Menu (shown in Figures 11.22 and 11.23), such as T to download all retrieved screens containing one or more of your search terms
- the destination you designated at the screen shown in Figure 11.24, or "???" if you did not designate a destination at that point

To display a summary of an OPD request so you can review the request, assign or change a destination, or discard the request:

1. Type the OPD request number (listed in the first column in Figure 11.25).

2. Press ENTER.

The monitor will then display a screen like that in Figure 11.26 on page 378. Follow the on-screen instructions for carrying out whichever task you want to accomplish.

For example, returning to Figure 11.25, if you wanted to designate downloading as the destination for OPD request 2 (which does not yet have a destination), you would type `2` and press ENTER. When the summary of OPD request 2 appears (Figure 11.26), you would type `dld` and press ENTER. The monitor would then redisplay Figure 11.26, but would show "Download to Disk" instead of "???" as the destination. On-screen instructions explain how to continue your online research session.

Summary of reading the law in LEXIS and WESTLAW

Figure 11.28 on pages 383–89 summarizes the procedures for reading the law in LEXIS, and Figure 11.29 on pages 390–98 summarizes the WESTLAW procedures.

Viewing Documents in LEXIS	
LEXIS Display Formats	
To display search terms surrounded on each side by 25 searchable words ("key word in context")	press KWIC
To display search terms surrounded on each side by the number of searchable words you want, from 1 to 999 ("variable key word in context")	press VAR KWIC to display 50 searchable words on each side of your search terms *or* type a number from 1 to 999 and then press VAR KWIC to see your search terms surrounded by that number of searchable words
To display the complete online text of a document	press FULL
To display the full text of just selected segments (*e.g.*, just the dissent segment)	press SEGMTS; then type the name of each segment you want to view (placing a comma between segment names), and press TRANSMIT
To display a citation list of retrieved documents	press CITE (or, on some keyboards, REFS)
Star Paging in LEXIS—displays various sets of page numbers available in LEXIS for certain documents	
To see star-page numbers	do nothing unless you have previously suppressed the display—the numbers automatically display throughout the document

(continues)

Figure 11.28. Quick Guide to Reading the Law in LEXIS

(continued)

Viewing Documents in LEXIS*—continued*	
To find out which sets of star-page numbers exist for the document you are viewing	type `p` and press TRANSMIT
To limit the display of multiple sets of star-page numbers to just one set	type `star` followed by the identification of the desired set of star-page numbers; then press TRANSMIT *Examples:* transmit `star us` to display just *U.S. Reports* page numbers transmit `star lexis` to display just LEXIS page numbers
To return to the standard display of star-page numbers	type `xstar` and press TRANSMIT
Moving Within a Document in LEXIS	
To move forward one screen	press NEXT PAGE
To move back one screen	press PREV PAGE
To move forward more than one screen†	type the number of screens you want to advance; then press NEXT PAGE
To move back more than one screen†	type the number of screens you want to move back; then press PREV PAGE
To return to the first screen	press FIRST PAGE
To move to a specific star page	type `p` followed by the desired star-page number, including its asterisks; then press TRANSMIT

To move to a specific part of an *A.L.R.* annotation	type `p` followed by an asterisk and the desired section number or part; then press TRANSMIT *Examples:* `p*3c` `p*index`
To move forward one line	press ROLL UP (available on the UBIQ keyboard)
To move back one line	press ROLL DOWN (available on the UBIQ keyboard)
Moving Between Documents in LEXIS	
To move forward one document in a collection of retrieved documents	press NEXT DOC (or, on some keyboards, NEXT CASE)
To move back one document in a collection of retrieved documents	press PREV DOC (or, on some keyboards, PREV CASE)
To move forward more than one document in a collection of retrieved documents	type the number of documents you want to advance; then press NEXT DOC (or, on some keyboards, NEXT CASE)
To move back more than one document in a collection of retrieved documents	type the number of documents you want to move back; then press PREV DOC (or, on some keyboards, PREV CASE)
To return to the first document in a collection of retrieved documents, or to the first screen of a citation list	press FIRST DOC (or, on some keyboards, FIRST CASE)

(continues)

† This technique does not work when you are viewing a citation list.

Figure 11.28. Quick Guide to Reading the Law in LEXIS (continued)

(continued)

Moving Between Documents in LEXIS*—continued*	
To move to a specific document in a collection of retrieved documents	type the document's identification number; then press TRANSMIT
To invoke "Browse" (to move to other statutory or administrative code sections, whether or not they appear in your collection of retrieved documents)	while viewing a statutory or administrative code section, type `b` and press TRANSMIT; then move anywhere in the code by using the navigating techniques already described
To leave "Browse"	type `b` and press TRANSMIT
To move between documents at different search levels	type the number of the search level you want to view, then press DIF LEVEL (or, on some keyboards, DISP DIF LEVEL); at that point, you can use any of the techniques for moving between documents

FOCUS in LEXIS*—Scanning for terms in a collection of retrieved documents, or in a document retrieved through LEXSEE or LEXSTAT*	
To transmit a FOCUS search request	type `focus` followed by the word or words you want the computer to scan for; then press TRANSMIT *Example:* `focus spine or spinal` *or* type `focus` and press TRANSMIT; when the monitor displays your original search request, modify it or type an entirely different request, then press TRANSMIT

To transmit a FOCUS search request to view occurrences of a citation identified by a LINK marker	type `focus` followed by an equal sign and the number in the LINK marker appearing in front of the citation you want to use in your FOCUS search; then press TRANSMIT *Example:* `focus =4` *or* type `focus` and press TAB to position the cursor under the desired LINK marker; then press TRANSMIT
To move within or between documents identified by FOCUS	use the techniques for moving in a collection of documents retrieved by an ordinary search request
To leave FOCUS	type `exit` and press TRANSMIT
Printing Search Results in LEXIS [††]	
To print the displayed screen	press PRINT (or, on some keyboards, PRINT SCREEN)
To automatically print each screen as it displays (on personal computers only)	invoke "session recording" by holding down ALT and pressing F2; then identify the recording session by transmitting `LPT1` or `LPT2` to designate your printer's port
To turn off automatic printing of displayed screens (on personal computers only)	hold down ALT and press F2

(continues)

[††] Printing options vary, depending on the computer hardware you use and your LEXIS subscription agreement. This discussion assumes you are printing locally, *i.e.,* on a printer at your office.

Figure 11.28. Quick Guide to Reading the Law in LEXIS (continued)

(continued)

Printing Search Results in LEXIS*[††]—*continued	
To print the displayed document	press PRINT DOC, designate where you want printing to occur, select the display format in which you want the document to print, type `y` to confirm you want to print the document, and press TRANSMIT; when you log off, select the option for printing
To print selected documents at a given search level	press PRINT ALL (or, on some keyboards, MAIL IT), press the key for the display format in which you want to print the documents, designate where you want printing to occur, transmit `sel`, specify the documents you want to print, type `y` to confirm you want to print the documents, and press TRANSMIT; when you log off, select the option for printing
To print all documents at a given search level	press PRINT ALL (or, on some keyboards, MAIL IT), press the key for the display format in which you want to print the documents, designate where you want printing to occur, type `y` to confirm you want to print the documents, and press TRANSMIT; when you log off, select the option for printing

Downloading Search Results in LEXIS†††	
To download screens automatically as they display	invoke "session recording" by holding down ALT and pressing F2
To turn off automatic downloading of displayed screens	hold down ALT and press F2
To download the displayed document	use the same procedure you would use to print the document (see above), but when you log off, select the option for downloading
To download selected documents at a given search level	use the same procedure you would use to print selected documents (see above), but when you log off, select the option for downloading
To download all documents at a given search level	use the same procedure you would use to print all documents (see above), but when you log off, select the option for downloading

†† Printing options vary, depending on the computer hardware you use and your LEXIS subscription agreement. This discussion assumes you are printing locally, *i.e.*, on a printer at your office.

††† This function is available only on a computer with a disk for storing information.

Figure 11.28. Quick Guide to Reading the Law in LEXIS (continued)

Viewing Documents in WESTLAW

WESTLAW Display Formats

To display the complete online text of a document, with your search terms highlighted	do nothing if you have not already selected a different display format—documents initially display in this format
To display the complete text of just selected fields (*e.g.*, just the headnote field)	type `f` and press ENTER; then type the name of each field you want to view (placing a comma between field names), and press ENTER
To cancel the display of selected fields and return to full-text display	type `xf` and press ENTER
To display a citation list of retrieved documents	type `l` and press ENTER

Star Paging in WESTLAW—displays various sets of page numbers available in WESTLAW for certain documents

To see star-page numbers	do nothing unless you have previously suppressed the display—the numbers automatically display throughout the document
To limit the display of multiple sets of star-page numbers to just one set	type `star` (or `st`) followed by the identification of the desired set of star-page numbers; then press ENTER *Examples:* transmit `star us` to display just *U.S. Reports* page numbers transmit `star wl` to display just WESTLAW page numbers
To cancel the display of all star-page numbers	type `xstar` (or `xst`) and press ENTER *or* use the Options Directory: type `options` (or `opt`) and press ENTER

To return to the standard display of star-page numbers as it existed before you customized or cancelled it	type `star` (or `st`) and press ENTER
Moving Within a Document in WESTLAW	
To select TERM mode for moving within a document	do nothing unless you have previously selected PAGE or BEST mode—the document will automatically display in TERM mode*
To switch to PAGE mode	type `p` and press ENTER
To switch to TERM mode	type `t` and press ENTER
To switch to BEST mode (available only with natural-language searching)	type `best` (or `b`) and press ENTER
To move to the next screen in the document	press ENTER while you are in PAGE mode, or press the PAGE DOWN or PgDn key
To move to the next screen that contains your search terms	press ENTER while you are in TERM mode
To move to the next screen in the statistically "best" portion of the document (if retrieved with a natural-language search request)	press ENTER while you are in BEST mode
To move to the previous screen in the document	type `p-` and press ENTER, or press the PAGE UP or PgUp key

(continues)

* This is true of documents retrieved by a Boolean or natural-language search request. Documents retrieved through FIND display in PAGE mode.

Figure 11.29. Quick Guide to Reading the Law in WESTLAW

(continued)

***Moving Within a Document in WESTLAW**—continued*	
To move to the previous screen that contained your search terms	type `t-` and press ENTER
To move to the previous screen in the statistically "best" portion of the document (if retrieved with a natural-language search request)	type `b-` and press ENTER
To move forward more than one screen	type `p+` followed by the number of screens you want to advance in the document, and then press ENTER; or type the number of screens you want to advance, and then press the PAGE DOWN or PgDn key
To move back more than one screen	type `p-` followed by the number of screens you want to move back in the document, and then press ENTER; or type the number of screens you want to move back, and then press the PAGE UP or PgUp key
To move forward half a screen**	type `h+` and press ENTER
To move back half a screen**	type `h-` and press ENTER
To move to a specific screen	type `p` followed by the number of the screen you want to view; then press ENTER
To move in a citation list to a screen where a specified document's citation will appear as the first one on the monitor	type `lr` followed by the document's rank number; then press ENTER

To move to a specific star page	type `star` (or `st`) followed by the desired star-page number, including an identification for the desired set of numbers if you need to distinguish among multiple sets; then press ENTER
	Examples: `star 458`
	`star us 458`
	`star wl 13`

To move from a case headnote to the corresponding text in the opinion	press the TAB key to position the cursor under the JUMP marker (a ">" symbol or a triangle) next to the headnote number; then press ENTER
To move to a case headnote from the part of an opinion dealing with the issue summarized in that headnote	press the TAB key to position the cursor under the JUMP marker (a ">" symbol or a triangle) next to the headnote's number in the text of the opinion; then press ENTER
Moving Between Documents in WESTLAW	
To move forward one document in a collection of retrieved documents	type `r` and press ENTER
To move back one document in a collection of retrieved documents	type `r-` and press ENTER
To move forward more than one document in a collection of retrieved documents	type `r+` followed by the number of documents you want to advance; then press ENTER

(continues)

** This technique does not work when you are viewing a citation list.

Figure 11.29. Quick Guide to Reading the Law in WESTLAW (continued)

(continued)

***Moving Between Documents in WESTLAW**—continued*	
To move back more than one document in a collection of retrieved documents	type `r-` followed by the number of documents you want to move back; then press ENTER
To move to a specific document in a collection of retrieved documents	type `r` followed by the document's rank number (or type the rank number alone); then press ENTER
To move from a document to the top of a citation list for the collection of retrieved documents	type `l` and press ENTER
To move from a document to the part of a citation list beginning with that document's citation	type `lr` and press ENTER
To move from a document to the part of a citation list beginning with another document's citation	type `lr` followed by that document's rank number; then press ENTER
To invoke DOCUMENTS IN SEQUENCE (to move to other statutory or administrative code sections, whether or not they appear in your collection of retrieved documents)	while viewing a statutory or administrative code section, type `d` and press ENTER
To move to the next section of a code while using DOCUMENTS IN SEQUENCE	type `d` and press ENTER
To move back one section in a code while using DOCUMENTS IN SEQUENCE	type `d-` and press ENTER

To move forward more than one section in a code while using DOCUMENTS IN SEQUENCE	type `d+` followed by the number of sections you want to advance; then press ENTER
To move back more than one section in a code while using DOCUMENTS IN SEQUENCE	type `d–` followed by the number of sections you want to move back; then press ENTER
To leave DOCUMENTS IN SEQUENCE and return to the code section you were viewing before invoking the feature	type `xd` and press ENTER
To leave DOCUMENTS IN SEQUENCE and move to a specific ranked document in your retrieved collection of code sections	type `r` followed by the section's rank number; then press ENTER
LOCATE in WESTLAW*—Scanning for terms in a retrieved collection of documents, or in a document retrieved through FIND*	
To transmit a LOCATE request	type `locate` (or `loc`) followed by the word or words you want the computer to scan for; then press ENTER *Example:* `locate spine or spinal` *or* type `locate` (or `loc`) and press ENTER; when the monitor displays a message to do so, type your LOCATE request and press ENTER *or* type `locate q` (or `loc q`) and press ENTER; when the monitor displays your original search request, make any modifications you want and press ENTER

(continues)

Figure 11.29. Quick Guide to Reading the Law in WESTLAW (continued)

(continued)

***LOCATE in WESTLAW**—continued*	
To modify a LOCATE request	type `locate` (or `loc`) and press ENTER; when the monitor displays your LOCATE request, make any modifications you want and press ENTER
To display a list of documents containing your LOCATE terms	type `Llocate` (or `Lloc`) and press ENTER
To move within or between documents identified by LOCATE	use techniques for moving in a collection of documents retrieved by an ordinary search request
To leave LOCATE	type `xloc` (or `xl`) and press ENTER
Printing Search Results in WESTLAW***	
To print a single line from the displayed screen (if you are using a WALT II terminal)	move the cursor to the line you want to print and press PRINT LINE
To print the displayed screen	press PRINT SCREEN (or, on some keyboards, the PRT SC key); depending on the keyboard you use, you might also need to press SHIFT at the same time
To automatically print each screen as it displays	hold down CONTROL (or, on some keyboards, the CTRL key) and press PRINT SCREEN (or, on some keyboards, the PRT SC key); on some keyboards, you press only ONLINE PRINT
To turn off automatic printing of displayed screens	hold down CONTROL (or, on some keyboards, the CTRL key) and press PRINT SCREEN (or, on some keyboards, the PRT SC key); on some keyboards, you press only ONLINE PRINT

To print the displayed document	type `pr` and press ENTER; when the monitor displays a menu of printing choices, type your selection and press ENTER; follow the on-screen instructions for designating a destination for your printing (If you prefer to designate a single printing destination that will apply throughout a search session, use the Options Directory: type `options` (or `opt`) and press ENTER.)
To print selected documents	follow the procedure explained under "To print the displayed document"
To print all documents	follow the procedure explained under "To print the displayed document"
To use the Offline Print Directory to review or discard a printing request, or to designate or change a destination for printing	type `opd` and press ENTER; then follow the on-screen instructions
Downloading Search Results in WESTLAWΔ	
To download the displayed screen	press F10 to display the WESTMATE menu; select the "File/Accessing" heading by either typing `f` or pressing ENTER; then select the "Store Screen to Disk" option
To download screens automatically as they display	press F10 to display the WESTMATE menu; select the "File/Accessing" heading by either typing `f` or pressing ENTER; then select the "Log Screens to Disk" option

(continues)

*** Printing options vary, depending on the computer hardware you use and your WESTLAW subscription agreement. This discussion assumes you are printing locally, *i.e.,* on a printer at your office.

Δ This function is available only on a computer with a disk for storing information.

Figure 11.29. Quick Guide to Reading the Law in WESTLAW (continued)

(continued)

Downloading Search Results in WESTLAW[Δ]*—continued*	
To turn off automatic downloading of displayed screens	press F10 to display the WESTMATE menu; select the "File/Accessing" heading by either typing `f` or pressing ENTER; then select the "Stop Disk Logging" option
To download the displayed document	type `pr` and press ENTER; when the monitor displays a menu of downloading choices, type your selection and press ENTER; follow the on-screen instructions for designating a disk as the destination for your downloading (If you prefer to designate a disk as the destination that will apply throughout a search session, use the Options Directory: type `options` (or `opt`) and press ENTER.)
To download selected documents	follow the procedure explained under "To download the displayed document"
To download all documents	follow the procedure explained under "To download the displayed document"
To use the Offline Print Directory to review or discard a downloading request, to designate downloading as the destination, or to change the destination to or from downloading	type `opd` and press ENTER; then follow the on-screen instructions

Δ This function is available only on a computer with a disk for storing information.

Figure 11.29. Quick Guide to Reading the Law in WESTLAW (continued)

CHAPTER 12

Using Computers in Updating the Law

Introduction. As in book-based legal research, once you have analyzed the authorities you have found, you need to update them. This step involves making sure the authorities you've determined apply to your problem still reflect valid law. Relying on cases that have been overruled or widely questioned, or on statutes or administrative regulations that have been amended or repealed, can invalidate the legal conclusions you have drawn or the legal arguments or theories you plan to present. Few things in legal advocacy can prove as devastating as asserting a position based on outdated law.

This chapter explains the many ways you can use LEXIS or WESTLAW to update the authorities that govern your problem.[237] These techniques include:

- using an online version of *Shepard's Citations* in LEXIS or WESTLAW
- verifying the citation and status of selected authorities through Auto-Cite in LEXIS or Insta-Cite in WESTLAW
- using LEXIS or WESTLAW as a citator (including the use of LEXCITE in LEXIS or QuickCite in WESTLAW) to search the text of online documents for references to the authorities whose validity you want to check

These and the other online updating techniques explained in this chapter complement one another; as you will see, comprehensive updating involves using a combination of techniques.

[237]Thorough updating entails checking not only the authorities on which you plan to rely, but the authorities on which your opponent relies. You might discover that your opponent's position is actually predicated on outdated law.

The steps you take to update authorities using LEXIS and WESTLAW are similar, although the commands differ between the two services. The rest of this chapter explains first the options and corresponding commands in LEXIS, and then those in WESTLAW.

Summary. A roundup of updating methods in LEXIS and WESTLAW appears at the end of the chapter (see pages 636–37).

Updating the Law Through LEXIS

Shepardizing cases through LEXIS

Introduction. Whether in a printed or an online version, *Shepard's Citations* (often referred to as "citators") serve the same purpose: to permit legal researchers to ascertain an authority's status. Chapter 6 of *The Legal Research Manual* explains how to use printed versions of *Shepard's Citations.*[238] If you understand how to use printed *Shepard's Citations*, using the online version will follow easily.

To use a Shepard's citator (that is, to "Shepardize"), you must have already found an authority about whose status you are curious. For purposes of Shepardizing, this known authority is called the cited authority; throughout the following explanation of online Shepardizing, the case of *State v. Yoder*, 49 Wis. 2d 430, 182 N.W.2d 539 (1971), will serve as the illustrative cited authority. The entries appearing in Shepard's tables for the cited authority in which you're interested (*i.e.*, that you are Shepardizing) are called the citing authorities; these authorities—such as cases, law review and *A.L.R.* articles, Attorney General Opinions—are citing to (*i.e.*, referring to) the item in whose treatment you're interested.

Figure 12.02 on page 407 shows the first screen of a Shepard's table for *State v. Yoder* as it appears online in LEXIS. Figure 12.01 on page 406 shows the table for *Yoder* as it appears in the main volume of a printed Shepard's citator. Although you will notice differences in the appearance of the Shepard's tables online and the appearance of their printed counterparts, you can accomplish online all the Shepardizing activities possible in the books:

- looking for cases, law review articles, and other authorities that cite the case
- checking the treatment of the case (that is, how other courts have evaluated the case—*e.g.*, explained it, distinguished it, overruled it—in the course of deciding later cases)

[238] Christopher G. Wren & Jill R. Wren, The Legal Research Manual: A Game Plan for Legal Research and Analysis 95–115 (2d ed. 1986).

- screening for later cases that have referred to a specific headnote or syllabus paragraph in the case you are Shepardizing
- determining the history of the case (*i.e.*, how the case was handled as it worked its way through the legal system)
- finding parallel citations (if any) of the case you are Shepardizing

Often, you can carry out these activities more efficiently online than in the printed *Shepard's Citations.*

A note of caution, however: currently, the online coverage of *Shepard's Citations* is not as comprehensive as the printed Shepard's coverage. At this time, the online versions of *Shepard's Citations* available through LEXIS do not allow you to Shepardize all the types of authorities (such as administrative regulations and municipal ordinances) you can update through the printed citators.[239]

Moreover, for some of the authorities you can Shepardize through LEXIS, the online version of Shepard's currently does not extend as far back in time as the printed version. For example, if you Shepardize the landmark case of *Marbury v. Madison,* 5 U.S. (1 Cranch) 137 (1803), you will now find *Ex Parte Republic of Peru,* 318 U.S. 578 (1943), listed in the online Shepard's as the earliest U.S. Supreme Court case citing *Marbury*; in the printed version of Shepard's, you will find *Cooper v. Telfair,* 4 U.S. (4 Dall.) 14 (1800), listed as the earliest U.S. Supreme Court case citing *Marbury.*[240]

So, when you Shepardize online, make sure you know the scope of Shepard's coverage for the authorities you plan to update. The monitor will show pertinent scope information when it displays the results of a Shepard's search; the scope information appears on the line labelled "Coverage" near the top of the screen, as illustrated in Figure 12.02 on page 407 and explained on pages 405–08. Through the online "help" feature available when you Shepardize in LEXIS, you can also find scope information about all the online Shepard's citators: to invoke "help" while using Shepard's online, type h and press TRANSMIT; then follow the on-screen instructions for using "help."

If the online version of a Shepard's citator does not provide the coverage you need, you will have to do some or all of your Shepardizing in the printed

[239] For a list of authorities you can Shepardize in printed citators, see CHRISTOPHER G. WREN & JILL R. WREN, THE LEGAL RESEARCH MANUAL: A GAME PLAN FOR LEGAL RESEARCH AND ANALYSIS 96 n.34 (2d ed. 1986).

[240] Why, you might ask, does a reference to *Marbury* appear in *Telfair,* which was decided three years before *Marbury*? In making a post-*Marbury* revision of 4 U.S. (Dall.), the court reporter added to *Telfair* an editorial footnote explaining that *Marbury* answered a question posed by Justice Chase in *Telfair.* Shepard's picked up the reference to *Marbury* from the footnote appended to *Telfair* but treated the reference as if it had occurred in the original decision. Thus, the Shepard's table for *Marbury* shows *Telfair* citing *Marbury,* even though the Court decided *Marbury* three years after *Telfair.*

Shepard's Citations. For instance, in the earlier example of online Shepard's coverage for U.S. Supreme Court cases citing *Marbury v. Madison*, you would miss 143 years' worth of citing cases—all those before 1943—if you Shepardized only online.

Of course, cases found through online Shepardizing often mention earlier cases not included as citing cases in online Shepard's tables. But later citing cases might not mention all the earlier citing cases. Consequently, the omission of the earlier citing cases from an online Shepard's table can, by cutting off part of the evolutionary trace of the case you are updating, still impede your full understanding of that case. Sometimes, for example, an earlier case not included in an online Shepard's table will set out a more complete discussion of the meaning of the case being updated, thus helping you gain insight into the contemporaneous understanding of the case. Similarly, the omission of earlier cases cuts off your access to Shepard's analysis codes accompanying those cases, thus denying you the opportunity to readily identify citing cases that have affected in certain ways (such as by distinguishing or limiting) the case you are updating. For instance, in the printed Shepard's table, an analysis code might draw your attention to a citing case that has distinguished the case you are updating; if that citing case is too early to be included in the online Shepard's table, you might not discover that your case has been distinguished on a point important to your research problem.

The following explanation takes you through the steps in Shepardizing a case in LEXIS. Figure 12.10 on pages 423–25 summarizes the steps.

Gaining access to Shepard's case tables in LEXIS. You can initiate a Shepard's search at nearly any time after logging on to LEXIS. You can begin Shepardizing as soon as the monitor displays the library menu; you do not need to select a library or file before starting to Shepardize. Or, you can wait until you have retrieved some documents from a file before you begin Shepardizing.

To retrieve a citator table through the Shepard's service in LEXIS, you use a search request based on the citation of the authority you want to Shepardize:

- If you are viewing the authority you want to Shepardize, simply type `shep` (or `sh`) and press TRANSMIT. The LEXIS computer will automatically "read in" to the search request the citation of your authority.

  Suppose you are viewing a case that has been reprinted in more than one reporter, and that therefore has parallel citations to, say, an official reporter and an unofficial West reporter. Which citation will the computer Shepardize? (Recall that you can get different Shepardizing results depending on which parallel citation you use to Shepardize.)[241] The computer will automatically read in to your "shep" command the citation to the official non-West reporter. For *Yoder*, that would be 49 Wis. 2d 430.[242]

If you retrieved the case through the LEXSEE feature explained on pages 238–43, however, the computer will Shepardize whichever citation you used with your LEXSEE command. So, if you had used `lexsee 182 nw2d 539` to retrieve *Yoder*, the computer would Shepardize 182 N.W.2d 539.

You can also transmit `shep` (or `sh`) while you are viewing the results of an Auto-Cite search.[243] If you do, the computer will Shepardize the citation used in your Auto-Cite request.

- You might want to Shepardize an authority you are *not* viewing—say, a case you see mentioned in another case you are looking at online, or a parallel citation of the authority you are viewing. To Shepardize an authority you are not viewing, you have two choices.

  To use the quicker method, type `shep` (or `sh`) followed by a space and the authority's citation; then press TRANSMIT. For the citation, type the volume number and abbreviation of the publication in which the authority appears and the page number on which the authority begins.

  For instance, to Shepardize *State v. Yoder*, 49 Wis. 2d 430, 182 N.W.2d 539 (1971), you could use any of the following requests:

```
shep 49 wis.2d 430
shep 49 wis2d 430
shep 49 wis. 2d 430
sh 182 n.w.2d 539
shep 182 nw2d 539
sh 182 nw2d 539
```

  As you can see, you must leave a space between the abbreviation and the numbers on each side of it. You have some flexibility, however, in typing the abbreviation. If you are uncertain about how to type an abbreviation, consult the LEXIS reference manual, which

[241] *See* CHRISTOPHER G. WREN & JILL R. WREN, THE LEGAL RESEARCH MANUAL: A GAME PLAN FOR LEGAL RESEARCH AND ANALYSIS 101, 104 (2d ed. 1986). For an example of different results in online Shepardizing, see pages 411–14.

[242] What if the case you are viewing has been reprinted only in a looseleaf reporter service? For example, *Schuchart & Associates, Professional Engineers, Inc. v. Solo Serve Corp.*, 220 U.S.P.Q. 170 (W.D. Tex. 1983), was not published in a West reporter or any official reporter, but was reprinted in BNA's *United States Patents Quarterly*. The "shep" (or "sh") command will also work with cases reprinted in looseleaf reporters whose citations can be Shepardized.

[243] Auto-Cite is explained at pages 422 and 426–37.

provides a list of abbreviations that will work in a Shepard's request.[244] You can also find a list of these abbreviations through the online "help" feature available when you Shepardize in LEXIS (type `h`, press TRANSMIT, and follow the on-screen instructions).

To use the second (and less direct) method of Shepardizing an authority you are not viewing, press the key labelled SELECT SERV. The monitor will display a list of services available in LEXIS, as shown in Figure 10.03 on page 241. To select the Shepard's service from that list, type `shep` and press TRANSMIT. A screen will then appear on which you can type the citation of the authority you want to Shepardize. To complete your Shepard's request, type your citation and press TRANSMIT.

- If you are viewing an authority and see the citation of a case you want to Shepardize, you can use the LINK feature (explained on page 244) to automate the use of Shepard's for updating that citation. To use LINK, type `shep` (or `sh`) followed by an equal sign and the number in the LINK marker preceding the citation you want to Shepardize, then press TRANSMIT. For example, transmit

```
sh =4
```

The computer will read in to your Shepard's request the citation associated with the LINK marker you selected.

Once you have entered the Shepard's service by transmitting a Shepard's request, you can Shepardize as many authorities as you want during the Shepard's session. You do not have to type `shep` (or `sh`) each time; just type and transmit a new citation when you want to Shepardize another authority.

Shepard's case tables in LEXIS. After you transmit a Shepard's request, the monitor displays the first screen of the first Shepard's table for the citation you transmitted. Figure 12.02 on page 407 shows a typical first screen. (Figure 12.03 shows the continuation of the table onto its second screen.) Just as with the printed citators, you need to be sure you have located the correct citator table when you Shepardize online. The heading on the first screen of an online citator table contains information that allows you to verify that you have transmitted the correct citation and, therefore, that the table you retrieved is appropriate for Shepardizing your authority.[245] As you can see in Figure 12.02, the heading information consists of these components:

[244] MEAD DATA CENTRAL, REFERENCE MANUAL FOR THE LEXIS/NEXIS SERVICES (undated looseleaf ed.) (Appendix H).

[245] The information in the heading verifies that the computer has conveniently carried out for you the first several steps you take when you Shepardize in printed citators—namely, selecting the proper set of *Shepard's Citations*, collecting all the necessary volumes in that set, finding the

- *Citations To*—This line of the heading identifies the citation being Shepardized. In Figure 12.02, the "Citations To" line indicates that the citing authorities in the table contain references to 49 Wis. 2d 430.
- *Series*—This line identifies the set of Shepard's citators from which the table was drawn. As with the printed version of *Shepard's Citations*, the online Shepard's service provides separate sets of citators for various authorities (*e.g.*, a set for U.S. Supreme Court decisions; a separate set for court decisions from each state; a set for each of West's regional reporters). The heading in Figure 12.02 identifies *Shepard's Wisconsin Citations* as the source of the table.
- *Division*—This line verifies that within the appropriate set of Shepard's citators, you have retrieved the correct collection of tables containing the specific table for Shepardizing your authority.

  As in the printed citators, the online Shepard's service provides a separate collection of tables for each series of a case reporter (*e.g.*, a collection of tables for Shepardizing cases published in the first series of *Wisconsin Reports*; a collection of tables for Shepardizing cases published in the second series of *Wisconsin Reports*; a collection of tables for Shepardizing cases published in the first series of *North Western Reporter*; a collection of tables for Shepardizing cases published in the second series of *North Western Reporter*). An online "division" corresponds to the collection of tables used to Shepardize cases published in a specific series of a case reporter.

  In Figure 12.02, the "Division" line indicates that the table is drawn from the collection of tables appropriate for Shepardizing cases that, like *Yoder*, are published in *Wisconsin Reports, Second Series*.
- *Coverage*—This line identifies the earliest and latest decision dates of citing cases found in the Shepard's volumes from which the displayed table was drawn. The citing authorities listed in the displayed table will have been issued during the period covered by the *Shepard's Citations* volumes listed in the "Coverage" line.

  When the "Coverage" line specifies (as it does in Figure 12.02) that coverage includes "All Shepard's Citations" or begins with the "First Shepard's Volume," you know you can Shepardize online as

---

correct tables in those volumes, and locating the specific table for Shepardizing your authority. *See* CHRISTOPHER G. WREN & JILL R. WREN, THE LEGAL RESEARCH MANUAL: A GAME PLAN FOR LEGAL RESEARCH AND ANALYSIS 97–104 (2d ed. 1986) (explaining these steps in book-based Shepardizing).

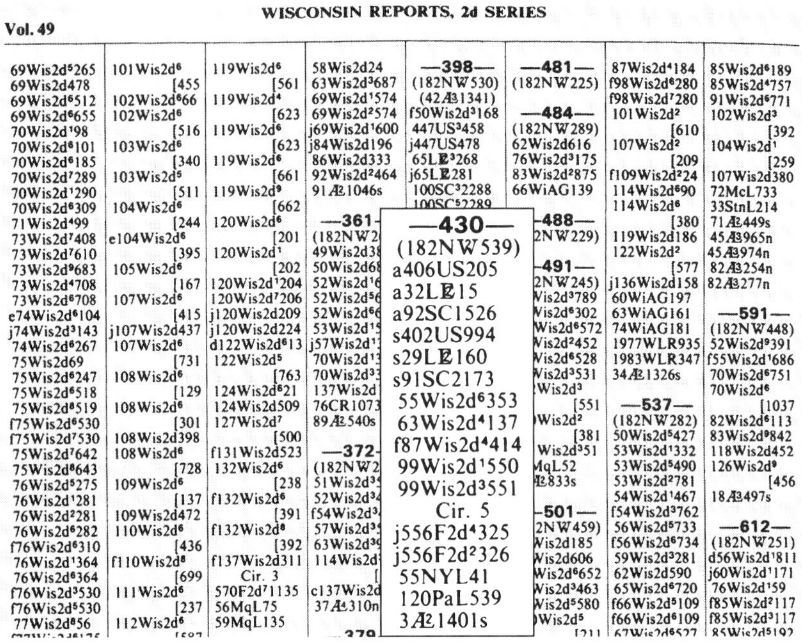

WISCONSIN REPORTS, 2d SERIES

Vol. 49

69Wis2d^{5}265
69Wis2d478
69Wis2d^{6}512
69Wis2d^{6}655
70Wis2d^{1}98
70Wis2d^{6}101
70Wis2d^{6}185
70Wis2d^{7}289
70Wis2d^{1}290
70Wis2d^{6}309
71Wis2d^{4}99
73Wis2d^{7}408
73Wis2d^{7}610
73Wis2d^{9}683
73Wis2d^{4}708
73Wis2d^{6}708
e74Wis2d^{6}104
j74Wis2d^{3}143
74Wis2d^{6}267
75Wis2d69
75Wis2d^{6}247
75Wis2d^{6}518
75Wis2d^{8}519
f75Wis2d^{6}530
f75Wis2d^{7}530
75Wis2d^{7}642
75Wis2d^{8}643
76Wis2d^{5}275
76Wis2d^{1}281
76Wis2d^{2}281
76Wis2d^{6}282
f76Wis2d^{6}310
76Wis2d^{1}364
76Wis2d^{6}364
f76Wis2d^{3}530
f76Wis2d^{5}530
77Wis2d^{8}56

101Wis2d^6
[455
102Wis2d^{6}66
102Wis2d^6
[516
103Wis2d^6
[340
103Wis2d^5
[511
104Wis2d^6
[244
e104Wis2d^6
[395
105Wis2d^6
[167
107Wis2d^6
[415
j107Wis2d437
107Wis2d^6
[731
108Wis2d^6
[129
108Wis2d^6
[301
108Wis2d398
108Wis2d^6
[728
109Wis2d^6
[137
109Wis2d472
110Wis2d^6
[436
f110Wis2d^8
[699
111Wis2d^6
[237
112Wis2d^6

119Wis2d^6
[561
119Wis2d^4
[623
119Wis2d^6
[623
119Wis2d^6
[661
119Wis2d^9
[662
120Wis2d^6
[201
120Wis2d^1
[202
120Wis2d^{1}204
120Wis2d^{7}206
j120Wis2d209
j120Wis2d224
d122Wis2d^{6}13
122Wis2d^5
[763
124Wis2d^{6}21
124Wis2d509
127Wis2d^7
[500
f131Wis2d523
132Wis2d^6
[238
f132Wis2d^6
[391
f132Wis2d^8
[392
f137Wis2d311
Cir. 3
570F2d^{7}1135
56MqL75
59MqL135

58Wis2d24
63Wis2d^{3}687
69Wis2d^{1}574
69Wis2d^{2}574
j69Wis2d^{1}600
j84Wis2d196
86Wis2d333
92Wis2d^{2}464
91Æ^{2}1046s

—361—
(182NW2
49Wis2d38
50Wis2d68
52Wis2d^{1}6
52Wis2d^{5}6
52Wis2d^{6}6
53Wis2d^{1}5
j57Wis2d^1
70Wis2d^1
70Wis2d^3
137Wis2d
76CR1073
89Æ^{2}540s

—372—
(182NW2
51Wis2d^3
52Wis2d^3
f54Wis2d^3
57Wis2d^3
63Wis2d^3
114Wis2d
[
c137Wis2d
37Æ^{4}310n

—398—
(182NW530)
(42Æ^{3}1341)
f50Wis2d^{3}168
447US^{3}458
j447US478
65LE^{3}268
j65LE281
100SC^{3}2288
100SC^{5}2289

—430—
(182NW539)
a406US205
a32LE15
a92SC1526
s402US994
s29LE160
s91SC2173
55Wis2d^{6}353
63Wis2d^{4}137
f87Wis2d^{4}414
99Wis2d^{1}550
99Wis2d^{3}551
Cir. 5
j556F2d^{4}325
j556F2d^{2}326
55NYL41
120PaL539
3Æ^{2}1401s

—481—
(182NW225)

—484—
(182NW289)
62Wis2d616
76Wis2d^{3}175
83Wis2d^{2}875
66WiAG139

—488—
2NW229)

—491—
2NW245)
Wis2d^{3}789
Wis2d^{6}302
Wis2d^{6}572
Wis2d^{2}452
Wis2d^{6}528
Wis2d^{3}531
Wis2d^3
[551
Wis2d^2
[381
Wis2d^{3}51
MqL52
Æ^{2}833s

—501—
2NW459)
Wis2d185
Wis2d606
Wis2d^{6}652
Wis2d^{3}463
Wis2d^{5}580
Wis2d^5
[211

87Wis2d^{4}184
f98Wis2d^{6}280
f98Wis2d^{7}280
101Wis2d^2
[610
107Wis2d^2
[209
f109Wis2d^{2}24
114Wis2d^{6}90
114Wis2d^6
[380
119Wis2d186
122Wis2d^2
[577
j136Wis2d158
60WiAG197
63WiAG161
74WiAG181
1977WLR935
1983WLR347
34Æ^{2}1326s

—537—
(182NW282)
50Wis2d^{5}427
53Wis2d^{1}332
53Wis2d^{5}490
53Wis2d^{2}781
54Wis2d^{1}467
f54Wis2d^{3}762
56Wis2d^{5}733
f56Wis2d^{6}734
59Wis2d^{3}281
62Wis2d590
65Wis2d^{6}720
f66Wis2d^{5}109
f66Wis2d^{6}109

85Wis2d^{6}189
85Wis2d^{4}757
91Wis2d^{6}771
102Wis2d^3
[392
104Wis2d^1
[259
107Wis2d380
72McL733
33StnL214
71Æ^{2}449s
45Æ^{3}965n
45Æ^{3}974n
82Æ^{3}254n
82Æ^{3}277n

—591—
(182NW448)
52Wis2d^{9}391
f55Wis2d^{1}686
70Wis2d^{6}751
70Wis2d^6
[1037
82Wis2d^{6}113
83Wis2d^{9}842
118Wis2d452
126Wis2d^9
[456
18Æ^{3}497s

—612—
(182NW251)
d56Wis2d^{1}811
j60Wis2d^{1}171
76Wis2d^{1}59
f85Wis2d^{2}117
f85Wis2d^{3}117

Source: Shepard's/McGraw-Hill, Inc. © 1988

Figure 12.01. Print Version of the Wis. 2d Table from *Shepard's Wisconsin Citations* for Shepardizing 49 Wis. 2d 430

far back in time as you could in the printed citators. This won't be true, however, if the message in the coverage line begins with a supplement, as in this example:

Shepard's 1943–1986 Supplements

This message indicates that the displayed table does not contain any citing cases decided before 1943. If coverage begins with a supplement and the date of the authority you are Shepardizing is earlier than the date of that supplement, the discrepancy indicates a gap in the online Shepard's coverage; to do a complete job of Shepardizing, you will have to augment your online Shepard's search with a search in the printed citator tables not found online.

The "Coverage" line indicates the latest date of coverage by identifying the most recent Shepard's supplement available online (which in Figure 12.02 is the September 1993 supplement).[246] From

[246] Shepard's periodically updates its printed citators with separate publications called "sup-

```
              (c) 1993 McGraw-Hill, Inc. - DOCUMENT 1 (OF 1)

CITATIONS TO: 49 Wis.2d 430
SERIES: Shepard's Wisconsin Citations
DIVISION: Wisconsin Reports, 2d Series
COVERAGE: All Shepard's Citations Through 09/93 Supplement.

NUMBER  ANALYSIS                CITING REFERENCE          SYLLABUS/HEADNOTE
------ ---------------- -------------------------- -----------------
  1    parallel citation        (182 N.W.2d 539)
  2    affirmed                 406 U.S. 205
  3    affirmed                  32 L.Ed.2d 15
  4    affirmed                  92 S.Ct. 1526
  5    same case                402 U.S. 994
  6    same case                 29 L.Ed.2d 160
  7    same case                 91 S.Ct. 2173
  8                              55 Wis.2d 353                 6
  9                              63 Wis.2d 137                 4
  10   followed                  87 Wis.2d 414                 4
  11                             99 Wis.2d 550                 1
--------------------------------------------------------------------------------
To see the text of a citing case, press the citing reference NUMBER and then
the ENTER key.
For further explanation, press the H key (for HELP) and then the ENTER key.
```

Source: Mead Data Central, Inc.; © 1993 Shepard's/McGraw-Hill, Inc.

Figure 12.02. First Screen of a Typical Shepard's Table in LEXIS (Showing the Wis. 2d Table from *Shepard's Wisconsin Citations* for Shepardizing 49 Wis. 2d 430)

```
              (c) 1993 McGraw-Hill, Inc. - DOCUMENT 1 (OF 1)
                              49 Wis.2d 430

NUMBER  ANALYSIS                CITING REFERENCE          SYLLABUS/HEADNOTE
------ ---------------- -------------------------- -----------------
  12                             99 Wis.2d 551                 3
  13                            143 Wis.2d 632
  14                            145 Wis.2d 43                  1
                                    Cir. 5
  15   dissenting opinion       556 F.2d 325                   4
  16   dissenting opinion       556 F.2d 326                   2
  --                             55 N.Y.U.L.Rev. 41
  --                            120 U.Pa.L.Rev. 539
  19   annot.supp                 3 A.L.R.2d 1401

--------------------------------------------------------------------------------
To see the text of a citing case, press the citing reference NUMBER and then
the ENTER key.
For further explanation, press the H key (for HELP) and then the ENTER key.
```

Source: Mead Data Central, Inc.; © 1993 Shepard's/McGraw-Hill, Inc.

Figure 12.03. Continuation of a Typical Shepard's Table in LEXIS (Showing the Wis. 2d Table from *Shepard's Wisconsin Citations* for Shepardizing 49 Wis. 2d 430)

the date of this supplement, you know you won't find in the table any citing authorities issued more recently than that date. (Because of the lag time inherent in the editorial process that produces a Shepard's table, the most recent citing authorities will likely be a month or two earlier than the date of the most recent supplement.)

Shepard's citators in LEXIS are updated when a new printed supplement is published, so the online and printed versions of a Shepard's citator should be equally current.

The part of the citator table that follows the heading contains all the information found in printed citator tables, though in an easier-to-read form. As Figure 12.02 shows, the information consists of:

- *Citing References*—In the middle of the table, under "Citing Reference," you will find a list of citations of the authorities that have referred to the authority being Shepardized. The citations in this list contain the same elements as the citations in the corresponding printed table: volume number, the abbreviation of the publication in which the citing authority appears, and the page number on which you will find a reference to the authority you are Shepardizing. For example, from Figure 12.03, you can determine that a reference to *Yoder* occurs at 556 F.2d 325.

  Sometimes you will encounter a citing authority in a form like "dk2 86–7598." A reference like this identifies a citing case by its docket number. Dk2 86–7598, for instance, identifies the citing authority as a case from the U.S. Court of Appeals for the Second Circuit with a docket number of 86–7598. This type of citation appears when Shepard's includes a citing case in an online citator table before the case receives a citation upon being published in a case reporter.

  As you read a Shepard's table, you might also find one or more citations in parentheses at the top of the "Citing Reference" column, such as 182 N.W.2d 539 in Figure 12.02. Such a parenthetical citation is a parallel citation of the case you are Shepardizing.
- *Analysis*—To the left of the list of citing authorities, in the column labelled "Analysis," you will frequently see comments indicating how citing authorities relate to the authority being Shepardized. For example, in Figure 12.02, the notation "affirmed" on the same

---

plements." For an explanation of Shepard's supplements, see CHRISTOPHER G. WREN & JILL R. WREN, THE LEGAL RESEARCH MANUAL: A GAME PLAN FOR LEGAL RESEARCH AND ANALYSIS 98 n.36 (2d ed. 1986).

line as 406 U.S. 205 indicates that this citing authority affirmed *Yoder*.

If no analysis comment appears next to a citing authority, the authority mentioning the case being Shepardized has simply cited it for one of its legal propositions, but provided no analytical discussion.

Figure 12.04 lists and explains the analysis comments you might find in an online Shepard's table. To see a listing of the comments while using the Shepard's service, press the SEGMTS key; to resume Shepardizing after viewing the list of analysis comments, press the FULL key. The analysis comments generally track the analyses you find in printed citators, but spell out the analyses rather than use the highly abbreviated codes (such as "a," "sc," or "f") appearing in the printed citator tables.

As Figure 12.04 shows, the analysis comments indicate one of two things: (1) how the case being Shepardized was handled as it worked its way through the legal system (the history of the case); or (2) how other courts have evaluated the case in the course of deciding later cases (the treatment of the case).

In the "Analysis" column, you might also see a comment that the reference to the case you are Shepardizing appears in an *A.L.R.* or *Lawyers' Edition* annotation or annotation supplement. An example of such a comment occurs in the last line of the Shepard's table in Figure 12.03.

- *Syllabus/Headnotes*—To the right of the list of citing authorities, in the column labelled "Syllabus/Headnote," you might see a number opposite a citing authority (such as the "4" opposite 556 F.2d 325 in Figure 12.03). A number in the "Syllabus/Headnote" column refers to the headnote or syllabus paragraph having that number in the case you are Shepardizing; the number in the "Syllabus/Headnote" column indicates that the citing case refers to the cited case for the point of law summarized in that headnote or syllabus paragraph. In our example, the portion of the case you find at 556 F.2d 325 cites *Yoder* for the point of law summarized in *Yoder*'s headnote number 4 in its Wis. 2d version.[247]

[247] In using the "Syllabus/Headnote" numbers, remember that different publishers of court decisions might assign different numbers to headnote or syllabus paragraphs dealing with the same point of law. For example, headnote 9 in the Wis. 2d version of a case (which is published by Lawyers Cooperative) will almost certainly deal with a different point of law than headnote 9, if there is one, in the N.W.2d version of that case (which is published by West). Consequently, whenever you attempt to match a "Syllabus/Headnote" number with a case headnote or syllabus paragraph number, you must make sure the headnote or syllabus paragraph number you are using is from the version of the case published in the reporter identified in the "Citations To" line in the heading of the displayed table.

History Comments

a	affirmed	Same case affirmed on appeal.
cc	connected case	Different case from case cited, but arising out of the same subject matter or intimately connected therewith.
Dm	dismissed	Appeal from same case dismissed.
m	modified	Same case modified on appeal.
r	reversed	Same case reversed on appeal.
s	same case	Same case as case cited.
Su	superseded	Substitution for former opinion.
v	vacated	Same case vacated.

Treatment Comments

c	criticised	Soundness of decision or reasoning in cited case criticized for reasons given.
d	distinguished	Case at bar different either in law or fact from case cited for reasons given.
e	explained	Statement of import of decision in cited case. Not merely a restatement of the facts.
Ex	examiner's decision	Examiner's decision.
f	followed	Cited as controlling.
ha	harmonized	Apparent inconsistency explained and shown not to exist.
j	dissenting opinion	Citation in dissenting opinion.
L	limited	Refusal to extend decision of cited case beyond precise issues involved.
Lp	limited in part	Limited in part.
o	overruled	Ruling in cited case expressly overruled.
p	parallel	Citing case substantially alike or on all fours with cited case in its law or facts.
q	questioned	Soundness of decision or reasoning in cited case questioned.
Va	valid	Valid.
Vo	void	Void or invalid.
Vp	void in part	Void or invalid in part.

Source: Adapted from the online list of analysis comments in LEXIS

Figure 12.04. Shepard's Analysis Comments in LEXIS

The "Syllabus/Headnote" numbers you find in an online citator table correspond to the small superscript numbers found in citations listed in printed citator tables.[248] Particularly in tables with lengthy lists of citing authorities, "Syllabus/Headnote" numbers, like the superscript numbers in printed citator tables, can save you from reading cases citing your case for points of law that might be irrelevant to your research problem.

[248] For an explanation of using the headnote feature in printed Shepard's citators, see CHRISTOPHER G. WREN & JILL R. WREN, THE LEGAL RESEARCH MANUAL: A GAME PLAN FOR LEGAL RESEARCH AND ANALYSIS 107–08 (2d ed. 1986).

- *Number*—Each entry in this column is a number you can use (as explained at pages 417 and 419) to retrieve the text of the citing authority identified by that number. For example, at the screen in Figure 12.02, you could type **10** and press the TRANSMIT key to retrieve the text of the case that contains the reference to *Yoder* at 87 Wis. 2d 414.

Finding all the citator tables in LEXIS for a case. Shepard's publishes a citator set for each state. State citators have separate tables for the different reporters (*e.g.*, the Wisconsin reporters, the North Western reporters) in which a case appears; if a reporter has more than one series (*e.g.*, Wis., Wis. 2d), a state citator will have separate tables for each series. In addition, Shepard's publishes citators corresponding to each regional reporter published by West; if a regional reporter has more than one series (*e.g.*, N.W., N.W.2d), a regional citator will have separate tables for each series.

As with Shepardizing in printed citators, each parallel citation for a case being Shepardized online will have a separate table of authorities citing the case. Returning to the example of *Yoder*, Shepardizing 49 Wis. 2d 430 will yield a table different from those yielded by Shepardizing 182 N.W.2d 539.

Although you might think that the citations found in the table for the parallel reference would simply duplicate the ones found in the table for the principal reference, that isn't a safe assumption. In a state's case citator, Shepard's does not include (in either the tables for the state reporter or for the regional reporter) references to any citing cases decided by courts in other states. Rather, any citing references from out-of-state cases would appear only in tables found in Shepard's regional citators.

For example, suppose a judge in Connecticut referred to *Yoder* in a decision. The Connecticut case, as a case decided by a non-Wisconsin state court, would not appear as a citing reference in either the Wis. 2d table or the N.W.2d table in *Shepard's Wisconsin Citations*. The Connecticut case would appear, however, as a citing reference in *Yoder*'s table in *Shepard's North Western Citations*, the Shepard's regional citator covering *Yoder*. So, if you had Shepardized *Yoder* only in *Shepard's Wisconsin Citations*, you would have missed the citing case from Connecticut (as well as any other cases citing *Yoder* that were decided by state courts outside Wisconsin), even if you had checked the N.W.2d table in the Wisconsin citator.

In short, to be absolutely sure your Shepardizing of a case is as thorough as possible, you need to Shepardize in all tables for all principal and parallel citations.

Figures 12.02, 12.03, 12.05, and 12.06 illustrate the point. Figures 12.02 and 12.03 show the two screens of the table retrieved when *Yoder* was Shepardized using 49 Wis. 2d 430. Figures 12.05 and 12.06 show the two screens

(c) 1993 McGraw-Hill, Inc. - DOCUMENT 1 (OF 2)

CITATIONS TO: 182 N.W.2d 539
SERIES: SHEPARD'S NORTHWESTERN REPORTER CITATIONS
DIVISION: NORTHWESTERN REPORTER, 2d SERIES
COVERAGE: First Shepard's Volume Through 09/93 Supplement.

NUMBER	ANALYSIS	CITING REFERENCE	SYLLABUS/HEADNOTE
1	parallel citation	(49 Wis.2d 430)	
2	affirmed	406 U.S. 205	
3	affirmed	32 L.Ed.2d 15	
4	affirmed	92 S.Ct. 1526	
5	same case	402 U.S. 994	
6	same case	29 L.Ed.2d 160	
7	same case	91 S.Ct. 2173	
8		198 N.W.2d 680	4
9		216 N.W.2d 200	1
10	followed	275 N.W.2d 104	1
11		299 N.W.2d 898	1

To see the text of a citing case, press the citing reference NUMBER and then the ENTER key.
For further explanation, press the H key (for HELP) and then the ENTER key.

(c) 1993 McGraw-Hill, Inc. - DOCUMENT 1 (OF 2)
182 N.W.2d 539

NUMBER	ANALYSIS	CITING REFERENCE	SYLLABUS/HEADNOTE
12		422 N.W.2d 163	1
13		426 N.W.2d 337	
14	dissenting opinion	556 F.2d 325	2
		Mich	
15		396 N.W.2d 422	1
		ND	
16		294 N.W.2d 890	5
		Calif	
17		124 Cal.Rptr. 85	
		Conn	
18		289 A.2d 924	
19	annot.supp	3 A.L.R.2d 1401	

To see the text of a citing case, press the citing reference NUMBER and then the ENTER key.
For further explanation, press the H key (for HELP) and then the ENTER key.

Source: Mead Data Central, Inc.; © 1993 Shepard's/McGraw-Hill, Inc.

Figure 12.05. A Typical Shepard's Table in LEXIS (Showing the N.W.2d Table from *Shepard's Northwestern Reporter Citations* for Shepardizing 182 N.W.2d 539)

(c) 1993 McGraw-Hill, Inc. - DOCUMENT 2 (OF 2)

CITATIONS TO: 182 N.W.2d 539
SERIES: Shepard's Wisconsin Citations
DIVISION: Northwestern Reporter, 2d Series (Wisconsin Cases)
COVERAGE: All Shepard's Citations Through 09/93 Supplement.

NUMBER	ANALYSIS	CITING REFERENCE	SYLLABUS/HEADNOTE
1	parallel citation	(49 Wis.2d 430)	
2	affirmed	406 U.S. 205	
3	affirmed	32 L.Ed.2d 15	
4	affirmed	92 S.Ct. 1526	
5	same case	402 U.S. 994	
6	same case	29 L.Ed.2d 160	
7	same case	91 S.Ct. 2173	
8		198 N.W.2d 680	4
9		216 N.W.2d 200	1
10	followed	275 N.W.2d 104	1
11		299 N.W.2d 898	1

To see the text of a citing case, press the citing reference NUMBER and then the ENTER key.
For further explanation, press the H key (for HELP) and then the ENTER key.

(c) 1993 McGraw-Hill, Inc. - DOCUMENT 2 (OF 2)
182 N.W.2d 539

NUMBER	ANALYSIS	CITING REFERENCE	SYLLABUS/HEADNOTE
12		422 N.W.2d 163	1
13		426 N.W.2d 337	
		Cir. 5	
14	dissenting opinion	556 F.2d 325	2

To see the text of a citing case, press the citing reference NUMBER and then the ENTER key.
For further explanation, press the H key (for HELP) and then the ENTER key.

Source: Mead Data Central, Inc.; © 1993 Shepard's/McGraw-Hill, Inc.

Figure 12.06. A Typical Shepard's Table in LEXIS (Showing the N.W.2d Table from *Shepard's Wisconsin Citations* for Shepardizing 182 N.W.2d 539)

of each table retrieved when *Yoder* was Shepardized using 182 N.W.2d 539. If you compare the tables, you see they contain different citing authorities.

Figures 12.05 and 12.06 also highlight that even for a single citation, Shepard's might have more than one table. As you can see from the "Series" line in the headings of these figures, tables for Shepardizing 182 N.W.2d 539 appear in *Shepard's Northwestern Reporter Citations* and in *Shepard's Wisconsin Citations*. And, as you can see by comparing the tables, they contain different citing authorities.

Retrieving multiple citator tables is not a phenomenon that occurs only when you Shepardize a case that appears in both a regional reporter and an individual state reporter. For instance, if you Shepardized *Segar v. Civiletti*, 508 F. Supp. 690, 26 Empl. Prac. Dec. ¶ 31,982 (D.D.C. 1981), the computer would retrieve a table from *Shepard's Federal Citations*, a table from *Shepard's Federal Labor Law Citations (Pt. 1)*, a table from *Shepard's Federal Law in Selected Law Reviews*, and a table from *Shepard's District of Columbia Citations*.

You can even retrieve multiple citator tables for a case that has only one citation you can Shepardize. For example, Shepardizing *Fraternal Order of Police, Lodge No. 5 v. Tucker*, 868 F.2d 74 (3d Cir. 1989), would yield a table from *Shepard's Federal Citations* and a table from *Shepard's Federal Labor Law Citations (Pt. 1)*.

Thus, if you want to ensure complete Shepardizing results, you will need to Shepardize each citation for the case you want to update and then review each table retrieved.

When you Shepardize in LEXIS, you can display a list of every table you retrieve for a given citation:

1. To see the list, press the CITE key. The monitor will display the heading information from each table. For instance, if you had Shepardized *Segar v. Civiletti*, 508 F. Supp. 690, pressing the CITE key would display a list of headings like that in Figure 12.07.
2. When you finish viewing the list, press the FULL key to redisplay the citator table you were viewing when you pressed the CITE key.

Moving within a Shepard's case table in LEXIS. Once you have displayed a Shepard's table, you can page through it (if it extends across more than one screen) by using standard LEXIS techniques for moving within a document:[249]

- The NEXT PAGE (or PgDn) key will move the display forward one screen at a time. The PREV PAGE (or PgUp) key will move the display back one screen at a time.

[249] See pages 332–33 for an explanation of these techniques.

```
                    SHEPARD'S CITATIONS - 4 DOCUMENTS
                   Copyright (c) 1993 McGraw-Hill, Inc.

CITATIONS TO: 508 F.Supp. 690

 1. SERIES:    SHEPARD'S FEDERAL CITATIONS
    DIVISION:  FEDERAL SUPPLEMENT
    COVERAGE:  All Shepard's Citations Through 09/93 Supplement.

 2. SERIES:    SHEPARD'S FEDERAL LABOR LAW CITATIONS (PT.1)
    DIVISION:  FEDERAL SUPPLEMENT (Labor Cases)
    COVERAGE:  Shepard's 1987 Volumes & Supplements Through 08/93 Supplement.

 3. SERIES:    SHEPARD'S FED. LAW IN SEL. LAW REV.
    DIVISION:  FEDERAL SUPPLEMENT
    COVERAGE:  First Shepard's Volume Through 08/93 Supplement.

 4. SERIES:    SHEPARD'S DISTRICT OF COLUMBIA CITATIONS
    DIVISION:  FEDERAL SUPPLEMENT (District of Columbia Cases)
    COVERAGE:  Shepard's Citing References From 1985 Through 08/93 Supplement.
```

Source: Mead Data Central, Inc.; © 1993 Shepard's/McGraw-Hill, Inc.

Figure 12.07. Typical List of Shepard's Tables in LEXIS for a Single Citation (508 F. Supp. 690)

- Used with a number, the NEXT PAGE (or PgDn) and PREV PAGE (or PgUp) keys will skip the display forward or back more than one screen at a time.
- The FIRST PAGE key will return the display to the first screen of the table.

Currently, the ROLL UP and ROLL DOWN keys, which normally move the display one line at a time, do not function in the online Shepard's service.

If you want to find out how many screens a table covers, type p and press TRANSMIT; the monitor will display a message telling you the number of LEXIS screens the table occupies.

Customizing the display of a Shepard's case table in LEXIS. While viewing a Shepard's table (especially one containing a lengthy list of citing authorities), you might want to focus on those authorities most likely to help you evaluate the case you are Shepardizing. For example, you might concentrate on citing authorities accompanied by an analysis comment (such as "explained," "distinguished," or "overruled") or by a "Syllabus/Headnote" number identifying a headnote or syllabus paragraph that summarizes a point of law in which you are interested.[250]

[250] Although Shepard's analysis comments and references to headnote or syllabus paragraph

When you Shepardize in LEXIS, you can instruct the computer to display only those citing authorities accompanied by a specific analysis comment, by a specific "Syllabus/Headnote" number, or by both criteria. To customize the display once you have retrieved a citator table, start by pressing the SEGMTS key. The monitor will display a screen like the one shown in Figure 12.08. At that point, you can customize the display in any of these ways:

- *By analysis comment.* Type the abbreviation of each analysis comment by which you want to screen citing authorities; use a comma between abbreviations. (If you want to display citing authorities that have *any* kind of analysis comment, you can just type **any**.) Then press TRANSMIT.

  For example, to restrict the display to citing authorities that overruled or questioned the case you are Shepardizing, you would type **o,q** and press TRANSMIT.

---

numbers can prove useful as screening devices, they represent editorial judgments that might not capture the nuance of the citing reference for your purposes. To understand fully the significance a citing reference holds for your research problem, you still need to read the citing authority for yourself rather than rely on Shepard's assessment. *See* CHRISTOPHER G. WREN & JILL R. WREN, THE LEGAL RESEARCH MANUAL: A GAME PLAN FOR LEGAL RESEARCH AND ANALYSIS 109–11 (2d ed. 1986).

```
You may restrict the display to those citations that Shepard's has designated
(by editorial analysis) as dealing with the history or treatment of the cited
case, or to those which refer to a specific paragraph of a syllabus or a
headnote of the cited case.

                       EDITORIAL ANALYSIS ABBREVIATIONS
  HISTORY OF CASE            TREATMENT OF CASE        TREATMENT OF CASE

  (  parallel citation       c  criticised            o  overruled
  a  affirmed                d  distinguished         p  parallel
  cc connected case          e  explained             q  questioned
  Dm dismissed               Ex examiner's decision   Va valid
  m  modified                f  followed              Vo void
  r  reversed                ha harmonized            Vp void in part
  s  same case               j  dissenting opinion
  Su superseded              L  limited
  v  vacated                 Lp limited in part

Please enter, separated by commas, the specific history or treatment
ABBREVIATIONS (or the word ANY for citations with any editorial analysis
abbreviation -- history or treatment) and the NUMBERS of the paragraphs for the
citations you want to display.
```

Source: Mead Data Central, Inc.; © 1993 Shepard's/McGraw-Hill, Inc.

Figure 12.08. Screen for Transmitting Choices for Customizing a Shepard's Table in LEXIS

- *By headnote or syllabus paragraph number.* Type the number of each headnote or syllabus paragraph by which you want to screen citing authorities; use a comma between numbers. Then press TRANSMIT.

  For example, to restrict the display to citing authorities that addressed the legal issues summarized in headnote or syllabus paragraphs numbered 4 or 6 in the case you are Shepardizing, you would type **4,6** and press TRANSMIT.

- *By a combination of analysis comment and headnote or syllabus paragraph number.* You can combine display restrictions in a single instruction. For example, to restrict the display to citing authorities that overruled or questioned the case you are Shepardizing, or that addressed the legal issues summarized in headnote or syllabus paragraphs numbered 4 or 6 in that case, you would type **o,q,4,6** and press TRANSMIT.

Changing your display criteria. You can change your display criteria as frequently as you want when viewing a citator table. Just press the SEGMTS key again, then type and transmit your new criteria.

Shortcut: Shepardizing more than one authority according to the same display criteria. If you want to Shepardize several authorities according to the same restrictive display criteria (*e.g.*, if you want to focus only on citing authorities that have overruled or questioned the cases you are Shepardizing), you can use shortcuts that save you from typing the restrictive criteria each time you Shepardize a new authority. Figure 12.09 explains these shortcuts.

Leaving a customized Shepard's display. When you finish viewing a customized Shepard's table, you can return to the original display, showing all the citing authorities in the table. To do that, press the FULL key.

Retrieving a citing authority from a Shepard's case table in LEXIS. While viewing a Shepard's table (whether in a full or restricted display), you might decide you want to see the text of an authority listed in the table as a citing reference. When you Shepardize in LEXIS, you can instruct the computer to retrieve the text of a citing authority:

1. Type that authority's retrieval number, found in the "Number" column.

2. Press TRANSMIT.

The computer will then use the corresponding citation from the "Citing Reference" column to retrieve (through a LEXSEE search) the authority you want

To Shepardize several authorities according to the same restrictive display criteria, you can use either of these shortcuts in LEXIS to avoid typing the restrictive criteria each time you Shepardize a new authority:

The Shortcut Command

1. Shepardize your first case as you normally would.
2. Press the SEGMTS key and transmit the restrictive display criteria you want, as you normally would.
3. When you finish viewing the restricted citator table for your first case, display a restricted citator table for your next case by typing its citation followed by a semicolon, by `.se` (which substitutes for the SEGMTS key), and by two more semicolons. Then transmit the instruction, which will take this form:

   ```
   556 f2d 310;.se;;
   ```

4. For each subsequent case you want to Shepardize using the same restrictive display criteria, transmit this shortcut instruction, using the citation for each new case.

The Display Restriction Menu

If you prefer not to type the shortcut command, LEXIS offers another technique that saves you from typing the restrictive criteria each time you Shepardize a new authority:

1. Shepardize your first case as you normally would.
2. Press the SEGMTS key and transmit the restrictive display criteria you want, as you normally would.
3. When you finish viewing the restricted citator table for your first case, type the citation for the next case you want to Shepardize, and press TRANSMIT.
4. Once a Shepard's table appears, press the SEGMTS key. The monitor will display a screen similar to the one shown in Figure 12.08 on page 416. At the top of the monitor, you will see the criteria you most recently used to restrict the display of a citator table.

   Then, if you simply press TRANSMIT, the computer will automatically use those criteria again to restrict the display of the table for the case you are now Shepardizing.
5. You can repeat this procedure for each subsequent case you want to Shepardize using the same restrictive display criteria.

Figure 12.09. Shortcuts for Restricting the Display of More Than One Shepard's Table in LEXIS

to view.[251] The monitor will display the citing authority in the KWIC format, highlighting the first reference to the authority you are Shepardizing. If you want to see the full text of the citing authority you retrieved, press the FULL key.

Retrieving a citing authority this way does not cause you to lose the citator table you had just been viewing, though the table disappears from sight while the monitor displays the text of the citing authority you selected. To switch from the text of this citing authority back to the citator table:

1. Type `resume shep` (or `res shep`).

2. Press TRANSMIT.

Once back at the table, if you want to select another citing authority to view, transmit its retrieval number. (If you want to select the same citing authority again, you can transmit `resume lexsee` (or `res lexsee`) instead of the retrieval number.)

For instance, if you were viewing the citator table shown in Figure 12.02 on page 407 and wanted to see the text of the U.S. Supreme Court case that affirms *Yoder* at 406 U.S. 205, you would type `2` and press TRANSMIT. The monitor would display the text of the Supreme Court's decision. To redisplay the citator table, you would type `resume shep` (or `res shep`) and press TRANSMIT. After redisplaying the citator table, you could view the text of 406 U.S. 205 again by transmitting `resume lexsee` (or `res lexsee`), or you could view the text of a different citing authority by transmitting its retrieval number.

Note that when you use a retrieval number to display a citing authority, you can, in turn, Shepardize that authority by transmitting `shep` (or `sh`) while viewing it.

Moving between Shepard's case tables in LEXIS. When a Shepard's search retrieves more than one citator table for a single citation (as occurred, for example, in Shepardizing the N.W.2d citation for *Yoder*),[252] LEXIS treats each table as a separate document. A message at the top of the monitor indicates how many tables were retrieved and which is being displayed; typical

[251] For a refresher on LEXSEE, see pages 238–43. Note that if the citing authority is not available in LEXIS or is not retrievable through LEXSEE, a retrieval number will not appear in the "Number" column, and this retrieval technique will not work.

In some situations, using a retrieval number might retrieve more than one authority. If the citing authority you want to retrieve has the same citation as another authority (as can occur, for example, when more than one short memorandum opinion appears on the same page of a case reporter), transmitting the retrieval number for your citing authority will retrieve not only your authority, but any other authority having the same citation.

[252] See page 414.

messages appear in Figure 12.05 on page 412 ("DOCUMENT 1 (OF 2)") and Figure 12.06 on page 413 ("DOCUMENT 2 (OF 2)").

You can move from one table to another by using standard LEXIS techniques for moving between documents:[253]

- The NEXT DOC and PREV DOC keys will move the display forward or back one table.
- Used with a number, the NEXT DOC and PREV DOC keys will skip the display forward or back more than one table at a time.
- The FIRST DOC key will return the display to the first screen of the first table.

Printing Shepard's case tables in LEXIS. You can print your Shepardizing results by using standard LEXIS printing techniques:[254]

- To print the screen you are viewing, press the key labelled PRINT SCREEN or PRINT.
- If you are working on a computer that has a disk for storing information, you can automatically print each screen as it displays. To do so, invoke "session recording" by holding down the ALT key and pressing the F2 key. Then identify the recording session by typing `LPT1` or `LPT2` to designate your printer's port, and press TRANSMIT.[255] When you want to turn off automatic printing of displayed screens, use the same keys you used to invoke the feature: hold down ALT and press F2 again.
- To print every table retrieved by a Shepard's search, press the key labelled PRINT ALL or MAIL IT. Then press the key for the format (FULL, SEGMTS, or CITE) in which you want the tables printed. Pressing FULL will yield a complete printout of each table; pressing SEGMTS will yield a printout of each table, abridged to show just the citing authorities that satisfy the restrictive criteria you indicate; pressing CITE will yield a list of the heading information from all the tables retrieved.

Note that you currently cannot print an individual citator table by using the PRINT DOC key, which normally allows you to print individual documents.

Downloading Shepard's case results in LEXIS. If you are using a computer with a storage disk, you can save ("download") your Shepardizing results to the disk, using standard LEXIS techniques for downloading:[256]

[253] See pages 334–36 for an explanation of these techniques.

[254] See pages 340–46 for an explanation of these techniques.

[255] The user manuals for your computer's hardware and software will indicate which printer port you should designate for this purpose.

[256] See pages 346–47 for an explanation of these techniques.

- When you are viewing a screen of a Shepard's table, you can download that screen, as well as subsequent individual screens as you display them, by using "session recording." To invoke session recording, hold down the ALT key and press the F2 key; press the same keys again to turn off the feature.
- You can also download all the tables retrieved by a Shepard's request. Press the PRINT ALL or MAIL IT key and follow the on-screen instructions for saving documents to disk. When you log off, follow the on-screen instructions for saving documents to disk. Downloading will occur after you log off.

Note that you currently cannot download an individual citator table by using the PRINT DOC key, which normally allows you to download individual documents.

Pausing during a Shepard's session in LEXIS to use LEXSEE, LEXSTAT, or Auto-Cite. During a Shepard's search session, you can retrieve a document by using LEXSEE or LEXSTAT, or you can implement an updating search in Auto-Cite.[257] To do so, simply follow the instructions for commencing a LEXSEE, LEXSTAT, or Auto-Cite search. To return to the Shepard's service from the service you invoked, type `resume shep` (or `res shep`) and press TRANSMIT.

Ending a Shepard's session in LEXIS. When you have Shepardized all the authorities you want, you end your Shepard's session either by pressing the EXIT SERV key or by typing `resume` (or `res`) and pressing TRANSMIT.

Pressing EXIT SERV will take you out of Shepard's (and out of any other service you might also have used) and return you to wherever you had been in LEXIS when you invoked a service.

Depending on the sequence of your research activities, transmitting `resume` (or `res`) will cause the computer either (1) to return you to your most recent research activity or (2) to present you with the "Resume Options" screen, where you can select from a list of your previous research activities the one to which you want to return. For example, suppose you had begun your online session by using a Boolean search to retrieve a case and then used Shepard's to update that case. Transmitting `resume` (or `res`) while viewing the Shepard's results would take you back to the case. On the other hand, if you had used a Boolean search to retrieve the case and then used two or more services before invoking Shepard's, transmitting `resume` (or `res`) while viewing your Shepard's result would produce the Resume Options screen.

Alternatively, if you invoked the Shepard's service while using the LEXSEE, LEXSTAT, or Auto-Cite service, you could resume using the other

[257] LEXSEE is explained at pages 238–43, LEXSTAT is explained at pages 243–44, and Auto-Cite is explained at pages 422 and 426–37.

service by transmitting `resume` (or `res`) followed by the name of the service to which you want to return—*e.g.*, `resume lexsee`, `resume lexstat`, `resume ac`.

Summary of Shepardizing a case through LEXIS. Figure 12.10 summarizes the steps and commands for using the Shepard's service in LEXIS.

Shepardizing other authorities through LEXIS

Currently, you cannot Shepardize online all the types of authorities (such as municipal ordinances) you can update through the printed citators.[258] Additional Shepard's citators will likely appear in LEXIS in the future, however. When they do, Mead Data Central will announce the availability of the new citators, which will almost certainly operate along the lines of the citators now online.

Using Auto-Cite in LEXIS to verify an authority's citation and status

Auto-Cite is a "citation verification service" available through LEXIS.[259] By transmitting a citation for a case, for an annotation in *American Law Reports* or *Lawyers' Edition 2d*, or for certain types of Internal Revenue Service documents, you can retrieve a report that indicates, among other things, the status of the case or other document. Auto-Cite is only available online; it does not have a printed counterpart.

The Auto-Cite report. You can display an Auto-Cite report in two presentation formats: outline or paragraph. Figure 12.11 on page 428 and Figure 12.12 on page 429 show the first two screens of a typical Auto-Cite report. Figure 12.11 shows in outline format the report for *State v. Yoder*, 49 Wis. 2d 430, 182 N.W.2d 539 (1971), and Figure 12.12 shows the same report in paragraph format. As the figures show, an Auto-Cite report provides the following information about a case.

A report begins with what Auto-Cite calls a *citation clause*, which you can use to double-check the accuracy of a case citation. For example, the citation clause in Figures 12.11 and 12.12 reads as follows:

State v. Yoder*1, 49 Wis. 2d 430, 182 N.W.2d 539 (1971)

(As explained below, the "*1" in this citation is a footnote linking *Wisconsin v. Yoder* with an annotation referring to the case.)

[258] For a list of authorities you can Shepardize in printed citators, see CHRISTOPHER G. WREN & JILL R. WREN, THE LEGAL RESEARCH MANUAL: A GAME PLAN FOR LEGAL RESEARCH AND ANALYSIS 96 n.34 (2d ed. 1986).

[259] WESTLAW offers a similar service, known as "Insta-Cite." See pages 544 and 552–64.

If you want to	Follow this procedure in LEXIS
Shepardize the authority you are viewing	type `shep` (or `sh`) and press TRANSMIT
Shepardize an authority you are not viewing	type `shep` (or `sh`) followed by a space and the authority's citation; then press TRANSMIT *Example:* `sh 49 wis.2d 430` *or* press the SELECT SERV key and follow the on-screen instructions
Shepardize an authority identified by a LINK marker, such as <=4>	type `shep` (or `sh`) followed by an equal sign and the number in the LINK marker appearing in front of the citation you want to Shepardize; then press TRANSMIT *Example:* `sh =4` *or* type `shep` (or `sh`) and press TAB to position the cursor under the desired LINK marker; then press TRANSMIT
Page through a citator table	press the NEXT PAGE, PREV PAGE, or FIRST PAGE key
Find out how many screens a table covers	type `p` and press TRANSMIT
Customize the display of a citator table	press the SEGMTS key and follow the on-screen instructions for transmitting your restrictive criteria (analysis comment, headnote or syllabus paragraph number, or a combination of these) *Example:* `o,q,4,6`

(continues)

Figure 12.10. Quick Guide to Shepardizing Cases through LEXIS

(continued)

If you want to	Follow this procedure in LEXIS
Display a list of citator tables retrieved for a citation	press the CITE key
Redisplay a complete citator table after displaying a customized table or a list of citator tables	press the FULL key
Retrieve the text of a citing authority from a citator table	type that authority's retrieval number, found in the "Number" column; then press TRANSMIT
Return to a citator table from the text of a citing authority	type `resume sh` (or `res sh`) and press TRANSMIT
Move between citator tables when Shepard's retrieves more than one table	press the NEXT DOC, PREV DOC, or FIRST DOC key
Print the screen you are viewing in a citator table	press the PRINT SCREEN or PRINT key
*Automatically print each screen as it displays	invoke "session recording" by holding down the ALT key and pressing the F2 key; then identify the recording session by typing **LPT1** or **LPT2** and pressing TRANSMIT to designate your printer's port
*Turn off automatic printing of displayed screens	hold down the ALT key and press the F2 key
Print every table retrieved by a Shepard's search	press the PRINT ALL or MAIL IT key and follow the on-screen instructions
*Automatically download each screen as it displays	invoke "session recording" by holding down the ALT key and pressing the F2 key

*Turn off automatic downloading of displayed screens	hold down the ALT key and press the F2 key
*Download every table retrieved by a Shepard's search	press the PRINT ALL or MAIL IT key and follow the on-screen instructions; when you log off, follow the on-screen instructions for saving documents to disk
Invoke another service during a Shepard's session	type a LEXSEE, LEXSTAT, or Auto-Cite request; then press TRANSMIT
Switch from the other service back to Shepard's	type `resume sh` (or `res sh`) and press TRANSMIT
End a Shepard's session	type `resume` (or `res`) and press TRANSMIT

End a Shepard's session and return to a specified service you have used	type `resume` (or `res`) and the name of the service; then press TRANSMIT
	Examples: `res lexsee`
	`res lexstat`
	`res ac`

End a Shepard's session and return to LEXIS	press the EXIT SERV key *or* type `resume lexis` (or `res lexis`); then press TRANSMIT
View an online list of publication abbreviations that work in a Shepard's request	type `h` while using Shepard's and press TRANSMIT; then follow the on-screen instructions
Find online help	type `h` while using Shepard's and press TRANSMIT; then follow the on-screen instructions

* This function is available only on a computer with a disk for storing information.

Figure 12.10. Quick Guide to Shepardizing Cases through LEXIS (continued)

Thus, a citation clause consists of:

- Case name
- Official or preferred citation for the case
- Parallel citations (if any) for the case
- Year of decision
- Court that decided the case—This information is omitted when the court's identity is apparent from the name of the reporter in the official or preferred citation. For example, the court is omitted from the Auto-Cite reports for *Yoder* because volume 49 of *Wisconsin Reports 2d* contains cases from only the Wisconsin Supreme Court. When the name of the reporter does not make clear which court decided the case, the Auto-Cite report includes the court's identity in the parenthetical with the year of decision. For instance, a citation clause for a case published in *Federal Supplement* would provide a parenthetical reference to the court because *Federal Supplement* contains cases from more than one U.S. District Court.

After the citation clause, the next portion of an Auto-Cite report contains information that updates the case. Updating information, which Auto-Cite refers to as *case status verification*, consists of:

- *Subsequent appellate history*—citations of subsequent appeals (if any) in the case, and the results of these appeals (*e.g.*, affirmed, reversed). Subsequent appellate history also encompasses any cases that have affected the precedential value of the decisions in those subsequent appeals.

  In the Auto-Cite reports for *Yoder*, the subsequent appellate history begins with a citation to the appeal from the Wisconsin Supreme Court's decision in *State v. Yoder*:

  > aff'd, Wisconsin v. Yoder*2, 406 U.S. 205,
  > 32 L. Ed. 2d 15, 92 S. Ct. 1526 (1972)

  (As explained below, the "*2" in this citation is a footnote linking *Wisconsin v. Yoder* with an annotation referring to the case.) The subsequent appellate history continues with citations to other cases the Auto-Cite editors believe have affected the precedential value of the U.S. Supreme Court's decision in *Wisconsin v. Yoder*:

  > (not followed by Madyun v. Franzen*3, 704
  > F.2d 954, 31 Fair Empl. Prac. Cas. (BNA) 817,
  > 31 Empl. Prac. Dec. (CCH) P 33576 (7th Cir.
  > Ill. 1983)

cert. denied, Madyun v. Franzen, 464 U.S. 996, 78 L. Ed. 2d 687, 104 S. Ct. 493, 33 Fair Empl. Prac. Cas. (BNA) 440, 32 Empl. Prac. Dec. (CCH) P 33926 (1983))

and (among conflicting authorities noted in Azeez v. Fairman, 795 F.2d 1296 (7th Cir. Ill. 1986))

- *Subsequent treatment history*—citations of other authorities (if any) that differ with or cast doubt on the validity of the case you are updating, and brief phrases describing how these later authorities have affected your case (*e.g.*, overruled, disapproved, diverged from, not followed, disagreed with, superseded by statute). These other authorities are not part of the direct appellate chain. They affect the precedential value of the case you are updating, *not* the precedential value of any decisions in appeals from that case; cases affecting decisions in appeals are identified under the "subsequent appellate history" section of the Auto-Cite report. The report for *Yoder* does not include any subsequent treatment history.

Through Auto-Cite's online "help" feature, you can view a listing of the Auto-Cite phrases for subsequent appellate and treatment histories and the definitions for those phrases: while using Auto-Cite, type h and press TRANSMIT; then follow the on-screen instructions.[260] An online list of the Auto-Cite phrases also appears in the ACGUID file in the GUIDE library. (For an explanation of GUIDE, see Appendix A.)

The final part of an Auto-Cite report contains additional information, referred to as *citation research* and consisting of:

- *Prior history*—citations of earlier decisions (if any) in the case, and the relationship of these decisions to the case in which you are interested. For example, the Auto-Cite report for *Segar v. Smith*, 738 F.2d 1249 (D.C. Cir. 1984), which is the appeal of *Segar v. Civiletti*, 508 F. Supp. 690 (D.D.C. 1981), includes the following prior history:

[260] Although an Auto-Cite report serves a valuable function by identifying other authorities that might have negatively affected the significance of the authority you are updating, the report reflects editorial judgments that might not capture for your purposes the nuances of the later authorities. To understand fully what an authority mentioned in an Auto-Cite report means for your research problem, you still need to read that authority for yourself.

```
Auto-Cite (R) Citation Service, (c) 1993 Lawyers Cooperative Publishing

49 WIS2D 430:                                         Screen 1 of 5

CITATION YOU ENTERED:

State v. Yoder*1, 49 Wis. 2d 430, 182 N.W.2d 539 (1971)

SUBSEQUENT APPELLATE HISTORY:

    aff'd, Wisconsin v. Yoder*2, 406 U.S. 205, 32 L. Ed. 2d 15, 92 S.
    Ct. 1526 (1972)

        (not followed by Madyun v. Franzen*3, 704 F.2d 954, 31 Fair Empl. Prac.
        Cas. (BNA) 817, 31 Empl. Prac. Dec. (CCH) P 33576 (7th Cir. Ill. 1983)

            cert. denied, Madyun v. Franzen, 464 U.S. 996, 78 L. Ed. 2d 687,
            104 S. Ct. 493, 33 Fair Empl. Prac. Cas. (BNA) 440, 32 Empl. Prac.
-------------------------------------------------------------------------------
Alternate presentation formats are available.
For further explanation, press the H key (for HELP) and then the TRANSMIT key.
To return to LEXIS, press the EXIT SERV key.  To resume prior citation research,
transmit RESUME followed by the service name (SHEPARDS).
```

```
49 WIS2D 430:                                         Screen 2 of 5

            Dec. (CCH) P 33926 (1983))

        and (among conflicting authorities noted in Azeez v. Fairman, 795 F.2d
        1296 (7th Cir. Ill. 1986))

ANNOTATIONS CITING THE CASE(S) INDICATED ABOVE WITH ASTERISK(S):

*1  Religious beliefs of parents as defense to prosecution for failure to
    comply with compulsory education law, 3 A.L.R.2d 1401, supp.

*2  Validity of state or local government regulation requiring private school
    to report attendance and similar information to government--post-Yoder
    cases, 8 A.L.R.5th 875, secs. 1-3.

    Criminal responsibility of parent for act of child, 12 A.L.R.4th 673, sec.
    9.

    Conditions at school as excusing or justifying nonattendance, 9 A.L.R.4th
    122, sec. 8.
-------------------------------------------------------------------------------
To return to LEXIS, press the EXIT SERV key.
```

Source: Mead Data Central, Inc.; © 1993 Lawyers Cooperative Publishing

Figure 12.11. First Two Screens of a Typical Auto-Cite Report in LEXIS in Outline Format (Reporting on *State v. Yoder*, 49 Wis. 2d 430, 182 N.W.2d 539)

```
Auto-Cite (R) Citation Service, (c) 1993 Lawyers Cooperative Publishing

49 WIS2D 430:                                            Screen 1 of 5

State v Yoder*1, 49 Wis 2d 430, 182 NW2d 539 (1971), affd Wisconsin v
Yoder*2, 406 US 205, 32 L Ed 2d 15, 92 S Ct 1526 (1972) (not followed by Madyun
v Franzen*3, 704 F2d 954, 31 BNA FEP Cas 817, 31 CCH EPD P 33576 (CA7 Ill
1983), cert den Madyun v Franzen, 464 US 996, 78 L Ed 2d 687, 104 S Ct 493, 33
BNA FEP Cas 440, 32 CCH EPD P 33926 (1983)) and (among conflicting authorities
noted in Azeez v Fairman, 795 F2d 1296 (CA7 Ill 1986))
  NO PRIOR HISTORY CITED

Annotations citing the case(s) indicated above with asterisk(s):

*1  Religious beliefs of parents as defense to prosecution for failure to
    comply with compulsory education law, 3 ALR2d 1401, supp.

*2  Validity of state or local government regulation requiring private school
------------------------------------------------------------------------------
Alternate presentation formats are available.
For further explanation, press the H key (for HELP) and then the TRANSMIT key.
To return to LEXIS, press the EXIT SERV key.  To resume prior citation research,
transmit RESUME followed by the service name (SHEPARDS).
```

```
49 WIS2D 430:                                            Screen 2 of 5

    to report attendance and similar information to government--post-Yoder
    cases, 8 ALR5th 875, secs. 1-3.

    Criminal responsibility of parent for act of child, 12 ALR4th 673, sec. 9.

    Conditions at school as excusing or justifying nonattendance, 9 ALR4th 122,
    sec. 8.

    What constitutes a private, parochial, or denominational school within
    statute making attendance at such school a compliance with compulsory
    school attendance law, 65 ALR3d 1222, sec. 9.

    Power of court or other public agency to order medical treatment over
    parental religious objections for child whose life is not immediately
    endangered, 52 ALR3d 1118.

    Religious beliefs of parents as defense to prosecution for failure to
    comply with compulsory education law, 3 ALR2d 1401, supp.

------------------------------------------------------------------------------
To return to LEXIS, press the EXIT SERV key.
```

Source: Mead Data Central, Inc.; © 1993 Lawyers Cooperative Publishing

Figure 12.12. First Two Screens of a Typical Auto-Cite Report in LEXIS in Paragraph Format (Reporting on *State v. Yoder*, 49 Wis. 2d 430, 182 N.W.2d 539)

PRIOR HISTORY:

Segar v. Civiletti, 508 F. Supp. 690, 25 Fair Empl. Prac. Cas. (BNA) 1452, 26 Empl. Prac. Dec. (CCH) P 31982 (D.D.C. 1981)

later proceeding, Segar v. Civiletti, 516 F. Supp. 314, 32 Fair Empl. Prac. Cas. (BNA) 1308, 26 Empl. Prac. Dec. (CCH) P 31806 (D.D.C. 1981)

and supplemental op., Segar v. Smith, 28 Fair Empl. Prac. Cas. (BNA) 935, 28 Empl. Prac. Dec. (CCH) P 32588 (D.D.C. 1982)

and aff'd in part and vacated in part, (BY CITATION YOU ENTERED)

- *Negative references*—citations of other cases (if any) to which your case makes express negative reference. For example, the Auto-Cite report for *Segar v. Smith*, 738 F.2d 1249 (D.C. Cir. 1984), includes the following:

CITATION YOU ENTERED MAKES NEGATIVE REFERENCE TO:

Rivera v. Wichita Falls, 665 F.2d 531, 27 Fair Empl. Prac. Cas. (BNA) 1352, 28 Empl. Prac. Dec. (CCH) P 32413 (5th Cir. Tex. 1982)

Pouncy v. Prudential Ins. Co., 668 F.2d 795, 28 Fair Empl. Prac. Cas. (BNA) 121, 28 Empl. Prac. Dec. (CCH) P 32451 (5th Cir. Tex. 1982)

- *Annotations*—citations of any *American Law Reports* or *Lawyers' Edition 2d* annotations that cite or analyze cases listed in other parts of an Auto-Cite report (except those listed in the "negative reference" section of the report). These annotations might lead you to helpful analyses of issues relevant to your research problem, as well as to other relevant authorities.

Auto-Cite uses asterisked numbers as footnotes to link cases with the annotations that have cited or analyzed them. For instance, in the Auto-Cite report for *Yoder*, you see "*1" in the citation to *State v. Yoder*, and "*2" in the citation to *Wisconsin v. Yoder*. Below, in the annotations section of the report, you see these asterisked numbers again: there, under "*1," you find an annotation

(3 A.L.R.2d 1401) that cites or analyzes *State v. Yoder*; under "*2," you find several annotations (*e.g.*, 8 A.L.R.5th 875 and 12 A.L.R.4th 673) that cite or analyze *Wisconsin v. Yoder*.

The following explanation takes you through the steps in using Auto-Cite. Figure 12.13 on pages 438–40 summarizes the explanation.

Gaining access to Auto-Cite in LEXIS. You can initiate an Auto-Cite search at nearly any time after logging on to LEXIS. You can begin using Auto-Cite as soon as the monitor displays the library menu; you do not need to select a library or file before carrying out an Auto-Cite search. Or, you can wait until you have retrieved some documents from a file before you begin using Auto-Cite.

To retrieve an Auto-Cite report, you use a search request based on the citation of the authority you want to update:

- If you are viewing the authority you want to update, simply type `ac` and press TRANSMIT. The LEXIS computer will automatically "read in" to the search request the citation of your authority. (You can also transmit `ac` while you are viewing a Shepard's table for the authority you are updating. If you do, the computer will automatically read in to your Auto-Cite request the citation used for your Shepard's search.)

  Suppose you are viewing a case that has been reprinted in more than one reporter, and which therefore has parallel citations. As with Shepardizing through LEXIS, the technique you used to retrieve the case will determine which citation the computer will use in the Auto-Cite search.[261] Unlike Shepard's, however, Auto-Cite does not produce different results depending on the citation used in the search instruction; if a case has more than one citation, Auto-Cite produces the same report for each parallel citation.
- If you want to retrieve an Auto-Cite report for an authority you are *not* viewing—say, a case you see mentioned in another case you are looking at online—you have two choices. To use the quicker method, type `ac` followed by a space and the citation of the authority you want to update; then press TRANSMIT.

  For the citation of a case or annotation, type the volume number and abbreviation of the publication in which the authority appears and the page number on which the authority begins. For instance, to retrieve the Auto-Cite report for *State v. Yoder*, 49 Wis. 2d 430, 182 N.W.2d 539 (1971), you could use any of the following requests:

[261] See pages 402–03.

```
ac 49 wis.2d 430
ac 49 wis2d 430
ac 49 wis. 2d 430
ac 182 n.w.2d 539
ac 182 nw2d 539
```

Similarly, to retrieve the Auto-Cite report for an annotation, you could type your request in any of these forms:

```
ac 12 a.l.r.4th 673
ac 12 alr4th 673
ac 12 a l r 4th 673
ac 66 l ed 2d 970
ac 66 l.ed2d 970
```

Some case reporters (such as the looseleaf services published by Commerce Clearing House) use years instead of volume numbers, and paragraph numbers instead of page numbers. Simply substitute those numbers in the Auto-Cite request. For example, to retrieve an Auto-Cite report for a case published at paragraph 15,846 in the 1978 volume of CCH's *National Labor Relations Board*, your request could read:

```
ac 1978 cchnlrb 15846
```

You can also use a LEXIS Cite to retrieve an Auto-Cite report.[262] Your request would take this form:

```
ac 1988 us lexis 2474
```

For Revenue Procedures and Revenue Rulings issued by the Internal Revenue Service, a different citation format (based on document numbers) applies to Auto-Cite requests, as these examples show:

```
ac revproc 85-47
ac rev proc 85-47
ac rp 85-47
ac revrul 83-137
ac rev rul 83-137
ac rev. rul. 83-137
```

An Auto-Cite request for an Internal Revenue Service document can also use a citation to the *Cumulative Bulletin* or the *Internal Revenue Bulletin*, using the conventional format for case reporters:

[262] LEXIS Cites are explained in Figure 10.02 on pages 239–40.

```
ac 1983-2 cb 41
ac 1983-2 cum. bull. 41
ac 1985-37 irb 10
ac 1985-37 intrevbull 10
```

As all these examples indicate, you have some flexibility in how you type an abbreviation in an Auto-Cite request, but you must leave a space on each side of the abbreviation and you must include any hyphens that are part of the citation. If you are uncertain about how to type an abbreviation, you can consult the LEXIS reference manual, which provides a list of abbreviations that will work in an Auto-Cite request.[263] You can also find a list of these abbreviations through the online "help" feature available when you use Auto-Cite: type `h` and press TRANSMIT; then follow the on-screen instructions. In addition, an online list of the abbreviations appears in the ACGUID file in the GUIDE library. (For an explanation of GUIDE, see Appendix A.)

To use the second (and less direct) method of retrieving an Auto-Cite report for an authority you are not viewing, press the key labelled SELECT SERV. The monitor will display a list of services available in LEXIS, as shown in Figure 10.03 on page 241. To select the Auto-Cite service from the list, type `ac` and press TRANSMIT. A screen will then appear on which you can type the citation of the authority you want to update; to complete your Auto-Cite request, type your citation and press TRANSMIT.

- If you are viewing an authority and see the citation of a case you want to update through Auto-Cite, you can use the LINK feature (explained on page 244) to automate the use of Auto-Cite for updating that citation. To use LINK, type `ac` followed by an equal sign and the number in the LINK marker preceding the citation for which you want to retrieve an Auto-Cite report, then press TRANSMIT. For example, transmit

```
ac =4
```

The computer will read in to your Auto-Cite request the citation associated with the LINK marker you selected.

- When you transmit an Auto-Cite request, you can specify the presentation format in which you want the computer to display the report. If you want to see the report in outline format (as in Figure

[263] MEAD DATA CENTRAL, REFERENCE MANUAL FOR THE LEXIS/NEXIS SERVICES (undated looseleaf ed.) (Appendix G).

12.11 on page 428), use `aco` in your Auto-Cite request instead of `ac`. To see the report in paragraph format (as in Figure 12.12 on page 429), use `acp`. Thus, if you transmitted `acp` while viewing an authority, the computer would display that authority's Auto-Cite report in paragraph format. Likewise, transmitting `acp` along with an authority's citation (*e.g.*, `acp 384 us 436`) would display that authority's Auto-Cite report in paragraph format.

If you use `ac` in your Auto-Cite request instead of specifying a presentation format, the computer will display the report in the most recent presentation format you requested during your online session. If you have not previously specified a format, the computer will display the report in the outline format.

Once you have entered the Auto-Cite service by transmitting an Auto-Cite request, you can retrieve Auto-Cite reports for as many authorities as you want during the Auto-Cite search session. You do not have to type `ac`, `aco`, or `acp` each time; just type and transmit a new citation when you want a report on another authority.

Moving within an Auto-Cite report in LEXIS. After you transmit an Auto-Cite request, the monitor displays the report for the citation you transmitted. You can page through the report (if it extends across more than one screen) by using standard LEXIS techniques for moving within a document:[264]

- The NEXT PAGE (or PgDn) key will move the display forward one screen at a time. The PREV PAGE (or PgUp) key will move the display back one screen at a time.
- Used with a number, the NEXT PAGE (or PgDn) and PREV PAGE (or PgUp) keys will skip the display forward or back more than one screen at a time.
- The FIRST PAGE key will return the display to the first screen of the table.

Currently, the ROLL UP and ROLL DOWN keys, which normally move the display one line at a time, do not function in the Auto-Cite service.

Retrieving an authority mentioned in an Auto-Cite report in LEXIS. If you decide while viewing an Auto-Cite report that you want to see the text of an authority listed in the report, you can instruct the computer to retrieve the authority's text:

1. Type a LEXSEE command.[265]

[264] See pages 332–33 for an explanation of these techniques.
[265] LEXSEE is explained at pages 238–43.

2. Press TRANSMIT.

The monitor will then display the authority you requested.

Retrieving an authority this way does not cause you to lose the Auto-Cite report you had just been viewing, though the report disappears from sight while the monitor displays the text of the authority you retrieved. To switch from the text of the authority back to the Auto-Cite report:

1. Type `resume ac` (or `res ac`).
2. Press TRANSMIT.

Once back at the report, if you want to select another authority to view, transmit another LEXSEE command. (If you want to select the same authority again, you can transmit `resume lexsee` or `res lexsee` instead.)

For instance, if you were viewing the Auto-Cite report shown in Figure 12.11 (on page 428) or 12.12 (on page 429) and wanted to see the text of the U.S. Supreme Court case that affirms *Yoder* at 406 U.S. 205, you could type `lexsee 406 us 205` and press TRANSMIT. The monitor would display the text of the Supreme Court's decision. To redisplay the Auto-Cite report, you would type `resume ac` (or `res ac`) and press TRANSMIT. After redisplaying the Auto-Cite report, you could view the text of 406 U.S. 205 again by transmitting `resume lexsee` (or `res lexsee`), or you could transmit a new LEXSEE command to view the text of a different authority mentioned in the report.

Note that when you retrieve an authority mentioned in an Auto-Cite report, you can, in turn, update that authority through Auto-Cite by typing `ac` and pressing TRANSMIT while viewing the authority.

Printing an Auto-Cite report in LEXIS. You can print an Auto-Cite report by using standard LEXIS techniques for printing:[266]

- To print the screen you are viewing, press the key labelled PRINT SCREEN or PRINT.
- If you are working on a computer that has a disk for storing information, you can automatically print each screen of an Auto-Cite report as it displays. To do so, invoke "session recording" by holding down the ALT key and pressing the F2 key; then identify the recording session by typing `LPT1` or `LPT2` to designate your printer's port and press TRANSMIT.[267]

  When you want to turn off automatic printing of displayed screens, use the same keys you used to invoke the feature: hold down ALT and press F2 again.

[266] See pages 340–46 for an explanation of these techniques.

[267] The user manuals for your computer's hardware and software will indicate which printer port you should designate for this purpose.

- To print the entire Auto-Cite report you are viewing, press the key labelled PRINT DOC. After you log off, the report will print in the display format (outline or paragraph) in effect when you pressed PRINT DOC.

Downloading an Auto-Cite report in LEXIS. If you are using a computer with a storage disk, you can save ("download") an Auto-Cite report to the disk, using standard LEXIS techniques for downloading:[268]

- When you are viewing a screen of an Auto-Cite report, you can download that screen, as well as subsequent individual screens as you display them, by using "session recording." To invoke session recording, hold down the ALT key and press the F2 key; press the same keys again to turn off the feature.
- You can also download an entire Auto-Cite report by pressing the PRINT DOC key. After you log off, the report will download in the display format (outline or paragraph) in effect when you pressed PRINT DOC.

Pausing during an Auto-Cite session to use LEXSEE, LEXSTAT, or Shepard's. During an Auto-Cite session, you can retrieve a document by using LEXSEE or LEXSTAT, or you can Shepardize an authority.[269] To do so, simply follow the instructions for commencing a LEXSEE, LEXSTAT, or Shepard's search. To return to the Auto-Cite service from the service you invoked, type `resume ac` (or `res ac`) and press TRANSMIT.

Ending an Auto-Cite session in LEXIS. When you have retrieved all the Auto-Cite reports you want, you end your Auto-Cite session either by pressing the EXIT SERV key or by typing `resume` (or `res`) and pressing TRANSMIT.

Pressing EXIT SERV will take you out of Auto-Cite (and out of any other service you might also have used) and return you to wherever you had been in LEXIS when you invoked a service.

Depending on the sequence of your research activities, transmitting `resume` (or `res`) will cause the computer either (1) to return you to your most recent research activity or (2) to present you with the "Resume Options" screen, where you can select from a list of your previous research activities the one to which you want to return. For example, suppose you had begun your online session by using a Boolean search to retrieve a case and then used Auto-Cite to update that case. Transmitting `resume` (or `res`) while viewing the Auto-Cite report would take you back to the case. On the other hand, if

[268] See pages 346–47 for an explanation of these techniques.

[269] LEXSEE is explained at pages 238–43, LEXSTAT is explained at pages 243–44, and Shepard's is explained at pages 400–22.

you had used a Boolean search to retrieve the case and then used two or more services before invoking Auto-Cite, transmitting `resume` (or `res`) while viewing the Auto-Cite report would produce the Resume Options screen.

Alternatively, if you invoked the Auto-Cite service while using the LEXSEE, LEXSTAT, or Shepard's service, you could resume using the other service by transmitting `resume` (or `res`) followed by the name of the service to which you want to return—*e.g.*, `resume lexsee`, `resume lexstat`, `resume shep`.

The role of Auto-Cite in updating in LEXIS. As you can see from this explanation of Auto-Cite and the previous section's explanation of Shepardizing online, Auto-Cite and Shepard's citators overlap as updating tools. (For updating purposes, Auto-Cite also overlaps with using LEXIS as a citator, a technique explained in the next section.) Despite their similar functions, however, you can obtain different results by using each of these techniques to update authorities.

Both Auto-Cite and Shepard's afford access to other authorities that have cited the authority you are updating. But where Shepard's provides comprehensive listings of citing authorities (no matter how routine the reason for the citing reference), Auto-Cite provides selective listings, focusing on authorities that have negatively affected the precedential value of the authority being updated. Even with a selective focus, however, the reach of an Auto-Cite report can extend beyond that of a Shepard's table: an Auto-Cite report might link a later authority with the one being updated even though the later authority does not expressly mention the earlier one and therefore does not appear in a Shepard's table.

For example, suppose *Case 1* has been effectively overruled by *Case 2* without the second case specifically mentioning the first case. If *Case 3* identifies *Case 2* as overruling *Case 1*, Auto-Cite editors are expected to spot the relationship, and the Auto-Cite report for *Case 1* should therefore identify *Case 2* as having overruled it. With Shepard's, however, because *Case 2* did not expressly mention *Case 1*, the Shepard's table will not identify *Case 2*.

In short, Auto-Cite and Shepard's complement each other. Each can give you updating results not obtained through the other, as shown by comparing the Shepard's and Auto-Cite results for *State v. Yoder*, 49 Wis. 2d 430. For example, the Shepard's table in Figures 12.02 and 12.03 on page 407 identifies some cases and law review articles not included in the Auto-Cite report for *Yoder* (Figure 12.11 or 12.12 on pages 428 and 429); conversely, the Auto-Cite report identifies some cases and *A.L.R.* annotations not included in the Shepard's table. If you want to ensure thorough updating in LEXIS, you'll need to use both Shepard's and Auto-Cite.

Summary of using Auto-Cite in LEXIS. Figure 12.13 summarizes the steps and commands for using the Auto-Cite service in LEXIS.

If you want to	Follow this procedure in LEXIS
Retrieve an Auto-Cite report for the authority you are viewing	type `ac` and press TRANSMIT
Retrieve an Auto-Cite report for an authority you are not viewing	type `ac` followed by a space and the authority's citation; then press TRANSMIT *Example:* `ac 49 wis.2d 430` *or* press the SELECT SERV key and follow the on-screen instructions
Retrieve an Auto-Cite report for an authority identified by a LINK marker, such as <=4>	type `ac` followed by an equal sign and the number in the LINK marker appearing in front of the authority for which you want to retrieve an Auto-Cite report; then press TRANSMIT *Example:* `ac =4` *or* type `ac` and press TAB to position the cursor under the desired LINK marker; then press TRANSMIT
Page through an Auto-Cite report	press the NEXT PAGE, PREV PAGE, or FIRST PAGE key
Retrieve the text of an authority mentioned in an Auto-Cite report	type a LEXSEE request; then press TRANSMIT
Return to an Auto-Cite report from the text of a retrieved authority	type `resume ac` (or `res ac`) and press TRANSMIT

Print the screen you are viewing	press the PRINT SCREEN or PRINT key
*Automatically print each screen as it displays	invoke "session recording" by holding down the ALT key and pressing the F2 key; then identify the recording session by typing LPT1 or LPT2 and pressing TRANSMIT to designate your printer's port
*Turn off automatic printing of displayed screens	hold down the ALT key and press the F2 key
Print the entire Auto-Cite report you are viewing	press the PRINT DOC key and follow the on-screen instructions
*Automatically download each screen as it displays	invoke "session recording" by holding down the ALT key and pressing the F2 key
*Turn off automatic downloading of displayed screens	hold down the ALT key and press the F2 key
Download the entire Auto-Cite report you are viewing	press the PRINT DOC key and follow the on-screen instructions; when you log off, follow the on-screen instructions for saving documents to disk
Invoke another service during an Auto-Cite session	type a LEXSEE, LEXSTAT, or Shepard's request; then press TRANSMIT

(continues)

* This function is available only on a computer with a disk for storing information.

Figure 12.13. Quick Guide to Auto-Cite in LEXIS

(continued)

If you want to	Follow this procedure in LEXIS
Switch from the other service back to Auto-Cite	type `resume ac` (or `res ac`) and press TRANSMIT
End an Auto-Cite session	type `resume` (or `res`) and press TRANSMIT

End an Auto-Cite session and return to a specified service you have used	type `resume` (or `res`) and the name of the service; then press TRANSMIT
	Examples: `res lexsee`
	`res lexstat`
	`res shep`

End an Auto-Cite session and return to LEXIS	press the EXIT SERV key *or* type `resume lexis` (or `res lexis`); then press TRANSMIT
View an online list of publication abbreviations that work in an Auto-Cite request	type `h` while using Auto-Cite and press TRANSMIT; then follow the on-screen instructions
Find online help	type `h` while using Auto-Cite and press TRANSMIT; then follow the on-screen instructions

Figure 12.13. Quick Guide to Auto-Cite in LEXIS (continued)

Using LEXIS as a citator[270]

Introduction. When you update authorities through LEXIS, you can take advantage of the computer's full-text searching capability and search the text of online documents for citations to the authorities in whose status you are interested. Generally characterized as using LEXIS as a citator, this method of locating later references to an authority involves using an ordinary Boolean search request in which at least some of the search terms reflect citation information about the authority you want to update.

To use this technique:

1. Formulate a search request based on the various citation forms you think have been used in later documents to refer to the authority you are updating.
2. Select a file containing the type of authorities (*e.g.*, federal cases, state cases, or law reviews) in which you want to search for citations to the authority you are updating.
3. Transmit your search request in that file, and scan the results to see how the later authorities deal with the authority you are updating. Using the KWIC display format (explained on pages 319–20) will help you scan faster.
4. If you have retrieved a significant percentage of documents that do not refer to the authority you are updating, or if you suspect you have bypassed pertinent documents, you can modify your search request and try again.

As this summary implies, using LEXIS as a citator is really nothing more than routine full-text searching. Thus, you apply the same principles and techniques earlier chapters present for formulating and modifying Boolean search requests and for reading search results.

Using LEXIS as a citator has some advantages over using Shepard's citators or Auto-Cite. First, this technique usually yields more comprehensive updating results than using Shepard's citators or Auto-Cite. Using LEXIS as a citator, you can update *any* authority: by typing in citation information, you can direct the computer to search for references to all kinds of authorities, including those (such as treatises or legal encyclopedias) you cannot update through Shepard's or Auto-Cite. Moreover, these updating references will sometimes appear in authorities (such as unpublished opinions) that Shepard's and Auto-Cite do not cover. And, using the LEXIS-as-citator technique, you

[270] LEXIS also offers LEXCITE, which automates the process of using LEXIS as a citator in some situations. See pages 461–66 for an explanation of LEXCITE.

might even capture references, if any, that have slipped by the editors who prepare the Shepard's tables or Auto-Cite reports.

In addition, you will usually obtain more current references than you can find through either Shepard's or Auto-Cite. Often, documents containing references to an authority you want to update will have been issued and added to the LEXIS database more recently than the most recent update of the pertinent Shepard's tables or Auto-Cite report.

Along with comprehensiveness, a second advantage of using LEXIS as a citator stems from the ability to modify your search request to link citation information with additional search terms. In this way, you can zero in on updating authorities that deal with particular facts or legal issues, or that satisfy some other criteria (such as having been decided by a certain judge or issued after a certain date). For instance, in connection with a research problem concerning the right of prisoners to practice their religion while incarcerated, suppose you were updating *Wisconsin v. Yoder*, a frequently cited Supreme Court case about freedom of religion. By adding appropriate search terms (*e.g.*, `prison**`, `inmate`) to your search request, you could focus your LEXIS updating search on authorities that cite *Yoder* in the context of similar facts.

Using LEXIS as a citator has some drawbacks, however. You confront the same challenges you face whenever you use a search request to search the text of authorities—contending with the computer's literalness, minimizing ambiguity in search terms, coping with nondistinctive search terms, and so on.[271] Consequently, you can bypass relevant updating authorities by failing to anticipate all the ways in which authors of later authorities might have written a citation to the authority you are updating. Similarly, you can bypass a relevant authority if its only citation to your authority contains a typographical error, as sometimes happens.

When you use LEXIS as a citator, you can also retrieve many documents you do *not* want—documents that have nothing to do with the authority you are updating. For example, using a search request like `state w/5 smith` to search for later citations to *State v. Smith* will likely turn up references to a large number of unrelated cases with that caption. By contrast, all the later references you locate through Shepard's or Auto-Cite will cite or deal with the authority in whose status you are interested.

The trick, then, is to strike a balance between the benefits and drawbacks of using LEXIS as a citator. As with formulating search requests for other purposes, no ironclad rules exist that guarantee success. The guidelines in the following paragraphs, however, can help you achieve the necessary balance.

Using LEXIS as a citator to search for references to cases. In anticipating the ways in which later authorities might have cited a case you are updating, you can take one of several approaches:

[271] See Chapter 7 for a discussion of formulating search requests.

- search for references to the case name, such as *Lewis v. United States* (see this page through page 445)
- search for references to the case citation, such as 445 U.S. 55 (see pages 445–48)
- search for references to either the case name *or* case citation (see page 448)
- search for references to both the case name *and* case citation (see pages 448–49)
- link other search terms with the citation information (see pages 449–50)

Searching for references to the case name. Because citations to a case will almost certainly include its name, you can locate references to the case you are updating if you search for occurrences of the case name in the text of other authorities. But your search request should not use the case name in a standard citation format—*e.g.*, "City of Phoenix v. Tanner." References to a given case often appear in a variety of formats. For instance, searching for "City of Phoenix v. Tanner" would not locate references citing the case as *Phoenix v. Tanner*. Similarly, one document might cite a case as *In the Matter of Application of Winn*, but another document might cite it as *In re Winn*.

In light of the potential variations on case names, you need to search for a name with an instruction that can accommodate different citation forms. As a general matter, you will want to use the "w/n" connector with a few key words from the case name. So, to search for references to *City of Phoenix v. Tanner*, your search request could read

```
phoenix w/5 tanner
```

The value you select for the "w/n" connector will depend on how far apart you anticipate the key words will appear. For example, in referring to a case normally cited as *United Public Employees, Local 390/400 v. City and County of San Francisco*, a judge might write the case name in its lengthier form, *United Public Employees, Local 390/400, SEIU, AFL-CIO, et al. v. City and County of San Francisco, et al.* The search request `("united public employees") w/5 ("san francisco")` would bypass this reference; here, "w/12" would be a better choice.

Usually, a value from 5 to 10 in the "w/n" connector will suffice, although potentially lengthy variations on a case name will indicate the need for a larger value. You can do a couple of things to anticipate whether an "n" value will likely be high enough to retrieve as many variations on your case name as possible, yet low enough to minimize retrieving documents in which the search terms occur dispersed and do not represent the name of your case. First, you can check the case caption (either in a printed case reporter or online) to be sure that, say, *Potts v. Smith* is not actually *Potts, Administrator de bonis non of May, to the Use of Wollerton v. Smith.* Second, you can select a fairly high "n" value, such as 15, for your first search and use smaller "n" values in succeeding search requests until you are satisfied with the results.

Regardless of the "n" value you select, however, you should expect to retrieve some documents that do not contain any references to the case you are updating. For example, using the search request

```
lewis w/5 ("united states" or "u. s." or u.s.)
```

to search the OMNI file in the STATES library for references to *Lewis v. United States*, 445 U.S. 55, will retrieve documents that do not cite the case but that contain one of these phrases:

> . . . and Mr. Alston C. **Lewis**. The **United States** Geological Survey maintained recording devices . . . .

> . . . the court relied upon the notable **United States** Supreme Court decisions of **Lewis** v. City of New Orleans . . . .

> . . . **United States** v. Alfred M. **Lewis**, Inc. . . .

> . . . the Constitution of the **United States**, including the Amendments thereto." (Missouri v. **Lewis** . . . .

Indeed, when performed during the preparation of this book, this search retrieved 2,447 cases. A sampling of 50 of those cases yielded only 4 that cited *Lewis v. United States*, 445 U.S. 55.

When searching for references to a case name, you should generally avoid using the "pre/n" connector, at least in your initial search request. As a case moves through the courts, the order of the parties' names can change; *Smith v. Jones* might become *Jones v. Smith* on appeal. In addition, writers occasionally reverse party names by mistake, inadvertently turning *ABC Co. v. XYZ Corp.* into *XYZ Corp. v. ABC Co.* If you had used the "pre/n" connector (which requires search terms to appear in a specified order), you would have missed some references in these situations.

Normally, though, citations to the case you are updating will have the parties' names in the order you expect. So, if you find the "w/n" connector retrieves an unmanageable number of documents having nothing to do with the case you are updating, you might want to try using the "pre/n" connector to focus the search on references to your case.

Regardless of the connector you use, your results might include documents retrieved because your search terms appear as, say, the names of lawyers in the case, not as party names. If so, you can add a restriction to confine your search to the "opinions" segment, where your search terms will more likely occur as part of a case name.[272]

In some instances, you can skip a connector altogether. If a case name includes an uncommon word, that word alone might suffice as the search request. Thus, if you wanted to locate references to *State v. Ziegenhagen*, simply transmitting `ziegenhagen` would likely locate references to that case and to little or nothing else.

Conversely, a case name—such as *Smith v. Brown* or *In re Jones*—might not include any distinctive words. Some party names—such as United States, Commissioner, State, People, or Commonwealth—recur frequently enough that you will probably encounter problems using them in an approach that relies on searching for references to only the name of a case. In these situations, to find references to the case you want without also finding an unwieldy number of unrelated references, you can take a different approach: try searching for references to the case citation (see below); try using the "and" connector to link party names with a corresponding citation (see pages 448–49); or try adding search terms reflecting relevant facts or issues (see pages 449–50).

Finally, keep in mind that a case name might change throughout the course of litigation. Parties might be added or dropped, or only some of the parties might be involved in an appeal. For example, *Segar v. Civiletti* became *Segar v. Smith* when the case moved to the United States Court of Appeals, and became *Meese v. Segar* in the United States Supreme Court. If you want to find references to decisions issued at each stage of the case you are updating, your search request will need to reflect any changes that have occurred in the case name. Thus, to find references to the various decisions in *Segar*, your search request could take this form:

```
segar w/5 (civiletti or smith or meese)
```

To determine whether a case name has changed, you can update the case through Auto-Cite (discussed on pages 422 and 426–37).

Searching for references to the case citation. You can use LEXIS to update a case by searching for references to its citation (*e.g.*, 725 F. Supp. 1407) in the text of other authorities. But, as with searching for references to a case name, your search request needs to accommodate variations in the way the case citation might appear.

Suppose you wanted to update *Lewis v. United States*, 445 U.S. 55. One writer might cite the case as "445 U.S. 55," another as "445 U.S. Reports 55," yet another as "445 U.S. Rep. 55." Likewise, a citation to a case reported in *Federal Supplement* might appear as "F. Supp.," "F.Supp.," or "Fed. Supp."

[272] See Chapter 5 for a discussion of field-restricted searching.

You can work around possible variations in references to a case reporter by omitting the name or abbreviation of the reporter from your search request and using just the volume and page numbers linked by the "pre/n" connector. So, to search for references to *In re Grand Jury Subpoena Duces Tecum Issued to Richard M. Nixon*, 360 F. Supp. 1 (D.D.C. 1973), you could use a search request like this:

```
360 pre/3 1
```

Because the order of the numbers is important, and because virtually every citation to a given case will put the volume number before the page number, the "pre/n" connector will normally prove more effective than the "w/n" connector.

Usually, a value from 2 to 6 in the "pre/n" connector will retrieve the references you want. The value you choose will depend on the number of words you might find in the name of the reporter. For example, if you were searching for references to a case reported in volume 13 of *Louisiana Reports* at page 512, the search request **13 pre/3 512** would locate references written as 13 La. 512 or 13 La. Rep. 512. For references to a case reported in volume 81 of *Maryland Appellate Reports* at page 527, you could use **81 pre/5 527**. And for references to a case reported in volume 21 of *Federal Rules Service 2d* at page 211, you could use **21 pre/6 211**.

As you consider the number of words a reporter name might contain, remember that spacing within a reporter abbreviation affects the number of words the LEXIS computer perceives. For instance, the author of an online document might have written the abbreviation for *New York Supplement, Second Series* as "N.Y.S.2d" (one word), as "N.Y.S. 2d" (two words), as "N.Y. Supp. 2d" (three words), or as "N. Y. S. 2d" (four words).

If the case you are updating has parallel citations, include in your search request any parallel citations you anticipate an author might have cited. Thus, to update *Lewis v. United States*, 445 U.S. 55, 100 S. Ct. 915, 63 L. Ed. 2d 198, 48 U.S.L.W. 4205, your search request could take this form to enhance comprehensiveness:

```
(445 pre/5 55) or (100 pre/5 915) or
(63 pre/5 198) or (48 pre/5 4205)
```

As this example indicates, you should keep looseleaf reporters (such as *United States Law Week*) in mind as parallel citations that might appear in documents that cite the case you are updating. For instance, *Missouri v. National Organization of Women*, 620 F.2d 1301 (8th Cir. 1980), identifies *Lewis* by its *United States Law Week* citation only.[273]

[273] Although not the case with *United States Law Week*, citations to some looseleaf reporters

Similarly, you might want to include a parallel citation based on a LEXIS or WESTLAW cite, on a docket number (to catch references to a case when it was available only as a slip opinion, before its publication in a case reporter), or on a citation to a legal newspaper (such as *New York Law Journal*), which might be the first publication to report a case. Thus, you could extend the comprehensiveness of your search for references to *Lewis* by anticipating slip-opinion citations based on its docket number (78–1595):

```
(445 pre/5 55) or (100 pre/5 915) or
(63 pre/5 198) or (48 pre/5 4205) or ("78-1595")
```

When you rely on a case citation in using LEXIS as a citator, you will often retrieve a substantial percentage of documents in which the references to the numbers in your search request have nothing to do with the citation to the case you are updating. The numbers might not even be part of a citation at all: for instance, using the search request **52 pre/5 31** to search the OMNI file in the STATES library for references to the U.S. Supreme Court case reported at 52 L. Ed. 2d 31 will retrieve a document that does not cite the case but that contains the phrase "Highway 105 South to Shelby County Highway **52** on Lee Street, thence Highway **31** South to Alabaster."

More often, though, the numbers in unrelated documents will refer to a citation, but for a different authority. For example, in updating *Lewis v. United States*, 445 U.S. 55, 100 S. Ct. 915, 63 L. Ed. 2d 198, 48 U.S.L.W. 4205, the search request

```
(445 pre/5 55) or (100 pre/5 915) or
(63 pre/5 198) or (48 pre/5 4205)
```

in the OMNI file in the STATES library will retrieve documents that contain these configurations of search terms:

> . . . Ex parte McDanal, 32 Ala.App. **445**, 27 So.2d 504; **55** C.J.S. Mandamus @ 272; . . .
>
> . . . Ingels v. Boteler, 9 Cir., **100** Fed. (2d) **915**.

---

use paragraph numbers rather than page numbers and include paragraph symbols or commas in these numbers. Because punctuation marks and symbols, such as "¶," affect how the computer perceives a number, your search request will sometimes need to include alternative formulations of a number (*e.g.*, ¶10,475 or 10475). Appendix G contains a summary of the rules governing how the LEXIS computer interprets punctuation marks and other symbols in connection with numbers.

To find out which looseleaf services number by paragraphs rather than pages, check THE BLUEBOOK: A UNIFORM SYSTEM OF CITATION Table T.16.

. . . C.I.T. Corp. v. Breckenridge (1944), **63** Cal.App.2d **198** . . . .

. . . Wigmore, Evidence @ **63**, at **198** . . . .

In fact, when performed during the preparation of this book, this search retrieved 396 cases. A sampling of 50 of those cases yielded only 14 that cited *Lewis.*

If searching for references to a case citation retrieves a high percentage of unrelated references, you can try searching for the citation in a standard citation format—*e.g.*, `("445 U.S. 55") or ("100 S. Ct. 915") or ("63 L. Ed. 2d 198") or ("48 U.S.L.W. 4205")`. Of course, when you do not allow for variations in the name of the reporter, you can bypass many references to the case you are updating. A better solution uses the "and" connector to link the citation with the name of the case (as explained below) or with search terms reflecting relevant facts or issues (as explained at pages 449–50).

Searching for references to either the case name or case citation. You can combine the two previous approaches in a single search request that looks for references to *either* the case name *or* the case citation. Thus, to update *Lewis v. United States*, 445 U.S. 55, 100 S. Ct. 915, 63 L. Ed. 2d 198, 48 U.S.L.W. 4205, your search request could take this form:

```
(lewis w/5 ("united states" or "u. s." or
u.s.)) or (445 pre/5 55) or (100 pre/5 915) or
(63 pre/5 198) or (48 pre/5 4205)
```

Using the "or" connector to link a case name with a case citation yields highly comprehensive results because the search request accommodates the largest number of possible variations in references to the case you are updating. For instance, when performed during the preparation of this book, the illustrative search request retrieved 2,763 cases in the OMNI file in the STATES library.

But with this approach, you will also get more unrelated references: by searching simultaneously for references to either the name or the citation for a case, you retrieve a combination of the unrelated references obtained when you search for each of these references separately. Thus, you increase the size of the collection from which you must cull the references to the case you are updating. For example, a sampling of 50 of the 2,763 cases retrieved by the illustrative search request yielded only 4 that cited *Lewis.*

Searching for references to both the case name and case citation. Instead of searching for documents that refer to either the name or citation information for a case, you can use the "and" connector to search for documents that refer to *both* the name *and* the case citation. Thus, to update *Lewis v. United States,*

445 U.S. 55, 100 S. Ct. 915, 63 L. Ed. 2d 198, 48 U.S.L.W. 4205, your search request could take this form:

```
(lewis w/5 ("united states" or "u. s." or
u.s.)) and ((445 pre/5 55) or (100 pre/5 915)
or (63 pre/5 198) or (48 pre/5 4205))
```

This approach rests on the assumption that any worthwhile updating reference will likely include both the name and citation of a case, especially if the reference involves an analysis that significantly affects the precedential value of the case being updated. This approach also assumes that if a document satisfies both the name component of the search request and the citation component, the document probably contains a reference to the case you are updating. Because the document must satisfy two criteria instead of one, the search request is less apt to retrieve unrelated documents. For instance, when performed during the preparation of this book, the illustrative search request retrieved 80 cases in the OMNI file in the STATES library, and all of the cases referred to *Lewis*.

Adding other search terms. With any of the previous approaches, you can add one or more search terms to the citation information to increase the likelihood of retrieving helpful references to the case you are updating. For instance, *Lewis v. United States*, 445 U.S. 55, 100 S. Ct. 915, 63 L. Ed. 2d 198, 48 U.S.L.W. 4205, addresses several issues, including: (1) whether someone being prosecuted for unlawful possession of a firearm by a felon can defend on the ground that the underlying felony conviction was invalid; and (2) for what purposes, if any, the government may use a felony conviction obtained against a defendant who did not have assistance of counsel. If you were just interested in uncounseled convictions and therefore wanted to update *Lewis* only with respect to the second issue, you could focus your search by adding appropriate search terms, as in these examples:

```
((445 pre/5 55) or (100 pre/5 915) or (63 pre/5
198) or (48 pre/5 4205)) and ((assist! w/3
counsel) or (uncounsel! w/3 convict***))
```

```
lewis and ((445 pre/5 55) or (100 pre/5 915) or
(63 pre/5 198) or (48 pre/5 4205)) and
((assist! w/3 counsel) or (uncounsel! w/3
convict***))
```

The search terms you link with your citation information can also include field restrictions limiting the search to updating references in, for instance, cases decided by a particular court or written by a particular judge.

If you have retrieved a large collection of updating references, you might want to add a date restriction to limit your search to recent authorities, on the assumption that these authorities will likely mention earlier authorities that have significantly affected the precedential value of the case you are updating. Your search request could take this form:

```
((445 pre/5 55) or (100 pre/5 915) or (63 pre/5
198) or (48 pre/5 4205)) and ((assist! w/3
counsel) or (uncounsel! w/3 convict***)) and
date aft 12-31-89
```

You can also use a date restriction to screen out documents issued before the decision date of the case you are updating; by definition, those documents cannot provide updating references to your case.[274] For an illustration of the effect of using a date restriction this way, see Figure 12.14 on pages 452–53. The figure shows the results of several paired searches for *Lewis v. United States*, one search without a date restriction and the other with a restriction based on the date of the *Lewis* decision (February 27, 1980).

Selecting an approach. When you use LEXIS as a citator to update cases, which of the preceding approaches will work best will depend on a variety of factors. For example, your choice of an approach might depend on whether the name of the case you are updating includes frequently occurring words, such as "Smith"; as search terms, such words will probably retrieve many authorities unrelated to your case. Or, the case you are updating might have several parallel citations; a search request based only on those citations could retrieve many authorities with references unrelated to the volume and page numbers for your case.

Although each research problem presents its own challenges, you can make certain choices that will usually enhance the effectiveness of using LEXIS as a citator. If your case includes at least one distinctive party name (*e.g.*, Ziegenhagen), a case-name search will often prove a productive way to start. (Even if the case name consists only of common words, such as "Smith" or "Commissioner," you still might want to start with a search request based solely on party names simply as a way of scoping out the number of authorities from which you will need to extract the references to the case you are updating.)

As a practical matter, you will also find that searching for both the case name and citation in a single search request proves effective. Although searching for either the name or citation can create problems (because you might retrieve an unmanageable number of unrelated authorities), searching simultaneously for *both* components maximizes the chance retrieved documents will refer to your case.

[274] But see note 240 on page 401 for a rare example to the contrary.

Regardless of the approach you use, combining citation information with other search terms (*e.g.*, a date restriction, or words reflecting relevant facts or issues) can help focus your search on relevant updating references, especially if earlier searches turned up unwieldy numbers of authorities.

Figure 12.14 suggests the kind of results you might obtain with the various approaches available when you use LEXIS as a citator to update cases. As you gain experience using LEXIS as a citator, you will develop a feel for the approaches that will work best for the cases you need to update.

Using LEXIS as a citator to search for references to statutes, administrative regulations, and constitutional provisions. As with cases, you can use LEXIS as a citator to update statutes, administrative regulations, and constitutional provisions. By updating these authorities, you discover how they have been treated by courts, legislatures, administrative agencies, and other participants in the legal system—for example, whether a statute has been amended or repealed by a legislature or interpreted by a court, whether a regulation has been judicially declared unconstitutional, or whether a constitutional provision has been analyzed in a law review article, Attorney General Opinion, or other source.

The technique for locating references to statutory-type authorities parallels the technique for locating references to cases:

1. Formulate a search request that includes citation information about the authority you want to update.

   Unlike a case citation, however, the citation information will usually consist exclusively of numbers. Even if a statutory-type authority has a name attached to it, authors citing the authority will often omit the name. For example, EPA Effluent Limitations Guidelines, 40 C.F.R. § 405.52 (1982) might be cited simply as 40 C.F.R. § 405.52 (1982).

2. Select a file containing the type of authorities (*e.g.*, federal cases, state cases, or law reviews) in which you want to search for citations to the authority you are updating.

3. Transmit your search request in that file, and scan the results to see how the later authorities deal with the authority you are updating. Using the KWIC display format (explained on pages 319–20) will help you scan faster.

4. If you have retrieved a significant percentage of documents that do not refer to the authority you are updating, or if you suspect you have bypassed pertinent documents, you can modify your search request and try again.

Approach	Sample Search Requests in LEXIS	Number of Documents Retrieved	Of First 50 Documents, Number With References to Case Being Updated	Of First 50 Documents, Percent With References to Case Being Updated
Case name	`lewis`	100,980	0	0%
With date restriction	`lewis and date aft 2/26/1980`	30,835	0	0%
Case name	`lewis w/5 "united states"`	1,232	7	14%
With date restriction	`(lewis w/5 "united states") and date aft 2/26/1980`	597	13	26%
Case name	`lewis w/5 ("united states" or u.s. or "u. s.")`	2,447	4	8%
With date restriction	`lewis w/5 ("united states" or u.s. or "u. s.") and date aft 2/26/1980`	971	7	14%
Case citation	`(445 pre/5 55) or (100 pre/5 915) or (63 pre/5 198) or (48 pre/5 4205)`	396	14	28%
With date restriction	`(445 pre/5 55) or (100 pre/5 915) or (63 pre/5 198) or (48 pre/5 4205) and date aft 2/26/1980`	178	23	46%
Case name or case citation	`(lewis w/5 ("united states" or u.s. or "u. s.")) or (445 pre/5 55) or (100 pre/5 915) or (63 pre/5 198) or (48 pre/5 4205)`	2,763	4	8%
With date restriction	`(lewis w/5 ("united states" or u.s. or "u. s.")) or (445 pre/5 55) or (100 pre/5 915) or (63 pre/5 198) or (48 pre/5 4205) and date aft 2/26/1980`	1,069	7	14%

Case name and case citation	(lewis w/5 ("united states" or u.s. or "u. s.")) and ((445 pre/5 55) or (100 pre/5 915) or (63 pre/5 198) or (48 pre/5 4205))	80	50	100%
With date restriction	(lewis w/5 ("united states" or u.s. or "u. s.")) and ((445 pre/5 55) or (100 pre/5 915) or (63 pre/5 198) or (48 pre/5 4205)) and date aft 2/26/1980	80	50	100%
Case citation and additional search terms	((445 pre/5 55) or (100 pre/5 915) or (63 pre/5 198) or (48 pre/5 4205)) and ((assist! w/3 counsel) or (uncounsel! w/3 convict***))	68	35	70%
With date restriction	((445 pre/5 55) or (100 pre/5 915) or (63 pre/5 198) or (48 pre/5 4205)) and ((assist! w/3 counsel) or (uncounsel! w/3 convict***)) and date aft 2/26/1980	51	47	94%
Case name and citation and additional search terms	lewis and ((445 pre/5 55) or (100 pre/5 915) or (63 pre/5 198) or (48 pre/5 4205)) and ((assist! w/3 counsel) or (uncounsel! w/3 convict***))	52	48	96%
With date restriction	lewis and ((445 pre/5 55) or (100 pre/5 915) or (63 pre/5 198) or (48 pre/5 4205)) and ((assist! w/3 counsel) or (uncounsel! w/3 convict***)) and date aft 2/26/1980	48	48	100%

Figure 12.14. LEXIS as Citator: Results of Searching in STATES Library, OMNI File for References to *Lewis v. United States*, 445 U.S. 55, 100 S. Ct. 915, 63 L. Ed. 2d 198, 48 U.S.L.W. 4205 (decided Feb. 27, 1980)

Citation form for statutory-type authorities. To use LEXIS to locate references to statutory-type authorities, you need to consider the standard citation forms, which vary from one jurisdiction to another, as these examples indicate:[275]

STATUTES

Statutory codes

29 U.S.C. § 1001 (1976)
Ala. Code § 1-1-1 (1980)
Del. Code Tit. 18, § 2720 (1987)
Fla. Stat. § 159.27 (1988)
N.Y. Civ. Rights Law § 8 (McKinney 1989)

Session laws

Employee Retirement Income Security Act of 1974, Pub. L. No. 93–406, 88 Stat. 829 (1974)
1989 Kan. Sess. Laws ch. 8
1988 Neb. Laws, L.B. 1054
1988 Va. Acts ch. 866

ADMINISTRATIVE REGULATIONS

Administrative codes

EPA Effluent Limitations Guidelines, 40 C.F.R. § 405.52 (1982)
902 Ky. Admin. Regs. 20:010
Mass. Admin. Code tit. 106, § 456.701
N.H. Code Admin. R. He-P 1901.04(e)
Tenn. Comp. R. & Regs. 0560-3-4-.05
Wis. Admin. Code § Ag 125.08 (Feb. 1987)

Administrative registers

47 Fed. Reg. 40,443 (1982)
Cal. Reg. Notice Reg. 84, No. 23
2 Okla. Reg. 02111 (1985)

CONSTITUTIONAL PROVISIONS

U.S. Const. art. III, § 2, cl. 3
U.S. Const. amend. XIV, § 1
Pa. Const. art. 5, § 9
Ind. Const. amend. 12

[275] For more details about citation form for statutory-type authorities, see THE BLUEBOOK: A UNIFORM SYSTEM OF CITATION 73–88, 90–93, 98, 165–218 (15th ed. 1991).

How the LEXIS computer treats symbols in numbers. As in the examples above, numbers in citations to statutes, regulations, or constitutional provisions sometimes contain punctuation marks or other symbols (*e.g.*, section symbols, hyphens, periods). In searching for such numbers in the text of documents, you need to consider how the computer will interpret symbols that might appear with the numbers. For instance, is "§1983" (without a space) equivalent to "§ 1983" (with a space)? Or do you need to include each version in your search request? Similarly, does the computer interpret the decimal point in "405.52" as marking the end of one search term and the beginning of a new one, so that the computer perceives "405" and "52" as separate search terms?

Appendix G explains the rules by which the LEXIS computer interprets punctuation marks and other symbols. Those rules form the basis for the following discussion.

Formulating your search request. When you use LEXIS as a citator to update a statute, regulation, or constitutional provision, your search request needs to accommodate various ways in which later authorities might have referred to the authority you are updating. For example, one authority might refer to "42 U.S.C. § 1983," another might refer to "42 U.S.C.A. §1983," another to "42 U.S. Code Ann. § 1983," and yet another to "section 1983 in the United States Code Annotated, Title 42."

To minimize the problem created by the variety of ways of identifying the publications in which statutory-type authorities appear, you will generally find it most effective to create a search request that includes pertinent numbers (*e.g.*, title number, section number) but omits the name or abbreviation of the publication. For instance, to search for references to 42 U.S.C. § 1983, your search request could take this form:

```
42 w/6 (§1983 or 1983)
```

In searching for statutory-type citations that include more than one number (such as 42 U.S.C. § 1983), using the "w/n" connector to link the numbers offers an advantage over the "pre/n" connector. Standard citation format specifies a particular order for the elements of citations to statutory-type authorities.[276] But references to these authorities often appear with the elements in a nonstandard order, as when a writer refers to "section 1983 in the United States Code Annotated, Title 42." The "w/n" connector, unlike the "pre/n" connector, will capture references in either standard or nonstandard order.[277]

[276] *See* THE BLUEBOOK: A UNIFORM SYSTEM OF CITATION Rules 11–14 (15th ed. 1991).

[277] You might also use a "w/n" connector to link a section number with a reference to a specific subsection. For instance, a writer could refer to "subsection b of section 12" instead of to "section 12(b)." The following search request would retrieve both of these references, along with references to "12b":

```
(12 w/3 b) or 12b
```

Of course, the greater flexibility of this search request also increases the likelihood of retrieving more references that have nothing to do with the subsection you are updating.

When you use the "w/n" connector to link a section number with a title or article number, an "n" value between 5 and 10 will usually suffice; the LEXIS reference manual recommends 10 as the "n" value.[278] The larger value accommodates greater variation in citation format, but the larger value can also retrieve more authorities in which the numbers do not refer to the authority you are updating. If you are unsure what "n" value to select, you might find it helpful to check *The Bluebook: A Uniform System of Citation*, which indicates standard formats for citing statutory-type authorities. Knowing the standard citation format for a specific authority can help you anticipate likely variations and, consequently, likely distances between the numbers you are looking for. As you consider what "n" value to use, remember that variations in spacing within a publication's abbreviation affect the number of words the computer perceives: for example, the computer sees "U.S.C." as one word and "U. S. C." as three words.

By omitting the name or abbreviation of the publication from your search request, you solve some retrieval problems. But you also need to consider the best way to use the remaining numbers in your search request; in the documents you are searching, these numbers might appear in a variety of configurations.

For example, suppose you want to find cases referring to section 302 in the federal copyright statute (Title 17 in the *United States Code*). If you used the search request `17 w/10 (§302 or 302)` in the COURTS file in the GENFED library, you would retrieve a large percentage of the references you want. But you would bypass a case like *Hasbro Bradley, Inc. v. Sparkle Toys, Inc.*, 780 F.2d 189 (2d Cir. 1985), in which the judge started his opinion by citing all of Title 17 (writing "17 U.S.C. § 101 et seq.") and then, in the remainder of the opinion, cited specific sections of the copyright statute (including section 302) without repeating the Title number.

In other instances, common citation practice might omit a standard citation element altogether. For instance, citations to the Internal Revenue Code, which appears in Title 26 of the *United States Code*, frequently omit any reference to Title 26; thus, instead of "26 U.S.C. § 61," a citation might read "I.R.C. § 61." If you search for the *United States Code* title number in citations to the Internal Revenue Code, you will likely bypass many relevant documents. As this example suggests, searching for references to statutes and similar authorities involves knowing which authorities are commonly cited in a nonstandard format.

Given the range of possible variations on citations to statutory-type authorities, you might need to experiment with multiple search strategies when

[278] MEAD DATA CENTRAL, REFERENCE MANUAL FOR THE LEXIS/NEXIS SERVICES 129–30 (undated looseleaf ed.).

you use LEXIS as a citator to update a statute or similar authority. You can try one or more of the following techniques:

- When the citation includes two numbers (such as title and section numbers for a statute or regulation, or article and section numbers for a constitutional provision), you can use both numbers and link them with the "w/n" connector. For example:

  ```
  17 w/10 (§302 or 302)
  ```

- When the citation includes a distinctive number that will likely occur only in references to the authority you are updating, you can search for just that number. For example:

  ```
  §974.06 or 974.06
  ```

- In addition to searching for numbers, you can use other search terms to provide a factual or legal context that increases the likelihood the numbers will refer to the authority you are updating. Thus, you might search for references to 17 U.S.C. § 302, a part of the federal copyright statute, using search requests such as these:

  ```
  (§302 or 302) w/25 copyright
  ```

  ```
  (17 w/10 (§302 or 302)) and copyright
  ```

  ```
  (17 w/10 (§302 or 302)) w/25 copyright
  ```

  Sometimes, a key phrase from the text of the authority you are updating can provide the needed context.

- As a last resort, you can try including the name or abbreviation of the publication in which the authority you are updating appears. For example, you might search for references to 28 U.S.C. § 1251 with a search request along these lines:

  ```
  28 w/10 (u.s.c. or "u. s. c." or
  u.s.c.a. or "u. s. c. a." or
  "u.s. code") w/10 (§1251 or 1251)
  ```

As you construct search requests to update statutory-type authorities, keep in mind a few other quirks (discussed below) concerning the format in which citations to these authorities might appear.

Renumbering. Through amendment, repeal, recodification, and other revisions, statutory-type provisions might be renumbered. For example, a legislature might reorganize a statutory code and renumber § 299.01 as § 799.01. In searching for references to these types of authorities, you should verify whether a provision has undergone a revision that has changed its citation.[279] If you want to ensure a comprehensive search, include each citation in your search request, as in:

```
§299.01 or 299.01 or §799.01 or 799.01
```

Non-code citations. A reference to a statute might cite something other than a statutory code. For instance, a writer might cite a federal statute by its public law or chapter number, its session law citation (in *Statutes at Large*), or its popular name (if it has one). Thus, a citation to section 1001 of the Employee Retirement Income Security Act might refer to the statute's *United States Code* citation (29 U.S.C. § 1001), its public law number (Pub. L. No. 93–406), its *Statutes at Large* citation (88 Stat. 832), or its popular name ("ERISA"). To enhance the likelihood of retrieving all references to this statute, your search request could include search terms based on each way of citing the statute:[280]

```
(29 w/10 (§1001 or 1001)) or "93-406" or
(88 pre/5 832) or "employee retirement" or
erisa or e.r.i.s.a. or "e. r. i. s. a."
```

This search would retrieve comprehensive results, but in most LEXIS files would also yield an unmanageable number of documents. A more practical search request would treat the popular name as a fact word that must occur in the document, thus providing context for the citation numbers:

```
((29 w/10 (§1001 or 1001)) or "93-406" or
(88 pre/5 832)) and ("employee retirement" or
erisa or e.r.i.s.a. or "e. r. i. s. a.")
```

If you still retrieve an unmanageable number of documents with a search request like this, you can further modify the search request by, say, adding a field restriction to limit the documents to those issued by a specific court.

Truncated citations. Suppose you want to update a specific subsection of a statute or regulation. A document with a discussion of that subsection might not contain a full citation to it. A discussion of a subsection with a number

[279] You can verify statutory renumberings by checking historical notes accompanying statutes in annotated codes or by checking cross-reference tables found in statutory codes. *See* CHRISTOPHER G. WREN & JILL R. WREN, THE LEGAL RESEARCH MANUAL: A GAME PLAN FOR LEGAL RESEARCH AND ANALYSIS 112 (2d ed. 1986). You might also learn about a renumbering when you read a case or other authority that discusses the statute in which you are interested. In addition, you can use the "section" segment in statutes in LEXIS to trace statutory renumberings, as explained on page 471.

[280] Note that the numbers in the *Statutes at Large* citation—88 and 832—are linked with "pre/n" rather than "w/n." Unlike references to code provisions, references to provisions in *Statutes at Large* rarely put the page number (here, 832) before the volume number (here, 88).

like 302(b)(2)(B) might actually cite only to 302(b)(2) or even to just 302(b). To accommodate possible truncations, you can begin with a broad version of the citation and narrow it if necessary. Thus, in the example, you could search for

```
302(b)
```

This search term will locate references to numbers with "302(b)" as their root, including

302(b)
302(b)(2)
302(b)(2)(B)

If you retrieve too many irrelevant references, you can narrow your focus by searching for

```
302(b)(2)
```

With this search term, you will locate references to numbers with "302(b)(2)" as their root, including

302(b)(2)
302(b)(2)(B)

You will not, however, locate references to just 302(b).[281]

Similarly (and especially in connection with administrative regulations), a discussion of a subsection with a number like 102.46(a) might cite the provision as ".46(a)" or "46(a)". Because LEXIS treats a period in the middle or beginning of a number as part of the number, each possible placement of the period creates a different word. To ensure you retrieve all references, your search request can include alternative ways in which a subsection might have been cited:

```
§102.46(a) or 102.46(a) or §46(a) or 46(a) or
§.46(a) or .46(a)
```

Roman numerals. When you search for references to provisions (such as articles or amendments in a constitution) that might be identified with Roman numerals, keep in mind the rules about how the LEXIS computer perceives Roman numerals and Arabic numbers and about how it perceives ordinal and

[281] You get these results because the LEXIS computer interprets parentheses in numbers as spaces. In effect, the computer treats numbers written with parentheses as phrase searches. Thus, a number like "302(b)(2)" is treated as a phrase consisting of the word "302," followed by the word "b," followed by the word "2." So long as a document contains the entire phrase, the computer will retrieve the document, regardless of what other words, if any, follow the phrase.

cardinal numbers. (See Appendix G.) For instance, the Fourteenth Amendment to the United States Constitution might be cited in any of these ways:

Amendment XIV
XIVth Amendment
Amend. 14
14th Amendment
Amendment Fourteen
Fourteenth Amendment

The following search request would retrieve any of these references:

```
(amendment or amend) w/10 (XIV or XIVth or
14 or 14th)
```

Using LEXIS as a citator to search for references to other kinds of authorities. You can use LEXIS as a citator to locate references to any kind of authority. You can search for references to such legal authorities as law review articles, congressional committee reports, or *A.L.R.* annotations, and to such nonlegal authorities as articles in medical journals. Through this technique, you can find references to authorities you cannot update by other means (such as by using Shepard's citators or Auto-Cite) and you can determine how judges and other legal writers currently view those authorities.

In searching for references of this sort, the same principles, challenges, and work-arounds already discussed for cases and statutory-type authorities come into play. You need to familiarize yourself with standard citation formats, anticipate likely variations, and then formulate a search request based on the possible ways of citing the authorities you want to update. If you are uncertain about the standard citation for an authority, *The Bluebook: A Uniform System of Citation* provides guidance.

The following examples suggest the range of authorities you can update by using LEXIS as a citator:

- You can retrieve references to *Restatement (Second) of Torts* § 623A with a search request like this:

  ```
  ((restatement or rest) w/10 tort)
  w/10 (§623a or 623a)
  ```

- You can retrieve references to Francis Wellman's book, *The Art of Cross-Examination*, with a search request like this:

  ```
  wellman w/10 cross-examination
  ```

- You can retrieve references to Rule 410 of the *Federal Rules of Evidence*, which deals with the admissibility of withdrawn pleas or of statements made during plea negotiations, with search requests like these:

```
((fed.r.evid. or "f. r. e." or f.r.e.
or fre or rule or evid) w/5 410) w/40
plea

410 w/25 (plea w/20 (admissib! or
admit! or admission))
```

Using LEXIS as a citator to update Shepardizing results. Because of the editorial time required to prepare the tables used in Shepardizing,[282] even the most recent citing references in a Shepard's citator will be several months old by the time the citator appears, whether in printed form or online. LEXIS, however, contains documents that have been issued more recently than those included in the most recent Shepard's citator. By adding a date restriction to your search request when you use LEXIS as a citator, you can focus your search on citing references that have not yet appeared in a Shepard's citator.

For example, suppose that on July 15, 1993 you were updating *Lewis v. United States*, 445 U.S. 55, 100 S. Ct. 915, 63 L. Ed. 2d 198 (1980). Searching for references to *Lewis* in documents issued during the six months preceding your search would update your Shepardizing and ensure that no gap occurs between your Shepardizing results and your LEXIS-as-citator results. You could use a search request along these lines:

```
(lewis w/5 ("united states" or u.s. or
"u. s.")) and ((445 pre/5 55) or (100 pre/5 915)
or (63 pre/5 198)) and date aft 1/15/1993
```

You can use this technique to update any authority you have Shepardized.

Automating LEXIS-as-citator searches by using LEXCITE

LEXIS offers LEXCITE as an automated method of creating LEXIS-as-citator search requests to locate references to various kinds of authorities you might want to update, including cases, law review articles, administrative agency decisions, and materials in the *Federal Register*. At this time, LEXCITE will locate references appearing in cases, law reviews, and *American Law Reports Annotated*.

A LEXCITE search involves transmitting a citation for the authority you are updating. The computer then automatically formulates a search request designed to locate references to that citation; if you are updating a case through

[282] See pages 400–22 for a discussion of Shepardizing in LEXIS.

LEXCITE, the request will also search automatically for references to some parallel citations and to the case name. In addition, the computer will search for references to your case in such forms as "id." or "supra" (which Mead Data calls "anaphoric" references).

In formulating a LEXCITE request, however, the computer makes certain assumptions (for example, which logic connectors and parallel citations to include), and those assumptions could result in a search request that might not be as well-suited for your purposes as the request you would formulate on your own. Consequently, for this and other reasons discussed at the end of this section, LEXCITE will not always serve as an adequate substitute for creating your own LEXIS-as-citator search requests (using techniques explained in the previous section).

Using LEXCITE. To perform a LEXCITE search, you first gain access to the LEXIS file in which you want to search for references to the authority you are updating. While in the file, you type and transmit a LEXCITE instruction at the same screen you use for typing and transmitting ordinary LEXIS search requests (see Figure 9.09 on page 200). If you have already transmitted a search request in the file, you treat the LEXCITE search as a modification of your existing search or as a new search. To transmit a LEXCITE search as a modification of the existing search request, transmit a command (*e.g.*, `m`, `m1`, `m2`) to modify your most recent search request; to transmit a LEXCITE search as a new search, press the NEW SEARCH key.[283]

For your LEXCITE instruction,

1. Type `lexcite` (or `lxcite`), followed by a citation enclosed in parentheses.
2. Press TRANSMIT.

The citation in a typical LEXCITE instruction consists of a volume number and abbreviation of the publication in which the authority appears and a page number from the authority. You can also use a LEXIS Cite in a LEXCITE instruction.[284]

For example, to conduct a LEXCITE search for references to *Lewis v. United States*, 445 U.S. 55, 100 S. Ct. 915, 63 L. Ed. 2d 198, 48 U.S.L.W. 4205, 1980 U.S. LEXIS 85, you could use any of the following LEXCITE instructions:

```
lexcite (445 u.s. 55)

lxcite (100 s ct 915)
```

[283] For a refresher on modifying search requests and using the NEW SEARCH key, see pages 167–72 and 183.

[284] Figure 10.02 on pages 239–40 explains LEXIS Cites.

```
lxcite(63 led2d 198)

lexcite(48 uslw 4205)

lxcite (1980 u.s. lexis 85)
```

As you can see, you have flexibility in how you punctuate and space within a publication's abbreviation, but you must leave a space on each side of the abbreviation. In addition, you must use an abbreviation that LEXCITE will recognize. If you transmit an unacceptable abbreviation, the monitor will display a message guiding you to an online list of abbreviations that work with LEXCITE.

If you want to view the list of approved abbreviations without first transmitting a LEXCITE instruction, you can see this list through the LEXIS online "help" feature. Currently, to gain access to this "LEXCITE Reporter Dictionary List":

1. Press the NEW SEARCH key to display the screen for typing and transmitting a new search request.
2. At that screen, type `h` and press TRANSMIT.
3. When the monitor displays the "help" menu, transmit `6` to select the tutorial labeled "Using Lexcite (tm) and LEXIS as a Citator," a choice that appears on the second page of the "help" menu.
4. When the tutorial menu appears on the screen, transmit `3` to select the online explanation about LEXCITE.
5. When the first screen of the explanation appears, transmit `e` to display an example of a LEXCITE search instruction.
6. Transmit `r` to display the list of abbreviations.
7. Follow the on-screen instructions to view the portion of the list containing the abbreviation you want to locate.
8. When you finish using the list, follow the on-screen instructions to exit from the "help" feature.

If you want to bypass the intervening "help" screens and go directly to the list of acceptable LEXCITE abbreviations, you can "stack" the preceding commands: after pressing the NEW SEARCH key, type `h;6;3;e;r` and press TRANSMIT. (Appendix I explains "stacking.")

If you transmit a LEXCITE instruction and the monitor displays a message indicating that LEXCITE does not recognize the reporter abbreviation in your request, consider the possibility that a parallel citation might work. For example, suppose you wanted to search for references to *Schuchart & Associates,*

Professional Engineers, Inc. v. Solo Serve Corp. in the COURTS file in the GENFED library. During the preparation of this book, using the citation "1983 Copr. L. Dec. P 25,593" (*Schuchart*'s citation in CCH's *Copyright Law Decisions*) in a LEXCITE instruction to retrieve those references produced a message that LEXCITE did not recognize the reporter abbreviation. The computer retrieved the references, however, with a LEXCITE instruction using the parallel citation to CCH's *Copyright Law Reporter* (Copy. L. Rep. 25,593);[285] using the citation to BNA's *United States Patents Quarterly* (220 U.S.P.Q. 170) also worked.

Once you transmit a LEXCITE instruction, the computer carries out the search and the monitor displays the results like ordinary LEXIS search results. You can then do anything you could do in LEXIS (*e.g.*, view or print the results, use LEXSEE to retrieve a document, Shepardize an authority).

After reviewing your LEXCITE results, you might want to run another search using LEXCITE. If so, you can transmit a command (*e.g.*, `m`, `m1`, `m2`) to modify your most recent search request, or you can press the NEW SEARCH key to begin a new search.

Embellishing LEXCITE. In addition to transmitting a LEXCITE instruction by itself, you can combine a LEXCITE instruction with other elements you might include in an ordinary LEXIS search request. Thus, you can add a date restriction or other field restriction to your LEXCITE instruction, or you can add search terms to create a factual or legal context in which the references to the authority you are updating should occur. You can also combine your LEXCITE instruction with another LEXCITE instruction.

For instance, suppose you want to avoid (to the extent possible) retrieving references that have already appeared in a Shepard's table. You could add a date restriction that limits the LEXCITE search to references occurring in cases decided within a period of four to six months before your search. So, if you had been updating *Lewis v. United States* in September 1993, your LEXCITE instruction might have taken this form:

```
lxcite (445 u.s. 55) and date aft 2/28/93
```

Or, suppose you want to locate cases in which courts have cited *Lewis v. United States* on the issue of uncounseled convictions (that is, convictions obtained without the assistance of an attorney). You could use a LEXCITE instruction like this:

```
lxcite (445 u.s. 55) and uncounsel!
```

[285] *Copyright Law Reporter* is a looseleaf service updated monthly, and *Copyright Law Decisions* is the annual compilation of a year's worth of *Copyright Law Reporter*.

Similarly, to search for cases that have cited both *Lewis* and *Miranda v. Arizona*, 384 U.S. 436, 86 S. Ct. 1602, 16 L. Ed. 2d 694, 1966 U.S. LEXIS 2817, you could combine LEXCITE instructions, as in these examples:

```
lxcite (445 u.s. 55) and lexcite (1966 u.s.
lexis 2817)

lexcite (100 s. ct. 915) and lexcite (16 l. ed.
2d 694)
```

After you view the results of a LEXCITE search, you can modify your LEXCITE instruction as you would an ordinary LEXIS request by, say, changing connectors or editing search terms.

The role of LEXCITE. LEXCITE simply amounts to an alternative method of transmitting an ordinary LEXIS-as-citator search request. Instead of requiring you to create the request, however, LEXCITE formulates it for you. In doing so, LEXCITE anticipates various ways in which the authority you are updating might have been cited, such as by a parallel citation, by "id." or "supra," or by a nonstandard reference like "Fed. Supp." instead of "F. Supp." LEXCITE thus simplifies using LEXIS as a citator.

LEXCITE has some limitations, however:

- LEXCITE only automates the procedure for searching for references to certain kinds of authorities. By contrast, using LEXIS as a citator allows you to find updating references to *any* kind of authority.
- Currently, you can only use LEXCITE to find updating references that appear in certain kinds of authorities.
- At this time, LEXCITE does not allow you to look at the search request the computer formulates in response to your LEXCITE instruction. Because you cannot know what the computer is searching for (*e.g.*, what parallel citations or nonstandard citation forms), you cannot know whether the computer has formulated a search request that fully achieves your updating goal.
- At this time, if the citation you use in a LEXCITE instruction applies to more than one case (as occurs, for example, with 387 N.Y.S.2d 426), the computer does not pause to ask for which of those cases you want LEXCITE to search. Instead, the computer will search for references to each of the cases, and your LEXCITE results can therefore include irrelevant references.
- Although LEXCITE searches for many parallel citations and nonstandard citation forms, LEXCITE currently does not search for citations to slip opinions or (undoubtedly for competitive reasons)

> WESTLAW Cites. If a reference to the authority you are updating uses only a citation for which LEXCITE will not search, LEXCITE will bypass that reference. For instance, searching in the WICASE file in the WISC library for references to *State v. Harris*, 119 Wis. 2d 612, 350 N.W.2d 633, using the LEXCITE instruction `lexcite(119 wis2d 612)` does not retrieve *State v. Farr*, 119 Wis. 2d 651, 350 N.W.2d 640, which identifies *Harris* only by its slip-opinion citation.

Despite these limitations, LEXCITE diminishes some of the difficulties of using LEXIS as a citator. Yet LEXCITE should not be seen as a complete replacement for using LEXIS as a citator.

For example, during the preparation of this book, using LEXCITE and a LEXIS-as-citator request yielded different results in searching the COURTS file in the GENFED library for references to Professor Wechsler's *Harvard Law Review* article, "Toward Neutral Principles of Constitutional Law." The LEXCITE instruction `lexcite(73 harv l rev 1)` retrieved 31 cases, while the LEXIS-as-citator request `wechsler w/10 neutral` retrieved 34 cases. The cases retrieved by the LEXCITE instruction included one case the LEXIS-as-citator request missed because of a typographical error in Professor Wechsler's name; the cases retrieved by the LEXIS-as-citator request included three cases the LEXCITE instruction missed because their references to the article cited only to a collection of articles republished in book form.[286] Similarly, in the US file in the GENFED library, the LEXIS-as-citator request `miranda and escobedo` retrieved 38 cases referring to both *Miranda v. Arizona* and *Escobedo v. Illinois*, while the LEXCITE instruction `lexcite(384 us 436) and lexcite(378 us 478)` retrieved 33 cases referring to both *Miranda* and *Escobedo*.

As these examples suggest, LEXCITE and LEXIS-as-citator complement rather than replace each other as techniques for updating.

Updating the law in LEXIS by using Easy Search

When you use LEXIS to update your research, you have the option of using the Easy Search feature to simplify the task.[287] Intended for novice or

[286] The LEXIS-as-citator request also retrieved one case containing "wechsler" within ten words of "neutral" but having nothing to do with Professor Wechsler's article.

[287] Long-time LEXIS users might notice similarities between the Easy Search feature and Legal Research Assistant, a component of the Easy Search software program Mead Data offers as part of its LEXIS/NEXIS Technology Series Research Software for MS-DOS. The Easy Search feature, which functions while you are logged on to LEXIS, derives from the Legal Research Assistant software that Mead Data developed so researchers could prepare search instructions offline, before logging on to LEXIS.

infrequent users of LEXIS, Easy Search provides a fill-in-the-blank method of implementing some of the updating techniques already explained in this chapter. (As explained in Chapter 10, you can also use Easy Search in the finding-the-law phase of a legal research project.)

Easy Search presents menus of updating activities (among other things) and asks you to specify the task the computer should perform. For the updating techniques available through Easy Search, you do not need to know an array of LEXIS commands; once you finish typing responses to the "plain English" prompts Easy Search displays, the computer translates your choices into LEXIS commands, carries out the updating task, and displays the results.

Easy Search is a relatively new feature, and the arrangement of the Easy Search menus has evolved since Mead Data added the feature to LEXIS. The basic menu-driven operation of Easy Search has remained unchanged, however.

Using Easy Search to update authorities in LEXIS. To use Easy Search, begin by selecting the Easy Search library (EASY) just as you would any other LEXIS library. When the monitor displays a screen listing the files in the EASY library, type the name of the file you want to select, then press the TRANSMIT key. Currently, the LEGAL file in the EASY library allows you to perform updating tasks in LEXIS (among other research activities). This discussion assumes that you will be using the LEGAL file.

After you select the LEGAL file, the monitor will display a menu from which you can select a category of documents to search. For updating activities, select the category designated "General Cases, Codes, Cite Verification." You will then see a screen similar to the one shown in Figure 12.15. As the figure indicates, you can then use Easy Search to update your research in several ways:

- You can Shepardize an authority. Select the menu choice "Verify a case using the Shepard's (R) or Auto-Cite (R) service."
- You can retrieve an Auto-Cite report. Select the menu choice "Verify a case using the Shepard's (R) or Auto-Cite (R) service."
- You can update an authority through LEXCITE. Select the menu choice "References to a case using the LEXCITE (R) feature."

To convey your menu choice:

1. Use the TAB key to move the cursor to the LINK marker next to the activity you want to select. Alternatively, type the number of the LINK marker corresponding to the activity you want to select. For example, to select "Verify a case using the Shepard's (R) or Auto-Cite (R) service," move the cursor to the LINK marker labelled "<=2>," or type `=2`.

```
LEVEL 1 - 1 OF 1 ITEM

EASY SEARCH - LEGAL
General Cases, Codes, Cite Verification

<=1> Specific case or ALR annotation
<=2> Verify a case using the Shepard's (R) or Auto-Cite (R) service
<=3> References to a case using the LEXCITE (R) feature
<=4> Find a statute or view a statutory table of contents

<=5> Main Menu   <=6> Sign Off
```

Source: Mead Data Central, Inc. © 1993

Figure 12.15. Menu for Selecting Updating Activities in the LEGAL File in the EASY Library in LEXIS

2. Press TRANSMIT.

After you select an updating technique, the monitor displays screens that ask you to respond to "plain English" prompts. These prompts guide you through typing a citation of the authority you want to update through Shepard's, Auto-Cite, or LEXCITE; if you update through LEXCITE, the on-screen prompts also guide you in selecting the LEXIS file in which you want the computer to search for updating references to your authority. After you type your responses and press TRANSMIT, Easy Search carries out your updating search.

Once you have finished checking the results of the updating search, you can return to the Easy Search menus by typing `.log` and pressing TRANSMIT.

The role of Easy Search in updating the law. For new or infrequent users, the menus and on-screen prompts in Easy Search can simplify using LEXIS to update research results: once you have typed your responses to the on-screen prompts, the computer constructs a search request (including segment restrictions where appropriate) and selects an appropriate library and file or service (such as Shepard's) for the search. Thus, Easy Search reduces the number of LEXIS commands and library and file names you have to know to use LEXIS.

At this time, however, Easy Search has some drawbacks for updating:

- Easy Search does not simplify Shepardizing to the point of automatically retrieving all available Shepard's tables for a case that has parallel citations, nor does the computer alert Easy Search users to the need to repeat the Shepardizing process for parallel citations. (Recall that you can get different Shepardizing results depending on which parallel citation you use to Shepardize.)[288] Consequently, Easy Search can mislead researchers unfamiliar with the online version of Shepard's into believing they have fully Shepardized when more can be done.

  To see how Shepardizing operates in Easy Search, try Shepardizing the U.S. Supreme Court case of *Lewis v. United States*, 445 U.S. 55, 100 S. Ct. 915, 63 L. Ed. 2d 198 (1980). No matter which citation you first transmit for Shepardizing through Easy Search, you will need to take additional steps to ensure that you retrieve the Shepard's tables based on the remaining parallel citations.
- When you use LEXCITE through Easy Search, you encounter the same LEXCITE limitations you find when you use LEXCITE without Easy Search (see pages 461–66). Moreover, Easy Search imposes an additional limitation by not allowing you to embellish the LEXCITE search as you normally can in LEXIS by, say, adding fact words or by combining multiple LEXCITE instructions in a single search request.
- For experienced LEXIS users, using the Easy Search menus will often prove slower than updating without the help of Easy Search.

Automating citation-updating in LEXIS through CheckCite

If you have access to a personal computer and a software program called CheckCite (available from Jurisoft, a division of Mead Data Central), you can automate the use of several online citation-updating features available through LEXIS—Shepard's, Auto-Cite, and LEXCITE. CheckCite allows you, while you are not connected to LEXIS, to prepare a list of citations the computer will update for you through LEXIS. CheckCite can compile the list by extracting the citations from an existing document (such as a brief or memorandum) prepared through a word-processing program; or, you can type citations directly into CheckCite. Through CheckCite, you tell the computer how to up-

[288] *See* CHRISTOPHER G. WREN & JILL R. WREN, THE LEGAL RESEARCH MANUAL: A GAME PLAN FOR LEGAL RESEARCH AND ANALYSIS 101, 104 (2d ed. 1986). For an example of different results in online Shepardizing, see pages 411–14.

date the citations on the CheckCite list—for example, whether to update a citation just through Shepard's, just through Auto-Cite, or through both, or whether Shepard's results should consist of citing references just from selected jurisdictions or just accompanied by certain kinds of analysis codes. After you indicate the information you want CheckCite to provide about your citations, CheckCite logs onto LEXIS, carries out the updating searches you requested, and delivers the results to a destination (such as a computer printer or storage disk) you specified through CheckCite.

If you need to conduct extensive online updating through LEXIS, using CheckCite could speed your updating efforts, reduce the time spent connected to LEXIS, and lower your online research costs. Your LEXIS customer-service representative can help you obtain CheckCite and a detailed reference manual explaining how to use the program.

Other tips for updating statutes through LEXIS

When you find a reference to a statute in a case or other authority, even a recent one, you cannot be sure the reference reflects the most up-to-date text of the statute; the provision might have subsequently been amended or repealed, for example. Even a provision you see in a statutory code file might not have incorporated recent legislative changes.

As with printed statutes, the text of which you update through such means as checking pocket parts and supplements accompanying statutory codes, you need to update the text of statutes you find online.[289] First, though, to get an idea of how much updating lies ahead, ascertain when legislative changes were last incorporated into the online text of the statute you want to update. To do that, you can check the online description of the file containing the statute: at the file menu, on-screen instructions explain how to gain access to the file description. The description will indicate the date of the online version of the statutory code. This information also usually appears near the top of the monitor when the statute is displayed. If you want to know when LEXIS will next incorporate changes into a statute, check the online GUIDE file for the statutory code containing that statute.[290] The updating schedule varies from jurisdiction to jurisdiction; because LEXIS obtains statutory codes from other publishers, online updates occur according to those publishers' schedules for updating their codes (*e.g.*, once a year).

Along with ascertaining the recency of updates to a statute, you can use the following LEXIS features to discover legislative changes.

[289] For a description of using pocket parts and supplements to update printed statutory codes, see CHRISTOPHER G. WREN & JILL R. WREN, THE LEGAL RESEARCH MANUAL: A GAME PLAN FOR LEGAL RESEARCH AND ANALYSIS 116–18 (2d ed. 1986).

[290] For an explanation of GUIDE, see Appendix A.

The "section" segment in statutory codes in LEXIS. The "section" segment of a statute in LEXIS normally contains just the section number and short title of a statutory provision. Figure 12.16 shows a section number and short title ("209.03. Reduction of county contributions") in a typical "section" segment.

When viewing a statute online, you might see that its "section" segment includes a statement that the provision has been repealed, amended, renumbered, or otherwise affected by legislative action. Figure 12.17 shows a "section" segment that includes a representative statement of legislative changes. Although any such change will already have been incorporated into the online text of the statute, you still might want to check the corresponding session law that effected the change to see whether the session law contains material (such as a preamble or statement of legislative intent) not incorporated in the code version of the statute. The "section" segment will often provide a citation to the session law implementing the change.

The "status" segment in statutory codes in LEXIS. When viewing a statute in LEXIS, you might also encounter the "status" segment, which is found in the *United States Code* file (USCS or USCODE in the GENFED library, or USCODE in the CODES library) and in most state statutory code files. In a federal statute, the "status" segment indicates the date through which

```
To be able to browse preceding or succeeding code sections, transmit B.  The
first page of the document you are currently viewing will be displayed in FULL.
--------------------------------------------------------------------------------

                        LEVEL 1 - 3 OF 1894 DOCUMENTS

                          ILLINOIS REVISED STATUTES

             CHAPTER 14.  ATTORNEY GENERAL AND STATE'S ATTORNEYS

                 STATE'S ATTORNEYS APPELLATE PROSECUTOR'S ACT

                  Ill. Rev. Stat. ch. 14, par. 209.03 (1988)

STATUS:
Repealed.  See 1990 Ill. ALS 86-1028, Section 4-3.
Affected.  See 1990 Ill. ALS 86-1028, Section 4-3, 4-3.            "status" segment
Amended.  See 1989 Ill. ALS 86-332, Section 1.
Repealed.  See 1989 Ill. ALS 86-962, Section 7-3001.
Affected.  See 1989 Ill. ALS 86-962, Section 7-3001, 7-3001.

209.03.  Reduction of county contributions   "section" segment
```

Source: Mead Data Central, Inc. © 1993

Figure 12.16. Typical "Status" and "Section" Segments in a LEXIS Statutory Code

```
To be able to browse preceding or succeeding code sections, transmit B.  The
first page of the document you are currently viewing will be displayed in FULL.
--------------------------------------------------------------------------------

                           LEVEL 1 - 1 OF 1 DOCUMENT

                           DEERING'S CALIFORNIA CODES
                       (c) 1991 Bancroft-Whitney Company

  *** THIS SECTION IS CURRENT THROUGH THE 1991 SUPPLEMENT (1990 SESSIONS) ***

GOVERNMENT CODE

                          Cal Gov Code @ 16102 (1991)

@ 16102. [Added by Stats 1969 ch 1526 @ 1, effective September 6, 1969,
operative January 1, 1969, as @ 16110, amended by Stats 1970 ch 450 @ 1,
effective July 17, 1970, amended and renumbered by Stats 1st Ex Sess 1971 ch 1 @
2.7, effective December 8, 1971, and repealed by Stats 1972 ch 1406 @ 4,
effective January 1, 1973.]

HISTORY:
  See @ 16111.
```

"section" segment

Source: Mead Data Central, Inc.; © 1982–1991, 1992 Bancroft-Whitney Company

Figure 12.17. Typical "Section" Segment Showing Statement of Legislative Changes in a LEXIS Statutory Code

any legislative changes have been incorporated into the statute, as illustrated in Figure 5.15 on page 138. To identify any legislative changes made to the statute after that date, you can search the PUBLAW file (the Advance Legislative Service file for the *United States Code*), as discussed on pages 473–76.

In a state statute, the "status" segment might indicate that the legislature has amended, repealed, or otherwise affected a statute since legislative changes were last added to its online text. Figure 12.16 shows an example. Legislative changes indicated in the "status" segment of a state statute have not yet been incorporated into the online statute, so you will need to locate the corresponding slip law, either in printed or online form. The "status" segment provides a citation that allows you to locate the slip law (*i.e.*, the first official text of the legislative enactment) that effected the change.

Typical citations in the "status" segment read along these lines:

> Amended. See 1989 Kan. SB 8
>
> Amended. See 1990 Cal ALS 56
>
> Affected. See 1989 Me. ALS 105, 1989 Me. Ch 105

As the first example indicates, a citation might refer you to just a slip law number. Or, as in the second example, a citation might refer you to just the slip law's LEXIS document number in an Advance Legislative Service file (discussed below). Or, as in the third example, a citation might refer you to both an Advance Legislative Service document number and a slip law number.

Advance Legislative Service ("ALS") in LEXIS. All of the statutory codes in LEXIS have a corresponding Advance Legislative Service file containing newly passed legislation (*i.e.*, slip laws). A jurisdiction's ALS file contains (among other things) the text of changes made to statutes, constitutions, and court rules. When a change to one of these types of authorities occurs in a jurisdiction, LEXIS adds to that jurisdiction's ALS file the document containing the text of the change; in addition, for state statutes, if there is a "status" segment in the corresponding code file, LEXIS simultaneously adds to that segment a cross-reference to the ALS update. Subsequently, LEXIS merges the contents of an ALS file into the corresponding federal or state statutory code file.

In effect, LEXIS provides ALS files to update online statutory codes between recompilations just as a publisher of a printed statutory code updates the code between recompilations by providing pocket parts, supplements, and a legislative advance sheet service (a supplemental publication containing slip laws issued between pocket parts).[291]

At the federal level, the PUBLAW file in either the GENFED or CODES library is the ALS file corresponding to the *United States Code*. At the state level, an ALS file in the CODES library is designated by a jurisdiction's postal abbreviation and the letters "ALS," such as "DEALS" for the Delaware ALS file; in a state library, such as the DEL library for Delaware, the ALS file is designated simply "ALS." The segments in ALS files vary somewhat from jurisdiction to jurisdiction, as does the frequency with which documents are added to these files (*e.g.*, weekly, or within 30 days after new legislation is enacted). But all ALS files serve the same purpose.

Using an ALS file in LEXIS. You can use an ALS file in any of several ways to update a statute:

- You can retrieve a document from an ALS file by using LEXSEE.[292] For example, suppose you were viewing a statute in the California statutory code file in LEXIS and saw a reference to "1990 Cal ALS 56" in the "status" segment. If you wanted to immediately view the legislative change, you could transmit the instruction

```
lexsee 1990 cal als 56
```

[291] Examples of printed legislative advance sheet services include *United States Code Congressional and Administrative News* ("USCCAN") and the advance pamphlets for the *United States Code Service*.

[292] For a refresher on LEXSEE, see pages 238–43.

to display the text of the slip law that affected the statute you were viewing.[293] After checking the slip law, using standard LEXIS techniques for moving within a document,[294] you could resume viewing the statute by transmitting `resume`.

If the "status" segment provides parallel citations for a single document in ALS, you can use any of the citations in your LEXSEE instruction. As in any LEXSEE search request, however, you must use a citation form that LEXSEE will recognize. If you encounter an error message that your LEXSEE instruction is not in proper form, you might need to omit some parts of the citation stated in the "status" segment. For example, a "status" segment might refer to "1989 Ariz. ALS 1 Sp. Sess. 4," a citation LEXSEE would not recognize; to use this citation with LEXSEE, you would transmit only "1989 ariz als 1."

- Suppose you do not have a citation to a legislative enactment that has affected a statute you are updating, perhaps because the statute does not have a "status" segment from which you can obtain this information. You can use an ALS file in a second way to verify the current text of your statute: gain access to the ALS file, then search the file for references to your statute. Thus, to update section 271.305 of the Nevada Revised Statutes, you could transmit the following search request in the NVALS file in the CODES library (or in the ALS file in the NEV library):

  ```
  §271.305 or 271.305
  ```

  This search request would retrieve any documents in the ALS file that refer to section 271.305. By reviewing these documents, you could determine whether the Nevada legislature has taken any action affecting this section.

  You might also want to conduct a broader search for references to multiple sections in the chapter or title of which the section you are updating is a part, especially if searching for just that section does not retrieve any documents. The legislature might have repealed or otherwise affected a range of sections, or even an entire chapter, without referring to the specific section you want to update.

[293] Don't be surprised if your LEXSEE instruction retrieves more than one document. Because of the way some legislatures number their enactments, several slip laws might share the same citation; for instance, the Texas legislature might hold several sessions a year, and it begins numbering enactments with "1" in each session. In this kind of situation, you'll need to page through the retrieved documents to find the one that affected the statute you are updating.

[294] Pages 332–33 explain these techniques.

In anticipation of this possibility in connection with section 271.305, you could carry out searches along these lines:

```
§271.3! or 271.3!

§271! or 271!
```

As you search ALS files for references to statutory code provisions you are updating, keep in mind a potential and unpredictable obstacle to comprehensiveness. Legislatures (especially Congress) sometimes modify statutes without referring to the codified versions. Instead, a legislature might modify a code provision by referring to and modifying an earlier session law that affected the code provision. In this situation, searching for a reference to the code provision will fail to locate the change.

Short of tediously including in your search request various terms representing each session law that conceivably could have affected the code provision you are updating, your best course is to check the cross-reference tables found in printed legislative advance sheet services that update printed versions of statutory codes. Although some delay inevitably occurs between the passage of a slip law and the publication of a legislative advance sheet, this printed updating tool will often correlate modifications of earlier session laws with their code counterparts sooner than those changes will be linked online with the corresponding code provisions in statutory code files.

- You can use an ALS file in a third way to update a statute. Regardless of whether a legislature has directly affected the language of the statute you want to update, the legislature might have affected another statute that interacts with, and thus indirectly affects, your statute. This situation can occur, for instance, when a legislature changes a statute containing a definition that applies in numerous other statutes in the code. To determine whether a statute has been indirectly affected by legislative action, you can select key words or phrases reflecting the statute's subject matter and search for references to those words or phrases in the corresponding ALS file.

In using ALS files, note that they cumulate. At this writing, even after ALS documents have been merged into the corresponding statutory code files, LEXIS retains these documents in the ALS files. Consequently, an ALS file might contain documents spanning several years of legislative activity, including documents effecting changes that have already been incorporated into the corresponding code. When you conduct a descriptive word search in an ALS file for references to a statutory code section or to key words or phrases, you can limit your search to a specific year. To do so, search with a restriction for date references in appropriate ALS segments, such as the "cite" or "heading" segment. For instance, because citations in the "cite" segment in an ALS document include the year of the legislative session in which the document was enacted, a search request to retrieve legislative changes made in 1989 could include a restriction like `cite(1989)`.

Summary of using ALS to update statutes in LEXIS. Figure 12.18 summarizes the techniques for using ALS files to update statutes.

Other tips for updating administrative regulations through LEXIS

As researchers familiar with the administrative-law arena will know, administrative agencies frequently change, rescind, or propose to change or rescind the text of their regulations. When an agency does so at the federal level and in many states, it publishes the change, rescission, or proposal in an administrative register (such as the *Federal Register*, issued daily by the federal government to update federal regulations). A change or rescission that appears in an administrative register supersedes the text in the corresponding administrative code (as well as any previous modifications published in the administrative register). An administrative register thus serves as a non-cumulative update that keeps the corresponding administrative code current between its periodic recompilations.

Just as you need to update the text of regulations in printed administrative codes by checking administrative registers, you need to update the text of regulations you find online.[295] A reference to an administrative regulation in even a recent case or other authority might not reflect the most up-to-date text of the regulation; the provision might have subsequently been revised or rescinded, for example. Even the regulation itself in an administrative code file might not have incorporated recent changes made by the promulgating agency.

To get an idea of how much updating lies ahead, start by ascertaining when changes were last incorporated into the online text of an administrative regulation. To do that for state regulations, check the online description of the administrative code file containing the regulation you want to update: at the file menu, on-screen instructions explain how to gain access to the file description. The description will indicate the date of the online version of the administrative code. To ascertain the revision date for a federal regulation, you can

[295] For a description of using printed administrative registers to update printed administrative codes, see CHRISTOPHER G. WREN & JILL R. WREN, THE LEGAL RESEARCH MANUAL: A GAME PLAN FOR LEGAL RESEARCH AND ANALYSIS 115–16 (2d ed. 1986).

If you want to	Follow this procedure in LEXIS

Retrieve a slip law when you know its citation	type `lexsee` (or `lxe`) followed by the citation of the slip law; then press TRANSMIT
	Example: To retrieve Chapter 105 of the Maine session laws for 1989, transmit one of these search requests:
	`lexsee 1989 me als 105`
	`lexsee 1989 me ch 105`

Return to the screen you were viewing before you invoked LEXSEE	type `resume` (or `res`) and press TRANSMIT

Retrieve slip laws that have affected the statutory code provision you are updating	gain access to the appropriate ALS file and search for references to the statutory code provision
	Example: To retrieve slip laws affecting section 271.305 of the Nevada Revised Statutes, gain access to the NVALS file in the CODES library (or the ALS file in the NEV library) and transmit a search request along these lines:
	`§271.305 or 271.305`
	`§271.3! or 271.3!`

Retrieve slip laws that might have indirectly affected the statutory code provision you are updating	gain access to the appropriate ALS file and search for key words or phrases reflecting the subject matter of the statutory code provision

Figure 12.18. Quick Guide to Updating Statutes Through LEXIS Advance Legislative Service ("ALS") Files

use the online description of the file in which the regulation is found, or you can use the "title" segment (discussed below) in the regulation itself.

Because LEXIS offers access (at this writing) to only nine state administrative codes and one state administrative register, the remaining discussion of online updating of regulations focuses on federal regulations. As LEXIS continues to add state administrative materials, you will likely be able to update state regulations by adapting the techniques used to update federal regulations.

The "title" and "source" segments in a *Code of Federal Regulations* file (CFR) in LEXIS.[296] In a regulation in a CFR file, the "title" segment identifies the name and number of the *Code of Federal Regulations* title (along with the subtitle) in which the *C.F.R.* provision is found. The "title" segment also provides the revision date for that *C.F.R.* title and, therefore, for all provisions in that title. Figure 12.19 shows a typical "title" segment from a regulation in a CFR file.

The schedule for revising the online version of the *Code of Federal Regulations* tracks the schedule for incorporating changes into the printed version: Titles 1 through 16 are revised as of January 1 each year; Titles 17 through 27, as of April 1 each year; Titles 28 through 41, as of July 1 each year; and Titles 42 through 50, as of October 1 each year. A statement in the "title" segment that, for example, a title has been "revised as of January 1, 1993" means the text includes any changes made through December 31, 1992.

Changes made during the period indicated in the "title" segment will already have been incorporated into the online text of the *Code of Federal Regulations* provision. Nevertheless, you still might want to check the *Federal Register* to see whether it contains material (such as an administrative agency's response to public comments about the provision) that did not make it into the text of the *Code of Federal Regulations* provision. The "source" segment in a regulation in a CFR file provides citations to *Federal Register* documents that implemented changes to the *Code of Federal Regulations* provision through the revision date shown in the "title" segment. Figure 12.19 shows a typical "source" segment.

To discover changes that have *not* yet been incorporated into the online version of an administrative code, you can use the following techniques.

Updating by retrieving a known document from the *Federal Register* file (FEDREG) in LEXIS. If you know the citation of a *Federal Register* document that updates a *Code of Federal Regulations* provision, you can retrieve the document by using a LEXSEE command. For example, if you know

[296] Many LEXIS files in addition to the CFR file in the GENFED or CODES library contain provisions from the *Code of Federal Regulations*. *See* pages 225–26. For example, environmental regulations also appear in the CFR file in the ENVIRN library, and labor regulations in the CFR file in the LABOR library.

```
To be able to browse preceding or succeeding code sections, transmit B.  The
first page of the document you are currently viewing will be displayed in FULL.
-------------------------------------------------------------------------------

                         LEVEL 1 - 1 OF 1 SECTION

                       TITLE 49 -- TRANSPORTATION;
                      REVISED AS OF OCTOBER 1, 1991
         SUBTITLE B -- OTHER REGULATIONS RELATING TO TRANSPORTATION

  CHAPTER III -- FEDERAL HIGHWAY ADMINISTRATION, DEPARTMENT OF TRANSPORTATION
          SUBCHAPTER B -- FEDERAL MOTOR CARRIER SAFETY REGULATIONS

                  PART 391 -- QUALIFICATIONS OF DRIVERS
                           SUBPART A -- GENERAL

             @ 391.1 Scope of the rules in this part; additional
                  qualifications; duties of carrier-drivers.

                              49 CFR 391.1

   (a) The rules in this part establish minimum qualifications for persons who
drive motor vehicles as, for, or on behalf of motor carriers. The rules in this
part also establish minimum duties of motor carriers with respect to the
```

"title" segment

```
                              49 CFR 391.1

qualifications of their drivers.

   (b) A motor carrier who employs himself as a driver must comply with both the
rules in this part that apply to motor carriers and the rules in this part that
apply to drivers.

   [35 FR 6460, Apr. 22, 1970, as amended at 53 FR 18057, May 19, 1988]

SOURCE: 35 FR 6460, Apr. 22, 1970.

AUTHORITY: 49 U.S.C. App. 2505; 49 U.S.C. 504 and 3102; 49 CFR 1.48.
```

"source" segment

Source: Mead Data Central, Inc. © 1993

Figure 12.19. Sample Document from CFR File in LEXIS

that a document published at 55 Fed. Reg. 3546 affects the *C.F.R.* provision you are updating, you can retrieve the document by transmitting any of the following search requests:

```
lexsee 55 fr 3546
lxe 55 fedreg 3546
lexsee 55 fed reg 3546
```

After checking the *Federal Register* document, you could transmit `resume` to return to wherever you were in your research when you transmitted your LEXSEE command.

Updating through the "cfr" segment in the *Federal Register* file (FEDREG) in LEXIS. If you do not know the citation of a *Federal Register* document that updates a *Code of Federal Regulations* provision, you can still determine whether an agency has affected the text of the regulation: search either a printed or online version of the *Federal Register* for references to the regulation.[297] To do this updating in LEXIS, you would search in the FEDREG file in either the GENFED or CODES library with a search request designed to retrieve documents that have affected the regulation since the last revision. The "cfr" segment in documents in FEDREG facilitates this search. This segment cross-references the *Federal Register* document to the *Code of Federal Regulations* by providing a citation to the *C.F.R.* title number and part number containing the regulation affected by the *Federal Register* document. Figure 12.20 shows a typical "cfr" segment.

Suppose you want to ascertain the current text of 49 C.F.R. § 391.15, and the version of the regulation you have was last revised as of October 1, 1988. Transmitting a search request in the following form in FEDREG would retrieve *Federal Register* documents affecting the regulation since that date:

```
cfr(49 pre/5 391) and (§391.15 or 391.15) and
date aft september 1988
```

The "cfr" segment restriction in this search request ensures the search will retrieve *Federal Register* documents affecting only the *C.F.R.* title and part number in which your regulation appears. Because the "cfr" segment does not cite to section numbers, the search request also includes an unrestricted search for the section number, which will normally appear somewhere in the text of a *Federal Register* document affecting the section. Because the FEDREG file contains (at this time) *Federal Register* documents dating back to July 1980, the date restriction ensures that retrieved documents will have been issued since the last revision of the regulation you are updating.

[297] For an explanation of updating the *C.F.R.* using printed updating materials, see CHRISTOPHER G. WREN & JILL R. WREN, THE LEGAL RESEARCH MANUAL: A GAME PLAN FOR LEGAL RESEARCH AND ANALYSIS 114–16 (2d ed. 1986).

```
LEVEL 1 - 1 OF 52 DOCUMENTS

DEPARTMENT OF TRANSPORTATION
Federal Highway Administration
AGENCY: Federal Highway Administration (FHWA), DOT.

49 CFR Parts 390 and 391
Qualifications of Drivers; Medical Examination     ]— "cfr" segment

[FHWA Docket No. MC-90-6]
RIN 2125-AC44

55 FR 13812

April 12, 1990

ACTION: Notice of proposed rulemaking (NPRM).

SUMMARY: The FHWA is seeking comments on a proposal to amend @ 391.43 of the
Federal Motor Carrier Safety Regulations (FMCSRs) to permit certain licensed
health care professionals to perform physical examinations of commercial motor
vehicle drivers. The FHWA is addressing this issue in response to numerous
```

Source: Mead Data Central, Inc. © 1993

Figure 12.20. Sample Document from FEDREG File in LEXIS

You might also want to conduct a broader search for references to the *C.F.R.* part in which the section you are updating is found, especially if a search for just that section does not retrieve any documents. An agency might have repealed or otherwise affected a range of sections, or even an entire *C.F.R.* part, without referring to the specific section you want to update. In anticipation of this possibility in connection with 49 C.F.R. § 391.15, you could carry out searches along these lines in FEDREG:

```
cfr(49 pre/5 391) and (§391.1! or 391.1!) and
date aft september 1988

cfr(49 pre/5 391) and date aft september 1988
```

Using the *Federal Register* file (FEDREG) in LEXIS to identify indirect changes to federal regulations. Finally, you can use the FEDREG file to determine whether an agency has indirectly affected the text of a regulation you want to update. For instance, an agency might change a regulation containing a definition that applies in numerous other regulations in the *Code of Federal Regulations*. To determine whether a regulation has been indirectly affected by agency action, you can select key words or phrases reflecting the regulation's subject matter and search for references to those words or phrases in the FEDREG file.

Similarly, a *Federal Register* document might include agency commentary citing the regulation you are updating even though the document itself does not modify your regulation (and the "cfr" segment therefore does not contain a reference to the *C.F.R.* title and part numbers of your regulation). To retrieve documents of this sort, you could omit a "cfr" segment restriction and search for the title and part numbers anywhere in a *Federal Register* document. Your search request would take this form:

```
(49 pre/5 391) and (§391.15 or 391.15) and
date aft september 1988
```

Summary of using the *Federal Register* file (FEDREG) to update federal administrative regulations in LEXIS. Figure 12.21 summarizes the techniques for updating federal administrative regulations through FEDREG.

Using the LSA file to update federal administrative regulations in LEXIS. In book-based research, the "List of C.F.R. Sections Affected" (known as "LSA") provides the starting point for updating a federal regulation when you know its *Code of Federal Regulations* citation.[298] Issued monthly as a separate pamphlet by the Government Printing Office (GPO), the LSA cross-references sections in the *Code of Federal Regulations* with the *Federal Register* documents containing changes made to the *C.F.R.* sections since the *C.F.R.* titles containing them were last recompiled.

LEXIS offers an online version of the LSA in the LSA file in the GENFED library. When you select the LSA file, you go directly to the text of the file, which begins with a table of contents called the LSA Guide, shown in Figure 12.22. Once in the LSA file, you can use any of three methods to locate *Federal Register* documents affecting your regulation:

- At the LSA Guide in Figure 12.22, transmit the page number for the *C.F.R.* title containing the regulation you want to update. The computer will then display the portion of the LSA table that lists *Federal Register* documents affecting regulations in the *C.F.R.* title you selected.

  Figure 12.23 depicts the first two screens of the listing for Title 5 from the LSA covering the period from January 2 through August 31, 1992. As the figure shows, an LSA table consists of three columns: the left column identifies the *C.F.R.* section affected by a *Federal Register* document, the middle column indicates how the section was affected, and the right column specifies where in the

[298] For a brief explanation of using the print version of LSA, see CHRISTOPHER G. WREN & JILL R. WREN, THE LEGAL RESEARCH MANUAL: A GAME PLAN FOR LEGAL RESEARCH AND ANALYSIS 115 (2d ed. 1986).

If you want to	Follow this procedure in LEXIS

Retrieve a *Federal Register* document when you know its citation	type `lexsee` (or `lxe`) followed by the citation of the *Federal Register* document; then press TRANSMIT
	Example: To retrieve 55 Fed. Reg. 3546, transmit one of these search requests:
	`lexsee 55 fr 3546`
	`lxe 55 fedreg 3546`
	`lexsee 55 fed reg 3546`

Retrieve *Federal Register* documents that have affected the *Code of Federal Regulations* provision you are updating	gain access to the FEDREG file and search the "cfr" segment for references to the *C.F.R.* title and part number containing the provision
	Example: To retrieve *Federal Register* documents affecting 49 C.F.R. § 391.15, gain access to FEDREG and transmit a search request along these lines:
	`cfr(49 pre/5 391) and (§391.15 or 391.15)`
	`cfr(49 pre/5 391) and (§391.1! or 391.1!)`

Retrieve *Federal Register* documents that might have indirectly affected the *Code of Federal Regulations* provision you are updating	gain access to the FEDREG file and search for key words or phrases reflecting the subject matter of the provision

Figure 12.21. Quick Guide to Updating Federal Administrative Regulations Through the *Federal Register* File (FEDREG) in LEXIS

```
                         LEVEL 1 - 1 OF 50 ITEMS

                    LSA-List of CFR Sections Affected

                               LSA GUIDE

The LSA Guide contains a list of CFR sections that have been affected.  To
review the CFR sections, type the page number listed to the right of the CFR
Title number and TRANSMIT.  For additional Titles press NEXT PAGE or type .np.

To Review-Type    To Review-Type    To Review-Type    To Review-Type

Title 1    3      Title 9    9      Title 15   15     Title 21   21
Title 3    4      Title 10   10     Title 16   16     Title 22   22
Title 4    5      Title 11   11     Title 17   17     Title 23   23
Title 5    6      Title 12   12     Title 18   18     Title 24   24
Title 7    7      Title 13   13     Title 19   19     Title 25   25
Title 8    8      Title 14   14     Title 20   20     Title 26   26

To search the MONTHLY LSA, press NEW SEARCH or type .ns; enter any term and
TRANSMIT.
```

```
                         LEVEL 1 - 2 OF 50 ITEMS

                    LSA-List of CFR Sections Affected

                               LSA GUIDE

The LSA Guide contains a list of CFR sections that have been affected.  To
review the CFR sections, type the page number listed to the right of the CFR
Title number and TRANSMIT.  For additional Titles press PREV PAGE or type .pp.

To Review-Type    To Review-Type    To Review-Type    To Review-Type

Title 27   27     Title 33   33     Title 39   39     Title 45   45
Title 28   28     Title 34   34     Title 40   40     Title 46   46
Title 29   29     Title 35   35     Title 41   41     Title 47   47
Title 30   30     Title 36   36     Title 42   42     Title 48   48
Title 31   31     Title 37   37     Title 43   43     Title 49   49
Title 32   32     Title 38   38     Title 44   44     Title 50   50

To search the MONTHLY LSA, press NEW SEARCH or type .ns; enter any term and
TRANSMIT.
```

Source: Mead Data Central, Inc. © 1993

Figure 12.22. Table of Contents for the LSA File in LEXIS

```
                        LEVEL 1 - 6 OF 50 ITEMS

                    LSA-List of CFR Sections Affected

                            August 31, 1992

         CHANGES JANUARY 2, 1992 THROUGH AUGUST 31, 1992

                              Monthly LSA

To view the full text of the FR (Federal Register) cite, use the LEXSEE (R)
feature, e.g., TRANSMIT LXE 57 FR 1665.  To perform a new search, press NEW
SEARCH or type .ns and TRANSMIT.  To return to the table of contents for the LSA
Guide, press FIRST DOC or type .fd.  To view the next document press NEXT DOC or
type .nd.

                   TITLE 5 - ADMINISTRATIVE PERSONNEL

Chapter I - Office of Personnel Management (Parts 1 - 1199)

    9                   Removal at 56 FR 18660 confirmed    ... 57 FR 10123
    212.301             Amended                             ... 57 FR 10123
    213                 Authority citation revised          ... 57 FR 17847
```

```
          TITLE 5; August 31, 1992; * DENOTES CURRENT MONTH'S CHANGES

    213.3102            (j) revised                         ... 57 FR 17847
    213.3202            Regulation at 56 FR 18661
                        confirmed                           ... 57 FR 10123
    213.3301 - 213.3302 Regulation at 56 FR 18660
                        confirmed                           ... 57 FR 10123
    213.3301b           Regulation at 56 FR 18660
                        confirmed                           ... 57 FR 10123
    214.201             Regulation at 56 FR 18661
                        confirmed                           ... 57 FR 10123
    294                 Authority citation revised          ... 57 FR 32150
    294.106             Revised                             ... 57 FR 32150
    294.107             (b) and (c) revised                 ... 57 FR 32150
    294.111             (b) revised                         ... 57 FR 32150
    294.112             Added                               ... 57 FR 32150
    297.501             (b)(8) heading revised and existing
                        text redesignated as (b)(8)(i);
                        (b)(8)(ii) added                    ... 57 FR 20956
    300.301             Removal at 56 FR 18661 confirmed    ... 57 FR 10123
    300.402             Revised                             ... 57 FR 10124
    305                 Removal at 56 FR 18661 confirmed    ... 57 FR 10123
    317                 Regulation at 56 FR 18661
                        confirmed                           ... 57 FR 10123
```

Source: Mead Data Central, Inc. © 1993

Figure 12.23. Part of the LSA Table in LEXIS (Showing Changes to Title 5 of the *Code of Federal Regulations*)

Federal Register you can find the document that effected the change.

If the *C.F.R.* section you are updating does not appear on the part of the LSA table that initially displays, you can page down through the table until you come to the portion that covers your regulation.

- You can use the FOCUS feature (explained on pages 336–40) to locate references to the regulation you are updating. For example, if you wanted to locate *Federal Register* documents affecting section 351.802 of Title 5 of the *C.F.R.*, you could transmit

```
focus "title 5" and 351.802
```

- You can press the NEW SEARCH key and transmit a search request, such as

```
"title 5" and 351.802
```

Given the way the LSA file is organized at this writing, a FOCUS search can prove more efficient than a search using the NEW SEARCH key. The LSA file contains not only the most recent monthly issue of the LSA, but issues from previous months. Because the LSA cumulates, however, you only need to check the most recent issue. FOCUS searches in only the most recent online issue of the LSA, but a search using the NEW SEARCH key searches all online monthly issues of the LSA. Thus, a FOCUS search will retrieve a comprehensive, cumulative online LSA table, while a search using the NEW SEARCH key will retrieve duplicative references from earlier LSA tables.

Regardless of the way you choose to search the LSA file, be sure that before using the file, you check the date of the online LSA and the date of the most recent recompilation of the *C.F.R.* title containing the regulation you are updating. Mead Data updates the LSA file within 24 to 48 hours after receiving from the GPO the computer tapes containing LSA data files. But any delay by the GPO in providing the tapes reduces the updating value of the LSA file. During the writing of this book, for instance, the most recent issue of the LSA in LEXIS in late June 1993 only covered changes through August 31, 1992. If you are updating a regulation found in a *C.F.R.* title recompiled more recently than the most recent online issue of the LSA, you would waste time using the LSA file to update the regulation; the regulation would already incorporate any changes listed in the online LSA.

The relationship between searching the LSA file and using other techniques for updating federal regulations online. Because the online LSA is a consolidated table of changes to the *Code of Federal Regulations*, using the LSA file to update a federal regulation can provide a convenient alternative to searching the FEDREG file with a "cfr" segment restriction to locate references to the regulation you are updating (as explained earlier). The LSA file does not, however, eliminate the need for searching the "cfr" segment. Because the GPO issues the LSA only once a month, while Mead Data updates the FEDREG file daily, you would still search the "cfr" segment of *Federal Register* documents issued since the date of the most recent LSA.

Updating through specialized and nonlegal files in LEXIS

LEXIS provides access to a wide assortment of files that highlight current activities in specialized areas of law (*e.g.*, banking, securities, tax, labor, environmental regulation, international trade). These specialized online materials often identify the most recent federal and state cases, statutes, and administrative regulations and decisions relevant to specific areas of practice. Many of these specialized libraries and files (such as Commerce Clearing House's *Tax Day-State* or the Bureau of National Affairs' *Environment Reporter*) consist of online versions of printed publications. Others (such as BNA's *Banking Daily* and *International Trade Daily*) appear only online. All of these specialized materials are updated regularly—often weekly, sometimes daily or even twice daily.

If you are updating an authority in an area of law for which a specialized library or file exists, you can search the specialized online materials for recent developments that have affected your authority. This updating technique is analogous to updating through printed looseleaf reporter services.[299]

When you update through specialized files in LEXIS (just as when you update through printed looseleaf reporters), you might find, for example, that an administrative agency rescinded the regulation you are updating or that a court invalidated a federal statute that served as the model for the state statute you are updating. To update in a specialized file, transmit a search request based on the citation of your authority (see pages 441–61) or on key words reflecting the subject matter of the authority you are updating (see Chapter 7).

To determine whether a specialized LEXIS file covers the subject of the authority you want to update, check the printed *LEXIS/NEXIS Library Contents and Alphabetical List* or *LEXIS Product Guide*. In addition, you can check the online descriptions available through the file menu of the appropriate topical library (such as the ENERGY library) or of a library consisting of specialty publications issued by a particular publisher (such as the BNA or CCH library).

For some research projects, you might want to extend your updating search to NEXIS, the companion service to LEXIS. NEXIS offers online ac-

[299] *See* CHRISTOPHER G. WREN & JILL R. WREN, THE LEGAL RESEARCH MANUAL: A GAME PLAN FOR LEGAL RESEARCH AND ANALYSIS 118–19 (2d ed. 1986).

cess to numerous non-law publications, such as *The New York Times*, *The Washington Post*, the *National Journal*, and *Business Week*, that often cover current developments in the law.[300] The *LEXIS/NEXIS Library Contents and Alphabetical List* provides additional information about NEXIS files.

Updating through the Hot Topics library (HOTTOP) in LEXIS

The HOTTOP library in LEXIS contains summaries of selected recent developments (such as the issuance of court decisions or the proposal of administrative regulations) in various areas of law practice. Topical areas covered in HOTTOP include taxation, intellectual property, natural resources, and ethics. To see whether HOTTOP covers an area of law in which you want to review recent developments, select the HOTLAW file in the HOTTOP library. The monitor will display a list of topics for which LEXIS provides notice of recent legal developments. On-screen prompts explain how to select a topic and how to view summaries under the topic. On-screen prompts also highlight some additional research options available in HOTLAW summaries, such as the ability to use pre-formulated search requests to retrieve the text of a summarized document or to search a file for documents related to an issue discussed in a HOTLAW summary.

Updating with the Electronic Clipping Service ("ECLIPSE") in LEXIS

For research projects that might last several days, weeks, months, or even years, you can use the ECLIPSE feature to save search requests you want the LEXIS computer to repeat automatically at regular intervals. For example, suppose you are involved in protracted litigation in which a federal administrative regulation plays a critical role. You could use ECLIPSE to search periodically in the *Federal Register* file (FEDREG) for changes in the text of the regulation. You could also use ECLIPSE to search, say, case-law files for federal court decisions interpreting or otherwise affecting the regulation.

Setting up an ECLIPSE search in LEXIS. To set up a search for ECLIPSE to perform, follow these steps:

1. Develop a search request, using appropriate search terms and connectors.

[300] For more about searching in nonlegal databases, see Chapter 13.

2. Select an appropriate file, conduct the search, and skim through the results to see whether they meet your needs. If necessary, modify your search request until you obtain satisfactory results.

3. Press the key labelled SELECT SERV to display the "Select Service" menu. At the menu (shown in Figure 10.03 on page 241), you'll see an entry for "ECLIPSE SERVICES" and sub-entries for saving and recalling search requests.

   (If you decide at this point, or at any other step in creating an ECLIPSE instruction, that you do not want to continue the procedure, you can stop by pressing the EXIT SERV key.)

4. Type **sav** and press TRANSMIT to begin the procedure for saving your search request as an ECLIPSE instruction.

   The monitor will display a screen like that in Figure 12.24. As the figure indicates, transmitting **sav** reads into your ECLIPSE instruction the search request itself, along with the name of the library and file in which you most recently performed the search (and in which ECLIPSE will repeat the search).

5. At the top of the screen like that in Figure 12.24, type a name for your search, then press TRANSMIT.

```
<--------------------------------------  [Type a name for your search,
                                          then press TRANSMIT.]
....5...10..

SELECTED LIBRARY:  GENFED                                      ┐
   SELECTED FILE:  COURTS                                      │
    SAVED SEARCH:  LEWIS AND (445 PRE/5 55) AND UNCOUNSEL!     ├─ search instructions
         RESULTS:  28                                          ┘
-------------------------------------------------------------------------------

        TO:                                          TRANSMIT:
        ---------------------------------------      ----------------------
        Save your current search request for         A reference NAME
        automatic updates                            of up to 12 characters


WARNING: Be sure that your search does not contain a Date segment restriction
that would preclude finding new CASES, such as: DATE BEF OCTOBER 3, 1993

To exit ECLIPSE SAVE, press the EXIT SERV key.
For further explanation, press the H key (for HELP) and then the ENTER key.
```

Source: Mead Data Central, Inc. © 1993

Figure 12.24. Screen for Naming an ECLIPSE Search in LEXIS

6. The monitor will display a screen asking you to indicate whether you want your ECLIPSE results stored in a computer at Mead Data Central or printed on a stand-alone printer. If you want to store the results in Mead Data's computer, type o (for "online system") and press TRANSMIT. If you want to print the results, type p (for "LEXIS/NEXIS printer") and press TRANSMIT.

7. The monitor will then display a screen asking you to choose the frequency with which you want ECLIPSE to update your search. Type d for daily updates, b for daily updates on business days only (Monday through Friday), w for weekly updates, or m for monthly updates; then press TRANSMIT. For weekly or monthly updates, ECLIPSE will run the search on the same day of the week or month that you initiated the instruction.

   In selecting an update frequency, keep in mind the updating schedule for the file in which ECLIPSE will search. It makes no sense to conduct a daily ECLIPSE search in a file updated only weekly or monthly, for example.

8. If you selected a printer as your option in Step 6, the monitor will next display a screen asking you to choose a display format for your ECLIPSE results. Press the desired display format key (KWIC, FULL, CITE, VAR KWIC, or SEGMTS). If you selected storage in Mead Data's computer as your option in Step 6, you will not be asked to select a display format at this point.

9. Next, the monitor will display your ECLIPSE instruction for you to review and confirm whether you want to save it. If you selected a printer as your option in Step 6, you will see a screen like the one in Figure 12.25; if you selected storage in Mead Data's computer as your option in Step 6, you will see a screen like the one in Figure 12.26.

   If you want to save your ECLIPSE instruction, transmit y (for "yes"). If you decide you do not want to save the ECLIPSE instruction, transmit n (for "no"). If you selected a printer as your option in Step 6, you have a third choice (shown in Figure 12.25): you can transmit r (for "report") to save the instruction *and* receive a printout of the results of the search request you just saved through ECLIPSE.

10. After you transmit y, r, or n, the monitor will display a screen prompting you to press the EXIT SERV key to return to the screen you were viewing before you invoked ECLIPSE.

```
            NAME:  UNCOUNSELED
SELECTED LIBRARY:  GENFED
   SELECTED FILE:  COURTS
    SAVED SEARCH:  LEWIS AND (445 PRE/5 55) AND UNCOUNSEL!
         RESULTS:  28
 DELIVERY OPTION:  LEXIS/NEXIS PRINTER
 UPDATE SCHEDULE:  WEEKLY
   REPORT FORMAT:  CITE
    FIRST UPDATE:  JUNE 23, 1993
--------------------------------------------------------------------------------


        TO:                                            ENTER:
        ---------------------------------------        --------------
        Save the search                                   Y
        Save the search and receive a report              R
        of the 28 INITIAL RESULTS
        Cancel the ECLIPSE SAVE                           N

For further explanation, press the H key (for HELP) and then the ENTER key.
```

Source: Mead Data Central, Inc. © 1993

Figure 12.25. Screen for Confirming Whether to Save an ECLIPSE Search in LEXIS (Stand-Alone Printer)

```
            NAME:  UNCOUNSELED
SELECTED LIBRARY:  GENFED
   SELECTED FILE:  COURTS
    SAVED SEARCH:  LEWIS AND (445 PRE/5 55) AND UNCOUNSEL!
         RESULTS:  28
 DELIVERY OPTION:  ONLINE SYSTEM
 UPDATE SCHEDULE:  WEEKLY
    FIRST UPDATE:  JUNE 23, 1993
--------------------------------------------------------------------------------


        TO:                                            ENTER:
        ---------------------------------------        -----------
        Save the search as it is shown above           Y (for YES)

        Cancel the ECLIPSE SAVE                        N (for NO)


For further explanation, press the H key (for HELP) and then the ENTER key.
```

Source: Mead Data Central, Inc. © 1993

Figure 12.26. Screen for Confirming Whether to Save an ECLIPSE Search in LEXIS (Online Storage)

You can set up more than one ECLIPSE search. For each ECLIPSE search you want to establish, repeat the steps above, giving each new search a unique name.

Modifying an ECLIPSE search in LEXIS. You can modify any or all aspects of an ECLIPSE search you have already saved. You can change the search request itself, the file in which to perform the search, the frequency with which the search will be updated, or (if you selected the printing option) the display format of the search results.

To modify an existing ECLIPSE search, follow the procedure for setting up an ECLIPSE search. Begin at Step 1 (above) by typing and transmitting the modified version of the ECLIPSE search you want to change. Thus, if your original ECLIPSE search consisted of `(lease w/10 apartment) and (plumbing or water)`, and you wanted to modify it to add `or heat or light or electric!`, you would transmit `(lease w/10 apartment) and (plumbing or water or heat or light or electric!)` as the modified ECLIPSE search request.

Continue the ECLIPSE procedure through Step 4. At Step 5, when the computer prompts you to name the search, type and transmit the *same* name you originally gave the search you are modifying.[301] Transmitting a name assigned to an existing ECLIPSE search causes the computer to display a message that a search already exists with that name. The message will also ask you to transmit `y` (for "yes") to confirm that you really want to replace the existing search with the new one, or `n` (for "no") if you do not. Replacing an existing search eliminates the search results ECLIPSE accumulated in connection with that search.

Checking the results of an ECLIPSE search in LEXIS. Each time ECLIPSE performs an updating search, it automatically stores the updated results in a computer at Mead Data Central (if you selected "online system" as your method for receiving updated ECLIPSE results) or prints the updated results on a stand-alone printer (if you selected "LEXIS/NEXIS printer" as your method for receiving results). Where printing occurs will depend on your computer hardware and on your contract with Mead Data.

If you have opted to have ECLIPSE results stored online, you will see a message when you log on to LEXIS notifying you when an ECLIPSE search has retrieved any new documents. When you see this message, you can retrieve your ECLIPSE results by following this procedure:

1. Press the SELECT SERV key to display the "Select Service" menu (shown in Figure 10.03 on page 241).

[301] The need to transmit the name of an existing search highlights the importance of keeping good notes when you use a computer in legal research. Chapter 14 provides tips for taking notes.

2. At the menu, type `rec` (for "recall a previously saved ECLIPSE search"), then press TRANSMIT.

   The monitor will display a list of the ECLIPSE searches for which you selected online storage when you set up the searches; the names of searches for which ECLIPSE has retrieved new results will appear highlighted. On-screen prompts will ask you which search you want to recall; after you specify the desired search, the monitor will display a screen like that in Figure 12.28.

   (If you change your mind at this point and decide you do not want to continue with your review of updated ECLIPSE results, press the EXIT SERV key.)

3. Type `r` (for "retrieve") and press TRANSMIT to retrieve updating results, which will consist of documents found since the last scheduled update.

   Transmitting `r` causes the computer to exit the ECLIPSE feature and to run the search in LEXIS. You might see a message asking whether you want your ECLIPSE search to override the most recent search request you transmitted in LEXIS (along with its search results). The monitor displays this message if you have performed a LEXIS search for which the results are still available for viewing at the time you invoke ECLIPSE. When this message appears, follow the on-screen instructions for designating your choice.

   If you want to return to ECLIPSE, press the SELECT SERV key and choose an ECLIPSE option from the "Select Service" menu.

Performing an ECLIPSE search in LEXIS between scheduled updates. Although setting up an ECLIPSE search involves establishing fixed intervals at which you will receive updated search results, you can, at your discretion, direct ECLIPSE to perform an updating search at *any* time. To carry out an interim search:

1. Press the SELECT SERV key to display the "Select Service" menu (shown in Figure 10.03 on page 241).

2. At the menu, type `rec` (for "recall a previously saved ECLIPSE search"), then press TRANSMIT.

   The monitor will display a list of your ECLIPSE searches, and on-screen prompts will ask you which search you want to recall. After you specify the desired search, the monitor will display a screen like that in Figure 12.27 or 12.28; the screen you see will depend on whether you selected online storage or printing on a stand-alone printer when you set up the ECLIPSE search.

```
           NAME:  UNCOUNSELED
SELECTED LIBRARY:  GENFED
   SELECTED FILE:  COURTS
    SAVED SEARCH:  LEWIS AND (445 PRE/5 55) AND UNCOUNSEL!
 DELIVERY OPTION:  LEXIS/NEXIS PRINTER
 UPDATE SCHEDULE:  WEEKLY
   REPORT FORMAT:  CITE
      DATE SAVED:  JUNE 16, 1993            PREVIOUS RESULTS: 28
     LAST UPDATE:  JUNE 23, 1993         LAST UPDATE RESULTS: 0
     NEXT UPDATE:  JUNE 30, 1993       TOTAL RESULTS (JUN. 23): 28
-------------------------------------------------------------------------------

          TO:                                         ENTER:
          -----------------------------------------   ---------
          See new results                               U
          See ALL results                               A
          Delete the search                             D
          Return to saved search list                   N
          View print options                            OPT

For further explanation, press the H key (for HELP) and then the ENTER key.
```

Source: Mead Data Central, Inc. © 1993

Figure 12.27. Screen for Executing or Deleting an ECLIPSE Search in LEXIS (Stand-Alone Printer)

```
           NAME:  UNCOUNSELED
SELECTED LIBRARY:  GENFED
   SELECTED FILE:  COURTS
    SAVED SEARCH:  LEWIS AND (445 PRE/5 55) AND UNCOUNSEL!
 DELIVERY OPTION:  ONLINE SYSTEM
 UPDATE SCHEDULE:  WEEKLY
      DATE SAVED:  JUNE 16, 1993

-------------------------------------------------------------------------------

TO:                                                         ENTER :
--------------------------------------------------------    ----------------
Retrieve new information for the saved search               R (for RETRIEVE)

Mark the saved search for deletion at the end of the day    D (for DELETE)

Return to your list of saved searches                       N (for NO)

For further explanation, press the H key (for HELP) and then the ENTER key.
```

Source: Mead Data Central, Inc. © 1993

Figure 12.28. Screen for Executing or Deleting an ECLIPSE Search in LEXIS (Online Storage)

(If you change your mind at this point and decide you do not want to continue with your ECLIPSE search, press the EXIT SERV key.)

3. Instruct the computer to retrieve updated ECLIPSE results. The instruction you transmit will depend on whether you selected online storage or printing on a stand-alone printer when you set up the ECLIPSE search.

   If you selected printing on a stand-alone printer, transmit `u` (for "updates") to obtain updating results consisting only of documents found since the last scheduled update. To obtain updating results consisting of all documents found since the ECLIPSE search was first set up, transmit `a` (for "all"). You can see these choices presented in Figure 12.27.

   If you selected online storage, you would simply transmit `r` (for "retrieve"), which will retrieve updating results consisting only of documents found since the last scheduled update. Figure 12.28 shows the screen that presents this option.

   Transmitting `u`, `a`, or `r` causes the computer to exit the ECLIPSE feature and to run the search in LEXIS. You might see a message asking whether you want your ECLIPSE search to override the most recent search request you transmitted in LEXIS (along with its search results). The monitor displays this message if you have performed a LEXIS search for which the results are still available for viewing at the time you invoke ECLIPSE. When this message appears, follow the on-screen instructions for designating your choice.

   If you want to return to ECLIPSE, press the SELECT SERV key and choose an ECLIPSE option from the "Select Service" menu.

Deleting an ECLIPSE search in LEXIS. You can delete an ECLIPSE search by following this procedure:

1. Press the SELECT SERV key to display the "Select Service" menu (shown in Figure 10.03 on page 241).

2. At the menu, type `rec` (for "recall a previously saved ECLIPSE search"), then press TRANSMIT.

   The monitor will display a list of your ECLIPSE searches, and on-screen prompts will ask you which search you want to recall for deletion. After you specify the desired search, the monitor will display a screen like that in Figure 12.27 or 12.28; the screen you see will depend on whether you selected online storage or printing on a stand-alone printer when you set up the ECLIPSE search.

3. Type `d` (for "delete") and press TRANSMIT. The computer will mark the search for deletion at the end of the day.

   You can still save the search from deletion if, before the end of the day, you transmit `rec` at the "Select Service" menu and then follow the on-screen instructions for restoring a deleted search.

Updating the Law Through WESTLAW

Shepardizing cases through WESTLAW[302]

Introduction. Whether in a printed or an online version, *Shepard's Citations* (often referred to as "citators") serve the same purpose: to permit legal researchers to ascertain an authority's status. Chapter 6 of *The Legal Research Manual* explains how to use printed versions of *Shepard's Citations.*[303] If you know how to use printed *Shepard's Citations*, using the online version will follow easily.

To use a Shepard's citator (that is, to "Shepardize"), you must have already found an authority about whose status you are curious. For purposes of Shepardizing, this known authority is called the cited authority; throughout the following explanation of online Shepardizing, the case of *State v. Yoder*, 49 Wis. 2d 430, 182 N.W.2d 539 (1971), will serve as the illustrative cited authority. The entries appearing in Shepard's tables for the cited authority in which you're interested (*i.e.*, that you are Shepardizing) are called the citing authorities; these authorities—such as cases, law review and *A.L.R.* articles, Attorney General Opinions—are citing to (*i.e.*, referring to) the item in whose treatment you're interested.

Figure 12.30 on page 503 shows the first screen of a Shepard's table for *State v. Yoder* as it appears online in WESTLAW. Figure 12.29 on page 502 shows the table for *Yoder* as it appears in the main volume of a printed Shepard's citator. Although you will notice differences in the appearance of the Shepard's tables online and the appearance of their printed counterparts, you can accomplish online all the Shepardizing activities possible in the books:

- looking for cases, law review articles, and other authorities that cite the case

[302] In addition to providing online access to *Shepard's Citations*, WESTLAW offers Shepard's PreView, a special citator service developed jointly by West Publishing Company and Shepard's/McGraw-Hill. Shepard's PreView provides advance notice of citations appearing in West reporters before the online or printed versions of *Shepard's Citations* incorporate those citing references. Pages 524 to 528 explain Shepard's PreView.

[303] CHRISTOPHER G. WREN & JILL R. WREN, THE LEGAL RESEARCH MANUAL: A GAME PLAN FOR LEGAL RESEARCH AND ANALYSIS 95–116 (2d ed. 1986).

- checking the treatment of the case (that is, how other courts have evaluated the case—*e.g.*, explained it, distinguished it, overruled it—in the course of deciding later cases)
- screening for later cases that have referred to a specific headnote or syllabus paragraph in the case you are Shepardizing
- determining the history of the case (*i.e.*, how the case was handled as it worked its way through the legal system)
- finding parallel citations (if any) of the case you are Shepardizing

Often, you can carry out these activities more efficiently online than in the printed *Shepard's Citations.*

A note of caution, however: currently, the online coverage of *Shepard's Citations* is not as comprehensive as the printed Shepard's coverage. At this time, the online versions of *Shepard's Citations* available through WESTLAW do not allow you to Shepardize all the types of authorities (such as municipal ordinances) you can update through the printed citators.[304]

Moreover, for some of the authorities you can Shepardize through WESTLAW, the online version of Shepard's currently does not extend as far back in time as the printed version. For example, if you Shepardize the landmark case of *Marbury v. Madison*, 5 U.S. (1 Cranch) 137 (1803), you will now find *Ex Parte Republic of Peru*, 318 U.S. 578 (1943), listed in the online Shepard's as the earliest U.S. Supreme Court case citing *Marbury*; in the printed version of Shepard's, you will find *Cooper v. Telfair*, 4 U.S. (4 Dall.) 14 (1800), listed as the earliest U.S. Supreme Court case citing *Marbury*.[305]

So, when you Shepardize online, make sure you know the scope of Shepard's coverage for the authorities you plan to update. The monitor will show pertinent scope information when it displays the results of a Shepard's search; the scope information appears on the line labelled "Coverage" near the top of the screen, as illustrated in Figure 12.30 on page 503 and explained on pages 504–05.

You can also use the "scope" command in WESTLAW to find scope information about an online Shepard's citator. While viewing a Shepard's table, type `scope` (or `sc`) and press ENTER; the monitor will display coverage

[304] For a list of authorities you can Shepardize in printed citators, see CHRISTOPHER G. WREN & JILL R. WREN, THE LEGAL RESEARCH MANUAL: A GAME PLAN FOR LEGAL RESEARCH AND ANALYSIS 96 n.34 (2d ed. 1986).

[305] Why, you might ask, does a reference to *Marbury* appear in *Telfair*, which was decided three years before *Marbury*? In making a post-*Marbury* revision of 4 U.S. (Dall.), the court reporter added to *Telfair* an editorial footnote explaining that *Marbury* answered a question posed by Justice Chase in *Telfair*. Shepard's picked up the reference to *Marbury* from the footnote appended to *Telfair* but treated the reference as if it had occurred in the original decision. Thus, the Shepard's table for *Marbury* shows *Telfair* citing *Marbury*, even though the Court decided *Marbury* three years after *Telfair*.

information for the citator containing the table you are viewing. (Alternatively, you can use the JUMP feature, explained on page 284: press the TAB key to position the cursor under the ">" symbol or triangle next to the word "SCOPE" at the bottom of the screen, and then press ENTER.) At any time while Shepardizing in WESTLAW, you can display coverage information about any online Shepard's citator by transmitting `scope` (or `sc`) followed by the abbreviation of the citator; for example, to see coverage information for *Shepard's Tennessee Citations*, you can type `sc tenn` and press ENTER.

If the online version of a Shepard's citator does not provide the coverage you need, you will have to do some or all of your Shepardizing in the printed *Shepard's Citations*. For instance, in the earlier example of online Shepard's coverage for U.S. Supreme Court cases citing *Marbury v. Madison*, you would miss 143 years' worth of citing cases—all those before 1943—if you Shepardized only online.

Of course, cases found through online Shepardizing often mention earlier cases not included as citing cases in online Shepard's tables. But later citing cases might not mention all the earlier citing cases. Consequently, the omission of the earlier citing cases from an online Shepard's table can, by cutting off part of the evolutionary trace of the case you are updating, still impede your full understanding of that case. Sometimes, for example, an earlier case not included in an online Shepard's table will set out a more complete discussion of the meaning of the case being updated, thus helping you gain insight into the contemporaneous understanding of the case. Similarly, the omission of earlier cases cuts off your access to Shepard's analysis codes accompanying those cases, thus denying you the opportunity to readily identify citing cases that have affected in certain ways (such as by distinguishing or limiting) the case you are updating. For instance, in the printed Shepard's table, an analysis code might draw your attention to a citing case that has distinguished the case you are updating; if that citing case is too early to be included in the online Shepard's table, you might not discover that your case has been distinguished on a point important to your research problem.

The following explanation takes you through the steps in Shepardizing a case through WESTLAW. Figure 12.43 on pages 545–51 summarizes the steps.

Gaining access to Shepard's case tables in WESTLAW. You can initiate a Shepard's search at nearly any time after logging on to WESTLAW. You can begin Shepardizing as soon as the monitor displays the WESTLAW Directory; you do not need to select a database before starting to Shepardize. Or, you can wait until you have retrieved some documents from a database before you begin Shepardizing.

To retrieve a case citator table through the Shepard's service in WESTLAW, you use a search request based on the citation of the authority you want to Shepardize:

- If you are viewing the case you want to Shepardize, simply type `shep` (or `sh`) and press ENTER. The WESTLAW computer will automatically "read in" to the search request the citation of your case.

  Suppose you are viewing a case that has been reprinted in more than one reporter, and that therefore has parallel citations to, say, an official reporter and an unofficial West reporter. Which citation will the computer Shepardize? (Recall that you can get different Shepardizing results depending on which parallel citation you use to Shepardize.)[306]

  If the case has a citation to a West reporter, the WESTLAW computer will automatically read in to your "shep" or "sh" command the West citation; for *Yoder*, that would be 182 N.W.2d 539. If the case does not have a West citation, transmitting `shep` or `sh` might cause the monitor to display a message that the case is an unpublished decision that cannot be Shepardized; however, you still might be able to Shepardize the case by using the technique explained below for Shepardizing an authority you are not viewing, *i.e.*, by transmitting `shep` or `sh` followed by a citation.[307]

  You can also transmit `shep` or `sh` while you are viewing the results of an Insta-Cite search[308] or a Shepard's PreView search.[309] Alternatively, you can use the JUMP feature; for example, while viewing the screen in Figure 12.38 on page 525, you could retrieve the case's Shepard's table by using the TAB key to position the cursor under the JUMP marker (">") in front of "Shepard's" at the bottom of the screen, and then pressing ENTER. Whether you type the command or use the JUMP feature, the computer will Shepardize the citation used in your Insta-Cite or Shepard's PreView request.

- If you want to Shepardize a case you are *not* viewing—say, a case you see mentioned in a law review article you are looking at online,

[306] *See* CHRISTOPHER G. WREN & JILL R. WREN, THE LEGAL RESEARCH MANUAL: A GAME PLAN FOR LEGAL RESEARCH AND ANALYSIS 101, 104 (2d ed. 1986). For an example of different results in online Shepardizing, see page 509.

[307] If a case does not have a West citation, you might have to track down a citation that can be Shepardized. Although the display of a case in WESTLAW will show parallel citations even if the case has not been published in a West reporter, WESTLAW might not display *all* the available parallel citations. The displayed citations might not be ones you can Shepardize, while a citation omitted from the display might be one you could Shepardize. Consequently, if the monitor displays a message that you cannot Shepardize a citation you obtained from WESTLAW, explore the possibility that another parallel citation exists that might work.

[308] Insta-Cite is explained at pages 544 and 552–64.

[309] Shepard's PreView is explained at pages 524–28.

or a parallel citation of the authority you are viewing—type `shep` (or `sh`) followed by the case's citation; then press ENTER. For the citation, type the volume number and abbreviation of the publication in which the case appears and a page number from the case. (If you transmit a page number other than the first page of the case, WESTLAW will determine the page on which the case begins and Shepardize based on that page number.)

For instance, to Shepardize *State v. Yoder*, 49 Wis. 2d 430, 182 N.W.2d 539, you could use any of the following requests:

```
sh 49 wis.2d 430
shep 49 wis2d 430
sh 49ws2d430
sh 49 wis. 2d 430
sh 49 wis.2d 431
sh 182 n.w.2d539
sh 182 nw2d 539
shep 182nw2d539
```

As you can see, you have considerable flexibility in typing your Shepard's request. If you are uncertain about what abbreviation to use, consult the *WESTLAW Reference Manual*, which provides a list of abbreviations that will work in a Shepard's request.[310] You can also find a list of these abbreviations online: type `pubs` and press ENTER anytime while using the Shepard's service; then follow the on-screen instructions. Abbreviations that work in a FIND or Insta-Cite instruction also work in a Shepard's request.

- If you are viewing an authority and see the citation of a case you want to Shepardize, you can use the JUMP feature (explained on page 284) to automate the use of Shepard's for updating that citation. To use JUMP, type `shep` (or `sh`), press the TAB key to position the cursor under the ">" symbol or triangle next to the citation you want to update, and then press ENTER. The computer will read in to your Shepard's request the citation on which you positioned the cursor.
- Sometimes, two or more cases will share the same citation (as occurs, for instance, when more than one case begins on the same page of a case reporter). When you Shepardize such a case in WESTLAW, the monitor will display a list of the cases that share the citation used in the Shepard's instruction. By following the on-

[310] WEST PUBLISHING COMPANY, WESTLAW REFERENCE MANUAL 343–59 (5th ed. 1993) (Appendix H).

screen prompts, you can select the number of the case you want to Shepardize.

To determine which number to select, check the case reporter to see where the printed version of the case appears in relation to any other case beginning on the same page. Alternatively, you can determine the order by transmitting a FIND instruction based on the case's citation.[311] For instance, if you transmit `fi 387 nys2d 426`, the monitor will display a list of the cases sharing that citation and indicate which case is first, which is second, and so on.

- When you Shepardize a case, you might retrieve citator tables from more than one Shepard's citator, as explained on pages 508–12. If you want to limit your Shepard's results to the table from a specific Shepard's citator, you can add to your Shepard's request a parenthetical abbreviation for the Shepard's citator from which you want to retrieve a table. For instance, to retrieve the Shepard's table for 508 F. Supp. 690 from only *Shepard's Federal Citations in Selected Law Reviews*, you would transmit:

```
sh 508 fsupp 690 (flrev)
```

At this time, WESTLAW does not provide an online list of citator abbreviations, but the information is available from WESTLAW reference attorneys at the telephone number listed in Appendix B.

Once you have entered the Shepard's service by transmitting a Shepard's command, you can Shepardize as many authorities as you want during the Shepard's search session. You do not have to type `shep` (or `sh`) each time; just type and transmit a new citation when you want to Shepardize another authority.

Shepard's case tables in WESTLAW. After you transmit a Shepard's request, the monitor displays the first screen of the first Shepard's table for the citation you transmitted. Figure 12.30 on page 503 shows a typical first screen. (Figure 12.31 shows the continuation of the table onto its second screen.) Just as with the printed citators, you need to be sure you have located the correct citator table when you Shepardize online. The heading on the first screen of an online citator table contains information that allows you to verify that you have transmitted the correct citation and, therefore, that the table you retrieved is appropriate for Shepardizing your authority:[312]

[311] For a refresher on FIND, see pages 279–84.

[312] The information in the heading verifies that the computer has conveniently carried out for you the first several steps you take when you Shepardize in printed citators—namely, selecting the proper set of *Shepard's Citations*, collecting all the necessary volumes in that set, finding the correct tables in those volumes, and locating the specific table for Shepardizing your authority. *See* CHRISTOPHER G. WREN & JILL R. WREN, THE LEGAL RESEARCH MANUAL: A GAME PLAN FOR LEGAL RESEARCH AND ANALYSIS 97–104 (2d ed. 1986) (explaining these steps in book-based Shepardizing).

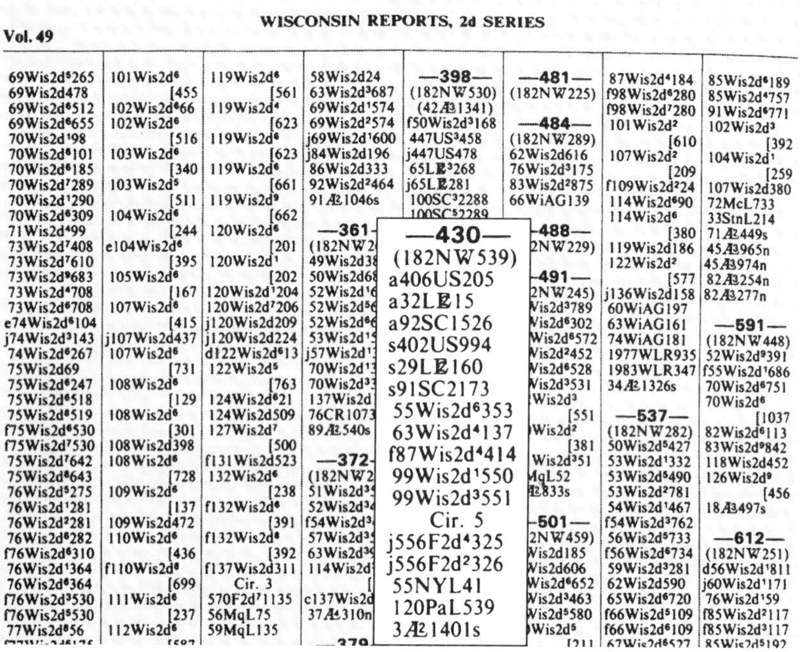

Vol. 49

WISCONSIN REPORTS, 2d SERIES

69Wis2d^{5}265
69Wis2d478
69Wis2d^{6}512
69Wis2d^{6}655
70Wis2d^{1}98
70Wis2d^{6}101
70Wis2d^{6}185
70Wis2d^{7}289
70Wis2d^{1}290
70Wis2d^{6}309
71Wis2d^{4}99
73Wis2d^{7}408
73Wis2d^{7}610
73Wis2d^{9}683
73Wis2d^{4}708
73Wis2d^{6}708
e74Wis2d^{6}104
j74Wis2d^{3}143
74Wis2d^{6}267
75Wis2d69
75Wis2d^{6}247
75Wis2d^{6}518
75Wis2d^{8}519
f75Wis2d^{6}530
f75Wis2d^{7}530
75Wis2d^{7}642
75Wis2d^{8}643
76Wis2d^{5}275
76Wis2d^{1}281
76Wis2d^{2}281
76Wis2d^{8}282
f76Wis2d^{6}310
76Wis2d^{1}364
76Wis2d^{6}364
f76Wis2d^{3}530
f76Wis2d^{5}530
77Wis2d^{8}56

101Wis2d^{6} [455
102Wis2d^{6}66
102Wis2d^{6} [516
103Wis2d^{6} [340
103Wis2d^{5} [511
104Wis2d^{6} [244
e104Wis2d^{6} [395
105Wis2d^{6} [167
107Wis2d^{6} [415
j107Wis2d437
107Wis2d^{6} [731
108Wis2d^{6} [129
108Wis2d^{6} [301
108Wis2d398
108Wis2d^{6} [728
109Wis2d^{6} [137
109Wis2d472
110Wis2d^{6} [436
f110Wis2d^{8} [699
111Wis2d^{6} [237
112Wis2d^{6}

119Wis2d^{6} [561
119Wis2d^{4} [623
119Wis2d^{6} [623
119Wis2d^{6} [661
119Wis2d^{9} [662
120Wis2d^{6} [201
120Wis2d^{1} [202
120Wis2d^{1}204
120Wis2d^{7}206
j120Wis2d209
j120Wis2d224
d122Wis2d^{6}13
122Wis2d^{5} [763
124Wis2d^{6}21
124Wis2d509
127Wis2d^{7} [500
f131Wis2d523
132Wis2d^{6} [238
f132Wis2d^{6} [391
f132Wis2d^{8} [392
f137Wis2d311
Cir. 3
570F2d^{7}1135
56MqL75
59MqL135

58Wis2d24
63Wis2d^{3}687
69Wis2d^{1}574
69Wis2d^{2}574
j69Wis2d^{1}600
j84Wis2d196
86Wis2d333
92Wis2d^{2}464
91A2 1046s

—361—
(182NW2
49Wis2d38
50Wis2d68
52Wis2d^{1}6
52Wis2d^{5}6
52Wis2d^{6}6
53Wis2d^{1}5
j57Wis2d^{1}
70Wis2d^{1}
70Wis2d^{3}
137Wis2d
76CR1073
89A2 540s

—372—
(182NW2
51Wis2d^{3}
52Wis2d^{3}
f54Wis2d^{3}
57Wis2d^{3}
63Wis2d^{3}
114Wis2d
[
c137Wis2d
37A4 310n

—398—
(182NW530)
(42A3 1341)
f50Wis2d^{3}168
447US^{3}458
j447US478
65LE^{3}268
j65LE281
100SC^{3}2288
100SC^{5}2289

—430—
(182NW539)
a406US205
a32LE15
a92SC1526
s402US994
s29LE160
s91SC2173
55Wis2d^{6}353
63Wis2d^{4}137
f87Wis2d^{4}414
99Wis2d^{1}550
99Wis2d^{3}551
Cir. 5
j556F2d^{4}325
j556F2d^{2}326
55NYL41
120PaL539
3A2 1401s

—481—
(182NW225)

—484—
(182NW289)
62Wis2d616
76Wis2d^{3}175
83Wis2d^{2}875
66WiAG139

—488—
2NW229)

—491—
2NW245)
Wis2d^{3}789
Wis2d^{6}302
Wis2d^{6}572
Wis2d^{2}452
Wis2d^{6}528
Wis2d^{3}531
Wis2d^{3} [551
Wis2d^{2} [381
Wis2d^{3}51
MqL52
A2 833s

—501—
2NW459)
Wis2d185
Wis2d606
Wis2d^{6}652
Wis2d^{3}463
Wis2d^{5}580
Wis2d^{5} [211

87Wis2d^{4}184
f98Wis2d^{6}280
f98Wis2d^{7}280
101Wis2d^{2} [610
107Wis2d^{2} [209
f109Wis2d^{2}24
114Wis2d^{6}90
114Wis2d^{6} [380
119Wis2d186
122Wis2d^{2} [577
j136Wis2d158
60WiAG197
63WiAG161
74WiAG181
1977WLR935
1983WLR347
34A2 1326s

—537—
(182NW282)
50Wis2d^{5}427
53Wis2d^{1}332
53Wis2d^{5}490
53Wis2d^{2}781
54Wis2d^{1}467
f54Wis2d^{3}762
56Wis2d^{5}733
f56Wis2d^{6}734
59Wis2d^{3}281
62Wis2d590
65Wis2d^{6}720
f66Wis2d^{5}109
f66Wis2d^{6}109

85Wis2d^{6}189
85Wis2d^{4}757
91Wis2d^{6}771
102Wis2d^{3} [392
104Wis2d^{1} [259
107Wis2d380
72McL733
33StnL214
71A2 449s
45A3 965n
45A3 974n
82A3 254n
82A3 277n

—591—
(182NW448)
52Wis2d^{9}391
f55Wis2d^{1}686
70Wis2d^{6}751
70Wis2d^{6} [1037
82Wis2d^{6}113
83Wis2d^{9}842
118Wis2d452
126Wis2d^{9} [456
18A3 497s

—612—
(182NW251)
d56Wis2d^{1}811
j60Wis2d^{1}171
76Wis2d^{1}59
f85Wis2d^{2}117
f85Wis2d^{3}117

Source: Shepard's/McGraw-Hill, Inc. © 1988

Figure 12.29. Print Version of the Wis. 2d Table from *Shepard's Wisconsin Citations* for Shepardizing 49 Wis. 2d 430

- *Citations To*—This line of the heading identifies the citation being Shepardized. In Figure 12.30, the "Citations To" line indicates that the citing authorities in the table contain references to 49 Wis. 2d 430.
- *Citator*—This line identifies the set of Shepard's citators from which the table was drawn. As with the printed *Shepard's Citations*, the online Shepard's service provides separate sets of citators for different authorities (*e.g.*, separate sets for various federal authorities; a separate set for authorities from each state; a set for each of West's regional reporters). The heading in Figure 12.30 identifies *Shepard's Wisconsin Citations* as the source of the table.
- *Division*—This line verifies that within the appropriate set of Shepard's citators, you have retrieved the correct collection of tables containing the specific table for Shepardizing your case.

As in the printed citators, the online Shepard's service provides a separate collection of tables for each series of a case reporter

```
                                    SHEPARD'S  (Rank 1 of 1)        Page 1 of 2
CITATIONS TO: 49 Wis.2d 430
CITATOR: WISCONSIN CITATIONS
DIVISION: Wisconsin Reports 2nd Series
COVERAGE: First Shepard's volume through Sept. 1993 Supplement
Retrieval                                    Headnote
   No.    --Analysis--- -----Citation-----      No.
    1 > Shep   Same Text ( 182 N.W.2d 539)
    2     A    Affirmed   406 U.S. 205
    3     A    Affirmed    32 L.Ed.2d 15
    4     A    Affirmed    92 S.Ct. 1526
    5     SC   Same Case  402 U.S. 994
    6     SC   Same Case   29 L.Ed.2d 160
    7     SC   Same Case   91 S.Ct. 2173
    8                      55 Wis.2d 343, 353     6
    9                      63 Wis.2d 130, 137     4
   10     F  Followed      87 Wis.2d 407, 414     4
   11                      99 Wis.2d 533, 550     1
   12                      99 Wis.2d 533, 551     3

   > Display only negative history and treatment code references (LOC NEG)
   > Insta-Cite    > Shepard's PreView    > QuickCite    > Commands    > SCOPE
Copyright (C) 1993 McGraw-Hill, Inc.; Copyright (C) 1993 West Publishing Co.
```

Source: West Publishing Company; © 1993 Shepard's/McGraw-Hill, Inc.

Figure 12.30. First Screen of a Typical Shepard's Case Table in WESTLAW (Showing the Wis. 2d Table from *Shepard's Wisconsin Citations* for Shepardizing 49 Wis. 2d 430)

```
                                    SHEPARD'S  (Rank 1 of 1)        Page 2 of 2
CITATIONS TO: 49 Wis.2d 430
CITATOR: WISCONSIN CITATIONS
DIVISION: Wisconsin Reports 2nd Series
Retrieval                                              Headnote
   No.    -----Analysis----- ---------Citation---------    No.
    1                      143 Wis.2d 624, 632
    2                      145 Wis.2d 24, 43              1

                                    Cir. 5
    3     J  Dissenting Opin  556 F.2d 310, 325           4
    4     J  Dissenting Opin  556 F.2d at 326             2
                               55 N.Y.U. L. Rev. at 41
                              120 U. Pa. L. Rev. at 539
          S  Anno Sup           3 A.L.R.2d at 1401

Copyright (C) 1993 McGraw-Hill, Inc.; Copyright (C) 1993 West Publishing Co.
```

Source: West Publishing Company; © 1993 Shepard's/McGraw-Hill, Inc.

Figure 12.31. Continuation of a Typical Shepard's Case Table in WESTLAW (Showing the Wis. 2d Table from *Shepard's Wisconsin Citations* for Shepardizing 49 Wis. 2d 430)

(*e.g.*, a collection of tables for Shepardizing cases published in the first series of *Wisconsin Reports*; a collection of tables for Shepardizing cases published in the second series of *Wisconsin Reports*; a collection of tables for Shepardizing cases published in the first series of *North Western Reporter*; a collection of tables for Shepardizing cases published in the second series of *North Western Reporter*). An online "division" corresponds to the collection of tables used to Shepardize cases published in a specific series of a case reporter.

In Figure 12.30, the "Division" line indicates that the table is drawn from the collection of tables appropriate for Shepardizing cases that, like *Yoder*, are published in *Wisconsin Reports, Second Series*.

- *Coverage*—This line provides information you can use to determine the earliest and latest decision dates of citing cases found in the Shepard's volumes from which the displayed table was drawn. The citing authorities listed in the displayed table will have been issued during the period covered by the citator volumes listed in the "Coverage" line.

  When the "Coverage" line specifies (as it does in Figure 12.30) that coverage begins with the "First Shepard's volume," you know you can Shepardize online as far back in time as you could in the printed citators.

  This won't be true, however, if the message in the coverage line begins with a supplement, as in this example:[313]

  1943–1988 Bound Supplement

  This message indicates that the displayed table does not contain any citing cases decided before 1943. If coverage begins with a supplement and the date of the case you are Shepardizing is earlier than the date of that supplement, the discrepancy indicates a gap in the online Shepard's coverage; to do a complete job of Shepardizing, you will have to augment your online Shepard's search with a search in the printed citators not found online.

  The message in the coverage line sometimes begins with a reference to a dated bound volume, such as:

  1979 Bound Volume

[313] Shepard's periodically updates its printed citators with separate publications called "supplements." For an explanation of Shepard's supplements, see CHRISTOPHER G. WREN & JILL R. WREN, THE LEGAL RESEARCH MANUAL: A GAME PLAN FOR LEGAL RESEARCH AND ANALYSIS 98 n.36 (2d ed. 1986).

To verify the online coverage in this situation, type **scope** (or **sc**) and press ENTER. (Or, use the TAB key to position the cursor under the JUMP marker in front of the word "SCOPE," and press ENTER.) The monitor will display a list of titles of the reporters from which citing references might appear in the Shepard's table and, for each reporter listed, will indicate the earliest volume that might contain a citing reference. On-screen prompts explain how to page through the list and how to resume Shepardizing.

The "Coverage" line indicates the latest date of coverage by identifying the most recent Shepard's supplement available online (which in Figure 12.30, for example, is the September 1993 supplement). From the date of this supplement, you know you won't find in the table any citing authorities issued more recently than that date. (Because of the lag time inherent in the editorial process that produces a Shepard's table, the most recent citing authorities will likely be a month or two earlier than the date of the most recent supplement. Using Shepard's PreView, explained on pages 524–28, can narrow the gap.)

Shepard's citators in WESTLAW are updated when a new printed supplement is published, so the online and printed versions of a Shepard's citator should be equally current.

The part of the citator table that follows the heading contains all the information found in printed citator tables, though in an easier-to-read form:

- *Citations*—In the middle of the table, under the label "Citation," you will find a list of citations of the authorities that have referred to the case being Shepardized. The citations in this list contain the same elements as the citations in the corresponding printed table: volume number, the abbreviation of the publication in which the citing authority appears, and the page number on which you will find a reference to the case you are Shepardizing. For example, from Figure 12.31, you can determine that a reference to *Yoder* occurs at 556 F.2d 326.

  A citation might include two page numbers, such as "556 F.2d 310, 325" in Figure 12.31. The first page number identifies the starting page of the case, and the second page number identifies a page containing a reference to the authority being Shepardized.

  Sometimes you will encounter a citing authority in a form like "dk2 86–7598." A reference like this identifies a citing case by its docket number. Dk2 86–7598, for instance, identifies the citing authority as a case from the U.S. Court of Appeals for the Second Circuit with a docket number of 86–7598. This type of citation appears when Shepard's includes a citing case in an online citator table before the case receives a citation upon being published in a case reporter. In some instances, you will see a citing authority identified by both a docket number and a citation: when the case obtains a citation, the citation might be added to the Shepard's table before Shepard's removes the docket number from the table. (If a docket number does not have an accompanying citation, you can check for one in the Shepard's PreView table for the case you are updating.)

As you read a Shepard's table, you might also find one or more citations in parentheses at the top of the "Citation" column, such as 182 N.W.2d 539 in Figure 12.30. Such a parenthetical citation is a parallel citation of the case you are Shepardizing.

- *Analysis*—To the left of the list of citing authorities, in the column labelled "Analysis," you will frequently see comments indicating how citing authorities relate to the case being Shepardized. For example, in Figure 12.30, the notation "affirmed" on the same line as 406 U.S. 205 indicates that this citing authority affirmed *Yoder*.

  If no analysis comment appears next to a citing authority, the authority mentioning the case being Shepardized has simply cited it for one of its legal propositions, but provided no analytical discussion.

  Figure 12.32 lists and explains the analysis comments you might find in an online Shepard's table for updating a case. To see an explanation of the comments while using Shepard's online, type `analysis` and press ENTER; to resume Shepardizing after viewing the list of comments, follow the on-screen instructions. The analysis comments generally track the analyses you find in printed citators, but spell out the analyses in addition to using the highly abbreviated codes (such as "a," "sc," or "f") appearing in the printed citator tables.

  As Figure 12.32 shows, the analysis comments indicate one of two things: (1) how the case being Shepardized was handled as it worked its way through the legal system (the history of the case); or (2) how other courts have evaluated the case in the course of deciding later cases (the treatment of the case).

  In the "Analysis" column, you might also see a comment that the reference to the case you are Shepardizing appears in an *A.L.R.* or *Lawyers' Edition* annotation or annotation supplement. An example of such a comment occurs in the last line of the Shepard's table in Figure 12.31.

History of Case

A	affirmed	Same case affirmed on appeal.
CC	connected case	Different case from case cited, but arising out of the same subject matter or intimately connected therewith.
CF	certiorari filed	Certiorari petition filed.
DE	denied	Denied.
DM	dismissed	Appeal from same case dismissed.
GR	granted	Granted.
IN	US cert den	Certiorari denied by U.S. Supreme Court.
	US cert dis	Certiorari dismissed by U.S. Supreme Court.
	US reh den	Rehearing denied by U.S. Supreme Court.
	US reh dis	Rehearing dismissed by U.S. Supreme Court.
M	modified	Same case modified on appeal.
MI	mandate issued	Mandate issued.
NP	not published	Not published.
PD	petition denied	Petition denied.
PG	petition granted	Petition granted.
R	reversed	Same case reversed on appeal.
S	superseded	Substitution for former opinion.
SC	same case	Same case as case cited.
V	vacated	Same case vacated.

Treatment of Case

C	criticized	Soundness of decision or reasoning in cited case criticized for reasons given.
D	distinguished	Case at bar different either in law or fact from case cited for reasons given.
E	explained	Statement of import of decision in cited case. Not merely a restatement of the facts.
EX	examiner's decision	Examiner's decision.
F	followed	Cited as controlling.
H	harmonized	Apparent inconsistency explained and shown not to exist.
J	dissenting opinion	Citation in dissenting opinion.
L	limited	Refusal to extend decision of cited case beyond precise issues involved.
O	overruled	Ruling in cited case expressly overruled.
P	parallel	Citing case substantially alike or on all fours with cited case in its law or facts.
Q	questioned	Soundness of decision or reasoning in cited case questioned.

Source: Adapted from West Publishing Company, WESTLAW Reference Manual 224 (5th ed. 1993) and WESTLAW's online list of analysis comments. Copyright © 1993 Shepard's/McGraw-Hill, Inc.

Figure 12.32. Shepard's Analysis Comments in WESTLAW for Cases

- *Headnote No.*—To the right of the list of citing authorities, in the column labelled "Headnote No.," you will frequently see a number opposite a citing authority (such as "4" opposite 556 F.2d 310, 325 in Figure 12.31). A number in the "Headnote No." column refers to the headnote or syllabus paragraph having that number in the case you are Shepardizing; the number in the "Headnote No." column indicates that the citing case refers to the cited case for the point of law summarized in that headnote or syllabus paragraph. In our example, the portion of the case you find at 556 F.2d 325 cites *Yoder* for the point of law summarized in *Yoder*'s headnote number 4 in its Wis. 2d version.[314]

  The numbers you find in the "Headnote No." column in an online citator table correspond to the small superscript numbers found in citations listed in printed citator tables.[315] Particularly in tables with lengthy lists of citing authorities, numbers in the "Headnote No." column, like the superscript numbers in printed citator tables, can save you from reading cases citing your case for points of law that might be irrelevant to your research problem.
- *Retrieval No.*—Each entry in this column is a number you can use (as explained at pages 519–21) to retrieve the text of the citing authority identified by that number. For example, at the screen in Figure 12.31, you could type 4 and press ENTER to retrieve the text of the case that contains the reference to *Yoder* at 556 F.2d 326.

Finding all the citator tables in WESTLAW for a case. Shepard's publishes a citator set for each state. State citators have separate tables for the different reporters (*e.g.*, the Wisconsin reporters, the North Western reporters) in which a case appears; if a reporter has more than one series (*e.g.*, Wis., Wis. 2d), a state citator will have separate tables for each series. In addition, Shepard's publishes citators corresponding to each regional reporter published by West; if a regional reporter has more than one series (*e.g.*, N.W., N.W.2d), a regional citator will have separate tables for each series.

[314] In using numbers from the "Headnote No." column, remember that different publishers of court decisions might assign different numbers to headnote or syllabus paragraphs dealing with the same point of law. For example, headnote 9 in the Wis. 2d version of a case (which is published by Lawyers Cooperative Publishing) will almost certainly deal with a different point of law than headnote 9, if there is one, in the N.W.2d version of that case (which is published by West). Consequently, whenever you attempt to match a number from the "Headnote No." column with a case headnote or syllabus paragraph number, you must make sure the headnote or syllabus paragraph number you are using is from the version of the case published in the reporter identified in the "Citations To" line in the heading of the displayed table.

[315] For an explanation of using the headnote feature in printed Shepard's citators, see CHRISTOPHER G. WREN & JILL R. WREN, THE LEGAL RESEARCH MANUAL: A GAME PLAN FOR LEGAL RESEARCH AND ANALYSIS 107–08 (2d ed. 1986).

As with Shepardizing in printed citators, each parallel citation for a case being Shepardized online will have a separate table of authorities citing the case. Returning to the example of *Yoder*, Shepardizing 49 Wis. 2d 430 will yield a table different from those yielded by Shepardizing 182 N.W.2d 539.

Although you might think that the citations found in the table for the parallel reference would simply duplicate the ones found in the table for the principal reference, that isn't a safe assumption. In a state's case citator, Shepard's does not include (in either the tables for the state reporter or for the regional reporter) references to any citing cases decided by courts in other states. Rather, any citing references from out-of-state cases would appear only in tables found in Shepard's regional citators.

For example, suppose a judge in Connecticut referred to *Yoder* in a decision. The Connecticut case, being a case decided by a non-Wisconsin state court, would not appear as a citing reference in either the Wis. 2d table or the N.W.2d table in *Shepard's Wisconsin Citations*. The Connecticut case would appear, however, as a citing reference in *Yoder*'s table in *Shepard's North Western Citations*, the Shepard's regional citator covering *Yoder*. So, if you had Shepardized *Yoder* only in *Shepard's Wisconsin Citations*, you would have missed the citing case from Connecticut (as well as any other cases citing *Yoder* that were decided by state courts outside Wisconsin), even if you had checked the N.W.2d table in the Wisconsin citator.

In short, to be absolutely sure your Shepardizing of a case is as thorough as possible, you need to Shepardize in all tables for all principal and parallel citations.

Figures 12.30, 12.31, 12.33, and 12.34 illustrate the point. Figures 12.30 and 12.31 show the two screens of the table retrieved when *Yoder* was Shepardized using 49 Wis. 2d 430. Figures 12.33 and 12.34 show the two screens of each table retrieved when *Yoder* was Shepardized using 182 N.W.2d 539. If you compare the tables, you see they contain different citing authorities.

When you are viewing a Shepard's table in WESTLAW for a case that has parallel citations, you will see a reminder to Shepardize each parallel citation. For example, in the *Yoder* table shown in Figure 12.30 (which corresponds to the version of *Yoder* published in *Wisconsin Reports, Second Series*), the parallel citation listed as the first entry in the table is preceded by a JUMP marker (">") and the notation "Shep." By using the TAB key to position the cursor under the JUMP marker and then pressing ENTER, you would retrieve the Shepard's tables for the *North Western Reporter* version of *Yoder*.

Figures 12.33 and 12.34 also highlight that even for a single citation, Shepard's might have more than one table. As you can see from the "Citator" line in the headings of these figures, tables for Shepardizing 182 N.W.2d 539 appear in *Shepard's Northwestern Reporter Citations* and in *Shepard's Wis-*

```
                                SHEPARD'S  (Rank 1 of 2)          Page 1 of 2
CITATIONS TO: 182 N.W.2d 539
CITATOR: NORTHWESTERN REPORTER CITATIONS
DIVISION: Northwestern Reporter 2nd Series
COVERAGE: First Shepard's volume through Aug. 1993 Supplement
Retrieval                                          Headnote
   No.    --Analysis-- -----Citation------            No.
    1 > Shep Same Text (49 Wis.2d 430)
    2      A  Affirmed  406 U.S. 205
    3      A  Affirmed   32 L.Ed.2d 15
    4      A  Affirmed   92 S.Ct. 1526
    5      SC Same Case 402 U.S. 994
    6      SC Same Case  29 L.Ed.2d 160
    7      SC Same Case  91 S.Ct. 2173
    8                   198 N.W.2d 675, 680            4
    9                   216 N.W.2d 197, 200            1
   10      F  Followed  275 N.W.2d 101, 104            1
   11                   299 N.W.2d 891, 898            1
   12                   422 N.W.2d 160, 163            1

   > Display only negative history and treatment code references (LOC NEG)
   > Insta-Cite   > Shepard's PreView    > QuickCite   > Commands   > SCOPE
Copyright (C) 1993 McGraw-Hill, Inc.; Copyright (C) 1993 West Publishing Co.
```

```
                                SHEPARD'S  (Rank 1 of 2)          Page 2 of 2
CITATIONS TO: 182 N.W.2d 539
CITATOR: NORTHWESTERN REPORTER CITATIONS
DIVISION: Northwestern Reporter 2nd Series
Retrieval                                                Headnote
   No.    -----Analysis----- ------Citation------           No.
    1                        426 N.W.2d 329, 337
    2     J  Dissenting Opin 556 F.2d 310, 325               2

                                  Mich
    3                        396 N.W.2d 373, 422             1

                                   ND
    4                        294 N.W.2d 883, 890             5

                                  Calif
    5                        124 Cal.Rptr. 68, 85

                                  Conn
    6                        289 A.2d 914, 924
          S  Anno Sup          3 A.L.R.2d at 1401

Copyright (C) 1993 McGraw-Hill, Inc.; Copyright (C) 1993 West Publishing Co.
```

Source: West Publishing Company; © 1993 Shepard's/McGraw-Hill, Inc.

Figure 12.33. A Typical Shepard's Case Table in WESTLAW (Showing the N.W.2d Table from *Shepard's Northwestern Reporter Citations* for Shepardizing 182 N.W.2d 539)

```
                                   SHEPARD'S  (Rank 2 of 2)        Page 1 of 2
CITATIONS TO: 182 N.W.2d 539
CITATOR: WISCONSIN CITATIONS
DIVISION: Northwestern Reporter 2nd Series
COVERAGE: First Shepard's volume through Sept. 1993 Supplement
Retrieval                                    Headnote
   No.     --Analysis-- ------Citation------    No.
    1 > Shep Same Text (  49 Wis.2d 430)
    2      A  Affirmed   406 U.S. 205
    3      A  Affirmed    32 L.Ed.2d 15
    4      A  Affirmed    92 S.Ct. 1526
    5      SC Same Case  402 U.S. 994
    6      SC Same Case   29 L.Ed.2d 160
    7      SC Same Case   91 S.Ct. 2173
    8                    198 N.W.2d 675, 680     4
    9                    216 N.W.2d 197, 200     1
   10      F  Followed   275 N.W.2d 101, 104     1
   11                    299 N.W.2d 891, 898     1
   12                    422 N.W.2d 160, 163     1

   > Display only negative history and treatment code references (LOC NEG)
   > Insta-Cite    > Shepard's PreView    > QuickCite    > Commands    > SCOPE
Copyright (C) 1993 McGraw-Hill, Inc.; Copyright (C) 1993 West Publishing Co.
```

```
                                   SHEPARD'S  (Rank 2 of 2)        Page 2 of 2
CITATIONS TO: 182 N.W.2d 539
CITATOR: WISCONSIN CITATIONS
DIVISION: Northwestern Reporter 2nd Series
Retrieval                                        Headnote
   No.     -----Analysis----- -----Citation-----    No.
    1                          426 N.W.2d 329, 337

                                    Cir. 5
    2     J  Dissenting Opin  556 F.2d 310, 325     2

Copyright (C) 1993 McGraw-Hill, Inc.; Copyright (C) 1993 West Publishing Co.
```

Source: West Publishing Company; © 1993 Shepard's/McGraw-Hill, Inc.

Figure 12.34. A Typical Shepard's Case Table in WESTLAW (Showing the N.W.2d Table from *Shepard's Wisconsin Citations* for Shepardizing 182 N.W.2d 539)

consin Citations. And, as you can see by comparing the tables, they contain different citing authorities.

Retrieving multiple citator tables is not a phenomenon that occurs only when you Shepardize a case that appears in a regional reporter in addition to an individual state reporter. For instance, if you Shepardized *Segar v. Civiletti*, 508 F. Supp. 690, 26 Empl. Prac. Dec. ¶31,982 (D.D.C. 1981), the computer would retrieve a table from *Shepard's Federal Reporter Citations*, a table from *Shepard's Federal Citations in Selected Law Reviews*, a table from *Shepard's District of Columbia Citations*, and a table from *Shepard's Federal Labor Law Citations*.

You can even retrieve multiple citator tables for a case that has only one citation you can Shepardize. For example, Shepardizing *Fraternal Order of Police, Lodge No. 5 v. Tucker*, 868 F.2d 74 (3d Cir. 1989), would yield a table from *Shepard's Federal Reporter Citations* and a table from *Shepard's Federal Labor Law Citations*.

Thus, if you want to ensure complete Shepardizing results, you will need to Shepardize each citation for the case you want to update and then review each table retrieved.

When you Shepardize in WESTLAW, you can display a list of every table you retrieve for a given citation. To see the list:

1. Type l (for "list").
2. Press ENTER. The monitor will display the name of each citator from which a table has been drawn. For instance, if you had Shepardized *Segar v. Civiletti*, 508 F. Supp. 690, transmitting l would display a list like that in Figure 12.35. (An arrow in the left margin will point to the table you were viewing when you instructed the computer to display the list.)
3. When you finish viewing a list, follow the on-screen instructions to continue with your Shepardizing.

Moving within a Shepard's case table in WESTLAW. Once you have displayed a Shepard's table, you can page through it (if it extends across more than one screen) by using standard WESTLAW techniques for moving within a document:[316]

- Press ENTER (or the PAGE DOWN or PgDn key) to move the display forward one screen at a time. Press the PAGE UP (or PgUp) key to move the display back one screen at a time.
- Type p+ or p− followed by a number and press ENTER to skip the display forward or back the designated number of screens. Alter-

[316] Pages 360–63 explain these techniques.

```
                              SHEPARD'S                     Only Page
CITATION: 508 F.Supp. 690

Shepard's results exist in the following Shepard's/McGraw-Hill citators:

     1. FEDERAL REPORTER CITATIONS
     2. FEDERAL CITATIONS IN SELECTED LAW REVIEWS
     3. DISTRICT OF COLUMBIA CITATIONS
=>   4. FEDERAL LABOR LAW CITATIONS


If you wish to:
  View the coverage in a particular citator, type its number and press ENTER
  Shepardize a document, type its citation and press ENTER
  Leave this Shepard's display, press ENTER

Copyright (C) 1993 McGraw-Hill, Inc.; Copyright (C) 1993 West Publishing Co.
```

Source: West Publishing Company; © 1993 Shepard's/McGraw-Hill, Inc.

Figure 12.35. Typical List of Shepard's Tables in WESTLAW for a Single Citation (508 F. Supp. 690)

natively, type a number and then press the PAGE DOWN (or PgDn) key or the PAGE UP (or PgUp) key.

- Type `p` followed by a number and press ENTER to move the display to the designated screen.

Transmitting `h+` or `h-`, which normally allows you to move forward or back half a screen within a document (see pages 361–62), currently does not work in the Shepard's service.

If your Shepard's result runs longer than 400 screens, the citator table will appear in "parts" containing up to 400 screens. Figure 12.36 shows a screen from a Shepard's table with more than 400 screens; the heading in the upper right of the screen indicates it appears in Part A of the table. You can move among "parts" of a Shepard's table this way:

- To move forward one "part" (say, from Part A to Part B), type `part` (or `pt`) and press ENTER.
- To move from the part you are viewing to any part you have already viewed, type `part` (or `pt`) followed by the letter for a "part," then press ENTER. For example, while viewing Part D, you could transmit `pt a` to move to Part A.

```
                                   SHEPARD'S  (Rank 1 of 3)      Page 1 of 400
CITATIONS TO: 384 U.S. 436                                       Part A
CITATOR: UNITED STATES CITATIONS
DIVISION: United States Supreme Court Reports
COVERAGE: 1943-1988 Bound Supplement through Aug. 1993 Supp; for more see SCOPE
Retrieval                                         Headnote
   No.    -----Analysis------ -----Citation-----     No.
    1 > Shep  Same Text       ( 16 L.Ed.2d 694)
    2 > Shep  Same Text       ( 86 S.Ct. 1602)
              Same Text       ( 10 A.L.R.3d 974)

                                   US Reh Den
    3                       in 385 U.S. 890
    4     SC  Same Case        382 U.S. 924
    5     SC  Same Case        383 U.S. 903
    6     SC  Same Case        342 F.2d 684
    7     SC  Same Case        394 F.2d 164
    8     SC  Same Case         98 Ariz. 18
    9     SC  Same Case        104 Ariz. 174
Note:  Your result exceeds 400 pages.  Enter PT to view the next part.
   > Display only negative history and treatment code references (LOC NEG)
   > Insta-Cite   > Shepard's PreView    > QuickCite    > Commands    > SCOPE
Copyright (C) 1993 McGraw-Hill, Inc.; Copyright (C) 1993 West Publishing Co.
```

Source: West Publishing Company; © 1993 Shepard's/McGraw-Hill, Inc.

Figure 12.36. A Typical Shepard's Case Table in WESTLAW Indicating the Table's Division into Parts

Customizing the display of a Shepard's case table in WESTLAW. While viewing a Shepard's table (especially one containing a lengthy list of citing authorities), you might want to focus on those authorities most likely to help you evaluate the case you are Shepardizing. For example, you might concentrate on citing authorities accompanied by an analysis comment (such as "explained," "distinguished," or "overruled") or by a number identifying a headnote or syllabus paragraph that summarizes a point of law in which you are interested.[317]

When you Shepardize in WESTLAW, you can instruct the computer to display only those citing authorities accompanied by a specific analysis comment or by a specific headnote number, decided by specific federal or state courts, or found in a specific publication (*e.g.*, a specific case reporter or law review). You can also customize a Shepard's table to display citing authorities satisfying a combination of these criteria.

[317] Although Shepard's analysis comments and references to headnote or syllabus paragraph numbers can prove useful as screening devices, they represent editorial judgments that might not capture the nuance of the citing reference for your purposes. To understand fully the significance a citing reference holds for your research problem, you still need to read the citing authority for yourself rather than rely on Shepard's assessment. *See* CHRISTOPHER G. WREN & JILL R. WREN, THE LEGAL RESEARCH MANUAL: A GAME PLAN FOR LEGAL RESEARCH AND ANALYSIS 109–11 (2d ed. 1986).

To customize the display once you have retrieved a citator table, you use the LOCATE feature. Start by typing `locate` (or `loc`) and pressing ENTER. The monitor will display a screen like the one shown in Figure 12.37. At that point, you can customize the display in any of these ways:

- *By analysis comment.* Type the code for the analysis comment by which you want to screen citing authorities, then press ENTER. For example, to restrict the display to citing authorities that questioned the case you are Shepardizing, you would type `q` and press ENTER.

  You can also customize a table according to categories of analysis codes. To display citing authorities that have *any* kind of analysis code (whether a history or treatment code), transmit `all` or `any`. To display citing authorities having any kind of history code, transmit `hist`. To display citing authorities having any kind of treatment code, transmit `tr`. To display citing authorities having negative codes (criticized, dismissed, distinguished, limited, modified, overruled, questioned, reversed, superseded, or vacated), transmit `neg`.

  If you want to see a list of analysis codes while using Shepard's through WESTLAW, type `analysis` and press ENTER. To resume

```
Please enter your LOCATE request.

     Note:  LOCATE allows you to restrict a Shepard's request by
            history/treatment codes, headnote numbers, court abbreviations
            state abbreviations, or publication abbreviations.

If you wish to:
   Submit a LOCATE request, type a code, number or abbreviation
     and press ENTER
   View a list of history/treatment codes with abbreviations, type ANALYSIS
     and press ENTER
   View a list of courts with abbreviations, type COURTS and press ENTER
   View a list of publications with abbreviations, type PUBS and press ENTER
   Continue, type SH and press ENTER
```


Figure 12.37. Screen for Transmitting Choices for Customizing a Shepard's Table in WESTLAW

Shepardizing after viewing the list of codes, follow the on-screen instructions. A comprehensive list of analysis codes appears in Figure 12.32 on page 507.

- *By headnote or syllabus paragraph number.* Type the number of the headnote or syllabus paragraph by which you want to screen citing authorities, then press ENTER. For example, to restrict the display to citing authorities that addressed the legal issues summarized in headnote or syllabus paragraph numbered 4 in the case you are Shepardizing, you would type `4` and press ENTER.
- *By federal or state court.* To display citing authorities decided by a particular federal court, type an appropriate abbreviation for the court, then press ENTER. For example, to display citing authorities from federal district and appellate courts in just the Ninth Circuit, you could type `cir9` and press ENTER. Similarly, to display citing authorities decided by the U.S. Claims Court, you could type `cl ct` and press ENTER. To see a list of federal court abbreviations you can use to customize a Shepard's display, transmit `courts` while you are using the Shepard's service through WESTLAW. To resume Shepardizing after viewing the list, follow the on-screen instructions.

  To display citing authorities decided by courts in a particular state, type the state's two-letter postal abbreviation, then press ENTER. So, for example, you would transmit `ma` to limit a Shepard's display to citing authorities decided by state courts in Massachusetts.[318]
- *By publication.* Type the abbreviation of the case reporter, law review, or other publication by which you want to screen citing

[318] The postal abbreviations for four states (Delaware, Indiana, Michigan, and South Carolina) coincide with four Shepard's analysis codes (DE, IN, MI, SC). Currently, when you use these states' abbreviations to customize a Shepard's display, the WESTLAW computer assumes you are using the abbreviations as analysis codes rather than as state abbreviations (although West might modify its WESTLAW software to change this assumption). So, if you transmit any of these abbreviations with the intention of customizing a Shepard's table along state lines, the computer will in fact customize the display according to analysis code. When a table does not contain citing authorities accompanied by the designated analysis code, the monitor will display a message that the table does not contain any citing authorities satisfying your instruction. The table, though, might actually contain citing authorities from the state you want.

To ensure the computer interprets the abbreviation in the sense you intend, you can use a field restriction in your LOCATE instruction. If you want the abbreviation to identify a state, transmit `st` followed by the abbreviation in parentheses; for example, transmit `st(mi)` to identify citing authorities from Michigan. If you want the abbreviation to identify an analysis code, transmit `an` followed by the abbreviation in parentheses; for example, transmit `an(mi)` to identify citing authorities accompanied by the analysis code for "mandate issued."

authorities; then press ENTER. For example, to restrict the display to citing authorities found in *Federal Supplement*, you could type **f.supp.** or **fsupp** and press ENTER. Similarly, transmitting **harv.l.rev.** would display only citing references found in the *Harvard Law Review*.

A publication's abbreviation as it appears in a Shepard's table will generally work in your instruction. When you type a publication abbreviation, you can omit punctuation, but you cannot have any spaces within the abbreviation. If the monitor displays a message indicating that the Shepard's table does not contain any citing references in the publication you designated, check to be sure you have transmitted the publication abbreviation in an acceptable format. You can find a list of acceptable abbreviations in the *WESTLAW Reference Manual*.[319]

If you want to limit the display to just certain volumes of a selected publication, you can add **>** or **aft** and a volume number to the publication abbreviation you transmit with your LOCATE request. For instance, you can transmit **>433us** or **aft433us** to limit the display to only those citing authorities appearing in *United States Reports* beginning with volume 434.

- *By a combination of display criteria.* You can combine display restrictions in a single instruction. For example, to restrict the display to citing authorities that have either overruled or questioned the case you are Shepardizing, you would type **o,q** and press ENTER. Likewise, to restrict the display to citing authorities that have addressed the legal issues summarized in headnote or syllabus paragraphs numbered either 4 or 6 in the case you are Shepardizing, you would type **4,6** and press ENTER.

  When all of your criteria come from the same category (*e.g.*, when they're all analysis codes or when they're all headnote numbers), the commas separating the criteria operate as "or" connectors. Thus, transmitting **o,q** displays citing authorities accompanied by either "o" or "q" in the analysis column of the Shepard's table. When your criteria come from different categories, the commas separating the criteria operate as "and" connectors. Thus, transmitting **q,4** displays only those citing authorities that are accompanied by "q" in the analysis column *and* by "4" in the headnote column.

  These connector rules also apply when you transmit multiple criteria from different categories, as with an instruction like

[319] WEST PUBLISHING COMPANY, WESTLAW REFERENCE MANUAL 361–74 (5th ed. 1993) (Appendix H).

`o,q,4,6`. A citing authority need satisfy only one criterion within a category, but must satisfy one criterion from each category. Here, for instance, the monitor would display citing authorities accompanied by either "o" or "q" in the analysis column and by either "4" or "6" in the headnote column.

Customizing a Shepard's display with a one-step instruction. When you customize a Shepard's table in WESTLAW, you might prefer not to transmit `locate` (or `loc`) and wait for the screen in Figure 12.37 to appear before you transmit your display criteria. If so, you can customize a Shepard's display this way:

1. Type `locate` (or `loc`) followed by the display criteria you want. Your all-in-one request will take the form shown in these examples:

```
loc q
loc 4,6
loc o,q,4,6
loc cir9
loc ny,ca
loc fsupp
```

2. Press ENTER.

This technique will not work, however, if your LOCATE request exceeds the space allocated for typing instructions on the Shepard's screen you are viewing when you begin using LOCATE. In that situation, you will have to use the technique explained earlier: transmit `locate` (or `loc`) without display criteria, then transmit your criteria when the screen in Figure 12.37 appears.

Changing your display criteria. You can change your display criteria as frequently as you want. To edit existing criteria:

1. Type `locate` (or `loc`).
2. Press ENTER. The monitor will display your most recent customizing instruction, which you can then revise and transmit.

To change most or all of your criteria, you might find it quicker simply to start over by transmitting a new request, using one of the techniques already discussed.

Shortcut: Shepardizing more than one authority according to the same display criteria. If you want to Shepardize several authorities according to the same restrictive display criteria (*e.g.*, to focus only on citing authorities that have overruled or questioned the cases you are Shepardizing), you can use a shortcut that saves you from typing the restrictive criteria each time you Shepardize a new authority. To do this:

1. Type `locate auto` or (`loc auto`) followed by whatever display criteria you want. Your request would take this form:

```
loc auto q
loc auto all
loc auto ny,ca
loc auto fsupp
```

2. Press ENTER.

From then on, until you revise or discard your LOCATE AUTO request, every citator table you retrieve during your WESTLAW session will display only the citing authorities that satisfy your LOCATE AUTO criteria.

To edit a LOCATE AUTO request, you can transmit `locate` (or `loc`) and then edit your existing LOCATE AUTO request when it appears on the monitor. Or, you can type `locate auto` (or `loc auto`) followed by new display criteria, and then press ENTER.

Leaving a customized Shepard's display. When you finish viewing a Shepard's case table you customized with a LOCATE request, you can return to the original display (showing all the citing authorities in the table). To do that:

1. Type `xloc` or `xl` (for "exit LOCATE").

2. Press ENTER.

To return to the original display (showing all the citing authorities in the table) when you finish viewing a Shepard's table you customized with a LOCATE AUTO request:

1. Type `xloc auto` or `xl auto`.

2. Press ENTER.

Alternatively, to exit a display customized with either a LOCATE or LOCATE AUTO request, you can press the TAB key to position the cursor under the JUMP marker (the ">" symbol or triangle) next to the phrase "Cancel LOCATE" at the bottom of the screen, then press ENTER.

Retrieving a citing authority from a Shepard's case table in WESTLAW. While viewing a Shepard's table (whether in a full or restricted display), you might decide you want to see the text of an authority listed in the table as a citing reference. When you Shepardize in WESTLAW, you can instruct the computer to retrieve the text of a citing authority. The technique you use depends on whether the authority you want to view has an accompanying number in the "Retrieval No." column of the Shepard's table. (See Figure 12.30 on page 503.)

If the citing authority has a retrieval number:

1. Type the retrieval number.

2. Press ENTER. The computer will then use the corresponding citation from the "Citation" column of the Shepard's table to retrieve the authority you want to view.

The monitor will display the citing authority in TERM mode, showing the first page of the authority, with the phrase "CITING CASE" highlighted at the top of the screen. Press ENTER to move to references to the citation in the form you Shepardized it. To move to a page that contains a reference, if any, to the citation in a different form (*e.g.*, "*Yoder*, *supra*," or "*Yoder*, 49 Wis. 2d at 435"), transmit that page's star number: type `star` (or `st`) followed by the number of the page you want to display, then press ENTER.[320] (You can save time using the star-paging feature if, when viewing a Shepard's table, you remember to note all the pages containing references to the case you are Shepardizing. For example, in Figure 12.31, you would note that the case reported at 556 F.2d 310 has references to *Yoder* at pages 325 and 326.) In addition, while viewing the citing authority, you can transmit a LOCATE request (such as `loc yoder`) to move to references to the case you are Shepardizing.

You can also retrieve a citing authority that does not have a retrieval number assigned to it in a Shepard's table. Instead of transmitting a retrieval number:

1. Type a FIND instruction based on the citation information in the Shepard's table.[321]

2. Press ENTER.

Once you retrieve a citing authority through FIND, you can transmit a star-page number to move to a page containing a reference to the case you are Shepardizing. If star paging is unavailable for the citing authority, you can use a LOCATE request to achieve the same result: while viewing the citing authority, transmit `locate` (or `loc`) followed by search terms identifying the case you are Shepardizing, *e.g.*, `loc yoder` or `loc 49 pre/5 430`.

Whether you retrieve a citing authority by its retrieval number or through FIND, you do not lose the citator table you had just been viewing; the table

[320] For a refresher on star paging in WESTLAW, see pages 356–58.

[321] For a refresher on FIND, see pages 279–84. Note that if the citing authority is not available online or is not retrievable through FIND, this technique will not work.

simply disappears from sight while the monitor displays the text of the citing authority you selected. To switch from the text of this citing authority back to the citator table:

1. Type gb (for "go back").

2. Press ENTER.

Once back at the table, if you want to select another citing authority to view, transmit its retrieval number or use a FIND instruction.

For instance, if you were viewing the citator table shown in Figure 12.30 and wanted to see the text of the U.S. Supreme Court case that affirms *Yoder* at 92 S. Ct. 1526, you would type 4 and press ENTER. The monitor would display the text of the Supreme Court's decision. To redisplay the citator table, you would type gb and press ENTER. After redisplaying the citator table, you could view the text of another citing authority by transmitting its retrieval number or using a FIND instruction.

Note that when you use a retrieval number or a FIND instruction to display a citing authority, you can, in turn, Shepardize that authority by transmitting sh while viewing it.

Moving between Shepard's case tables in WESTLAW. When a Shepard's search retrieves more than one citator table for a single citation (as occurred, for example, in Shepardizing the N.W.2d citation for *Yoder*),[322] WESTLAW treats each table as a separate document. A message at the top of the monitor indicates how many tables were retrieved and which is being displayed; thus, "Rank 1 of 2" in Figure 12.33 on page 510 indicates you are viewing the first of two tables.

You can move from one table to another by using standard WESTLAW techniques for moving between documents:[323]

- Transmit r (for "rank") to move the display forward one table.
- Transmit r followed by a number to move the display to the table having that document number. For example, transmit r4 to display the fourth table.
- Transmit r+ or r− followed by a number to skip the display forward or back the specified number of tables.

Printing Shepard's case tables in WESTLAW. You can print your Shepardizing results by using standard WESTLAW printing techniques:[324]

[322] See Figures 12.33 and 12.34 on pages 510 and 511.
[323] Pages 364–67 explain these techniques.
[324] Pages 371–79 explain these techniques.

- To print a single line of the screen you are viewing (if you are using a WALT II terminal), move the cursor to the line you want to print and press the PRINT LINE key.
- To print the screen you are viewing, press the key labelled PRINT SCREEN (or, on some keyboards, the key labelled PRT SC); depending on the keyboard you use, you might need to hold down the SHIFT key while you press PRINT SCREEN (or PRT SC).
- To print each screen automatically as it displays, hold down the key labelled CONTROL (or CTRL) while you press PRINT SCREEN (or PRT SC); on some keyboards, you press only the key labelled ON-LINE PRINT. To cancel automatic screen printing, press the same keys again.
- For other printing choices—*i.e.*, to print some or all screens from a table, or to print some or all tables—type pr (for "print offline") while viewing a Shepard's table, then press ENTER. The monitor will display the WESTLAW Offline Printing and Downloading Menu, from which you can choose which Shepard's results you want printed after you log off WESTLAW.

You can also use the Offline Print Directory to review or discard a printing request, or to designate or change a destination for printing. To do so, type opd and press ENTER; then follow the on-screen instructions.

Downloading Shepard's case results in WESTLAW. If you are using a computer with a storage disk, you can save ("download") your Shepardizing results to the disk, using standard WESTLAW techniques for downloading.[325]

- When you are viewing a screen of a Shepard's table, you can download that screen. Press the F10 function key; when the monitor displays the WESTMATE menu, select the "File/Accessing" heading by either typing f or pressing ENTER. Then select the "Store Screen to Disk" option.
- When you are viewing a Shepard's table, you can download screens automatically as they display. Press the F10 function key; when the monitor displays the WESTMATE menu, select the "File/Accessing" heading by either typing f or pressing ENTER. Then select the "Log Screens to Disk" option. To stop downloading screens automatically, press F10 to display the WESTMATE menu, select the "File/Accessing" heading again, and then select the "Stop Disk Logging" option.

[325] Pages 379–82 explain these techniques.

- You can also download some or all screens from a table, or some or all tables. Type pr (for "print offline") while viewing a Shepard's table, then press ENTER; when the monitor displays the WESTLAW Offline Printing and Downloading Menu (which allows you to select what you want to store), transmit your choice. Downloading will occur after you log off.

In addition, you can use the Offline Print Directory to review or discard a downloading request, to designate downloading as the destination, or to change the destination to or from downloading. To do so, type opd and press ENTER; then follow the on-screen instructions.

Pausing during a Shepard's session in WESTLAW to use FIND, Shepard's PreView, or Insta-Cite. During a Shepard's search session, you can retrieve a document by using FIND, or you can implement an updating search in Shepard's PreView or Insta-Cite.[326] To do so, simply follow the instructions for commencing a FIND, Shepard's PreView, or Insta-Cite search. To return to the Shepard's service from the feature or service you invoked, type gb (for "go back") and press ENTER.

Alternatively, to use Shepard's PreView or Insta-Cite to update the authority for which you are viewing a Shepard's table, you can use the JUMP feature. For example, while viewing the screen in Figure 12.30 on page 503, you could retrieve the Shepard's PreView or Insta-Cite results for 49 Wis. 2d 430 by using the TAB key to position the cursor under the appropriate JUMP marker (">") at the bottom of the screen, and then pressing ENTER. To go back to Shepard's, you could transmit gb.

Ending a Shepard's session and returning to FIND, Shepard's PreView, or Insta-Cite. As noted earlier, you can Shepardize at nearly any point during an online research session. (See page 498.) If you invoked the Shepard's service while using the FIND feature or the Shepard's PreView or Insta-Cite service, you can resume using that other feature or service by typing gb and pressing ENTER.

Suppose, however, you used more than a single service or feature before invoking Shepard's. If you want to return to the service or feature you were using immediately before invoking Shepard's, type gb and press ENTER. To return to any other service or feature, type map and press ENTER to display a list of your previous research activities; then follow the on-screen instructions to select the service or feature to which you want to return. (Alternatively, you could transmit gb repeatedly until you arrive at the earlier stage in your research to which you want to return.)

[326] See pages 279–84 for an explanation of the FIND feature, pages 524–28 for an explanation of Shepard's PreView, and pages 544 and 552–64 for an explanation of Insta-Cite.

Thus, if you had carried out searches using FIND, Shepard's PreView, Insta-Cite, and Shepard's (in that order), you could return from Shepard's to Insta-Cite simply by transmitting `gb`. To return to a document you were viewing through FIND or to return to Shepard's PreView, however, you would transmit `map` and make your selection from the on-screen list of research activities. (Or, you could transmit multiple "gb" commands.)

Ending a Shepard's session and returning to WESTLAW. If you had been viewing the WESTLAW Directory or the results of a WESTLAW search just before invoking Shepard's, you could return to WESTLAW by transmitting `gb`. Alternatively, you could use a shortcut "map" command that bypasses the map list: transmit `map1` to return directly to the WESTLAW Directory, or `map2` to return directly to your most recent WESTLAW search results (if any).

Summary of Shepardizing a case through WESTLAW. Figure 12.43 on pages 545–51 summarizes the steps and commands for using the Shepard's service in WESTLAW.

Shepard's PreView: updating Shepard's case results in WESTLAW

Shepard's PreView serves as an online supplement to Shepard's citators. When you are updating a case in WESTLAW, you can use Shepard's PreView to identify references to the case that have appeared in recently published volumes of West reporters but that have not yet been included in the online or printed tables of *Shepard's Citations*. Citing references appear in Shepard's PreView weeks, even months, before the information becomes available in the regular Shepard's citators.

Figure 12.38 depicts the first screen of a typical table retrieved through Shepard's PreView. As the illustration shows, a PreView table:

- lists West reporter citations of authorities that have cited the case being updated
- provides retrieval numbers you can use to display the citing authorities

Although Shepard's PreView operates as an online extension of Shepard's citators, Shepard's PreView differs in a few significant respects. First, citing references come only from West reporters; if a case that cites the one you are updating has not been published by West, you will not find the citing case through Shepard's PreView. Second, Shepard's PreView tables do not provide Shepard's analysis comments (*e.g.*, overruled, questioned, followed) or cross-references to headnote numbers in the case being updated. Third, even for a case with parallel citations, all the citing references to the case appear in a

```
                         SHEPARD'S PREVIEW                  Page 1 of 16
Citations to:  326 U.S. 310
               International Shoe Co. v. State of Washington, Office
               of Unemployment Compensation and Placement
               (U.S.Wash.  1945)

Retrieval
   No.      ------Citation------
            ( 66 S.Ct. 154)          Same Text
            ( 90 L.Ed. 95)           Same Text

                 Cir. DC
    1       145 F.R.D. 8, 9

                 Cir. 1
    2       982 F.2d 686, 690
    3       987 F.2d 39, 43
    4       987 F.2d 39, 46
    5       818 F.Supp. 486, 489

Note:  Citing references are only from West Reporters.
       > Insta-Cite     > Shepard's     > QuickCite     > Commands     > SCOPE
Copyright (C) 1993 Shepard's/McGraw-Hill, Inc. and West Publishing Company
```

Source: West Publishing Company; © 1993 Shepard's/McGraw-Hill, Inc. and West Publishing Company

Figure 12.38. First Screen of a Typical Shepard's PreView Table in WESTLAW

single table, regardless of the citation you use to retrieve the table; you will not find multiple tables, or divisions within a table, as often occurs in Shepard's (see pages 508–12).

Gaining access to Shepard's PreView in WESTLAW. As with Shepard's, you can initiate a Shepard's PreView search at nearly any time after logging on to WESTLAW. You can begin PreViewing as soon as the monitor displays the WESTLAW Directory, or you can wait until you have retrieved some documents.

To retrieve a PreView table, you use a Shepard's-style search request based on the citation of the case you want to update:

- If you are viewing the case you want to update (or if you are viewing a Shepard's table or Insta-Cite report for that case), simply type sp (for "Shepard's PreView") and press ENTER. Alternatively, if you are viewing a Shepard's table or Insta-Cite report for the case you want to PreView, you can use the JUMP feature. For example, while viewing the screen in Figure 12.30 on page 503, you could retrieve the case's PreView table by using the TAB key to position the cursor under the JUMP marker (">") in front of "Shepard's PreView" at the bottom of the screen, and then pressing ENTER. Whether you type the command or use the JUMP feature, the computer will automatically "read in" to the search request the citation of your case.

- If you want to update a case you are *not* viewing, type sp followed by the case's citation; then press ENTER. For the citation, type the volume number and abbreviation of the publication in which the case appears and a page number from the case. (If you transmit a page number other than the first page of the case, WESTLAW will determine the page on which the authority begins.)

  For instance, to PreView *International Shoe Co. v. Washington*, 326 U.S. 310, 66 S. Ct. 154, 90 L. Ed. 95, you could use any of the following requests:

  ```
  sp 326 us 310
  sp 66 sct 154
  sp 90 led 95
  sp 326us310
  ```

  As with a Shepard's search request, you have considerable flexibility in typing your PreView request. If you are uncertain about what abbreviation to use, check the *WESTLAW Reference Manual*[327] or transmit pubs anytime after invoking PreView and follow the on-screen instructions. Abbreviations that work in a Shepard's, Insta-Cite, or FIND instruction also work in a PreView request.

- If you are viewing an authority and see the citation of a case you want to update through Shepard's PreView, you can use the JUMP feature (explained on page 284) to automate the use of Shepard's PreView for updating that citation. To use JUMP, type sp, press the TAB key to position the cursor under the ">" symbol or triangle next to the citation you want to update, and then press ENTER. The computer will read in to your Shepard's PreView request the citation on which you positioned the cursor.

When two or more cases share the citation used in a PreView request, the monitor will display a list of those cases. Follow the on-screen instructions to select the one you want to update.

Once you have invoked Shepard's PreView, you can PreView as many cases as you want during the PreView search session. You do not have to type sp each time; when you want to PreView another case, just type and transmit its citation.

[327] WEST PUBLISHING COMPANY, WESTLAW REFERENCE MANUAL 375–78 (5th ed. 1993) (Appendix I).

Moving within a Shepard's PreView table in WESTLAW. After displaying a PreView table, you can page through it (if it extends across more than one screen) as you would through a Shepard's table:

- Press the ENTER key (or the PAGE DOWN or PgDn key) to move the display forward one screen at a time. Press the PAGE UP (or PgUp) key to move the display back one screen at a time.
- Type `p+` or `p-` followed by a number and press ENTER to skip the display forward or back the designated number of screens. Alternatively, type a number and then press the PAGE DOWN (or PgDn) key or the PAGE UP (or PgUp) key.
- Type `p` followed by a number and press ENTER to move the display to the designated screen.

Customizing the display of a Shepard's PreView table in WESTLAW. As with Shepard's, you can use the LOCATE feature to customize the display of a PreView table. In PreView, however, you can customize only by the courts that issued the citing cases or by the West reporters that contain the citing cases. For instance, to restrict the display to citing cases found in *Federal Supplement*, you could transmit a request like one of these:

```
locate fsupp
loc f.supp
```

Or, to restrict the display to citing cases found in either *Federal Supplement* or *Federal Reporter, Second Series*, you could transmit

```
loc fsupp,f2d
```

To view a list of publication abbreviations you can use to customize a PreView table, type `scope` and press ENTER while using PreView. To resume PreViewing after checking the list of abbreviations, follow the on-screen instructions.

If you want a display restriction to remain in effect throughout a PreView session, transmit a LOCATE AUTO request as you would in Shepard's:

```
loc auto fsupp,f2d
```

You can edit a LOCATE or LOCATE AUTO request by typing `locate` (or `loc`) and pressing ENTER, then editing the instruction when it appears on the screen. Or, you can start over by transmitting a new LOCATE or LOCATE AUTO request.

When you finish viewing a PreView table for which you customized the display, you can exit the LOCATE feature and redisplay the full table by typing `xloc` (or `xl`). If you had a LOCATE AUTO restriction in effect, transmit `xloc auto` (or `xl auto`) instead.

Retrieving a citing case from a Shepard's PreView table in WESTLAW. If you want to see the text of a citing case listed in a PreView table, you can transmit its retrieval number, just as you would in Shepard's. You can then page through the retrieved case the same way you would page through a case retrieved from a Shepard's table. To return to the PreView table, transmit **gb** (for "go back").

Printing and downloading Shepard's PreView results in WESTLAW. To save PreView results, follow the procedures (explained on pages 521–23) for printing or downloading Shepard's results.

Leaving Shepard's PreView. When you want to invoke another WESTLAW feature or service during a Shepard's PreView session, or when you want to end a PreView session, follow the procedures (explained on pages 523–24) that you would use for the same purpose in Shepard's.

Shepardizing statutes through WESTLAW

Introduction. As with updating cases, you can use an online version of *Shepard's Citations* to update federal statutes and (as of this writing) statutes from a handful of states. If you know how to use printed *Shepard's Citations* to update a statute, updating a statute with the online version of *Shepard's Citations* will follow easily.[328]

Figure 12.40 on page 531 shows the first two screens of a Shepard's table for 42 U.S.C. § 303 as it appears online in WESTLAW. Figure 12.39 on page 530 shows the corresponding part of the table as it appears in a printed Shepard's citator. Although you will notice differences in the appearance of the Shepard's tables online and the appearance of their printed counterparts, you can accomplish online the same Shepardizing activities possible in the books. You can discover how a statute has subsequently been treated by courts and by the legislature that enacted it—for example, whether the statute has been amended or repealed by the legislature, or has been interpreted by a court. In addition, you can discover when the statute has been cited in other selected sources, such as law review articles, administrative decisions, and Attorney General Opinions. Often, you can carry out these activities more efficiently online than in the printed *Shepard's Citations.*

The following explanation takes you through the steps in Shepardizing a statute in WESTLAW. Figure 12.43 on pages 545 to 551 summarizes the steps.

Gaining access to Shepard's statute tables in WESTLAW. You can initiate a Shepard's search at nearly any time after logging on to WESTLAW.

[328]Chapter 6 of *The Legal Research Manual* explains how to use printed versions of *Shepard's Citations* to update statutes. CHRISTOPHER G. WREN & JILL R. WREN, THE LEGAL RESEARCH MANUAL: A GAME PLAN FOR LEGAL RESEARCH AND ANALYSIS 111–13 (2d ed. 1986).

You can begin Shepardizing as soon as the monitor displays the WESTLAW Directory; you do not need to select a database before starting to Shepardize. Or, you can wait until you have retrieved some documents from a database before you begin Shepardizing.

To retrieve a statute citator table through the Shepard's service in WESTLAW, you use a search request based on the citation of the statute you want to Shepardize:

- If you are viewing the statute you want to Shepardize, simply type **shep** (or **sh**) and press ENTER. The WESTLAW computer will automatically "read in" to the search request the citation of your statute.
- If you want to Shepardize a statute you are *not* viewing—say, a statute you see mentioned in a law review article you are looking at online—type **shep** (or **sh**) followed by the statute's citation; then press ENTER. For instance, to Shepardize 42 U.S.C. § 1983, you could use any of the following requests:

  ```
  sh 42 usc 1983
  shep 42 usc 1983
  sh 42usc1983
  sh 42 u.s.c. s 1983
  ```

  As you can see, you have considerable flexibility in typing your Shepard's request. If you are uncertain about how to type a statutory citation that Shepard's will recognize, you can view an online list of acceptable formats: type **pubs** and press ENTER while using the Shepard's service; then follow the on-screen instructions.
- If you are viewing an authority and see the citation of a statute you want to Shepardize, you can use the JUMP feature (explained on page 284) to automate the use of Shepard's for updating that citation. To use JUMP, type **shep** or **sh**, press the TAB key to position the cursor under the ">" symbol or triangle next to the citation you want to update, and then press ENTER. The computer will read in to your Shepard's request the citation on which you positioned the cursor.
- When you Shepardize a statute online, as when you use a printed Shepard's citator to update a statute, you need to be sure you are using the Shepard's table corresponding to the edition of the code containing the statute in which you are interested. Unless instructed otherwise, WESTLAW will Shepardize the version of the statute that appears in the current edition of the statutory code. If you want to Shepardize a version of the statute from an earlier edition of the

UNITED STATES CODE '82 Ed.

T. 42 § 301

630F2d1336	546F2d870	48ABA35	**§§ 301 to**	**§ 302**	318FS910	**Subd. 3**	82St16 §103
639F2d544	573F2d29	48ABA41	**1397f**	et seq.	**Subd. 10**	R95St816	93St19
650F2d183	615F2d1289	61ABA1065	Cir. DC	Cir. 9	L79St421	**Subd. 4**	301US619
657F2d1123	634F2d1309	64ABA1256	655F2d402	129F2d402	Cir. 6	A81St821	319US310
659F2d929	639F2d649	65ABA211	684F2d981	**§ 302**	363FS897	L86St919	327US360
673F2d1114	698F2d1068	67ABA1275	Cir. 2	79St415	Cir. 8	A95St871	363US603
676F2d355	713F2d601	68ABA1569	733F2d1038	80St1077	318FS910	**¶A**	367US394
679F2d1321	728F2d1292	AgD§ 7.11	741F2d6	Rs86St1329	**¶A**	Cir. 3	375US254
686F2d1345	38FS865	1LE1596s	611FS1412	A95St816	A79St418	670F2d1295	404US290
713F2d1433	41FS367	1LE1865s	Cir. 6	327US360		ABA347	422US760
722F2d1497	66FS306	1LE2088n	750F2d507	90LE728		**Cl. 4**	422US1051
733F2d1339	125FS263	8LE894s	Cir. 11	66SC644		St2337	424US323
734F2d1381	361FS681	24LE925s	711F2d1022	Cir. D		**Subsec. b**	432US424
739F2d1470	380FS780	27LE935s	**§§ 301 to 1397**	498F2d10		**Subd. 1**	434US391
751F2d987	385FS962	35LE735s	Cir. 8	99FS734		Cir. 5	449US168
765F2d872	404FS1194	39LE992n	724F2d712	Cir. 2		F2d327	451US514
44FS686	431FS419	40LE783s	**§§ 301 to 1396**	448F2d21		F2d135	457US572
45FS277	450FS544	42LE946s	Cir. 3	Cir. 3		**Subd. 2**	463US1328
46FS662	456FS609	43LE833s	599FS949	270FS176		**¶A**	464US879
52FS230	474FS813	43LE854n	608FS500	Cir. 5		Cir. 5	81LE1307
66FS619	487FS592	45LE804n	610FS1095	556F2d32		F2d327	87LE1420
67FS268	565FS813	47LE975s	98FRD712	Cir. 9		F2d136	90LE718
69FS109	569FS632	50LE928s	**§§ 301 to 1305**	127FS118		**§ 304**	4LE1437
69FS679	575FS324	51LE862n	Cir. 1	Cir. 1		t420	6LE922
70FS666	586FS905	53LE1295n	508FS326	315FS297		St821	11LE308
78FS682	596FS1294	61LE910s	**§§ 301 to 427**	75A3 1168		6St1329	30LE455
78FS882	600FS835	60A2 1070s	Cir. 2	**Subsec.**		C1363	45LE522
84FS671	602FS334	65A2 1182s	259FS369	A86St1329		Cir. 1	45LE704
84FS675	Cir. 11	88A2 493s	**§§ 301 to 306**	A95St816		F2d808	47LE26
84FS677	702F2d951	91A2 1212n	429US186	Cir. 2		F2d25	53LE456
101FS351	720F2d1252	5A3 1040s	50LE394	369FS819		Cir. 2	54LE631
127FS118	721F2d1298	8A3 696s	97SC431	Cir. 6		F2d211	66LE372
138FS943	724F2d917	11A3 1134s	Cir. DC	462FS235		FS868	68LE411
146FS789	738F2d1152	17A3 381n	655F2d403	Cir. 9		Cir. 5	73LE231
198FS705	739F2d566	22A3 44n	Cir. 5	449F2d45		F2d329	77LE1433
313FS1213	747F2d1415	22A3 440s	736F2d1045	**Subd. 1**		FS1304	78LE217
356FS754	754F2d956	22A3 1081s	Cir. 7	Cir. 2		Cir. 8	79LE156
356FS955	773F2d1154	23A3 1034s	608FS1325	303FS341		FS659	79LE882
371FS961	Cir. Fed.	38A3 613s	**§ 301**	359FS969		Cir. 9	81LE92

§ 303
et seq.
415US679
39LE682
§ 303
79St350
79St420
Rs86St1329
Cir. 2
C473F2d926
372FS1363
Subsec. a
A79St353
81St821 §204
A86St919
A88St2337
Subd. 1
A79St414
79St423
R95St816

Figure 12.39. Print Version of the United States Code Table from *Shepard's United States Citations* for Shepardizing 42 U.S.C. § 303

statutory code, add the year of the code parenthetically to your Shepard's request, as here:

```
sh 42 usc 303 (1976)
```

To see a list of the versions of the statute for which the online Shepard's service has citing references, type `ed` (for "Directory of Editions") and press ENTER while viewing the Shepard's result for that statute.

- When you Shepardize a statute online, you might retrieve citator tables from more than one Shepard's citator, as explained on page 537. If you want to limit your Shepard's results to the table from a specific Shepard's citator, you can add to your Shepard's request a parenthetical abbreviation for the Shepard's citator from which you want to retrieve a table. For instance, to retrieve the Shepard's table for 42 U.S.C. § 1983 from only *Shepard's United States Citations*, you would transmit:

```
                                SHEPARD'S  (Rank 1 of 5)         Page 1 of 5
CITATIONS TO: 42 USC s 303
CITATOR: UNITED STATES CITATIONS
DIVISION: United States Code
COVERAGE: First Shepard's volume through Aug. 1993 Supplement
Retrieval
   No.     -----Analysis----- -----Citation------
                                 TITLE 42
                               s 303 et seq.
    1                        415 U.S. 651, 679
    2                         39 L.Ed.2d 662, 682

                                   s 303
                            79 Stat. 350
                            79 Stat. 420
          RS  Repeal & super 86 Stat. 1329

Note:  Use FIND to view the statute's historical notes.  To view a list of
       the other editions with citing references, type ED and press ENTER.

Copyright (C) 1993 McGraw-Hill, Inc.; Copyright (C) 1993 West Publishing Co.
```

```
                                SHEPARD'S  (Rank 1 of 5)         Page 2 of 5
CITATIONS TO: 42 USC s 303
CITATOR: UNITED STATES CITATIONS
DIVISION: United States Code
Retrieval
   No.     -----Analysis----- -------Citation--------
                                     s 303
                                    Cir. 2
    1     C   Constitutional  473 F.2d 923, 926
    2                         372 F.Supp. 1360, 1363

                                   Subsec. a
          A   Amended        79 Stat. 353
                             81 Stat. 821 s 204
          A   Amended        86 Stat. 919
          A   Amended        88 Stat. 2337

                                    Subd. 1
          A   Amended        79 Stat. 414
                             79 Stat. 423
          R   Repealed       95 Stat. 816

Copyright (C) 1993 McGraw-Hill, Inc.; Copyright (C) 1993 West Publishing Co.
```

Source: West Publishing Company; © 1993 Shepard's/McGraw-Hill, Inc.

Figure 12.40. First Two Screens of a Typical Shepard's Statute Table in WESTLAW (Showing the United States Code Table from *Shepard's United States Citations* for Shepardizing 42 U.S.C. § 303)

```
sh 42 usc 1983 (us)
```

At this time, WESTLAW does not provide an online list of citator abbreviations, but the information is available from WESTLAW reference attorneys at the telephone number listed in Appendix B.

Once you have entered the Shepard's service by transmitting a Shepard's command, you can Shepardize as many authorities as you want during the Shepard's search session. You do not have to type `shep` or `sh` each time; just type and transmit a new citation when you want to Shepardize another authority.

Shepard's statute tables in WESTLAW. After you transmit a Shepard's request, you will see either of the following:

- If your initial Shepard's table consists of fewer than 10 screens, the monitor will display the first screen of that table (as in Figure 12.40).
- If your initial Shepard's table runs 10 or more screens, the monitor will display a table of contents (such as the one in Figure 12.41) for that table.

  Like the citator tables in printed Shepard's volumes for updating statutes, the online counterparts contain internal headings desig-

```
                                 SHEPARD'S  (Rank 1 of 5)
CITATIONS TO: 42 USC s 1983                                       Part A
CITATOR: UNITED STATES CITATIONS                       Pages in this part: 400
DIVISION: United States Code

                              Table of Contents                  Only Page

  1. TITLE 42, s 1983 et seq.
  2. TITLE 42, ss 1983 to 1988
  3. TITLE 42, ss 1983 to 1986
  4. TITLE 42, ss 1983 to 1985
  5. TITLE 42, s 1983

If you wish to:
   View the first page in the Shepard's result that contains citing references
     to a listed subsection, type its retrieval number and press ENTER
Note:  Your result exceeds 400 pages.  Enter PT to view the next part.
Copyright (C) 1993 McGraw-Hill, Inc.; Copyright (C) 1993 West Publishing Co.
```

Source: West Publishing Company; © 1993 Shepard's/McGraw-Hill, Inc.

Figure 12.41. Typical Table of Contents for a Shepard's Statute Table in WESTLAW

nating the subsections or range of statutory sections that the citing authorities have addressed. For example, the authorities listed under the heading "Subsec. a" in Figure 12.40 refer to subsection (a) of 42 U.S.C. § 303. The table of contents for an online Shepard's table will list the subsections or ranges of statutory sections cited in the Shepard's results.

If you want to see the table of contents for a Shepard's result containing fewer than 10 screens, or if you want to return to a table of contents, type `toc` and press ENTER while viewing the Shepard's table.

When a Shepard's citator table runs more than 400 screens (as in Figure 12.41), the computer divides the table into 400-screen chunks called "parts," each identified by a letter (Part A, Part B, and so on). Each lettered part has its own table of contents.

Once in a citator table, you need to be sure (just as when using a printed citator) that you have located the correct citator table for the statute you are Shepardizing. The heading on the first screen of an online citator table (such as the one in Figure 12.40) contains information that allows you to verify that you have transmitted the correct citation and, therefore, that the table you retrieved is appropriate for Shepardizing your statute:[329]

- *Citations To*—This line of the heading identifies the citation being Shepardized. In Figure 12.40, the "Citations To" line indicates that the citing authorities in the table contain references to 42 U.S.C. § 303.
- *Citator*—This line identifies the set of Shepard's citators from which the table was drawn. As with the printed *Shepard's Citations*, the online Shepard's service provides separate sets of citators for different authorities (*e.g.*, separate sets for various federal authorities, separate sets for state authorities). The heading in Figure 12.40 identifies *Shepard's United States Citations* as the source of the table.
- *Division*—This line verifies that within the appropriate set of Shepard's citators, you have retrieved the correct collection of tables for Shepardizing your statute. Like printed Shepard's citators, the

[329] The information in the heading verifies that the computer has conveniently carried out for you the first several steps you take when you Shepardize in printed citators—namely, selecting the proper set of *Shepard's Citations*, collecting all the necessary volumes in that set, finding the correct tables in those volumes, and locating the specific table for Shepardizing your authority. *See* CHRISTOPHER G. WREN & JILL R. WREN, THE LEGAL RESEARCH MANUAL: A GAME PLAN FOR LEGAL RESEARCH AND ANALYSIS 97–104, 111 (2d ed. 1986) (explaining these steps in book-based Shepardizing).

online Shepard's service provides collections of tables for Shepardizing cases and collections of tables for Shepardizing statutes. In Figure 12.40, the "Division" line indicates that the table is drawn from the collection of tables appropriate for Shepardizing statutes in the *United States Code*.

- *Coverage*—This line provides information you can use to determine the earliest and latest dates of citing authorities found in the Shepard's volumes from which the displayed table was drawn. The citing authorities listed in the displayed table will have been issued during the period covered by the citator volumes listed in the "Coverage" line.

  When the "Coverage" line specifies (as it does in Figure 12.40) that coverage begins with the "First Shepard's volume," you know you can Shepardize online as far back in time as you could in the printed citators.

  The "Coverage" line also indicates the latest date of coverage by identifying the most recent Shepard's supplement available online (which in Figure 12.40, for example, is the August 1993 supplement).[330] From the date of this supplement, you know you won't find in the table any citing authorities issued more recently than that date. (Because of the lag time inherent in the editorial process that produces a Shepard's table, the most recent citing authorities will likely be a month or two earlier than the date of the most recent supplement. You can use a WESTLAW-as-citator search, explained on pages 595–96, to narrow the gap.)

  To see additional information that can help you verify the coverage of an online citator, type `scope` (or `sc`) and press ENTER while viewing a Shepard's table from that citator. The monitor will display a list of titles of the case reporters, law reviews, and other authorities from which citing references might appear in the Shepard's table and, for each authority listed, will indicate the earliest volume that might contain a citing reference. On-screen prompts explain how to page through the list and how to resume Shepardizing.

  Shepard's citators in WESTLAW are updated when a new printed supplement is published, so the online and printed versions of a Shepard's citator should be equally current.

[330] Shepard's periodically updates its printed citators with separate publications called "supplements." For an explanation of Shepard's supplements, see CHRISTOPHER G. WREN & JILL R. WREN, THE LEGAL RESEARCH MANUAL: A GAME PLAN FOR LEGAL RESEARCH AND ANALYSIS 98 n.36 (2d ed. 1986).

The portion of the citator table that follows the heading contains all the information found in printed citator tables, though in an easier-to-read form:

- *Citations*—In the column labelled "Citation," you will find a list of citations of the authorities that have referred to the statute being Shepardized. For example, from Figure 12.40, you can determine that a reference to 42 U.S.C. § 303 occurs at 372 F. Supp. 1363. (As this reference also illustrates, citations to case reporters usually include two page numbers. The first page number identifies the starting page of the case, and the second page number identifies a page containing a reference to the authority being Shepardized.)
- *Analysis*—To the left of the list of citing authorities, in the column labelled "Analysis," you will frequently see comments indicating how citing authorities relate to the statute being Shepardized. For example, in Figure 12.40, the notation "Constitutional" on the same line as 473 F.2d 923, 926 indicates that this citing authority upheld the constitutionality of 42 U.S.C. § 303. The notation "Amended" on the same line as 79 Stat. 353 indicates that this citing authority amended 42 U.S.C. § 303(a).

  If no analysis comment appears next to a citing authority, the authority mentioning the statute being Shepardized has simply cited it, without affecting or analyzing it.

  Figure 12.42 lists and explains the analysis comments you might find in an online Shepard's table for updating a statute. To see an explanation of the comments while using Shepard's online, type `analysis` and press ENTER; to resume Shepardizing after viewing the list of comments, follow the on-screen instructions. The analysis comments track the analyses you find in printed citators, but spell out the analyses in addition to using the highly abbreviated codes (such as "Rs," "Sg," or "L") appearing in the printed citator tables.

  As Figure 12.42 shows, the analysis comments indicate one of two things: (1) how the statute being Shepardized has been affected by legislative action (*e.g.*, whether the statute has been repealed); or (2) how courts have treated the statute (*e.g.*, whether a court has declared the statute unconstitutional).

  In the "Analysis" column, you might also see the comment "Anno" or "Anno Sup," indicating that the reference to the statute you are Shepardizing appears in an *A.L.R.* or *Lawyers' Edition* annotation or annotation supplement.
- *Retrieval No.*—Each entry in this column is a number you can use (as explained at pages 541–43) to retrieve the text of the citing authority identified by that number.

Operation of Statute: Legislative

A	(amended)	Statute amended.
AD	(added)	New section added.
AN	(amended and renumbered)	Statute amended and sections renumbered.
AR	(amended and re-enacted)	Statute amended and re-enacted.
AU	(added and renumbered)	New section added and sections renumbered.
E	(extended)	Provisions of an existing statute extended in their application to a later statute, or allowance of additional time for performance of duties required by a statute within a limited time.
L	(limited)	Provisions to an existing statute declared not to be extended in their application to a later statute.
R	(repealed)	Abrogation of an existing statute.
RE	(re-enacted)	Statute re-enacted.
RN	(renumbered)	Renumbering of existing sections.
RP	(repealed in part)	Abrogation of part of an existing statute.
RR	(repealed and re-enacted)	Abrogation of an existing statute and statute re-enacted.
RS	(repealed and superseded)	Abrogation of an existing statute and substitution of new legislation therefor.
RV	(revised)	Statute revised.
S	(superseded)	Substitution of new legislation for an existing statute expressly abrogated.
SP	(superseded in part)	Substitution of new legislation for part of an existing statute not expressly abrogated.
SG	(supplementing)	New matter added to an existing statute.
SD	(suspended)	Statute suspended.
SN	(suspended in part)	Statute suspended in part.
VA	(validated)	Statute validated.

Operation of Statute: Judicial

C	Constitutional.
U	Unconstitutional.
UP	Unconstitutional in part.
VA	Valid.
V	Void or invalid.
VP	Void or invalid in part.

Source: Adapted from WEST PUBLISHING COMPANY, WESTLAW REFERENCE MANUAL 243–44 (5th ed. 1993) and WESTLAW's online list of analysis comments.

Figure 12.42. Shepard's Analysis Comments in WESTLAW for Statutes

Finding all the citator tables in WESTLAW for a statute. Shepard's publishes a citator set for each state and for federal authorities. Each jurisdiction's citator set has tables for Shepardizing statutes from that jurisdiction. In addition, state citator sets have tables for the United States Constitution and the *United States Code*; those tables list citations of that state's court decisions and legislative acts citing federal constitutional and statutory provisions. Finally, because a citing reference might identify a version of a statute as it appears in a specific edition of a statutory code, Shepard's statute citators provide separate tables for each edition of a statutory code.

Consequently, thorough Shepardizing (whether in printed citators or online) can entail checking more than a single Shepard's table for a statute, and for Shepardizing federal statutes, can entail checking tables in federal and state citators.

When you Shepardize a statute through WESTLAW, the computer automatically retrieves all online citator tables containing citing references to the statute you are updating. To see a list of the tables you retrieve for a given citation:

1. Type l (for "list").
2. Press ENTER. The monitor will display the name of each citator from which a table has been drawn. The screen will look similar to the list, illustrated in Figure 12.35 on page 513, that you can display when you Shepardize a case through WESTLAW. (An arrow in the left margin will point to the table you were viewing when you instructed the computer to display the list.)
3. When you finish viewing a list, follow the on-screen instructions to continue with your Shepardizing.

While viewing a Shepard's table for a statute, you can also see a list of the versions of the statute for which the online Shepard's service has citing references. To do so:

1. Type ed (for "Directory of Editions").
2. Press ENTER.
3. When you finish viewing the directory, follow the on-screen instructions to continue with your Shepardizing.

Moving within a Shepard's statute table in WESTLAW. Once you have displayed a Shepard's table, you can page through it (if it extends across more than one screen) by using standard WESTLAW techniques for moving within a document:[331]

[331] Pages 360–63 explain these techniques.

- Press ENTER (or the PAGE DOWN or PgDn key) to move the display forward one screen at a time. Press the PAGE UP (or PgUp) key to move the display back one screen at a time.
- Type `p+` or `p-` followed by a number and press ENTER to skip the display forward or back the designated number of screens. Alternatively, type a number and then press the PAGE DOWN (or PgDn) key or the PAGE UP (or PgUp) key.
- Type `p` followed by a number and press ENTER to move the display to the designated screen.

Transmitting `h+` or `h-`, which normally allows you to move forward or back half a screen within a document (see pages 361–62), currently does not work in the Shepard's service.

If the display of your Shepard's result begins with a table of contents (which appears when a Shepard's result exceeds nine screens), you move past the table of contents and into the citator table by transmitting the identification number of the internal heading for the portion of the table you want to view. For instance, at the screen shown in Figure 12.41 on page 532, you would transmit `4` to see the portion of the citator table containing references to authorities that have cited sections 1983 to 1985 of Title 42 of the *United States Code*.

If your Shepard's result runs longer than 400 screens, the citator table will appear in "parts" containing up to 400 screens. To move among "parts":

- To move forward one "part" (say, from Part A to Part B), type `part` (or `pt`) and press ENTER.
- To move from the part you are viewing to any part you have already viewed, type `part` (or `pt`) followed by the letter for a "part," then press ENTER. For example, while viewing Part D, you could transmit `pt a` to move to Part A.

Customizing the display of a Shepard's statute table in WESTLAW. While viewing a Shepard's table (especially one containing a lengthy list of citing authorities), you might want to instruct the computer to display only those citing authorities that satisfy certain criteria most likely to help you evaluate the statute you are Shepardizing. For example, you might concentrate on citing authorities accompanied by an analysis comment like "repealed."

You can use the LOCATE feature to customize the display once you have retrieved a Shepard's statute table. Start by typing `locate` (or `loc`) and pressing ENTER. The monitor will display a screen like the one shown in Figure 12.37 on page 515. At that point, you can customize the display in any of these ways:

- *By analysis comment.* Type the code for the analysis comment by which you want to screen citing authorities, then press ENTER. For example, to restrict the display to citing authorities that have amended the statute you are Shepardizing, you would type `a` and press ENTER.

  You can also customize a table according to categories of analysis codes. To display citing authorities that have *any* kind of analysis code, transmit `all` or `any`. To display citing authorities having any kind of code reflecting legislative activity (such as amendment), transmit `hist` (for "history"). To display citing authorities having any kind of code reflecting judicial activity (such as upholding a statute's constitutionality), transmit `tr` (for "treatment"). To display citing authorities having negative codes (such as "repealed," "superseded," or "unconstitutional"), transmit `neg`.

  If you want to see a list of analysis codes while using Shepard's through WESTLAW, type `analysis` and press ENTER. To resume Shepardizing after viewing the list of codes, follow the on-screen instructions. A list of analysis codes for statutes appears in Figure 12.42 on page 536.
- *By court.* To display citing authorities decided by a particular court, type an appropriate abbreviation for the court, then press ENTER. For example, to display citing authorities from federal district and appellate courts in just the Ninth Circuit, you could type `cir9` and press ENTER. To see a list of court abbreviations you can use to customize a Shepard's display, transmit `courts` while you are using the Shepard's service through WESTLAW. To resume Shepardizing after viewing the list, follow the on-screen instructions.
- *By publication.* Type the abbreviation of the case reporter, law review, or other publication by which you want to screen citing authorities; then press ENTER. For example, to restrict the display to citing authorities found in *United States Reports*, you could type `u.s.` or `us` and press ENTER. Similarly, transmitting `a.l.r.fed.` would display only citing references found in the *American Law Reports Federal.*

  A publication's abbreviation as it appears in a Shepard's table will generally work in your instruction. When you type a publication abbreviation, you can omit punctuation, but you cannot have any spaces within the abbreviation. If the monitor displays a message indicating that the Shepard's table does not contain any citing references in the publication you designated, check to be sure you have transmitted the publication abbreviation in an acceptable format. You can find a list of acceptable abbreviations in the *WESTLAW Reference Manual*.[332]

If you want to limit the display to just certain volumes of a selected publication, you can add `>` or `aft` and a volume number to the publication abbreviation you transmit with your LOCATE request. For instance, you can transmit `>433us` or `aft433us` to limit the display to only those citing authorities appearing in *United States Reports* beginning with volume 434.

- *By a combination of display criteria.* You can combine display restrictions in a single instruction. For example, to restrict the display to citing authorities that have either amended or repealed the statute you are Shepardizing, you would type `a,r` and press ENTER.

  When all of your criteria come from the same category (*e.g.*, when they're all analysis codes or when they're all court abbreviations), the commas separating the criteria operate as "or" connectors. Thus, transmitting `a,r` displays citing authorities accompanied by either "a" or "r" in the analysis column of the Shepard's table. When your criteria come from different categories, the commas separating the criteria operate as "and" connectors. Thus, transmitting `c,u.s.` displays only those citing cases accompanied by "c" in the analysis column *and* by "U.S." in the citation column.

Customizing a Shepard's display with a one-step instruction. When you customize a Shepard's table in WESTLAW, you might prefer not to transmit `locate` (or `loc`) and wait for a new screen to appear before you transmit your display criteria. If so, you can customize a Shepard's display this way:

1. Type `locate` (or `loc`) followed by the display criteria you want. Your all-in-one request will take this form:

```
loc a
locate u.s.
loc c,u.s.
```

2. Press ENTER.

Changing your display criteria. You can change your display criteria as frequently as you want. To edit existing criteria:

1. Type `locate` (or `loc`).
2. Press ENTER. The monitor will display your most recent customizing instruction, which you can then revise and transmit.

[332] WEST PUBLISHING COMPANY, WESTLAW REFERENCE MANUAL 361–74 (5th ed. 1993) (Appendix H).

Or, you can just transmit `locate` (or `loc`) followed by your new display criteria.

Shortcut: Shepardizing more than one authority according to the same display criteria. If you want to Shepardize several authorities according to the same restrictive display criteria (*e.g.*, to focus only on citing authorities that have amended the statutes you are Shepardizing), you can avoid typing the restrictive criteria each time you Shepardize a new authority. To do this:

1. Type `locate auto` (or `loc auto`) followed by whatever display criteria you want. Your request would take this form:

```
loc auto a
loc auto all
loc auto u.s.
```

2. Press ENTER.

From then on, until you discard or edit your LOCATE AUTO request, every citator table you retrieve during your WESTLAW session will display only the citing authorities that satisfy your LOCATE AUTO criteria.

To edit a LOCATE AUTO request, you can transmit `locate` (or `loc`) and then edit your existing LOCATE AUTO request when it appears on the monitor. Or, you can type `locate auto` (or `loc auto`) followed by new display criteria, then press ENTER.

Leaving a customized Shepard's display. When you finish viewing a Shepard's statute table you customized with a LOCATE request, you can return to the original display (showing all the citing authorities in the table). To do that:

1. Type `xloc` or `xl` (for "exit LOCATE").

2. Press ENTER.

To return to the original display when you finish viewing a Shepard's table you customized with a LOCATE AUTO request:

1. Type `xloc auto` or `xl auto`.

2. Press ENTER.

Retrieving a citing authority from a Shepard's statute table in WESTLAW. While viewing a Shepard's table (whether in a full or restricted display), you might decide you want to see the text of an authority listed in the table as a citing reference. When you Shepardize in WESTLAW, you can instruct the computer to retrieve the text of a citing authority. The technique you use depends on whether the authority you want to view has an accompanying number in the "Retrieval No." column of the Shepard's table. (See Figure 12.40 on page 531.)

If the citing authority has a retrieval number:

1. Type the retrieval number.
2. Press ENTER. The computer will then use the corresponding citation from the "Citation" column of the Shepard's table to retrieve the authority you want to view.

The monitor will display the citing authority in TERM mode, showing the first page of the authority, with the phrase "CITING CASE" highlighted at the top of the screen. To move to references to the statute you are Shepardizing, press ENTER.

You can also retrieve a citing authority that does not have a retrieval number assigned to it in a Shepard's table. Instead of transmitting a retrieval number:

1. Type a FIND instruction based on the citation information in the Shepard's table.[333]
2. Press ENTER.

Once you retrieve a citing authority through FIND, you can transmit a star-page number to move to a page containing a reference to the statute you are Shepardizing.[334] (You can save time using the star-paging feature if, when viewing a Shepard's table, you remember to note all the pages containing references to the statute you are Shepardizing.) If star paging is unavailable for the citing authority, you can use a LOCATE request to achieve the same result: while viewing the citing authority, transmit `locate` (or `loc`) followed by search terms identifying the statute you are Shepardizing. For example, transmit `loc 42 w/6 303` to see references to 42 U.S.C. § 303.

Whether you retrieve a citing authority by its retrieval number or through FIND, you do not lose the citator table you had just been viewing; the table simply disappears from sight while the monitor displays the text of the citing authority you selected. To switch from the text of this citing authority back to the citator table:

1. Type `gb` (for "go back").
2. Press ENTER.

Once back at the table, if you want to select another citing authority to view, transmit its retrieval number or use a FIND instruction.

[333] For a refresher on FIND, see pages 279–84. Note that if the citing authority is not available online or is not retrievable through FIND, this technique will not work.

[334] For a refresher on star paging in WESTLAW, see pages 356–58.

Note that when you use a retrieval number or a FIND instruction to display a citing authority, you can, in turn, Shepardize that authority by transmitting `sh` while viewing it.

Moving between Shepard's statute tables in WESTLAW. When a Shepard's search retrieves more than one citator table for a single citation (as occurs, for example, in Shepardizing 42 U.S.C. § 303),[335] WESTLAW treats each table as a separate document. A message at the top of the monitor indicates how many tables were retrieved and which is being displayed; thus, "Rank 1 of 5" in Figure 12.40 on page 531 indicates you are viewing the first of five tables.

You can move from one table to another by using standard WESTLAW techniques for moving between documents:[336]

- Transmit `r` (for "rank") to move the display forward one table.
- Transmit `r` followed by a number to move the display to the table having that document number. For example, transmit `r4` to display the fourth table.
- Transmit `r+` or `r-` followed by a number to skip the display forward or back the specified number of tables.

Printing and downloading Shepard's statute tables in WESTLAW. To save your results when you Shepardize statutes, follow the procedures (explained on pages 521–23) for printing or downloading your results when you Shepardize cases.

Pausing during a Shepard's session in WESTLAW to use FIND, Shepard's PreView, or Insta-Cite. During a Shepard's search session, you can retrieve a document by using FIND, or you can implement an updating search in Shepard's PreView or Insta-Cite.[337] To do so, simply follow the instructions for commencing a FIND, Shepard's PreView, or Insta-Cite search. To return to the Shepard's service from the feature or service you invoked, type `gb` (for "go back") and press ENTER.

Ending a Shepard's session and returning to FIND, Shepard's PreView, or Insta-Cite. As noted earlier, you can Shepardize at nearly any point during an online research session. (See pages 528–29.) If you invoked the Shepard's service while using the FIND feature or the Shepard's PreView or Insta-Cite service, you can resume using that other feature or service by typing `gb` and pressing ENTER.

[335] See Figure 12.40 on page 531.

[336] Pages 364–67 explain these techniques.

[337] See pages 279–84 for an explanation of the FIND feature, pages 524–28 for an explanation of Shepard's PreView, and pages 544 and 552–64 for an explanation of Insta-Cite.

Suppose, however, you used more than a single service or feature before invoking Shepard's. If you want to return to the service or feature you were using immediately before invoking Shepard's, type **gb** and press ENTER. To return to any other service or feature, type **map** and press ENTER to display a list of your previous research activities; then follow the on-screen instructions to select the service or feature to which you want to return. (Alternatively, you could transmit **gb** repeatedly until you arrive at the earlier stage in your research to which you want to return.)

Thus, if you had carried out searches using FIND, Shepard's PreView, Insta-Cite, and Shepard's (in that order), you could return from Shepard's to Insta-Cite simply by transmitting **gb**. To return to a document you were viewing through FIND or to return to Shepard's PreView, however, you would transmit **map** and make your selection from the on-screen list of research activities. (Or, you could transmit multiple "gb" commands.)

Ending a Shepard's session and returning to WESTLAW. If you had been viewing the WESTLAW Directory or the results of a WESTLAW search just before invoking Shepard's, you could return to WESTLAW by transmitting **gb**. Alternatively, you could use a shortcut "map" command that bypasses the map list: transmit **map1** to return directly to the WESTLAW Directory, or **map2** to return directly to your most recent WESTLAW search results (if any).

Summary of Shepardizing a statute through WESTLAW. Figure 12.43 summarizes the steps and commands for updating an authority by using the Shepard's service in WESTLAW.

Shepardizing other authorities through WESTLAW

Currently, you cannot Shepardize online all the types of authorities (such as municipal ordinances) you can update through the printed citators.[338] Additional Shepard's citators will likely appear in WESTLAW in the future, however. When they do, West Publishing will announce the availability of the new citators, which will almost certainly operate along the lines of the citators now online.

Using Insta-Cite in WESTLAW to verify a case's citation and status

Insta-Cite is a "citation verification service" available through WESTLAW.[339] By transmitting a citation for a case, you can retrieve a report that

[338] For a list of authorities you can Shepardize in printed citators, see CHRISTOPHER G. WREN & JILL R. WREN, THE LEGAL RESEARCH MANUAL: A GAME PLAN FOR LEGAL RESEARCH AND ANALYSIS 96 n.34 (2d ed. 1986).

[339] LEXIS offers a similar service, known as Auto-Cite. *See* pages 422 and 426–37.

If you want to	Follow this procedure in WESTLAW
Shepardize the authority you are viewing	type `shep` (or `sh`) and press ENTER
Shepardize an authority you are not viewing	type `shep` (or `sh`) followed by the authority's citation; then press ENTER *Example:* `sh 49 wis.2d 430` `sh 42 u.s.c. s 1983`
Shepardize an authority when you see its citation accompanied by a JUMP marker (a ">" symbol or a triangle)	type `shep` (or `sh`), press the TAB key to position the cursor under the JUMP marker, and then press ENTER
Retrieve an authority's citator table from a specific Shepard's citator	type `shep` (or `sh`) followed by the authority's citation and, in parentheses, the abbreviation of the desired Shepard's citator; then press ENTER *Example:* `sh 508 fsupp 690 (flrev)` `sh 42 usc 1983 (us)`
Shepardize a statute as it appears in an edition other than the current edition of the statutory code	type `shep` (or `sh`) followed by the statute's citation and, in parentheses, the desired year; then press ENTER *Example:* `sh 42 usc 303 (1976)`

(continues)

Figure 12.43. Quick Guide to Shepardizing Cases and Statutes through WESTLAW

(continued)

If you want to	Follow this procedure in WESTLAW
Page through a citator table	• press ENTER (or PAGE DOWN or PgDn) to move forward one screen; press PAGE UP (or PgUp) to move back one screen • type `p` followed by a number and press ENTER to move to the designated screen • type `p+` or `p-` followed by a number, and then press ENTER to skip forward or back the designated number of screens; alternatively, type a number and then press PAGE DOWN (or PgDn) or PAGE UP (or PgUp) • type `part` (or `pt`) and press ENTER to move forward one part • type `part` (or `pt`) followed by the letter for a part, then press ENTER to move to a part you have already viewed
Customize the display of a citator table	type `locate` (or `loc`) followed by your restrictive criteria (analysis comment, headnote or syllabus paragraph number, court, publication, or a combination of these); then press ENTER *Example:* `loc o,q,4,6`
Redisplay a complete citator table after displaying a customized table	type `xloc` (or `xl`) and press ENTER
Automatically customize the display of all citator tables	type `locate auto` (or `loc auto`) followed by your restrictive criteria (such as analysis comments); then press ENTER *Example:* `loc auto all`
Redisplay a complete citator table after automatically customizing the display	type `xloc auto` (or `xl auto`) and press ENTER

Retrieve the text of a citing authority from a citator table	type that authority's retrieval number, found in the "Retrieval No." column; then press ENTER *or* for a citing authority that does not have a retrieval number, type a FIND request using the authority's citation; then press ENTER
Return to a citator table from the text of a citing authority	type **gb** and press ENTER
Move between citator tables when Shepard's retrieves more than one table	• type **r** (for "rank") and press ENTER to move forward one table • type **r** followed by a number and press ENTER to move to the designated table • type **r+** or **r–** followed by a number; then press ENTER to skip forward or back the designated number of tables
Display a list of citator tables retrieved for a citation	type **l** and press ENTER
Redisplay a citator table after displaying a list of tables	type the number (shown on the list) for the citator containing the table; then press ENTER
Print a single line from the screen you are viewing in a citator table (if you are using a WALT II terminal)	move the cursor to the line you want to print and press the PRINT LINE key
Print the screen you are viewing in a citator table	press the PRINT SCREEN (or PRT SC) key; on some keyboards, you might also need to hold down the SHIFT key

(continues)

Figure 12.43. Quick Guide to Shepardizing Cases and Statutes through WESTLAW (continued)

(continued)

If you want to	Follow this procedure in WESTLAW
Print each screen automatically as you view it in a citator table	hold down the CONTROL (or CTRL) key and press the PRINT SCREEN (or PRT SC) key; on some keyboards, you press only the ONLINE PRINT key
Turn off automatic printing of displayed screens	hold down the CONTROL (or CTRL) key and press the PRINT SCREEN (or PRT SC) key; on some keyboards, you press only the ONLINE PRINT key
Print some or all screens from a retrieved citator table after you log off	type **pr** and press ENTER; then follow the on-screen instructions
Print some or all retrieved citator tables after you log off	type **pr** and press ENTER; then follow the on-screen instructions
*Download the screen you are viewing in a citator table	press F10 to display the WESTMATE menu; select the "File/Accessing" heading by either typing **f** or pressing ENTER; then select the "Store Screen to Disk" option
*Download each screen automatically as you view it in a citator table	press F10 to display the WESTMATE menu; select the "File/Accessing" heading by either typing **f** or pressing ENTER; then select the "Log Screens to Disk" option
*Turn off automatic downloading of displayed screens	press F10 to display the WESTMATE menu; select the "File/Accessing" heading by either typing **f** or pressing ENTER; then select the "Stop Disk Logging" option
*Download some or all screens from a retrieved citator table after you log off	type **pr** and press ENTER; then follow the on-screen instructions
*Download some or all retrieved citator tables after you log off	type **pr** and press ENTER; then follow the on-screen instructions

Invoke another service or feature during a Shepard's session	type a FIND, Shepard's PreView, or Insta-Cite request; then press ENTER
Switch from the other service or feature back to Shepard's	type **gb** and press ENTER
Switch from Shepard's to any other service or feature you have used during your Shepard's session (if you have used more than one other service or feature)	type **map** and press ENTER; then make your selection from the list displayed on the monitor *or* transmit **gb** repeatedly until you arrive at the research activity you want to return to
Switch from Shepard's to the service or feature you most recently used during your Shepard's session	type **gb** and press ENTER
End a Shepard's session and return to WESTLAW	type **map1** and press ENTER to return to the WESTLAW Directory *or* type **map2** and press ENTER to return to your most recent WESTLAW search results (if any)

(continues)

* This function is available only on a computer with a disk for storing information.

Figure 12.43. Quick Guide to Shepardizing Cases and Statutes through WESTLAW (continued)

(continued)

If you want to	Follow this procedure in WESTLAW
Update Shepard's case results through Shepard's PreView	type `sp` and press ENTER to update the case or Shepard's table you are viewing *or* type `sp` followed by a case citation and press ENTER to update a case you are not viewing *or* if you are viewing another authority and see the case citation accompanied by a JUMP marker (a ">" symbol or a triangle), type `sp`, press the TAB key to position the cursor under the JUMP marker, and then press ENTER
View a list of Shepard's commands and accompanying explanations	type `cmds` and press ENTER while in the Shepard's service
View a list of publication abbreviations that work in a Shepard's request	type `pubs` and press ENTER while in the Shepard's service
View an explanation of Shepard's analysis comments	type `analysis` and press ENTER

Determine the coverage of a Shepard's citator while you are viewing one of its tables (*e.g.*, to determine the earliest volume of a case reporter in which a citing reference might appear in a citator table)	type `scope` (or `sc`) and press ENTER
Determine the coverage of a Shepard's citator when you are not viewing one of its tables (*e.g.*, to determine the earliest volume of a case reporter in which a citing reference might appear in a citator table)	while in the Shepard's service, type `scope` (or `sc`) followed by the abbreviation of the citator; then press ENTER and follow the on-screen instructions *Example:* To see coverage information for *Shepard's Tennessee Citations,* type `sc tenn` and press ENTER
Display the table of contents for the part you are viewing of a Shepard's statute table	type `toc` and press ENTER
Display a list (a "Directory of Editions") of the versions of a statute for which the online Shepard's service has citing references	while viewing a Shepard's table for the statute, type `ed` and press ENTER

Figure 12.43. Quick Guide to Shepardizing Cases and Statutes through WESTLAW (continued)

indicates, among other things, the status of the case. Insta-Cite is only available online; it does not have a printed counterpart.

The Insta-Cite report. Figures 12.44 and 12.45 show typical Insta-Cite reports: Figure 12.44 shows the report for *State v. Yoder*, 49 Wis. 2d 430, 182 N.W.2d 539 (1971), and Figure 12.45 shows the report for *Blackwelder v. Safnauer*, 689 F. Supp. 106 (N.D.N.Y. 1988). As the figures show, an Insta-Cite report provides the following information about a case.

Each screen of a report begins with a citation line that identifies the citation used in the Insta-Cite request. At the top left corner of Figure 12.44, for example, you see "CITATION: 49 Wis.2d 430," indicating that the report was retrieved by using 49 Wis. 2d 430 in the Insta-Cite request.

After the citation line, the monitor displays the body of the Insta-Cite report, consisting of numbered entries for individual cases or court orders. The numbered entries include the following "citation verification" information for the case being updated, allowing you to double-check the accuracy of its citation:[340]

- Case name

[340] At this writing, Insta-Cite provides citation verification for federal cases decided since 1754 and for state cases decided since 1879.

```
                                INSTA-CITE                          Only Page
CITATION: 49 Wis.2d 430
                              Direct History

=>   1  State v. Yoder, 49 Wis.2d 430, 182 N.W.2d 539 (Wis., Jan 08, 1971)
            (NO. STATE 92-94)
          Certiorari Granted by
     2  Wisconsin v. Yoder, 402 U.S. 994, 91 S.Ct. 2173, 29 L.Ed.2d 160
            (U.S.Wis., May 24, 1971) (NO. 1536)
          AND Judgment Affirmed by
     3  Wisconsin v. Yoder, 406 U.S. 205, 92 S.Ct. 1526, 32 L.Ed.2d 15
            (U.S.Wis., May 15, 1972) (NO. 70-110)
            (> Additional Negative Indirect History)

   > View additional negative indirect history on Shepard's
   > Shepard's  > Shepard's PreView   > QuickCite  > Commands    > SCOPE
  (C) Copyright West Publishing Company 1993
```

Source: West Publishing Company © 1993

Figure 12.44. A Typical Insta-Cite Report in WESTLAW (Reporting on *State v. Yoder*, 49 Wis. 2d 430, 182 N.W.2d 539)

```
                                INSTA-CITE              Page    1 of     2
CITATION: 689 F.Supp. 106
                              Direct History

=>    1  Blackwelder v. Safnauer, 689 F.Supp. 106, 57 USLW 2023,
             48 Ed. Law Rep. 418 (N.D.N.Y., Jun 17, 1988) (NO. 86-CV-1208)
           Reconsideration Denied by
      2  Blackwelder v. Safnauer, 1988 WL 85938 (N.D.N.Y., Aug 15, 1988)
             (NO. 86-CV-1208)
           Order Affirmed by
      3  Blackwelder v. Safnauer, 866 F.2d 548, 51 Ed. Law Rep. 764
             (2nd Cir.(N.Y.), Jan 23, 1989) (NO. 597, 88-7766)

=>    4  Blackwelder v. Safnauer, 689 F.Supp. 106, 57 USLW 2023,
             48 Ed. Law Rep. 418 (N.D.N.Y., Jun 17, 1988) (NO. 86-CV-1208)
           Appeal Dismissed by
      5  Blackwelder v. Safnauer, 866 F.2d 548, 51 Ed. Law Rep. 764
             (2nd Cir.(N.Y.), Jan 23, 1989) (NO. 597, 88-7766)

     > Shepard's  > Shepard's PreView  > QuickCite  > Commands   > SCOPE
(C) Copyright West Publishing Company 1993
```

```
                                INSTA-CITE              Page    2 of     2
CITATION: 689 F.Supp. 106

Related References
      6  Matter of Blackwelder, 139 Misc.2d 776, 528 N.Y.S.2d 759,
             46 Ed. Law Rep. 1214 (N.Y.Sup., Apr 27, 1988) (NO. 8197)

                          Negative Indirect History

  Disagreement Recognized by
      7  Jeffery v. O'Donnell, 702 F.Supp. 516, 51 Ed. Law Rep. 463
             (M.D.Pa., Aug 24, 1988) (NO. CIV. 86-1560)
             ( > Additional History)


                             Secondary Sources

Corpus Juris Secundum (C.J.S.) References
         16A C.J.S. Constitutional Law Sec.519 Note 88.1 (Pocket Part)
         79 C.J.S. Schools and School Dist. Sec.468 Note 2 (Pocket Part)

(C) Copyright West Publishing Company 1993
```

Source: West Publishing Company © 1993

Figure 12.45. A Typical Insta-Cite Report in WESTLAW (Reporting on *Blackwelder v. Safnauer*, 689 F. Supp. 106)

- Official or preferred citation for the case
- Parallel citations (if any) for the case
- Court that decided the case
- Date of decision
- Docket number

An entry that corresponds to the citation used in an Insta-Cite request will appear with the case name highlighted and preceded by an arrow (as in the first entry in Figure 12.44).

The entries include authorities that fall into one of four categories with respect to the case being updated:

- *Direct history*—citations of prior or subsequent decisions (if any) in the case. The prior or subsequent decisions involve the same parties, facts, and issues as those in the case being updated.

  In the Insta-Cite report for *State v. Yoder* (Figure 12.44), an example of a "direct history" entry is the United States Supreme Court's decision (entry 3 in the figure) affirming the Wisconsin Supreme Court's decision (entry 1).

  As of this writing, an Insta-Cite report will provide direct history citations when you update a federal case decided from 1754 to the present or a state case decided from 1879 to the present.
- *Negative indirect history*—citations of decisions that are not part of the direct history of the case being updated but that negatively affect the precedential value of the case being updated.[341]

  For instance, Figure 12.45 refers to *Jeffery v. O'Donnell*, a case that in the opinion of the Insta-Cite editors has some negative impact on the precedential value of *Blackwelder* and is, therefore, part of *Blackwelder*'s "negative indirect history."

  As of this writing, if the precedential value of the case you are updating has been affected by decisions issued from 1972 to the present, those decisions will appear in the Insta-Cite report. So, if

[341] Long-time users of Insta-Cite should note that in mid-1991, WESTLAW rearranged "negative indirect history" coverage. Until then, an Insta-Cite report automatically displayed citations to decisions that negatively affected the precedential value of decisions that themselves negatively affected the precedential value of the case being updated. For example, suppose a federal district court decided *Case 1*, another federal district court issued a decision (*Case 2*) criticizing *Case 1*, and a third federal court issued a decision (*Case 3*) criticizing *Case 2*. Before mid-1991, the Insta-Cite report for *Case 1* would have automatically displayed not only a reference to *Case 2* (because it negatively affected *Case 1*), but a reference to *Case 3* (because it negatively affected *Case 2*).

Now, the Insta-Cite report for *Case 1* would automatically display a reference to *Case 2* but not to *Case 3*. If you want to see whether Insta-Cite reports any decisions that cast doubt on *Case 2*, you will need to retrieve the Insta-Cite report for *Case 2*.

you were updating a 1960 case that was overruled by a 1965 decision, the Insta-Cite report would *not* tell you the case had been overruled; you would have to use another updating technique, such as Shepardizing. On the other hand, if the 1960 case had been overruled by a 1975 decision, you would learn that from the Insta-Cite report.

To identify pre-1972 cases that negatively affect the case you are updating through Insta-Cite, you can use the JUMP marker (the ">" symbol or triangle) preceding the phrase "View additional negative indirect history on Shepard's," which appears at the bottom of the first screen in an Insta-Cite report for a case decided before 1972. (The phrase appears, for example, in Figure 12.44.) Press the TAB key to position the cursor under that JUMP marker, then press ENTER. In response, the computer will retrieve information from the Shepard's table corresponding to the citation you used in your Insta-Cite request; the Shepard's information will be limited to updating references accompanied by the Shepard's analysis comments "criticized," "distinguished," "limited," "overruled," or "questioned."

- *Related references*—citations of decisions involving the same parties and facts as those in the case being updated, but resolving different legal issues. Thus, although an entry designated "related reference" involves the case being updated, the entry does not affect the case's precedential value. An example of a related reference appears in entry 6 in Figure 12.45.

  Insta-Cite reports provide related references issued after August 1983.
- *Secondary sources*—citations in *Corpus Juris Secundum* to the case being updated. Typical references to *C.J.S.* (West's legal encyclopedia) appear at the end of the Insta-Cite report in Figure 12.45.

Analysis phrases. Between entries in an Insta-Cite report you will find analysis phrases, which explain the relationships among the entries. For instance, in Figure 12.44, the analysis phrases track *State v. Yoder*, 49 Wis. 2d 430, through the following developments: after the Wisconsin Supreme Court decided *State v. Yoder* (entry 1), the United States Supreme Court granted certiorari review (entry 2) and in a subsequent decision (entry 3), affirmed the Wisconsin Supreme Court's decision.

As this example illustrates, unless an analysis phrase starts with "AND," the phrase describes how one entry affects the entry immediately above. Thus, in Figure 12.44, the phrase between entries 1 and 2—"Certiorari Granted by"—describes how entry 2 affected entry 1.

When an analysis phrase starts with "AND," the entry after the phrase does not affect the entry immediately above, but one farther up. To spot which entry is affected in this situation, begin at the phrase that starts with "AND." Then read back through the entries until you come to an analysis phrase that does not start with "AND." The entry immediately above that phrase will be the one the phrase starting with "AND" refers to. For example, in Figure 12.44, the phrase "AND Judgment Affirmed by" indicates that the United States Supreme Court's decision in entry 3 affirmed the Wisconsin Supreme Court's decision in entry 1, *not* the United States Supreme Court's order in entry 2.

The *WESTLAW Reference Manual*[342] lists the analysis phrases that appear most frequently in Insta-Cite reports and defines the most commonly used phrases that reflect the precedential value of cases being updated through Insta-Cite.[343]

The following explanation takes you through the steps in using Insta-Cite. Figure 12.46 on pages 566–69 summarizes the steps.

Gaining access to Insta-Cite in WESTLAW. You can initiate an Insta-Cite search at nearly any time after logging on to WESTLAW. You can begin using Insta-Cite as soon as the monitor displays the WESTLAW Directory; you do not need to select a database before carrying out an Insta-Cite search. Or, you can wait until you have retrieved some documents from a database before you begin using Insta-Cite.

To retrieve an Insta-Cite report, you use a search request based on the citation of the case you want to update:

- If you are viewing the case you want to update, simply type `ic` and press ENTER. The WESTLAW computer will automatically "read in" to the search request the citation of your case. (You can also transmit `ic` while you are viewing a Shepard's or Shepard's PreView table for the case you are updating. Alternatively, you can use the JUMP feature; for example, while viewing the screen in Figure 12.38 on page 525, you could retrieve the case's Insta-Cite report by using the TAB key to position the cursor under the JUMP marker (">") in front of "Insta-Cite" at the bottom of the screen, and then pressing ENTER. Whether you type the command or use the JUMP feature, the computer will automatically read in to your

[342] WEST PUBLISHING COMPANY, WESTLAW REFERENCE MANUAL 336–42 (5th ed. 1993) (Appendix G).

[343] Although an Insta-Cite report serves a valuable function by identifying other authorities that might have affected the significance of the authority you are updating, the report reflects editorial analyses that might not capture for your purposes the nuances of the later authorities. To understand fully what an authority mentioned in an Insta-Cite report means for your research problem, you still need to read that authority for yourself.

Insta-Cite request the citation used in your Shepard's or Shepard's PreView request.)

Suppose you are viewing a case that has been reprinted in more than one reporter, and which therefore has parallel citations. Unlike the situation that occurs when you Shepardize a case having more than one citation, Insta-Cite just produces a single report for the case.[344]

- If you want to retrieve an Insta-Cite report for a case you are *not* viewing—say, a case you see mentioned in a law review article you are looking at online—type `ic` followed by the citation of the case you are updating; then press ENTER.

  For the citation, type the volume number and abbreviation of the publication in which the case appears and a page number from the case. (If you transmit a page number other than the first page of the case, WESTLAW will determine the page on which the case begins and retrieve the Insta-Cite report based on that page number.)

  For instance, to retrieve the Insta-Cite report for *State v. Yoder*, 49 Wis. 2d 430, 182 N.W.2d 539, you could use any of the following requests:

```
ic 49 wis.2d 430
ic 49 wis2d 432
ic 49 wis. 2d 430
ic 182 n.w.2d 539
ic182 nw2d 539
```

  Some case reporters (such as the looseleaf services published by Commerce Clearing House) use years instead of volume numbers, and paragraph numbers instead of page numbers. Simply substitute those numbers in the Insta-Cite request. For example, to retrieve an Insta-Cite report for a case published at paragraph 25,593 in the 1983 volume of CCH's *Copyright Law Decisions*, your request could read:

```
ic 1983 copr.l.dec. 25593
```

  You can also use a WESTLAW Cite to retrieve an Insta-Cite report.[345] Your request would take this form:

[344] For an example of how Shepardizing parallel citations for a single case can produce different Shepard's results, see page 509.

[345] WESTLAW Cites are explained in Figure 10.08 on pages 281–82.

`ic 1988 wl 13280`

As all these examples indicate, you have considerable flexibility in how you type an Insta-Cite request. (You must, however, include any hyphens that are part of the citation, *e.g.*, `ic 56 aftr2d 85-5979`.) If you are uncertain about how to type an abbreviation, you can consult the *WESTLAW Reference Manual*, which provides a list of abbreviations that will work in an Insta-Cite request.[346] You can also find a list of these abbreviations online: while using Insta-Cite, type `pubs` and press ENTER; then follow the on-screen instructions.

After you transmit an Insta-Cite request, if the monitor displays a message indicating that Insta-Cite does not recognize the reporter abbreviation you used, consider the possibility that a parallel citation might work.

You might also encounter a situation in which two or more cases share the citation you used in your Insta-Cite request. In that event, the monitor will display a list of the cases; by following the on-screen instructions, you can select the case you want to update.

- If you are viewing an authority and see the citation of a case you want to update through Insta-Cite, you can use the JUMP feature (explained on page 284) to automate the use of Insta-Cite for updating that citation. To use JUMP, type `ic`, press the TAB key to position the cursor under the ">" symbol or triangle next to the citation you want to update, and then press ENTER. The computer will read in to your Insta-Cite request the citation on which you positioned the cursor.

Retrieving additional Insta-Cite reports. Once you have entered the Insta-Cite service by transmitting an Insta-Cite request, you can retrieve Insta-Cite reports for as many cases as you want during the Insta-Cite search session. You do not have to type `ic` each time; just type and transmit a new citation when you want a report on another case.

If you want to retrieve an Insta-Cite report for an authority listed in an Insta-Cite report you are viewing, you do not even need to type a citation. Instead:

1. Type `ic` followed by the Insta-Cite report's entry number corresponding to the case for which you want to retrieve an Insta-Cite report.

[346] WEST PUBLISHING COMPANY, WESTLAW REFERENCE MANUAL 327–36 (5th ed. 1993) (Appendix G).

2. Press ENTER.

The monitor will display the new Insta-Cite report.

Retrieving an Insta-Cite report by using an entry number does not cause you to lose the Insta-Cite report you had just been viewing, though the previous report disappears from sight while the monitor displays the later Insta-Cite report. To switch back to the previous Insta-Cite report:

1. Type **gb** (for "go back").

2. Press ENTER.

Or, if you have retrieved several Insta-Cite reports by using entry numbers, you can return to any of the reports by typing **map** and pressing ENTER to display a "map" list of research results you can review.

For example, if you were viewing the Insta-Cite report shown in Figure 12.44 on page 552 and wanted to see the Insta-Cite report for the U.S. Supreme Court case that affirms *Yoder* at 406 U.S. 205, you would type **ic 3** and press ENTER. The monitor would display the new Insta-Cite report. To redisplay the Insta-Cite report shown in Figure 12.44, you would type **gb** and press ENTER.

Moving within an Insta-Cite report in WESTLAW. After you transmit an Insta-Cite request and the monitor displays the report for the citation you transmitted, you can page through the report (if it extends across more than one screen) by using standard WESTLAW techniques for moving within a document:[347]

- Press ENTER (or the PAGE DOWN or PgDn key) to move the display forward one screen at a time. Press the PAGE UP (or PgUp) key to move the display back one screen at a time.
- Type **p+** or **p–** followed by a number and press ENTER to skip the display forward or back the designated number of screens. Alternatively, type a number and then press the PAGE DOWN (or PgDn) key or the PAGE UP (or PgUp) key.
- Type **p** followed by a number and press ENTER to move the display to the designated screen.

Transmitting **h+** or **h–**, which normally allows you to move forward or back half a screen within a document (see pages 361–62), currently does not work in the Insta-Cite service.

Customizing the display of an Insta-Cite report in WESTLAW. If you only want to view certain parts of an Insta-Cite report, you can use the following LOCATE requests to customize the display of the report you have retrieved:

[347] Pages 360–63 explain these techniques.

- `locate hist` (or `loc hist`)—limits the display to "direct history," "negative indirect history," and "related references"
- `locate dir` (or `loc dir`)—limits the display to "direct history" and "related references"
- `locate indir` (or `loc indir`)—limits the display to "negative indirect history"
- `locate sec` (or `loc sec`)—limits the display to "secondary sources"

You can combine display restrictions in a single request (such as `loc indir,sec`) and you can switch from one display restriction to another by simply transmitting a new LOCATE request.

A LOCATE request will only customize the display of the Insta-Cite report you were viewing when you transmitted the request. If you want to use the same restriction or restrictions to automatically customize the display of subsequent Insta-Cite reports, you can use a LOCATE AUTO command. For instance, the request

```
loc auto sec
```

will automatically restrict the display of each Insta-Cite report to the "secondary sources" section until you revise or discard the LOCATE AUTO request.

When you finish viewing an Insta-Cite report customized with a LOCATE or LOCATE AUTO request, you can return to the original display (showing all entries in the report):

1. If you used LOCATE to customize the Insta-Cite report, type `xloc` or `xl` (for "exit LOCATE"). If you customized with LOCATE AUTO, type `xloc auto` or `xl auto` (for "exit LOCATE AUTO").
2. Press ENTER.

When you transmit `xloc auto` or `xl auto`, the instruction cancels the display restriction not only for the Insta-Cite report you were viewing at that time, but for any reports you subsequently retrieve.

Retrieving an authority mentioned in an Insta-Cite report in WESTLAW. While viewing an Insta-Cite report, you can instruct the computer to retrieve the text of an authority listed in the report:

1. Type the Insta-Cite report's entry number corresponding to the authority you want to retrieve.
2. Press ENTER.

The monitor will display the authority you requested, showing it with the phrase "HISTORY CASE" highlighted at the top of the screen. To switch from the text of the authority back to the Insta-Cite report, type gb (for "go back") and press ENTER. Once back at the report, if you want to select another entry to view, transmit its number.

For instance, if you were viewing the Insta-Cite report shown in Figure 12.44 on page 552 and wanted to see the text of the U.S. Supreme Court case that affirms *Yoder* at 406 U.S. 205, you would type 3 and press ENTER. The monitor would display the text of the Supreme Court's decision. To redisplay the Insta-Cite report, you would type gb and press ENTER. After redisplaying the Insta-Cite report, you could view the text of another entry by transmitting its number.

Note that when you retrieve an authority mentioned in an Insta-Cite report, you can, in turn, update that authority through Insta-Cite by typing ic and pressing ENTER while viewing the authority.

Printing an Insta-Cite report in WESTLAW. You can print an Insta-Cite report by using standard WESTLAW printing techniques:[348]

- To print a single line of the screen you are viewing (if you are using a WALT II terminal), move the cursor to the line you want to print and press the PRINT LINE key.
- To print the screen you are viewing, press the key labelled PRINT SCREEN (or, on some keyboards, the key labelled PRT SC); depending on the keyboard you use, you might need to hold down the SHIFT key while you press PRINT SCREEN (or PRT SC).
- To print each screen automatically as it displays, hold down the key labelled CONTROL (or CTRL) while you press PRINT SCREEN (or PRT SC); on some keyboards, you press only the key labelled ON-LINE PRINT. To cancel automatic screen printing, press the same keys again.
- To print screens from a report after you log off WESTLAW, rather than at the time you view them, type pr (for "print offline") while viewing the report, then press ENTER. The monitor will display the WESTLAW Offline Printing and Downloading Menu, at which you can choose the screens you want printed after logging off.

You can also use the Offline Print Directory to review or discard a printing request, or to designate or change a destination for printing. To do so, type opd and press ENTER; then follow the on-screen instructions.

Downloading an Insta-Cite report in WESTLAW. If you are using a computer with a storage disk, you can save ("download") an Insta-Cite report to your disk, using standard WESTLAW techniques for downloading:[349]

[348] Pages 371–79 explain these techniques.
[349] Pages 379–82 explain these techniques.

- When you are viewing a screen of an Insta-Cite report, you can download that screen. Press the F10 function key; when the monitor displays the WESTMATE menu, select the "File/Accessing" heading by either typing f or pressing ENTER. Then select the "Store Screen to Disk" option.
- When you are viewing an Insta-Cite report, you can download screens automatically as they display. Press the F10 function key; when the monitor displays the WESTMATE menu, select the "File/Accessing" heading by either typing f or pressing ENTER. Then select the "Log Screens to Disk" option. To stop downloading screens automatically, press F10 to display the WESTMATE menu, select the "File/Accessing" heading again, and then select the "Stop Disk Logging" option.
- You can also download screens from a report after you log off WESTLAW, rather than at the time you view them. Type pr (for "print offline") while viewing the report, then press ENTER. The monitor will display the WESTLAW Offline Printing and Downloading Menu, at which you can choose the screens you want downloaded after logging off.

In addition, you can use the Offline Print Directory to review or discard a downloading request, to designate downloading as the destination, or to change the destination to or from downloading. To do so, type opd and press ENTER; then follow the on-screen instructions.

Pausing during an Insta-Cite session to use Shepard's, Shepard's PreView, or FIND in WESTLAW. During an Insta-Cite search session, you can use Shepard's or Shepard's PreView to update an authority,[350] or you can retrieve a document by using FIND.[351] To do so, simply follow the instructions for commencing a Shepard's, Shepard's PreView, or FIND search. To return to Insta-Cite from the service or feature you invoked, type gb (for "go back") and press ENTER.

Alternatively, to use Shepard's or Shepard's PreView to update the authority for which you are viewing an Insta-Cite report, you can use the JUMP feature. For example, while viewing the screen in Figure 12.44 on page 552, you could retrieve the Shepard's or Shepard's PreView results for 49 Wis. 2d 430 by using the TAB key to position the cursor under the appropriate JUMP marker (">") at the bottom of the screen, and then pressing ENTER. To go back to Insta-Cite, you could transmit gb.

[350] See pages 496–524 and 528–44 for an explanation of Shepard's, and pages 524–28 for an explanation of Shepard's PreView.

[351] See pages 279–84 for an explanation of FIND.

Ending an Insta-Cite session and returning to Shepard's, Shepard's PreView, or FIND. As noted earlier, you can carry out an Insta-Cite search at nearly any point during an online research session. (See page 556.) If you invoked Insta-Cite while using the Shepard's or Shepard's PreView service or the FIND feature, you can resume using the other service or feature by typing **gb** and pressing ENTER.

Suppose, however, you had used more than a single service or feature before invoking Insta-Cite. If you want to return to the service or feature you were using immediately before invoking Insta-Cite, type **gb** and press ENTER. To return to any other service or feature, type **map** and press ENTER to display a list of your previous research activities; then follow the on-screen instructions to select the service or feature to which you want to return. (Alternatively, you could transmit **gb** repeatedly until you arrive at the earlier stage in your research you want to return to.)

Thus, if you had carried out searches using FIND, Shepard's, Shepard's PreView, and Insta-Cite (in that order), you could return to Shepard's PreView simply by transmitting **gb**. To return to a document you were viewing through FIND or to return to Shepard's or Shepard's PreView, however, you would transmit **map** and make your selection from the on-screen list of research activities. (Or, you could transmit multiple "gb" commands.)

Ending an Insta-Cite session and returning to WESTLAW. If you had been viewing the WESTLAW Directory or the results of a WESTLAW search just before invoking Insta-Cite, you could return to WESTLAW by typing **gb** and pressing ENTER. Alternatively, you could use a shortcut "map" command that bypasses the map list: transmit **map1** to return directly to the WESTLAW Directory, or **map2** to return directly to your most recent WESTLAW search results (if any).

The role of Insta-Cite in updating in WESTLAW. As you can see from this explanation of Insta-Cite and the previous sections' explanation of Shepardizing online, Insta-Cite and Shepard's citators overlap as updating tools. (For updating purposes, Insta-Cite also overlaps with using WESTLAW as a citator, a technique explained in the next section.) Despite their similar functions, however, you can obtain different results by using each of these techniques to update authorities.

Both Insta-Cite and Shepard's afford access to other authorities that have cited the authority you are updating. But where Shepard's provides comprehensive listings of citing authorities (no matter how routine the reason for the citing reference), Insta-Cite provides selective listings, focusing on authorities that have negatively affected the precedential value of the authority being updated. Even with a selective focus, however, the reach of an Insta-Cite report can extend beyond that of a Shepard's table: an Insta-Cite report might link an authority with the one being updated even though the later authority does not expressly mention the earlier one and therefore does not appear in a Shepard's table.

For example, suppose *Case 1* has been effectively overruled by *Case 2* without the second case specifically mentioning the first case. If *Case 3* identifies *Case 2* as overruling *Case 1*, Insta-Cite editors are expected to spot the relationship, and the Insta-Cite report for *Case 1* should therefore identify *Case 2* as having overruled it. With Shepard's, however, because *Case 2* did not expressly mention *Case 1*, the Shepard's table will not identify *Case 2*.

In short, Insta-Cite and Shepard's complement one another; each can give you updating results not obtained through the other. For example, the Shepard's table in Figures 12.30 and 12.31 on page 503 identifies some cases and law review articles not included in the Insta-Cite report in Figure 12.44 on page 552. Conversely, an Insta-Cite report, such as the one in Figure 12.45 on page 553, often identifies secondary sources not included in the corresponding Shepard's table. If you want to ensure thorough updating in WESTLAW, you'll need to use both Shepard's (including Shepard's PreView) and Insta-Cite.

Summary of using Insta-Cite in WESTLAW. Figure 12.46 summarizes the steps and commands for Insta-Cite.

Using WESTLAW as a citator[352]

Introduction. When you update authorities through WESTLAW, you can take advantage of the computer's full-text searching capability and search the text of online documents for citations to the authorities in whose status you are interested. Generally characterized as using WESTLAW as a citator, this method of locating later references to an authority involves using an ordinary search request in which at least some of the search terms reflect citation information about the authority you want to update.

If you search for updating references in databases that allow natural-language searching (as most do), you can formulate your search request either with Boolean terms and connectors or with natural language. As an updating vehicle, however, natural-language searching has some shortcomings, as explained on pages 583–84: the 100-document limitation can preclude comprehensive updating, and the use of statistical relevance as the retrieval mechanism means you cannot always know whether the computer has identified the most recent authorities that might have affected the authority you are updating.

To use WESTLAW as a citator:

[352] WESTLAW also offers QuickCite, which automates some of the process of using WESTLAW as a citator. See pages 596–603 for an explanation of QuickCite.

1. Formulate a search request based on the various citation forms you think have been used in later documents to refer to the authority you are updating.

2. Select a database containing the type of authorities (*e.g.*, federal cases, state cases, or law reviews) in which you want to search for citations to the authority you are updating.

   At this point, if you plan to search with a Boolean request, you might also consider implementing the TERMS display option, which will cause retrieved documents with the greatest number of different search terms to display first.[353] Scanning these documents at the outset will often help you quickly determine the effectiveness of your search request. Later, you can switch to the AGE display order, which will allow you to conveniently identify the most recent updating references.

3. Type and transmit your search request in the database you selected, and scan the results to see how the later authorities deal with the authority you are updating. Using TERM mode (explained on pages 358–59) will help you scan faster.

4. If you have retrieved a significant percentage of documents that do not refer to the authority you are updating, or if you suspect you have bypassed pertinent documents, you can modify your search request and try again.

As this summary implies, using WESTLAW as a citator is really nothing more than routine full-text searching. Thus, you apply the same principles and techniques earlier chapters present for formulating and modifying search requests and for reading search results.

Using WESTLAW as a citator has some advantages over using Shepard's citators, Shepard's PreView, or Insta-Cite. First, this technique—especially when implemented with Boolean searching—can yield more comprehensive updating results than using Shepard's citators, Shepard's PreView, or Insta-Cite. Using WESTLAW as a citator, you can update *any* authority: by typing in citation information, you can direct the computer to search for references to all kinds of authorities, including those (such as treatises or legal encyclopedias) you cannot update through Shepard's, Shepard's PreView, or Insta-Cite. Moreover, these updating references will sometimes appear in authorities that Shepard's, Shepard's PreView, and Insta-Cite do not cover. And, using the WESTLAW-as-citator technique, you might even capture references, if

[353] See page 353 for an explanation of the TERMS display option.

If you want to	Follow this procedure in WESTLAW
Retrieve an Insta-Cite report for the authority you are viewing	type `ic` and press ENTER
Retrieve an Insta-Cite report for an authority you are not viewing	type `ic` followed by the authority's citation; then press ENTER *Example:* `ic 49 wis.2d 430`
Retrieve an Insta-Cite report for an authority when you see its citation accompanied by a JUMP marker (a ">" symbol or a triangle)	type `ic`, press the TAB key to position the cursor under the JUMP marker, and then press ENTER
Retrieve an Insta-Cite report for an authority identified in the Insta-Cite report you are viewing	type `ic` followed by the number corresponding to the entry for which you want to retrieve an Insta-Cite report
Return to the previous Insta-Cite report	type `gb` and press ENTER
Page through an Insta-Cite report	• press ENTER (or PAGE DOWN or PgDn) to move forward one screen; press PAGE UP (or PgUp) to move back one screen • type `p` followed by a number and press ENTER to move to the designated screen • type `p+` or `p-` followed by a number, and then press ENTER to skip forward or back the designated number of screens; alternatively, type a number and then press PAGE DOWN (or PgDn) or PAGE UP (or PgUp)

Customize the display of an Insta-Cite report	type `locate` (or `loc`) followed by your restrictive criteria; then press ENTER *Examples:* `loc hist` `loc indir,sec`
Redisplay a complete Insta-Cite report after displaying a customized report	type `xloc` (or `xl`) and press ENTER
Retrieve the text of an authority mentioned in the Insta-Cite report you are viewing	type the number corresponding to the entry you want to retrieve; then press ENTER
Return to the Insta-Cite report from the text of the retrieved authority	type `gb` and press ENTER
Print a single line from the screen you are viewing in an Insta-Cite report (if you are using a WALT II terminal)	move the cursor to the line you want to print and press the PRINT LINE key
Print the screen you are viewing in an Insta-Cite report	press the PRINT SCREEN (or PRT SC) key; on some keyboards, you might also need to hold down the SHIFT key
Print each screen automatically as you view it in an Insta-Cite report	hold down the CONTROL (or CTRL) key and press the PRINT SCREEN (or PRT SC) key; on some keyboards, you press only the ONLINE PRINT key
Turn off automatic printing of displayed screens	hold down the CONTROL (or CTRL) key and press the PRINT SCREEN (or PRT SC) key; on some keyboards, you press only the ONLINE PRINT key
Print some or all screens from an Insta-Cite report after you log off	transmit `pr` and press ENTER; then follow the on-screen instructions

(continues)

Figure 12.46. Quick Guide to Insta-Cite in WESTLAW

(continued)

If you want to	Follow this procedure in WESTLAW
*Download the screen you are viewing in an Insta-Cite report	press F10 to display the WESTMATE menu; select the "File/Accessing" heading by either typing **f** or pressing ENTER; then select the "Store Screen to Disk" option
*Download each screen automatically as you view it in an Insta-Cite report	press F10 to display the WESTMATE menu; select the "File/Accessing" heading by either typing **f** or pressing ENTER; then select the "Log Screens to Disk" option
*Turn off automatic downloading of displayed screens	press F10 to display the WESTMATE menu; select the "File/Accessing" heading by either typing **f** or pressing ENTER; then select the "Stop Disk Logging" option
*Download some or all screens from an Insta-Cite report after you log off	type **pr** and press ENTER; then follow the on-screen instructions
Invoke another service or feature during an Insta-Cite session	type a Shepard's, Shepard's PreView, or FIND request; then press ENTER
Switch from the other service or feature back to Insta-Cite	type **gb** and press ENTER

Switch from Insta-Cite to any other service or feature you have used during your Insta-Cite session (if you have used more than one other service or feature)	type **map** and press ENTER; then make your selection from the list displayed on the monitor *or* transmit **gb** repeatedly until you arrive at the research activity you want to return to
Switch from Insta-Cite to the service or feature you most recently used during your Insta-Cite session	type **gb** and press ENTER
End an Insta-Cite session and return to WESTLAW	type **map1** and press ENTER to return to the WESTLAW Directory *or* type **map2** and press ENTER to return to your most recent WESTLAW search results (if any)
View an online list of Insta-Cite commands and accompanying explanations	type **cmds** and press ENTER while using Insta-Cite
View an online list of publication abbreviations that work in an Insta-Cite request	type **pubs** and press ENTER while using Insta-Cite

* This function is available only on a computer with a disk for storing information.

Figure 12.46. Quick Guide to Insta-Cite in WESTLAW (continued)

any, that have slipped by the editors who prepare the Shepard's and Shepard's PreView tables or Insta-Cite reports.

In addition, particularly with Boolean searching, you can obtain more current references than you can find through Shepard's, Shepard's PreView, or Insta-Cite. Often, documents containing references to an authority you want to update will have been issued and added to the WESTLAW database more recently than the most recent update of the pertinent Shepard's or Shepard's PreView tables or Insta-Cite report.

Along with comprehensiveness, a second advantage of using WESTLAW as a citator stems from the ability to modify your search request to link citation information with additional search terms. In this way, you can zero in on updating authorities that deal with particular facts or legal issues, or that satisfy some other criteria (such as having been decided by a certain judge or issued after a certain date). For instance, in connection with a research problem concerning the right of prisoners to practice their religion while incarcerated, suppose you were updating *Wisconsin v. Yoder*, a frequently cited Supreme Court case about freedom of religion. By adding appropriate search terms (*e.g.*, `prison**`, `inmate`) to your search request, you could focus your WESTLAW updating search on authorities that cite *Yoder* in the context of similar facts.

Using WESTLAW as a citator has some drawbacks, however. You confront the same challenges you face whenever you use a search request to search the text of authorities, *i.e.*, contending with the computer's literalness, minimizing ambiguity in search terms, coping with nondistinctive search terms, and so on[354] (although using natural language for WESTLAW-as-citator searching sometimes automatically minimizes these difficulties, as explained later). Consequently, you can bypass relevant updating authorities by failing to anticipate all the ways in which authors of later authorities might have written a citation to the authority you are updating. Similarly, you can bypass a relevant authority if its only citation to your authority contains a typographical error, as sometimes happens.

When you use WESTLAW as a citator, you can also retrieve many documents you do *not* want—documents that have nothing to do with the authority you are updating. For example, using a search request like `state w/5 smith` to search for later citations to *State v. Smith* will likely turn up references to a large number of unrelated cases with that caption. By contrast, all the later references you locate through Shepard's, Shepard's PreView, or Insta-Cite will cite or deal with the authority in whose status you are interested.

The trick, then, is to strike a balance between the benefits and drawbacks of using WESTLAW as a citator. As with formulating search requests for other

[354] See Chapter 7 for a discussion of formulating search requests.

purposes, no ironclad rules exist that guarantee success. The guidelines in the following paragraphs, however, can help you achieve the necessary balance.

Using WESTLAW as a citator with Boolean searches for references to cases. In anticipating the ways in which later authorities might have cited a case you are updating, you can take one of several approaches:

- search for references to the case name, such as *Lewis v. United States* (see this page through page 574)
- search for references to the case citation, such as 445 U.S. 55 (see pages 574–77)
- search for references to either the case name *or* case citation (see page 577)
- search for references to both the case name *and* case citation (see page 578)
- link other search terms with the citation information (see pages 578–79)

Boolean searching for references to the case name. Because citations to a case will almost certainly include its name, you can locate references to the case you are updating if you search for occurrences of the case name in the text of other authorities. But your search request should not use the case name in a standard citation format—*e.g.*, "City of Phoenix v. Tanner." References to a given case often appear in a variety of formats. For instance, searching for "City of Phoenix v. Tanner" would not locate references citing the case as *Phoenix v. Tanner.* Similarly, one document might cite a case as *In the Matter of Application of Winn*, but another document might cite it as *In re Winn.*

In light of the potential variations on case names, you need to search for a name with an instruction that can accommodate different citation forms. As a general matter, you will want to use the "w/n" or "/s" connector with a few key words from the case name. So, to search for references to *City of Phoenix v. Tanner*, you could use one of these search requests:

```
phoenix w/5 tanner
phoenix /s tanner
```

When you use the "w/n" connector, the value you select will depend on how far apart you anticipate the key words will appear. For example, in referring to a case normally cited as *United Public Employees, Local 390/400 v. City and County of San Francisco*, a judge might write the case name in its lengthier form, *United Public Employees, Local 390/400, SEIU, AFL-CIO, et al. v. City and County of San Francisco, et al.* The search request `("united public employees") w/5 ("san francisco")` would bypass this reference; here, "w/12" would be a better choice.

Usually, a value from 5 to 10 in the "w/n" connector will suffice, although potentially lengthy variations on a case name might indicate the need for a larger value. You can do a couple of things to anticipate whether an "n" value will likely be high enough to retrieve as many variations on your case name as possible, yet low enough to minimize retrieving documents in which the search terms occur dispersed and do not represent the name of your case. First, you can check the case caption (either in a printed case reporter or online) to be sure that, say, *Potts v. Smith* is not actually *Potts, Administrator de bonis non of May, to the Use of Wollerton v. Smith.* Second, you can select a fairly high "n" value, such as 15, for your first search and use smaller "n" values in succeeding search requests until you are satisfied with the results.

Regardless of the "n" value you select, however, you should expect to retrieve some documents that do not contain any references to the case you are updating. For example, using the search request

```
lewis w/5 ("united states" or u.s.)
```

to search the ALLSTATES database for references to *Lewis v. United States*, 445 U.S. 55, will retrieve documents that do not cite the case but that contain one of these phrases:

> . . . and Mr. Alston C. **Lewis**. The **United States** Geological Survey maintained recording devices . . . .
>
> . . . the court relied upon the notable **United States** Supreme Court decisions of **Lewis** v. City of New Orleans . . . .
>
> . . . **United States** v. Alfred M. **Lewis**, Inc. . . .
>
> . . . Constitution of the **United States**. People v. **Lewis**, 413 Ill. 116 . . . .

Indeed, when performed during the preparation of this book, this search retrieved 2,082 cases. A sampling of 50 of those cases yielded only 12 that cited *Lewis v. United States*, 445 U.S. 55.

If you prefer, you can use the "/s" connector instead of "w/n." Because the parties' names in a case citation will almost certainly appear in the same sentence, using "/s" avoids your having to guess an appropriate "n" value. But "/s" can increase the number of irrelevant references you retrieve. In a long sentence, your search terms might appear widely separated and thus not relate to one another in the way you intend. For example, using the search request

```
lewis /s ("united states" or u.s.)
```

to search the ALLSTATES database for references to *Lewis v. United States*, 445 U.S. 55, retrieves irrelevant documents in which the search terms appear in lengthy sentences like this one:

> See also, 2 N. Singer, Statutory Construction, s 42.06, at 456 (4th ed.1986); People v. **Lewis**, 180 Cal.App.3d 816, 225 Cal.Rptr. 782 (4th Dist.1986); People v. Masry, 179 Cal.App.3d 1149, 225 Cal.Rptr. 174 (4th Dist.1986); People v. Holland, 708 P.2d 119 (Colo.1985); State v. Norton, 675 P.2d 577 (Utah 1983), cert. denied, 466 U.S. 942, 104 S.Ct.1923 (1984); **United States** ex rel. Massarella v. Elrod, 682 F.2d 688, 689 (7th Cir.1982), cert. denied, 460 **U.S.** 1037, 103 S.Ct. 1426427 (1983); Dobbert v. Florida . . . .

When performed during the preparation of this book, this search retrieved 4,422 cases, more than double the number retrieved using "w/5" as the connector. A sampling of 50 of those cases yielded none that cited *Lewis*. (In addition, because the computer processes "/s," as well as "+s," "/p," and "+p," more slowly than other connectors, using "/s" can significantly increase the cost of your search.)[355]

When searching for references to a case name, you should generally avoid using the "pre/n," "+n," or "+s" connectors, at least in your initial search request. As a case moves through the courts, the order of the parties' names can change; *Smith v. Jones* might become *Jones v. Smith* on appeal. In addition, writers occasionally reverse party names by mistake, inadvertently turning *ABC Co. v. XYZ Corp.* into *XYZ Corp. v. ABC Co.* If you had used a "pre/n," "+n," or "+s" connector (each of which requires search terms to appear in a specified order), you would have missed some references in these situations.

Normally, though, citations to the case you are updating will have the parties' names in the order you expect. So, if you find the "w/n" or "/s" connector retrieves an unmanageable number of documents having nothing to do with the case you are updating, you might want to try using a "pre/n", "+n," or "+s" connector to focus the search on references to your case.

Regardless of the connector you use, your results might include documents retrieved because your search terms appear as, say, the names of lawyers in the case, not as party names. If so, you can add a restriction to confine your search to the "opinion" field, where your search terms will more likely occur as part of a case name.[356]

[355] See page 57 n.59.

[356] See Chapter 5 for a discussion of field-restricted searching.

In some instances, you can skip a connector altogether. If a case name includes an uncommon word, that word alone might suffice as the search request. Thus, if you wanted to locate references to *State v. Ziegenhagen*, simply transmitting `ziegenhagen` would likely locate references to that case and to little or nothing else.

Conversely, a case name—such as *Smith v. Brown* or *In re Jones*—might not include any distinctive words. Some party names—such as United States, Commissioner, State, People, or Commonwealth—recur frequently enough that you will probably encounter problems using them in an approach that relies on searching for references to only the name of a case. In these situations, to find references to the case you want without also finding an unwieldy number of unrelated references, you can take a different approach: try searching for references to the case citation (see below); try using the "and" connector to link party names with a corresponding citation (see page 578); or try adding search terms reflecting relevant facts or issues (see pages 578–79).

Finally, keep in mind that a case name might change throughout the course of litigation. Parties might be added or dropped, or only some of the parties might be involved in an appeal. For example, *Segar v. Civiletti* became *Segar v. Smith* when the case moved to the United States Court of Appeals, and became *Meese v. Segar* in the United States Supreme Court. If you want to find references to decisions issued at each stage of the case you are updating, your search request will need to reflect any changes that have occurred in the case name. Thus, to find references to the various decisions in *Segar*, your search request could take one of these forms:

```
segar w/5 (civiletti or smith or meese)
segar /s (civiletti or smith or meese)
```

To determine whether a case name has changed, you can update the case through Insta-Cite (explained on pages 544 and 552–64.)

Boolean searching for references to the case citation. You can use WESTLAW to update a case by searching the text of other authorities for references to its citation (*e.g.*, 725 F. Supp. 1407). But, as with searching for references to a case name, your search request needs to accommodate variations in the way the case citation might appear.

Suppose you wanted to update *Lewis v. United States*, 445 U.S. 55. One writer might cite the case as "445 U.S. 55," another as "445 U.S. Reports 55," yet another as "445 U.S. Rep. 55." Likewise, a citation to a case reported in *Federal Supplement* might appear as "F. Supp.," "F.Supp.," or "Fed. Supp." For cases in WESTLAW that have been published in West reporters, West editors put citations in standard form. Standardized citations do not appear, however, in cases in WESTLAW that are online in the form of slip opinions or that are not scheduled for publication in West reporters.

You can work around possible variations in references to a case reporter by omitting the name or abbreviation of the reporter from your search request and using just the volume and page numbers linked by the "pre/n" or "+n" connector. So, to search for references to *In re Grand Jury Subpoena Duces Tecum Issued to Richard M. Nixon*, 360 F. Supp. 1 (D.D.C. 1973), you could use search requests like these:

```
360 pre/3 1

360 +3 1
```

Because the order of the numbers is important, and because virtually every citation to a given case will put the volume number before the page number, the "pre/n" or "+n" connector will normally prove more effective than the "w/n" or "/s" connector.

Usually, a value from 2 to 6 in the "pre/n" or "+n" connector will retrieve the references you want. The value you choose will depend on the number of words you might find in the name of the reporter. For example, if you were searching for references to a case reported in volume 13 of *Louisiana Reports* at page 512, the search request `13 pre/3 512` would locate references written as 13 La. 512 or 13 La. Rep. 512. For references to a case reported in volume 81 of *Maryland Appellate Reports* at page 527, you could use `81 pre/5 527`. And for references to a case reported in volume 21 of *Federal Rules Service 2d* at page 211, you could use `21 pre/6 211`.

As you consider the number of words a reporter name might contain, remember that spacing within a reporter abbreviation affects the number of words the WESTLAW computer perceives. For instance, the abbreviation for *New York Supplement, Second Series* might be written as "N.Y.S.2d" (one word), as "N.Y.S. 2d" (two words), as "N.Y. Supp. 2d" (three words), or as "N. Y. S. 2d" (four words).

If the case you are updating has parallel citations, include in your search request any parallel citations you anticipate an author might have cited. Thus, to update *Lewis v. United States*, 445 U.S. 55, 100 S. Ct. 915, 63 L. Ed. 2d 198, 48 U.S.L.W. 4205, your search request could take this form to enhance comprehensiveness:

```
(445 pre/5 55) or (100 pre/5 915) or (63 pre/5
198) or (48 pre/5 4205)
```

As this example indicates, you should keep looseleaf reporters, such as *United States Law Week*, in mind as parallel citations that might appear in documents that cite the case you are updating. It is especially important to include as part of your search request any citations to looseleaf reporters if you want to retrieve cases appearing online as slip opinions (before other citations might be available) or cases that are not published in West reporters. In these instances, West editors will not have enhanced the cases by replacing citations to nonpreferred sources (such as looseleaf reporters) with citations to preferred sources (such as *Supreme Court Reporter* or *Lawyers' Edition 2d*); the only reference to an authority you are updating might therefore consist of its looseleaf reporter citation.[357]

Similarly, you might want to include a parallel citation based on a WESTLAW or LEXIS cite, on a docket number (to catch references to a case when it was available only as a slip opinion, before its publication in a case reporter), or on a citation to a legal newspaper (such as *New York Law Journal*), which might be the first publication to report a case. Thus, you could extend the comprehensiveness of your search for references to *Lewis* by anticipating slip-opinion citations based on its docket number (78–1595):

```
(445 pre/5 55) or (100 pre/5 915) or (63 pre/5
198) or (48 pre/5 4205) or ("78-1595")
```

When you rely on a case citation in using WESTLAW as a citator, you will often retrieve a substantial percentage of documents in which the references to the numbers in your search request have nothing to do with the citation to the case you are updating. The numbers might not even be part of a citation at all: for instance, using the search request `52 pre/5 31` to search the ALLSTATES database for references to the U.S. Supreme Court case reported at 52 L. Ed. 2d 31 will retrieve a document that does not cite the case but that contains the phrase "the claimant was **52** years old and had **31** years of service with this employer."

More often, though, the numbers in unrelated documents will refer to a citation, but for a different authority. For example, in updating *Lewis v. United States*, 445 U.S. 55, 100 S. Ct. 915, 63 L. Ed. 2d 198, 48 U.S.L.W. 4205, the search request

[357] Note that when you search for references to looseleaf reporters, your search terms might include paragraph numbers. Although not the case with *United States Law Week*, citations to some looseleaf reporters use paragraph numbers rather than page numbers. To find out which looseleaf services number by paragraphs rather than pages, check Table T.16 in THE BLUEBOOK: A UNIFORM SYSTEM OF CITATION (15th ed. 1991).

Some paragraph numbers in citations to looseleafs will include commas. The WESTLAW computer automatically treats as equivalent a number with a comma and the same number without a comma, so you can use either form in your search request. In addition, you can omit the paragraph symbol (¶) from your search request. The WESTLAW computer automatically converts the paragraph symbol to the letter "P" and inserts a space between the character and the number. For example, "¶10,475" becomes "P 10,475," leaving the number as a search term independent of the paragraph symbol or letter "P."

Appendix H summarizes the rules governing how the WESTLAW computer interprets punctuation marks and other symbols in connection with numbers.

```
(445 pre/5 55) or (100 pre/5 915) or (63 pre/5
198) or (48 pre/5 4205)
```

in the ALLSTATES database will retrieve documents that contain these configurations of search terms:

> . . . City of Westminster v. Church, 167 Colo. 1, 9, **445** P.2d 52, **55** . . . .
>
> . . . Ingels v. Boteler, 9 Cir., **100** F.2d **915**.
>
> . . . C.I.T. Corp. v. Breckenridge (1944), **63** Cal.App.2d **198** . . . .
>
> . . . Wigmore, Evidence s **63**, at **198** . . . .

If searching for references to a case citation retrieves a high percentage of unrelated references, you can try searching for the citation in a standard citation format—*e.g.*, `("445 U.S. 55") or ("100 S. Ct. 915") or ("63 L. Ed. 2d 198") or ("48 U.S.L.W. 4205")`. Of course, when you do not allow for variations in the name of the reporter, you can bypass references to the case you are updating. A better solution uses the "and" connector to link the citation with the name of the case (as explained at page 578) or with search terms reflecting relevant facts or issues (as explained at pages 578–79).

Boolean searching for references to either the case name or case citation. You can combine the two previous approaches in a single search request that looks for references to *either* the case name *or* the case citation. Thus, to update *Lewis v. United States*, 445 U.S. 55, 100 S. Ct. 915, 63 L. Ed. 2d 198, 48 U.S.L.W. 4205, your search request could take this form:

```
(lewis w/5 ("united states" or u.s.)) or (445
pre/5 55) or (100 pre/5 915) or (63 pre/5 198)
or (48 pre/5 4205)
```

Using the "or" connector to link a case name with a case citation yields highly comprehensive results because the search request accommodates the largest number of possible variations in references to the case you are updating. For instance, when performed during the preparation of this book, the illustrative search request retrieved 2,464 cases in the ALLSTATES database.

But with this approach, you will also get more unrelated references: by searching simultaneously for references to either the name or the citation for a case, you retrieve a combination of the unrelated references obtained when you search for each of these references separately. Thus, you increase the size of the collection from which you must cull the references to the case you are updating.

Boolean searching for references to both the case name and case citation. Instead of searching for documents that refer to either the name or citation information for a case, you can use the "and" connector to search for documents that refer to *both* the name *and* the case citation. Thus, to update *Lewis v. United States*, 445 U.S. 55, 100 S. Ct. 915, 63 L. Ed. 2d 198, 48 U.S.L.W. 4205, your search request could take this form:

```
(lewis w/5 ("united states" or u.s.)) and
((445 pre/5 55) or (100 pre/5 915) or (63 pre/5
198) or (48 pre/5 4205))
```

This approach rests on the assumption that any worthwhile updating reference will likely include both the name and citation of a case, especially if the reference involves an analysis that significantly affects the precedential value of the case being updated. This approach also assumes that if a document satisfies both the name component of the search request and the citation component, the document probably contains a reference to the case you are updating. Because the document must satisfy two criteria instead of one, the search request is less apt to retrieve unrelated documents. For instance, when performed during the preparation of this book, the illustrative search request retrieved 84 cases in the ALLSTATES database, and all of them referred to *Lewis*.

Adding other search terms. With any of the previous approaches, you can add one or more search terms to the citation information to increase the likelihood of retrieving helpful references to the case you are updating. For instance, *Lewis v. United States*, 445 U.S. 55, 100 S. Ct. 915, 63 L. Ed. 2d 198, 48 U.S.L.W. 4205, addresses several issues, including: (1) whether someone being prosecuted for unlawful possession of a firearm by a felon can defend on the ground that the underlying felony conviction was invalid; and (2) for what purposes, if any, the government may use a felony conviction obtained against a defendant who did not have assistance of counsel. If you were just interested in uncounseled convictions and therefore wanted to update *Lewis* only with respect to the second issue, you could focus your search by adding appropriate search terms, as in these two examples:

```
((445 pre/5 55) or (100 pre/5 915) or (63 pre/5
198) or (48 pre/5 4205)) and ((assist! w/3
counsel) or (uncounsel! w/3 convict***))
```

```
lewis and ((445 pre/5 55) or (100 pre/5 915) or
(63 pre/5 198) or (48 pre/5 4205)) and
((assist! w/3 counsel) or (uncounsel! w/3
convict***))
```

The search terms you link with your citation information can also include field restrictions limiting the search to updating references in, for instance, cases decided by a particular court or written by a particular judge.

If you have retrieved a large collection of updating references, you might want to add a date restriction to limit your search to recent authorities, on the assumption that these authorities will likely mention earlier authorities that have significantly affected the precedential value of the case you are updating. Your search request could take this form:

```
((445 pre/5 55) or (100 pre/5 915) or (63 pre/5
198) or (48 pre/5 4205)) and ((assist! w/3
counsel) or (uncounsel! w/3 convict***)) and
date(aft 12-31-89)
```

You can also use a date restriction to screen out documents issued before the decision date of the case you are updating; by definition, those documents cannot provide updating references to your case.[358] For an illustration of the effect of using a date restriction this way, see Figure 12.47. The figure shows the results of several paired searches for *Lewis v. United States*, one search without a date restriction and the other with a restriction based on the date of the *Lewis* decision (February 27, 1980).

Selecting an approach. When you use WESTLAW as a citator with Boolean searching to update cases, which of the preceding approaches will work best will depend on a variety of factors. For example, your choice of an approach might depend on whether the name of the case you are updating includes frequently occurring words, such as "Smith"; as search terms, such words will probably retrieve many authorities unrelated to your case. Or, the case you are updating might have several parallel citations; a search request based only on those citations could retrieve many authorities with references unrelated to the volume and page numbers for your case.

Although each research problem presents its own challenges, you can make certain choices that will usually enhance the effectiveness of using WESTLAW as a citator. If your case includes at least one distinctive party name (*e.g.*, Ziegenhagen), a case-name search will often prove a productive way to start. (Even if the case name consists only of common words, such as "Smith" or "Commissioner," you still might want to start with a search request based solely on party names simply as a way of scoping out the number of authorities from which you will need to extract the references to the case you are updating.)

As a practical matter, you will usually find that searching for both the case name and citation in a single search request proves effective. Although

[358] But see note 305 on page 497 for a rare example to the contrary.

Approach	Sample Search Requests in WESTLAW	Number of Documents Retrieved	Of First 50 Documents, Number With References to Case Being Updated*	Of First 50 Documents, Percent With References to Case Being Updated*
Case name	`lewis`	89,373	0	0%
With date restriction	`lewis and date(aft 2/26/1980)`	29,875	0	0%
Case name	`lewis w/5 "united states"`	1,088	8	16%
With date restriction	`(lewis w/5 "united states") and date(aft 2/26/1980)`	553	15	30%
Case name	`lewis w/5 ("united states" or u.s.)`	2,082	12	24%
With date restriction	`lewis w/5 ("united states" or u.s.) and date(aft 2/26/1980)`	963	16	32%
Case citation	`(445 pre/5 55) or (100 pre/5 915) or (63 pre/5 198) or (48 pre/5 4205)`	466	50	100%
With date restriction	`(445 pre/5 55) or (100 pre/5 915) or (63 pre/5 198) or (48 pre/5 4205) and date(aft 2/26/1980)`	195	50	100%
Case name or case citation	`(lewis w/5 ("united states" or u.s.)) or (445 pre/5 55) or (100 pre/5 915) or (63 pre/5 198) or (48 pre/5 4205)`	2,464	50	100%
With date restriction	`(lewis w/5 ("united states" or u.s.)) or (445 pre/5 55) or (100 pre/5 915) or (63 pre/5 198) or (48 pre/5 4205) and date(aft 2/26/1980)`	1,074	50	100%

Case name and case citation	(lewis w/5 ("united states" or u.s.)) and ((445 pre/5 55) or (100 pre/5 915) or (63 pre/5 198) or (48 pre/5 4205))	84	50	100%
With date restriction	(lewis w/5 ("united states" or u.s.)) and ((445 pre/5 55) or (100 pre/5 915) or (63 pre/5 198) or (48 pre/5 4205)) and date(aft 2/26/1980)	84	50	100%
Case citation and additional search terms	((445 pre/5 55) or (100 pre/5 915) or (63 pre/5 198) or (48 pre/5 4205)) and ((assist! w/3 counsel) or (uncounsel! w/3 convict***))	60	50	100%
With date restriction	((445 pre/5 55) or (100 pre/5 915) or (63 pre/5 198) or (48 pre/5 4205)) and ((assist! w/3 counsel) or (uncounsel! w/3 convict***)) and date(aft 2/26/1980)	52	50	100%
Case name and citation and additional search terms	lewis and ((445 pre/5 55) or (100 pre/5 915) or (63 pre/5 198) or (48 pre/5 4205)) and ((assist! w/3 counsel) or (uncounsel! w/3 convict***))	51	50	100%
With date restriction	lewis and ((445 pre/5 55) or (100 pre/5 915) or (63 pre/5 198) or (48 pre/5 4205)) and ((assist! w/3 counsel) or (uncounsel! w/3 convict***)) and date(aft 2/26/1980)	51	50	100%

* The numbers in this column might change if the results were evaluated in AGE display order instead of TERMS display order. For example, if you used the AGE display order to view the 466 cases retrieved by the seventh search request in the chart, you would find that 22 of the first 50 documents, not 50 of the first 50, refer to the case being updated.

The TERMS display order can significantly speed up the task of identifying relevant documents in a large collection of retrieved documents. But note that with TERMS display order, you cannot necessarily infer that the percentage of relevant cases found in, say, the first 50 retrieved cases applies to the entire collection. Because the TERMS display order causes retrieved documents with the greatest number of different search terms to display first, you will likely encounter a higher percentage of relevant cases among the first 50 documents in the collection than among, say, the last 50.

Figure 12.47. WESTLAW as Citator: Results of Boolean Searching in ALLSTATES Database (TERMS Display Order) for References to *Lewis v. United States*, 445 U.S. 55, 100 S. Ct. 915, 63 L. Ed. 2d 198, 48 U.S.L.W. 4205 (decided Feb. 27, 1980)

searching for either the name or citation can create problems (because you might retrieve an unmanageable number of unrelated authorities), searching simultaneously for *both* components maximizes the chance retrieved documents will refer to your case.

Regardless of the approach you use, combining citation information with other search terms (*e.g.*, a date restriction, or words reflecting relevant facts or issues) can help focus your search on relevant updating references, especially if earlier searches turned up unwieldy numbers of authorities.

Figure 12.47 suggests the kind of results you might obtain with the various approaches available when you use WESTLAW as a citator to update cases. As you gain experience using WESTLAW as a citator, you will develop a feel for the approaches that will work best for the cases you need to update.

Using WESTLAW as a citator with natural-language searches for references to cases. If you use natural language in your WESTLAW-as-citator searches for references to cases you want to update, you can locate those references by adapting the approaches used in Boolean WESTLAW-as-citator searches. For instance, to locate references to the case reported at page 915 in volume 100 of *Supreme Court Reporter*, you could search with a natural-language search request like `100 s.ct. 915` instead of a Boolean search request like `100 pre/5 915`.

Of the available approaches (*e.g.*, searching for references to a case name, searching for references to a case citation), search requests for a case citation or for a case citation combined with fact words operate the most effectively if you use natural language to identify updating references to cases. Thus, to identify updating references to *Lewis v. United States*, 445 U.S. 55, you could use a natural-language search request like this:

```
445 u.s. 55
```

If you wanted to identify updating references to *Lewis* that deal with a specific issue in that case (such as the government's use of uncounseled felony convictions), you could include appropriate fact words in your natural-language search request:

```
445 u.s. 55 uncounseled conviction
```

When a natural-language search request includes a sequence of search terms consisting of a number followed by a case reporter abbreviation followed by another number (such as `445 u.s. 55`), the natural-language feature normally recognizes the sequence as a citation. This recognition triggers an automatic search for updating references that include not only the citation in your search request, but parallel citations (such as "100 S. Ct. 915" for *Lewis*) and anaphoric citations (like "id.") to the case being updated. So, natural-language searches can retrieve citations that Boolean WESTLAW-as-citator searches would bypass unless you specifically included those citations in your Boolean search request. A natural-language updating search, however, does not automatically recognize *all* possible ways in which an author of an updating authority might have identified the case you are updating. For example, at this writing, the natural-language feature does not automatically search for docket numbers or LEXIS Cites; if you wanted to retrieve these kinds of updating references, you would need to include the citations in your natural-language search request.

In addition to extending an updating search to most, if not all, parallel citations, natural-language updating searches offer another benefit. Because the natural-language feature recognizes search terms like `445 u.s. 55` as a citation to a specific case, natural-language searches for a case citation will not retrieve the kind of irrelevant references you can retrieve with Boolean WESTLAW-as-citator searches. For example, you will not retrieve references to a different case or to numbers having nothing to do with any case citation, as can happen when you search with a Boolean request like `445 pre/5 55`.

Caveat. Despite these benefits of using natural language in WESTLAW-as-citator search requests, natural-language searching will not work as well as Boolean searching in many updating situations:

- Updating normally requires comprehensive results. But the current 100-document limitation in the natural-language feature can preclude retrieving all updating references. Unless you know for certain that the database in which you are searching contains 100 or fewer documents that refer to the case you are updating, you cannot know whether you have retrieved all the updating references.
- Because natural-language algorithms retrieve documents based on statistical relevance,[359] you cannot be certain (again, unless the database does not contain more than 100 updating documents) that your search has retrieved the most significant updating references. For example, a case that overrules the case you are updating might mention your case so few times that the updating authority does not qualify for inclusion among the 100 most statistically relevant documents available through natural-language searching.
- Similarly, retrieving documents based on statistical criteria can result in the computer not retrieving the most recent references to the case you are updating. Unless you know that the database you are searching contains no more than 100 updating documents, you cannot be certain your natural-language search has provided you with an up-to-date view of the treatment of the case you are updating.

[359] See pages 21 and 25–26.

- Displaying retrieved documents in reverse chronological order provides the quickest way of identifying the most current updating references. Currently, however, the natural-language feature only displays retrieved documents based on a calculation of each document's statistical relevance. Consequently, when a natural-language updating search retrieves a large number of documents that cite the case you are updating, you might have to work harder to isolate the most recent documents.

In short, if you formulate a WESTLAW-as-citator search request with natural language, you face a higher risk of failing to obtain comprehensive updating results than you face with Boolean WESTLAW-as-citator requests. The extent of the risk will vary from search to search, and can be difficult—if not impossible—to predict. Nonetheless, a natural-language updating search will sometimes retrieve documents a Boolean search misses (and vice versa). Consequently, you might want to try both Boolean and natural-language updating searches if you want the most assurance possible that you have obtained comprehensive results through your WESTLAW-as-citator updating.

Using WESTLAW as a citator with Boolean searches for references to statutes, administrative regulations, and constitutional provisions. As with cases, you can use WESTLAW as a citator to update statutes, administrative regulations, and constitutional provisions. By updating these authorities, you discover how they have been treated by courts, legislatures, administrative agencies, and other participants in the legal system—for example, whether a statute has been amended or repealed by a legislature or interpreted by a court, whether a regulation has been judicially declared unconstitutional, or whether a constitutional provision has been analyzed in a law review article, Attorney General Opinion, or other source.

The technique for using Boolean searches to locate references to statutory-type authorities parallels the technique for using Boolean searches to locate references to cases:

1. Formulate a search request that includes citation information about the authority you want to update.

   Unlike a case citation, however, the citation information will usually consist exclusively of numbers. Even if a statutory-type authority has a name attached to it, authors citing the authority will often omit the name. For example, EPA Effluent Limitations Guidelines, 40 C.F.R. § 405.52 (1982) might be cited simply as 40 C.F.R. § 405.52 (1982).

2. Select a database containing the type of authorities (*e.g.*, federal cases, state cases, or law reviews) in which you want to search for citations to the authority you are updating.

At this point, also consider implementing the TERMS display option, which will cause retrieved documents with the greatest number of different search terms to display first.[360] Scanning these documents at the outset will often help you quickly determine the effectiveness of your search request.

3. Type and transmit your search request in the database you selected, and scan the results to see how the later authorities deal with the authority you are updating. Using TERM mode (explained on pages 358–59) will help you scan faster.

4. If you have retrieved a significant percentage of documents that do not refer to the authority you are updating, or if you suspect you have bypassed pertinent documents, you can modify your search request and try again.

Citation form for statutory-type authorities. To use WESTLAW to locate references to statutory-type authorities, you need to consider the standard citation forms, which vary from one jurisdiction to another, as these examples indicate:[361]

STATUTES

Statutory codes

29 U.S.C. § 1001 (1976)
Ala. Code § 1-1-1 (1980)
Del. Code Tit. 18, § 2720 (1987)
Fla. Stat. § 159.27 (1988)
N.Y. Civ. Rights Law § 8 (McKinney 1989)

Session laws

Employee Retirement Income Security Act of 1974,
Pub. L. No. 93-406, 88 Stat. 829 (1974)
1989 Kan. Sess. Laws ch. 8
1988 Neb. Laws, L.B. 1054
1988 Va. Acts ch. 866

[360] See page 353 for an explanation of the TERMS display option.

[361] For more details about citation form for statutory-type authorities, see THE BLUEBOOK: A UNIFORM SYSTEM OF CITATION 73–88, 90–93, 98, 165–218 (15th ed. 1991).

ADMINISTRATIVE REGULATIONS

Administrative codes

EPA Effluent Limitations Guidelines, 40 C.F.R. § 405.52 (1982)
902 Ky. Admin. Regs. 20:010
Mass. Admin. Code tit. 106, § 456.701
N.H. Code Admin. R. He-P 1901.04(e)
Tenn. Comp. R. & Regs. 0560-3-4-.05
Wis. Admin. Code § Ag 125.08 (Feb. 1987)

Administrative registers

47 Fed. Reg. 40,443 (1982)
Cal. Reg. Notice Reg. 84, No. 23
2 Okla. Reg. 02111 (1985)

CONSTITUTIONAL PROVISIONS

U.S. Const. art. III, § 2, cl. 3
U.S. Const. amend. XIV, § 1
Pa. Const. art. 5, § 9
Ind. Const. amend. 12

How the WESTLAW computer treats symbols in numbers. As in the examples above, numbers in citations to statutes, regulations, or constitutional provisions sometimes contain punctuation marks or other symbols (*e.g.*, section symbols, hyphens, periods). In searching for such numbers in the text of documents, you need to consider how the computer will interpret symbols that might appear with the numbers. For instance, is "§1983" (without a space) equivalent to "§ 1983" (with a space)? Or do you need to include each version in your search request? Similarly, does the computer interpret the decimal point in "405.52" as marking the end of one search term and the beginning of a new one, so that the computer perceives "405" and "52" as separate search terms?

Appendix H explains the rules by which the WESTLAW computer interprets punctuation marks and other symbols. Those rules form the basis for the following discussion.

Formulating your Boolean search request. When you use WESTLAW as a citator to update a statute, regulation, or constitutional provision, your search request needs to accommodate various ways in which later authorities might have referred to the authority you are updating. For example, one authority might refer to "42 U.S.C. § 1983," another might refer to "42 U.S.C.A. s1983," another to "42 U.S. Code Ann. s. 1983," and yet another to "section 1983 in the United States Code Annotated, Title 42."

To minimize the problem created by the variety of ways of identifying the publications in which statutory-type authorities appear, you will generally find it most effective to create a search request that includes pertinent numbers (*e.g.*, title number, section number) but omits the name or abbreviation of the publication. For instance, to search for references to 42 U.S.C. § 1983, your search request could take this form:

```
42 w/10 (1983 or s1983)
```

The search term **s1983** in this search request increases the comprehensiveness of the search. For cases in WESTLAW that have been published in West reporters, West editors put citations in standard form. So, in those cases, you would not see a non-standard citation form like one with the letter "s" adjoining a section number, as in "42 U.S.C.A. s1983." However, cases in WESTLAW that are online in the form of slip opinions or that are not scheduled for publication in West reporters might contain nonstandard citations. If you want to retrieve these kinds of cases, your search request should include search terms that will find nonstandard references to the statutory-type authority you are updating.

In searching for statutory-type citations that include more than one number (such as 42 U.S.C. § 1983), using the "w/n" connector to link the numbers offers an advantage over the "pre/n" or "+n" connector. Standard citation format specifies a particular order for the elements of citations to statutory-type authorities.[362] But references to these authorities often appear with the elements in a nonstandard order, as when a writer refers to "section 1983 in the United States Code Annotated, Title 42." The "w/n" connector, unlike the "pre/n" or "+n" connector, will capture references in either standard or nonstandard order.[363]

When you use the "w/n" connector to link a section number with a title or article number, an "n" value between 5 and 10 will usually suffice.[364] The larger value accommodates greater variation in citation format, but the larger value can also retrieve more authorities in which the numbers do not refer to

[362] *See* THE BLUEBOOK: A UNIFORM SYSTEM OF CITATION Rules 11–14 (15th ed. 1991).

[363] You might also use a "w/n" connector to link a section number with a reference to a specific subsection. For instance, a writer could refer to "subsection b of section 12" instead of to "section 12(b)." The following search request would retrieve both of these references, along with references to "12b":

```
(12 w/3 b) or 12b
```

Of course, the greater flexibility of this search request also increases the likelihood of retrieving more references that have nothing to do with the subsection you are updating.

[364] *Cf.* WEST PUBLISHING COMPANY, WESTLAW REFERENCE MANUAL 267 (5th ed. 1993) (recommending an "n" value of 5). But that number could bypass some variations on a statute's citation. For instance, transmitting **42 w/5 (1983 or s1983)** would not retrieve a reference to "section 1983 in the United States Code Annotated, Title 42."

the authority you are updating. If you are unsure what "n" value to select, you might find it helpful to check *The Bluebook: A Uniform System of Citation*, which indicates standard formats for citing statutory-type authorities. Knowing the standard citation format for a specific authority can help you anticipate likely variations and, consequently, likely distances between the numbers you are looking for. As you consider what "n" value to use, remember that variations in spacing within a publication's abbreviation affect the number of words the computer perceives: for example, the computer sees "USC" as one word and "U. S. C." as three words.

By omitting the name or abbreviation of the publication from your search request, you solve some retrieval problems. But you also need to consider the best way to use the remaining numbers in your search request; in the documents you are searching, these numbers might appear in a variety of configurations.

For example, suppose you want to find cases referring to section 302 in the federal copyright statute (Title 17 in the *United States Code*). If you used the search request `17 w/10 (302 or s302)` in the ALLFEDS database, you would retrieve a large percentage of the references you want. But you would bypass a case like *Hasbro Bradley, Inc. v. Sparkle Toys, Inc.*, 780 F.2d 189 (2d Cir. 1985), in which the judge started his opinion by citing all of Title 17 (writing "17 U.S.C. § 101 et seq.") and then, in the remainder of the opinion, cited specific sections of the copyright statute (including section 302) without repeating the Title number.

In other instances, common citation practice might omit a standard citation element altogether. For instance, citations to the Internal Revenue Code, which appears in Title 26 of the *United States Code*, frequently omit any reference to Title 26; thus, instead of "26 U.S.C. § 61," a citation might read "I.R.C. § 61." If you search for the *United States Code* title number in citations to the Internal Revenue Code, you will likely bypass many relevant documents. As this example suggests, searching for references to statutes and similar authorities involves knowing which authorities are commonly cited in a nonstandard format.

Given the range of possible variations on citations to statutory-type authorities, you might need to experiment with multiple search strategies when you use WESTLAW as a citator to update a statute or similar authority. You can try one or more of the following Boolean searching techniques:

- When the citation includes two numbers (such as title and section numbers for a statute or regulation, or article and section numbers for a constitutional provision), you can use both numbers and link them with the "w/n" connector. For example:

```
17 w/10 (302 or s302)
```

- When the citation includes a distinctive number that will likely occur only in references to the authority you are updating, you can search for just that number. For example:

```
974.06 or s974.06
```

- In addition to searching for numbers, you can use other search terms to provide a factual or legal context that increases the likelihood the numbers will refer to the authority you are updating. Thus, you might search for references to 17 U.S.C. § 302, a part of the federal copyright statute, using search requests such as these:

```
(302 or s302) w/25 copyright

(17 w/10 (302 or s302)) and copyright

(17 w/10 (302 or s302)) w/25 copyright
```

  Sometimes, a key phrase from the text of the authority you are updating can provide the needed context.

- If searching the full text of cases for numbers in a citation retrieves an unmanageable number of irrelevant references, you can restrict your search to the headnote field. There, as explained on pages 94–95, a number usually refers to a statutory-type authority, not to, say, a street number or a party's age. So, if you wanted to retrieve references to 17 U.S.C. § 302, you could use a search request like this:

```
he(17 w/10 302)
```

  Because West editors standardize the format of citations found in headnotes and leave a space between the section symbol and the section number, you do not need to include an alternative search term like `s302` in a request restricted to the headnote field.

  Remember, though, that not all cases in WESTLAW contain headnotes (see page 85 n.80). By restricting a search to that field, you can bypass relevant cases (such as slip opinions and cases never published in West reporters) that do not have headnotes.

- As a last resort, you can try including the name or abbreviation of the publication in which the authority you are updating appears. For example, you might search for references to 28 U.S.C. § 1251 with a search request along these lines:

```
28 w/10 (u.s.c. or u.s.c.a. or "u.s.
code") w/10 (1251 or s1251)
```

As you construct search requests to update statutory-type authorities, keep in mind a few other quirks (discussed below) concerning the format in which citations to these authorities might appear.

Renumbering. Through amendment, repeal, recodification, and other revisions, statutory-type provisions might be renumbered. For example, a legislature might reorganize a statutory code and renumber § 299.01 as § 799.01. In searching for references to these types of authorities, you should verify whether a provision has undergone a revision that has changed its citation.[365] If you want to ensure a comprehensive search, include each citation in your search request, as in:

```
299.01 or s299.01 or 799.01 or s799.01
```

Non-code citations. A reference to a statute might cite something other than a statutory code. For instance, a writer might cite a federal statute by its public law or chapter number, its session law citation (in *Statutes at Large*), or its popular name (if it has one). Thus, a citation to section 1001 of the Employee Retirement Income Security Act might refer to the statute's *United States Code* citation (29 U.S.C. § 1001), its public law number (Pub. L. No. 93-406), its *Statutes at Large* citation (88 Stat. 832), or its popular name ("ERISA"). To enhance the likelihood of retrieving all references to this statute, your search request could include search terms based on each way of citing the statute:[366]

```
(29 w/10 (1001 or s1001)) or 93-406 or
(88 pre/5 832) or "employee retirement" or
e.r.i.s.a.
```

This search would retrieve comprehensive results, but in most WESTLAW databases would also yield an unmanageable number of documents. A more practical search request would treat the popular name as a fact word that must occur in the document, thus providing context for the citation numbers:

[365] You can verify statutory renumberings by checking historical notes accompanying statutes in annotated codes or by checking cross-reference tables found in statutory codes. *See* CHRISTOPHER G. WREN & JILL R. WREN, THE LEGAL RESEARCH MANUAL: A GAME PLAN FOR LEGAL RESEARCH AND ANALYSIS 112 (2d ed. 1986). You might also learn about a renumbering when you read a case or other authority that discusses the statute in which you are interested. In addition, you can use the "credit" or "historical notes" field in statutes in WESTLAW to trace statutory renumberings, as explained on pages 610–11.

[366] Note that the numbers in the *Statutes at Large* citation—88 and 832—are linked with "pre/n" rather than "w/n." Unlike references to code provisions, references to provisions in *Statutes at Large* rarely put the page number (here, 832) before the volume number (here, 88).

```
((29 w/10 (1001 or s1001)) or 93-406 or (88
pre/5 832)) and ("employee retirement" or
e.r.i.s.a.)
```

If you still retrieve an unmanageable number of documents with a search request like this, you can further modify the search request by, say, adding a field restriction to limit the documents to those issued by a specific court.

Truncated citations. Suppose you want to update a specific subsection of a statute or regulation. A document with a discussion of that subsection might not contain a full citation to it. A discussion of a subsection with a number like 302(b)(2)(B) might actually cite only to 302(b)(2) or even to just 302(b). To accommodate possible truncations, you can begin with a broad version of the citation and narrow it if necessary. Thus, in the example, you could search for

```
302(b)
```

This search term will locate references to numbers with "302(b)" as their root, including

302(b)
302(b)(2)
302(b)(2)(B)

If you retrieve too many irrelevant references, you can narrow your focus by searching for

```
302(b)(2)
```

With this search term, you will locate references to numbers with "302(b)(2)" as their root, including

302(b)(2)
302(b)(2)(B)

You will not, however, locate references to just 302(b).

Similarly (and especially in connection with administrative regulations), a discussion of a subsection with a number like 102.46(a) might cite the provision as ".46(a)" or "46(a)." To ensure you retrieve all references, your search request can include alternative ways in which a subsection might have been cited:

```
102.46(a) or s102.46(a) or .46(a) or s.46(a)
```

Because WESTLAW treats ".46(a)" as equivalent to "46(a)" (see page 720 in Appendix H), you only need to include one of these versions in your search request.

Roman numerals. When you search for references to provisions (such as articles or amendments in a constitution) that might be identified with Roman numerals, keep in mind the rules about how the WESTLAW computer perceives Roman numerals and Arabic numbers and about how it perceives ordinal and cardinal numbers. (See Appendix H.) For instance, in a case, the Fourteenth Amendment to the United States Constitution might be cited in any of these ways:

Amendment XIV
XIVth Amendment
Amend. 14
14th Amendment
Amendment Fourteen
Fourteenth Amendment

The following search request would retrieve any of these references:

```
(amendment or amend) w/10 (XIV or XIVth or
14 or 14th)
```

Using WESTLAW as a citator with natural-language searches for references to statutes, administrative regulations, and constitutional provisions. In most databases, you can use natural language in your WESTLAW-as-citator search requests for references to statutory-type authorities you want to update. If you do, you need to consider the variety of citation formats that authors of updating authorities use to refer to statutory-type authorities, just as you need to consider those variations when you use Boolean WESTLAW-as-citator search requests (as explained in the preceding paragraphs). For example, authors might refer to a federal statute just by its *United States Code* citation, just by its public law number, or just by a *Statutes at Large* citation.

When a natural-language search request includes a sequence of search terms consisting of a number followed by the abbreviation of a federal statutory-type publication followed by another number, the natural-language feature normally recognizes the sequence as a citation. Because of this recognition, the search is more likely than a Boolean WESTLAW-as-citator search to retrieve a collection of documents in which the top-ranked documents contain references to the citation being updated, rather than references to the numbers in contexts unrelated to the citation. So, a natural-language search request for references to a *United States Code* provision could take this form:

```
42 u.s.c. 1983
```

Similarly, you could search for references to the *Code of Federal Regulations* with a natural-language search request like this:

```
40 c.f.r. 61.147
```

Or, you could locate references to the *Federal Register* by using a natural-language search request like this:

`47 fed.reg. 40443`

Although the natural-language feature can lessen some of the challenges posed by the various ways in which later authorities might refer to a federal statutory-type provision, natural-language searching does not address all of these challenges. You still need to consider obstacles like renumbered statutes, non-code citations (such as session law citations), truncated citations (such as references to section 302(b) as shorthand for section 302(b)(2)(B)), or references like "17 U.S.C. § 101 et seq." instead of "17 U.S.C. § 302." These situations present you with the same problems you encounter when you use Boolean WESTLAW-as-citator search requests, and the solutions in formulating natural-language updating search requests are often the same as those used in Boolean searching (covered earlier). For example, if you think a federal statute might have been cited just by its public law number, you could add that number to your natural-language search request.

Currently, when you use a combination of search terms that corresponds to a citation of a state statutory-type authority, the natural-language feature does not automatically recognize these search terms as a citation. For example, at this writing, the natural-language feature does not recognize `del. code tit. 18 sec. 2720` in a search request as a reference to a Delaware statute. Consequently, if you use natural language to search for updating references to a state statute, administrative regulation, or constitutional provision, you might have to experiment at the outset to discover what combination of search terms will best identify references to these kinds of state authorities. For instance, if you are updating an authority identified by a number (such as "744.441" or "12-61-302" or "12.55.125") likely to occur only as a reference to that authority, the number by itself might prove an effective search term. By contrast, if you are updating an authority identified by a number likely to occur in a variety of settings, you might be able to provide the necessary context for the authority's identifying number by adding search terms that reflect the authority's subject matter; or, you could try including as part of your search request a key phrase from the authority.

Caveat. Using natural language to search for updating references to federal or state statutes, administrative regulations, or constitutional provisions presents the same drawbacks (highlighted on pages 583–84) as those encountered in using natural language to update cases. The current 100-document limitation can preclude comprehensive updating, and the use of statistical relevance as the retrieval mechanism means you cannot always know whether the computer has identified the most recent authorities that might have affected the authority you are updating.

Using WESTLAW as a citator to search for references to other kinds of authorities. You can use WESTLAW as a citator to locate references to any kind of authority. You can use Boolean or natural-language requests to search for references to such legal authorities as law review articles, congressional committee reports, or *A.L.R.* annotations, and to such nonlegal authorities as articles in medical journals. Through this technique, you can find references to authorities you cannot update by other means (such as by using Shepard's citators or Insta-Cite) and you can determine how judges and other legal writers currently view those authorities.

In searching for references of this sort, the same principles, challenges, and work-arounds already discussed for cases and statutory-type authorities come into play. You need to familiarize yourself with standard citation formats, anticipate likely variations, and then formulate a search request based on the possible ways of citing the authorities you want to update. If you are uncertain about the standard citation for an authority, *The Bluebook: A Uniform System of Citation* provides guidance.

The following examples suggest the range of authorities you can update by using WESTLAW as a citator.

- You can retrieve references to *Restatement (Second) of Torts* § 623A with a Boolean search request like this:

```
((restatement or rest) w/10 tort)
w/10 (623a or s623a)
```

- You can retrieve references to Francis Wellman's book, *The Art of Cross-Examination*, with a Boolean search request like this:

```
wellman w/10 cross-examination
```

- You can retrieve references to Rule 410 of the *Federal Rules of Evidence*, dealing with the admissibility of withdrawn pleas or of statements made during plea negotiations, with Boolean search requests like these:

```
((fed.r.evid. or f.r.e. or rule or
evid) w/5 410) w/35 plea

op(410 w/35 (plea w/25 (admissib! or
admit! or admission)))

he(evid.rule w/5 410)
```

When you search for an evidentiary, procedural, or court rule, restricting your Boolean search to the headnote field can reduce the number of irrelevant references you retrieve (as explained on pages

94–95). Remember, though, that a headnote restriction will bypass cases (such as slip opinions and cases never published in West reporters) that do not have headnotes.

You can also use natural-language search requests to perform updating searches for authorities like these. For example, if you wanted to retrieve references to Wellman's book on cross-examination, you could transmit

```
wellman "art of cross-examination"
```

But, as with using natural language in WESTLAW-as-citator searches for cases and statutory-type authorities, the natural-language feature's current 100-document limitation and statistical retrieval method can keep you from obtaining comprehensive results when you update treatises, articles, and other kinds of authorities. (See pages 583–84.)

Using WESTLAW as a citator to update Shepardizing results. Because of the editorial time required to prepare the tables used for Shepardizing,[367] even the most recent citing references in a Shepard's citator will be several months old by the time the citator appears, whether in printed form or online; the references in a Shepard's PreView table will be more recent but still not current.[368] WESTLAW, however, contains documents that have been issued more recently than those included in the most recent Shepard's citator or Shepard's PreView table.

Thus, you can supplement your Shepardizing results by using WESTLAW as a citator to update an authority. You can do this more readily if you can isolate those references that have not yet appeared in a Shepard's or Shepard's PreView table. With Boolean searching, if you display the results of your WESTLAW-as-citator search request in AGE order (explained on page 353), this task is relatively simple: because the most recent documents will display first, you can just begin with the first document and continue scanning documents until you encounter ones you have already identified by Shepardizing.

If you select TERMS or PUBLICATION as the order for displaying Boolean search results, or if you search with natural language, documents will not display in reverse chronological order. When using the TERMS or PUBLICATION display order (explained on page 353) or natural language, you can isolate citing references that have not yet appeared in a Shepard's citator or Shepard's PreView table if you include a date restriction in your search request when you use WESTLAW as a citator.

For example, suppose that on July 15, 1993 you were updating *Lewis v. United States*, 445 U.S. 55, 100 S. Ct. 915, 63 L. Ed. 2d 198 (1980). Searching for references to *Lewis* in documents issued during the six months preceding

[367] See pages 496–524 and 528–44 for a discussion of Shepardizing in WESTLAW.
[368] See pages 524–28 for a discussion of Shepard's PreView.

your search would update your Shepardizing and ensure that no gap occurs between your Shepardizing results and your WESTLAW-as-citator results. You could use a Boolean search request along these lines:

```
(lewis w/5 ("united states" or u.s.)) and
((445 pre/5 55) or (100 pre/5 915) or
(63 pre/5 198)) and date(aft 1/15/1993)
```

If you used a natural-language search request, you could transmit `445 u.s. 55` combined with a date restriction added with the "res" command.

You can use search requests like these to update any authority you have Shepardized. If you implement this updating technique with the natural-language feature, however, you run a risk that the feature's current 100-document limitation will prevent you from obtaining comprehensive results.

Automating WESTLAW-as-citator searches by using QuickCite

WESTLAW offers QuickCite as an automated method of creating Boolean WESTLAW-as-citator search requests to locate references to cases you want to update. QuickCite is designed to obtain more recent updating results than you can get through Shepard's or Shepard's PreView (discussed earlier in this chapter). If you prefer, though, you can broaden QuickCite's reach to overlap with, or even duplicate, Shepard's or Shepard's PreView.

A QuickCite search involves transmitting a citation for the case you are updating. The computer then automatically formulates a Boolean search request designed to locate references to that citation, to some parallel citations, and to the case name. In formulating a QuickCite request, however, the computer makes certain assumptions (for example, which logic connectors and parallel citations to include), and those assumptions could result in a search request that might not be as well-suited for your purposes as the request you would formulate on your own. Consequently, for this and other reasons discussed at the end of this section, QuickCite will not always serve as an adequate substitute for creating your own WESTLAW-as-citator search requests (using techniques explained in the previous section).

Using QuickCite. You can initiate a QuickCite search any time after you log on to WESTLAW:

- If you want to use QuickCite to update the case you are viewing, simply type `qc` and press ENTER. The computer will "read in" to the QuickCite instruction a citation for the case. If a reporter citation appears at the upper left corner of the display of the case, the computer will select that citation for the QuickCite instruction; if a reporter citation does not appear in that location, the computer will use the case's WESTLAW Cite in the QuickCite instruction.[369]

You can also transmit `qc` while you are viewing the results of a Shepard's, Shepard's PreView, or Insta-Cite search.[370] Alternatively, you can use the JUMP feature; for example, while viewing the screen in Figure 12.44 on page 552, you could initiate a QuickCite search by using the TAB key to position the cursor under the JUMP marker (">") in front of "QuickCite" at the bottom of the screen, and then pressing ENTER. Whether you type the command or use the JUMP feature, the computer will read in to the QuickCite instruction a reporter citation or WESTLAW Cite for the case whose results you are viewing.

- If you want to use QuickCite to update a case you are *not* viewing, type `qc` followed by the citation of that case, then press ENTER. For the citation, type the volume number and abbreviation of the publication in which the authority appears and a page number from the authority; you can also use a WESTLAW Cite in a QuickCite instruction. For instance, to conduct a QuickCite search for references to *Patterson v. Illinois*, 487 U.S. 285, 108 S. Ct. 2389, 101 L.Ed. 2d 261, 56 U.S.L.W. 4733, 1988 WL 62992, you could use any of the following instructions:

```
qc 487 us 285
qc 487us285
qc 108 s.ct. 2389
qc108sct2389
qc 101 l. ed. 2d 261
qc 1988 wl 62992
```

As you can see, you have considerable flexibility in typing your QuickCite instruction. If you are uncertain about what abbreviation to use, try using an abbreviation that works in an instruction for FIND, Shepard's, or Insta-Cite.

After you transmit a "qc" instruction, the monitor might display a message indicating that QuickCite does not recognize the reporter abbreviation in your instruction. If this occurs, consider the possibility that a parallel citation might work.

You might also encounter a situation in which two or more cases share the citation you used in your QuickCite instruction, as occurs,

[369] WESTLAW Cites are explained in Figure 10.08 on pages 281–82.

[370] Pages 496–544 explain Shepard's and Shepard's PreView, and pages 544 and 552–64 explain Insta-Cite.

for example, with 387 N.Y.S.2d 426. In that event, the monitor will display a list of the cases, and you can follow the on-screen instructions to select the one you want to update.

- If you are viewing an authority and see the citation of a case you want to update through QuickCite, you can use the JUMP feature (explained on page 284) to automate the use of QuickCite for updating that citation. To use JUMP, type **qc**, press the TAB key to position the cursor under the ">" symbol or triangle next to the citation you want to update, and then press ENTER. The computer will read in to your QuickCite instruction the citation on which you positioned the cursor.

After you transmit a "qc" instruction, the computer will formulate a Boolean search request and display a screen like the one shown in Figure 12.48, which offers several choices for telling the computer how to carry out the QuickCite search:

- If you do not want to change the QuickCite request the computer formulated, press ENTER. The computer will run the search in the ALLSTATES database if you are updating a state case, or in the ALLFEDS database if you are updating a federal case.

```
                                  QuickCite
Citation:  1983 WL 1147
           Schuchart & Associates v. Solo Serve Corp. (W.D.Tex., Jun 28, 1983)

Command                  Result
Press ENTER . . . . . Updates Shepard's and Shepard's PreView by retrieving
                         documents added to ALLFEDS after 5/83 that cite this
                         decision.
ALL . . . . . . . . . Retrieves all ALLFEDS documents that cite this
                         decision.
Database Identifier . Retrieves documents added to WESTLAW after 5/83 that
(e.g., SCT)              cite this decision in the selected database.
Q . . . . . . . . . . Displays the QuickCite query for editing in ALLFEDS.

   Note:  Your previous research will be discarded when you select a
          QuickCite command.  For comprehensive citator information, also
          use Insta-Cite (IC), Shepard's (SH) and Shepard's PreView (SP).


If you wish to:
   Select a QuickCite command, type the command and press ENTER
   Go back to the previously accessed service, type GB and press ENTER
   Obtain further information on QuickCite, type HELP and press ENTER
```

Source: West Publishing Company © 1993

Figure 12.48. Typical Menu of Choices for Updating with QuickCite in WESTLAW

In addition to selecting a default database, the computer will include in the QuickCite request an "added date" restriction (or, in some situations, a "date" restriction). The date in the "added date" field refers to the date WESTLAW added the document to its database, not the date the document was issued. See Figure 12.49. The date the document was issued appears in the "date" field.

Each document in WESTLAW has a field, designated "added date," that contains the date on which the document was added to the WESTLAW service. Although not visible on the monitor, this "added date" can be used in a field restriction to confine a search to only those documents added to WESTLAW on, before, or after a designated date.*

For example, suppose you had run the following search request on October 15, 1993:

```
(apartment w/10 lease) and (plumbing or water)
```

At some later point, to update your search by finding documents added to WESTLAW since October 15, you could repeat the search with an "added date" restriction, using the field name or its abbreviation ("ad"):

```
(apartment w/10 lease) and (plumbing or water) and added
date(after 10/14/1993)

(apartment w/10 lease) and (plumbing or water) and
ad(after 10/14/1993)
```

By using an "added date" one day earlier than the date you last ran your search, you ensure that your search results will include any documents that might have been added on the same day you last ran your search request, but that were added after you ran the search.

Although not an updating technique, you can also use the "added date" field if you want to know what search results you would have obtained as of some date in the past. To do so, use an "added date" to restrict your search to documents added to WESTLAW before a designated date:

```
(apartment w/10 lease) and (plumbing or water) and added
date(before 10/5/1993)

(apartment w/10 lease) and (plumbing or water) and
ad(before 10/5/1993)
```

---

* The "added date" field differs from the "date" field. The "date" field contains the date on which the document was created or issued (*e.g.*, the date on which a case was decided), not the date on which the document was added to WESTLAW.

Figure 12.49. The "Added Date" Field for Updating in WESTLAW

The "added date" restriction is designed to retrieve only the most recent references to the case you are updating and to avoid (to the extent possible) retrieving authorities that have already appeared in a Shepard's or Shepard's PreView table for the case you are updating. If you are updating a case that has been reported in a West case reporter, the computer is programmed to assume the case can be updated through Shepard's and Shepard's PreView; the computer will therefore formulate a QuickCite request with an "added date" restriction roughly limiting the search to cases added to WESTLAW too recently to have been included yet in a Shepard's or Shepard's PreView table.

If you are updating a case that has *not* been reported in a West case reporter, the computer will use either an "added date" restriction or a "date" restriction. The choice depends initially on the date the court decided the case you are updating. For a case decided on or after January 1, 1984, the computer will formulate a QuickCite request with an "added date" restriction. For a case decided before January 1, 1984, the computer will formulate a QuickCite request with an "added date" restriction if the citation the computer includes in the QuickCite request can be updated through Shepard's or Shepard's PreView; if the citation cannot be updated that way, the computer will formulate a QuickCite request with a "date" restriction, which will retrieve all cases decided since the decision date of the case you are updating.

- If you do not want the computer to include an "added date" or "date" restriction in your QuickCite request, type `all` and press ENTER. Instead of retrieving only the most recent references to the case you are updating, the computer will retrieve any references in a default database—the ALLFEDS database if you are updating a federal case, or the ALLSTATES database if you are updating a state case.

  Transmitting `all` to eliminate the "added date" or "date" restriction can increase the number of irrelevant references the computer will retrieve. Without the "added date" or "date" restriction, the computer could retrieve some references satisfying your QuickCite request that appear in cases issued before the case you are updating was decided.

- If you want to run the QuickCite search in a database other than the default database (ALLFEDS if you are updating a federal case or ALLSTATES if you are updating a state case), type the database identifier (such as PA-CS for Pennsylvania cases), then press ENTER. The computer will run your QuickCite search in the database you designate, using an "added date" or "date" restriction to retrieve only the most recent references to the case you are updating.

- If you want to view or edit the search request the computer formulated in response to your "qc" instruction, type **q** (for "query") and press ENTER. The monitor will display the QuickCite request. At that point, you can run the QuickCite search by pressing ENTER, or you can edit the request and then transmit the edited version by pressing ENTER.

  If you edit the request, the modifications you can make include changing or removing the "added date" or "date" restriction, and adding other search terms to create a factual or legal context in which the references to the case you are updating should occur.

After you transmit a QuickCite request, the computer leaves the QuickCite feature and carries out the search as an ordinary Boolean search. When the monitor displays the results of the search you initiated through QuickCite, you can do anything you could ordinarily do in WESTLAW (*e.g.*, view or print the results, use FIND to retrieve another document, Shepardize an authority). If you want to initiate another search through QuickCite, type another "qc" instruction and press ENTER.

Examples of QuickCite requests. To illustrate using QuickCite to update a case that has *not* been published in a West reporter, suppose you were viewing the version of *Schuchart & Associates, Professional Engineers, Inc. v. Solo Serve Corp.*, 220 U.S.P.Q. 170, 1983 Copr. L. Dec. ¶ 25,593, 1983 WL 1147 (W.D. Tex. 1983), that you retrieved from the DCTU database, which contains unpublished opinions from U.S. District Courts. If you typed **qc**, the computer would formulate this QuickCite request (using a space for the "or" connector):

```
(SCHUCHART +3 ASSOCIATES /S SOLO +3 SERVE)
"1983 WL 1147" & DATE(AFT 5/1983)
```

Because the DCTU display of *Schuchart* does not show a case reporter citation at the upper left corner of the screen, the computer includes the WESTLAW Cite in the QuickCite request; the computer does not include the citations to the looseleaf reporters. Also, because a WESTLAW Cite cannot be Shepardized, the computer does not exclude from its search those cases whose citations have already appeared in a Shepard's or Shepard's PreView table; instead, the computer includes a "date" restriction that results in a search for all cases in the ALLFEDS database issued since the federal district court in Texas issued its decision in *Schuchart*.

The computer formulates a different QuickCite request if you transmit one of *Schuchart*'s looseleaf reporter citations. Transmitting **qc 1983** `copr.l.dec. 25593` (to retrieve references to the *Copyright Law Decisions* citation for *Schuchart*) yields this QuickCite request:

```
(SCHUCHART +3 ASSOCIATES /S SOLO +3 SERVE)
"1983 COPR.L.DEC. P 25593" & DATE(AFT 5/1983)
```

Transmitting `qc 220 u.s.p.q. 170` in May 1993 to retrieve references to the *United States Patents Quarterly* citation for *Schuchart* generated this QuickCite request:[371]

```
(SCHUCHART +3 ASSOCIATES /S SOLO +3 SERVE)
"220 U.S.P.Q. 170" & ADDED DATE(AFT 1/1993)
```

As an example of using QuickCite to update a case that *has* been published in a West case reporter, suppose that in May 1993 you had been viewing the United States Supreme Court case of *Patterson v. Illinois*, 487 U.S. 285, 108 S. Ct. 2389, 101 L.Ed. 2d 261, 56 U.S.L.W. 4733, 1988 WL 62992 (1988). Transmitting `qc` would have yielded this QuickCite request:

```
PATTERSON & "487 U.S. 285" "108 S.CT. 2389" &
ADDED DATE(AFT 1/1993)
```

Because the display of *Patterson* shows the case's *Supreme Court Reporter* citation in the upper left corner of the screen, the computer included that citation in the QuickCite request; in this instance, the computer also included the parallel citation to the official reporter (*United States Reports*), but not the WESTLAW Cite or other non-West reporter citations (such as those for *Lawyers' Edition 2d* or *United States Law Week*). In addition, because the citations included in the QuickCite request can be Shepardized, the computer inserted an "added date" restriction to exclude from the search those cases that had already appeared in a Shepard's or Shepard's PreView table.

The role of QuickCite. QuickCite simply amounts to an alternative method of transmitting an ordinary Boolean WESTLAW-as-citator search request. Instead of requiring you to create the request, however, QuickCite formulates it for you. QuickCite thus simplifies using WESTLAW as a citator.

QuickCite has some limitations, however:

- At this time, QuickCite only automates the procedure for searching for references to cases. You cannot use QuickCite to search for references to other kinds of authorities, such as statutes or administrative regulations.

[371] The computer would also have formulated this QuickCite request if you had simply transmitted `qc` while viewing the version of *Schuchart* appearing in the USPQ database, where the upper left corner of the *Schuchart* display shows a citation to *United States Patents Quarterly*.

- An automatically formulated QuickCite request might not include all parallel citations to the case you are updating. Nor will the request include the slip-opinion citation, the WESTLAW Cite once the case has been published in a West reporter, or (undoubtedly for competitive reasons) a LEXIS Cite. If, as in the *Patterson* example, a QuickCite request uses the "and" connector to require the presence of a citation, QuickCite will bypass references in which the case you are updating is identified only by a citation not included in the QuickCite request (such as, in the *Patterson* example, by the *Lawyers' Edition 2d* or *United States Law Week* citation).
- In formulating a request, QuickCite might not select the most efficient connectors. For instance, the "/s" connector, such as the one QuickCite selected in the *Schuchart* example, could significantly slow the computer's search in comparison to a search using a "w/n" connector.[372]

You can compensate for QuickCite's shortcomings by reviewing the automatically formulated search request before you transmit it. If the request does not fully accomplish your updating goal, you can edit the request by, for example, including missing citations, changing a connector, removing or modifying an "added date" or "date" restriction, or adding search terms based on the facts or issues of your research problem. Of course, extensive editing largely undermines the automation QuickCite was designed to accomplish.

If you use QuickCite, keep in mind that WESTLAW could change the assumptions the computer makes in formulating QuickCite requests. Reviewing your QuickCite requests before instructing the computer to carry them out will help you spot changes in the way QuickCite formulates requests and help you obtain the results you intend. Also, remember that QuickCite is designed principally to supplement Shepard's and Shepard's PreView, and you should use those services to ensure comprehensive updating.

Updating the law in WESTLAW by using EZ ACCESS

In WESTLAW, you have the option of using EZ ACCESS to update your research in certain kinds of authorities—currently, federal and state cases and federal statutes. Intended for novice or infrequent users of WESTLAW, EZ ACCESS provides a fill-in-the-blank method of implementing the techniques already explained in this chapter for using WESTLAW to update your research. (As explained in Chapter 10, you can also use EZ ACCESS in the finding-the-law phase of a legal research project.)

[372] See page 57 n.59 for a discussion of how the "/s," "+s," "/p," and "+p" connectors can slow the WESTLAW computer's search and increase the researcher's online costs.

EZ ACCESS presents menus of updating tasks (among other things) and asks researchers to specify which ones the computer should perform. With EZ ACCESS, you do not need to know an array of commands to use WESTLAW; once you type a response to the "plain English" prompts EZ ACCESS displays, the computer translates your choices into WESTLAW commands, carries out the updating task, and displays the results. Thus, EZ ACCESS allows you to update in WESTLAW by remembering just one command: **ez**.

In exchange for this convenience, however, you can lose comprehensiveness in your updating results and control over the updating process. As explained at the end of this section, experienced online researchers can find that EZ ACCESS diminishes the effectiveness and efficiency of their updating in WESTLAW.

Gaining access to EZ ACCESS. After you log on to WESTLAW, you can invoke EZ ACCESS at any point during your research:

1. Type **ez**.

2. Press ENTER.

The monitor will display a screen like the one shown in Figure 12.50. To update your research, select "Insta-Cite, Shepard's, Shepard's PreView or QuickCite" as your EZ ACCESS choice.

COPR. (C) 1993 West Publishing Co. All Rights Reserved

***** WELCOME TO EZ ACCESS *****

EZ ACCESS is West Publishing Company's easy-to-use menu driven research system. You can quickly retrieve information by making a selection from a list of options. When you are unsure of the next step, type **EZ** to see available choices.

What would you like to do?

Retrieve cases, statutes or other documents using:

1. A Title or Citation
2. A West Topic and Key number
3. Significant words

Retrieve references to your document citation using:

4. Insta-Cite, Shepard's, Shepard's PreView or QuickCite

Leave EZ ACCESS, type 5 and press ENTER

Type a **number** and press **ENTER**

Source: West Publishing Company © 1993

Figure 12.50. Opening Screen for EZ ACCESS in WESTLAW

If you prefer, you can use the Options Directory (explained at pages 197–99) to invoke EZ ACCESS automatically as part of the WESTLAW sign-on procedure. If you implement that option, the first screen you will see after you log on to WESTLAW will be the "Welcome to EZ ACCESS" screen (Figure 12.50) instead of the WESTLAW Directory screen (Figure 9.07 on page 196).

Getting help in using EZ ACCESS. While using EZ ACCESS, you might find yourself unsure of what to do next. By transmitting **ez** again, you can display a menu of EZ ACCESS choices that will help you decide what your next step should be. For additional information about using EZ ACCESS, you can also consult WESTLAW's publication entitled *Guide to EZ ACCESS.*

Initiating your updating through EZ ACCESS. Once you have gained access to EZ ACCESS and selected "Insta-Cite, Shepard's, Shepard's PreView or QuickCite" from the menu in Figure 12.50, the monitor will display a screen with an instruction to indicate the type of authority—case or statute—you want to update.

Updating cases through EZ ACCESS. If you choose to update a case, the monitor will display a screen asking you to type a case citation. After you type a citation and press ENTER, the monitor will display a screen like that in Figure 12.51, giving you the choices of updating a case by using:

```
REFERENCES:  Reference Options

The case law citation you requested references to is:

        Lewis v. U. S., 445 U.S. 55, 100 S.Ct. 915, 63 L.Ed.2d 198
         (U.S.Va., Feb 27, 1980) (NO. 78-1595)

        What would you like to do?

                  1. Insta-Cite for current case history
                  2. Shepard's for complete case commentary
                  3. Shepard's PreView to update Shepard's
                  4. QuickCite for the most current citing cases

        Type a number and press ENTER


               For additional options, type EZ and press ENTER
```

Source: West Publishing Company © 1993

Figure 12.51. Screen for Selecting an Updating Technique in EZ ACCESS in WESTLAW

- Shepard's
- Shepard's PreView
- Insta-Cite
- QuickCite

Using Shepard's through EZ ACCESS to update a case. When you select "Shepard's for complete case commentary" at the menu in Figure 12.51, the computer will retrieve Shepard's tables.

Using Shepard's PreView through EZ ACCESS to update a case. When you select "Shepard's PreView to update Shepard's" at the menu in Figure 12.51, the computer will retrieve the Shepard's PreView table for your citation. The computer uses West reporter citations to retrieve Shepard's PreView tables. If you transmit a non-West citation, the computer will convert that citation to a West citation (if one exists) and retrieve the Shepard's PreView table based on the West citation. If a parallel West citation does not exist, the monitor will display a message that a Shepard's PreView table is not available for your citation.

Using Insta-Cite through EZ ACCESS to update a case. When you select "Insta-Cite for current case history" at the menu in Figure 12.51, the computer will retrieve the Insta-Cite report for the case you are updating.

Performing a QuickCite search through EZ ACCESS to update a case. When you select "QuickCite for the most current citing cases" at the menu in Figure 12.51, the monitor displays a screen that asks you to select the database you want to search for references to the case you are updating. After you select a database, the computer formulates a QuickCite search request and retrieves any authorities that satisfy the search request. In formulating the QuickCite search request, the computer operates as it does when you use QuickCite (explained on pages 596–603) without the aid of EZ ACCESS.

As explained on page 603, a search request created by QuickCite can bypass relevant authorities. A QuickCite search request in EZ ACCESS has the same drawback, and for the same reasons.

Updating statutes through EZ ACCESS. If you choose to update a statute through EZ ACCESS, the monitor will display a screen asking you to type your statutory citation. After you type a citation and press ENTER, the monitor will ask you to confirm that you want to Shepardize that citation, currently your only option for updating a statute through EZ ACCESS.

Running subsequent updating searches through EZ ACCESS. When you choose an updating technique through EZ ACCESS, the computer leaves the EZ ACCESS feature and carries out the updating search as if you had initiated it without EZ ACCESS. So, for example, if you select Shepard's as your updating choice in EZ ACCESS, the computer will leave EZ ACCESS, enter the Shepard's service, and carry out your search as though you had gained access to the Shepard's service on your own and transmitted a Shepard's command there.

Once the monitor displays the results of an updating search you initiated through EZ ACCESS, you can do anything you could ordinarily do (*e.g.*, view or print the results, or retrieve a document mentioned in your updating results).

If you want to initiate another updating search through EZ ACCESS, type `ez` again and press ENTER. If you were updating a statute, the monitor will display a menu of choices for continuing in EZ ACCESS. If you were updating a case, the monitor will redisplay a modified version of the screen shown in Figure 12.51. The modified screen will allow you to continue updating the case you were most recently updating through EZ ACCESS, but only by using techniques you have not already selected. So, for instance, if you have already used Insta-Cite to update your case through EZ ACCESS, that option will disappear from the menu of choices shown in Figure 12.51. If you want to update a different case, type `ez` again, press ENTER, and follow the on-screen instructions to return to the "Welcome to EZ ACCESS" screen (Figure 12.50).

Leaving EZ ACCESS. As just noted, you leave EZ ACCESS whenever you implement an updating technique through EZ ACCESS. You might, however, gain access to EZ ACCESS and then decide not to use the feature to update your research after all. In that situation, you can leave EZ ACCESS by selecting "Return to WESTLAW" from an EZ ACCESS menu. If you are not viewing a menu that offers this choice, transmitting `ez` will move you to a menu that does.

The role of EZ ACCESS in updating the law. For new or infrequent users, EZ ACCESS can simplify using WESTLAW to update research results. The EZ ACCESS menus let you use Shepard's, Shepard's PreView, Insta-Cite, and QuickCite without knowing the commands you would otherwise need to type to gain access to these features. But at this time, EZ ACCESS has some pitfalls for updating, especially for those inexperienced with CALR:

- EZ ACCESS does not simplify Shepardizing to the point of automatically retrieving all available Shepard's tables for a case that has parallel citations, nor does the computer always alert EZ ACCESS users to the need to repeat the Shepardizing process for parallel citations. (Recall that you can get different Shepardizing results depending on which parallel citation you use to Shepardize.)[373] Consequently, EZ ACCESS can mislead researchers unfamiliar with the online version of Shepard's into believing they have fully Shepardized when more can be done.

[373] *See* CHRISTOPHER G. WREN & JILL R. WREN, THE LEGAL RESEARCH MANUAL: A GAME PLAN FOR LEGAL RESEARCH AND ANALYSIS 101, 104 (2d ed. 1986). For an example of different results in online Shepardizing, see page 509.

For example, suppose you are updating a case that has not been published in a West reporter but has been published in more than one non-West publication (such as in two looseleaf services) that can be Shepardized. In this situation, Shepardizing a citation through EZ ACCESS will retrieve only the Shepard's table for the citation you transmitted. To Shepardize another citation for the case, you will have to return to the "Welcome to EZ ACCESS" screen (Figure 12.50) and start over with the updating process.

Or, suppose you are updating a case that has been published in a West reporter and in one or more non-West publications that can be Shepardized (as occurs, for example, with U.S. Supreme Court cases). If you Shepardize one of the non-West citations through EZ ACCESS, the computer will retrieve the Shepard's tables for the citation to the West reporter's version of the case. When you finish viewing the Shepard's tables EZ ACCESS retrieved, you will need to transmit `ez` again to display a menu allowing you to Shepardize a parallel citation. After that, if you want to see the Shepard's tables for yet another parallel citation, transmitting `ez` again will not display another menu inviting you to Shepardize a parallel citation; instead, you will see a menu like the one in Figure 12.51 but without offering Shepardizing as a choice. You will have to transmit `ez` again to return to a screen offering the choice of updating another citation.

When you transmit the West citation for a case that has a citation to a West reporter and to one or more non-West publications that can be Shepardized, the computer will retrieve the Shepard's tables for the West citation. After you finish viewing those tables, transmitting `ez` again will not bring you to a menu offering you the opportunity to do additional Shepardizing. Instead, to Shepardize the non-West citations, you will have to transmit `ez` once more to return to a screen offering the choice of updating another citation.

To see how Shepardizing operates in EZ ACCESS, try Shepardizing the U.S. Supreme Court case of *Lewis v. United States*, 445 U.S. 55, 100 S. Ct. 915, 63 L. Ed. 2d 198 (1980). No matter which citation you first transmit for Shepardizing through EZ ACCESS, you will need to take additional steps (sometimes with no on-screen reminders) to ensure that you retrieve the Shepard's tables based on the remaining parallel citations.

- When you use QuickCite through EZ ACCESS (just as when you use QuickCite independently of EZ ACCESS), the search request the computer formulates could bypass some relevant authorities by failing to account for all the ways in which the case you are updating could be cited. This drawback to QuickCite is discussed on page 603.

- For experienced WESTLAW users, wending through the EZ ACCESS menus will almost always prove slower than updating without the help of EZ ACCESS.
- Because of its simplicity and automation, EZ ACCESS invites researchers who do not understand how online updating works to use WESTLAW for this purpose. But, as suggested by the discussion on pages 564–65 and 570–96, using WESTLAW effectively as a citator calls for understanding such points as how logic connectors work, what factors can affect the selection of search terms (*e.g.*, a term's ambiguity or lack of distinctiveness), and how the computer's literalness affects its response to search instructions. Similarly, to Shepardize comprehensively, you need to be sure you have retrieved all the relevant Shepard's tables for the authority you are updating. EZ ACCESS, however, is designed for users least likely to know how to evaluate the effectiveness of a WESTLAW-as-citator search request or to know, because of unfamiliarity with online Shepardizing, whether more steps need to be taken to retrieve all the relevant online Shepard's tables. Thus, EZ ACCESS could encourage WESTLAW use by those most likely to find online updating a waste of time and money, whether through EZ ACCESS or otherwise.

Automating citation-updating in WESTLAW through WEST*Check*

If you have access to a personal computer and a software program called WEST*Check* (available from West Publishing Company), you can automate the use of online citation-updating features—Shepard's, Shepard's PreView, Insta-Cite, and QuickCite. WEST*Check* allows you, while you are not connected to WESTLAW, to prepare a list of citations the computer will update for you through WESTLAW. WEST*Check* can compile the list by extracting the citations from an existing document (such as a brief or memorandum) prepared through a word-processing program; or, you can type citations directly into WEST*Check*. Through WEST*Check*, you tell the computer how to update the citations on the WEST*Check* list—for example, whether to update a citation just through Shepard's, just through Shepard's PreView, just through Insta-Cite, or through some combination of the three, or whether Shepard's results should consist of citing references just from selected jurisdictions or just accompanied by certain kinds of analysis codes. After you indicate the information you want WEST*Check* to provide about your citations, WEST-*Check* logs onto WESTLAW, carries out the updating searches you requested, and delivers the results to a destination (such as a computer printer or storage disk) you specified through WEST*Check*.

If you need to conduct extensive online updating through WESTLAW, using WEST*Check* could speed your updating efforts, reduce the time spent connected to WESTLAW, and lower your online research costs. Your WEST-LAW customer-service representative can help you obtain WEST*Check* and a detailed reference manual explaining how to use the program.

Other tips for updating statutes through WESTLAW

When you find a reference to a statute in a case or other authority, even a recent one, you cannot be sure the reference reflects the most up-to-date text of the statute; the provision might have subsequently been amended or repealed, for example. Even a provision you see in a statutory code database might not have incorporated recent legislative changes.

As with printed statutes, the text of which you update through such means as checking pocket parts and supplements accompanying statutory codes, you need to update the text of statutes you find online.[374] First, though, to get an idea of how much updating lies ahead, ascertain when legislative changes were last incorporated into the online text of the statute you want to update. For some statutes, this information appears near the top of the monitor when the statute is displayed. You can also find this information by using the "scope" command: if you are in the database containing the statute you want to update, simply type `scope` (or `sc`) and press ENTER; otherwise, type `scope` (or `sc`) followed by the name of the database containing the statute, then press ENTER. The monitor will display a description of the database, including the date of the online version of the statutory code. The schedule for incorporating changes into statutory codes varies from jurisdiction to jurisdiction.

Along with ascertaining the recency of updates to a statute, you can use the following WESTLAW features to discover legislative changes.

The "credit" and "historical notes" fields in statutory codes in WEST-LAW. The "credit" field of a statute in WESTLAW summarizes the history of changes to the statute; the "historical notes" field often contains the same information, along with a more detailed explanation of the nature of the changes. When viewing a statute online, you might see that these fields include notations that the provision has been repealed, amended, renumbered, or oth-

[374] For a description of using pocket parts and supplements to update printed statutory codes, see CHRISTOPHER G. WREN & JILL R. WREN, THE LEGAL RESEARCH MANUAL: A GAME PLAN FOR LEGAL RESEARCH AND ANALYSIS 116–18 (2d ed. 1986).

erwise affected by legislative action. These fields will also provide citations to the session laws that implemented the changes. Although any such changes will already have been incorporated into the online text of the statute, you still might want to check the corresponding session laws that effected the changes to see whether the session laws contain material (such as a preamble or statement of legislative intent) that was not incorporated into the code version of the statute.

Figure 12.52 shows a credit field that includes a representative statement of legislative changes.

Sometimes, references to the repeal of a statute or a subsection of a statute will appear in the "text" field of that statute.

Legislative service databases and UPDATE in WESTLAW. All of the statutory codes in WESTLAW have a corresponding legislative service database containing newly passed legislation (*i.e.*, slip laws). A jurisdiction's current legislative service database contains, among other things, the text of changes made to statutes, constitutions, and (in some states) court rules during the current calendar year. When a change to one of these types of authorities occurs in a jurisdiction, WESTLAW adds to that jurisdiction's legislative service database the document containing the text of the change; subsequently,

```
CA BUS & PROF  §  6322.1        R 4 OF 8          P 4 OF 6          CA-ST         Page
 TEXT

 not exceed the monetary jurisdiction of small claims court.
  (c) Notwithstanding the provisions of any other section, any increase or
 decrease in costs of law library fees in any county shall not be effective
 until January 1 of the year next following adoption by the board of supervisors
 or the law library board of trustees of the increase or decrease, except that
 any fee increase adopted by a board of supervisors in 1990 in accordance with
 subdivision (a) or (b) may be immediately implemented in accordance with the
 resolution of the board of supervisors.

                          1990 Main Volume Credit(s)

 (Added by Stats.1947, c. 932, p. 2156, § 1.  Amended by Stats.1957, c. 86, p.
 664, § 1;  Stats.1961, c. 39, p. 947, § 1;  Stats.1968, c. 199, p. 493, § 1;
 Stats.1972, c. 890, p. 1585, § 1;  Stats.1974, c. 647, p. 1510, § 1;
 Stats.1980, c. 64, p. 171, § 1.)

                          1993 Pocket Part Credit(s)

 (Amended by Stats.1990, c. 56 (S.B.1609), § 1, eff. April 20, 1990.)
```

"credit" field

Source: West Publishing Company © 1993

Figure 12.52. Typical "Credit" Field Showing Statement of Legislative Changes in a WESTLAW Statutory Code Provision

WESTLAW merges the contents of a current legislative service database into the corresponding statutory code database.

In effect, WESTLAW provides legislative service databases to update online statutory codes between recompilations just as a publisher of a printed statutory code updates the code between recompilations by providing pocket parts, supplements, and a legislative advance sheet service (a supplemental publication containing slip laws issued between pocket parts).[375]

At the federal level, the US-PL database is the legislative service database corresponding to the *United States Code*. At the state level, a legislative service database is designated by a jurisdiction's postal abbreviation and the suffix "-LEGIS," such as "CA-LEGIS" for the California legislative service database. The frequency with which documents are added to legislative service databases varies from jurisdiction to jurisdiction (*e.g.*, weekly, or within 30 days after new legislation is enacted). But all legislative service databases serve the same purpose.

At the end of each calendar year, WESTLAW transfers documents from the current legislative service database into an historical legislative service database with a year appended as part of the database name. For instance, in connection with New York statutes, at the end of 1989, WESTLAW transferred NY-LEGIS documents into an historical database designated as NY-LEGIS89. NY-LEGIS then remained empty until WESTLAW began adding new slip laws passed in 1990.

Using a legislative service database and UPDATE in WESTLAW. You can use a legislative service database in any of several ways to update a statute:

- If you know the citation of a slip law that has affected the statute you are updating, you can use the FIND feature to retrieve that slip law if it appears in the current legislative service database for the statutory code containing the statute you are updating.[376] For example, suppose that in December 1992 you had been updating 16 U.S.C. § 1433 and knew that Public Law 102–587 (enacted in November 1992) had affected that statute. You could have retrieved the slip law from US-PL by transmitting the following FIND instruction:

  ```
  fi uspl 102-587
  ```

  After checking the slip law, using standard WESTLAW techniques for moving within a document,[377] you could have transmitted **gb**

[375] Examples of legislative advance sheet services include *United States Code Congressional and Administrative News* ("USCCAN") and the advance pamphlets for the *United States Code Service*.

[376] For a refresher on FIND, see pages 279–84.

[377] Pages 360–63 explain these techniques.

to go back to the point in your research at which you transmitted your FIND instruction.

As an alternative to using FIND, you can also retrieve an updating slip law by searching for its citation in the "citation" field of the appropriate current legislative service database. So, in the preceding example, you could have retrieved the slip law by transmitting the following search request in the US-PL database:

```
ci(102-587)
```

- If you do not know the citation of a relevant slip law, you can retrieve a document from a legislative service database by using the UPDATE feature. While viewing a statutory code provision you want to update, you might see a message along these lines at the top of the screen:

```
This document has been amended.
Use > UPDATE to retrieve the
amending document(s).
```

An UPDATE message like this indicates that the current legislative service database corresponding to the code database contains at least one slip law that has affected the statute you are viewing. You can transmit **update** to retrieve any updating slip laws, the changes in which will not yet have been incorporated into the statute. Alternatively, you can retrieve the updating material by using the JUMP feature: press the TAB key to position the cursor under the JUMP marker (the ">" symbol or triangle) in front of "UPDATE" in the message, and then press ENTER. After retrieving the updating material, you can view it, using standard WESTLAW techniques for moving within and between documents.[378] After checking the updating material, you can resume viewing the statute by typing **gb** (for "go back") and pressing ENTER.

- Sometimes, a document in a legislative service database affects a statutory code provision, but WESTLAW has not established an UPDATE linkage between the two documents. In that situation, you cannot retrieve the slip law by transmitting **update** while viewing the affected statute. The monitor will display a message that although UPDATE found no documents, the legislative service database might contain documents affecting the statute. If this occurs, you can use a legislative service database in another way to verify the current text of your statute: gain access to the current

[378] Pages 360–67 explain these techniques.

legislative service database, then search the database for references to your statute.

In most legislative service databases, WESTLAW editorially enhances slip laws, notably by adding to a slip law's "citation" field cross-references to statutory code provisions affected by the slip law. Such a cross-reference will display on the monitor at the point where the slip law's text affects a statutory provision. Figure 12.53 illustrates this enhancement, showing a cross-reference to 5 U.S.C.A. § 1201 embedded in Public Law 101-12. You can locate this kind of cross-reference by restricting your search to the "citation" field in a legislative service database. For example, to locate slip laws affecting 5 U.S.C. § 1201, you could transmit a search request like one of these in the US-PL database:

```
ci(5 pre/20 1201)

ci(5 +s 1201)
```

The choice of connectors in these search requests is designed to increase the likelihood of retrieving slip laws in which the cross-

```
PL 101-12, 1989 S 20        R 1 OF 1        P 3 OF 59      US-PL89        Page
  Sec. 2
(Cite as: 103 Stat 16)
  make disclosures described in such section 2302(b)(8)) from reprisal.
   (b) Purpose.--The purpose of this Act is to strengthen and improve protection
 for the rights of Federal employees, to prevent reprisals, and to help
 eliminate wrongdoing within the Government by--
   (1) mandating that employees should not suffer adverse consequences as a
  result of prohibited personnel practices;  and
   (2) establishing--
    (A) that the primary role of the Office of Special Counsel is to protect
   employees, especially whistleblowers, from prohibited personnel practices;
    (B) that the Office of Special Counsel shall act in the interests of
   employees who seek assistance from the Office of Special Counsel;  and
    (C) that while disciplining those who commit prohibited personnel practices
   may be used as a means by which to help accomplish that goal, the protection
   of individuals who are the subject of prohibited personnel practices remains
   the paramount consideration.

                         << 5 USCA § 1201 >>  ]— a typical cross-reference

 SEC. 3. MERIT SYSTEMS PROTECTION BOARD;  OFFICE OF SPECIAL COUNSEL;  INDIVIDUAL
   RIGHT OF ACTION.
```

Source: West Publishing Company © 1993

Figure 12.53. Typical Cross-Reference in a Slip Law in a WESTLAW Legislative Service Database (US-PL) to a Statutory Code Provision Affected by the Slip Law

reference to the statute being updated appears in a string citation, as in this example:

```
<< 15 USCA §§ 3311, 3312, 3313,
3314, 3315, 3316, 3317, 3318,
3319, 3320, 3331, 3332, 3333 >>
```

To retrieve slip laws that have not been editorially enhanced with embedded citations to affected sections, you can also perform an unrestricted search for statutory references appearing anywhere in a legislative service database. Thus, to update 5 U.S.C. § 1201, you could transmit the following search request in the US-PL database:

```
5 w/10 (1201 or s1201)
```

You might also want to conduct a broader search for references to multiple sections in the chapter or title of which the section you are updating is a part, especially if searching for just that section does not retrieve any documents. The legislature might have repealed or otherwise affected a range of sections, or even an entire chapter, without referring to the specific section you want to update. In anticipation of this possibility in connection with, say, section 43A.14 of the Minnesota statutes, you could carry out searches along these lines in the MN-LEGIS database:

```
43A.1! or s43A.1!

43A! or s43A!
```

As you search legislative service databases for references to statutory code provisions you are updating, keep in mind a potential and unpredictable obstacle to comprehensiveness. Legislatures (especially Congress) sometimes modify statutes without referring to the codified versions. Instead, a legislature might modify a code provision by referring to and modifying an earlier session law that affected the code provision. In this situation, searching for a reference to the code provision will fail to locate the change.

Short of tediously including in your search request various terms representing each session law that conceivably could have affected the code provision you are updating, your best course is to check cross-reference tables found in printed legislative advance sheet services that update printed versions of statutory codes. Although some delay inevitably occurs between the passage of a slip law and the publication of a legislative advance sheet, this printed updating tool will often correlate modifications of earlier session laws with their code counterparts sooner than UPDATE will link those changes with the corresponding code provisions in statutory code databases.

- Finally, you can use a legislative service database by searching for words relevant to the statute you are updating. Regardless of whether a legislature has directly affected the language of the statute you want to update, the legislature might have affected another statute that interacts with, and thus indirectly affects, your statute. This situation can occur, for instance, when a legislature changes a statute containing a definition that applies in numerous other statutes in the code. To determine whether a statute has been indirectly affected by legislative action, you can select key words or phrases reflecting the statute's subject matter and search for references to those words or phrases in the corresponding legislative service database.

Summary of using legislative service databases and UPDATE to update statutes in WESTLAW. Figure 12.54 on pages 618–19 summarizes the techniques for bringing statutes up to date by using legislative service databases and the UPDATE feature.

Other tips for updating administrative regulations through WESTLAW

As researchers familiar with the administrative-law arena will know, administrative agencies frequently change, rescind, or propose to change or rescind the text of their regulations. When an agency does so at the federal level and in many states, it publishes the change, rescission, or proposal in an administrative register (such as the *Federal Register*, issued daily by the federal government to update federal regulations). A change or rescission that appears in an administrative register supersedes the text in the corresponding administrative code (as well as any previous modifications published in the administrative register). An administrative register thus serves as a noncumulative update that keeps the corresponding administrative code current between its periodic recompilations.

Just as you need to update the text of regulations in printed administrative codes by checking administrative registers, you need to update the text of regulations you find online.[379] A reference to an administrative regulation in

[379] For a description of using printed administrative registers to update printed administrative codes, see CHRISTOPHER G. WREN & JILL R. WREN, THE LEGAL RESEARCH MANUAL: A GAME PLAN FOR LEGAL RESEARCH AND ANALYSIS 115–16 (2d ed. 1986).

even a recent case or other authority might not reflect the most up-to-date text of the regulation; the provision might have subsequently been revised or rescinded, for example. Even the regulation itself in an administrative code database might not have incorporated recent changes made by the promulgating agency.

To get an idea of how much updating lies ahead, start by ascertaining when changes were most recently incorporated into the online text of an administrative regulation. To do that, use the "scope" command: if you are in an administrative code database containing the regulation you want to update, simply type `scope` (or `sc`) and press ENTER; otherwise, type `scope` (or `sc`) followed by the name of an administrative code database containing the regulation, then press ENTER.[380] The monitor will display a description of the database, including the date of the online version of the code. Changes made before the date indicated in the scope description will already have been incorporated into the online text of the administrative code provision you are updating.

Along with ascertaining the recency of updates to an administrative code provision, you can use the following WESTLAW features to discover changes made by administrative agencies. Because WESTLAW offers access (at this writing) to only six state administrative codes and three state administrative registers, most of the remaining discussion of online updating of regulations focuses on federal regulations. You can update existing online state administrative materials, however, by adapting the techniques used to update federal regulations. As WESTLAW continues to add state administrative codes and registers, the same techniques will likely work there as well.

The "credit," "superior-feature," and "notes" fields in administrative code databases in WESTLAW. In a document in a state administrative code database, the "credit" field, the "superior-feature" field (if available), and sometimes the "notes" field contain information about the history of changes to the code provision; in a document in a *Code of Federal Regulations* database (such as CFR, FCIV-CFR, or FFIN-CFR), the "credit" field contains this information. In a state administrative code database, the "credit" and "superior-feature" fields will sometimes provide a citation to the state administrative register document that implemented the change; in a CFR database, the "credit" field will provide a citation to the *Federal Register* document that implemented the change. Although any such changes will already have been incorporated into the online text of the code provision you are updating, you still might want to check the corresponding administrative register document

[380] Many WESTLAW databases in addition to the CFR database contain provisions from the *Code of Federal Regulations*. See page 271. For example, civil rights regulations also appear in the FCIV-CFR database, and financial services regulations in the FFIN-CFR database.

If you want to	Follow this procedure in WESTLAW

Retrieve a slip law when you know its citation, if the slip law appears in a current legislative service database	type `find` (or `fi`) followed by the citation of the slip law; then press ENTER
	Example: To retrieve Public Law 102-587 so long as it appears in the US-PL database, transmit
	`fi uspl 102-587`
	or
	search for the citation in the citation field of the appropriate current legislative service database
	Example: To retrieve Public Law 102-587 so long as it appears in the US-PL database, transmit
	`ci(102-587)`

Return to the screen you were viewing before you invoked FIND	type `gb` and press ENTER

Retrieve slip laws that have affected the statutory code provision you are viewing	type `update` and press ENTER
Return, after using UPDATE, to the statutory code provision you were viewing	type `gb` and press ENTER

Retrieve slip laws that have affected the statutory code provision you are updating if UPDATE is unavailable or when you do not want to use UPDATE	gain access to the appropriate current legislative service database and search for references to the statutory code provision
	Example: To retrieve from the US-PL database slip laws affecting 5 U.S.C. § 1201, transmit a request along these lines:
	`ci(5 pre/20 1201)`
	`ci(5 +s 1201)`
	`5 w/10 (1201 or s1201)`

Retrieve slip laws that might have indirectly affected the statutory code provision you are updating	gain access to the appropriate current legislative service database and search for key words or phrases reflecting the subject matter of the statutory code provision

Figure 12.54. Quick Guide to Updating Statutes Through WESTLAW Legislative Service Databases and the UPDATE Feature

to see whether it contains material (such as an administrative agency's response to public comments about the provision) that did not make it into the text of the code provision.

Figure 12.55 shows a "credit" field that includes a representative statement of agency changes.

To discover changes that have *not* yet been incorporated into the online version of an administrative code, you can use the following techniques.

Updating by using FIND to retrieve a known administrative register document in WESTLAW. If you know the citation of a *Federal Register* document that updates a *Code of Federal Regulations* provision, you can retrieve the document with a FIND instruction. For example, if you know that a document published at 55 Fed. Reg. 3546 affects the *Code of Federal Regulations* provision you are updating, you can retrieve the document by transmitting the following instruction:

```
fi 55 fr 3546
```

After checking the document, you can type `gb` (for "go back") and press ENTER to return to the screen you were viewing before you invoked FIND.

Using UPDATE to retrieve administrative register documents in WESTLAW. If you are viewing a provision in a *Code of Federal Regulations* database, you can retrieve *Federal Register* documents updating that provision: type `update` and press ENTER. The computer will retrieve pertinent *Federal Register* documents issued since West last updated (by incorporating changes published in the *Federal Register*) the online version of the *C.F.R.* title containing the provision you are updating. After checking the updating documents from the *Federal Register*, you can resume viewing your *C.F.R.* provision by typing `gb` (for "go back") and pressing ENTER.

Although the UPDATE feature simplifies the task of updating regulations, UPDATE has a couple limitations. First, the documents UPDATE retrieves might not be as recent as the documents you could retrieve by searching in the FR database (as explained below). UPDATE relies on linkages created between *C.F.R.* provisions and *Federal Register* documents when West editors add to *Federal Register* documents cross-references to *C.F.R.* provisions affected by those documents; because of the quantity of *Federal Register* documents, it can take West editors several weeks to establish the UPDATE linkages for federal regulations. By contrast, West updates the FR database daily. Second, UPDATE just retrieves *Federal Register* documents (such as final rules) that change the text of *C.F.R.* provisions; UPDATE does not retrieve *Federal Register* documents (such as proposed rules or notices of hearings) that might prove useful in ascertaining a regulation's current or projected status.

```
Citation              Rank(R)          Page(P)          Database        Mode
49 CFR s 391.1        R 1 OF 1         P 1 OF 2         CFR             Page
 49 C.F.R. s 391.1

                        CODE OF FEDERAL REGULATIONS
                         TITLE 49--TRANSPORTATION
             SUBTITLE B--OTHER REGULATIONS RELATING TO TRANSPORTATION
     CHAPTER III--FEDERAL HIGHWAY ADMINISTRATION, DEPARTMENT OF TRANSPORTATION
              SUBCHAPTER B--FEDERAL MOTOR CARRIER SAFETY REGULATIONS

                    PART 391--QUALIFICATIONS OF DRIVERS
                            SUBPART A--GENERAL

 s 391.1 Scope of the rules in this part;  additional qualifications;  duties of
   carrier-drivers.

  (a) The rules in this part establish minimum qualifications for persons who
 drive motor vehicles as, for, or on behalf of motor carriers.  The rules in
 this part also establish minimum duties of motor carriers with respect to the
 qualifications of their drivers.
  (b) A motor carrier who employs himself as a driver must comply with both the
 rules in this part that apply to motor carriers and the rules in this part that
 apply to drivers.
```

```
49 CFR s 391.1        R 1 OF 1         P 2 OF 2         CFR             Page

 [53 FR 18057, May 19, 1988]

                    PART 391--QUALIFICATIONS OF DRIVERS

  Authority: 49 U.S.C. App. 2505;  49 U.S.C. 504 and 3102;  49 CFR 1.48.

  Source:  35 FR 6460, Apr. 22, 1970;  39 FR 32561, Sept. 9, 1974;  51 FR 12621,
 April 14, 1986;  51 FR 17571, May 13, 1986;  53 FR 18056, May 19, 1988;  54 FR
 7191, Feb. 17, 1989, unless otherwise noted.

 49 C. F. R. s 391.1
 49 CFR s 391.1
END OF DOCUMENT
```

"credit" field (bracketing "[53 FR 18057, May 19, 1988]")

"credit" field (bracketing the Authority and Source lines)

Source: West Publishing Company © 1993

Figure 12.55. Typical "Credit" Field Summary of Changes Made to a *Code of Federal Regulations* Provision in WESTLAW

Consequently, when you update federal regulations, UPDATE does not eliminate the need to search the FR database, using the following techniques.

Updating through the "prelim" field in the *Federal Register* database in WESTLAW. If you do not know the citation of a *Federal Register* document that updates a *Code of Federal Regulations* provision, or if you want to supplement your use of the UPDATE feature, you can search either a printed or online version of the *Federal Register* to determine whether an agency has affected the text of the regulation.[381] To do this updating in WESTLAW, you would search in the FR database with a search request designed to retrieve documents that have affected the regulation since the last revision. The "prelim" field (abbreviated "pr") in documents in the FR database facilitates this search. Among other things, this field cross-references the *Federal Register* document to the *Code of Federal Regulations* by providing a citation to the *C.F.R.* title number and part number containing the regulation affected by the *Federal Register* document. (The "prelim" field also specifies the nature of the *Federal Register* document, identifies the issuing agency and any sub-agency, lists agency docket numbers related to the document, and provides other miscellaneous information relevant to the document.) Figure 12.56 shows the portion of a typical "prelim" field that contains the cross-reference to the *C.F.R.*

Suppose you want to ascertain the current text of 49 C.F.R. § 391.15, and the version of the regulation you have was last revised as of October 1, 1988. Transmitting a search request like one of these in the FR database would retrieve *Federal Register* documents affecting the regulation since that date:

```
pr(49 pre/20 391) and (391.15 or s391.15) and
date(aft september 1988)

pr(49 +s 391) and (391.15 or s391.15) and
date(aft september 1988)
```

The "prelim" field restriction in this search request ensures the search will retrieve *Federal Register* documents affecting only the *C.F.R.* title and part number in which your regulation appears. The choice of connectors in the "prelim" field restriction is designed to increase the likelihood of retrieving *Federal Register* documents in which the "prelim" field's cross-reference to the regulation being updated appears in a string citation, as in this example:

```
49 CFR Parts 106, 107, 171, 172, 173,
174, 175, 176, 177, 178, 179, and 180
```

[381] For a brief explanation of updating the *C.F.R.* using printed updating materials, see CHRISTOPHER G. WREN & JILL R. WREN, THE LEGAL RESEARCH MANUAL: A GAME PLAN FOR LEGAL RESEARCH AND ANALYSIS 114–16 (2d ed. 1986).

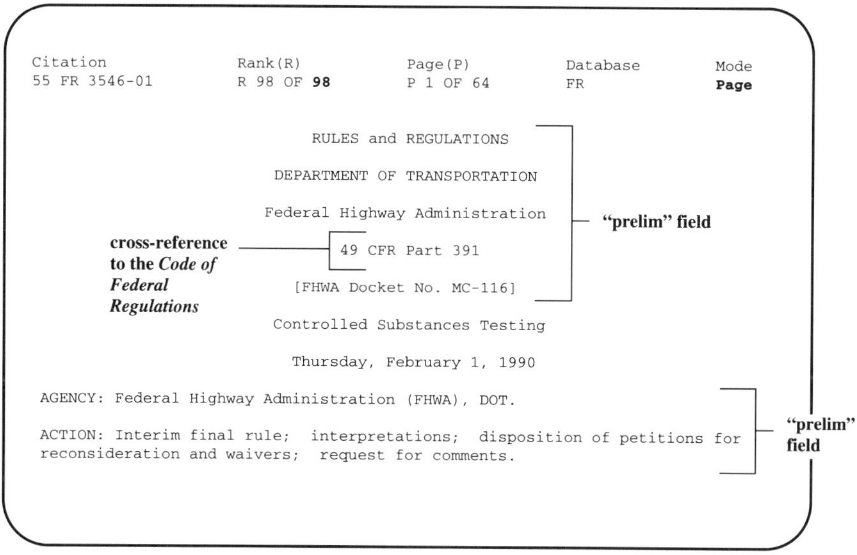

Source: West Publishing Company © 1993

Figure 12.56. Portion of a Typical "Prelim" Field in the FR Database in WESTLAW Showing a Cross-Reference to the *Code of Federal Regulations*

Because the "prelim" field does not cite to section numbers, the search request also includes an unrestricted search for the section number, which will normally appear somewhere in the text of a *Federal Register* document affecting the section. Lastly, the illustrative search request includes a date restriction: because the FR database (at this time) contains *Federal Register* documents dating back to July 1980, the date restriction ensures that retrieved documents will have been issued since the last revision of the regulation you are updating.

You might also want to conduct a broader search for references to the *C.F.R.* part in which the section you are updating is found, especially if a search for just that section does not retrieve any documents. An agency might have repealed or otherwise affected a range of sections, or even an entire *C.F.R.* part, without referring to the specific section you want to update. In anticipation of this possibility in connection with 49 C.F.R. § 391.15, you could carry out searches along these lines in the FR database:

```
pr(49 pre/5 391) and (391.1! or s391.1!) and
date(aft september 1988)

pr(49 pre/5 391) and date(aft september 1988)
```

Using the FR database in WESTLAW to identify indirect changes to federal administrative regulations. Finally, you can use the FR database to determine whether an agency has indirectly affected the text of a regulation you want to update. For instance, an agency might change a regulation containing a definition that applies in numerous other regulations in the *Code of Federal Regulations*. To determine whether a regulation has been indirectly affected by agency action, you can select key words or phrases reflecting the regulation's subject matter and search for references to those words or phrases in the FR database.

Similarly, a *Federal Register* document might include agency commentary citing the regulation you are updating even though the document itself does not modify your regulation (and the "prelim" field therefore does not contain a reference to the *C.F.R.* title and part numbers of your regulation). To retrieve documents of this sort, you could omit a "prelim" field restriction and search for the title and part numbers anywhere in a *Federal Register* document. Your search request would take this form:

```
(49 pre/5 391) and (391.15 or s391.15) and
date(aft september 1988)
```

Summary of using the FR database to update federal administrative regulations in WESTLAW. Figure 12.57 summarizes the techniques for updating federal administrative regulations through FR.

Updating through specialized and nonlegal databases in WESTLAW

WESTLAW provides access to a wide assortment of databases that highlight current activities in specialized areas of law (*e.g.*, banking, securities, tax, labor, environmental regulation, international trade). These specialized online materials often identify the most recent federal and state cases, statutes, and administrative regulations and decisions relevant to specific areas of practice. Many of these specialized databases (such as Commerce Clearing House's *Tax Day: State* or the Bureau of National Affairs' *Environment Reporter*) consist of online versions of printed publications. Others (such as BNA's *Banking Daily* and *International Trade Daily*) appear only online. All of these specialized materials are updated regularly—often weekly, sometimes daily or even three times a day.

If you are updating an authority in an area of law for which a specialized database exists, you can search the specialized online materials for recent developments that have affected your authority. This technique is analogous to updating through printed looseleaf reporter services.[382]

[382] *See* CHRISTOPHER G. WREN & JILL R. WREN, THE LEGAL RESEARCH MANUAL: A GAME PLAN FOR LEGAL RESEARCH AND ANALYSIS 118–19 (2d ed. 1986).

If you want to	Follow this procedure in WESTLAW
Retrieve a *Federal Register* document when you know its citation	type `find` (or `fi`) followed by the citation of the *Federal Register* document; then press ENTER *Example:* To retrieve 55 Fed. Reg. 3546, transmit `fi 55 fr 3546`
Return to the screen you were viewing before you invoked FIND	type `gb` and press ENTER
Use UPDATE to retrieve *Federal Register* documents that have affected the *Code of Federal Regulations* provision you are viewing	type `update` and press ENTER
Return, after using UPDATE, to the *Code of Federal Regulations* provision you were viewing	type `gb` and press ENTER

Retrieve *Federal Register* documents that have affected the *Code of Federal Regulations* provision you are updating if UPDATE is unavailable or when you do not want to use UPDATE	gain access to the FR database and search the "prelim" field for references to the *C.F.R.* title and part number containing the provision
	Example: To retrieve *Federal Register* documents affecting 49 C.F.R. § 391.15, gain access to FR and transmit a search request along these lines:
	`pr(49 +s 391) and (391.15 or s391.15)`
	`pr(49 +s 391) and (391.1! or s391.1!)`

Retrieve *Federal Register* documents that might have indirectly affected the *Code of Federal Regulations* provision you are updating	gain access to the FR database and search for key words or phrases reflecting the subject matter of the provision

Figure 12.57. Quick Guide to Updating Federal Administrative Regulations Through the WESTLAW *Federal Register* Database and the UPDATE Feature

When you update through specialized databases in WESTLAW (just as when you update through printed looseleaf reporters), you might find, for example, that an administrative agency rescinded the regulation you are updating or that a court invalidated a federal statute that served as the model for the state statute you are updating. To update in a specialized database, transmit a WESTLAW-as-citator search request based on the citation of your authority (see pages 564–65 and 570–96) or on key words reflecting the subject matter of the authority you are updating (see Chapter 7).

To determine whether a specialized database covers the subject of the authority you want to update, check the printed *Database List*, *WESTLAW DataBasics*,[383] or the online WESTLAW Directory. The *WESTLAW DataBasics* descriptions of specialized databases also offer tips for searching the databases, including whether special commands apply.[384]

For some research projects, you might want to extend your updating search to nonlegal database services such as DIALOG and VU/TEXT, which are available through "gateway" connections in WESTLAW. "Gateway" database services offer online access to numerous non-law publications, such as *The New York Times*, *The Washington Post*, the *National Journal*, and *Business Week*, that often cover current developments in the law.[385] The *Database List*, *WESTLAW DataBasics*, and the online WESTLAW Directory provide additional information about gateway services.

Updating through WESTLAW's Highlights and Bulletin databases

WESTLAW offers several databases containing editor-prepared summaries of selected cases, statutes, and administrative materials recently added to WESTLAW. Because summaries are added at least daily, you can use these databases to identify significant new developments that might have affected your research. Currently, these databases include:

- WESTLAW Bulletin (WLB), which contains summaries of recent state and federal authorities on a range of topics
- WESTLAW Supreme Court Bulletin (WLB-SCT), which contains summaries of recent actions taken by the U.S. Supreme Court

[383] West Publishing Company, WESTLAW DataBasics (1993).

[384] For example, in some specialized databases, you can use the "read" command to view the most recent documents, or the "list" command to view the headlines of those documents. In addition, in some specialized databases, you do not initially retrieve documents by transmitting a search request: as soon as you gain access to the database, the most recent document will automatically display; if you want to run a search request, you type s and press ENTER. *See* West Publishing Company, WESTLAW Reference Manual 128–29 (5th ed. 1993).

[385] For more about searching in nonlegal databases, see Chapter 13.

- WESTLAW State Bulletin databases (identified by "WSB-" followed by a state's postal abbreviation), which contain summaries of recent developments in a particular state's law
- WESTLAW Topical Highlights databases (identified by the prefix "WTH-"), which contain summaries of recent authorities in particular areas of law. For example, WTH-MDML covers medical malpractice, WTH-ENV covers environmental law, and WTH-PL covers products liability. To see whether a Topical Highlights database covers the subject of the authority you want to update, check the printed *Database List*, *WESTLAW DataBasics*, or the online WESTLAW Directory.

The *WESTLAW DataBasics* descriptions of the WESTLAW Highlights and Bulletin databases also offer tips for searching these databases, including whether special commands apply.[386]

Updating through the Personal Directory of Queries ("PDQ") in WESTLAW

For research projects that might last several days, weeks, months, or even years, you will often want to update your research by repeating search requests that yielded useful results. If you develop a successful search request you think you will want to repeat, you can avoid reformulating and retyping it each time if you use WESTLAW's Personal Directory of Queries ("PDQ") to save the request for later use. In addition to saving your search so you can run it whenever you choose, PDQ can also operate as a clipping service in any WESTLAW database that has an "added date" field (explained in Figure 12.49 on page 599). As a clipping service, PDQ will automatically repeat your search at specified intervals, looking for just those documents that have been added to WESTLAW since the last time you ran the search through PDQ.

For example, suppose you are involved in protracted litigation in which a federal administrative regulation plays a critical role. Say that on October 10, you updated the regulation by running a search request in the *Federal Register* database (FR). Because you want to check periodically for changes in the text of the regulation, you could save the search request in PDQ. A week later, PDQ could run the request again to see if any changes have occurred since October 10. You could also use PDQ to save requests for searching, say, case-law files for recent federal court decisions interpreting or otherwise affecting the regulation.

[386] *See* WEST PUBLISHING COMPANY, WESTLAW DATABASICS 670, 673, 674 (1993).

As you use PDQ to update research results, keep in mind the updating schedule for the databases in which you are running your searches. It makes no sense, for example, to run the same PDQ search daily in a database updated only weekly or monthly.

Because natural-language search requests do not operate well for updating (see pages 583–84), the following discussion focuses on saving Boolean (terms-and-connectors) search requests in PDQ. If you want to use PDQ with a natural-language request, you transmit the same PDQ commands used with Boolean requests. At this writing, however, the PDQ natural-language screens do not offer the opportunity afforded by PDQ terms-and-connectors screens to instruct PDQ to repeat your search automatically.

Setting up a search request in PDQ in WESTLAW. Start by invoking PDQ:

1. Type pdq.

2. Press ENTER. If you do not have any search requests currently saved in PDQ, the monitor will display the "Welcome to PDQ" screen (Figure 12.58). If you do have search requests currently saved in PDQ, the monitor will display a directory of saved PDQ search requests. Figure 12.59 shows a typical PDQ Directory.

```
                       Welcome to PDQ
              Your Personal Directory of Queries
There are no entries in your Personal Directory of Queries.

PDQ allows you to create or save queries for use at a later date.  PDQ also
allows you to run queries automatically on a regular basis.  Results will be
delivered to the destination you specify.  The PDQ Directory lists the queries
you have saved in the order in which you added them.

Each query is numbered sequentially.  You may view a PDQ entry by entering its
number or name.

Each entry name can be up to ten characters long.  An entry name cannot contain
a semicolon (;).  For example, MONOPOLY and MONOPOLY1 are valid entry names,
but MONOPOLY;1 and ANTIMONOPOLY are not valid entry names.


If you wish to:
   Add your most recent query to PDQ, type ADD and press ENTER
   Create a query to save in PDQ, type CREATE and press ENTER
   Go back to the previously accessed service, type GB and press ENTER
   Receive further information on PDQ, type HELP and press ENTER
```

Source: West Publishing Company © 1993

Figure 12.58. Welcome Screen for WESTLAW'S Personal Directory of Queries (PDQ)

```
                              PDQ DIRECTORY                      Only Page

Entry Name        Database         Query                            Next Run
   1 PLUMBING     OH-CS            (APARTMENT W/10 LEASE) & (P...   REQUEST
   2 ELECTRIC     OH-CS            (APARTMENT W/10 LEASE) & (P...   REQUEST
   3 HOUSE        OH-CS            ((APARTMENT    HOUSE) W/5 L...   REQUEST
   4              ALLFEDS          (LEWIS W/5 ("UNITED STATES"...   REQUEST




 If you wish to:
   Add your most recent query, type ADD and press ENTER
   Add a query without first running it, type CREATE and press ENTER
   View an entry, type its number and press ENTER
   View the list of PDQ commands, type CMDS and press ENTER
   Go back to the previously accessed service, type GB and press ENTER
```

Source: West Publishing Company © 1993

Figure 12.59. Sample PDQ Directory in WESTLAW

If you change your mind at this point and decide you do not want to save your search request, type **gb** (for "go back") and press ENTER.

After invoking PDQ, the steps for saving a search request in PDQ differ slightly, depending on whether you want PDQ to "add" a search request (*i.e.*, to save the search you most recently performed in WESTLAW) or whether you want PDQ to "create" a search request (*i.e.*, to save a search you have not just performed):

1. If your most recent search request yielded satisfactory results and you want to save the request in PDQ for future use, type **add** and press ENTER.

   If you want to set up a search request in PDQ without running the search immediately before saving it as a PDQ entry, type **create tc** to create a Boolean (terms-and-connectors) search request, then press ENTER.[387] Alternatively, you can transmit just **create**; the computer will select the search method (terms-and-connectors or natural-language) designated in your WESTLAW

[387] If you wanted to create a plain-English search request using the WESTLAW natural-language feature, you could transmit **create nat**.

Options Directory or, if you have already searched WESTLAW during your online session, the search method you used in your most recent search.

After you transmit an "add" instruction, the monitor will display screens like those in Figure 12.60. As the figure indicates, transmitting **add** reads your most recent search request into PDQ, reads in the name of the database in which you most recently performed the search, and reads in choices about how PDQ will perform the search and display the results (such as how frequently PDQ will repeat the search).

After you transmit a "create" instruction to save a new search, the monitor will display screens similar to those in Figure 12.60. The computer will read in to your PDQ entry less information, though, than when you transmit "add" to save your most recent search.

2. At the screen like that in Figure 12.60, type the instructions you want the computer to follow when it runs your PDQ search and displays the results.

   If you are adding an existing search request to PDQ and do not want to make any changes to the instructions in your PDQ entry, simply type **pdq** and press ENTER. The monitor will display the PDQ Directory with your newly saved search listed as an entry.

   If you need to supply missing instructions for your PDQ entry, or if you want to modify instructions, you can do so at this point. Note that you move the cursor from one section of the screen to another by using the TAB key, either after typing instructions in some part of your entry or to skip past some part of the entry you do not want to change.

   To see information about the options available for some aspect of the PDQ entry (such as the format options for displaying results of the search), use the HOME or TAB key to move the cursor to the upper left corner of the screen. There, type the number corresponding to the option in which you're interested (*e.g.*, **9** in Figure 12.60 to see information about display formats), then press ENTER.

   You can type instructions about your PDQ search in any numbered area of the screen shown in Figure 12.60. For example:

   - You can name your search, if you want. The PDQ Directory displays saved search requests, but a long request might not display in full. If you save several similar requests in PDQ, naming the requests can help you quickly distinguish among PDQ entries when you return to the directory.

```
                         PDQ ENTRY 1                    Page 1 of 2

1. Entry Name:  PLUMBING                           Saved:  12/03/92
2. Database Identifier:  OH-CS                  Last Run:  12/03/92
3. Query:                                 Search Method:  Terms Search
(APARTMENT W/10 LEASE) & (PLUMBING WATER)



4. Added Date: 12/02/92
-------------------------- AUTOMATIC RUN SETTINGS ------------------------------
5. Next Run:
6. Client ID:  ABDUL/ELJOHN RENTALS
7. Frequency:  Upon Request
8. Delivery:   Attached Printer
9. Format:     List of All Citations

                  Press TAB to move the cursor
If you wish to:
   Leave PDQ and run this query, type RUN and press ENTER
   View available choices for a setting, type its number and press ENTER
   View a different page, type P followed by its number and press ENTER
   View your PDQ Directory, type PDQ and press ENTER
```

```
                         PDQ ENTRY 1                    Page 2 of 2
10. Automatic Update:  On
11. Ranking:  Database Default
12. Star Paging:  On
13. Maximum Lines Per Query:  2500
14. Restrict the Display of the Result to Specific Fields:

15. Locate Terms:




16. Comments:




                  Press TAB to move the cursor
If you wish to:
   Leave PDQ and run this query, type RUN and press ENTER
   View available choices for a setting, type its number and press ENTER
   View a different page, type P followed by its number and press ENTER
   View your PDQ Directory, type PDQ and press ENTER
```

Source: West Publishing Company © 1993

Figure 12.60. Sample Screens for Setting Up, Editing, Performing, or Deleting a PDQ Terms-and Connectors Search in WESTLAW

To name a request in PDQ, type the name on the line labelled "Entry Name."

- To identify the database in which to run the search request, type the name of the database on the line labelled "Database Identifier."
- Type your search request, or changes to it, in the section labelled "Query."
- The lines labelled "Added Date" and "Automatic Update" work in tandem as a mechanism for targeting your PDQ search on documents recently added to WESTLAW.

  If you leave "Automatic Update" unchanged at its default setting, which is "on," the computer will automatically supply a date on the line labelled "Added Date." The computer will use that date in an "added date" field restriction to focus the next PDQ search on documents added to WESTLAW since the PDQ search was last performed. (Figure 12.49 on page 599 explains the "added date" field.) Because the computer selects a date for the "added date" restriction one day earlier than the date the PDQ search was last performed, the restriction ensures your PDQ search results will include any documents that might have been added on the same day the search was last run, but that were added after the search was run. Also, with "Automatic Update" set at "on," the computer will automatically update the "added date" each time PDQ runs your search.

  In short, you will normally want to leave the "Automatic Update" setting at "on" and let the computer automatically supply a date for the "Added Date" line. This way, your PDQ searches will just retrieve recently added documents.
- You can change the interval at which PDQ will repeat your search (*e.g.*, daily, weekly, monthly, upon request). Use the HOME or TAB key to move the cursor to the upper left corner of the screen. There, type the number corresponding to the line labelled "Frequency" and press ENTER to display a list of available intervals. From the list, you can select a new updating interval by transmitting its identification number. If you select an interval other than "upon request," the computer will insert a date on the line labelled "Next Run."
- If you want to change the date on which the computer will next run your PDQ search, type the new date on the line labelled "Next Run." If you subsequently change the interval at which you want PDQ to repeat your search, the computer will auto-

matically insert a new "next run" date consistent with the new interval you choose.

- To change the instructions the computer will follow in delivering results of your PDQ search, type your new instructions on the line labelled "Delivery." Destinations to which the computer can send the results will vary depending on the equipment you use. Possible destinations include a printer, a computer disk, or a fax machine. Or, instead of instructing the computer to send results automatically to a specified destination, you can instruct the computer to notify you when you sign on to WESTLAW whether any PDQ searches have retrieved new results.
- You can change several instructions about how the computer will display the results of a PDQ search. Typing a new instruction on the line labelled "Format" will change the display format (*e.g.*, citation list or complete documents). Typing a new instruction on the line labelled "Ranking" will change the order in which retrieved documents will display (*e.g.*, in TERMS order). Typing a new instruction on the line labelled "Star Paging" will change whether star-page numbers (if available) will appear in documents PDQ retrieves. Typing an instruction in the section labelled "Restrict the Display of the Result to Specific Fields" allows you to restrict the display of retrieved documents to selected fields (*e.g.*, headnote, synopsis).
- You can instruct the computer to use the LOCATE feature (explained on pages 367 and 369–71) to isolate a subset of documents retrieved when PDQ automatically runs your search. To do so, type your LOCATE terms in the section labelled "Locate Terms."
- If you want to add reminders to yourself about your PDQ search request, you can type your notes in the section labelled "Comments."

3. At this point, if you change your mind and decide you don't want to save the search request in PDQ, use the HOME or TAB key to move the cursor to the upper left corner of the monitor. Then type **del** (for "delete") and press ENTER.

   If you want to go ahead and save your PDQ entry, you have a couple choices. You can save the search request but remain in PDQ: use the HOME or TAB key to move the cursor to the upper left corner of the monitor, then type **pdq** and press ENTER; the monitor will redisplay the PDQ Directory (Figure 12.59). Alternatively, you can save the search request and simultaneously leave PDQ, using any one of several avenues. Use the HOME or TAB key to move the cursor to the upper left corner of the monitor, then do one of the following:

- Type gb (for "go back") and press ENTER to return to the screen you were viewing before you invoked PDQ.
- Type q and press ENTER if you want to return to WESTLAW's query entry screen (Figure 9.10 or Figure 9.11 on pages 201 and 202).

  The monitor will display the request you just saved in PDQ. At that point, you can run the search request again, edit it and then run it, or transmit a new search request. None of these actions will affect the PDQ version of the saved search request.
- Type s or run and press ENTER if you want to return to WESTLAW and have the saved search request run automatically.

  If you want to run the saved search in a different database, transmit sdb followed by the abbreviation of the new database. The computer will run the search in the new database without affecting the database instruction in your PDQ entry.

Currently, you can save as many as 100 search requests in PDQ. For each request you want to save, repeat the steps above.

Modifying a saved search request through PDQ in WESTLAW. Once you have saved a search request in PDQ, you can modify the request at any time. To do so:

1. Type pdq and press ENTER to display your PDQ Directory (Figure 12.59).
2. Type the name or entry number of the saved search you want to modify, then press ENTER. The monitor will display a screen like that in Figure 12.60, showing the PDQ entry you selected.
3. Use the TAB key to move the cursor to whatever part of the entry you want to modify, then type your changes. For example, you could change the database in which to run the search.
4. Once you have made your changes, use the HOME or TAB key to move the cursor to the upper left corner of the monitor. From there, you can continue your research by following one of the avenues explained earlier in step 3 (beginning on page 633) under "Setting up a search request in PDQ."

Checking the results of a PDQ search in WESTLAW. Whenever PDQ runs a search, the computer delivers the search results in the manner you specified on the "Delivery" line of your PDQ entry screen. For example, for the PDQ search shown in Figure 12.60, the computer will send the search results to an attached printer. Other available destinations, which will vary depending on the equipment you use, include a computer disk or a fax machine.

Instead of instructing the computer to send results automatically to a specified destination, you can instruct the computer to notify you when you sign on to WESTLAW whether any PDQ searches have retrieved new results. To do so, designate "Notify at Sign On" as the "Delivery" option in your PDQ entry. If a PDQ search retrieves new results while that option remains in effect, you will see a message when you log on to WESTLAW informing you that PDQ has new search results available for you to view. To look at these results:

1. Type `pdq` and press ENTER to display your PDQ Directory (Figure 12.59). You will see an arrow pointing to PDQ searches that have retrieved new results.
2. Type `s` or `run` followed by the name or entry number of the PDQ search that retrieved the results you want to view, then press ENTER.

Performing a PDQ search in WESTLAW between scheduled updates. If you choose to have PDQ repeat a search at a specified interval (such as daily, weekly, or monthly) instead of "upon request," you still might want to run that search between the scheduled updating intervals. To carry out an interim search:

1. Type `pdq` and press ENTER to display your PDQ Directory (Figure 12.59).
2. At the directory, type `s` or `run` followed by the name or entry number of the PDQ search you want to run, then press ENTER.

   If you first want to verify that you are selecting the right search, you can transmit the search's name or entry number at the PDQ Directory. The computer will display the PDQ entry for that search. Once you see that you selected the correct search, use the HOME or TAB key to move the cursor to the upper left corner of the monitor; there, type `s` or `run` and press ENTER.

Deleting a saved search request from PDQ in WESTLAW. To delete a search request you have saved in PDQ:

1. Type `pdq` and press ENTER to display your PDQ Directory (Figure 12.59).
2. At the directory, type `del` followed by the name or entry number of the PDQ search you want to delete, then press ENTER. Or, you can delete several PDQ searchcs at once by transmitting their

entry numbers in a single instruction like `del 1,3,5` or `del 1-10`.

If you have multiple entries in your PDQ Directory, deleting an entry will cause the computer to renumber subsequent entries.

A shortcut for typing PDQ commands in WESTLAW. If you want to speed up the transmission of your PDQ commands, you can combine separate commands into a single typed instruction (a technique sometimes called "stacking" commands). When you stack commands, you do not need to wait for the monitor to display screens that would otherwise appear after you transmit individual commands. For instance, when setting up a search request in PDQ, you could transmit `pdq add` as a single instruction instead of transmitting `pdq`, waiting for the next screen to appear, and then transmitting `add`. Similarly, you could transmit `pdq create`. Appendix J explains how stacking works in WESTLAW and offers more examples of stacked commands.

Summary of updating the law in LEXIS and WESTLAW

As this chapter indicates, both LEXIS and WESTLAW offer similar updating capabilities. Each CALR service offers:

- *Shepard's Citations*
- a service for verifying an authority's citation and status (Auto-Cite in LEXIS, and Insta-Cite in WESTLAW)
- the ability to search the text of documents for references to the authority you are updating (*i.e.*, using LEXIS or WESTLAW as a citator, including the use of LEXCITE in LEXIS and QuickCite in WESTLAW)
- access to slip laws and session laws that update statutory codes
- access to administrative registers that update administrative codes
- access to a wide assortment of legal and nonlegal LEXIS files and WESTLAW databases that highlight current activities, especially in specialized areas of law
- the ability to save successful search requests to use again in updating earlier results (ECLIPSE in LEXIS, and PDQ in WESTLAW)

These techniques often complement each other. For example, using an online version of *Shepard's Citations* to update a case can yield a comprehensive list of references to the case, but not alert you to authorities that have affected the precedential value of your case without expressly mentioning it. Auto-Cite and Insta-Cite, on the other hand, often identify authorities that indirectly affect precedential value, but neither Auto-Cite nor Insta-Cite offers comprehensive listings of citing references like those found in a Shepard's table. When you use LEXIS or WESTLAW as a citator, you can update *any* kind of authority and you can find updating references in a wide range of citing authorities, which will often be more recent than those found through *Shepard's Citations*, Auto-Cite, or Insta-Cite. But using a CALR service as a citator also means that (because of problems such as ambiguity in search terms) your results will often include references having nothing to do with the authority you are updating.[388] Thus, effective updating in LEXIS or WESTLAW frequently involves using a combination of updating techniques.

If your research project requires a particularly high degree of thoroughness, you can also extend your updating to using both LEXIS and WESTLAW. As indicated by the sample screens from the Auto-Cite and Insta-Cite reports for *State v. Yoder* (Figure 12.11 on page 428 and Figure 12.44 on page 552), similar updating techniques in the two CALR services can yield differing results. Likewise, although the *Shepard's Citations* tables you retrieve in LEXIS and WESTLAW will contain the same citing authorities, WESTLAW enhances its *Shepard's Citations* coverage with Shepard's PreView. With other updating techniques, the results you achieve in LEXIS and WESTLAW can diverge because a document in one CALR service might contain typographical or other data-entry errors not found in the corresponding document in the other service and because LEXIS and WESTLAW sometimes differ in the authorities they make available.[389]

Closing thoughts on updating the law

Whichever techniques and whichever CALR service you use, updating online, like updating in books, is simply one phase of legal research. In learning computer-assisted legal research, as in learning book-based research, it is analytically useful to isolate updating as a separate phase of the research process (following the phases of finding the law and reading the law).[390] Learning online updating as a separate phase of online research highlights the updating capabilities of the CALR services.

[388] Using LEXCITE in LEXIS, or using QuickCite in WESTLAW, to search for updating references avoids many of the problems associated with using a CALR service as a citator. But you can only use LEXCITE or QuickCite to locate updating references to certain kinds of authorities; moreover, LEXCITE and QuickCite introduce other difficulties that, for some researchers, can offset the benefits these features offer.

[389] For a discussion of data-entry errors, see page 665 n.412.

[390] *See* CHRISTOPHER G. WREN & JILL R. WREN, THE LEGAL RESEARCH MANUAL: A GAME PLAN FOR LEGAL RESEARCH AND ANALYSIS 120, 122 (2d ed. 1986).

In practice, of course, legal research does not always proceed in a linear fashion with all your "finding" preceding all your "reading," preceding all your "updating," and ending there. Thus, when you research online, you might Shepardize a case, then use LEXSEE, FIND, or the retrieval number in the Shepard's table to move directly to a citing case listed in the citator table. After scanning that case, you could (if the case proved relevant) immediately update it through, say, Shepard's, Auto-Cite, or Insta-Cite. From there, you could use LEXSEE, FIND, or a retrieval number to retrieve and scan still another case or other authority cited in the Shepard's, Auto-Cite, or Insta-Cite results. In turn, you could update that authority, and continue the process.

In short, when you use computers in legal research, you can follow a variety of paths to search for answers to research problems. Regardless of the paths you choose, however, the research process remains the same as in book-based research—a cycle of finding the law, reading the law, and updating the law, a cycle that repeats until you decide it should stop.

CHAPTER 13

Incorporating Nonlegal Databases into Computer-Assisted Legal Research

Introduction. Researchers often find nonlegal materials useful in the fact-gathering stage of legal research. To fill this need, numerous database vendors offer computer access to a burgeoning array of nonlegal materials concerning business and finance, science and medicine, the social sciences, and current events. Increasingly, Mead Data Central and West Publishing Company have made nonlegal databases available through the LEXIS and WESTLAW services.

The seemingly endless collection of materials available through nonlegal databases includes such diverse items as daily newspapers, national news magazines, business newsletters and trade journals, corporate financial reports, and scientific and technical papers presented at conferences of professional associations. Nonlegal databases thus afford you the opportunity to tap into an immense reservoir of facts, often unavailable in a library's print collection.[391] The kinds of data you might find include:

- information about clients, parties, and witnesses (*e.g.*, whether an expert witness has made speeches to professional organizations or had articles published in professional journals in the area of claimed expertise)

[391] Although a bit dated, two articles from *Trial* magazine provide a good feel for the range of information available through nonlegal databases and for the uses to which legal researchers can put the information. *See* Adolph J. Levy, *Online Computer Databases: Finding Data on Adverse Witnesses, Defendants, and Defective Products*, TRIAL, Jan. 1987, at 18; John J. McGonagle, Jr., *The Electronic Law Library: The Expanding Role of Computerized Research*, TRIAL, Sept. 1983, at 40.

- information about a product that has injured a client (*e.g.*, industrial or military design or performance standards for the product, names of firms that manufacture similar products)
- names of persons or organizations that have patented devices
- trademark applications and registrations
- unpublished scientific and technical papers about research in progress
- newspaper articles about lawsuits settled out of court, including names of participating attorneys you can contact for more information
- financial evaluations of thousands of companies (*e.g.*, Standard & Poor's profiles), including projected earnings, dividends, and company operations
- stock market prices
- international currency exchanges

As this list suggests, you confront in nonlegal databases an enormous amount of information. To extract from this mass the information you will find helpful, you need a strategy for searching.

Search strategy

A successful search strategy begins with "a healthy respect for your opponent—the vast quantity of information that's out there."[392] This awareness dictates the first task in searching a nonlegal database: narrowing your subject to a manageable area of inquiry.

> Assume, for example, that you need information about the effects of a particular chemical in the workplace to support a claim filed by an employee claiming damages for an illness allegedly due to that chemical. You must understand before you start that you will have access to literally thousands of pieces of information. In other words, you could get too much information. Ask the following questions (each of which is answerable through database searches):
>
> - What is the real name of the compound? What other names are used to describe it? Who makes it? For what else is it used?
> - Do you want information from the U.S. only?
> - How much time do you want to cover? Before the incident only, only after it, or both? How far back?

[392] ALFRED GLOSSBRENNER, HOW TO LOOK IT UP ONLINE 89 (1987). Much of the following discussion draws, with permission, on Chapter 5 of Glossbrenner's book.

> - Are you interested in its effects, in whether anyone has been sued because of it, whether hearings have been held on it, or whether the Food and Drug Administration, the Environmental Protection Agency, etc., have take[n] any action?
> - What kinds of information do you want: regulatory clearances and restrictions, medical studies, environmental evaluations, toxicological analyses?
> - Do you want to know about treatment for the claimed illness, about diagnosing it, about its frequency, or about all of these?
>
> These questions must be thought out *before* you begin any search so that it can be conducted properly. Once you are on-line, you cannot just pause to puzzle out what to do with your search results. A two-minute pause could cost you [several dollars in the database vendor's access charges or other fees]. In addition, if you do not have an adequate search strategy, you will not get the right results. You may get too much, too little, too much detail, or not enough.[393]

After narrowing your topic, your next task consists of selecting the database or databases in which to conduct your search. Because many nonlegal databases are made up of files corresponding to various publications and organizations, it often helps in choosing an appropriate database to ascertain what publications or organizations are likely to make available the kind of information in which you are interested. Also consider what kind of focus each publication or organization is apt to bring to the subject. To illustrate, suppose you want to locate information about industrial robots, especially regarding their use in automobile assembly lines.

> *Business Week*, *Scientific American*, *Automotive Industry*, and *The New York Times*[, among others,] could all be expected to publish information on industrial robots. And you know, almost without thinking about it, that each one is going to take a different angle on the story.
>
> *Business Week* would probably supply lots of business-oriented, industry-impact statistics. It might also single out a few key robot manufacturing firms and interview their executives. *Scientific American* might mention the economic implications as well, but it would focus on the technical aspects of how such robots work. As a trade journal, *Automotive Industry* could be expected to contain performance statistics, operating costs, announcements of planned installations, and labor union reaction to specific robot-related issues. The *Times* coverage would be similar to that in *Business Week*, and though it wouldn't be as deep, it would undoubtedly cover "impact on society" issues.

[393] John J. McGonagle, Jr., *The Electronic Law Library: The Expanding Role of Computerized Research*, TRIAL, Sept. 1983, at 40, 44–45 (emphasis in original).

> Certainly there would be some overlap in the kinds of coverage, but in general, this kind of logic is sound. If you know from years of reading *Business Week* that it could be expected to produce exactly the kind of article you want, it surely makes sense to search a database that covers *Business Week* and comparable publications.[394]

Thus, the names of publications or organizations that make available relevant information provide a double-faceted guide for identifying suitable databases: if you do not find a file for your publication or organization in a database, you might not want to choose that database for your search; on the other hand, if a database does contain a file for your publication or organization, the database might also contain other files with useful information from comparable publications or organizations. Consequently, once you know the publications or organizations that make available the kind of information you consider pertinent, you can identify suitable databases by determining which databases include those publications or information from those organizations, or that include comparable publications or information. (If you do not know which publications or organizations serve as significant sources of information about your subject, you can obtain advice from librarians, professors, or other experts.)

Learning about the contents of nonlegal databases

To find out the coverage of a nonlegal database (and its format, *e.g.*, text, summaries, citations, or statistics), check a database directory. For nonlegal databases available through LEXIS, you can get information from:

- Mead Data's printed directories—the *LEXIS/NEXIS Library Contents and Alphabetical List*, the *NEXIS and Related Services Alphabetical List*, the *LEXIS Product Guide*, and the *NEXIS Product Guide*
- online descriptions available through the LEXIS file menu and the GUIDE file for the NEXIS service

For WESTLAW:

- Information about nonlegal databases provided through WESTLAW by third-party vendors appears in the entries under "Gateway Databases" in the printed *WESTLAW Database List*. For additional information about a gateway database mentioned in the *WESTLAW Database List*, you can refer to *WESTLAW DataBasics*.

[394] ALFRED GLOSSBRENNER, HOW TO LOOK IT UP ONLINE 91 (1987).

- Information about DIALOG databases available through WESTLAW appears in *WESTLAW DataBasics* and in the WESTLAW publication *Guide to DIALOG Databases on WESTLAW.*
- For nonlegal databases listed in the online WESTLAW Directory, you can find online coverage information by typing **scope** (or **sc**) followed by the identifier of a nonlegal database, then pressing ENTER.

In addition, both Mead Data and West Publishing frequently issue press releases and brochures about nonlegal databases that are useful for researching in certain specialized areas (such as products liability or personal injury) and that are available through, respectively, LEXIS or WESTLAW. These publications highlight the contents of the databases and often provide tips for searching them for specific types of information.

To locate information about nonlegal databases not available through LEXIS or WESTLAW, check at your library for a directory of databases, such as the *Gale Directory of Databases*, published by Gale Research. Because new nonlegal databases frequently enter the pool of thousands of nonlegal databases, and because existing databases sometimes vanish, referring to a current directory will also help you keep abreast of changes in the availability of online sources of information.[395] Checking a directory's subject index for a reference to your subject area can turn up names of databases that cover your subject, along with references to locations in the directory where you can read brief descriptions of the databases. Database descriptions often indicate which publications and organizations the database covers. If a directory's database description does not provide this information, you can check the reference manuals or promotional literature for the databases you found listed in the directory's subject index. You can also obtain assistance in selecting suitable databases by asking a librarian, a database vendor's customer service representative, or an information broker (*i.e.*, an individual or firm that specializes in searching databases for clients).[396]

As you survey nonlegal databases in considering which to search, you will discover overlapping coverage. In those instances, to decide which databases will best meet your needs, compare the characteristics of the overlapping databases: for instance, one database might provide information in the form

[395] Some directories are also available in online versions. Because checking the printed and online versions of database directories can yield differing lists of appropriate databases, you might want to refer to both versions when possible. For an explanation of why you can obtain divergent results, see ALFRED GLOSSBRENNER, HOW TO LOOK IT UP ONLINE 452–53 (1987).

[396] *The Burwell Directory of Information Brokers*, edited by Helen P. Burwell and Carolyn N. Hill, provides one source of information about information brokers.

of citations or summaries, while another might provide the same information in the form of the full text of documents. In addition, how far back in time a database's coverage extends and how frequently the database is updated serve as important criteria.[397]

Determining the nonlegal databases to which you have access

Once you have decided which databases you want to search, you need to determine how you will gain access to them. As noted earlier, many nonlegal databases, including "gateway" databases, are available through LEXIS and WESTLAW. (When LEXIS or WESTLAW affords access to another vendor's database service, the CALR service is said to function as a "gateway" to the third-party service.) LEXIS offers access to nonlegal information through several database services, such as NEXIS (for general nonlegal information) and MEDIS (for medical and health care information). WESTLAW provides access to nonlegal information through such services as DIALOG (for general nonlegal information), VU/TEXT (for newspaper and wire service coverage), and Dow Jones News/Retrieval (principally for business and financial information).

In addition, you can gain access to other nonlegal databases if your library subscribes to databases separately from LEXIS and WESTLAW. If your library does not subscribe to a particular database you want to search, try gaining access through an association or consortium of database users (such as a bar association) or by contacting an information broker.

Organizing your search

At this point—before going online to search the database you have selected—pause and organize your search. By doing so, you will enhance the efficiency and effectiveness of your search and minimize its cost. If you are not already familiar with the database you plan to search, organizing your search begins with acquainting yourself with the database's search protocol.

For nonlegal databases you can search through LEXIS (such as files in the NEXIS or MEDIS services), the commands, logic connectors, and rules for expressing search terms are largely the same as those used to search LEXIS.

[397] Although selecting a database focuses on determining what material the database *includes*, also keep in mind that an online version of a publication might *exclude* material that appears in its printed version (assuming a printed version exists). For example, articles in the printed version of *The Washington Post* that are copyrighted by another source might not appear in the online version of the *Post*.

When you gain access to DIALOG through WESTLAW,[398] you can use WESTLAW Boolean search protocol to search DIALOG databases.[399] When you gain access to nonlegal databases available through WESTLAW but provided by an online database service other than DIALOG (such as VU/TEXT or Dow Jones News/Retrieval), you use that service's search protocol instead of WESTLAW's commands, logic connectors, and rules for expressing search terms.

If you gain access to nonlegal databases through services other than LEXIS (or NEXIS) or WESTLAW, you will find that the rules for formulating and executing search requests generally differ from the LEXIS or WESTLAW rules. The reference manuals for these other nonlegal databases will explain the databases' search protocols. Because so many protocols exist, and because the quality of reference manuals varies widely, orienting yourself to a new search protocol will proceed more easily if you know what to look for in a manual. Asking and answering the following questions when you read a reference manual will help you extract the necessary information:[400]

- *What equivalencies, universal characters, and root expanders can you use to express search terms?* For example, various protocols

[398] At this writing, WESTLAW actually offers two ways of gaining access to and using DIALOG. First, as part of the standard WESTLAW subscription agreement, you can gain access to DIALOG databases while using WESTLAW and then use standard WESTLAW Boolean commands to search in DIALOG (an arrangement called "DIALOG on WESTLAW"). Second, you can choose to have your WESTLAW subscription include another way of using DIALOG. With this option, you can gain access to DIALOG databases while using WESTLAW; however, you use DIALOG commands rather than WESTLAW commands to search the DIALOG databases (an arrangement called "Gateway DIALOG"). In effect, under this option, DIALOG functions independently of WESTLAW except for the convenience to the researcher of being able to gain access to DIALOG without having to log off WESTLAW.

[399] Although you can use the WESTLAW Boolean search protocol for searching in DIALOG, the computer executes searches a bit differently there from the way the search would run in a WESTLAW-created database. Currently, for example:

- The computer converts the "/s" connector to "w/10," the " + s" connector to " + 10," and the "/p" connector to "/30."
- The computer does not automatically search some fields, instead searching them only if you include a field restriction in your search request.
- In some fields, the computer will only search for phrases, rather than for individual words. So, for example, to locate articles by Molly Ivins by searching in a "phrase-indexed" DIALOG field containing authors' names, you might need to search for `au("ivins, molly")` instead of just `au(ivins)`.

For search tips, including whether some fields in a DIALOG database are not searched automatically or whether a database contains phrase-indexed fields, check the "scope" description for that database: type `scope` (or `sc`) followed by the DIALOG database identifier, then press ENTER.

[400] This checklist is drawn, with permission, from ALFRED GLOSSBRENNER, HOW TO LOOK IT UP ONLINE 111–12 (1987).

make symbols such as the asterisk (*), the question mark (?), the dollar sign ($), and the pound sign (#) available as universal characters or root expanders.

- *What logic connectors can you use to link search terms?* Connectors (sometimes called "operators") representing the core logic relationships (and, or, but not) are generally available. The protocol might also include proximity connectors to allow you to establish required distances between search terms.
- *How can you search for a phrase?* One protocol, for instance, uses a special command called "stringsearch." Other protocols rely on particular spacing or punctuation to trigger a phrase search.
- *How do you specify the fields, if any, to which you want to restrict your search?* Different databases often have different names for fields containing the same kind of information. In addition, search protocols use various ways of specifying field restrictions in search requests—*e.g.*, using an "at" symbol (@) with the field's identification number.
- *What formats can you choose for displaying search results on the monitor, and what items of information are displayed in each format?* For example, the search protocol for a database of newspaper articles might allow you to display entire articles, just the portions containing your search terms, or only the headlines.
- *What options are available for storing your search results?* If you want to preserve the results of your search, you might be able to have your computer's printer reproduce the results on paper, have the database vendor send you a printout of the results, or (if you are using a computer with a disk for storing information) capture the results by downloading them to your computer's disk for viewing or printing later.
- *How do you log on to the database and enter a particular file?* For example, you might need to type a command like `begin`. You might use a file number or an abbreviation for the file name. Or you might make a selection from a menu of choices displayed on the monitor.
- *How do you start your search?* One protocol might require you to use a command like `find` or `S`. Another protocol might simply give you an on-screen instruction to type in your search terms.
- *How do you exit a file, log off the database, and stop the vendor's online charges from running?* For example, you might type a command like `off`, `logoff`, or `disc` (for "disconnect").

> "The quickest way to double the cost of your search is to wait until you're ready to leave a system before you go rooting through the system manual to find out how to get off. Always note the exit before entering the theater."[401]

Once you are familiar with the protocol of the database you want to search, you finish preparing for online searching by taking the following steps:

- Select your search terms. The nature of the material you will be searching will affect your choices. For example, articles in *Business Week* and *Scientific American* about the same subject will almost certainly use different terminology to express similar ideas. You need to choose search terms appropriate to the material you search.
- Determine which logic connectors, if any, to use.
- Choose the fields, if any, to which to restrict your search. You might not want to use a field restriction in your search request. For example, if you were searching in a database of newspaper articles for information about a particular subject, you would probably not want to include in your search request a restriction to the field containing authors' names. By contrast, if you were searching in a database of book titles for a book about which you knew only the author's name, you would include a restriction to the field containing authors' names.

  If you use a field restriction, you'll need to understand what kind of information the field contains. For instance, if you want to search newspaper headlines for a particular term, you will obtain misleading search results if you choose as a field restriction the "title" field in a file in which that field contains titles of individuals (*e.g.*, senator, mayor) rather than titles of documents. You can verify the contents of database fields by checking the vendors' reference manuals or other literature, or by referring to the vendors' online "help" files.[402]
- Write out your search request.
- Make sure you know the display options available and the method of exiting files and logging off the database.

[401] ALFRED GLOSSBRENNER, HOW TO LOOK IT UP ONLINE 112 (1987).

[402] For additional caveats about using field restrictions in searching nonlegal databases, see Nina Cascio, *NEXIS for Academic Law Librarians*, LEGAL REFERENCE SERVICES Q., Spring/Summer 1986, at 47, 57.

The online sequence

Having completed your preparation for online searching, you commence your search. The following steps, which parallel those in searching LEXIS or WESTLAW, constitute the search sequence:

1. Log on to the database service.
2. Gain access to a file.
3. Transmit your search request.
4. Evaluate the results you obtain.
5. If necessary, modify your search request and transmit the modified request. Continue this cycle until you obtain results you consider satisfactory.
6. Preserve your search results by taking notes, by producing a computer-generated printout or requesting one from the vendor, or by downloading the results to your computer's disk.
7. Exit the file.
8. If appropriate, select a different file and repeat your search, or try a new search.
9. Log off the database.

Closing thoughts on finding nonlegal information online

"Ultimately, the only way to become an effective searcher [in nonlegal databases] is to become familiar with the databases and online systems that focus on your fields of interest."[403] Because you confront thousands of nonlegal databases as potential sources of information, proficiency at searching all of them is an unrealistic objective. For legal researchers, proficiency in using every nonlegal database is also unnecessary: the major half-dozen or so nonlegal databases (such as NEXIS, DIALOG, VU/TEXT, or Dow Jones News/Retrieval) offer a comprehensive store of information. Thus, the most realistic approach, especially when you're starting out, is to search just a few databases until you become knowledgeable about their contents, organization, and search protocols; then, if you need to, you can gradually increase the number of nonlegal databases you can search successfully.

Finally, as you search for nonlegal information, don't overlook the legal files and databases in LEXIS and WESTLAW as potential sources. Although

[403] ALFRED GLOSSBRENNER, HOW TO LOOK IT UP ONLINE 94 (1987).

LEXIS and WESTLAW serve as repositories of documents primarily reflecting legal doctrines, the following examples illustrate how you can use CALR services to locate facts.

> [I]f you have a case involving a Jeep rollover, simply searching for cases that mention both "Jeep" and "rollover," or "rolled over" might produce what you need. The cases you find may set forth safety standards [and] names of experts, . . . as well as the names of plaintiffs' counsel to contact for more information.[404]

Or, suppose you want to locate an expert witness to testify on behalf of a client. Some nonlegal databases contain files exclusively devoted to listing experts on various subjects. But you might be able to identify experts simply by searching case law on LEXIS or WESTLAW: combining such search terms as **"expert witness"**, **expert**, **testimony**, or **opinion** with search terms relating to a desired area of expertise (*e.g.*, **"genetic engineering"**, **"accident reconstruction"**) might retrieve cases in which an expert has offered an opinion.

In short, by searching nonlegal and legal databases, you can locate facts on virtually any topic relevant to a legal research problem.

[404] Adolph J. Levy, *Online Computer Databases: Finding Data on Adverse Witnesses, Defendants, and Defective Products*, TRIAL, Jan. 1987, at 18, 21.

PART IV

More Tips for Effectively Using Computers in Legal Research

Part IV covers the following subjects:

- tips about keeping a record of your online searches and their results (Chapter 14)
- guidelines for determining when your online search is complete (Chapter 15)
- a summary of the strengths and weaknesses of CALR services, and advice about integrating computer-assisted legal research with legal research in books (Chapter 16)

CHAPTER 14

Taking Notes: Keeping a Record of Your Search Session

Previous chapters explain how to develop search requests and use a computer in gathering facts and in finding, reading, and updating the law. Your online research efforts will be undermined, however, without a way of keeping track of those efforts and the results you obtain.

During a computerized search, as when you research in books and other printed materials, you might examine dozens or scores of sources. Without good notes, you can end up backtracking and duplicating your earlier, unrecorded efforts. But unlike backtracking in printed materials, a duplication that wastes the researcher's time, backtracking during online research also runs up unnecessary charges for redundant use of the databases.

When you do your research in a computer database, note-taking also acquires added importance because some of the sources you check online will not have a printed counterpart. Your record of your online search results could prove the only means for reviewing your results after you log off.

A useful record of a LEXIS or WESTLAW search session will include the following information about each search request you transmit:

- the search request as transmitted
- the LEXIS libraries and files or WESTLAW databases you search, or the service (such as Shepard's) in which you carry out a research task
- the date on which you perform the search
- the results of the search (for example, the number of documents you retrieve, or a list of citations)

- each modification you make to a search request (including the date you run the modified request, the libraries, files, or databases in which you run it, and the results obtained)

By keeping track of your search requests, of the libraries, files, or databases you search, and of the results you achieve, you not only preserve information that helps avoid duplicating earlier research, you can see which search requests work well, which requests prove ineffective or inefficient, and which files or databases yield useful results for your research purposes. From this information, you can begin to detect patterns that will guide you in future online search sessions.

The strategies that lead to good note-taking in book-based legal research (*e.g.*, organizing notes by issue, recording useful case headnote numbers) also apply in computer-assisted legal research.[405] When you use a computer in legal research, you can take advantage of several techniques to implement these note-taking strategies to preserve a record of your LEXIS or WESTLAW session:

- If you use a worksheet like the one in Figure 9.18 on pages 214–17 when you formulate your search requests, and then keep copies of the completed worksheets, you will create from the outset a record of the searches you perform. Your worksheet for a search request can become the cover sheet for other information you record about that search.
- After you have performed a descriptive-word search and retrieved a collection of documents containing your search terms, you can see an online summary of your search request and the documents it retrieved.

  In LEXIS, type `r` (for "request") and press TRANSMIT to see a screen like the one in Figure 14.01; if you have been searching a file for which the computer reports the results by separating documents into different groups, as in Figure 11.01 on page 319, you might need to transmit `r` a second time to advance to the screen that will show your search levels.

  In WESTLAW, type `g` (for "glance") and press ENTER to see a summary of your search; a screen like the one in Figure 14.02 will display if you are reviewing a Boolean search, and a comparable screen will display if you are reviewing a natural-language search.

[405] For an explanation of these strategies, see Chapter 7 in CHRISTOPHER G. WREN & JILL R. WREN, THE LEGAL RESEARCH MANUAL: A GAME PLAN FOR LEGAL RESEARCH AND ANALYSIS (2d ed. 1986).

```
       DATE:  JUNE 16, 1993
     CLIENT:  ABDUL/ELJOHN RENTALS
    LIBRARY:  OHIO
       FILE:  COURTS

Your search request is:
 (APARTMENT W/10 LEASE) AND (PLUMBING OR WATER)

Number of CASES found with your search request through:
   LEVEL   1...       40

To display the next screen of text of the CASE you were viewing, press the NEXT
PAGE key.

To redisplay the screen of text of the CASE you were viewing, press the ENTER
key.

For further explanation, press the H key (for HELP) and then the ENTER key.
```

Source: Mead Data Central, Inc. © 1993

Figure 14.01. Screen in LEXIS for Reviewing Your Current Search Request and a Summary of Its Results

```
THE CURRENT DATABASE IS OH-CS
YOUR QUERY:
(APARTMENT W/10 LEASE)  &  (PLUMBING    WATER)

    23 documents satisfy your query.

If you wish to:
   View the current document, press ENTER
   Edit your query, type Q and press ENTER
```

Source: West Publishing Company © 1993

Figure 14.02. Screen in WESTLAW for Reviewing Your Current Search Request and a Summary of Its Results

If you want to preserve the information on the screen, you can print the displayed screen, as explained in Chapter 11.

- Citation lists (such as those in Figure 11.08 on page 326 or Figure 11.18 on page 352) provide a convenient means for preserving a record of documents you have retrieved. By printing or downloading a list of those documents' citations, as explained in Chapter 11, you avoid the expense of printing or downloading the full text of each document. After you log off LEXIS or WESTLAW and stop incurring charges, you can use the citation list to locate the full text of authorities in printed sources.

  In addition, if you perform the same online search later to update your research, you can compare the list of your earlier results with the list of your more recent results to spot authorities added to the database since your previous search.

- You can also use the printing or downloading techniques explained in Chapter 11 to preserve results other than citation lists. For instance, printing or downloading a single screen of an authority, a Shepard's table, or an Auto-Cite or Insta-Cite report provides a quick and convenient way to take notes, especially if you would otherwise need to copy lengthy quotations or lists by hand. Printing or downloading is particularly well-suited to saving research results not available to you in printed form.

- If you use a personal computer with the Windows version of the LEXIS 2000 Research Software and a Windows version of a word-processing program, you can retrieve documents from LEXIS in one window and run your word processor simultaneously in another window. If you want to save text from a document you retrieve through LEXIS, you can copy that text directly from the LEXIS document into a document (such as a memo or brief) in your word processor.

  Similarly, West Publishing offers a Windows version of its WESTMATE software that allows you to copy text from documents in WESTLAW into a document in a Windows word-processing program.

- If you expect to repeat a search request at some point, you can store the request in the Electronic Clipping Service (ECLIPSE) in LEXIS or the Personal Directory of Queries (PDQ) in WESTLAW. In LEXIS, ECLIPSE will keep a record of the search request, the library and file searched, when the search was last performed, and the number of documents retrieved. In WESTLAW, PDQ will keep a record of the search request, the database searched, and the date the search was last performed; in addition, PDQ lets you store personal notes about your search. Chapter 12 explains how to use ECLIPSE and PDQ.

- In LEXIS, after retrieving search results you want to save, you can use the LOG feature to store those results until the end of the day. At this writing, LOG allows you to store up to 999 searches a day. For each search you save through LOG, the computer will keep a record of the search request, the library and file searched, and the number of documents retrieved. Throughout the day, you can return as often as you want to the results of any search stored in LOG.

  To store results in LOG after you run a Boolean search, type `.keep` and press TRANSMIT. Currently, for searches performed through LEXSEE, LEXSTAT, Shepard's, or Auto-Cite, the computer automatically stores those results in LOG.

  To view your log of stored search results, type `.log` and press TRANSMIT. While viewing the log, you can return to the results of a logged search by typing an equal sign followed by the identification number that LOG assigns to the search, and then pressing TRANSMIT; for example, you would transmit `=3` to return to the results of the third search in your log. Alternatively, you can return to your search results by pressing TAB to position the cursor under the LOG identification number, and then pressing TRANSMIT.[406]

  If you want to delete a logged search while viewing your log, transmit `.del` followed by the LOG identification number of the search. Transmit `.delall` if you want to delete, with a single command, all results stored in your log. Currently, the computer also deletes a search from LOG when you use LOG to return to the results of the search.

- When you log off LEXIS or WESTLAW, you can instruct the computer to save, for a designated period, the results of your most recent search. If you use this option, the computer will store your search request, keep track of the LEXIS library and file or WESTLAW database in which you last performed the search, and (if you log back on before the designated period expires) allow you to return directly to the collection of documents you retrieved.

These techniques, by helping you keep a careful record of your online research activities, will minimize wasted effort and money, and go a long way toward ensuring that your research is complete, properly focused, and useful.

[406] The alternative of pressing TAB to select the results you want to view through LOG does not exist with versions earlier than version 2.7 of the LEXIS/NEXIS Technology Series Research Software for MS-DOS.

CHAPTER 15

When to Stop

Whether you do legal research by using computers or books, or both, the research process remains the same. You need to develop your facts and legal issues, and then find, read, and update legal authorities relevant to your research problem.

Your research cannot continue endlessly, however, and you will eventually come to ask yourself, "Is it time to stop?"

Whether you use computers or books (or a combination of them), the same guidelines apply in deciding when to end a legal research project. These guidelines include balancing the thoroughness of the results you have obtained against the diminishing usefulness of new results you uncover as you continue your research. The guidelines also include developing a sense of confidence that you have discovered whether gaps exist in the law and, if so, that you can make sensible arguments as to how those gaps should be filled or how they are likely to be filled.[407]

When you use a computer to search LEXIS or WESTLAW (or any other online database), you will come to ask yourself an additional question: "Is it time to stop searching online?" As with the question of when to conclude a research project, some guidelines—highlighted in this chapter—exist that can help you decide when to terminate a CALR search.

Stop when you achieve your goal. The decision to end an online search session depends in part on the scope of the research activity that prompted you to go online. For instance, if you went online just to Shepardize a case, you would log off after retrieving the Shepard's results. In contrast, if you logged on with the goal of finding authorities through descriptive-word searching, you might run several searches before concluding you had accomplished your online research goal.

[407] *See* CHRISTOPHER G. WREN & JILL R. WREN, THE LEGAL RESEARCH MANUAL: A GAME PLAN FOR LEGAL RESEARCH AND ANALYSIS 129–30 (2d ed. 1986).

Be wary of stopping a Boolean descriptive-word search if you have not retrieved any *irrelevant* documents. In connection with online descriptive-word searching, one frequently suggested standard recommends that online searchers who retrieve a large number of documents through Boolean search requests modify their searches and stop when a search request retrieves about 30 documents. A numerical standard for deciding when to stop a Boolean search might appear to provide a practical solution to the problem of retrieving more documents than you can manage, and might seem analogous to your goal in book-based research, where you also want to deal with a manageable number of relevant authorities.

But a purely numerical standard in online searching overlooks a critical point. In book-based research, you pare your research leads by scanning authorities for their relevance to your research problem. For example, faced with a large collection of summaries in a case digest, you would not decide to stop reading the summaries just because you reached the 30th one. Rather, you would scan the summaries, constantly weighing the relevance of the summaries you have already read against each succeeding summary as you scan it, until you had narrowed the summaries to a collection you could manage. In contrast, when you narrow a collection of documents online, you normally effect that reduction without a chance to assess (even briefly) the relevance of all the individual documents. For instance, to reduce the number of documents retrieved online, you can use increasingly restrictive logic connectors in your Boolean search request, a technique that narrows the search based on the position of terms in documents and that does not necessarily correlate with relevance.[408] Or, for example, you can edit search terms to reduce the number of documents retrieved, a technique that normally jettisons relevant documents (as explained on pages 19–20).

When deciding whether you have reached a good stopping point in a Boolean descriptive-word search, instead of making a decision based just on the number of documents retrieved, consider applying a guideline that focuses on the ratio of relevant and irrelevant documents in the retrieved collection. As explained in Appendix M, you can evaluate the effectiveness of a Boolean search request by using two measurements: recall, which "measures how well

[408] Two simplified search requests illustrate the point. During the preparation of this book, transmitting `(lease w/10 apartment) and date(aft 12/31/85)` retrieved 92 cases from the COURTS file in the OHIO library in LEXIS, while transmitting `(lease w/5 apartment) and date(aft 12/31/85)` retrieved 63 cases. In WESTLAW, the first search request retrieved 73 cases from the OH-CS database, while the second request retrieved 32 cases. Although the change from `w/10` to `w/5` created more manageable collections of documents, changing the distance between search terms by five words does not appear to correlate with any known principle of legal or logical relevance. Most likely, some of the 29 cases dropped by the modification in LEXIS, and some of the 41 cases dropped by the modification in WESTLAW, would have proved relevant to the issue on which the search results were sought.

[the request] retrieves *all* the relevant documents," and precision, which measures "how well the [request] retrieves *only* the relevant documents."[409]

Because an inverse relationship exists between recall and precision, you can use the precision measurement to infer how well you have done in retrieving all the documents you wanted to find. The precision of your search therefore provides a helpful guideline for deciding when to stop. In nearly every instance, you can safely assume that when your Boolean search results contain a high percentage of relevant documents (*i.e.*, when precision is high), your search has bypassed a substantial percentage of the relevant documents in the database (*i.e.*, recall is low).

In short, although the natural inclination might be to terminate a Boolean descriptive-word search when most of the documents it retrieves are relevant, high-precision search results actually suggest that the researcher might want to continue searching if the goal is to achieve comprehensive results from the online search. In fact, some experienced researchers recommend that to retrieve a satisfactory percentage of the relevant documents in a database, about half the documents a Boolean search request retrieves should be irrelevant.[410] You might decide to strive for a different percentage of irrelevant documents in your search results. But if you keep in mind that high-precision results normally indicate you have missed a large percentage of relevant documents, you can make a more informed decision about whether to stop your Boolean search or to continue your online efforts to locate more authorities.

In WESTLAW, if you search with natural language, you do not encounter the need to cull relevant documents from an unmanageably large collection of retrieved documents. A natural-language search request will retrieve no more than the number of documents you instruct it to retrieve (with an allowable maximum currently set at 100 documents); moreover, the statistical probability formulas natural language uses to identify relevant documents will normally place at the top of the retrieved collection those documents with the greatest probable relevance. When you search with natural language, however, you typically give up comprehensiveness as a research goal: by definition, the 100-document limitation means that your results cannot be comprehensive unless 100 or fewer documents in the database hold relevance to your research issue.

Stop if you aren't progressing in your online search. You might find that despite your best efforts, your online search is not accomplishing what you want. Lack of progress could occur for several reasons.

[409] David C. Blair & M.E. Maron, *An Evaluation of Retrieval Effectiveness for a Full-Text Document-Retrieval System*, 28 COMM. ASS'N COMPUTING MACHINERY 289, 290 (1985) (emphasis in original).

[410] *See* James A. Sprowl, *WESTLAW vs LEXIS: Computer-Assisted Legal Research Comes of Age*, 15 PROGRAM: AUTOMATED LIBRARY AND INFORMATION SYSTEMS 132, 135 (1981).

If you researched your problem in books before logging on to a CALR service, and if your online search does not uncover any additional authorities, you have probably found everything you are apt to find; spending more time online will likely amount to spinning your wheels. Even if you are finding new authorities online, you still might want to end your CALR session if these authorities do not add anything significant to your knowledge. For instance, you might be incurring online charges but only finding documents containing repetitive recitations of legal principles with which you are already familiar.

On other occasions, your searches might not yield any relevant documents at all. If you encounter that obstacle, your search requests might not appropriately reflect the concepts you want to locate; if your initial online efforts at modifying your requests do not quickly harvest a better crop of documents, logging off will allow you to reassess your research problem or the appropriateness of your search instructions. Or, not finding any relevant documents could mean the CALR service you are using does not contain any helpful authorities. Given the millions of documents in LEXIS and WESTLAW, this situation will likely occur infrequently. But if you feel sufficiently comfortable with your online search skills and knowledgeable about the subject you are researching, you could reasonably conclude you would have retrieved a relevant document if the CALR service contained it. Staying online will probably just increase your search cost without any corresponding benefit.

Conversely, your search might retrieve a lot of documents, but with many of them irrelevant and with the collection too large to screen for useful documents. If modifying your search request does not improve your results, your research problem might not be appropriate for online searching. As explained on pages 154–57, ambiguous search terms, words that recur frequently in documents, or concepts that lie "between the lines" of a document's text can foil online searchers. In these situations, you will likely enjoy greater success if you stop your online searching and continue your research in printed materials.

Stop before you overspend. Many researchers gain their introduction to LEXIS and WESTLAW in a setting (such as a school) where the user does not pay to search the CALR services. In other settings, however, the cost of using a CALR service is a key factor in deciding when to terminate an online session. The significance of cost will vary from one research problem to another, but the steady accrual of online charges during a search session requires the researcher to calculate how much online information to buy for a specific research problem.

Stop if you are hoping to find something by a stroke of luck. Sometimes serendipity plays a role in successful legal research, although the "lucky find" usually follows as a byproduct of a good research game plan. For example, a researcher who has selected an appropriate topic in a printed case digest might notice in the topic's scope note some cross-references to other helpful topics the researcher might not have considered. The people who compile, edit, and index printed research materials use cross-references, topical outline organization, and other editorial features that not only keep researchers on track but that seed the research path with authorities likely to prove relevant to researchers investigating an issue in a given area of law.

In contrast, CALR databases provide few such editorial guideposts. Consequently, although an online searcher can sometimes stumble onto relevant information, the opportunities for serendipitous discoveries are fewer, and the likelihood of making those discoveries far less. So, if you find yourself scouting around online in the hope you will hit on relevant documents, consider the possibility that your research results will not justify the CALR vendor's charges for your search. Logging off so you can browse in printed materials could permit you to acquire the information needed to make an online search session a cost-effective research option.

CHAPTER 16

Assessing the Role of Computers in Legal Research

"The good news is that [the computer] gives you exactly what you ask for. The bad news is that it gives you *exactly* what you ask for."
—*Attorney Jacob P. Hart*[411]

As the variety of sources available online has multiplied, and as the legal community's access to CALR services has expanded, LEXIS and WESTLAW have emerged as increasingly useful research companions to printed materials. Indeed, some researchers see the CALR services as substitutes for using printed materials to find, read, and update legal authorities.

As with anything else, though, a mix of advantages and disadvantages attends the use of computers in legal research. Consequently, to use a computer effectively in legal research, you need to sort out the claims made about computer-assisted research so you can decide whether you should use a CALR service as part of a sound strategy for researching a particular problem and, if so, at what point in your research to do so.

In explaining how to use LEXIS and WESTLAW in finding, reading, and updating the law, earlier chapters have touched on benefits and drawbacks of computerizing these tasks and have noted the parallels between accomplishing research tasks online and in printed materials. This chapter considers in more

[411] Jacob P. Hart, *What Ever Happened to Carbon Paper?*, ALI-ABA CLE REV., Apr. 28, 1989, at 1, 8 (emphasis in original).

detail the strengths and weaknesses of computer-assisted legal research and how to incorporate online searching into an overall research strategy.

Factors to weigh in deciding whether to use a CALR service

The benefits asserted for computer-assisted legal research generally fall into these categories:

- flexibility
- comprehensiveness
- speed
- convenience
- cost-effectiveness
- currency

As you develop a research strategy, consider whether these characteristics would actually benefit your research efforts.

Would a CALR service offer valuable flexibility for your research? Because LEXIS and WESTLAW allow you to retrieve documents by searching their text for specified words rather than by searching in professionally prepared indexes for references to those documents, LEXIS and WESTLAW afford an almost infinitely adaptable capability to create indexing criteria for locating documents. This flexibility lets you carry out specialized searches that would normally prove impracticable in printed materials. For instance, you can easily index LEXIS or WESTLAW to retrieve all the dissents written by a specific judge about a specific issue during a specific time span. Or, if you know a distinctive phrase from a relevant authority but don't have its citation, you can search for the authority in LEXIS or WESTLAW by using the distinctive words as your indexing criteria.

The ability to index a database any way you like also lets you circumvent the constraints sometimes attributed to printed indexes: a limited universe of terms and concepts under which someone else has indexed information; the need to anticipate correctly the index headings and terms to examine; the lag between the first occurrences of novel legal issues and the creation of appropriate new index categories to accommodate those issues; and the possibility of not finding information because it has been misindexed or not indexed at all. Because you become the indexer when you search LEXIS or WESTLAW for relevant terms, you will not fail to find a document as a result of any deficiencies in a printed index. (Of course, unlike in book-based research, a document in LEXIS or WESTLAW could be "lost" to you if it contains a typographical error in a word you have used as a search term or if the document suffers from other data-entry errors.)[412]

The almost limitless flexibility available when you search LEXIS or WESTLAW results because the computer will obediently search for anything you request—it is "an extremely efficient idiot."[413] This flexibility can benefit your research in many situations, but will not enhance your results in every research problem. If you need to use search terms that have more than a single meaning or that occur frequently in online documents, your online search can easily locate an unmanageable number of documents having nothing to do with the issue you are researching. In addition, if you want suggestions for other avenues of research, you will need to examine retrieved documents, and in doing so, you might have to sort through many irrelevant documents in order to find any that offer useful information.

The satisfaction of being able to retrieve documents by searching for words in the documents' text can make it easy to forget that in using this search technique, you give up benefits you enjoy when you use professionally prepared indexes. Because an index explicitly links scattered but conceptually related pieces of information, an index minimizes the likelihood you will waste time poring over irrelevant authorities; instead, you can examine index entries covering ideas pertinent to your research problem and be pointed only to authorities likely to prove relevant, in some fashion, to that problem. When you search online, you can only guess that if certain words appear in retrieved authorities, those words will reflect the ideas raised by your research problem.[414]

[412] "Users of computerized legal research systems [such as LEXIS and WESTLAW] should be aware that computers have inherent problems. For example, typographical errors and the use of acronyms can cause computer users to miss cases; readers of hard copy equivalents do not necessarily miss cases because of such minor errors." Kelly Warnken, *A Study in LEXIS and WESTLAW Errors*, LEGAL ECON., July/Aug. 1987, at 38, 58. Warnken's article describes various data-entry errors discovered in LEXIS and WESTLAW, such as misspellings, inadvertent omissions of pages of text, accidental failure to include a document in a database, and dividing in two a case that was undivided in the printed version. *See also* ALFRED GLOSSBRENNER, HOW TO LOOK IT UP ONLINE 107 (1987) ("The question of quality is something that the [database] industry doesn't talk much about. But the fact is that due to data-entry errors, most databases are littered with landmines that can easily blow up in an unsuspecting searcher's face. . . . However such mistakes happen, there is virtually no way to catch them. How can you think of every possible misspelling of a name or a word?"); *id.* at 107–08.

[413] THOMAS MANN, A GUIDE TO LIBRARY RESEARCH METHODS 90 (1987).

[414] Researchers familiar with Plato's *Republic* might detect a similarity between, on the one hand, simulating concepts for the computer by translating them into search terms the computer can locate and, on the other hand, Plato's allegory of the cave. Much as an inhabitant of Plato's cave had to guess at the identity of unseen objects by viewing the objects' shadows on the cave wall, an online searcher needs to rely on search requests that, in effect, amount to "word shadows" that the searcher guesses are the best approximations of the desired "objects" (*i.e.*, the desired legal concepts). *See* THE REPUBLIC OF PLATO 193–94 (Allan Bloom trans., 1968).

Moreover, through cross-references and the careful selection of main entries and sub-entries, good professionally prepared indexes suggest other useful avenues of inquiry a researcher might have overlooked. In short, professionally prepared indexes help ensure that as you conduct your search, you will not only spend most of your time looking at authorities that hold some relevance for your research problem, but that you will not miss any critical authorities.

Whether the flexibility LEXIS and WESTLAW offer will prove useful for your research problem will depend in part on whether you think your problem would benefit if you created your own index. If the information you seek is not indexed in the way you want (for example, if you're looking for all dissents by a certain judge) or if the printed resources available to you have poor indexes, searching a CALR service might allow you to retrieve helpful information you otherwise could not find.

What effect would using a CALR service have on the comprehensiveness of your research? In LEXIS or WESTLAW, you have access to millions of documents obtained from an enormous range of suppliers and addressing every conceivable subject. With the availability of all these online documents, you can search for, say, every case that mentions "gallium arsenide" or "surrogate motherhood." For these reasons, LEXIS and WESTLAW are often described as tools for conducting comprehensive research.

But focusing on the quantity of documents available online and the ability to search them all can distract from the important question facing the researcher: "Will I locate all the documents I need for *my* research problem?" Some stumbling blocks can keep you from reaching this goal.

Despite the millions of documents online, the ones you need might be missing from a CALR service. Examples of authorities not available in LEXIS or WESTLAW currently include municipal ordinances, materials in many state administrative registers, most contemporary treatises, and early editions of secondary sources (such as law reviews and treatises) useful in conducting legal research requiring historical investigation. Moreover, online materials with printed counterparts sometimes do not contain the complete contents of the printed versions. Copyright restrictions, for instance, can prevent the online inclusion of some portions of printed source material.

The nature of the issue you want to research can also operate as an impediment to comprehensiveness when your online search is based on the wording of relevant documents. When the idea you want to locate can be expressed in a variety of ways, you can bypass relevant online documents if your search request does not include the words that authors of those documents used to express the idea. Similarly, you can miss documents when the concept in which you are interested is just implicit in the text of relevant authorities.[415]

[415] *See* page 157 n.121 and accompanying text.

Ironically, the very capability that LEXIS and WESTLAW offer for using Boolean logic to search comprehensively can also prevent you from conducting thorough research. A Boolean search might retrieve more documents (some relevant and some irrelevant) than you can examine. Reducing the number of retrieved documents to a manageable number (either by modifying your search request or by taking a sampling of documents from the retrieved collection) will almost certainly cause you to lose or bypass some relevant documents.[416] Thus, even when a Boolean search retrieves all the documents relevant to your research problem, if these documents are numerous, the large number of retrieved documents could keep you from obtaining the full benefit of the comprehensiveness of the search results.

For obtaining complete online research results, natural-language searching (available in WESTLAW) can prove an even less suitable vehicle than Boolean searching in LEXIS or WESTLAW. Because the natural-language feature currently limits search results to 100 or fewer documents, the computer will not cause you to overlook relevant documents hidden among more documents than you can reasonably expect to review. As the document limitation implies, however, the natural-language feature is not designed to ensure comprehensive search results. Rather, natural-language searching in WESTLAW offers a way of conveniently identifying through statistical analysis the most relevant documents in a larger pool of potentially relevant documents. And, although a natural-language search might retrieve some relevant documents that a comparable Boolean search would bypass, the natural-language search might also fail to retrieve some relevant documents that the Boolean search would have found, even when the pool of potentially relevant documents does not exceed 100.

Traditionally, legal researchers have prized comprehensiveness. In theory, comprehensive research means obtaining every relevant authority, however tangential; in practice, comprehensiveness means research extensive enough to leave the researcher confident of not having missed any authorities critical to the research problem. If you seek comprehensiveness in the theoretical sense, your research strategy will encompass all available means, including online searching. If your goal is comprehensiveness in the practical sense, whether you decide to search online will depend on a variety of factors, such as whether you have access to a library of printed materials containing the authorities crucial to your issue and whether you feel confident in your ability to create a search request that will retrieve the authorities you need from a CALR service. If comprehensiveness is not the goal of your search (as when you only need to find a representative authority standing for a well-settled

[416] Appendices M and N explain why this occurs with Boolean searching. *See also* page 659.

legal doctrine), whether you search online might turn on nothing more than personal preference for using a computer instead of a book.

Would a CALR service speed your research? Because of the variety of materials online, you can often use LEXIS or WESTLAW to gain immediate access to documents you could otherwise obtain only after the delay entailed in travelling some distance to a library, or to several libraries. Even when you have ready access to information in printed form, the computer in some situations can still speed up retrieving the information. For example, the computer can often retrieve Shepard's tables faster than you can retrieve them from the hardbound *Shepard's Citations* volumes and accompanying paperbound supplements and then turn to the appropriate tables in those volumes.

In addition, the computer can accomplish in minutes (or even seconds) certain tasks that in printed materials could take hours (even days) or that might not even be possible to complete in a reasonable time. For instance, the computer will almost certainly speed your efforts when you conduct a search such as one to see whether any state's statutes mention the "horizontal gaze nystagmus" test.

But the dazzling rapidity with which the computer puts researchers in contact with documents does not mean you will always research a problem faster with a computer than with printed materials. When you use a computer to search for documents based on words they contain, the need to winnow irrelevant retrieved documents can offset the benefit of the computer's speed at document retrieval, sometimes slowing your research compared to how it would have proceeded in printed materials. Indeed, to enhance the likelihood of retrieving all (or nearly all) of the online documents relevant to your issue, you might need a search request that will retrieve a collection of documents in which as many as half will be irrelevant to your research goal.[417] You can use the KWIC or VAR KWIC display mode in LEXIS or the TERM mode in WESTLAW to accelerate your review of the text immediately surrounding your search terms in a retrieved document, but often that review will not enable you to decide whether the document has relevance for your research problem. Without reading more than the text near your search terms, you might not be able to tell (even if the search terms as used in the retrieved authority have the meaning you intended) whether the facts or issues in that authority actually have any bearing on the problem you are researching.

In addition, as fast as a computer can retrieve a document, sometimes you will be able to retrieve the same document just as fast, or faster, from a nearby printed source. One lawyer who wanted to retrieve a certain Alaska Supreme Court case clocked the time it took to log on to a CALR service, transmit search instructions, retrieve the case, and print its 34 pages of typewritten text

[417] *See* page 660 n.410 and accompanying text.

on a laser printer connected to his computer. He then clocked the time needed to walk from his office to the library, turn to the case in the correct volume of the case reporter, and photocopy the 19 typeset pages the case occupied in the printed reporter. He found that performing these tasks took about two minutes longer when he used the computer (about 8 minutes 45 seconds) than when he used the book (about 6 minutes 40 seconds).[418]

Would a CALR service lend convenience to your research? By placing an enormous array of information as close as your computer terminal, LEXIS and WESTLAW bring to legal research a significant element of convenience. If a resource you need is not on the shelf of a nearby library, there's a good chance you can find the material in LEXIS or WESTLAW. Moreover, no matter how many other researchers might be seeking the information when you are, everyone has simultaneous access to the same material; documents are never "checked out" of the electronic library. And, the electronic libraries are always open (except for limited periods one night a week when the vendors make access to their databases unavailable, or on occasions when technical difficulties or power outages prevent you from gaining access).

When you use LEXIS or WESTLAW, you can perform some research tasks more conveniently than you can in printed sources. Some online versions of printed publications are consolidated in a way that eliminates the need with the printed versions to check multiple volumes, including supplements or pocket parts. For example, when you use *Shepard's Citations* through LEXIS or WESTLAW, each Shepard's table you retrieve merges into a single listing the entries from the main hardbound volumes and from any paperbound supplements. Likewise, the annotation articles in the online version of *American Law Reports Annotated* incorporate changes found in the printed *A.L.R.* pocket parts. In addition, if you want to search for authorities from multiple jurisdictions, the CALR services allow you to carry out your search with a single search request and avoid the need to check multiple printed volumes for the authorities you want. And if you know you will need to repeat a search, you can automate the subsequent searches by saving the original search request in the Electronic Clipping Service (ECLIPSE) in LEXIS or in the Personal Directory of Queries (PDQ) in WESTLAW.

But to take advantage of the conveniences offered through LEXIS or WESTLAW, you need to learn the rules for communicating your search instructions to the CALR computers, you need to familiarize yourself with the organization and contents of each CALR service you want to use, and you

[418] HENRY H. PERRITT, JR., HOW TO PRACTICE LAW WITH COMPUTERS 66–67 (Supp. 1990). The experiment also included a period of about 9 minutes 20 seconds for downloading the case from the CALR service; printing occurred from the downloaded file. Because downloading from a CALR service is not a necessary prelude to printing a document, our summary omits the time attributed to downloading.

need to keep abreast of the frequent additions to (and occasional deletions from) the materials available through the CALR services. Although some search instructions (such as `sh` to begin a search in online Shepard's tables) are straightforward, instructions for locating other information can require a more detailed understanding of how search terms and logic connectors operate. Some researchers might enjoy the challenge of selecting and arranging search terms and logic connectors to create effective search requests: "construct[ing] your query or search request . . . can actually be fun if you like puzzles or word games."[419] If you lack an enthusiasm for puzzles or word games, however, you might not view a CALR service as bringing convenience to your research efforts.

Using the Easy Search feature to search in LEXIS or using the EZ ACCESS feature to search in WESTLAW can reduce the number of commands you need to remember. But many researchers will find the constraints of these features too confining to compensate for their ease of use.

In WESTLAW, you can search many databases with natural-language search requests, which do not require you to understand how to use logic connectors to link search terms. But natural-language searching, though simple, does not supplant Boolean (terms-and-connectors) searching; indeed, you can accomplish some research tasks in WESTLAW only by using Boolean techniques.[420] In addition, once you transmit a natural-language search request, you need to know the same WESTLAW commands for viewing and updating the documents you retrieve as you need to know for viewing and updating documents you retrieve with Boolean searching.

The literalness with which the computer responds to search instructions can also detract from the convenience of ready access to vast quantities of information. You can find yourself wading through many retrieved documents that contain the words you specified in your search request but that have nothing to do with the idea in which you were interested.

Would a CALR service make a cost-effective contribution to your research? Among the reasons offered for using LEXIS and WESTLAW is the assertion that CALR services provide a cost-effective way to perform legal research. Savings result in part, the argument goes, because researchers can locate information faster with a computer.

As mentioned earlier, though, using a CALR service will not always speed your research. In particular, if you have to spend much online time modifying search requests or sorting through a collection of retrieved documents to weed out irrelevant ones, your research can proceed slowly, with online charges mounting quickly. "On-line searching can be absolutely fantastic or it can be

[419] Jordan J. Breslow, *Lawyers On Line*, PC WORLD, Oct. 1985, at 216, 220.
[420] *See* pages 71–73.

a dead loss—and you pay either way."[421] Moreover, as costs accrue while you remain logged on to a CALR service, you could feel pressure to rush your judgments about the relevance of documents you retrieve, possibly causing you to remove from further consideration an authority you would have retained if you'd had more time to consider it. If you think your research would benefit if you could ponder your results in a less hurried fashion as they unfold, you might not consider LEXIS or WESTLAW a cost-effective option.

Savings also result, the argument continues, because the online availability of legal materials makes it possible to avoid the cost of purchasing and storing expensive printed sources. In evaluating this aspect of the cost-effectiveness claim for CALR, it helps to keep in mind the difference between the "sunk" cost of printed research materials and the recurring cost of a CALR service. Once you buy a book or other printed source, you do not incur any additional charge each time you use it; indeed, with each use, the publication earns back part of its cost and therefore becomes an increasingly inexpensive investment. With a CALR service, however, because you incur new charges each time you use it, the cost of using the service is always on the rise. Thus, the online versions of infrequently used legal materials can often serve as cost-effective substitutes for the corresponding print versions, while print versions of frequently used sources might prove more cost-effective than their online counterparts.

To help ensure that the cost of your computer-assisted legal research does not outweigh the value of the results you obtain, you should be aware of how the vendors of the CALR services compute their charges.[422] CALR vendors offer a variety of subscription arrangements for their customers, and the terms of their contracts are subject to change. Nonetheless, you can ask certain questions to assess a CALR service's pricing structure:

- Will I incur a separate charge for each database or file I search? If so, will the charge vary for different databases or files?
- Will I incur a separate charge each time I transmit a search request? Will I be charged each time I transmit a modification to a search request? If so, will the charge be the same for each transmission, whether a new search or a modification?

[421] David Coursey, *The Cost of Information: How Does a 50 Cent Newspaper Turn Into a $20 On-Line Search?*, INFOWORLD, Aug. 5, 1991, at 40, 40 (quoting Barbara Quint, editor of *Database Searcher*).

[422] One librarian has described how a researcher's lack of familiarity with the pricing for online searching contributed to a CALR bill "that probably exceed[ed] the annual income" of the client for whom the online research was done. John S. Rosenberg, *Online Legal Research: Tips, Tricks, Traps*, LAW LIBR. LIGHTS, May/June, 1987, at 2, 17. *See also* SUSAN K. BOYD, AMERICAN BAR ASS'N, THE ABA'S FIRST SECTION: ASSURING A QUALIFIED BAR 125 (1993) ("alarmed law firms [have seen] graduates run up a $200 [CALR] bill with a client who is not going to pay it").

- Will I incur a separate charge for using information provided by a third-party vendor (such as Shepard's, Auto-Cite, or DIALOG)?
- Will I incur a separate charge for printing or downloading information?
- Will I incur a separate charge for the time spent logged on to the CALR service?

Two billing methods have predominated for CALR services: "transaction-based" billing, which bases charges mainly on the number of transactions (*e.g.*, searches) a researcher performs, and "time-based" billing, which bases charges mainly on the amount of time spent logged on to the CALR service.[423] At this writing, Mead Data primarily uses transaction-based billing for LEXIS, while West Publishing primarily uses time-based billing for WESTLAW. By knowing the billing practices of the CALR services to which you have access, you can estimate which service would be less expensive to use for researching a problem. For example, if your research problem will require several searches but not much time online, using WESTLAW might be the less expensive choice; on the other hand, if you need to perform only one or two searches but need to stay online to review the results, LEXIS might offer a more economical route.[424]

Would a CALR service provide the most up-to-date authorities for your research? Mead Data and West Publishing continually add authorities to their CALR services, often adding documents the day they are issued. For example, you can find United States Supreme Court cases in LEXIS or WESTLAW within hours after the Court announces them. Some LEXIS files and WESTLAW databases are even updated throughout the day. In general, primary authorities (*e.g.*, cases, statutes, administrative regulations) will appear online before or at the same time they appear in printed form. If you need prompt access to the most recent authorities, searching LEXIS or WESTLAW will be an essential part of your research strategy.

But just because a source is available in LEXIS or WESTLAW does not mean the information is the most recent you can find. Some kinds of documents (such as state attorney general opinions) that researchers generally use relatively infrequently do not appear online as quickly as documents for which more demand exists. For instance, in late March 1992, the most recent Ala-

[423] A third approach—charging a fixed monthly fee for unlimited use—has attracted support as a way of helping online searchers control their CALR costs. *See, e.g.*, Richard Leiter, *The Future of CALR in Law Firms*, TRENDS IN LAW LIBR. MGMT. & TECH., Sept. 1988, at 1, 3. Fixed-fee billing has even been suggested as a "demand" that LEXIS and WESTLAW subscribers should make in their contract negotiations. *See Making Legal Research a 90's Product*, COMPUTER COUNS., Nov. 1991, at 7, 7.

[424] For other suggestions for cutting the cost of using databases, see Glenn A. Deig, *Affordable On-Line Research: It Does Exist!*, COMPUTER COUNS., Dec. 1991, at 1.

bama Attorney General opinion in LEXIS was dated September 26, 1989, and the most recent one in WESTLAW was dated March 30, 1990, even though the Alabama Attorney General had issued opinions as recently as the last week of March 1992. In addition, because of delays in obtaining documents for inclusion online, a CALR service sometimes will not even have the most current coverage of materials in high demand.

When you search online, verify the currency of the file or database you are using. That way, you will know whether the CALR service contains the most recent authorities available. You might find you need to turn to an offline source for current information.

The decision to use a computer in legal research

In any legal research problem, the researcher needs to figure out how to make the best use of the research tools available. For researchers with access to a CALR service, the factors discussed in the preceding section—flexibility, comprehensiveness, speed, convenience, cost-effectiveness, and currency—provide a backdrop for deciding whether to use a computer in a legal research project and, if so, at what point. By making your best guess about how these factors will play out in the context of your legal research problem, you can decide whether using a computer might prove faster, more convenient, more economical, or otherwise better than relying only on offline materials for a particular task.

The guess you make will result from viewing the factors through the filter of the environment in which you will research a specific problem. For example:

- Is there an offline version of the material you want and, if so, is that version readily available to you?

  For example, although you might have ready access to a printed reporter for your state's cases, you might lack access to cases from other states. Likewise, you might need a copy of a case the United States Supreme Court decided just a few hours earlier or a copy of a case not scheduled for publication in a printed reporter.

  For most information offered by a CALR service, an offline version exists. Occasionally, however, a CALR service offers a resource not available offline. For instance, Auto-Cite tables in LEXIS and Insta-Cite tables in WESTLAW provide updating tools that do not have offline counterparts.
- If you have ready access to an offline version of the material you want to search, is the material indexed in a way that gives you access to the information you need?

You might want to retrieve information in a way not feasible using printed sources, such as finding all the cases argued by a particular attorney or all the statutes containing a specific word or phrase. Perhaps you want to retrieve a case you have read and all you can remember is a catchy phrase it contains. Or, after checking appropriate headings in printed indexes, you might want to try creating your own index terms to see if they will locate additional relevant authorities. In situations like these, a CALR service might allow you to find information you could not locate through printed indexes.

- If you have ready access to an offline version of the material you want to search, is the material available online in a format that is easier to use? Using the online version of *Shepard's Citations*, for instance, can prove more convenient when it avoids the need to check multiple printed Shepard's volumes.
- If you want to find online documents based on the language they contain, can you create a search request that will achieve your goal?

  The likelihood of retrieving a manageable collection containing as many relevant documents as possible and as few irrelevant ones as possible improves if you can anticipate the words that appear in relevant documents. The likelihood improves further if those words are not ambiguous, if they are searchable, and if (unlike words such as "complaint" or "waiver") they do not appear frequently in authorities unrelated to the issue you are researching.

In short, your decision to use a CALR service will depend on how you assess the costs and benefits a CALR service will introduce into *your* legal research project. Obviously, if you feel sure that using a computer will get you better results at less cost than using printed materials, the sensible decision is to use a CALR service as part of your research strategy. At the other extreme, if you feel sure that using a computer will increase your costs without improving your research, a decision to use a CALR service would be difficult to justify.

Most decisions about using a CALR service are less clear-cut.[425] For example, you might think that using a CALR service would improve your re-

[425] A study commissioned and publicized by Mead Data Central takes a different view, suggesting that most of the time, the decision is clear-cut in favor of using a CALR service. The 1991 report of the study drew the following conclusions from the results of 77 research sessions (called "studies" in the report) in which researchers looked for cases in printed materials and in

search over what you could accomplish in offline materials, but that using a CALR service would also increase your costs. In that situation, your decision will probably turn on whether you consider the likely improvement important enough to justify the extra cost.

Which to use: LEXIS or WESTLAW?

If you decide to use a CALR service in your legal research, another question materializes: LEXIS or WESTLAW, or both? If you have access to only one of the services, the question answers itself. If you have access to both services, consider these factors:

- the information included in each service
- the anticipated charge for performing your research in each service
- your preference for using one service rather than the other

As earlier chapters show, LEXIS and WESTLAW exhibit remarkable similarities in the types and quantities of materials available online, in the tasks the services allow you to perform, and in the way the computers carry out search instructions. Moreover, as Mead Data and West Publishing continue to compete for business from the same pool of customers, the characteristics of each service grow increasingly to resemble those of the other. Many differ-

---

LEXIS:

- "In 88.3% of the studies LEXIS research was completed in less time."
- "In 76.6% of the studies LEXIS research located more relevant cases."
- "In 67.5% of the studies, LEXIS found more relevant cases in less time."
- "In 58.4% of the studies the total cost of LEXIS research was less than the cost of manual research."

RICHARD C. REED & ALTMAN WEIL PENSA, PRODUCTIVITY AND QUALITY OF WORK PRODUCT WITH COMPUTER-ASSISTED LEGAL RESEARCH: A STUDY BY ALTMAN WEIL PENSA 1 (1991).

The report has been greeted with some skepticism, however. One commentator wrote that the "report distributed by MDC has scant supporting detail and inspires little confidence in its methodology. It still seems doubtful that WESTLAW or LEXIS will find *significant* cases that could not have been found in an evenly matched manual search." John Doyle, *Aiming at the Databases*, TRENDS IN LAW LIBR. MGMT. & TECH., Apr. 1991, at 4, 4 (emphasis in original). A law librarian whose law firm participated in the study wrote an article expressing his doubts about the study's methodology and the report's conclusions. He noted that, for example, the study participants always conducted research in printed materials before replicating the research in LEXIS. Consequently, researchers knew what they were looking for in LEXIS, although they "were asked to 'pretend' that when they sat down at the computer they had done no prior research." Richard Leiter, *Altman Weil Pensa Concludes the First "Second and a Half" Party Study of the Effectiveness of CALR Vis-A-Vis Manual Research*, 22 AM. ASS'N LAW LIBR. NEWSL. 444, 444 (1991).

ences fall into the "bells and whistles" category, such as different names for almost indistinguishable functions (like Mead Data calling a feature "FOCUS" and West calling its comparable feature "LOCATE").

Some distinctions can matter, however, in deciding which service to use. Although LEXIS and WESTLAW offer nearly identical access to the text of cases, statutes, administrative regulations, and other primary authorities, some significant differences occur in the coverage of secondary sources and in editorial enhancements to the text of primary authorities. For example, at this writing, if you want online access to articles in *American Law Reports Annotated*, you must use LEXIS. If you want the most current updating possible through Shepard's, you will need to turn to WESTLAW, which offers Shepard's PreView; on the other hand, the updating coverage available through Auto-Cite in LEXIS is more extensive than the updating coverage available through Insta-Cite in WESTLAW.[426] In the area of primary authorities, WESTLAW, because of its ties to West Publishing Company, offers some editorial additions to primary authorities (such as the Key Number headnotes in cases) that are not available in LEXIS.

Pricing can also affect your choice between LEXIS and WESTLAW. If you can perform the same research task less expensively in one of the services without sacrificing quality, presumably you will opt to use that service.

Sometimes, the choice between LEXIS and WESTLAW will simply depend on your preference. For instance, you might find the commands in one service easier to use, you might prefer the way one service displays information on the monitor, or you might favor one service's way of organizing documents into files or databases or of using segments or fields to structure documents.

Of course, your research goal might lead you to use both LEXIS and WESTLAW, especially if your project requires a high level of comprehensiveness. Despite the similarities of the services, you can obtain different results from searching each service. These disparities can occur because of differences in the kinds of materials online, because of differences in the schedules for adding documents to the services, or because of typographical or other errors in online documents.[427]

[426] At this writing, an Auto-Cite report includes earlier citations than you can find in an Insta-Cite report to cases outside the appellate chain for the case you are updating and that have affected the precedential value of that case. For example, the Auto-Cite report for *Dalehite v. United States*, 346 U.S. 15 (1953), lists the citation of the United States Supreme Court case characterized as overruling *Dalehite* in 1955. This information does not appear in the Insta-Cite report for *Dalehite*. In addition, an Auto-Cite report includes citations to *American Law Reports* and *Lawyers' Edition 2d* annotations that mention the case you are updating.

[427] *See* note 412 on page 665.

Incorporating online database services into your legal research strategy

As you can see from the preceding sections of this chapter, deciding to use a CALR service (and which one) is no different from deciding to use any other legal research tool. As when you select an offline research tool, you consider the research activity you want to perform, and then evaluate the resources available for accomplishing that activity: in thinking about a CALR service, ask whether it can assist you with gathering facts relevant to your research problem, with finding the law, with reading the law, or with updating the law.

Gathering your facts. In the fact-gathering stage of legal research, you can turn to thousands of databases containing nonlegal information about business, finance, medicine, science, and other disciplines. For instance, you can find out whether a client or potential client has been in the news, you can evaluate the credibility of expert witnesses by reviewing articles they have written, you can collect facts about opposing parties or counsel, you can learn what patents or other licenses a company holds, or you can evaluate a products liability case.

The array of newspapers, magazines, wire services, and other sources of information available through LEXIS and WESTLAW easily outstrips the range of nonlegal information you will find in a typical library of offline materials. Much fact gathering will continue to occur as a result of searching out offline documents such as hospital records in a personal injury case, police reports in a criminal case, or survey maps in a boundary dispute. Nonetheless, computer databases provide rich veins of information you can mine in the fact-gathering stage of your legal research.

Finding the law. In the law-finding stage of your legal research, you can implement in either printed or online resources the law-finding approaches summarized on pages 312 to 316. Two approaches, however, usually work more efficiently and effectively when you use books or other printed resources. First, you might want to use the "generalized" law-finding approach (*e.g.*, checking legal encyclopedias, treatises, or law reviews) to orient yourself to an unfamiliar area of the law before researching in cases, statutes, and other primary authorities. Lack of familiarity with the core terms or concepts in the new area of law will likely hinder you in constructing effective search requests for finding background information online; in an unfamiliar area of law, you will often proceed more efficiently by searching printed materials and taking advantage of their scope notes, index cross-references, and other editorial features designed to guide readers to information about which they know little.

Second, if your research turns on the legal definition of a word or phrase, you could find it cumbersome to implement online the "words and phrases" approach for finding the law: you could easily retrieve an overwhelming number of documents that mention your word or phrase without defining it. By contrast, checking the printed *Words and Phrases* volumes or the "Words and Phrases" topic entry or volume in a case digest will point you only to cases containing definitions of the word or phrase you want.

Even when you use a law-finding approach that works well online, you will normally not use online materials exclusively. Usually, if you use a CALR service in the law-finding stage of your legal research, you will mix printed with online materials to achieve an appropriate blend of resources that will allow you to research your problem completely and most quickly, conveniently, and cost-effectively.

Thus, for example, you might find a useful case while researching in LEXIS or WESTLAW; after logging off, you could check the table of cases in a printed case digest to determine the topic and number under which the case has been indexed, then turn to that part of the digest to locate other useful cases. Conversely, you might find a useful West topic and Key Number while researching in a West digest and use that information as the basis for a search in WESTLAW for cases indexed under the same topic and Key Number in West digests to which you do not have access.

In short, at the law-finding stage of your research, searching in online materials can complement your search in offline materials. By using a computer in your law-finding, you might locate some authorities that were not indexed the way you anticipated in printed indexes. On the other hand, using the indexes in offline sources will usually provide greater assurance that you have found most, if not all, of the authorities central to your research problem and that you have not overlooked essential authorities.[428]

[428] *Cf.* David C. Blair & M.E. Maron, *An Evaluation of Retrieval Effectiveness for a Full-Text Document-Retrieval System*, 28 COMM. ASS'N COMPUTING MACHINERY 289, 295 (1985) ("it is impossibly difficult for users [of databases] to predict the exact words, word combinations, and phrases that are used by *all* (or most) relevant documents" (emphases in original)); Daniel P. Dabney, *The Curse of Thamus: An Analysis of Full-Text Legal Document Retrieval*, 78 LAW LIBR. J. 5, 35 (1986) ("The Blair and Maron study shows that full-text retrieval systems have a severe limitation. They do not provide comprehensive (or even adequate) retrieval of documents by subject.").

These analyses concerned Boolean searching with requests consisting of search terms and connectors, so the conclusions do not apply equally to natural-language searching. Nonetheless, natural-language searching, like Boolean searching, requires researchers to guess correctly the language that appears in relevant documents. So, as with Boolean searching, natural-language searching poses a challenge you do not face when you use printed research tools like case digests, which organize information by concept rather than by the language in the digested authorities and which provide cross-references and other editorial aids designed to lead you to relevant information.

Reading the law. After you retrieve documents in LEXIS or WESTLAW, you generally skim at least parts of them to make a tentative assessment of the documents' relevance. But normally you will not remain connected to LEXIS or WESTLAW to read in detail the documents you found online. When you read documents online, the charges for being connected to the CALR service continue to mount.

In any event, reading on paper is more efficient than reading on a computer monitor.[429] Paper offers other unique advantages as well: you can read printed text on the commuter train or attach "Post-It" notes to pages you want to highlight. Although the computer offers tremendous capacity for storing and sorting information, paper remains the leading medium for displaying information. Indeed, after spending years attempting to develop the "paperless office," computer scientists at Xerox Corporation's Palo Alto Research Center (the legendary think tank credited with inventing the personal computer) concluded that the "paperless office" could never be accomplished because "sometimes paper is just the right medium."[430]

Thus, when you find useful information online, your best course will often consist of recording citation information (by writing it down, by printing or downloading a citation list, or by printing or downloading any other screens containing the citation information you need); logging off; then retrieving the documents in printed form to analyze them offline. If you lack access to a printed version, or if an offline version does not exist, you might print or download the documents in full so you can read them after you log off.

Updating the law. Whether you use printed or online materials to update authorities, you have a range of updating techniques from which to choose. Some of the techniques listed on page 636 for online updating have book-based counterparts; for example, you can Shepardize a case by using *Shepard's Citations* in either a printed or online version, or you can update a federal administrative regulation by checking either a printed or online version of *Federal Register*. Some updating techniques are unique to CALR services: you will only find Auto-Cite reports in LEXIS and Insta-Cite reports in WESTLAW; you will only find Shepard's PreView in WESTLAW; and only a CALR service will allow you to update an authority with a comprehensive search for references to it in the text of documents. As in other stages of legal research, the goal in updating authorities is to coordinate your offline and online resources to accomplish your purpose as completely, conveniently, quickly, and economically as possible.

[429] *See* note 202 on page 318 and accompanying text.

[430] Laura Myers, *Xerox Invents Software That Lets Faxed Paper Instruct PCs*, AP, May 23, 1992 (AM cycle), *available in* LEXIS, Nexis library, Wires file (quoting Z Smith, inventor at Xerox Palo Alto Research Center). *See also* note 202 on page 318.

Epilogue

> "Societies have always been shaped more by the nature of the media by which [people] communicate than by the content of the communication."[431]

> "[A] rapidly changing communications environment cannot leave the legal system untouched."[432]

> "A tool used as extensively as the computer cannot help influencing how we think."[433]

Although the vast majority of information available in a CALR service does not differ from the information available in offline resources, the computer allows researchers to bypass professionally prepared indexes and to create their own paths through the data, sometimes locating information that might otherwise have remained undiscovered. And, as with any new technology that profoundly alters the relationship between people and information, the use of computers in legal research carries potentially far-reaching implications. A single researcher using a computer will not have much impact on the legal profession, but thousands of people using computers in legal research can create an environment that affects the way law is created, thought about, communicated, and practiced.

The impact of user indexing on access to the law. The widespread use of computers to retrieve legal authorities based on words in their text diminishes the leveling effect that has resulted from the profession's reliance on a common indexing system. Indexes channel researchers dealing with similar facts and legal issues to a common pool of authorities; a researcher's level of skill at using the indexes affects mainly the amount of time required to find relevant authorities, not whether the researcher will find those authorities. When professionally indexed printed resources provided the only realistic avenue for locating legal authorities to support an assertion, all participants in a legal proceeding could, with a sufficient amount of diligence, reasonably expect to locate all or nearly all of the same authorities. But different researchers looking online for authorities addressing the same issue can create entirely different indexes and locate disparate pools of authorities; each researcher's results will depend on his or her skill at indexing online documents.

[431] MARSHALL MCLUHAN & QUENTIN FIORE, THE MEDIUM IS THE MASSAGE: AN INVENTORY OF EFFECTS 8 (Bantam Books ed., 1967).

[432] M. ETHAN KATSH, THE ELECTRONIC MEDIA AND THE TRANSFORMATION OF LAW 48 (1989).

[433] James Dickey, novelist and poet, quoted in CHRON. HIGHER EDUC., June 8, 1988, at B3. For a broad discussion of the ways technology can affect how people think, see DONALD A. NORMAN, THINGS THAT MAKE US SMART: DEFENDING HUMAN ATTRIBUTES IN THE AGE OF THE MACHINE (1993).

The need to develop and maintain indexing skills (as well as familiarity with online search commands, knowledge of the continually changing contents of online services, and awareness of the costs of searching) raises, in turn, the question of whether online searching will become the domain of specialists within the legal community. Some law offices, recognizing the difficulty lawyers face in trying both to practice law and to keep up the skills and knowledge necessary for competent online searching, have hired law librarians or other information specialists to serve as in-house experts to whom those who need to do computer-assisted legal research can turn for advice.[434]

As the use of CALR services spreads, and in some places supplants the use of printed research tools, the special skills required to use the databases (and the possible need for assistance from specialists) will make gaining access to the law more difficult for some groups. Clients who cannot afford to hire lawyers in firms with the resources to devote to keeping on top of database searching, as well as laypeople who want to do their own legal research, will find their access to the law diminished in comparison to the access that would have been available through printed materials.

The effect of user indexing on legal doctrine. Along with affecting access to the law, CALR services could affect the development of the law itself. Some commentators have suggested that user indexing will lead to innovations in legal doctrine, while others have suggested that user indexing will impede innovation in legal thinking. Under one view, the opportunity to use nearly any word or phrase to index legal information liberates the researcher from thinking about the law according to the organization established by professionally prepared indexes; this liberation frees the researcher to create new ways of looking at legal information and thus to develop innovative arguments for changing the law.[435] A different view holds that user indexing limits innovation because the researcher must specify particular words in the text of documents; this characteristic of online searching induces researchers to think in narrow, literal ways about law instead of thinking in creative ways that lead to change.[436]

In a similar vein, by requiring researchers to focus on the language used in online documents, CALR services could prompt judges, legislators, and other authors of legal documents to write, or ultimately to think, less creatively.

[434] "Many lawyers, busy with the practice of law, do not search [legal databases] effectively or efficiently. . . . It is not hard to imagine the number of errors made by endusers [such as lawyers] when professional librarians experience frustration about keeping up with their own expert searching skills." DEBORAH S. PANELLA, BASICS OF LAW LIBRARIANSHIP 38–39 (1991).

[435] *See, e.g.*, Jean Stefancic, *Listen to the Voices: An Essay on Legal Scholarship, Women, and Minorities*, LEGAL REFERENCE SERVICES Q., Nos. 3/4, 1991, at 141, 146.

[436] *Id. See also* Steven A. Childress, *The Hazards of Computer-Assisted Research to the Legal Profession*, 55 OKLA. B.J. 1531, 1534 (1984).

The literalness of the computer's retrieval technique places a premium on consistency in phrasing and on the use of words in their literal rather than metaphorical senses.[437] As more legal documents find their way online, whether in CALR services or in in-house databases of legal documents like briefs and memos, the authors of those documents might start composing documents in predictable language designed to enhance the likelihood they will be found by an online searcher.[438] If legal writers start writing in a boilerplate fashion, their thinking could become similarly crimped, leading to rigidity in the law.

Thus, legal decisionmakers and advocates need to guard against this possible undesirable consequence of using CALR services:

> By forcing the user to find cases by reference to specific words and phrases, the computer prevents him from approaching the issue-at-hand from a general perspective, past the boundaries of matched facts and issues. The lawyer will find the case that is "on all fours" with the instant legal issue and some cases with similar fact patterns. But will he be able to see the issue as more than a specific-fact or a category-of-law question?
>
> The problem is ultimately one of professional creativity. Law is more than words and rules which must be matched. The result of a mistaken view of the professional "completeness" of computer-assisted research may be a type of tunnel-vision, limiting the lawyer to arguments based on cases and fact-specific rules rather than on analogies, broad policies, and imagination; powerful dicta from "nonrelevant" opinions will be missed and, worse, unsought-for or ignored.
>
> . . . .
>
> The costs in the short-run may be more limited lawyers, stale arguments, and dependence on prior creativity. . . . The long-run offers a worse picture as the law itself begins to reflect this smaller outlook and a rigid definition of "relevance."[439]

[437] For example, one researcher has recounted looking for cases involving a riding stable's liability for injuries sustained when a rider fell from one of the stable's horses. The researcher turned up some irrelevant cases because the judges used "horse" metaphorically, as in "[p]ublic policy is an unruly horse." *See* JOHN E. KINSOCK, LEGAL DATABASES ONLINE: LEXIS AND WESTLAW 41 (1985).

[438] *Id.* at 46.

[439] Steven A. Childress, *The Hazards of Computer-Assisted Research to the Legal Profession*, 55 OKLA. B.J. 1531, 1534 (1984) (footnote omitted). *Cf.* George M. Jenks, *Technological Gimmicks Come and Go, but Libraries Persist*, CHRON. HIGHER EDUC., Sept. 30, 1987, at B3 ("Will the ability to find specific bits of information [by searching a computer database] mean that scholars may be wearing blinders? That they may lose a breadth of vision that the serendipity of reading a book may provide?"). *See also Data Retrieval May Be Hazardous to Legal Health*, LAW & COMPUTER TECH., Jan./Feb. 1975, at 25, 25:

> Electronic data retrieval applied to the field of law could distort legal thinking [and] adversely affect the concept of precedent and the lawmaking ability of judges. . . , according to a study

Effects on individual researchers. The availability of CALR services can affect individual legal researchers in other ways, too. By making a vast and constantly growing quantity of legal and nonlegal data available at the touch of a computer key, CALR services put legal researchers in the middle of the information explosion. Legal researchers thus face the challenge of figuring out how to gain control over all this data—how to organize it, how to sort the irrelevant from the relevant, and how to mold the remaining data into useful information.

Before computers introduced the library without covers, indexes provided the principal organizing frameworks for understanding the underlying data.[440] When researchers use a CALR service to search the text of online documents, their search requests serve as the frameworks for organizing the information in the database. Online searchers working in a subject area about which they know little, however, can find that the lack of a professionally prepared index leaves them adrift in data without guidance for initiating or pursuing their online searches for information.

Thus, when you research online, you need to beware of the possibility, which always exists when you use computer technology to receive information, that you will be "more promptly but less judiciously informed."[441] In the context of computer-assisted legal research, when you create your own index to retrieve authorities by searching for language they contain, the computer will retrieve documents quickly. But in bypassing professionally prepared indexes, you could find it harder to acquire a sense of how ideas fit together in the subject area you are researching. Researchers using printed indexes not only find references to relevant information, but learn something about the organization of the subject area being investigated, namely, how others have perceived that subject and how opposing parties might view it.[442]

> prepared for Canada's Department of Communications.
>
> . . . .
>
> Electronic legal retrieval systems have been developed with little regard for how lawyers actually think, according to the study, and to the extent they reflect a lawyer's thought processes, they may do so accidentally. In addition, retrieval systems may impose certain alien logical structures on the verbal symbols of law and thereby affect legal thought and "ultimately, substantive law."

But see Jerome S. Rubin, *Fear and Trembling in the Groves of Academe*, LAW & COMPUTER TECH., Mar./Apr. 1975, at 51 (response by president of Mead Data Central).

[440] Without frameworks, "we have no way of knowing what things mean. . . . [W]e are . . . adrift in a sea of facts. . . . Without [frameworks], people have no idea what to do with information. They cannot even tell what is information and what is not." Neil Postman, *Learning by Story*, ATLANTIC MONTHLY, Dec. 1989, at 119, 122–23 (book reviews).

[441] Barbara Wallraff, *The Literate Computer*, ATLANTIC MONTHLY, Jan. 1988, at 64, 71.

[442] For other observations about how user-created indexes undercut shared perceptions of the organization of the law, see M. ETHAN KATSH, THE ELECTRONIC MEDIA AND THE TRANSFORMATION OF LAW 221–23 (1989).

Finally, the simple fact that CALR services make it *possible* for legal researchers to search through enormous amounts of information can easily evolve into a sense that all this information *must* be searched. If, for example, you lack access to the printed version of informal opinions of the attorney general of a neighboring state but can search them online, should you?

Traditionally, the decision whether to conduct a particular search has depended not on whether the search could be performed, but on whether the researcher believed the search was likely to uncover information that would contribute significantly to resolving the research problem. When researching in printed materials, the researcher must draw a line at some point and decide to stop looking for additional authorities; with CALR services providing the ability to search more materials than are normally available in a typical book-based law library, the researcher could feel that deciding where to draw the line has become more difficult.[443]

Conclusion

The goal of legal research is to resolve a legal problem. To reach that goal, you need to know when to select a particular problem-solving tool and how to use it.

[443] For some, a heightened uncertainty about whether to search a computer database could stem in part from concern that deciding not to search online might be viewed as malpractice. The issue in malpractice, however, focuses on the lawyer's knowledge, not the research tool from which the lawyer acquired that knowledge. Lawyers are expected to know "those plain and elementary principles of law which are commonly known by well informed attorneys, and to discover those additional rules of law which, although not commonly known, may readily be found by standard research techniques." *Smith v. Lewis*, 13 Cal. 3d 349, 358, 530 P.2d 589, 595, 118 Cal. Rptr. 621, 627 (1975).

So, if a lawyer learns the appropriate legal rules by researching in offline materials, the failure to conduct online research will not matter. Conversely, if a lawyer searches online but fails to discover the relevant law, the simple fact of having searched online will not shield the lawyer from malpractice liability if the rules could have been discovered through research in offline materials.

To the extent a researcher conducts online searches without regard to whether they are likely to uncover anything significant—searching online just because the databases exist, because of unfounded concern over malpractice, or because an opposing party might be searching online—the use of a CALR service adds to the client's costs without necessarily adding to the researcher's knowledge. When that occurs on a wide scale, the public's access to legal services becomes less affordable. *See, e.g.*, Daniel P. Dabney, *The Curse of Thamus: An Analysis of Full-Text Legal Document Retrieval*, 78 LAW LIBR. J. 5, 38–39 (1986).

For summaries of the evolving malpractice issues raised by the increasing availability and acceptance of computer-assisted legal research, see Simon Chester, *Electronic Malpractice: Does Reasonable Competence Require Computer Research?*, LAW PRAC. MGMT., Nov./Dec. 1991, at 23; Laura A. O'Connell, *Legal Malpractice: Does the Lawyer Have a Duty to Use Computerized Research?*, 35 FED'N INS. COUNS. Q. 77 (1984).

As the preceding pages have indicated, LEXIS and WESTLAW are not perfect tools. Like other legal research tools, CALR services have not only strengths that can advance a legal researcher's efforts, but weaknesses that can hinder them. The great value LEXIS and WESTLAW offer researchers is the ability to get at information in a new way that complements traditional book-based research. With access to legal information now available through printed *and* computerized resources, researchers can enhance their abilities by using a comprehensive research strategy that minimizes the weaknesses of each kind of resource while capitalizing on its strengths.

PART V

Appendices

APPENDIX A

Sources of Information About LEXIS Libraries and Files

To search successfully in LEXIS, you need to know the names and coverage of the libraries and files you can use. Several sources—printed, online, and telephonic—provide this information.

Printed Sources

To help you plan a successful search, Mead Data Central provides printed reference materials you can check for information about LEXIS libraries and files before you log on:

- The *LEXIS Product Guide* provides descriptions of libraries and their associated files, including the names and contents of segments. Mead Data updates this publication periodically.
- The *LEXIS/NEXIS Library Contents and Alphabetical List*, published periodically, lists library and file names, their abbreviations, and some information about dates of coverage.
- Mead Data's newsletters and press releases provide updates about LEXIS libraries and files, along with search tips and information about new features Mead Data has added to LEXIS. Newsletters include *LEXIS Brief* (distributed primarily to law firms), *LEXIS In-House* (distributed to Mead Data's corporate counsel subscribers), *LEXIS Liaison* (distributed to Mead Data's government subscribers), *LEXIS Bench Brief* (for courts), *LEXIS Update* (distributed to law librarians in the private sector), *Advantage* (for sponsors of membership groups), *LEXIS/NEXIS Insight* (distributed primarily to Mead Data's business and accounting subscribers), and *LEXIS News for Accounting Professionals.* Your law library might keep these newsletters and press releases on file.

Once you log on, you can obtain more current information online.

Online Sources

DEBUT. When you log on to LEXIS, the monitor displays announcements of new additions and other changes to the service; a typical display appears in Figure 9.03 on page 193. To see more detailed information about these changes, you can press the key labelled SELECT SERV (for "select a service"), then type **debut** and press TRANSMIT.[444] A screen like that in Figure A.01 will appear. On-screen instructions explain how to use DEBUT; when you finish, press the EXIT SERV key to exit the DEBUT service.

Library and file menus. The LEXIS library and file menus (discussed on pages 194–96) offer up-to-date descriptions of all libraries and files, whether recently added or longstanding. As Figure 9.05 on page 195 shows, the library menu lists a page number after the name of each library; when you are viewing this menu, you can opt to see a description of a library by typing its page number and pressing TRANSMIT. After reviewing the information, you can do any of the following:

- see the next screen or previous screen of library descriptions by pressing the NEXT PAGE (or PgDn) or PREV PAGE (or PgUp) key, respectively
- return to the initial screen of the library descriptions by pressing the FIRST PAGE key

[444] For a brief explanation of Mead Data Central's use of the term "service," see page 240 n.148.

```
WELCOME TO DEBUT!

To learn more about any of these topics, type the corresponding
number and press TRANSMIT.


1. Automate private litigation support and work product libraries
   through the LEXIS service with LEXIS Private Database Services.

2. Search NYTEXT in the LEGIS library for full text of all published versions
   of bills pending in the New York state legislature. Type 2 and press ENTER.

3. For more information on dual column print and print appearance
   enhancements, type 3 and press ENTER.

4. For more information on the new Easy Search (TM) library, type 4 and
   press ENTER.

5. Search JET; BLKENT; ESSENC; and EBONY in the MARKET library. For a brief
   description of these new files, type 5 and press ENTER.
------------------------------------------------------------------

To return to the list of select services, press the SELECT SERV key.
To return to your research, press the EXIT SERV key.
```

Source: Mead Data Central, Inc. © 1993

Figure A.01. "Welcome to DEBUT" Screen in LEXIS

- return to the initial screen of the library menu by pressing the CHG LIB key
- gain access to a library by typing its name and pressing TRANSMIT

Similarly, when you are viewing the LEXIS file menu (as in Figure 9.06 on page 195) in the library you selected, you can choose to see a description of a file by typing the page number listed next to the file in the menu and pressing TRANSMIT. After reviewing the information, you can do any of the following:

- see the next screen or previous screen of file descriptions by pressing the NEXT PAGE (or PgDn) or PREV PAGE (or PgUp) key, respectively
- return to the initial screen of file descriptions by pressing the FIRST PAGE key
- return to the initial screen of the file menu by pressing the CHG FILE key
- return to the initial screen of the library menu by pressing the CHG LIB key
- gain access to a file by typing its name and pressing TRANSMIT

SEGMTS key. LEXIS provides online information about segments you can search in various files. Once you have gained access to a LEXIS file, you can press the SEGMTS key to see a list of segments available for searching in that file. An illustrative list appears in Figure 11.06 on page 324.

GUIDE. In many libraries, LEXIS provides a file named GUIDE. A GUIDE file provides online descriptions of the files in the library of which the GUIDE file is a part. For instance, the GUIDE file for the CODES library contains descriptions of the files in CODES. A typical GUIDE description does the following:

- identifies the name of the library and file covered by the description
- lists other libraries and files in which the described file also appears
- notes the LEXIS schedule for updating the file
- indicates the kinds of materials included in the file, as well as the kinds of materials excluded from the file
- describes what constitutes a document in the file
- provides a sample document showing the segments that make up a document
- offers sample search requests to use in the file

You can gain access to a GUIDE file either by going through a GUIDE library made up of all available GUIDE files, or by selecting a GUIDE file in some other library. Thus, you can proceed in either of these ways:

- At the library menu (shown in Figure 9.05 on page 195), select the GUIDE library by typing `guide` and pressing TRANSMIT. Once in the library, follow the on-screen instructions for selecting the GUIDE file that describes the LEXIS file about which you want more information.
- If you have already selected another library (*e.g.*, GENFED, CODES), check the file menu (shown in Figure 9.06 on page 195) for a GUIDE file, which will contain descriptions for the files in that library. To select the GUIDE file, type `guide` and press TRANSMIT, then follow the on-screen instructions for selecting the GUIDE description you want.

The CNTNTS file. In the GUIDE library, LEXIS provides the CNTNTS file, which serves as an online index to the LEXIS/NEXIS service.[445] CNTNTS lists alphabetically the materials available in LEXIS and identifies the libraries and files in which those materials appear. CNTNTS also indicates the abbreviations you use to gain access to libraries and files, and provides (for some files) information about dates of coverage. CNTNTS can help you if you want to determine whether LEXIS includes, say, materials dealing with Colorado insurance law: you could look in the online index under "C," where you would find that these materials appear in several files, including the Colorado file (COLO) in the insurance law library (INSRLW).

To gain access to the CNTNTS file, first go to the GUIDE library (transmit `guide` at the library menu shown in Figure 9.05 on page 195). When the first screen of the GUIDE library appears, select the CNTNTS file by transmitting `cntnts`. Figure A.02 shows the screen that will then appear; instructions on that screen explain how to locate information in the file.

Customer Service

To ask a LEXIS customer service representative or reference attorney for assistance in using the LEXIS service, you can call 1-800-543-6862. Mead Data also offers this assistance through a telecommunications number for the deaf: 1-800-732-5306.

[445] The information found in the CNTNTS file formerly appeared in the online *Index to MDC Libraries*, previously part of the tutorial service (TUTOR) in LEXIS.

```
                              LEVEL 1 - 1 OF 25 DOCUMENTS

You have chosen the CNTNTS file.  This file contains an alphabetical listing by
publication or source name of material available on the LEXIS/NEXIS(R) service.
Library, file and coverage information for each publication or source is also
included.

There are two ways to effectively use this file:

1.  Perform a LEXIS/NEXIS search. Press the NEW SEARCH key or type and enter
".ns".  Then TRANSMIT your search terms.

                                          or

2.  Scroll through the letters of the alphabet as you would an index.  To find
publication or source names beginning with a specific letter, type the number
opposite that letter and TRANSMIT.  To return to this page, TRANSMIT ".fd".

     A - 2      E - 6      I - 10      M - 14      Q - 18      U   -  22
     B - 3      F - 7      J - 11      N - 15      R - 19      V   -  23
     C - 4      G - 8      K - 12      O - 16      S - 20      W   -  24
     D - 5      H - 9      L - 13      P - 17      T - 21      XYZ -  25
```

Source: Mead Data Central, Inc. © 1993

Figure A.02. First Screen of the CNTNTS File in the GUIDE Library in LEXIS

APPENDIX B

Sources of Information About WESTLAW Databases

To search successfully in WESTLAW, you need to know the names and coverage of the databases you can use. Several sources—printed, online, and telephonic—provide this information.

Printed Sources

To help you plan a successful search, West Publishing Company provides printed reference materials you can check for information about WESTLAW databases before you log on:

- *WESTLAW DataBasics* provides detailed descriptions of selected WESTLAW databases, including the names and contents of fields.[446] In *WESTLAW DataBasics*, you will also find search tips and information about dates of coverage.
- The *WESTLAW Database List*, which West publishes periodically, provides a comprehensive listing of databases, their identifiers, and their years of coverage.
- West's newsletters and press releases provide updates about WESTLAW databases, along with search tips and information about new features West has added to WESTLAW. Newsletters include *Password* (for all WESTLAW users) and *Class Actions* (for students). Your law library might keep these newsletters and press releases on file.

Once you log on, you can obtain more current information online.

Online Sources

NEW database. When you log on to WESTLAW, the monitor displays announcements of new additions and other changes to the service; a typical display appears in Figure 9.04 on page 193. You can view more detailed

[446] West Publishing Company, WESTLAW DataBasics (1993).

information about these changes when you advance to the WESTLAW directory screen (Figure 9.07 on page 196), which is the next screen the monitor will display. There, if you type **new** and press ENTER, you will gain access to the NEW database, which contains descriptions of databases and other features recently added to, or updated in, WESTLAW. (If you want to switch to the NEW database when you are already in another database, type **db new** and press ENTER.) On-screen instructions explain how to use the NEW database.

To leave the NEW database and return to the WESTLAW directory, type **db** and press ENTER. If you want to leave the NEW database and go directly to a different database without returning to the directory, type **db** followed by the identifier of the other database, then press ENTER.

WESTLAW Directory. WESTLAW's online directory (discussed on pages 196–97) makes available the names and identifiers of all WESTLAW databases, whether recently added or longstanding. When you are viewing the directory, you can opt to see this information by typing **p** followed by the page number listed in the directory next to the subject matter in which you are interested, and then pressing ENTER. For example, referring to Figure 9.07 on page 196, you would type **p309** and press ENTER to see information about databases concerning environmental law.

The monitor will then display the first page of the directory that lists the databases in the area you selected. The first screen in Figure B.01 on page 696 illustrates the monitor's appearance. At this point, you can elect to see a list of the databases and their identifiers in the category you chose: to see the list, press the PAGE DOWN key if the kind of documents in which you are interested are listed on the next page; otherwise, type **p** followed by the listed page number, then press ENTER. The monitor will display a screen like the second one in Figure B.01; there, for example, you can see that the identifier for the database containing United States Supreme Court cases about environmental law is FENV-SCT. After reviewing the information, you can do any of the following:

- see the next screen of the directory by pressing ENTER or PAGE DOWN, or see the previous screen by transmitting **p-** or pressing PAGE UP
- move to a specific screen of the directory by typing **p** followed by the page number of the screen you want to view, and then pressing ENTER
- return to the initial screen of the directory either by typing **p1** and pressing ENTER, or by typing **db** and pressing ENTER
- gain access to a database by typing its identifier and pressing ENTER

IDEN database. If you just need to know an identifier to gain access to a WESTLAW database, you can search the IDEN database, which contains a

```
____WESTLAW DIRECTORY WELCOME SCREEN________________________________P1_______
 ____ENVIRONMENTAL LAW DATABASES                                      P309_____

xxxxxxxxxxxxxxxxxxxxxxxxxxxxxxxxxxxxxxxxxxxxxxxxxxxxxxxxxxxxxxxxxxxxxxxxxxxxxxxx
Environmental Law databases contain documents that relate to environmental
protection and conservation.  Among the subjects included are radioactive, solid
and toxic waste management, pollution, clean air and water acts, and the impact
of administrative and zoning law on the environment.
xxxxxxxxxxxxxxxxxxxxxxxxxxxxxxxxxxxxxxxxxxxxxxxxxxxxxxxxxxxxxxxxxxxxxxxxxxxxxxxx
 ------------------------------------   ---------------------------------------
 INDEX TO ENVIRONMENTAL LAW DATABASES   INDEX TO ENVIRONMENTAL DATABASES CONT.
 Federal Databases --                   State Databases --
  Administrative Law ..... Next Page     Administrative Law ...... Enter P318
  Case Law .............. Next Page      Case Law ................ Enter P319
  Statutes & Regulations . Enter P311   Texts & Periodicals ...... Enter P319
 Historical Databases  ... Enter P522   ---------------------------------------
 Specialized Databases ... Enter P312
  DIALOG Databases ....... Enter P317
 ------------------------------------
If you wish to:
   Select a database, type its identifier, e.g., FENV-USCA and press ENTER
   View information about a database, type SCOPE followed by its identifier
     and press ENTER
```

```
____WESTLAW DIRECTORY WELCOME SCREEN________________________________P1_______
 ____ENVIRONMENTAL LAW DATABASES                                      P310______

          FEDERAL DATABASES                         FEDERAL DATABASES
         ADMINISTRATIVE LAW                             CASE LAW
 FENV-EPA    E.P.A. Decisions               FENV-CS    Federal Cases
  FENV-FIFRA Fed. Insecticide, Fungicide     FENV-SCT   Supreme Court
              & Rodenticide Act Dec.         FENV-CTA   Courts of Appeals
  FENV-RCRA  Fed. Resource Conservation      FENV-DCT   District Court
              & Recovery Act Decisions
  FENV-TSCA  Federal Toxic Substance
              Control Act Decisions
 FENV-GCM    E.P.A. Gen. Counsel Memo.
 FENV-NR     News Releases
 FENV-ORW    Ocean Res. & Wildlife Rptr


If you wish to:
   Select a database, type its identifier, e.g., FENV-GCM and press ENTER
   View information about a database, type SCOPE followed by its identifier
     and press ENTER
   View the Index to Environmental Law Databases, type P309 and press ENTER
```

Source: West Publishing Company © 1993

Figure B.01. First and Second Pages of the Directory for Environmental Law Databases in WESTLAW

list of databases and their identifiers. To gain access to this database from the WESTLAW directory, type `iden` and press ENTER. (If you want to switch to the IDEN database when you are already in another database, type `db iden` and press ENTER.) On-screen instructions explain how to use the IDEN database.

To obtain information from IDEN, you transmit a search request as you would in any other database. By using search terms that describe a particular area of law or type of document, you can instruct the computer to locate identifiers for all databases covering that area of law or containing that type of document. For instance, if you wanted to see the names and identifiers for any databases covering labor law, you would type the search request `labor` and press ENTER. Or, if you wanted to see a list of the names and identifiers for any databases containing, say, Pennsylvania cases, you could type `pennsylvania w/5 cases` (or you could type `"pennsylvania cases"` as a phrase search) and press ENTER. After you transmit your search request, the monitor will display the first page of the complete list of WESTLAW databases. To move to each screen on which your search terms appear in the relationship specified in your search request, press ENTER.

When you finish searching the IDEN database, you can do either of the following:

- return to the WESTLAW Directory by typing `db` and pressing ENTER
- switch directly to a different database by typing `db` followed by the identifier of the other database, and then pressing ENTER

"Scope" command. If you know the identifier of a database, you can go directly to an online description of the database's contents (including its fields) by typing `scope` (or `sc`) followed by a space and the identifier, then pressing ENTER. Thus, to ascertain the coverage of the U.S. Supreme Court database, you would type `scope sct` (or `sc sct`) and press ENTER. If you are already in a database and want to determine its contents, just type `scope` (or `sc`) without an identifier, then press ENTER. On-screen instructions explain how to view the information displayed by the "scope" command and how to return to your research.

"F" command. Once you are in a database, you can view a list of its fields by typing `f` and pressing ENTER. For example, Figure 11.16 on page 350 depicts the list of fields the "f" command generates in a case-law database.

Customer Service

To ask a WESTLAW representative for assistance in using the WESTLAW service, you can call these numbers:

- Customer service: 1-800-937-8529
- Telecommunications for the deaf: 1-800-333-4656
- Reference attorneys: 1-800-REF-ATTY (1-800-733-2889)
  1-800-688-6363

APPENDIX C

Non-Searchable Words in LEXIS

Noise Words[†]					
all	ever	him	said	thereof	we
also	from	his	she	thereon	were
am	had	however	so	thereto	what
an	hardly	i.e.	should	therewith	when
and	has	if	some	these	where
any	have	into	such	they	whereby
are	having	is	than	this	wherein
as	he	it	that	those	whether
at	hence	its	the	thus	which
be	her	me	their	to	who
because	here	nor	them	too	whom
been	hereby	of	then	unto	whose
could	herein	on	there	us	why
did	hereof	onto	thereby	very	with
do	hereon	or	therefore	viz	would
does	hereto	our	therefrom	was	you
e.g.	herewith	really	therein		

[†] Source: Mead Data Central, Reference Manual for the LEXIS/NEXIS Services (undated looseleaf ed.) (Appendix E); Mead Data Central, LEXIS-NEXIS User's Guide 4-5 to 4-6 (1990 & Supp. 1991).

Reserved Words[††]					
and	gtr	but not	*lexsee*	*a/c*	*auto*cite*
and not	lss	>	*lxe*	*a*c*	*auto-cite*
or	bef	<	*shep*	*autocite*	*m1*
equ	aft	=	*shepards*	*auto/cite*	*m*
			ac		

[††] Source: Mead Data Central, Reference Manual for the LEXIS/NEXIS Services 39 (undated looseleaf ed.); Mead Data Central, LEXIS-NEXIS User's Guide 4-4 (1990 & Supp. 1991). Any italicized word in this list is considered a reserved word only if it appears as the *first* word in your search request. If one of these italicized words appears anywhere else in a search request, LEXIS treats the word as searchable.

APPENDIX D

Non-Searchable Words in Boolean Searching in WESTLAW

Stop Words*					
about	because	however	out	these	what
above	before	if	over	this	when
after	between	in	since	those	where
also	but	into	such	through	whether
although	by	mr.	than	thus	which
an	either	now	that	to	while
and	for	of	the	under	with
as	from	on	then	until	within
at	further	or	there	upon	without
be	here	other	therefore		

* Source: WEST PUBLISHING COMPANY, WESTLAW REFERENCE MANUAL 313 (5th ed. 1993).

APPENDIX E

Automatic Equivalencies in LEXIS

A.D.	AD
A.E.C.	AEC
A.G.	AG
A.L.R.	ALR
A.R.R.	ARR
AFFD	AFF'D
AFFG	AFF'G
AFFIRMED	AFF'D
AFFIRMING	AFF'G
ALABAMA	ALA
ALAS.	ALASKA
AMENDED	AMD
AMENDING	AMG
ANONYMOUS	ANON
APPENDICES	APPENDIX
APRIL	APR
ARIZONA	ARIZ
ARKANSAS	ARK
AUGUST	AUG
AVENUE	AVE
B.F.P.	BFP
B.T.A.	BTA
C.A.	CCA
C.B.	CB
C.C.A.	CCA
C.C.P.A.	CCPA
C.F.R.	CFR
C.I.A.	CIA
C.I.F.	CIF
C.O.D.	COD
C.P.A.	CPA
C.P.L.	CPL
C.P.L.R.	CPLR
CA	CCA
CAL	CALIF
CALIFORNIA	CALIF
CERTIORARI	CERT
CHAPTER	CH
CIRCUIT	CIR
COLORADO	COLO
CONNECTICUT	CONN
D.A.	DA
D.O.D.	DOD
D.O.T.	DOT
DAKOTA	DAK
DECEMBER	DEC
DELAWARE	DEL
DIES	DIE
E.O.	EO
E.P.T.L.	EPTL
EFFECTIVE	EFF
EIGHT	8
EIGHTEEN	18
EIGHTEENTH	18TH
EIGHTH	8TH
EIGHTIETH	80TH
EIGHTY	80
ELEVEN	11
ELEVENTH	11TH
EXHIBIT	EXH
F	FED
F.A.A.	FAA
F.A.A.A.	FAAA
F.B.I..	FBI
F.C.C.	FCC
F.D.A.	FDA
F.D.I.C.	FDIC
F.I.C.A.	FICA
F.M.C.	FMC
F.O.B.	FOB
F.P.C.	FPC
F.R.	FR
F.R.D.	FRD
F.T.C.	FTC
FEBRUARY	FEB
FIFTEEN	15
FIFTEENTH	15TH
FIFTH	5TH
FIFTIETH	50TH
FIFTY	50
FIRST	1ST
FIVE	5
FLORIDA	FLA
FORTIETH	40TH
FORTY	40
FOUR	4
FOURTEEN	14
FOURTEENTH	14TH
FOURTH	4TH
FRIDAY	FRI
G.C.M.	GCM
GEORGIA	GA
GOES	GO
H.E.W.	HEW
H.U.D.	HUD
I.C.C.	ICC
I.R.B.	IRB
I.R.C.	IRC
I.R.S.	IRS
INDIANA	IND

(continues)

Source: MEAD DATA CENTRAL, REFERENCE MANUAL FOR THE LEXIS/NEXIS SERVICES (undated looseleaf ed.) (Appendix D).

(continued)

INDICES	INDEX
JANUARY	JAN
JULY	JUL
JUNE	JUN
KANSAS	KAN
KENTUCKY	KY
LB	LBS
LOUISIANA	LA
M.T.	MT
MANUSCRIPT	MS
MARCH	MAR
MARYLAND	MY
MATRICES	MATRIX
MEMO	MEMORANDA
MEMORANDUM	MEMORANDA
MICHIGAN	MICH
MIMEOGRAPH	MIM
MINNESOTA	MINN
MISSOURI	MO
MONDAY	MON
MONTANA	MONT
MOTION	MOT
N.A.S.A.	NASA
N.L.R.B.	NLRB
N.Y.	NY
NEBRASKA	NEB
NEVADA	NEV
NINE	9
NINETEEN	19
NINETEENTH	19TH
NINETIETH	90TH
NINETY	90
NINTH	9TH
NOVEMBER	NOV
O.D.	OD
O.E.O.	OEO
OCTOBER	OCT
OKLAHOMA	OKLA
ONE	1
P.L.	PL
PARAGRAPH	PARA
PENNSYLVANIA	PA
PERMANENT	PERM
POUND	LBS
R.S.	RS
REGULATION	REG
REHEADING	REH
REVD	REV'D
REVERSED	REV'D
REVERSING	REV'G
REVG	REV'G
S.C.A.	SCA
S.C.P.A.	SCPA
S.M.	SM
S.P.R.	SPR
S.S.T.	SST
SATURDAY	SAT
SEC	§
SECOND	2ND
SECTION	§
SEPTEMBER	SEPT
SEVEN	7
SEVENTEEN	17
SEVENTEENTH	17TH
SEVENTH	7TH
SEVENTIETH	70TH
SEVENTY	70
SIX	6
SIXTEEN	16
SIXTEENTH	16TH
SIXTH	6TH
SIXTIETH	60TH
SIXTY	60
SUBDIV	SUBD
SUBDIVISION	SUBD
SUBSEC	§§
SUBSECTION	§§
SUNDAY	SUN
SUPPLEMENT	SUPP
T.C.	TC
T.C.M.	TCM
T.D.	TD
T.I.R.	TIR
TEMPORARY	TEMP
TEN	10
TENNESSEE	TENN
TENTH	10TH
TEXAS	TEX
THIRD	3RD
THIRTEEN	13
THIRTEENTH	13TH
THIRTIETH	30TH
THIRTY	30
THURSDAY	THUR
TITLE	TIT
TREASURY	TREA
TUESDAY	TUE
TWELFTH	12TH
TWELVE	12
TWENTIETH	20TH
TWENTY	20
TWO	2
U.C.C.	UCC
U.S.C.	USC
U.S.C.A.	USCA
U.S.C.M.A.	USCMA
VERMONT	VT
VERTICES	VERTEX
VIRGINIA	VA
VOLUME	VOL
WEDNESDAY	WED
WILLFUL	WILFUL
WISCONSIN	WIS
WYOMING	WYO

Note. Because of a computer programming error, the equivalency for "reh" is "reheading" instead of "rehearing."

APPENDIX F

Automatic Equivalencies in Boolean Searching in WESTLAW

States

Alabama	=Ala
Alaska	=Alas
Arizona	=Ariz
Arkansas	=Ark
California	=Cal
	=Calif
Colorado	=Colo
Connecticut	=Conn
Dakota	=Dak
Delaware	=Del
Florida	=Fla
Georgia	=Ga
Indiana	=Ind
Kansas	=Kan
Kentucky	=Ky
Louisiana	=La
Michigan	=Mich
Minnesota	=Minn
Missouri	=Mo
Montana	=Mont
Nebraska	=Neb
Nevada	=Nev
Oklahoma	=Okla
Pennsylvania	=Pa
Tennessee	=Tenn
Texas	=Tex
Vermont	=Vt
Virginia	=Va
Wisconsin	=Wis
Wyoming	=Wyo

Numbers

one	=1	first	=1st
two	=2	second	=2nd
three	=3	third	=3rd
four	=4	fourth	=4th
five	=5	fifth	=5th
six	=6	sixth	=6th
seven	=7	seventh	=7th
eight	=8	eighth	=8th
nine	=9	ninth	=9th
ten	=10	tenth	=10th
eleven	=11	eleventh	=11th
twelve	=12	twelfth	=12th
thirteen	=13	thirteenth	=13th
fourteen	=14	fourteenth	=14th
fifteen	=15	fifteenth	=15th
sixteen	=16	sixteenth	=16th
seventeen	=17	seventeenth	=17th
eighteen	=18	eighteenth	=18th
nineteen	=19	nineteenth	=19th
twenty	=20	twentieth	=20th
thirty	=30	thirtieth	=30th
forty	=40	fortieth	=40th
fifty	=50	fiftieth	=50th
sixty	=60	sixtieth	=60th
seventy	=70	seventieth	=70th
eighty	=80	eightieth	=80th
ninety	=90	ninetieth	=90th

Calendar Abbreviations

Monday	=Mon
Tuesday	=Tues
Wednesday	=Wed
Thursday	=Thurs
Friday	=Fri
Saturday	=Sat
Sunday	=Sun
January	=Jan
February	=Feb
March	=Mar
April	=Apr
June	=Jun
July	=Jul
August	=Aug
September	=Sept
October	=Oct
November	=Nov
December	=Dec

Legal Terms

affirmed	=affd
	=aff'd
affirming	=affg
	=aff'g
amended	=amd
amending	=amg
certiorari	=cert
reversed	=revd
	=rev'd
reversing	=revg
	=rev'g

(continues)

Source: WEST PUBLISHING COMPANY, WESTLAW REFERENCE MANUAL 315–17 (5th ed. 1993).

(continued)

Other Common Abbreviations and Spelling Variations

anonymous	= anon	permanent	= perm	superçede	= supersede
avenue	= ave	pound	= lb	superceded	= superseded
chapter	= ch		= lbs	superceding	= superseding
circuit	= cir	puerto	= porto	supplement	= supp
effective	= eff	regulation	= reg	temporary	= temp
exhibit	= exh		= regs	title	= tit
judgement	= judgment	section	= sec	treasury	= treas
manuscript	= ms		= secs	volume	= vol
memorandum	= memo	subdivision	= subd		= vols
	= memoranda		= subdiv	willful	= wilful
mimeograph	= mim		= subds	willfully	= wilfully
motion	= mot	subpoena	= subpena		
paragraph	= para	subsection	= subsec		
	= paras		= subsecs		

APPENDIX G

How the LEXIS Computer Interprets Punctuation and Other Symbols in Words and Numbers

In searching the text of documents in LEXIS for terms that contain punctuation marks or other symbols, you need to consider how the computer will interpret these characters. For instance, is "§1983" (without a space) equivalent to "§ 1983" (with a space)? Or do you need to include each version in your search request? This appendix explains the rules by which the LEXIS computer interprets punctuation marks and other symbols.

In understanding these rules, it helps to remember these points about spacing:

- A space represents the start of a new word. (See page 16 n.10.)
- In certain contexts, the computer treats some symbols as spaces.
- If the computer encounters consecutive spaces, the computer treats those spaces as a single space.
- When the LEXIS computer encounters a space (or a symbol it treats as a space), the computer can fill the space with noise words (explained on pages 28–29) or with symbols it treats as a space. So, searching for the phrase `"time date"` will retrieve phrases such as "time, however, and to date."

The rules discussed in this appendix have remained virtually unchanged since the inception of LEXIS. Keep in mind, however, the possibility that LEXIS could change them. If you retrieve results that conflict with the following rules, re-examine your search request to make sure you have not transmitted an erroneous instruction. If your search request does not appear to contain any errors, a LEXIS customer service representative can assist you in discovering the reason for your unexpected search results.

Ampersand &

The LEXIS computer treats the ampersand as a space. For example, `"kornstein, veisz wexler"` will retrieve "Kornstein, Veisz & Wexler" (as well as "Kornstein, Veisz and Wexler").

Apostrophe ’

When you use an apostrophe to create the possessive form of a search term, such as `court's`, the LEXIS computer will retrieve both the possessive and nonpossessive forms (here, “court’s” and “court”). Likewise, `court` will retrieve either “court” or “court’s”. (See page 34.)

When an apostrophe does not create the possessive form, the LEXIS computer treats the apostrophe as a necessary character in the word. Thus, `o'hara` will retrieve “o’hara” but not “ohara,” and `ohara` will retrieve “ohara” but not “o’hara.” In this situation, to ensure a comprehensive search for a word that might be spelled with or without an apostrophe, include each version in your search request:

```
o'hara or ohara
```

Asterisk *

When you place an asterisk in a search term, the LEXIS computer treats the symbol as a universal character substituting for any character at that location in the search term. (See pages 36–38.) The computer does not search for the asterisk.

Suppose, though, you want to search for a phrase that contains an asterisk, perhaps as an indication of omitted words (as in “but voluntarily * * * chose”). When you include a freestanding asterisk as part of a phrase search, such as `"but voluntarily * * * chose"`, the LEXIS computer treats the symbol as an invalid search term and terminates the search so you can edit the request by removing the asterisks.

When you remove the asterisks, the computer will carry out the search and treat asterisks in the text of documents as spaces. So, `"but voluntarily chose"` will retrieve a document containing the phrase “but voluntarily * * * chose”.

“At” symbol @

The LEXIS computer treats the “at” symbol as equivalent to the section symbol (§). (See below.)

Braces { }

The LEXIS computer treats braces in a search request as invalid characters. If you include braces in your search request, the computer will terminate the search and the monitor will display an error message indicating a faulty transmission.

Brackets [ ]

The LEXIS computer treats brackets like parentheses. (See below.)

Colon :

The LEXIS computer treats a colon in the middle of a number (as in “143:24”) as part of the number, not as a space separating one search term from another. So, LEXIS reads a number like "143:24" as one word. Searching for `143:24` will retrieve that number but not "143" or "24."

In all other situations (*e.g.*, as a lead-in to a listing), the computer treats a colon as a space.

Comma ,

The LEXIS computer treats a comma in the middle of a number as part of the number. Searching for `40,443` will not retrieve "40443", nor will `40443` retrieve "40,443." For a comprehensive search for a number that might be written with or without a comma, include both alternatives in your search request:

```
40,443 or 40443
```

When the LEXIS computer encounters a comma in other contexts (such as after a word in a sentence), the computer treats the comma as a space.

Dollar sign $

The LEXIS computer treats the dollar sign as a space. For example, `$1000` will retrieve either "$1000" or "1000", and `1000` will retrieve either "1000" or "$1000". So, if you are searching for a number that might be written with or without a dollar sign abutting it, you can use either form in your search request.

Exclamation mark !

When you place an exclamation mark at the end of a search term, the LEXIS computer treats the exclamation mark as a universal character substituting for an unlimited number of characters following the root of the search term. (See pages 38–39.) The computer does not search for the exclamation mark.

Suppose, though, you want to search for a phrase that contains an exclamation mark (such as "words 'No! Collect"). When an exclamation mark appears in the text of a document, the LEXIS computer treats the symbol as a space; therefore, you can omit the exclamation mark from the phrase search in your search request. For example, the phrase search `"words no collect"` will retrieve "words 'No! Collect".

Hyphen -

The LEXIS computer treats a hyphen in a number as a space separating one search term from another, rather than as part of the number. So, searching for `1-1-1` will retrieve either "1-1-1" or "1 1 1"; likewise, searching for `1 1 1` will retrieve references to either "1 1 1" or "1-1-1."

When you use LEXSEE, LEXSTAT, Auto-Cite, or Shepard's, however, the computer treats a hyphen in a number as part of the number, not as a space that starts a new word.[447] When you use one of these services, if a number in a citation includes a hyphen, you must include the hyphen as part of the citation in your search request.

In a search term consisting of letters, the LEXIS computer treats a hyphen as a space separating one search term from another. Thus,

`post-conviction` will retrieve post-conviction
post conviction

Likewise, searching for `post conviction` will retrieve either "post conviction" or "post-conviction." Of course, the author of a document might have written "postconviction." To ensure you locate documents containing any of the three possible spellings, use a search request containing "postconviction" as an alternative to either "post-conviction" or "post conviction." Your LEXIS search request would take either of the following forms:

`post-conviction or postconviction`

`post conviction or postconviction`

Paragraph symbol ¶

When a paragraph symbol appears in a document, the LEXIS computer substitutes the letter "P". Consequently, a reference to "¶130.5" in a printed document would appear as "P130.5" in LEXIS. The LEXIS computer treats a "P" standing in for the paragraph symbol as a searchable character. So, when a paragraph symbol "P" abuts a paragraph number (as in "P130.5"), the computer treats the symbol as part of the number. Searching for `p130.5` will retrieve "P130.5" but not "130.5", and `130.5` will retrieve "130.5" but not "P130.5". A paragraph number might be written with or without a space between the paragraph symbol and paragraph number (or even without a paragraph symbol), so you should anticipate the possible alternatives in your search request. Thus, a search request for paragraph 130.5 could take this form:

`130.5 or p130.5`

This search request will retrieve "P 130.5," "P130.5," or just "130.5."

Parentheses ( )

The LEXIS computer treats parentheses as spaces. So, searching for `12(b)` will retrieve either "12(b)" or "12 b"; likewise, searching for `12 b` will retrieve either "12 b" or "12(b)."

Note, though, that because "12(b)" and "12 b" are each treated as two words, neither will retrieve the single word "12b". For a comprehensive search

[447] See pages 238–43 for a discussion of LEXSEE, pages 243–44 for a discussion of LEXSTAT, pages 422 and 426–37 for a discussion of Auto-Cite, and pages 400–22 for a discussion of Shepard's.

for a number that might be written with or without parentheses, include both alternatives in your search request, as here:

```
12(b) or 12b
```

This search request will retrieve references to "12(b)", "12 b," or "12b."

Parentheses in search requests can also indicate the order for processing connectors (see pages 66–67, 158–59, and 161) or the presence of a segment restriction (see page 77).

Percent sign %

When the percent sign abuts a number, the LEXIS computer treats the symbol as part of the number; you must include the symbol in your search term to retrieve references to it. For example, `100%` will retrieve "100%" but not "100", and `100` will retrieve "100" but not "100%". For a comprehensive search for a number that might be written with or without a percent sign abutting it, include both alternatives in your search request:

```
100% or 100
```

Period .

The LEXIS computer treats a period at the beginning of a number (as in ".704") or in the middle of a number (as in "405.52") as part of the number, not as a space separating one search term from another. Searching for `.704` will retrieve ".704" but not "704", and searching for `704` will retrieve "704" but not ".704". For a comprehensive search for a number (such as the number of a statutory or administrative code provision) that might be written with or without a decimal point, include both alternatives in your search request:

```
.704 or 704
```

Note that when you search for a number that begins with a decimal point, some of the references you retrieve might include a leading zero (as in "0.704"). The computer automatically treats these forms as equivalent.

A period at the end of a number is treated as a space, not as part of the number. So, in formulating search requests, you can safely omit periods from the end of numbers.

When you use a period at the beginning or end of a string of letters, the computer treats the period as a space. A period in the middle of a string of letters (such as an acronym like "A.I.D.S.") is treated as part of the search term, not as a space separating one search term from another. So, searching for `a.i.d.s.` will retrieve "A.I.D.S." but not "AIDS", and `aids` will retrieve "AIDS" but not "A.I.D.S." To ensure a comprehensive search, include the possible alternatives in your search request:

```
a.i.d.s. or aids or "a i d s"
```

Plus sign +

The LEXIS computer treats the plus sign as a space. For example,

`2+2`	will retrieve	2+2 2 -- two two, two two of them at two 2. There are two
`"jaguar xke 2 2"`	will retrieve	Jaguar XKE 2 2 Jaguar XKE 2+2

A plus sign in a search request denominates a logic connector in LEXIS when used in the "+n" connector. (See pages 50–51.)

Pound or number sign #

When a pound or number sign abuts a number (as in "#10"), the LEXIS computer treats the symbol as part of the number. Searching for `#10` will retrieve "#10" but not "10", and searching for `10` will retrieve "10" but not "#10". For a comprehensive search for a number that might be written with or without a pound or number sign abutting it, include both alternatives in your search request:

```
#10 or 10
```

Question mark ?

The LEXIS computer treats the question mark as a space. For example, `"is that your answer do you want to look at it"` will retrieve "Is that your answer? Do you want to look at it?"

Quotation marks " "

You can use quotation marks in a search request to indicate a phrase search for the search terms enclosed in the quotation marks, as explained on pages 51–53.

When the LEXIS computer encounters a quotation mark in a document, the computer treats the symbol as a space. If you want to search for a phrase that has quotation marks within it (such as "interpretation of 'discretionary' is erroneous"), your search request can either include or omit the internal quotation marks. For example, to locate documents containing the phrase "interpretation of 'discretionary' is erroneous," you could use any of these requests:

```
"interpretation of "discretionary" is erroneous"

"interpretation of discretionary is erroneous"

interpretation of "discretionary" is erroneous

interpretation of discretionary is erroneous
```

Section symbol §

When a section symbol abuts a section number (as in "§1001"), the LEXIS computer treats the section symbol as part of the number. Searching for `§1001` will retrieve "§1001" but not "1001", and `1001` will retrieve "1001" but not "§1001". A section number might be written with or without a space between the section symbol and section number (or even without a section symbol), so you should anticipate the possible alternatives in your search request. Thus, a search request for section 1001 could take this form:

```
1001 or §1001
```

This search request will retrieve "§1001," "§ 1001," or just "1001."

If your keyboard does not have a key for the section symbol, you can use the "@" symbol, which LEXIS treats as equivalent to "§". In this instance, your search request would read:

```
1001 or @1001
```

Semicolon ;

When you use a semicolon in a search request, the LEXIS computer treats the semicolon as a separator between "stacked" commands. Appendix I explains how to stack commands in LEXIS.

But suppose you want to search for a phrase that contains a semicolon (such as "prosecution for gambling; a note given"). Omitting the semicolon from your phrase search will retrieve the phrase because the LEXIS computer treats semicolons in documents as spaces. Therefore, `"prosecution for gambling a note given"` will retrieve a document containing the phrase "prosecution for gambling; a note given."

Slash /

When a slash appears in a word, such as `plaintiff/appellee`, the LEXIS computer treats the slash as a space. For example,

`plaintiff/appellee`	will retrieve	plaintiff/appellee plaintiff appellee plaintiff-appellee
`plaintiff/`	will retrieve	plaintiff/appellee plaintiff-appellee plaintiff/respondent plaintiff
`/appellee`	will retrieve	plaintiff/appellee plaintiff-appellee defendant/appellee appellee

`time/date`	will retrieve	time/date time, the date time--on the date time, however, and to date

A slash in a search request denominates a logic connector in LEXIS when used in the "w/n," "/n," "pre/n," "w/seg," "not w/n," or "not w/seg" connector. (See pages 48–51 and 53–54.)

Alphabetic characters in numbers

In addition to considering how the LEXIS computer treats punctuation marks and other symbols in numbers, knowing the following rules about alphabetic characters in numbers will help you formulate effective search requests.

Roman numerals. The LEXIS computer does not treat Roman numerals as automatic equivalents of their Arabic counterparts. Thus, searching for the Roman numeral `XIV` will not retrieve the Arabic number "14". For a comprehensive search for a citation (such as a citation to a constitutional provision) that might be written with either a Roman or Arabic number, include both forms in your search request:

```
xiv or 14
```

Ordinal and cardinal numbers. The LEXIS computer does not treat ordinal numbers as automatic equivalents of their cardinal counterparts. So, searching for the cardinal number `14` will not retrieve the ordinal number "14th". Likewise, searching for `XIV` will not retrieve "XIVth". For a comprehensive search for a citation (such as a citation to a constitutional provision) that might be written with either a cardinal or ordinal number, include both forms in your search request:

```
14 or 14th or XIV or XIVth
```

LEXIS does, however, treat some cardinal numbers in their numeric form (*e.g.*, "14") as automatically equivalent to their alphabetic counterparts (*e.g.*, "fourteen"). In those instances, you only need to include one form in your search request. Similarly, LEXIS treats some ordinal numbers in their numeric form (*e.g.*, "14th") as automatically equivalent to their alphabetic counterparts (*e.g.*, "fourteenth"). Appendix E provides a list of automatic equivalents in LEXIS.

Reminder

As you formulate search requests that call into play the preceding rules governing how the LEXIS computer treats symbols in search terms, keep in mind that more than one rule might apply. For instance, when you search for a paragraph number greater than 999, you need to consider the rule for the paragraph symbol and the rule for the comma. Thus, a comprehensive search for paragraph number 10,475 would take this form:

```
10,475 or 10475 or p10,475 or p10475
```

APPENDIX H

How the WESTLAW Computer Interprets Punctuation and Other Symbols in Words and Numbers

In searching the text of documents in WESTLAW for terms that contain punctuation marks or other symbols, you need to consider how the computer will interpret these characters. For instance, is "§1983" (without a space) equivalent to "§ 1983" (with a space)? Or do you need to include each version in your search request? This appendix explains the rules by which the WESTLAW computer interprets punctuation marks and other symbols.

In understanding these rules, it helps to remember these points about spacing:

- A space represents the start of a new word. (See page 16 n.10.)
- In certain contexts, the computer treats some symbols as spaces.
- If the computer encounters consecutive spaces, the computer treats those spaces as a single space.

The rules discussed in this appendix have remained virtually unchanged since the inception of WESTLAW. Keep in mind, however, the possibility that WESTLAW could change them. If you retrieve results that conflict with the following rules, re-examine your search request to make sure you have not transmitted an erroneous instruction. If your search request does not appear to contain any errors, a WESTLAW customer service representative can assist you in discovering the reason for your unexpected search results.

Ampersand &

When you use an ampersand in a search request (except as part of a phrase), the computer treats the symbol as the "and" connector. (See pages 45–46.)

If you include an ampersand as part of a phrase in your search request (as in `"kornstein, veisz & wexler"`), the computer will treat the ampersand as an invalid character and terminate the search so you can edit the request by removing the ampersand. When you run the search without the ampersand (such as `"kornstein, veisz wexler"`), the computer will retrieve documents containing the phrase with the ampersand (here, "Kornstein, Veisz & Wexler").

But the request "kornstein, veisz wexler" will not retrieve documents in which the word "and" appears in place of the ampersand, as in "Kornstein, Veisz and Wexler." For a comprehensive search, you can use a request like "kornstein, veisz wexler" or "kornstein, veisz and wexler".

Apostrophe '

When you use an apostrophe to create the possessive form of a search term, such as collier's, the WESTLAW computer will search for the apostrophe. Thus, collier's will retrieve "collier's," but not "collier" (although collier will retrieve either "collier" or "collier's," as explained on page 34).

When an apostrophe does not create the possessive form, the computer simply ignores the apostrophe. For example,

o'hara	will retrieve	o'hara ohara
ohara	will retrieve	ohara o'hara

Thus, you do not need to include both forms in your search request.

Asterisk *

When you place an asterisk in a search term, the WESTLAW computer treats the symbol as a universal character substituting for any character at that location in the search term. (See pages 36–38.) The computer does not search for the asterisk.

Suppose, though, you want to search for a phrase that contains an asterisk, perhaps as an indication of omitted words (as in "but voluntarily * * * chose"). When you include a freestanding asterisk as part of a phrase search, such as "but voluntarily * * * chose", the WESTLAW computer treats the symbol as an invalid character and terminates the search so you can edit the request by removing the asterisks.

When you remove the asterisks, the computer will carry out the search and treat asterisks in the text of documents as spaces. So, "but voluntarily chose" will retrieve a document containing the phrase "but voluntarily * * * chose".

"At" symbol @

If an "@" symbol abuts characters that follow it (as in "@135344"), the WESTLAW computer treats the symbol as part of the word; you must include the symbol in your search term to retrieve references to it. For example, @135344 will retrieve "@135344" but not "135344"; likewise, 135344 will retrieve "135344" but not "@135344."

Braces { }

The WESTLAW computer treats braces in a search request as invalid characters. If you include braces in your search request, the computer will terminate the search so you can edit the request by removing the braces.

Brackets [ ]

If you transmit a number (or a string of numbers and letters) containing brackets, the WESTLAW computer will convert the brackets to parentheses in your search request. For example, if you transmit `12[b][6]`, the computer will search for "12(b)(6)" instead. As a result, the computer will bypass any references in documents to the version of the number with brackets.

Suppose, however, you want to search for, say, "12[b][6]." When a bracket occurs in a number in the text of a document, the computer treats the bracket as a space separating one term from another, not as part of the number. So, to retrieve "12[b][6]," you could transmit the phrase search

```
"12 b 6"
```

Or you could transmit a search request using a proximity connector that requires the three terms to appear sequentially, as here:

```
12 pre/1 b pre/1 6
```

If you are searching for a number that might be written with brackets or parentheses, including each alternative in your search request will ensure comprehensiveness:

```
12(b)(6) or 12b(6) or 12(b)6 or 12b6 or "12 b 6"
```

In a string of letters in a document, brackets are ignored by the WESTLAW computer. Searching for `"subject to certain exceptions a decision"` will retrieve documents with the phrase "subject to [certain exceptions], a decision." If you include brackets as part of a phrase search in your search request, such as `"subject to [certain exceptions], a decision"`, the computer will treat the brackets as invalid characters in the phrase and terminate the search so you can edit the request by removing the brackets.

Colon :

The WESTLAW computer treats a colon in the middle of a number (*e.g.*, "10:15") in a search request as part of the number, not as a space separating one search term from another. So, WESTLAW reads a search term like `10:15` as one word. Searching for `10:15` will therefore retrieve that number but not "10" or "15."

The computer treats a colon in the middle of a number in a document as a space. So, you can also retrieve a number like "10:15" by searching for just the number on one side of the colon, but you will generally retrieve irrelevant references as well. For example:

`10:15`	will retrieve	10:15
`10`	will retrieve	10 10:15, 10:30, etc. 4:10, 9:10, etc.
`15`	will retrieve	15 10:15, 8:15, etc. 15:438, 15:441, etc.

You might want to search for a phrase—like "noble aspirations: our unwillingness"—that contains a colon. If you include the colon in the search request, as in `"noble aspirations: our unwillingness"`, the computer will generate an error message (possibly false) that the colon and the word preceding it do not appear together in the database. You can, however, avoid this difficulty by omitting the colon from your search request. For example, the request `"noble aspirations our unwillingness"` will retrieve documents containing the phrase "noble aspirations: our unwillingness."

Comma ,

The WESTLAW computer ignores a comma in the middle of a number. Searching for `40,443` is the same as searching for "40443", and vice versa. So, if you are searching for a number that might be written with or without a comma, you can use either form in your search request.

When the WESTLAW computer encounters a comma in other contexts (such as after a word in a sentence), the computer treats the comma as a space.

Dollar sign $

If a dollar sign abuts other characters (as in "$10,000"), the WESTLAW computer treats the symbol as part of the word; you must include the symbol in your search term to retrieve references to it. For example, `$10000` will retrieve "$10,000" or "$10000" but not "10,000" or "10000"; likewise, `10000` will retrieve "10,000" or "10000" but not "$10,000" or "$10000". So, for a comprehensive search for a number that might be written with or without a dollar sign abutting it, include both alternatives in your search request:

```
$10000 or 10000
```

Exclamation mark !

When you place an exclamation mark at the end of a search term, the WESTLAW computer treats the exclamation mark as a universal character substituting for an unlimited number of characters following the root of the search term. (See pages 38–39.) The computer does not search for the exclamation mark.

Suppose, though, you want to search for a phrase that contains an exclamation mark, such as "Helm hard down! luff! luff!" The WESTLAW computer ignores exclamation marks that appear in documents. So, you could transmit either `"helm hard down! luff! luff!"` or `"helm hard down luff luff"` as your phrase search to retrieve a document containing the phrase "helm hard down! luff! luff!"

Hyphen -

The WESTLAW computer treats a hyphen in a number as part of the number, not as a space separating one search term from another. So, WESTLAW reads a number like "1-1-1" as one word. Searching for `1-1-1` will therefore retrieve that number but not "1 1 1" or "1."

When you use a hyphen in a search term consisting of letters, such as `post-conviction`, the hyphen "normalizes" the search term so the computer will automatically search for variations of the term. (Pages 34–36 explain normalization.) Thus, in WESTLAW

`post-conviction`	will retrieve	post-conviction
		post conviction
		postconviction

Paragraph symbol ¶

The WESTLAW computer does not recognize the paragraph symbol in the text of documents. The computer is programmed to display a paragraph symbol as a "P" on the monitor, but not to find a "P" that stands in for a paragraph symbol. Consequently, you should ignore paragraph symbols when you formulate your search requests.

For example, suppose you want to find references to paragraph 34556 in volume 101 of *Labor Cases*. The phrase search `"101 Lab.Cas. P 34556"` in the ALLFEDS database will yield a message that the database does not contain any documents satisfying your search request. However, transmitting `101 pre/5 34556` or the phrase search `"101 Lab.Cas. 34556"` will retrieve references to "101 Lab.Cas. P 34556."

Inconsistencies in how paragraph symbols appear in the underlying documents received by West Publishing, or inconsistencies in how those documents are transcribed for inclusion in the WESTLAW database, sometimes cause a "P" substituting for a paragraph symbol to turn out unpredictably to be a searchable character. In those instances, if you use a phrase search that omits the "P," you can bypass relevant references. Consequently, when you search for references that might include a paragraph symbol or a "P" standing in for the symbol, using a proximity connector (as in `101 pre/5 34556`) offers an advantage over a phrase search (such as `"101 Lab.Cas. 34556"`). The proximity connector allows you to link relevant search terms without wondering whether to include the "P."

Parentheses ( )

The WESTLAW computer treats parentheses in a number, or in a string of numbers and letters, as part of the number. So, WESTLAW reads a number like "12(b)(6)" as one word. Searching for `12(b)(6)` will therefore retrieve that number but not variations like "12b(6)" or "12(b)6." For a comprehensive search for a number that might be written with or without parentheses, include each alternative in your search request, as here:

```
12(b)(6) or 12b(6) or 12(b)6 or 12b6
```

In a string of letters in a document, parentheses are ignored by the WESTLAW computer. Searching for `"vice lords including petitioner in jackson's murder"` will retrieve documents with the phrase "Vice Lords (including petitioner) in Jackson's murder."

If you include parentheses as part of a phrase search—as in `"vice lords (including petitioner) in jackson's murder"`—the computer will treat the parentheses as invalid characters in the phrase and terminate the search so you can edit the request.

Note that the computer treats parentheses as invalid characters only when they occur in a phrase search, that is, in a phrase set off by quotation marks. When you use parentheses in a search request but not in a phrase search, the computer treats the parentheses as indicating either the order for processing connectors (see pages 66–67, 158–59, and 161) or the presence of a field restriction (see page 77). In a natural-language search request, parentheses identify search terms that operate as synonyms (see pages 175 and 177).

Percent sign %

When the percent sign abuts a number, the WESTLAW computer treats the symbol as part of the number; you must include the symbol in your search term to retrieve references to it. For example, `100%` will retrieve "100%" but not "100"; likewise, `100` will retrieve "100" but not "100%". So, for a comprehensive search for a number that might be written with or without a percent sign abutting it, include both alternatives in your search request:

```
100% or 100
```

When you include a freestanding percent sign as part of a phrase search, such as `"100 % of the time"`, the WESTLAW computer treats the symbol as an invalid character and terminates the search so you can edit the request by removing the percent sign.

If a freestanding percent sign in a search request is not part of a phrase search (for example, `apartment % house`), the computer treats the symbol as the "but not" logic connector. (See pages 46–47.)

Period .

The WESTLAW computer treats a period at the beginning of a number (as in ".704") as a space separating one search term from another, not as part of the number. Searching for `.704` will retrieve "704", and searching for `704` will retrieve ".704". So, you can use either form in your search request.

Note that when you search for a number that begins with a decimal point, WESTLAW will not automatically retrieve references that begin with a leading zero (*e.g.*, "0.704"). If you want to retrieve references to both forms, you should include both alternatives in your search request:

```
.704 or 0.704
```

A period in the middle of a number (as in "260.185") in a search request is treated as part of the number, not as a space separating one search term from another. Because WESTLAW treats a search term like `260.185` as one word, searching for `260.185` will retrieve that number but not "260" or "185."

In order to retrieve a number like "260.185," however, you do not need to transmit the entire number. The computer treats a period in the middle of a number in a document as a root expander for the number to the left of the period. So, you can transmit just `260` and retrieve any decimal number having "260" as its root (such as "260.181," "260.185"). Thus,

`260.185`	will retrieve	260.185
`260`	will retrieve	260 260.181, 260.185, etc.

When you use a period in a search term containing only letters, such as an abbreviation (like `fed.r.evid.`) or an acronym (like `a.i.d.s.`), you obtain a result different from the one you obtain with periods in a search term containing numbers. With letters, a period "normalizes" the search term so the computer will automatically search for variations of the term. (Pages 34–36 explain normalization.) Thus, in WESTLAW

`a.i.d.s.`	will retrieve	a.i.d.s a. i. d. s. aids a i d s

Plus sign +

The WESTLAW computer treats a plus sign as a space or as equivalent to the word "plus." For example:

`2+2`	will retrieve	2+2 2 plus 2
`"jaguar xke 2 2"`	will retrieve	Jaguar XKE 2 2 Jaguar XKE 2+2

A plus sign in a search request denominates a logic connector in WESTLAW when used in the "+n," "+s," or "+p" connector. (See pages 50–51 and 55–56.)

Pound or number sign #

The WESTLAW computer does not recognize the pound or number sign in the text of documents. The computer is programmed to display the symbol on the monitor, but not to find it in response to a search request. Consequently, you should not include a pound or number sign in your search requests as a way of retrieving documents containing this symbol.

The "#" symbol can serve a different purpose in a search request in WESTLAW, however. When you place the symbol at the beginning of a search term, the symbol turns off the automatic search for certain plurals and equivalents of that term, as explained on page 31 n.28 and page 32 n.30. So, the search term `#damage` will retrieve "damage" but not "damages"; the search term `#sec` will retrieve "SEC" but not "section."

Question mark ?

If you include a question mark after a single search term or after a phrase (as in `"is that your answer?"`), the computer will treat the question mark as an invalid character and terminate the search so you can edit the request by removing the question mark. Searching for `"is that your answer"` will retrieve the phrase "Is that your answer?"

When you search for a phrase in WESTLAW, the phrase must be contained in a single sentence. The WESTLAW computer sees a question mark in a document as ending a sentence. Consequently, if you want to search for language like "Is that your answer? Do you want to look at it?", you cannot simply omit the question marks and transmit `"is that your answer do you want to look at it"`. Instead, you need to construct phrase searches in which each phrase contains words found in just one sentence, as in `"is that your answer" w/5 "do you want to look at it"`.

Quotation marks " "

When you use quotation marks in a search request, you trigger a phrase search for the search terms enclosed in the quotation marks, as explained on pages 51–53.

Suppose the phrase you want to search for already has quotation marks within it (such as "act protects 'reasonable' trespasses"). What happens if you include the internal quotation marks in your search request, as in `"act protects "reasonable" trespasses"`? Because the WESTLAW computer interprets search terms between consecutive quotation marks in a search request as separate phrases, the computer carries out this request as though you had transmitted `"act protects" or reasonable or trespasses`, using a space between the phrases as the alternative form of the "or" connector (see pages 44–45). Obviously, this search differs quite a bit from what you had in mind. To get the result you intend, you can simply omit the internal quotation marks from your search request (because the computer treats quotation marks in documents as spaces). So, if you transmit the phrase search `"act protects reasonable trespasses"`, the computer will retrieve documents containing the phrase with the word "reasonable" enclosed in quotation marks.

Section symbol §

The WESTLAW computer does not recognize the section symbol in the text of documents. The computer is programmed to display section symbols on the monitor, but not to find them in response to search requests. To retrieve references that might contain a section symbol (such as "42 U.S.C. § 1983"), transmit a search request like `42 w/10 1983` or the phrase search `"42 U.S.C. 1983"`.

Sometimes (principally in cases that have not been published in a West reporter), citations use an "s" in place of the section symbol; a citation might read "42 U.S.C. s 1983" (with a space) or "42 U.S.C. s1983" (without a space) instead of "42 U.S.C. § 1983." Because the computer treats "s1983" as different from "1983," the search request `42 w/10 1983` would not retrieve documents in which the only statutory references consisted of "42 U.S.C. s1983." To ensure a comprehensive search, you can use a search request that takes the form `42 w/10 (1983 or s1983)`.

Semicolon ;

When you use a semicolon in a phrase search, the WESTLAW computer treats the semicolon as a searchable character and requires its presence in a document. On the other hand, if you omit a semicolon from the phrase in your search request, the computer will still locate documents in which the semicolon appears in the phrase corresponding to the one used in the search request. For example, searching for the phrase `"prosecution for gambling a note given"` will retrieve the phrase "prosecution for gambling; a note given".

You can also use a semicolon in a search request to combine separate search commands into a single "stacked" instruction, as explained in Appendix J.

Slash /

When a slash appears in the middle or at the end of a word, such as `plaintiff/appellee`, the WESTLAW computer treats the slash as a space or ignores it. For example:

`plaintiff/appellee`	will retrieve	plaintiff/appellee plaintiff appellee
`plaintiff/`	will retrieve	plaintiff/appellee plaintiff/respondent
`date/time`	will retrieve	date/time dates, times,
`a/k/a`	will retrieve	a/k/a aka

A slash in a search request denominates a logic connector in WESTLAW when used in the "w/n," "/n," "pre/n," "/s," or "/p" connector. (See pages 48–51 and 55–56.)

Alphabetic characters in numbers

In addition to considering how the WESTLAW computer treats punctuation marks and other symbols in numbers, knowing the following rules about alphabetic characters in numbers will help you formulate effective search requests.

Roman numerals. In statutory and administrative code databases, a one-way equivalency exists between Arabic and Roman numbers. For instance, transmitting the Arabic number `25` as a search term will retrieve either "25" or the Roman numeral "XXV", although the search term `xxv` will retrieve only "XXV", not "25". Consequently, in code databases, using Arabic numbers as search terms works more effectively than using Roman numerals.

In other databases, no automatic equivalency exists between Arabic numbers and their Roman-numeral counterparts. For example, transmitting the Arabic number `14` will not retrieve the Roman numeral "XIV". For a comprehensive search for a citation (such as a citation to a constitutional provision) that might be written with either a Roman or Arabic number, include both forms in your search request:

```
xiv or 14
```

Ordinal and cardinal numbers. The WESTLAW computer does not treat ordinal numbers as automatic equivalents of their cardinal counterparts. So, searching for the cardinal number `14` will not retrieve the ordinal number "14th". Likewise, searching for `XIV` will not retrieve "XIVth". For a comprehensive search for a citation (such as a citation to a constitutional provision) that might be written with either a cardinal or ordinal number, include both forms in your search request:

```
14 or 14th or XIV or XIVth
```

WESTLAW does, however, treat some cardinal numbers in their numeric form (*e.g.*, "14") as automatically equivalent to their alphabetic counterparts (*e.g.*, "fourteen"). In those instances, you only need to include one form in your search request. Similarly, WESTLAW treats some ordinal numbers in their numeric form (*e.g.*, "14th") as automatically equivalent to their alphabetic counterparts (*e.g.*, "fourteenth"). Appendix F provides a list of automatic equivalents in WESTLAW.

The effect of punctuation marks on how the WESTLAW computer counts words

When you use the "w/n," "/n," "pre/n," or "+n" connector in a search request, the WESTLAW computer, in determining the distance between words, looks as though it sometimes (but not always) counts punctuation marks in documents as words. Two researchers have written about this phenomenon:

> [A] period at the end of a sentence is counted as a word, though a period within a sentence, such as the period in "v.", will not be counted. Similarly, punctuation such as [semicolons, commas, parentheses, or colons] appear to be counted as words if they are followed by a carriage return, but are not counted as words if they occur within a paragraph.[448]

When you examine the documents you retrieve, the results might make you wonder how the computer counted the number of words between your search terms. The word count might differ from what you expected because, in certain situations, West Publishing uses a special kind of space (called a "word space") after punctuation marks in the online document. Although you cannot tell when you are viewing a word space in a WESTLAW document, the computer recognizes this kind of space and counts it as a word.

The word space exists to allow the WESTLAW computer to process the "/s," "+s," "/p," and "+p" connectors, which require the computer to distinguish among the variety of functions a single punctuation mark can perform in a document. For example, a period can (among other things) end a sentence, end a paragraph, end an abbreviation, serve as a decimal point in a number, appear as part of an acronym, or appear as part of an ellipsis. When a punctuation mark ends a sentence or paragraph, a word space follows the punctuation mark. As a result, when you use the "/s" or "+s" connector, the computer can recognize when your search terms appear in the same sentence, and when you use the "/p" or "+p" connector, the computer can spot when your search terms appear in the same paragraph.

[448] *See* Nick Triffin & Edie Adams, *Database Trivia?*, 3 TRENDS IN LAW LIBR. MGMT. & TECH., Nov. 1990, at 6, 6. Triffin and Adams also provide examples of passages in documents that search requests using the "w/n" connector will or will not retrieve, depending on whether the WESTLAW computer counts punctuation marks in the passages as words.

APPENDIX I

Using "Dot" Commands and the "Short Cut" Feature in LEXIS

The "dot" commands. For most of the keys specifically designated on LEXIS keyboards to carry out CALR functions, LEXIS provides an alternative known as a "dot" command. A dot command consists of a period (the "dot") followed by two letters that identify the function the computer should perform. Whenever the discussion in this book says to press a LEXIS function key, you can type its corresponding dot command and press TRANSMIT instead. Figure I.01 on page 726 lists the LEXIS dot commands in alphabetical order; Figure I.02 on page 727 arranges these commands by function.

With some function keys, you can type a number and press the function key to perform the function the specified number of times. For example, to skip four screens forward from the screen you are viewing, you can type `4` and press the NEXT PAGE key. You can achieve the same result if you type the dot command followed by the number you want to use, then press TRANSMIT. Thus, rather than typing `4` and pressing NEXT PAGE, you can type `.np4` and press TRANSMIT.

Stacking commands: the "short cut" feature in LEXIS. You can combine into a single instruction various dot commands and other commands you type without a period (such as `m` to modify a search). The resulting instruction bypasses the screens you would otherwise have to view before you could transmit your next command. LEXIS refers to this technique as its "short cut" feature; some people also describe it as "stacking" commands. The shortcut feature can reduce the time spent online and, therefore, the cost of online research. Researchers typically find that stacking commands proves most useful, however, after having gained experience with LEXIS and grown comfortable with the structure of its libraries and files and with the commands and procedures for searching them.

You can begin stacking commands any time after logging on to LEXIS. To construct a shortcut instruction, type your first command, a semicolon, your next command, a semicolon, and so on; then press TRANSMIT. For example, although not all shortcut instructions contain this many stacked commands, you could construct an instruction that begins with your client identifier, then

LEXIS Function Key	LEXIS "Dot" Command
CHG FILE	.cf
CHG LIB	.cl
CITE	.ci
n DIF LEVEL or *n* DISP DIF LEVEL	.dl*n*
EXIT FOCUS	.ef
EXIT SERV	.es
FIRST DOC	.fd
FIRST PAGE	.fp
FOCUS	.fo
FULL	.fu
KWIC	.kw
MAIL IT or PRINT ALL	.mi
NEW SEARCH	.ns
NEXT DOC	.nd
NEXT PAGE	.np
PREV DOC	.pd
PREV PAGE	.pp
PRINT ALL or MAIL IT	.mi
PRINT DOC	.pr
PRINT SCREEN	.sp
SEGMTS	.se
SELECT SERV	.ss
SIGN OFF	.so
VAR KWIC	.vk
n VAR KWIC	.vk*n*

Notes:
n = a number you type
Not all LEXIS keyboards will have all the function keys listed here.

Figure I.01. Quick Guide to LEXIS Dot Commands in Alphabetical Order

LEXIS Function Key	LEXIS "Dot" Command
Selecting a library or file	
CHG FILE	.cf
CHG LIB	.cl
Retrieving documents	
NEW SEARCH	.ns
Displaying retrieved documents	
FULL	.fu
KWIC	.kw
VAR KWIC	.vk
n VAR KWIC	.vk*n*
CITE	.ci
SEGMTS	.se
Moving within a displayed document	
FIRST PAGE	.fp
NEXT PAGE	.np
PREV PAGE	.pp
Moving between retrieved documents	
n DIF LEVEL or *n* DISP DIF LEVEL	.dl*n*
FIRST DOC	.fd
NEXT DOC	.nd
PREV DOC	.pd
Searching within retrieved documents	
FOCUS	.fo
EXIT FOCUS	.ef
Storing the results of a search	
MAIL IT or PRINT ALL	.mi
PRINT DOC	.pr
PRINT SCREEN	.sp
Entering and leaving a service	
SELECT SERV	.ss
EXIT SERV	.es
Logging off LEXIS	
SIGN OFF	.so

Notes:
n = a number you type
Not all LEXIS keyboards will have all the function keys listed here.

Figure I.02. Quick Guide to LEXIS Dot Commands Arranged by Function

selects a library and file, states your search request, and ends by designating a display format for retrieved documents.

To illustrate, suppose you were doing research on a lawsuit Megacorp Company filed against your client, Acme Dynamite, for selling allegedly defective dynamite that injured Wile E. Coyote, a Megacorp employee. After you transmitted your LEXIS identification number, you could use the following shortcut instruction to identify your client, gain access to the STATES library, search in the OMNI file for cases dealing with strict product liability for defectively manufactured dynamite, and then display the retrieved documents in the KWIC display format:

```
           library     search request
   client     |         file   |
     |        |          |     |
     ↓        ↓          ↓     ↓
     acme;states;omni;((strict! w/3 liab!) w/25 ((dynamite or
     explosive) w/10 defectiv!)) and (injur! or damag!);.kw
                                                          ↑
                                                          |
                                                   display format
```

Once you have performed a search—using a shortcut instruction or not—you can use a shortcut instruction to repeat the search in a different file in the same library. To do so, type a shortcut instruction that will switch you to the file you want to search, type two semicolons after the name of the new file, and then press TRANSMIT. So, to run the preceding search in, say, the Illinois (ILL) file in the STATES library, you could transmit this shortcut instruction:

```
.cf;ill;;
↑  ↑    ↑
|  |    repeat search
|  |
|  file name
|
change file
```

You can also use a shortcut instruction to run the same search in a file in a different library, such as the COURTS file in the GENFED library:

```
.cl;genfed;courts;;
↑  ↑      ↑       ↑
|  |      |       repeat search
|  |      |
|  |      file name
|  |
|  library name
|
change library
```

Moreover, you can designate a display format, such as CITE:

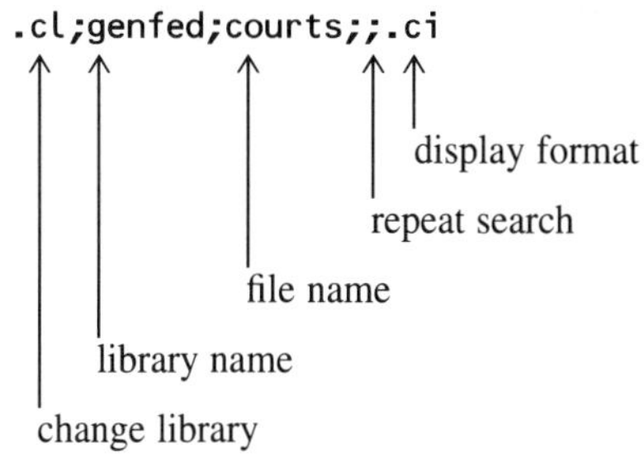

Figure I.03 sets out some common scenarios in which a shortcut instruction can speed up your online searching. For more examples, see Chapter 18 of the *LEXIS-NEXIS User's Guide*.[449]

[449] MEAD DATA CENTRAL, LEXIS-NEXIS USER'S GUIDE 18-1 to 18-2 (1990 & 1991 Supp.).

If you want to	Configuration in LEXIS	Example
Transmit a search request at the screen for identifying your client	*client*;*library name*;*file name*;*search request*;*display format*	`smith;genfed;us;445 pre/5 55;.kw`
Add a modification to the end of your current search request	`m;`*modification*	`m;and uncounsel!`
Switch to a new file in the same library	`.cf;`*file name*	`.cf;allcde`
Switch to a new file in the same library and repeat your previous search request	`.cf;`*file name*`;;`	`.cf;9th;;`
Switch to a new library	`.cl;`*library name*	`.cl;genfed`
Switch to a new file in a different library	`.cl;`*library name*;*file name*	`.cl;genfed;us`
Switch to a new file in a different library and repeat your previous search request	`.cl;`*library name*;*file name*`;;`	`.cl;codes;uscode;;`
Move to the next page of the displayed document and show the screen in a specified format	`.np;`*display format*	`.np;.vk`
Move to the previous page of the displayed document and show the screen in a specified format	`.pp;`*display format*	`.pp;.vk`

Note: Italicized words represent information the researcher supplies.

Figure I.03. Examples of Short-Cut Instructions in LEXIS

APPENDIX J

Stacking Commands in WESTLAW

In WESTLAW, you can often combine separate commands into a single instruction, a technique WESTLAW sometimes refers to as "stacking" commands. When you stack commands, you bypass the screens you would otherwise have to view before you could transmit your next command. For example, if you transmit **db**, **sdb**, or **qdb**, you need to wait for the WESTLAW Directory (shown in Figure 9.07 on page 196) to display before you can transmit the identifier of the database you want to select. But as explained on pages 182–83, you can combine **db**, **sdb**, or **qdb** with a database identifier (such as ID-CS), as in the following "stacked" instruction for selecting the database containing Idaho cases:

```
db id-cs
↑  ↑
|  |
|  database identifier
|
select a database
```

With this instruction, you bypass the WESTLAW Directory screen and go directly to the selected database.

Thus, stacking can reduce the time spent online and, therefore, the cost of online research. Researchers typically find that stacking commands proves most useful, however, after having gained experience with WESTLAW and grown comfortable with the structure of its databases and with the commands and procedures for searching them.

The following examples illustrate other opportunities for stacking commands when you use WESTLAW. Note that sometimes you use a semicolon to combine WESTLAW commands in a stacked instruction, and other times not.

Combining a database selection with a search request. At the WESTLAW Directory (shown in Figure 9.07 on page 196) or at the screen for typing your search request (Figure 9.10 on page 201 or Figure 9.11 on page 202), you can select a database and transmit your search request in a single instruction. For instance, to select the database of U.S. Supreme Court cases and then search it for cases referring to *Miranda v. Arizona* and *Escobedo v. Illinois*, you could transmit this stacked instruction:

```
db sct miranda & escobedo
↑  ↑   ↑
|  |   search request
|  database identifier
select a database
```

You can also transmit a stacked instruction like this while viewing a document in WESTLAW, but when a document is displayed, the amount of space available for typing search instructions will vary.

Combining a star-page command with FIND. Pages 279–84 explain how to retrieve a document with the FIND feature. If you want to retrieve a case with a FIND instruction (such as `fi 110 sct 2841`) and begin viewing the case at a particular star page (such as star page 2849), you can transmit a stacked instruction like this:

```
fi 110 sct 2841;st 2849
↑                ↑
|                command for viewing a star page
FIND instruction
```

Combining commands for offline printing and downloading. You can use a stacked instruction to combine the separate commands involved when you use the Offline Printing and Downloading Menu (illustrated in Figures 11.22 and 11.23 on page 373) for printing or downloading search results. For instance, you might want to download the first page of documents 4 through 7 in your collection of retrieved documents. If so, you could transmit this stacked instruction:

```
pr;f4-7;dld
↑  ↑    ↑
|  |    This command indicates the destination for printing or
|  |    downloading—here, downloading to a disk on your
|  |    personal computer.
|  This command indicates the portion of the results you want
|  to print or download—here, the first page of documents
|  4 through 7.
This command signals the computer that you will be printing
or downloading your search results.
```

You can also add another semicolon and a command to indicate what you want to do after you transmit your printing or downloading instruction. So, if you wanted to continue your research by next switching to the database containing U.S. Supreme Court cases, you could transmit:

```
pr;f4-7;dld;db sct
```

- `sct` — database identifier
- `db` — select a database
- `dld` — destination for printing or downloading
- `f4-7` — results to print or download
- `pr` — printing or downloading command

If the screen you are viewing when you type your stacked instruction provides enough typing space, you can even extend the stacked instruction to include the search you want to perform after you transmit your printing or downloading instruction. So, if you were viewing the results of a search in the database of California unannotated statutes and wanted to download those results, then switch to the database of U.S. Supreme Court cases to search for references to *Miranda* and *Escobedo*, you could transmit a stacked instruction like this:

```
pr;f4-7;dld;db sct miranda & escobedo
```

- `miranda & escobedo` — search request
- `sct` — database identifier
- `db` — select a database
- `dld` — destination for printing or downloading
- `f4-7` — results to print or download
- `pr` — printing or downloading command

Combining commands for using the WESTLAW Personal Directory of Queries (PDQ). Pages 627 to 636 explain how to set up, modify, run, and delete PDQ entries. You can combine the separate PDQ commands for these activities in a single stacked instruction. For example:

- To set up your most recent search as a PDQ request and then return to the screen you were viewing before invoking PDQ, transmit

```
pdq add;gb
```

- `gb` — go back to the screen you were viewing before invoking PDQ
- `add` — set up and save the PDQ search
- `pdq` — invoke PDQ

- To set up your most recent search as a PDQ request and then return to WESTLAW's query entry screen, transmit

```
pdq add;q
↑   ↑   ↑
|   |   return to the WESTLAW query entry screen
|   set up and save the PDQ search
invoke PDQ
```

- To set up as a PDQ request a search you have not just performed, transmit

```
pdq create
↑   ↑
|   set up and save the PDQ search
invoke PDQ
```

- To retrieve the second search request in your PDQ Directory for modification, transmit

```
pdq;2
↑   ↑
|   retrieve the second PDQ search
invoke PDQ
```

You can transmit the name of the saved search instead of its entry number, if you prefer.

- To run the second search request in your PDQ Directory, transmit

```
pdq;2;s
↑   ↑ ↑
|   | run the search
|   retrieve the second PDQ search
invoke PDQ
```

You can transmit the name of the saved search instead of its entry number, if you prefer.

- To run the second search request in your PDQ Directory, but in a database different from the one you specified in the PDQ entry, transmit

```
pdq;2;sdb XXX
↑   ↑ ↑
|   | run the search in a specified database (type a
|   | database identifier in place of XXX)
|   |
|   retrieve the second PDQ search
|
invoke PDQ
```

You can transmit the name of the saved search instead of its entry number, if you prefer.

- To delete the third search request in your PDQ Directory, transmit

```
pdq;3;del
↑   ↑ ↑
|   | delete the search
|   |
|   retrieve the third PDQ search
|
invoke PDQ
```

You can transmit the name of the saved search instead of its entry number, if you prefer.

If you are already viewing the PDQ Directory, you can omit **pdq** from the beginning of a stacked PDQ instruction. Thus, to delete your third PDQ entry, you could transmit the following instruction while viewing the PDQ Directory:

```
3;del
↑ ↑
| delete the search
|
retrieve the third PDQ search
```

Or, to run your second PDQ entry, you could transmit the following instruction while viewing the PDQ Directory:

```
2;s
↑ ↑
| run the search
|
retrieve the second PDQ search
```

APPENDIX K

Quick Guide to Keys and Commands for Using LEXIS

The following figure lists the function keys you can use to perform LEXIS tasks on a LEXIS 2000 keyboard, on a UBIQ keyboard, or on an IBM PC or IBM-compatible keyboard equipped with a template identifying the keys for performing specific LEXIS functions. The final column of the figure lists the commands you can type on any of these keyboards as an alternative to pressing function keys to carry out LEXIS tasks.

Figure 9.12 on page 208 shows the layout of the LEXIS 2000 keyboard, Figure 9.14 on page 210 shows the arrangement of the UBIQ keyboard, and Figure 9.13 on page 209 depicts the LEXIS template for an IBM PC or IBM-compatible keyboard.

Task You Want to Perform	LEXIS 2000 Keyboard	UBIQ Keyboard	IBM PC or Compatible Keyboard (with template)†	Keyboard or "Dot" Command (all keyboards)

Selecting a Library or File in LEXIS

Task You Want to Perform	LEXIS 2000 Keyboard	UBIQ Keyboard	IBM PC or Compatible Keyboard (with template)†	Keyboard or "Dot" Command (all keyboards)
Display the library menu	CHG LIB	CHG LIB	CHG LIB F10	.cl
Switch to a specified library	.cl;*library*	.cl;*library*	.cl;*library*	.cl;*library*
Display the file menu for the current library	CHG FILE	CHG FILE	CHG FILE F9	.cf
Switch to a specified file in the current library	.cf;*file*	.cf;*file*	.cf;*file*	.cf;*file*
Switch to a specified file in a different library	.cl;*library*;*file*	.cl;*library*;*file*	.cl;*library*;*file*	.cl;*library*;*file*

Retrieving Documents in LEXIS

Task You Want to Perform	LEXIS 2000 Keyboard	UBIQ Keyboard	IBM PC or Compatible Keyboard (with template)†	Keyboard or "Dot" Command (all keyboards)
Begin a new search	NEW SEARCH	NEW SEARCH	NEW SRCH F8	.ns
Display the current search request	r	r	r	r
Cancel a search	STOP	STOP	STOP ALT F10	
Modify the search request	MODIFY	m	MODIFY ALT F8	m

Modify the search request at search level n[††]	*n* MODIFY	`m`*n* *n*`m`	*n* MODIFY *n* ALT F8	`m`*n* *n*`m`
Retrieve a document using LEXSEE	*citation* LEXSEE *citation* F7	`lxe` *citation* `lexsee` *citation*	*citation* LEXSEE *citation* CTRL F3	`lxe` *citation* `lexsee` *citation*

Return to a document retrieved through LEXSEE	RESUME LEXSEE
	SHIFT F7
		`res lxe`
		`resume lxe`
		`res lexsee`
		`resume lexsee`
			`res lxe`
			`resume lxe`
			`res lexsee`
			`resume lexsee`
				`res lxe`
				`resume lxe`
				`res lexsee`
				`resume lexsee`

Retrieve a document using LEXSTAT	*citation* LEXSTAT *citation* F8	`lxt` *citation* `lexstat` *citation*	*citation* LEXSTAT *citation* CTRL F4	`lxt` *citation* `lexstat` *citation*

Return to a document retrieved through LEXSTAT	RESUME LEXSTAT
	SHIFT F8
		`res lxt`
		`resume lxt`
		`res lexstat`
		`resume lexstat`
			`res lxt`
			`resume lxt`
			`res lexstat`
			`resume lexstat`
				`res lxt`
				`resume lxt`
				`res lexstat`
				`resume lexstat`

Return to LEXIS after using LEXSEE or LEXSTAT	RESUME LEXIS F9	`res lexis` `resume lexis`	RESUME LEXIS CTRL F6	`res lexis` `resume lexis`

(continues)

Notes:
On a keyboard that has keys (such as CHG LIB) labelled for specified functions, you can either press those keys or type the corresponding command listed in the final column of this chart.
file = the name of a file, such as TENN
library = the name of a library, such as STATES
star-page I.D. = an identification of a set of star-page numbers, such as "us" for star-page numbers in *U.S. Reports*
citation = a citation, such as "487 us 285"

[†] The commands in this column operate in version 2.7 of LEXIS/NEXIS Technology Series Research Software for MS-DOS.
[††] n = a number from 1 to 255

(continued)

Task You Want to Perform	LEXIS 2000 Keyboard	UBIQ Keyboard	IBM PC or Compatible Keyboard (with template)†	Keyboard or "Dot" Command (all keyboards)

Displaying Retrieved Documents in LEXIS

Task You Want to Perform	LEXIS 2000 Keyboard	UBIQ Keyboard	IBM PC or Compatible Keyboard (with template)†	Keyboard or "Dot" Command (all keyboards)
Display the complete online text of each document	FULL	FULL	FULL F6	`.fu`
Display each document so it shows 25 searchable words on each side of your search terms	KWIC	KWIC	KWIC F5	`.kw`
Display each document so it shows 50 searchable words on each side of your search terms	VAR KWIC	VAR KWIC	VAR KWIC SHIFT F5	`.vk`
Display a document so it shows *n* searchable words on each side of your search terms†††	*n* VAR KWIC	*n* VAR KWIC	*n* VAR KWIC *n* SHIFT F5	`.vk`*n*
Display the list of a document's segments available for customized viewing	SEGMTS	SEGMTS	SGMTS SHIFT F10	`.se`
Display the citation list of retrieved documents	CITE	CITE	CITE F7	`.ci`
Show the number of screens in the displayed document	`p`	`p`	`p`	`p`

Limit the display of multiple sets of star-page numbers to just one set	*star-page I.D.* ENTER STAR *star-page I.D.* F2	`st` *star-page I.D.* `star` *star-page I.D.*	*star-page I.D.* ENTER STAR *star-page I.D.* ALT F5	`st` *star-page I.D.* `star` *star-page I.D.*
Return to the standard display of star-page numbers	EXIT STAR SHIFT F2	`xst` `xstar`	EXIT STAR ALT F7	`xst` `xstar`

Moving Within a Displayed Document in LEXIS

Move forward one screen in the displayed document	NEXT PAGE	NEXT PAGE	NEXT PG (or PgDn) F1	`.np`
Skip ahead *n* screens in the displayed document[†††]	*n* NEXT PAGE	*n* NEXT PAGE	*n* NEXT PG (or *n* PgDn) *n* F1	`.np`*n*
Move back one screen in the displayed document	PREV PAGE	PREV PAGE	PREV PAGE (or PgUp) F2	`.pp`
Skip back *n* screens in the displayed document[†††]	*n* PREV PAGE	*n* PREV PAGE	*n* PREV PG (or *n* PgUp) *n* F2	`.pp`*n*
Move forward one line in the displayed document		ROLL UP		
Move back one line in the displayed document		ROLL DOWN		
Return to the first screen in the displayed document	FIRST PAGE	FIRST PAGE	FIRST PG SHIFT F6	`.fp`
Move to star-page *n*	*n* P* *n* F1	`p*`*n*	*n* P* *n* ALT F6	`p*`*n*

(continues)

[†] The commands in this column operate in version 2.7 of LEXIS/NEXIS Technology Series Research Software for MS-DOS.
[†††] n = a number from 1 to 999

(continued)

Task You Want to Perform	LEXIS 2000 Keyboard	UBIQ Keyboard	IBM PC or Compatible Keyboard (with template)[†]	Keyboard or "Dot" Command (all keyboards)

Searching Within Retrieved Documents in LEXIS

Task You Want to Perform	LEXIS 2000 Keyboard	UBIQ Keyboard	IBM PC or Compatible Keyboard (with template)[†]	Keyboard or "Dot" Command (all keyboards)
Implement a FOCUS search	FOCUS F4	`focus` `.fo`	FOCUS CTRL F7	`focus` `.fo`
Exit FOCUS	EXIT FOCUS SHIFT F4	`exit` `.ef`	EXIT FOCUS CTRL F8	`exit` `.ef`

Moving Between Documents in LEXIS

Task You Want to Perform	LEXIS 2000 Keyboard	UBIQ Keyboard	IBM PC or Compatible Keyboard (with template)[†]	Keyboard or "Dot" Command (all keyboards)
Move to the next document in a retrieved collection	NEXT DOC	NEXT DOC	NEXT DOC F3	`.nd`
Skip ahead *n* documents in a retrieved collection[†††]	*n* NEXT DOC	*n* NEXT DOC	*n* NEXT DOC *n* F3	`.nd`*n*
Move to the previous document in a retrieved collection	PREV DOC	PREV DOC	PREV DOC F4	`.pd`
Skip back *n* documents in a retrieved collection[†††]	*n* PREV DOC	*n* PREV DOC	*n* PREV DOC *n* F4	`.pd`*n*
Move to document number *n* in a retrieved collection	*n*	*n*	*n*	*n*
Return to the first document in a retrieved collection, or to the first screen of a citation list	FIRST DOC	FIRST DOC	FIRST DOC SHIFT F7	`.fd`

Move to documents at a different search level (level *n*)[††]	*n* DIF LEVEL	*n* DISP DIF LEVEL	*n* DIF LEV *n* SHIFT F8	.dl*n*
Invoke "Browse" to move to other sections of a statutory or administrative code	b	b	b	b
Exit "Browse"	b	b	b	b

Updating Search Results in LEXIS

Shepardize the authority you are viewing	SHEP F6	sh shep	SHEP CTRL F2	sh shep
Shepardize an authority you are not viewing	*citation* SHEP *citation* F6	sh *citation* shep *citation*	*citation* SHEP *citation* CTRL F2	sh *citation* shep *citation*
Customize the display of a Shepard's table	SEGMTS	SEGMTS	SGMTS SHIFT F10	.se
Cancel customization of a Shepard's table	FULL	FULL	FULL F6	.fu
Return to a retrieved Shepard's table after using another service	RESUME SHEP SHIFT F6	res sh resume sh res shep resume shep	res sh resume sh res shep resume shep	res sh resume sh res shep resume shep

(continues)

[†] The commands in this column operate in version 2.7 of LEXIS/NEXIS Technology Series Research Software for MS-DOS.
[††] *n* = a number from 1 to 255
[†††] *n* = a number from 1 to 999

(continued)

Task You Want to Perform	LEXIS 2000 Keyboard	UBIQ Keyboard	IBM PC or Compatible Keyboard (with template)[†]	Keyboard or "Dot" Command (all keyboards)

Updating Search Results in LEXIS—*continued*

Task You Want to Perform	LEXIS 2000 Keyboard	UBIQ Keyboard	IBM PC or Compatible Keyboard (with template)[†]	Keyboard or "Dot" Command (all keyboards)
Retrieve the Auto-Cite report for the case you are viewing	AUTO-CITE F5	ac	AUTO-CITE CTRL F1	ac
Retrieve the Auto-Cite report for a case you are not viewing	*citation* AUTO-CITE *citation* F5	ac *citation*	*citation* AUTO-CITE *citation* CTRL F1	ac *citation*
Return to a retrieved Auto-Cite report after using another service	RESUME AC SHIFT F5	res ac resume ac	res ac resume ac	res ac resume ac
Use LEXCITE to retrieve documents that refer to a specific citation	lexcite(*citation*)	lexcite(*citation*)	lexcite(*citation*)	lexcite(*citation*)
Save a search request as an ECLIPSE search to run again later	SAVE ECLIPSE F3	.ss;sav	SAVE ECLIPSE ALT F3	.ss;sav
Recall an ECLIPSE search	RECALL ECLIPSE SHIFT F3	.ss;rec	RECALL ECLIPSE ALT F4	.ss;rec
Return to LEXIS after using an updating service	RESUME LEXIS F9	res lexis resume lexis	RESUME LEXIS CTRL F6	res lexis resume lexis

Printing or Downloading the Results of a Search in LEXIS [Δ]

Print the displayed screen	PRINT SCREEN	PRINT	SHIFT PrtSc	
Print or download the displayed document	PRINT DOC F12	PRINT DOC	PRINT DOC SHIFT F3	.pr
Print or download selected documents or all retrieved documents	PRINT ALL F11	MAIL IT	PRINT ALL SHIFT F4	.mi
Automatically print or download each screen as it displays	SESSION RECORD SHIFT F11		SESS REC ALT F2	
Turn off automatic printing or downloading of displayed screens	SESSION RECORD SHIFT F11		SESS REC ALT F2	

Miscellaneous Tasks in LEXIS

Display online help in LEXIS	h	h	h	h
Display the elapsed time for the current search session	t	t	t	t
Change the client name or identification	c	c	c	c

(continues)

[†] The commands in this column operate in version 2.7 of LEXIS/NEXIS Technology Series Research Software for MS-DOS.
[Δ] Downloading is unavailable on a UBIQ terminal.

(continued)

Task You Want to Perform	LEXIS 2000 Keyboard	UBIQ Keyboard	IBM PC or Compatible Keyboard (with template)[†]	Keyboard or "Dot" Command (all keyboards)

Miscellaneous Tasks in LEXIS—*continued*

Task You Want to Perform	LEXIS 2000 Keyboard	UBIQ Keyboard	IBM PC or Compatible Keyboard (with template)[†]	Keyboard or "Dot" Command (all keyboards)
Display the "Select Service" menu to select a service (*e.g.*, ECLIPSE)	SELECT SERV F10	SELECT SERV	SELECT SERV SHIFT F1	.ss
Exit a service (*e.g.*, ECLIPSE)	EXIT SERV SHIFT F10	EXIT SERV	EXIT SERV SHIFT F2	.es
Return to LEXIS from another service (*e.g.*, from LEXSEE)	RESUME LEXIS F9	res lexis resume lexis	RESUME LEXIS CTRL F6	res lexis resume lexis
Return to a previous step in your research (*e.g.*, from Shepard's to LEXSEE)	RESUME SHIFT F9	res resume	RESUME CTRL F5	res resume
Type the section symbol	§ SHIFT '	§ SHIFT 0	@ CTRL u	@
Order copies of public records documents and searches from LEXIS Document Services	LEXDOC SHIFT F1	lexdoc	LEXDOC CTRL F10	lexdoc

Obtain up-to-the-minute price quotes on U.S. stocks, bonds, and mutual funds, and on Canadian securities (at library menu only)	QUOTE SHIFT F12	quote	QUOTE CTRL F9	quote
Temporarily return to DOS while remaining logged on to LEXIS	ALT d		ALT d	
Log off LEXIS	SIGN OFF	SIGN OFF	SIGN OFF ALT F9	.so
Display LEXIS/NEXIS Technology Series Research Software's online ("local") help	ALT h		ALT h	
Exit from LEXIS/NEXIS Technology Series Research Software	ALT q		ALT q	

† The commands in this column operate in version 2.7 of LEXIS/NEXIS Technology Series Research Software for MS-DOS.

APPENDIX L

Quick Guide to Keys and Commands for Using WESTLAW

The following figure lists the function keys you can use to perform WESTLAW tasks on a WALT PC keyboard, on a WALT II keyboard, or on an IBM PC or IBM-compatible keyboard equipped with a template identifying the keys for performing specific WESTLAW functions. The final column of the figure lists the commands you can type on any of these keyboards as an alternative to pressing function keys to carry out WESTLAW tasks.

Figure 9.15 on page 211 shows the layout of the WALT PC keyboard, Figure 9.17 on page 213 shows the arrangement of the WALT II keyboard, and Figure 9.16 on page 212 depicts the WESTLAW template for an IBM PC or IBM-compatible keyboard.

Task You Want to Perform	WALT PC Keyboard	WALT II Keyboard	IBM PC or Compatible Keyboard (with template)*	Keyboard Command (all keyboards)

Selecting a Database in WESTLAW

Task You Want to Perform	WALT PC Keyboard	WALT II Keyboard	IBM PC or Compatible Keyboard (with template)*	Keyboard Command (all keyboards)
Display the WESTLAW Directory	CHANGE DB	CHANGE DATABASE	db	db
Switch to a specified database	*database* CHANGE DB	*database* CHANGE DATA-BASE	db *database*	db *database*
Return to the WESTLAW Directory	CHANGE DB 1 MAP 1 F2	CHANGE DATABASE 1 MAP	db 1 MAP 1 SHIFT F8	db map1
Show the coverage of the current database	SCOPE	SCOPE	SCOPE SHIFT F9	sc scope
Show the coverage of a specified database	*database* SCOPE	*database* SCOPE	*database* SCOPE *database* SHIFT F9	sc *database* scope *database*
Display a list of the databases and services (*e.g.*, Shepard's, FIND) you used most recently	MAP F2	MAP	MAP SHIFT F8	map

Setting WESTLAW Options

Task You Want to Perform	WALT PC Keyboard	WALT II Keyboard	IBM PC or Compatible Keyboard (with template)*	Keyboard Command (all keyboards)
Customize certain default settings in WESTLAW (*e.g.*, display order for search results)	OPTIONS	opt options	opt options	opt options

Retrieving Documents in WESTLAW

Switch to natural-language searching	nat	nat	nat	nat
Switch to terms-and-connectors searching	tc	tc	tc	tc
Begin a new search	s	s	s	s
Cancel a search	x	x	x	x
Interrupt a Boolean search	i	i	i	i
Display a summary of your search (showing your search request and the number of documents it retrieved)	g	g	g	g
Run the same search in a different database	sdb	sdb	sdb	sdb

(continues)

Notes:
On a keyboard that has keys labelled for specified functions (such as CHANGE DATABASE), you can either press those keys or type the corresponding command listed in the final column of this chart.
database = the name of a database, such as TN-CS
citation = a citation, such as "487 us 285"
terms = a word or phrase
n = a number you type
star-page I.D. = an identification of a set of star-page numbers, such as "us" for star-page numbers in *U.S. Reports*
field = the name of a field

* The commands in this column operate in version 4.5 of WESTMATE Communications Software for DOS.

(continued)

Task You Want to Perform	WALT PC Keyboard	WALT II Keyboard	IBM PC or Compatible Keyboard (with template)*	Keyboard Command (all keyboards)

Retrieving Documents in WESTLAW—*continued*

Task You Want to Perform	WALT PC Keyboard	WALT II Keyboard	IBM PC or Compatible Keyboard (with template)*	Keyboard Command (all keyboards)
Run the same search in a specified database	sdb *database*	sdb *database*	sdb *database*	sdb *database*
Modify the search request	q	q	q	q
Modify the search request and run it in a different database	qdb	qdb	qdb	qdb
Modify the search request and run it in a specified database	qdb *database*	qdb *database*	qdb *database*	qdb *database*
Display information about broadening a Boolean search	expand	expand	expand	expand
Display information about narrowing a Boolean search	restrict	restrict	restrict	restrict
Invoke the WESTLAW thesaurus for adding synonyms to a search request	thes	thes	thes	thes
Add a field restriction to a natural-language search request	res	res	res	res

Retrieve a document using FIND	*citation* FIND *citation* F9	*citation* FIND	*citation* FIND *citation* SHIFT F7	fi *citation* find *citation*
Exit FIND	GO BACK F3 MAP F2	GO BACK MAP	GO BACK F8 MAP SHIFT F8	gb map
Return to your most recent WESTLAW search results (if any)	2 MAP 2 F2	2 MAP	2 MAP 2 SHIFT F8	map2
Display a list of searches saved in your Personal Directory of Queries	PDQ	PDQ	pdq	pdq
Display the Related Materials directory showing materials (*e.g.*, legislative or court-issued amendments, historical notes, annotations) related to the displayed statute, court rule, or legislative service document	rm	rm	rm	rm
Retrieve general materials (*e.g.*, references, historical notes, annotations, disposition tables) applicable to the statutory title, chapter, or subchapter containing the displayed statute or court rule	gm	gm	gm	gm

(continues)

* The commands in this column operate in version 4.5 of WESTMATE Communications Software for DOS.

(continued)

Retrieving Documents in WESTLAW—*continued*

Task You Want to Perform	WALT PC Keyboard	WALT II Keyboard	IBM PC or Compatible Keyboard (with template)*	Keyboard Command (all keyboards)
Retrieve references (*e.g.*, library references, related administrative code sections, law review commentaries) related to the displayed unannotated statute or court rule	re refs	re refs	re refs	re refs
Retrieve annotations (*i.e.*, Notes of Decisions) for the displayed unannotated statute or court rule	an annos	an annos	an annos	an annos
Retrieve annotated statutory documents amended or repealed by the displayed legislative service document or court order	st-ann	st-ann	st-ann	st-ann
Retrieve unannotated statutory documents amended or repealed by the displayed legislative service document or court order	stat	stat	stat	stat

Retrieve court rules affected by the displayed court order	ru rules	ru rules	ru rules	ru rules
Invoke EZ ACCESS for finding search results	EZ ACCESS	EZ ACCESS	EZ ACCESS SHIFT F2	ez
Display additional choices while in EZ ACCESS	EZ ACCESS	EZ ACCESS	EZ ACCESS SHIFT F2	ez
Invoke Black's Law Dictionary	di	DICTIONARY	di	di
Find the definition for a specified word or phrase in Black's Law Dictionary	di *terms*	*terms* DICTIONARY	di *terms*	di *terms*

Displaying Retrieved Documents in WESTLAW

Display the complete online text of each document	[occurs automatically]	[occurs automatically]	[occurs automatically]	[occurs automatically]
Display the citation list of retrieved documents	L list	CITE LIST	CITE LIST SHIFT F7	L list
Display the citation list beginning with the citation of the document with rank number *n*	Lr*n*	Lr*n*	Lr*n*	Lr*n*
Display the list of a document's fields available for customized viewing	f	FIELDS	f	f

(continues)

* The commands in this column operate in version 4.5 of WESTMATE Communications Software for DOS.

(continued)

Task You Want to Perform	WALT PC Keyboard	WALT II Keyboard	IBM PC or Compatible Keyboard (with template)*	Keyboard Command (all keyboards)

Displaying Retrieved Documents in WESTLAW—*continued*

Task You Want to Perform	WALT PC Keyboard	WALT II Keyboard	IBM PC or Compatible Keyboard (with template)*	Keyboard Command (all keyboards)
Restrict the display to a specified field	`f` *field*	*field* FIELDS	`f` *field*	`f` *field*
Cancel the display of a field list or of a field-restricted display	`xf`	`xf`	`xf`	`xf`
Limit the display of multiple sets of star-page numbers to just one set	*star-page I.D.* STAR	*star-page I.D.* STAR	*star-page I.D.* STAR *star-page I.D.* F2	`st` *star-page I.D.* `star` *star-page I.D.*
Cancel the display of all star-page numbers	`xst` `xstar`	`xst` `xstar`	`xst` `xstar`	`xst` `xstar`
Redisplay all star-page numbers	STAR	STAR	STAR F2	`st` `star`

Moving Within a Displayed Document in WESTLAW

Task You Want to Perform	WALT PC Keyboard	WALT II Keyboard	IBM PC or Compatible Keyboard (with template)*	Keyboard Command (all keyboards)
Select TERM mode for moving within a document	`t`	`t`	`t`	`t`
Select PAGE mode for moving within a document	`p`	`p`	`p`	`p`

Select BEST mode for moving within a document	b best	b best	b best	b best
Show the next screen in the displayed document (TERM mode)	ENTER t	ENTER t	ENTER t	ENTER t
Show the previous screen in the displayed document (TERM mode)	t–	t–	t–	t–
Move to screen *n* in the displayed document (PAGE mode)	p*n*	p*n*	p*n*	p*n*
Show the next screen in the displayed document (PAGE mode)	ENTER PAGE DOWN NEXT PAGE	ENTER NEXT PAGE	ENTER PAGE DOWN or PgDn NEXT PAGE F3	ENTER p
Skip ahead *n* screens in the displayed document (PAGE mode)	*n* PAGE DOWN *n* NEXT PAGE	*n* NEXT PAGE	*n* PAGE DOWN or *n* PgDn *n* NEXT PAGE *n* F3	p+*n*
Show the previous screen in the displayed document (PAGE mode)	PAGE UP PREV PAGE	PREV PAGE	PAGE UP or PgUp PREV PAGE SHIFT F3	p–
Skip back *n* screens in the displayed document (PAGE mode)	*n* PAGE UP *n* PREV PAGE	*n* PREV PAGE	*n* PAGE UP or *n* PgUp *n* PREV PAGE *n* SHIFT F3	p–*n*

(continues)

* The commands in this column operate in version 4.5 of WESTMATE Communications Software for DOS.

(continued)

Moving Within a Displayed Document in WESTLAW—*continued*

Task You Want to Perform	WALT PC Keyboard	WALT II Keyboard	IBM PC or Compatible Keyboard (with template)*	Keyboard Command (all keyboards)
Move half a screen forward in the displayed document (PAGE mode)	h+	h+	h+	h+
Move half a screen back in the displayed document (PAGE mode)	h–	h–	h–	h–
Show the next screen in the statistically "best" portion of the displayed document (BEST mode)	ENTER	ENTER	ENTER	ENTER
Show the previous screen in the statistically "best" portion of the displayed document (BEST mode)	b–	b–	b–	b–
Move to star-page *n*	*n* STAR	*n* STAR	*n* STAR *n* F2	st *n* star *n*
Move to star-page *n* of a specific publication if you need to distinguish star-page sets	*star-page I.D. n* STAR	*star-page I.D. n* STAR	*star-page I.D. n* STAR *star-page I.D. n* F2	st *star-page I.D. n* star *star-page I.D. n*

Searching Within Retrieved Documents in WESTLAW

Invoke the LOCATE feature	LOCATE F4	LOCATE	LOCATE SHIFT F5	loc locate
Search for selected terms in retrieved documents	*terms* LOCATE *terms* F4	*terms* LOCATE	*terms* LOCATE *terms* SHIFT F5	loc *terms* locate *terms*
Display a list of documents containing your LOCATE terms	Lloc Llocate	Lloc Llocate	Lloc Llocate	Lloc Llocate
Exit LOCATE	xloc xlocate	xloc xlocate	xloc xlocate	xloc xlocate

Moving Between Documents in WESTLAW

Move to the next document in a retrieved collection	NEXT DOC	NEXT DOC	NEXT DOC F4	r
Skip ahead *n* documents in a retrieved collection	*n* NEXT DOC	*n* NEXT DOC	*n* NEXT DOC *n* F4	r+*n*
Move to the previous document in a retrieved collection	PREV DOC	PREV DOC	PREV DOC SHIFT F4	r–

(continues)

* The commands in this column operate in version 4.5 of WESTMATE Communications Software for DOS.

(continued)

Moving Between Documents in WESTLAW—*continued*

Task You Want to Perform	WALT PC Keyboard	WALT II Keyboard	IBM PC or Compatible Keyboard (with template)*	Keyboard Command (all keyboards)
Skip back *n* documents in a retrieved collection	*n* PREV DOC	*n* PREV DOC	*n* PREV DOC *n* SHIFT F4	r–*n*
Move to the document with rank number *n* in a retrieved collection	*n* r*n*	*n* r*n*	*n* r*n*	*n* r*n*
Invoke DOCUMENTS IN SEQUENCE to move to other statutory or administrative code sections	d	d	d	d
Move to the next section of a statutory or administrative code while using DOCUMENTS IN SEQUENCE	d	d	d	d
Skip ahead *n* sections in a statutory or administrative code while using DOCUMENTS IN SEQUENCE	d+*n*	d+*n*	d+*n*	d+*n*
Move to the previous section of a statutory or administrative code while using DOCUMENTS IN SEQUENCE	d–	d–	d–	d–

Skip back *n* sections in a statutory or administrative code while using DOCUMENTS IN SEQUENCE	d–*n*	d–*n*	d–*n*	d–*n*
Exit DOCUMENTS IN SEQUENCE	xd	xd	xd	xd

Updating Search Results in WESTLAW

Shepardize the authority you are viewing	SHEPARDIZE F6	SHEPARDIZE	SHEPARDIZE F6	sh shep
Shepardize an authority you are not viewing	*citation* SHEPARDIZE *citation* F6	*citation* SHEPARDIZE	*citation* SHEPARDIZE *citation* F6	sh *citation* shep *citation*
Customize a retrieved Shepard's table	LOCATE F4	LOCATE	LOCATE SHIFT F5	loc locate
Cancel customization of a Shepard's table	xloc xlocate	xloc xlocate	xloc xlocate	xloc xlocate
Retrieve the Shepard's PreView table for the authority you are viewing	SHEP PREVIEW F7	SHEPARD'S PREVIEW	SHEPARD'S PREVIEW SHIFT F6	sp
Retrieve the Shepard's PreView table for an authority you are not viewing	*citation* SHEP PREVIEW *citation* F7	*citation* SHEPARD'S PRE-VIEW	*citation* SHEPARD'S PRE-VIEW *citation* SHIFT F6	sp *citation*

(continues)

* The commands in this column operate in version 4.5 of WESTMATE Communications Software for DOS.

(continued)

Task You Want to Perform	WALT PC Keyboard	WALT II Keyboard	IBM PC or Compatible Keyboard (with template)*	Keyboard Command (all keyboards)

Updating Search Results in WESTLAW—*continued*

Task You Want to Perform	WALT PC Keyboard	WALT II Keyboard	IBM PC or Compatible Keyboard (with template)*	Keyboard Command (all keyboards)
Retrieve the Insta-Cite report for the case you are viewing	INSTA-CITE F5	INSTA-CITE	INSTA-CITE F5	ic
Retrieve the Insta-Cite report for a case you are not viewing	*citation* INSTA-CITE *citation* F5	*citation* INSTA-CITE	*citation* INSTA-CITE *citation* F5	ic *citation*
Use QuickCite to retrieve documents that refer to a specific citation	*citation* QUICK CITE *citation* F8	*citation* QUICK CITE	qc *citation*	qc *citation*
Invoke EZ ACCESS for updating search results	EZ ACCESS	EZ ACCESS	EZ ACCESS SHIFT F2	ez
Display additional choices while in EZ ACCESS	EZ ACCESS	EZ ACCESS	EZ ACCESS SHIFT F2	ez
Retrieve legislation or court rules amending or repealing the displayed statute or court rule	UPDATE F11	update	update	update
Save a search request as a PDQ search to run again later	PDQ	PDQ	pdq	pdq

Recall a PDQ search to review, run, or modify	PDQ	PDQ	pdq	pdq
Exit Shepard's, Shepard's PreView, Insta-Cite, or other updating service	GO BACK F3 MAP F2	GO BACK MAP	GO BACK F8 MAP SHIFT F8	gb map
Return to your most recent WESTLAW search results (if any) after updating	2 MAP 2 F2	2 MAP	2 MAP 2 SHIFT F8	map2
Return to the WESTLAW Directory after updating	1 MAP 1 F2	1 MAP	1 MAP 1 SHIFT F8	map1

Printing the Results of a Search in WESTLAW

Print the line on which the cursor rests		PRINT LINE		
Print the displayed screen on an attached printer	PRINT SCREEN	PRINT SCREEN	SHIFT PrtSc SHIFT PrtScr	SHIFT PrtSc SHIFT PrtScr
Automatically print each screen as it displays	CONTROL PRINT-SCREEN	ONLINE PRINT	CONTROL PrtSc CTRL PrtScr	CONTROL PrtSc CTRL PrtScr
Cancel automatic printing of displayed screens	CONTROL PRINT-SCREEN	ONLINE PRINT	CONTROL PrtSc CTRL PrtScr	CONTROL PrtSc CTRL PrtScr

(continues)

* The commands in this column operate in version 4.5 of WESTMATE Communications Software for DOS.

(continued)

Task You Want to Perform	WALT PC Keyboard	WALT II Keyboard	IBM PC or Compatible Keyboard (with template)*	Keyboard Command (all keyboards)

Printing the Results of a Search in WESTLAW—*continued*

Task You Want to Perform	WALT PC Keyboard	WALT II Keyboard	IBM PC or Compatible Keyboard (with template)*	Keyboard Command (all keyboards)
Select any other printing choice (*e.g.*, print the displayed document, print selected screens, print selected documents)	OFFLINE PRINT F12	OFFLINE PRINT	OFFLINE PRINT SHIFT F10	pr
Display the Offline Print Directory of printing requests	opd	opd	opd	opd

Downloading the Results of a Search in WESTLAW

Task You Want to Perform	WALT PC Keyboard	WALT II Keyboard	IBM PC or Compatible Keyboard (with template)*	Keyboard Command (all keyboards)
Download the displayed screen	MENU f s F10 f s		MENU f s F10 f s	
Automatically download each screen as it displays	MENU f L F10 f L		MENU f L F10 f L	
Cancel automatic downloading of displayed screens	MENU f L F10 f L		MENU f L F10 f L	

Select any other downloading choice (*e.g.*, download the displayed document, download selected screens, download selected documents)	OFFLINE PRINT F12 `pr`		OFFLINE PRINT SHIFT F10 `pr`	
Display the Offline Print Directory of downloading requests	`opd`		`opd`	

Miscellaneous Tasks in WESTLAW

Return to the WESTLAW Directory from another service (*e.g.*, Shepard's)	1 MAP 1 F2	1 MAP	1 MAP 1 SHIFT F8	`map1`
Display online help in WESTLAW	HELP F1	HELP	HELP F1	`h` `help`
Display the elapsed time for the current search session	`time`	`time`	`time`	`time`
Change the client name or identification	`client`	`client`	`client`	`client`
Erase all characters from the cursor to the end of the typing area	DEL EOF	DEL EOF	DEL EOF F9	

(continues)

* The commands in this column operate in version 4.5 of WESTMATE Communications Software for DOS.

(continued)

Miscellaneous Tasks in WESTLAW—*continued*

Task You Want to Perform	WALT PC Keyboard	WALT II Keyboard	IBM PC or Compatible Keyboard (with template)*	Keyboard Command (all keyboards)
Erase all characters in the typing area	HOME, then DEL EOF	CLEAR	HOME, then DEL EOF HOME, then F9	
Log off WESTLAW	SIGN OFF	OFF	`off`	`off`
Display the WESTMATE menu for gaining access to WESTLAW	RESTART		START SHIFT F1	
Display the WESTMATE menus for carrying out WESTLAW functions	MENU F10		MENU F10	
Display WESTMATE software's online ("local") help while WESTMATE access menu is displayed	HELP F1		HELP F1	
Exit WESTMATE software at WESTMATE access menu	`quit`		`quit` ALT F1	

* The commands in this column operate in version 4.5 of WESTMATE Communications Software for DOS.

APPENDIX M

Fashioning Effective Boolean Search Requests: Recall and Precision

In technical terms, a Boolean search request's performance can be evaluated through two principal measurements. The first measurement—"recall"—indicates what percentage of all relevant documents in the database the search request retrieves. The second measurement—"precision"—indicates what percentage of the retrieved documents is relevant.

For example, suppose a database of 1,000 documents contains 100 documents you would consider relevant to your research problem. If your search request retrieves 60 of those 100 relevant documents, the recall measurement for your request would be 60 per cent. If your search request also retrieves 180 irrelevant documents along with the 60 relevant documents (for a total of 240 retrieved documents), the precision measurement for your search request would be 25 percent—that is, 60 relevant documents out of 240 retrieved documents. Thus, your search request would have a relatively high level of recall (retrieving 6 out of every 10 potentially relevant documents) and a relatively low level of precision (with only one out of every four documents retrieved being relevant).

As this example suggests, when recall increases, precision decreases; when recall decreases, precision increases. So, when your Boolean search results show a high degree of recall (that is, when you retrieve a high percentage of the relevant documents in the database), you can also expect that your search results will show a low degree of precision (that is, you will have to sort through a lot of irrelevant documents to cull out the relevant ones).[450]

This inverse relationship underlies the challenge of computer-assisted legal research. Ideally, a search request would have both high recall and high precision: you would retrieve a high percentage of the potentially relevant documents contained in the database, *and* a high percentage of the retrieved documents would be relevant. In practice, however, the trade-off between re-

[450] "A well-known and well-documented rule of thumb in text retrieval [such as computer-assisted legal research] is that increased recall is gained only at the expense of a loss of precision, and vice versa." Jon Bing, *Performance of Legal Text Retrieval Systems: The Curse of Boole*, 79 LAW LIBR. J. 187, 196 (1987).

call and precision never disappears when you search a database for legal concepts. Consequently, as you construct Boolean search requests, you must decide how to strike a balance between precision and recall. Through an awareness of the need to do so, you are in a better position to fashion your search requests in ways that mitigate the worst consequences of this characteristic of full-text database searching. For example, knowing that high precision indicates low recall, you might decide to broaden the sweep of your search request if most of the documents it retrieves are relevant; these results suggest you have failed to retrieve many other documents that would also prove relevant to your research project. Chapters 7 and 8 explain techniques for constructing and modifying search requests to enhance their effectiveness.

APPENDIX N

The Blair & Maron Study: Important Findings for Database Searchers

In 1985, two computer scientists, David C. Blair and M.E. Maron, surprised many database searchers by showing that even search requests constructed by knowledgeable searchers can fail to retrieve relevant documents far more frequently than users of databases had previously realized.[451] Blair and Maron's findings hold significance for computer-assisted legal research because the scientists examined the effectiveness of using search terms and connectors to retrieve documents with search requests like the Boolean search requests used to retrieve information from LEXIS, WESTLAW, and other CALR databases. Moreover, Blair and Maron worked with a database that shared many characteristics of a CALR service.

In their controlled study, Blair and Maron evaluated CALR-like searches of a database consisting of documents totalling 350,000 pages of text, a small collection compared to those in LEXIS or WESTLAW and therefore presumably easier to search successfully than LEXIS or WESTLAW. The search requests in the study were constructed by legal assistants and supervising lawyers who were thoroughly acquainted with the contents of the documents in the database. A search was considered successful when the supervising lawyer concluded it had retrieved 75 per cent of the relevant documents in the database—in the language of "precision" and "recall" (see Appendix M), when the lawyer believed the search had a recall measurement of 75 per cent.

Blair and Maron followed up these apparently successful Boolean searches to determine the actual, as opposed to presumed, effectiveness. Their study revealed that although an average of 79 out of every 100 documents a search request retrieved proved relevant (a fairly high level of precision), the searches, on average, retrieved only 20 out of every 100 relevant documents in the database, *not* the 75 out of every 100 documents the researchers had thought they were retrieving.

The findings of the Blair & Maron study suggest two cautionary notes. First, even experienced users of CALR services can encounter difficulty in

[451] David C. Blair & M.E. Maron, *An Evaluation of Retrieval Effectiveness for a Full-Text Document-Retrieval System*, 20 COMM. ASS'N COMPUTING MACHINERY 289 (1985).

accurately estimating how comprehensive a search has been. "The total number of relevant documents found by a search usually can be determined, but the number of relevant documents in a collection *not* found by a search is seldom known."[452]

Second, the results of the Blair & Maron study highlight the need to guard against being lulled into a false sense of comprehensiveness by search results in which a high percentage of the retrieved documents is relevant. High-precision search results tend to reinforce a natural, if subconscious, inclination to conclude that a highly precise search has also retrieved a high percentage of all the relevant documents in the database. As Appendix M explains, though, just the opposite is probably true. Knowing that, you can make an informed decision about whether to broaden your search, either online or in books, to locate more authorities pertaining to your research problem.[453]

[452] Daniel P. Dabney, *The Curse of Thamus: An Analysis of Full-Text Legal Document Retrieval* 78 LAW LIBR. J. 5, 16 (1986) (emphasis in original).

[453] For additional discussion about Blair and Maron's study and its implications for CALR database searching, see Robert C. Berring, *Full-Text Databases and Legal Research: Backing into the Future*, 1 HIGH TECH. L.J. 27 (1986); Jon Bing, *Performance of Legal Text Retrieval Systems: The Curse of Boole*, 79 LAW LIBR. J. 187 (1987); David C. Blair & M.E. Maron, *Full-Text Information Retrieval: Further Analysis and Clarification*, 26 INFO. PROCESSING & MGMT. 437 (1990); Daniel P. Dabney, *A Reply to West Publishing Company and Mead Data Central on The Curse of Thamus*, 78 LAW LIBR. J. 349 (1986); Daniel P. Dabney, *The Curse of Thamus: An Analysis of Full-Text Legal Document Retrieval,* 78 LAW LIBR. J. 5, 16 (1986); Jo McDermott, *Another Analysis of Full-Text Legal Document Retrieval*, 78 LAW LIBR. J. 337 (1986); Craig E. Runde & William H. Lindberg, The Curse of Thamus: *A Response*, 78 LAW LIBR. J. 345 (1986); Gerard Salton, *Another Look at Automatic Text-Retrieval Systems*, 20 COMM. ASS'N COMPUTING MACHINERY 648 (1986). *See also* John Doyle, *Aiming at the Databases: Retrieval Effectiveness of Legal Databases*, 3 TRENDS IN LAW LIBR. MGMT. & TECH., May 1990, at 3.

APPENDIX O

Another Viewpoint: Learn With BOOK*

By R.J. Heathorn

A new aid to rapid—almost magical—learning has made its appearance. Indications are that if it catches on all the electronic gadgets will be so much junk.

The new device is known as Built-in Orderly Organised Knowledge. The makers generally call it by its initials, BOOK.

Many advantages are claimed over the old-style learning and teaching aids on which most people are brought up nowadays. It has no wires, no electric circuit to break down. No connection is needed to an electricity power point. It is made entirely without mechanical parts to go wrong or need replacement.

Anyone can use BOOK, even children, and it fits comfortably into the hands. It can be conveniently used sitting in an armchair by the fire.

How does this revolutionary, unbelievably easy invention work? Basically BOOK consists only of a large number of paper sheets. These may run to hundreds where BOOK covers a lengthy programme of information. Each sheet bears a number in sequence, so that the sheets cannot be used in the wrong order.

To make it even easier for the user to keep the sheets in the proper order they are held firmly in place by a special locking device called a "binding."

Each sheet of paper presents the user with an information sequence in the form of symbols, which he absorbs optically for automatic registration on the brain. When one sheet has been assimilated a flick of the finger turns it over and further information is found on the other side.

By using both sides of each sheet in this way a great economy is effected, thus reducing both the size and cost of BOOK. No buttons need to be pressed to move from one sheet to another, to open or close BOOK, or to start it working.

BOOK may be taken up at any time and used by merely opening it. Instantly it is ready for use. Nothing has to be connected up or switched on. The user may turn at will to any sheet, going backwards or forwards as he pleases. A sheet is provided near the beginning as a location finder for any required information sequence.

A small accessory, available at trifling extra cost, is the BOOKmark. This enables the user to pick up his programme where he left off on the previous learning session. BOOKmark is versatile and may be used in any BOOK.

The initial cost varies with the size and subject matter. Already a vast range of BOOKS is available, covering every conceivable subject and adjusted to different levels of aptitude. One BOOK, small enough to be held in the hands, may contain an entire learning schedule.

Once purchased, BOOK requires no further upkeep cost; no batteries or wires are needed, since the motive power, thanks to an ingenious device patented by the makers, is supplied by the brain of the user.

BOOKS may be stored on handy shelves and for ease of reference the programme schedule is normally indicated on the back of the binding.

Altogether the Built-in Orderly Organised Knowledge seems to have great advantages with no drawbacks. We predict a big future for it.

* "Learn With BOOK" is reprinted by permission of *Punch*. Originally published May 9, 1962.

INDEX

Information about computer-assisted legal research features and activities can also be located through the Detailed Table of Contents on pages xv–xxix.

In this index, the letter "n" after a page number indicates that the information appears in a footnote beginning on that page. References to "Quick Guides" identify summaries organized in chart form.

Symbols

A

C

E

Also refer to Detailed Table of Contents

G

H

J

K

L

M

N

O

P

Q

R

S

T

U

V